Being and Time

Martin Heidegger

Must Have Books
503 Deerfield Place
Victoria, BC
V9B 6G5
Canada
trava2911@gmail.com

ISBN: 9781774640661

Dedicated to

EDMUND HUSSERL

in friendship and admiration

Todtnauberg in Baden, Black Forest
8 April 1926

CONTENTS

DIVISION TWO: DASEIN AND TEMPORALITY

TRANSLATORS' PREFACE

MORE than thirty years have passed since *Being and Time* first appeared, and it has now become perhaps the most celebrated philosophical work which Germany has produced in this century. It is a very difficult book, even for the German reader, and highly resistant to translation, so much so that it has often been called 'untranslatable'. We feel that this is an exaggeration.

Anyone who has struggled with a philosophical work in translation has constantly found himself asking how the author himself would have expressed the ideas which the translator has ascribed to him. In this respect the 'ideal' translation would perhaps be one so constructed that a reader with reasonable linguistic competence and a key to the translator's conventions should be able to retranslate the new version into the very words of the original. Everybody knows that this is altogether too much to demand; but the faithful translator must at least keep this ahead of him as a desirable though impracticable goal. The simplest compromise with the demands of his own langugage is to present the translation and the original text on opposite pages; he is then quite free to choose the most felicitous expressions he can think of, trusting that the reader who is shrewd enough to wonder what is really happening can look across and find out. Such a procedure would add enormously to the expense of a book as long as *Being and Time*, and is impracticable for other reasons. But on any page of Heidegger there is a great deal happening, and we have felt that we owe it to the reader to let him know what is going on. For the benefit of the man who already has a copy of the German text, we have indicated in our margins the pagination of the later German editions, which differs only slightly from that of the earlier ones. All citations marked with 'H' refer to this pagination. But for the reader who does not have the German text handy, we have had to use other devices.

As long as an author is using words in their ordinary ways, the translator should not have much trouble in showing what he is trying to say. But Heidegger is constantly using words in ways which are by no means ordinary, and a great part of his merit lies in the freshness and penetration which his very innovations reflect. He tends to discard much of the traditional philosophical terminology, substituting an elaborate vocabulary of his own. He occasionally coins new expressions from older roots, and he takes full advantage of the ease with which the German language lends itself to the formation of new compounds. He also uses familiar expressions in new ways. Adverbs, prepositions, pronouns, conjunctions are made to do service as nouns; words which have undergone a long history of semantical change are used afresh in their older senses; specialized modern idioms are generalized far beyond the limits within which they would ordinarily be applicable. Puns are by no means uncommon and frequently a key-word may be used in several senses, successively or even simultaneously. He is especially fond of ringing the changes on words with a common stem or a common prefix. He tends on the whole to avoid personal constructions, and often uses abstract nouns ('Dasein', 'Zeitlichkeit', 'Sorge', 'In-der-Welt-sein', and so forth) as subjects of sentences where a personal subject would ordinarily be found. Like Aristotle or Wittgenstein, he likes to talk about his words, and seldom makes an innovation without explaining it; but sometimes he will have used a word in a special sense many times before he gets round to the explanation; and he may often use it in the ordinary senses as well. In such cases the reader is surely entitled to know what word Heidegger is actually talking about, as well as what he says about it; and he is also entitled to know when and how he actually uses it.

We have tried in the main to keep our vocabulary under control, providing a German-English glossary for the more important expressions, and a rather full analytical index which will also serve as an English-German glossary. We have tried to use as few English terms as possible to represent the more important German ones, and we have tried not to to use these for other purposes than those we have specifically indicated. Sometimes we have had to coin new terms to correspond to Heidegger's. In a number of cases there are two German terms at the author's disposal which he has chosen to differentiate, even though they may be synonyms in ordinary German usage; if we have found only one suitable English term to correspond to them, we have sometimes adopted the device of capitalizing it when it represents the German word to which it is etymologically closer: thus 'auslegen' becomes 'interpret', but 'interpretieren' becomes 'Interpret'; 'gliedern' becomes 'articulate', but 'artikulieren' becomes 'Articulate'; 'Ding' becomes 'Thing', but 'thing' represents 'Sache' and a number of other expressions. In other cases we have coined a new term. Thus while 'tatsächlich' becomes 'factual', we have introduced 'factical' to represent 'faktisch'. We have often inserted German expressions in square brackets on the occasions of their first appearance or on that of their official definition. But we have also used bracketed expressions to call attention to departures from our usual conventions, or to bring out etymological connections which might otherwise be overlooked.

In many cases bracketing is insufficient, and we have introduced footnotes of our own, discussing some of the more important terms on the occasion of their first appearance. We have not hesitated to quote German sentences at length when they have been ambiguous or obscure; while we have sometimes taken pains to show where the ambiguity lies, we have more often left this to the reader to puzzle out for himself. We have often quoted passages with verbal subtleties which would otherwise be lost in translation. We have also called attention to a number of significant differences between the earlier and later editions of Heidegger's work. The entire book was reset for the seventh edition; while revisions were by no means extensive, they went beyond the simple changes in punctuation and citation which Heidegger mentions in his preface. We have chosen the third edition (1931) as typical of the earlier editions, and the eighth (1957) as typical of the later ones. In general we have preferred the readings of the eighth edition, and our marginal numbering and cross-references follow its pagination. Heidegger's very valuable footnotes have been renumbered with roman numerals and placed at the end of the text where we trust they will be given the attention they deserve. Hoping that our own notes will be of immediate use to the reader, we have placed them at the bottoms of pages for easy reference, indicating them with arabic numerals.

In general we have tried to stick to the text as closely as we can without sacrificing intelligibility; but we have made numerous concessions to the reader at the expense of making Heidegger less Heideggerian. We have, for instance, frequently used personal constructions where Heidegger has avoided them. We have also tried to be reasonably flexible in dealing with hyphenated expressions. Heidegger does not seem to be especially consistent in his use of quotation marks, though in certain expressions (for instance, the word 'Welt') they are very deliberately employed. Except in a few footnote references and some of the quotations from Hegel and Count Yorck in the two concluding chapters, our single quotation marks represent Heidegger's double ones. But we have felt free to introduce double ones of our own wherever we feel that they may be helpful to the reader. We have followed a similar policy with regard to italicization. When Heidegger uses italics in the later editions (or spaced type in the earlier ones), we have generally used italics; but in the relatively few cases where we have felt that some emphasis of our own is needed, we have resorted to wide spacing. We have not followed Heidegger in the use of italics for proper names or for definite articles used demonstratively to introduce restrictive relative clauses. But we have followed the usual practice of italicizing words and phrases from languages other than English and German, and have italicized titles of books, regardless of Heidegger's procedure.

We have received help from several sources. Miss Marjorie Ward has collated the third and eighth editions, and made an extremely careful study of Heidegger's vocabulary and ours, which has saved us from innumerable inconsistencies and many downright mistakes; there is hardly a page which has not profited by her assistance. We are also indebted to several persons who have helped us in various ways: Z. Adamczewski, Hannah Arendt, J. A. Burzle, C. A. Campbell, G. M. George, Fritz Heider, Edith Kern, Norbert Raymond, Eva Schaper, Martin Scheerer, John Wild. If any serious errors remain, they are probably due to our failure to exploit the time and good nature of these friends and colleagues more unmercifully. We are particularly indebted to Professor R. Gregor Smith who brought us together in the first place, and who, perhaps more than anyone else, has made it possible for this translation to be presented to the public. We also wish to express our appreciation to our publishers and to Max Niemeyer Verlag, holders of the German copyright, who have shown extraordinary patience in putting up with the long delay in the preparation of our manuscript.

We are particularly grateful to the University of Kansas for generous research grants over a period of three years, and to the University of Kansas Endowment Association for enabling us to work together in Scotland.

AUTHOR'S PREFACE TO THE SEVENTH GERMAN EDITION

THIS treatise first appeared in the spring of 1927 in the *Jahrbuch für Phänomenologie und phänomenologische Forschung* edited by Edmund Husserl, and was published simultaneously in a special printing.

The present reprint, which appears as the seventh edition, is unchanged in the text, but has been newly revised with regard to quotations and punctuation. The page-numbers of this reprint agree with those of the earlier editions except for minor deviations.[1]

While the previous editions have borne the designation 'First Half', this has now been deleted. After a quarter of a century, the second half could no longer be added unless the first were to be presented anew. Yet the road it has taken remains even today a necessary one, if our Dasein is to be stirred by the question of Being.

For the elucidation of this question the reader may refer to my *Einführung in die Metaphysik*, which is appearing simultaneously with this reprinting under the same publishers.[2] This work presents the text of a course of lectures delivered in the summer semester of 1935.

[1] See Translators' Preface, p. 15.
[2] Max Niemeyer Verlag, Tübingen, 1953. English translation by Ralph Manheim, Yale University Press and Oxford University Press, 1959.

... δῆλον γὰρ ὡς ὑμεῖς μὲν ταῦτα (τί ποτε βούλεσθε σημαίνειν ὁπόταν ὃν φθέγγησθε) πάλαι γιγνώσκετε, ἡμεῖς δὲ πρὸ τοῦ μὲν ᾠόμεθα, νῦν δ' ἠπορή-καμεν ...

'For manifestly you have long been aware of what you mean when you use the expression "*being*". We, however, who used to think we understood it, have now become perplexed.'[1]

Do we in our time have an answer to the question of what we really mean by the word 'being'?[1] Not at all. So it is fitting that we should raise anew *the question of the meaning*[2] *of Being*. But are we nowadays even perplexed at our inability to understand the expression 'Being'? Not at all. So first of all we must reawaken an understanding for the meaning of this question. Our aim in the following treatise is to work out the question of the meaning of *Being* and to do so concretely. Our provisional aim is the Interpretation[3] of *time* as the possible horizon for any understanding whatsoever of Being.[4]

But the reasons for making this our aim, the investigations which such a purpose requires, and the path to its achievement, call for some introductory remarks.

---

[1] 'seiend'. Heidegger translates Plato's present participle ὄν by this present participle of the verb 'sein' ('to be'). We accordingly translate 'seiend' here and in a number of later passages by the present participle 'being'; where such a translation is inconvenient we shall resort to other constructions, usually subjoining the German word in brackets or in a footnote. The participle 'seiend' must be distinguished from the infinitive 'sein', which we shall usually translate either by the infinitive 'to be' or by the gerund 'being'. It must also be distinguished from the important substantive 'Sein' (always capitalized), which we shall translate as 'Being' (capitalized), and from the equally important substantive 'Seiendes', which is directly derived from 'seiend', and which we shall usually translate as 'entity' or 'entities'. (See our note 6, H. 3 below.)

[2] 'Sinn.' In view of the importance of the distinction between 'Sinn' and 'Bedeutung' in German writers as diverse as Dilthey, Husserl, Frege and Schlick, we shall translate 'Sinn' by 'meaning' or 'sense', depending on the context, and keep 'signification' and 'signify' for 'Bedeutung' and 'bedeuten'. (The verb 'mean' will occasionally be used to translate such verbs as 'besagen', 'sagen', 'heissen' and 'meinen', but the noun 'meaning' will be reserved for 'Sinn'.) On 'Sinn', see H. 151, 324; on 'Bedeutung', etc., see H. 87, and our note 47 ad loc.

[3] Heidegger uses two words which might well be translated as 'interpretation': 'Auslegung' and 'Interpretation'. Though in many cases these may be regarded as synonyms, their connotations are not quite the same. 'Auslegung' seems to be used in a broad sense to cover any activity in which we interpret something 'as' something, whereas 'Interpretation' seems to apply to interpretations which are more theoretical or systematic, as in the exegesis of a text. See especially H. 148 ff. and 199 f. We shall preserve this distinction by writing 'interpretation' for 'Auslegung', but 'Interpretation' for Heidegger's 'Interpretation', following similar conventions for the verbs 'auslegen' and 'interpretieren'.

[4] '... als des möglichen Horizontes eines jeden Seinsverständnisses überhaupt ...' Throughout this work the word 'horizon' is used with a connotation somewhat different from that to which the English-speaking reader is likely to be accustomed. We tend to think of a horizon as something which we may widen or extend or go beyond; Heidegger, however, seems to think of it rather as something which we can neither widen nor go beyond, but which provides the limits for certain intellectual activities performed 'within' it.

INTRODUCTION

EXPOSITION OF THE QUESTION OF THE MEANING OF BEING

I

THE NECESSITY, STRUCTURE, AND PRIORITY OF THE QUESTION OF BEING

¶ *1. The Necessity for Explicitly Restating the Question of Being*

THIS question has today been forgotten. Even though in our time we deem it progressive to give our approval to 'metaphysics' again, it is held that we have been exempted from the exertions of a newly rekindled γιγαντομαχία περὶ τῆς οὐσίας. Yet the question we are touching upon is not just a n y question. It is one which provided a stimulus for the researches of Plato and Aristotle, only to subside from then on *as a theme for actual investigation.*[1] What these two men achieved was to persist through many alterations and 'retouchings' down to the 'logic' of Hegel. And what they wrested with the utmost intellectual effort from the phenomena, fragmentary and incipient though it was, has long since become trivialized.

Not only that. On the basis of the Greeks' initial contributions towards an Interpretation of Being, a dogma has been developed which not only declares the question about the meaning of Being to be superfluous, but sanctions its complete neglect. It is said that 'Being' is the most universal and the emptiest of concepts. As such it resists every attempt at definition. Nor does this most universal and hence indefinable concept require any definition, for everyone uses it constantly and already understands what he means by it. In this way, that which the ancient philosophers found continually disturbing as something obscure and hidden has taken on a clarity and self-evidence such that if anyone continues to ask about it he is charged with an error of method.

At the beginning of our investigation it is not possible to give a detailed

---

[1] '... *als thematische Frage wirklicher Untersuchung*'. When Heidegger speaks of a question as 'thematisch', he thinks of it as one which is taken seriously and studied in a systematic manner. While we shall often translate this adjective by its cognate, 'thematic', we may sometimes find it convenient to choose more flexible expressions involving the word 'theme'. (Heidegger gives a fuller discussion on H. 363.)

account of the presuppositions and prejudices which are constantly reimplanting and fostering the belief that an inquiry into Being is unnecessary. They are rooted in ancient ontology itself, and it will not be possible to interpret that ontology adequately until the question of Being has been clarified and answered and taken as a clue—at least, if we are to have regard for the soil from which the basic ontological concepts developed, and if we are to see whether the categories have been demonstrated in a way that is appropriate and complete. We shall therefore carry the discussion of these presuppositions only to the point at which the necessity for restating the question about the meaning of Being become plain. There are three such presuppositions.

1. First, it has been maintained that 'Being' is the 'most universal' concept: τὸ ὄν ἐστι καθόλου μάλιστα πάντων.[1] *Illud quod primo cadit sub apprehensione est ens, cuius intellectus includitur in omnibus, quaecumque quis apprehendit.* 'An understanding of Being is already included in conceiving anything which one apprehends as an entity.'[1,ii] But the 'universality' of 'Being' is not that of a *class* or *genus*. The term 'Being' does not define that realm of entities which is uppermost when these are Articulated conceptually according to genus and species: οὔτε τὸ ὄν γένος.[iii] The 'universality' of Being 'transcends' any universality of genus. In medieval ontology 'Being' is designated as a '*transcendens*'. Aristotle himself knew the unity of this transcendental 'universal' as a *unity of analogy* in contrast to the multiplicity of the highest generic concepts applicable to things. With this discovery, in spite of his dependence on the way in which the ontological question had been formulated by Plato, he put the problem of Being on what was, in principle, a new basis. To be sure, even Aristotle failed to clear away the darkness of these categorial interconnections. In medieval ontology this problem was widely discussed, especially in the Thomist and Scotist schools, without reaching clarity as to principles. And when Hegel at last defines 'Being' as the 'indeterminate immediate' and makes this definition basic for all the further categorial explications of his 'logic', he keeps looking in the same direction as ancient ontology,

---

1 ' ". . . was einer am Seienden erfasst" '. The word 'Seiendes', which Heidegger uses in his paraphrase, is one of the most important words in the book. The substantive 'das Seiende' is derived from the participle 'seiend' (see note 1, p. 19), and means literally 'that which is'; 'ein Seiendes' means 'something which is'. There is much to be said for translating 'Seiendes' by the noun 'being' or 'beings' (for it is often used in a collective sense). We feel, however, that it is smoother and less confusing to write 'entity' or 'entities'. We are well aware that in recent British and American philosophy the term 'entity' has been used more generally to apply to almost anything whatsoever, no matter what its ontological status. In this translation, however, it will mean simply 'something which *is*'. An alternative translation of the Latin quotation is given by the English Dominican Fathers, *Summa Theologica*, Thomas Baker, London, 1915: 'For that which, before aught else, falls under apprehension, is *being*, the notion of which is included in all things whatsoever a man apprehends.'

except that he no longer pays heed to Aristotle's problem of the unity of Being as over against the multiplicity of 'categories' applicable to things. So if it is said that 'Being' is the most universal concept, this cannot mean that it is the one which is clearest or that it needs no further discussion. It is rather the darkest of all.

2. It has been maintained secondly that the concept of 'Being' is   4
indefinable. This is deduced from its supreme universality,[iv] and rightly so, if *definitio fit per genus proximum et differentiam specificam.* 'Being' cannot indeed be conceived as an entity; *enti non additur aliqua natura*: nor can it acquire such a character as to have the term "entity" applied to it. "Being" cannot be derived from higher concepts by definition, nor can it be presented through lower ones. But does this imply that 'Being' no longer offers a problem? Not at all. We can infer only that 'Being' cannot have the character of an entity. Thus we cannot apply to Being the concept of 'definition' as presented in traditional logic, which itself has its foundations in ancient ontology and which, within certain limits, provides a quite justifiable way of defining "entities". The indefinability of Being does not eliminate the question of its meaning; it demands that we look that question in the face.

3. Thirdly, it is held that 'Being' is of all concepts the one that is self-evident. Whenever one cognizes anything or makes an assertion, whenever one comports oneself towards entities, even towards oneself,[1] some use is made of 'Being'; and this expression is held to be intelligible 'without further ado', just as everyone understands "The sky *is* blue', 'I *am* merry', and the like. But here we have an average kind of intelligibility, which merely demonstrates that this is unintelligible. It makes manifest that in any way of comporting oneself towards entities as entities—even in any Being towards entities as entities—there lies *a priori* an enigma.[2] The very fact that we already live in an understanding of Being and that the meaning of Being is still veiled in darkness proves that it is necessary in principle to raise this question again.

Within the range of basic philosophical concepts—especially when we come to the concept of 'Being'—it is a dubious procedure to invoke self-evidence, even if the 'self-evident' (Kant's 'covert judgments of the common reason')[3]

[1] '. . . in jedem Verhalten zu Seiendem, in jedem Sich-zu-sich-selbst-verhalten . . .' The verb 'verhalten' can refer to any kind of behaviour or way of conducting oneself, even to the way in which one relates oneself to something else, or to the way one refrains or holds oneself back. We shall translate it in various ways.
[2] 'Sie macht offenbar, dass in jedem Verhalten und Sein zu Seiendem als Seiendem a priori ein Rätsel liegt.' The phrase 'Sein zu Seiendem' is typical of many similar expressions in which the substantive 'Sein' is followed by the preposition 'zu'. In such expressions we shall usually translate 'zu' as 'towards': for example, 'Being-towards-death', 'Being towards Others', 'Being towards entities within-the-world'.
[3] ' "die geheimen Urteile der gemeinen Vernunft" '.

is to become the sole explicit and abiding theme for one's analytic—
'the business of philosophers'.

By considering these prejudices, however, we have made plain not only
that the question of Being lacks an *answer*, but that the question itself is
obscure and without direction. So if it is to be revived, this means that
we must first work out an adequate way of *formulating* it.

¶ 2. *The Formal Structure of the Question of Being*

The question of the meaning of Being must be *formulated*. If it is a
fundamental question, or indeed *the* fundamental question, it must be
made transparent, and in an appropriate way.[1] We must therefore
explain briefly what belongs to any question whatsoever, so that from this
standpoint the question of Being can be made visible as a *very special* one
with its own distinctive character.

Every inquiry is a seeking [Suchen]. Every seeking gets guided beforehand by what is sought. Inquiry is a cognizant seeking for an entity both
with regard to the fact t h a t it is and with regard to its Being as it is.[2]
This cognizant seeking can take the form of 'investigating' ["Untersuchen"],
in which one lays bare that which the question is about and ascertains its
character. Any inquiry, as an inquiry about something, has *that which is
asked about* [sein *Gefragtes*]. But all inquiry about something is somehow a
questioning of something [Anfragen bei . . .]. So in addition to what is
asked about, an inquiry has *that which is interrogated* [ein *Befragtes*]. In
investigative questions—that is, in questions which are specifically theoretical—what is asked about is determined and conceptualized. Furthermore, in what is asked about there lies also *that which is to be found out by
the asking* [das *Erfragte*]; this is what is really intended:[3] with this the
inquiry reaches its goal. Inquiry itself is the behaviour of a questioner, and
therefore of an entity, and as such has its own character of Being. When one
makes an inquiry one may do so 'just casually' or one may formulate the

[1] '. . . dann bedarf solches Fragen der angemessenen Durchsichtigkeit'. The adjective
'durchsichtig' is one of Heidegger's favourite expressions, and means simply 'transparent',
'perspicuous', something that one can 'see through'. We shall ordinarily translate it by
'transparent'. See H. 146 for further discussion.

[2] '. . . in seinem Dass- und Sosein'.

[3] '. . . das eigentlich Intendierte . . .' The adverb 'eigentlich' occurs very often in this
work. It may be used informally where one might write 'really' or 'on its part', or in a
much stronger sense, where something like 'genuinely' or 'authentically' would be more
appropriate. It is not always possible to tell which meaning Heidegger has in mind. In the
contexts which seem relatively informal we shall write 'really'; in the more technical
passages we shall write 'authentically', reserving 'genuinely' for 'genuin' or 'echt'. The
reader must not confuse this kind of 'authenticity' with the kind, which belongs to an
'authentic text' or an 'authentic account'. See H. 42 for further discussion. In the present
passage, the verb 'intendieren' is presumably used in the medieval sense of 'intending', as
adapted and modified by Brentano and Husserl.

2/16/23

question explicitly. The latter case is peculiar in that the inquiry does not become transparent to itself until all these constitutive factors of the question have themselves become transparent.

The question about the meaning of Being is to be *formulated*. We must therefore discuss it with an eye to these structural items.

Inquiry, as a kind of seeking, must be guided beforehand by what is sought. So the meaning of Being must already be available to us in some way. As we have intimated, we always conduct our activities in an under-standing of Being. Out of this understanding arise both the explicit question of the meaning of Being and the tendency that leads us towards its conception. We do not *know* what 'Being' means. But even if we ask, 'What *is* "Being"?', we keep within an understanding of the 'is', though we are unable to fix conceptionally what that 'is' signifies. We do not even know the horizon in terms of which that meaning is to be grasped and fixed. *But this vague average understanding of Being is still a Fact.*

However much this understanding of Being (an understanding which is already available to us) may fluctuate and grow dim, and border on mere acquaintance with a word, its very indefiniteness is itself a positive pheno-menon which needs to be clarified. An investigation of the meaning of **6** Being cannot be expected to give this clarification at the outset. If we are to obtain the clue we need for Interpreting this average understanding of Being, we must first develop the concept of Being. In the light of this concept and the ways in which it may be explicitly understood, we can make out what this obscured or still unillumined understanding of Being means, and what kinds of obscuration—or hindrance to an explicit illumination—of the meaning of Being are possible and even inevitable.

Further, this vague average understanding of Being may be so infil-trated with traditional theories and opinions about Being that these remain hidden as sources of the way in which it is prevalently understood. What we seek when we inquire into Being is not something entirely unfamiliar, even if proximally[1] we cannot grasp it at all.

In the question which we are to work out, *what is asked about* is Being— that which determines entities as entities, that on the basis of which

---

[1] 'zunächst'. This word is of very frequent occurrence in Heidegger, and he will discuss his use of it on H. 370 below. In ordinary German usage the word may mean 'at first', 'to begin with', or 'in the first instance', and we shall often translate it in such ways. The word is, however, cognate with the adjective 'nah' and its superlative 'nächst', which we shall usually translate as 'close' and 'closest' respectively; and Heidegger often uses 'zunächst' in the sense of 'most closely', when he is describing the most 'natural' and 'obvious' experiences which we have at an uncritical and pre-philosophical level. We have ventured to translate this Heideggerian sense of 'zunächst' as 'proximally', but there are many border-line cases where it is not clear whether Heidegger has in mind this special sense or one of the more general usages, and in such cases we have chosen whatever expression seems stylistically preferable.

[woraufhin] entities are already understood, however we may discuss them in detail. The Being of entities 'is' not itself an entity. If we are to understand the problem of Being, our first philosophical step consists in not μῦθόν τινα διηγεῖσθαι,ᵛ in not 'telling a story'—that is to say, in not defining entities as entities by tracing them back in their origin to some other entities, as if Being had the character of some possible entity. Hence Being, as that which is asked about, must be exhibited in a way of its own, essentially different from the way in which entities are discovered. Accordingly, *what is to be found out by the asking*—the meaning of Being—also demands that it be conceived in a way of its own, essentially contrasting with the concepts in which entities acquire their determinate signification.

In so far as Being constitutes what is asked about, and "Being" means the Being of entities, then entities themselves turn out to be *what is interrogated*. These are, so to speak, questioned as regards their Being. But if the characteristics of their Being can be yielded without falsification, then these entities must, on their part, have become accessible as they are in themselves. When we come to what is to be interrogated, the question of Being requires that the right way of access to entities shall have been obtained and secured in advance. But there are many things which we designate as 'being' ["seiend"], and we do so in various senses. Everything we talk about, everything we have in view, everything towards which we comport ourselves in any way, is being; what we are is being, and so is how we are. Being lies in the fact that something is, and in its Being as it is; in Reality; in presence-at-hand; in subsistence; in validity; in Dasein; in the 'there is'.[1] In *which* entities is the meaning of Being to be discerned? From which entities is the disclosure of Being to take its departure? Is the starting-point optional, or does some particular entity have priority when we come to work out the question of Being? Which entity shall we take for our example, and in what sense does it have priority?

If the question about Being is to be explicitly formulated and carried through in such a manner as to be completely transparent to itself, then any treatment of it in line with the elucidations we have given requires us to explain how Being is to be looked at, how its meaning is to be understood and conceptually grasped; it requires us to prepare the way for choosing the right entity for our example, and to work out the genuine way of access to it. Looking at something, understanding and conceiving it, choosing, access to it—all these ways of behaving are constitutive for our inquiry, and therefore are modes of Being for those particular entities

---

[1] 'Sein liegt im Dass- und Sosein, in Realität, Vorhandenheit, Bestand, Geltung, Dasein, im "es gibt".' On 'Vorhandenheit' ('presence-at-hand') see note 1, p. 48, H. 25. On 'Dasein', see note 1, p. 27.

which we, the inquirers, are ourselves. Thus to work out the question of Being adequately, we must make an entity—the inquirer—transparent in his own Being. The very asking of this question is an entity's mode of *Being*; and as such it gets its essential character from what is inquired about—namely, Being. This entity which each of us is himself and which includes inquiring as one of the possibilities of its Being, we shall denote by the term "*Dasein*".[1] If we are to formulate our question explicitly and transparently, we must first give a proper explication of an entity (Dasein), with regard to its Being.

Is there not, however, a manifest circularity in such an undertaking? If we must first define an entity *in its Being*, and if we want to formulate the question of Being only on this basis, what is this but going in a circle? In working out our question, have we not 'presupposed' something which only the answer can bring? Formal objections such as the argument about 'circular reasoning', which can easily be cited at any time in the study of first principles, are always sterile when one is considering concrete ways of investigating. When it comes to understanding the matter at hand, they carry no weight and keep us from penetrating into the field of study.

But factically[2] there is no circle at all in formulating our question as we have described. One can determine the nature of entities in their Being without necessarily having the explicit concept of the meaning of Being at one's disposal. Otherwise there could have been no ontological knowledge heretofore. One would hardly deny that factically there has been such knowledge.[3] Of course 'Being' has been presupposed in all ontology up till now, but not as a *concept* at one's disposal—not as the sort of thing we are seeking. This 'presupposing' of Being has rather the character of taking a look at it beforehand, so that in the light of it the entities presented to us get provisionally Articulated in their Being. This guiding

8

[1] The word 'Dasein' plays so important a role in this work and is already so familiar to the English-speaking reader who has read about Heidegger, that it seems simpler to leave it untranslated except in the relatively rare passages in which Heidegger himself breaks it up with a hypthen ('Da-sein') to show its etymological construction: literally 'Being-there'. Though in traditional German philosophy it may be used quite generally to stand for almost any kind of Being or 'existence' which we can say that something *has* (the 'existence' of God, for example), in everyday usage it tends to be used more narrowly to stand for the kind of Being that belongs to *persons*. Heidegger follows the everyday usage in this respect, but goes somewhat further in that he often uses it to stand for any *person* who has such Being, and who is thus an 'entity' himself. See H. 11 below.

[2] 'faktisch'. While this word can often be translated simply as 'in fact' or 'as a matter of fact', it is used both as an adjective and as an adverb and is so characteristic of Heidegger's style that we shall as a rule translate it either as 'factical' or as 'factically', thus preserving its connection with the important noun 'Faktizität' (facticity'), and keeping it distinct from 'tatsächlich' ('factual') and 'wirklich' ('actual'). See the discussion of 'Tatsächlichkeit' and 'Faktizität' in Sections 12 and 29 below (H. 56, 135).

[3] '. . . deren faktischen Bestand man wohl nicht leugnen wird'.

activity of taking a look at Being arises from the average understanding of Being in which we always operate and *which in the end belongs to the essential constitution*[1] *of Dasein itself.* Such 'presupposing' has nothing to do with laying down an axiom from which a sequence of propositions is deductively derived. It is quite impossible for there to be any 'circular argument' in formulating the question about the meaning of Being; for in answering this question, the issue is not one of grounding something by such a derivation; it is rather one of laying bare the grounds for it and exhibiting them.[2]

In the question of the meaning of Being there is no 'circular reasoning' but rather a remarkable 'relatedness backward or forward' which what we are asking about (Being) bears to the inquiry itself as a mode of Being of an entity. Here what is asked about has an essential pertinence to the inquiry itself, and this belongs to the ownmost meaning [eigensten Sinn] of the question of Being. This only means, however, that there is a way—perhaps even a very special one—in which entities with the character of Dasein are related to the question of Being. But have we not thus demonstrated that a certain kind of entity has a priority with regard to its Being? And have we not thus presented that entity which shall serve as the primary example to be *interrogated* in the question of Being? So far our discussion has n o t demonstrated Dasein's priority, nor has it shown decisively whether Dasein may possibly or even necessarily serve as the primary entity to be interrogated. But indeed something like a priority of Dasein has announced itself.

¶ *3. The Ontological Priority of the Question of Being*

When we pointed out the characteristics of the question of Being, taking as our clue the formal structure of the question as such, we made it

---

[1] 'Wesensverfassung'. 'Verfassung' is the standard word for the 'constitution' of a nation or any political organization, but it is also used for the 'condition' or 'state' in which a person may find himself. Heidegger seldom uses the word in either of these senses; but he does use it in ways which are somewhat analogous. In one sense Dasein's 'Verfassung' is its 'constitution', the way it is constituted, '*sa condition humaine*'. In another sense Dasein may have several 'Verfassungen' as constitutive 'states' or factors which enter into its 'constitution'. We shall, in general, translate 'Verfassung' as 'constitution' or 'constitutive state' according to the context; but in passages where 'constitutive state' would be cumbersome and there is little danger of ambiguity, we shall simply write 'state'. These states, however, must always be thought of as constitutive and essential, not as temporary or transitory stages like the 'state' of one's health or the 'state of the nation'. When Heidegger uses the word 'Konstitution', we shall usually indicate this by capitalizing 'Constitution'.

[2] '. . . weil es in der Beantwortung der Frage nicht um eine ableitende Begründung, sondern um aufweisende Grund-Freilegung geht.' Expressions of the form 'es geht . . . um—' appear very often in this work. We shall usually translate them by variants on '—is an issue for . . .'.

clear that this question is a peculiar one, in that a series of fundamental considerations is required for working it out, not to mention for solving it. But its distinctive features will come fully to light only when we have delimited it adequately with regard to its function, its aim, and its motives.

Hitherto our arguments for showing that the question must be restated have been motivated in part by its venerable origin but chiefly by the lack of a definite answer and even by the absence of any satisfactory formulation of the question itself. One may, however, ask what purpose this question is supposed to serve. Does it simply remain—or *is* it at all—a mere matter for soaring speculation about the most general of generalities, *or is it rather, of all questions, both the most basic and the most concrete?*

Being is always the Being of an entity. The totality of entities can, in accordance with its various domains, become a field for laying bare and delimiting certain definite areas of subject-matter. These areas, on their part (for instance, history, Nature, space, life, Dasein, language, and the like), can serve as objects which corresponding scientific investigations may take as their respective themes. Scientific research accomplishes, roughly and naïvely, the demarcation and initial fixing of the areas of subject-matter. The basic structures of any such area have already been worked out after a fashion in our pre-scientific ways of experiencing and interpreting that domain of Being in which the area of subject-matter is itself confined. The 'basic concepts' which thus arise remain our proximal clues for disclosing this area concretely for the first time. And although research may always lean towards this positive approach, its real progress comes not so much from collecting results and storing them away in 'manuals' as from inquiring into the ways in which each particular area is basically constituted [Grundverfassungen]—an inquiry to which we have been driven mostly by reacting against just such an increase in information.

The real 'movement' of the sciences takes place when their basic concepts undergo a more or less radical revision which is transparent to itself. The level which a science has reached is determined by how far it is *capable* of a crisis in its basic concepts. In such immanent crises the very relationship between positively investigative inquiry and those things themselves that are under interrogation comes to a point where it begins to totter. Among the various disciplines everywhere today there are freshly awakened tendencies to put research on new foundations.

Mathematics, which is seemingly the most rigorous and most firmly constructed of the sciences, has reached a crisis in its 'foundations'. In the controversy between the formalists and the intuitionists, the issue is one of obtaining and securing the primary way of access to what are supposedly the objects of this science. The relativity theory of *physics* arises from the tendency to exhibit the interconnectedness of Nature as it is 'in itself'. As a theory of the conditions under which we have access to Nature itself, it seeks to preserve the changelessness of the laws of motion by ascertaining all relativities, and thus comes up against the question of the structure of its own given area of study—the problem of matter. In *biology* there is an awakening tendency to inquire beyond the definitions which mechanism and vitalism have given for "life" and "organism", and to define anew the kind of Being which belongs to the living as such. In those *humane sciences which are historiological in character*,[1] the urge towards historical actuality itself has been strengthened in the course of time by tradition and by the way tradition has been presented and handed down: the history of literature is to become the history of problems. *Theology* is seeking a more primordial interpretation of man's Being towards God, prescribed by the meaning of faith itself and remaining within it. It is slowly beginning to understand once more Luther's insight that the 'foundation' on which its system of dogma rests has not arisen from an inquiry in which faith is primary, and that conceptually this 'foundation' not only is inadequate for the problematic of theology, but conceals and distorts it.

Basic concepts determine the way in which we get an understanding beforehand of the area of subject-matter underlying all the objects a science takes as its theme, and all positive investigation is guided by this understanding. Only after the area itself has been explored beforehand in a corresponding manner do these concepts become genuinely demonstrated and 'grounded'. But since every such area is itself obtained from the domain of entities themselves, this preliminary research, from which the basic concepts are drawn, signifies nothing else than an interpretation of those entities with regard to their basic state of Being. Such research must run ahead of the positive sciences, and it *can*. Here the work of Plato and Aristotle is evidence enough. Laying the foundations for the sciences in this way is different in principle from the kind of 'logic' which limps along after, investigating the status of some science as it chances to find it, in order to discover its 'method'. Laying the foundations, as we have described it, is rather a productive logic—in the sense that it leaps ahead,

---

[1] 'In den *historischen Geisteswissenschaften* . . .' Heidegger makes much of the distinction between 'Historie' and 'Geschichte' and the corresponding adjectives 'historisch' and 'geschichtlich'. 'Historie' stands for what Heidegger calls a 'science of history'. (See H. 375, 378.) 'Geschichte' usually stands for the kind of 'history' that actually *happens*. We shall as a rule translate these respectively as 'historiology' and 'history', following similar conventions in handling the two adjectives. See especially Sections 6 and 76 below.

as it were, into some area of Being, discloses it for the first time in the constitution of its Being, and, after thus arriving at the structures within it, makes these available to the positive sciences as transparent assignments for their inquiry.[1] To give an example, what is philosophically primary is neither a theory of the concept-formation of historiology nor the theory of historiological knowledge, nor yet the theory of history as the Object of historiology; what is primary is rather the Interpretation of authentically historical entities as regards their historicality.[2] Similarly the positive outcome of Kant's *Critique of Pure Reason* lies in what it has contributed towards the working out of what belongs to any Nature whatsoever, not in a 'theory' of knowledge. His transcendental logic is an *a priori* logic for the subject-matter of that area of Being called "Nature".

But such an inquiry itself—ontology taken in the widest sense without favouring any particular ontological directions or tendencies—requires a further clue. Ontological inquiry is indeed more primordial, as over against the ontical[3] inquiry of the positive sciences. But it remains itself naïve and opaque if in its researches into the Being of entities it fails to discuss the meaning of Being in general. And even the ontological task of constructing a non-deductive genealogy of the different possible ways of Being requires that we first come to an understanding of 'what we really mean by this expression "Being" '.

The question of Being aims therefore at ascertaining the *a priori* conditions not only for the possibility of the sciences which examine entities as entities of such and such a type, and, in so doing, already operate with an understanding of Being, but also for the possibility of those ontologies themselves which are prior to the ontical sciences and which provide their foundations. *Basically, all ontology, no matter how rich and firmly compacted a system of categories it has at its disposal, remains blind and perverted from its ownmost aim, if it has not first adequately clarified the meaning of Being, and conceived this clarification as its fundamental task.*

Ontological research itself, when properly understood, gives to the question of Being an ontological priority which goes beyond mere resumption of a venerable tradition and advancement with a problem that has hitherto been opaque. But this objectively scientific priority is not the only one.

[1] '. . . als durchsichtige Anweisungen des Fragens . . .'

[2] '. . . sondern die Intepretation des eigentlich geschichtlich Seienden auf seine Geschichtlichkeit'. We shall translate the frequently occurring term 'Geschichtlichkeit' as 'historicality'. Heidegger very occasionally uses the term 'Historizität', as on H. 20 below, and this will be translated as 'historicity'.

[3] While the terms 'ontisch' ('ontical') and 'ontologisch' ('ontological') are not explicitly defined, their meanings will emerge rather clearly. Ontological inquiry is concerned primarily with *Being*; ontical inquiry is concerned primarily with *entities* and the facts about them.

¶ *4. The Ontical Priority of the Question of Being*

Science in general may be defined as the totality established through an interconnection of true propositions.[1] This definition is not complete, nor does it reach the meaning of science. As ways in which man behaves, sciences have the manner of Being which this entity—man himself— possesses. This entity we denote by the term "*Dasein*". Scientific research is not the only manner of Being which this entity can have, nor is it the one which lies closest. Moreover, Dasein itself has a special distinctiveness as compared with other entities, and it is worth our while to bring this to view in a provisional way. Here our discussion must anticipate later analyses, in which our results will be authentically exhibited for the first time.

Dasein is an entity which does not just occur among other entities. Rather it is ontically distinguished by the fact that, in its very Being, that Being is an *issue* for it. But in that case, this is a constitutive state of Dasein's Being, and this implies that Dasein, in its Being, has a relationship towards that Being—a relationship which itself is one of Being.[2] And this means further that there is some way in which Dasein understands itself in its Being, and that to some degree it does so explicitly. It is peculiar to this entity that with and through its Being, this Being is disclosed to it. *Understanding of Being is itself a definite characteristic of Dasein's Being.* Dasein is ontically distinctive in that it *is* ontological.[3]

Here "Being-ontological" is not yet tantamount to "developing an ontology". So if we should reserve the term "ontology" for that theoretical inquiry which is explicitly devoted to the meaning of entities, then what we have had in mind in speaking of Dasein's "Being-ontological" is to be designated as something "pre-ontological". It does not signify simply "being-ontical", however, but rather "being in such a way that one has an understanding of Being".

That kind of Being towards which Dasein can comport itself in one way or another, and always does comport itself somehow, we call "*existence*" [*Existenz*]. And because we cannot define Dasein's essence by citing a "what" of the kind that pertains to a subject-matter [eines sachhaltigen Was], and because its essence lies rather in the fact that in each case it

---

[1] '. . . das Ganze eines Begründungszusammenhanges wahrer Sätze . . .' See H. 357 below.

[2] 'Zu dieser Seinsverfassung des Daseins gehört aber dann, dass es in seinem Sein zu diesem Sein ein Seinsverhältnis hat.' This passage is ambiguous and might also be read as: '. . . and this implies that Dasein, in its Being towards this Being, has a relationship of Being.'

[3] '. . . dass es ontologisch *ist*'. As 'ontologisch' may be either an adjective or an adverb, we might also write: '. . . that it *is* ontologically'. A similar ambiguity occurs in the two following sentences, where we read 'Ontologisch-sein' and 'ontisch-seiend' respectively.

has its Being to be, and has it as its own,[1] we have chosen to designate this entity as "Dasein", a term which is purely an expression of its Being [als reiner Seinsausdruck].

Dasein always understands itself in terms of its existence—in terms of a possibility of itself: to be itself or not itself. Dasein has either chosen these possibilities itself, or got itself into them, or grown up in them already. Only the particular Dasein decides its existence, whether it does so by taking hold or by neglecting. The question of existence never gets straightened out except through existing itself. The understanding of oneself which leads *along this way* we call *"existentiell"*.[2] The question of existence is one of Dasein's ontical 'affairs'. This does not require that the ontological structure of existence should be theoretically transparent. The question about that structure aims at the analysis [Auseinanderlegung] of what constitutes existence. The context [Zusammenhang] of such structures we call *"existentiality"*. Its analytic has the character of an understanding which is not existentiell, but rather *existential*. The task of an existential analytic of Dasein has been delineated in advance, as regards both its possibility and its necessity, in Dasein's ontical constitution.

So far as existence is the determining character of Dasein, the ontological analytic of this entity always requires that existentiality be considered beforehand. By "existentiality" we understand the state of Being that is constitutive for those entities that exist. But in the idea of such a constitutive state of Being, the idea of Being is already included. And thus even the possibility of carrying through the analytic of Dasein depends on working out beforehand the question about the meaning of Being in general.

Sciences are ways of Being in which Dasein comports itself towards entities which it need not be itself. But to Dasein, Being in a world is something that belongs essentially. Thus Dasein's understanding of Being pertains with equal primordiality both to an understanding of something like a 'world', and to the understanding of the Being of those entities which become accessible within the world.[3] So whenever an ontology takes for its theme entities whose character of Being is other than that of Dasein, it has its own foundation and motivation in Dasein's own ontical structure, in which a pre-ontological understanding of Being is comprised as a definite characteristic.

---

[1] '. . . dass es je sein Sein als seiniges zu sein hat . . .'

[2] We shall translate 'existenziell' by 'existentiell', and 'existenzial' by 'existential' There seems to be little reason for resorting to the more elaborate neologisms proposed by other writers.

[3] '. . . innerhalb der Welt . . .' Heidegger uses at least three expressions which might be translated as 'in the world': 'innerhalb der Welt', 'in der Welt', and the adjective (or adverb) 'innerweltlich'. We shall translate these respectively by 'within the world', 'in the world', and 'within-the-world'.

Therefore *fundamental ontology*, from which alone all other ontologies can take their rise, must be sought in the *existential analytic of Dasein.*

Dasein accordingly takes priority over all other entities in several ways. The first priority is an *ontical* one: Dasein is an entity whose Being has the determinate character of existence. The second priority is an *ontological* one: Dasein is in itself 'ontological', because existence is thus determinative for it. But with equal primordiality Dasein also possesses—as constitutive for its understanding of existence—an understanding of the Being of all entities of a character other than its own. Dasein has therefore a third priority as providing the ontico-ontological condition for the possibility of any ontologies. Thus Dasein has turned out to be, more than any other entity, the one which must first be interrogated ontologically.

But the roots of the existential analytic, on its part, are ultimately *existentiell*, that is, *ontical*. Only if the inquiry of philosophical research is itself seized upon in an existentiell manner as a possibility of the Being of each existing Dasein, does it become at all possible to disclose the existentiality of existence and to undertake an adequately founded onto-logical problematic. But with this, the ontical priority of the question of being has also become plain.

Dasein's ontico-ontological priority was seen quite early, though Dasein itself was not grasped in its genuine ontological structure, and did not even become a problem in which this structure was sought. Aristotle says: ἡ ψυχὴ τὰ ὄντα πώς ἐστιν.[vi] "Man's soul is, in a certain way, entities." The 'soul' which makes up the Being of man has αἴσθησις and νόησις among its ways of Being, and in these it discovers all entities, both in the fact that they are, and in their Being as they are—that is, always in their Being. Aristotle's principle, which points back to the ontological thesis of Parmenides, is one which Thomas Aquinas has taken up in a characteristic discussion. Thomas is engaged in the task of deriving the *'transcendentia'*—those characters of Being which lie beyond every possible way in which an entity may be classified as coming under some generic kind of subject-matter (every *modus specialis entis*), and which belong necessarily to anything, whatever it may be. Thomas has to demonstrate that the *verum* is such a *transcendens*. He does this by invoking an entity which, in accordance with its very manner of Being, is properly suited to 'come together with' entities of any sort whatever. This distinctive entity, the *ens quod natum est convenire cum omni ente*, is the soul (*anima*).[vii] Here the priority of 'Dasein' over all other entities emerges, although it has not been ontologically clarified. This priority has obviously nothing in common with a vicious subjectivizing of the totality of entities.

By indicating Dasein's ontico-ontological priority in this provisional manner, we have grounded our demonstration that the question of Being is ontico-ontologically distinctive. But when we analysed the structure of this question as such (Section 2), we came up against a distinctive way in which this entity functions in the very formulation of that question. Dasein then revealed itself as that entity which must first be worked out in an ontologically adequate manner, if the inquiry is to become a transparent one. But now it has been shown that the ontological analytic of Dasein in general is what makes up fundamental ontology, so that Dasein functions as that entity which in principle is to be *interrogated* beforehand as to its Being.

If to Interpret the meaning of Being becomes our task, Dasein is not only the primary entity to be interrogated; it is also that entity which already comports itself, in its Being, towards what we are asking about when we ask this question. But in that case the question of Being is nothing other than the radicalization of an essential tendency-of-Being which belongs to Dasein itself—the pre-ontological understanding of Being.

15

II

THE TWOFOLD TASK IN WORKING OUT THE QUESTION OF BEING. METHOD AND DESIGN OF OUR INVESTIGATION

¶ *5. The Ontological Analytic of Dasein as Laying Bare the Horizon for an Interpretation of the Meaning of Being in General*

IN designating the tasks of 'formulating' the question of Being, we have shown not only that we must establish which entity is to serve as our primary object of interrogation, but also that the right way of access to this entity is one which we must explicitly make our own and hold secure. We have already discussed which entity takes over the principal role within the question of Being. But how are we, as it were, to set our sights towards this entity, Dasein, both as something accessible to us and as something to be understood and interpreted?

In demonstrating that Dasein in ontico-ontologically prior, we may have misled the reader into supposing that this entity must also be what is given as ontico-ontologically primary not only in the sense that it can itself be grasped 'immediately', but also in that the kind of Being which it possesses is presented just as 'immediately'. Ontically, of course, Dasein is not only close to us—even that which is closest: we *are* it, each of us, we ourselves. In spite of this, or rather for just this reason, it is ontologically that which is farthest. To be sure, its ownmost Being is such that it has an understanding of that Being, and already maintains itself in each case as if its Being has been interpreted in some manner. But we are certainly not saying that when Dasein's own Being is thus interpreted pre-ontologically in the way which lies closest, this interpretation can be taken over as an appropriate clue, as if this way of understanding Being is what must emerge when one's ownmost state of Being is considered[1] as an ontological theme. The kind of Being which belongs to Dasein is rather such that, in understanding its own Being, it has a tendency to do so in terms of that entity towards which it comports itself proximally and in a way which is essentially constant—in terms of the 'world'. In Dasein itself, and therefore in its own understanding of Being, the way the world is

---

[1] 'Besinnung'. The earliest editions have 'Bestimmung' instead.

understood is, as we shall show, reflected back ontologically upon the way 16
in which Dasein itself gets interpreted.

Thus because Dasein is ontico-ontologically prior, its own specific state
of Being (if we understand this in the sense of Dasein's 'categorial
structure') remains concealed from it. Dasein is ontically 'closest' to itself
and ontologically farthest; but pre-ontologically it is surely not a stranger.

Here we have merely indicated provisionally that an Interpretation of
this entity is confronted with peculiar difficulties grounded in the kind of
Being which belongs to the object taken as our theme and to the very
behaviour of so taking it. These difficulties are not grounded in any short-
comings of the cognitive powers with which we are endowed, or in the
lack of a suitable way of conceiving—a lack which seemingly would not
be hard to remedy.

Not only, however, does an understanding of Being belong to Dasein,
but this understanding develops or decays along with whatever kind of
Being Dasein may possess at the time; accordingly there are many ways in
which it has been interpreted, and these are all at Dasein's disposal.
Dasein's ways of behaviour, its capacities, powers, possibilities, and vicissitudes, have been studied with varying extent in philosophical psychology,
in anthropology, ethics, and 'political science', in poetry, biography, and
the writing of history, each in a different fashion. But the question remains
whether these interpretations of Dasein have been carried through with
a primordial existentiality comparable to whatever existentiell primordiality they may have possessed. Neither of these excludes the
other but they do not necessarily go together. Existentiell interpretation can demand an existential analytic, if indeed we conceive of
philosophical cognition as something possible and necessary. Only when
the basic structures of Dasein have been adequately worked out with
explicit orientation towards the problem of Being itself, will what we
have hitherto gained in interpreting Dasein get its existential justification.

Thus an analytic of Dasein must remain our first requirement in the
question of Being. But in that case the problem of obtaining and securing
the kind of access which will lead to Dasein, becomes even more a burning
one. To put it negatively, we have no right to resort to dogmatic constructions and to apply just any idea of Being and actuality to this entity, no
matter how 'self-evident' that idea may be; nor may any of the 'categories' which such an idea prescribes be forced upon Dasein without
proper ontological consideration. We must rather choose such a way of
access and such a kind of interpretation that this entity can show itself in
itself and from itself [an ihm selbst von ihm selbst her]. And this
means that it is to be shown as it is *proximally and for the most part*—

possess, only because historicality is a determining characteristic for Dasein in the very basis of its Being. If this historicality remains hidden from Dasein, and as long as it so remains, Dasein is also denied the possibility of historiological inquiry or the discovery of history. If historiology is wanting, this is not evidence *against* Dasein's historicality; on the contrary, as a deficient mode[1] of this state of Being, it is evidence for it. Only because it is 'historical' can an era be unhistoriological.

On the other hand, if Dasein has seized upon its latent possibility not only of making its own existence transparent to itself but also of inquiring into the meaning of existentiality itself (that is to say, of previously inquiring into the meaning of Being in general), and if by such inquiry its eyes have been opened to its own essential historicality, then one cannot fail to see that the inquiry into Being (the ontico-ontological necessity of which we have already indicated) is itself characterized by historicality. The ownmost meaning of Being which belongs to the inquiry into Being a s a n historical inquiry, gives u s the assignment [Anweisung] o f inquiring into the history of that inquiry itself, that is, of becoming historiological. In working out the question of Being, we must heed this assignment, so that by positively making the past our own, we may bring ourselves into full possession of the ownmost possibilities of such inquiry. The question of the meaning of Being must be carried through by explicating Dasein beforehand in its temporality and historicality; the question thus brings itself to the point where it understands itself as historiological.

Our preparatory Interpretation of the fundamental structures of Dasein with regard to the average kind of Being which is closest to it (a kind of Being in which it is therefore proximally historical as well), will make manifest, however, not only that Dasein is inclined to fall back upon its world (the world in which it is) and to interpret itself in terms of that world by its reflected light, but also that Dasein simultaneously falls prey to the tradition of which it has more or less explicitly taken hold.[2] This tradition keeps it from providing its own guidance, whether in

---

[1] 'defizienter Modus'. Heidegger likes to think of certain characteristics as occurring in various ways or 'modes', among which may be included certain ways of 'not occurring' or 'occurring only to an inadequate extent' or, in general, occurring 'deficiently'. It is as if zero and the negative integers were to be thought of as representing 'deficient modes of being a positive integer'.

[2] '. . . das Dasein hat nicht nur die Geneigtheit, an seine Welt, in der es ist, zu verfallen and reluzent aus ihr her sich auszulegen, Dasein verfällt in eins damit auch seiner mehr oder minder ausdrücklich ergriffenen Tradition.' The verb 'verfallen' is one which Heidegger will use many times. Though we shall usually translate it simply as 'fall', it has the connotation of *deteriorating, collapsing,* or *falling down.* Neither our 'fall back upon' nor our 'falls prey to' is quite right: but 'fall upon' and 'fall on to', which are more literal, would be misleading for 'an . . . zu verfallen'; and though 'falls to the lot of' and 'devolves upon' would do well for 'verfällt' with the dative in other contexts, they will not do so well here.

inquiring or in choosing. This holds true—and by no means least—for that understanding which is rooted in Dasein's ownmost Being, and for the possibility of developing it—namely, for ontological understanding.

When tradition thus becomes master, it does so in such a way that what it 'transmits' is made so inaccessible, proximally and for the most part, that it rather becomes concealed. Tradition takes what has come down to us and delivers it over to self-evidence; it blocks our access to those primordial 'sources' from which the categories and concepts handed down to us have been in part quite genuinely drawn.[1] Indeed it makes us forget that they have had such an origin, and makes us suppose that the necessity of going back to these sources is something which we need not even understand. Dasein has had its historicality so thoroughly uprooted by tradition that it confines its interest to the multiformity of possible types, directions, and standpoints of philosophical activity in the most exotic and alien of cultures; and by this very interest it seeks to veil the fact that it has no ground of its own to stand on. Consequently, despite all its historiological interests and all its zeal for an Interpretation which is philologically 'objective' ["sachliche"], Dasein no longer understands the most elementary conditions which would alone enable it to go back to the past in a positive manner and make it productively its own.

We have shown at the outset (Section 1) not only that the question of the meaning of Being is one that has not been attended to and one that has been inadequately formulated, but that it has become quite forgotten in spite of all our interest in 'metaphysics'. Greek ontology and its history —which, in their numerous filiations and distortions, determine the conceptual character of philosophy even today—prove that when Dasein understands either itself or Being in general, it does so in terms of the 'world', and that the ontology which has thus arisen has deteriorated [verfällt] to a tradition in which it gets reduced to something self-evident —merely material for reworking, as it was for Hegel. In the Middle Ages this uprooted Greek ontology became a fixed body of doctrine. Its systematics, however, is by no means a mere joining together of traditional pieces into a single edifice. Though its basic conceptions of Being have been taken over dogmatically from the Greeks, a great deal of unpretentious work has been carried on further within these limits. With the peculiar character which the Scholastics gave it, Greek ontology has, in its essentials, travelled the path that leads through the *Disputationes metaphysicae* of Suarez to the 'metaphysics' and transcendental philosophy of modern times, determining even the foundations and the aims of Hegel's

[1] In this passage Heidegger juxtaposes a number of words beginning with the prefix 'über-'; 'übergibt' ('transmits'); 'überantwortet' ('delivers over'); 'das Überkommene' ('what has come down to us'); 'überlieferten' ('handed down to us').

'logic'. In the course of this history certain distinctive domains of Being have come into view and have served as the primary guides for subsequent problematics: the *ego cogito* of Descartes, the subject, the "I", reason, spirit, person. But these all remain uninterrogated as to their Being and its structure, in accordance with the thoroughgoing way in which the question of Being has been neglected. It is rather the case that the categorial content of the traditional ontology has been carried over to these entities with corresponding formalizations and purely negative restrictions, or else dialectic has been called in for the purpose of Interpreting the substantiality of the subject ontologically.

If the question of Being is to have its own history made transparent, then this hardened tradition must be loosened up, and the concealments which it has brought about[1] must be dissolved. We understand this task as one in which by taking *the question of Being as our clue*, we are to destroy the traditional content of ancient ontology until we arrive at those primordial experiences in which we achieved our first ways of determining the nature of Being—the ways which have guided us ever since.

In thus demonstrating the origin of our basic ontological concepts by an investigation in which their 'birth certificate' is displayed, we have nothing to do with a vicious relativizing of ontological standpoints. But this destruction is just as far from having the *negative* sense of shaking off the ontological tradition. We must, on the contrary, stake out the positive possibilities of that tradition, and this always means keeping it within its *limits*; these in turn are given factically in the way the question is formulated at the time, and in the way the possible field for investigation is thus bounded off. On its negative side, this destruction does not relate itself towards the past; its criticism is aimed at 'today' and at the prevalent way of treating the history of ontology, whether it is headed towards doxography, towards intellectual history, or towards a history of problems. But to bury the past in nullity [Nichtigkeit] is not the purpose of this destruction; its aim is *positive*; its negative function remains unexpressed and indirect.

The destruction of the history of ontology is essentially bound up with the way the question of Being is formulated, and it is possible only within such a formulation. In the framework of our treatise, which aims at working out that question in principle, we can carry out this destruction only with regard to stages of that history which are in principle decisive.

In line with the positive tendencies of this destruction, we must in the first instance raise the question whether and to what extent the

---

[1] '. . . der durch sie gezeitigten Verdeckungen.' The verb 'zeitigen' will appear frequently in later chapters. See H. 304 and our note ad loc.

Interpretation of Being and the phenomenon of time have been brought together thematically in the course of the history of ontology, and whether the problematic of Temporality required for this has ever been worked out in principle or ever could have been. The first and only person who has gone any stretch of the way towards investigating the dimension of Temporality or has even let himself be drawn hither by the coercion of the phenomena themselves is Kant. Only when we have established the problematic of Temporality, can we succeed in casting light on the obscurity of his doctrine of the schematism. But this will also show us *why* this area is one which had to remain closed off to him in its real dimensions and its central ontological function. Kant himself was aware that he was venturing into an area of obscurity: 'This schematism of our understanding as regards appearances and their mere form is an art hidden in the depths of the human soul, the true devices of which are hardly ever to be divined from Nature and laid uncovered before our eyes.'[1] Here Kant shrinks back, as it were, in the face of something which must be brought to light as a theme and a principle if the expression "Being" is to have any demonstrable meaning. In the end, those very phenomena which will be exhibited under the heading of 'Temporality' in our analysis, are precisely those *most covert* judgments of the 'common reason' for which Kant says it is the 'business of philosophers' to provide an analytic.

In pursuing this task of destruction with the problematic of Temporality as our clue, we shall try to Interpret the chapter on the schematism and the Kantian doctrine of time, taking that chapter as our point of departure. At the same time we shall show why Kant could never achieve an insight into the problematic of Temporality. There were two things that stood in his way: in the first place, he altogether neglected the problem of Being; and, in connection with this, he failed to provide an ontology with Dasein as its theme or (to put this in Kantian language) to give a preliminary ontological analytic of the subjectivity of the subject. Instead of this, Kant took over Descartes' position quite dogmatically, notwithstanding all the essential respects in which he had gone beyond him. Furthermore, in spite of the fact that he was bringing the phenomenon of time back into the subject again, his analysis of it remained oriented towards the traditional way in which time had been ordinarily understood; in the long run this kept him from working out the phenomenon of a 'transcendental determination of time' in its own structure and function. Because of this double effect of tradition the decisive *connection* between *time* and the '*I think*' was shrouded in utter darkness; it did not even become a problem.

In taking over Descartes' ontological position Kant made an essential omission: he failed to provide an ontology of Dasein. This omission was a decisive one in the spirit [im Sinne] of Descartes' ownmost Tendencies. With the *'cogito sum'* Descartes had claimed that he was putting philosophy on a new and firm footing. But what he left undetermined when he began in this 'radical' way, was the kind of Being which belongs to the *res cogitans*, or—more precisely—the *meaning of the Being of the 'sum'*.[1] By working out the unexpressed ontological foundations of the *'cogito sum'*, we shall complete our sojourn at the second station along the path of our destructive retrospect of the history of ontology. Our Interpretation will not only prove that Descartes had to neglect the question of Being altogether; it will also show why he came to suppose that the absolute 'Being-certain' ["Gewisssein"] of the *cogito* exempted him from raising the question of the meaning of the Being which this entity possesses.

Yet Descartes not only continued to neglect this and thus to accept a completely indefinite ontological status for the *res cogitans sive mens sive animus* ['the thing which cognizes, whether it be a mind or spirit']: he regarded this entity as a *fundamentum inconcussum*, and applied the medieval ontology to it in carrying through the fundamental considerations of his *Meditationes*. He defined the *res cogitans* ontologically as an *ens*; and in the medieval ontology the meaning of Being for such an *ens* had been fixed by understanding it as an *ens creatum*. God, as *ens infinitum*, was the *ens i n c r e a t u m*. But createdness [Geschaffenheit] in the widest sense of something's having been produced [Hergestelltheit], was an essential item in the structure of the ancient conception of Being. The seemingly new beginning which Descartes proposed for philosophizing has revealed itself as the implantation of a baleful prejudice, which has kept later generations from making any thematic ontological analytic of the 'mind' ["Gemütes"] such as would take the question of Being as a clue and would at the same time come to grips critically with the traditional ancient ontology.

Everyone who is acquainted with the middle ages sees that Descartes is 'dependent' upon medieval scholasticism and employs its terminology. But with this 'discovery' nothing is achieved philosophically as long as it remains obscure to what a profound extent the medieval ontology has influenced the way in which posterity has determined or failed to determine the ontological character of the *res cogitans*. The full extent of this cannot be estimated until both the meaning and the limitations of the ancient ontology have been exhibited in terms of an orientation directed

[1] We follow the later editions in reading *'der Seinssinn des "sum"'*. The earlier editions have an anacoluthic 'den' for 'der'.

towards the question of Being. In other words, in our process of destruction we find ourselves faced with the task of Interpreting the basis of the ancient ontology in the light of the problematic of Temporality. When this is done, it will be manifest that the ancient way of interpreting the Being of entities is oriented towards the 'world' or 'Nature' in the widest sense, and that it is indeed in terms of 'time' that its understanding of Being is obtained. The outward evidence for this (though of course it is *merely* outward evidence) is the treatment of the meaning of Being as παρουσία or οὐσία, which signifies, in ontologico-Temporal terms, 'presence' ["Anwesenheit"].[1] Entities are grasped in their Being as 'presence'; this means that they are understood with regard to a definite mode of time—the *'Present'*[2]

The problematic of Greek ontology, like that of any other, must take its clues from Dasein itself. In both ordinary and philosophical usage, Dasein, man's Being, is 'defined' as the ζῷον λόγον ἔχον—as that living thing whose Being is essentially determined by the potentiality for discourse.[3] λέγειν is the clue for arriving at those structures of Being which belong to the entities we encounter in addressing ourselves to anything or speaking about it [im Ansprechen und Besprechen]. (Cf. Section 7 B.) This is why the ancient ontology as developed by Plato turns into 'dialectic'. As the ontological clue gets progressively worked out—namely, in the 'hermeneutic' of the λόγος—it becomes increasingly possible to grasp the problem of Being in a more radical fashion. The 'dialectic', which has been a genuine philosophical embarrassment, becomes superfluous. That

---

[1] The noun οὐσία is derived from one of the stems used in conjugating the irregular verb εἶναι, ('to be'); in the Aristotelian tradition it is usually translated as 'substance', though translators of Plato are more likely to write 'essence', 'existence', or 'being'. Heidegger suggests that οὐσία is to be thought of as synonymous with the derivative noun παρουσία ('being-at', 'presence'). As he points out, παρουσία has a close etymological correspondence with the German 'Anwesenheit', which is similarly derived from the stem of a verb meaning 'to be' (Cf. O.H.G. 'wesan') and a prefix of the place or time at which ('an-'). We shall in general translate 'Anwesenheit' as 'presence', and the participle 'anwesend' as some form of the expression 'have presence'.

[2] 'die "Gegenwart"'. While this noun may, like παρουσία or 'Anwesenheit', mean the *presence* of someone *at* some place or on some occasion, it more often means the *present*, as distinguished from the past and the future. In its etymological root-structure, however, it means a *waiting-towards*. While Heidegger seems to think of all these meanings as somehow fused, we shall generally translate this noun as 'the Present', reserving 'in the present' for the corresponding adjective 'gegenwärtig'.

[3] The phrase ζῷον λόγον ἔχον is traditionally translated as 'rational animal', on the assumption that λόγος refers to the faculty of *reason*. Heidegger, however, points out that λόγος is derived from the same root as the verb λέγειν ('to talk', 'to hold discourse'); he identifies this in turn with νοεῖν ('to cognize', 'to be aware of', 'to know'), and calls attention to the fact that the same stem is found in the adjective διαλεκτικός ('dialectical'). (See also H. 165 below.) He thus interprets λόγος as 'Rede', which we shall usually translate as 'discourse' or 'talk', depending on the context. See Section 7 B below (H. 32 ff.) and Sections 34 and 35, where 'Rede' will be defined and distinguished both from 'Sprache' ('language') and from 'Gerede' ('idle talk') (H. 160 ff.).

is *why* Aristotle 'no longer has any understanding' of it, for he has put it on a more radical footing and raised it to a new level [aufhob]. λέγειν itself—or rather νοεῖν, that simple awareness of something present-at-hand in its sheer presence-at-hand,[1] which Parmenides had already taken to guide him in his own interpretation of Being—has the Temporal structure of a pure 'making-present' of something.[2] Those entities which show themselves in this and for it, and which are understood as entities in the most authentic sense, thus get interpreted with regard to the Present; that is, they are conceived as presence (οὐσία).[3]

Yet the Greeks have managed to interpret Being in this way without any explicit knowledge of the clues which function here, without any acquaintance with the fundamental ontological function of time or even any understanding of it, and without any insight into the reason why this function is possible. On the contrary, they take time itself as one entity among other entities, and try to grasp it in the structure of its Being, though that way of understanding Being which they have taken as their horizon is one which is itself naïvely and inexplicitly oriented towards time.

Within the framework in which we are about to work out the principles of the question of Being, we cannot present a detailed Temporal Interpretation of the foundations of ancient ontology, particularly not of its loftiest and purest scientific stage, which is reached in Aristotle. Instead we shall give an interpretation of Aristotle's essay on time,[ii] which may be chosen as providing a way of *discriminating* the basis and the limitations of the ancient science of Being.

Aristotle's essay on time is the first detailed Interpretation of this

---

[1] '. . . von etwas Vorhandenem in seiner puren Vorhandenheit . . .' The adjective 'vorhanden' means literally 'before the hand', but this signification has long since given way to others. In ordinary German usage it may, for instance, be applied to the stock of goods which a dealer has 'on hand', or to the 'extant' works of an author; and in earlier philosophical writing it could be used, like the word 'Dasein' itself, as a synonym for the Latin '*existentia*'. Heidegger, however, distinguishes quite sharply between 'Dasein' and 'Vorhandenheit', using the latter to designate a kind of Being which belongs to things *other* than Dasein. We shall translate 'vorhanden' as 'present-at-hand', and 'Vorhandenheit' as 'presence-at-hand'. The reader must be careful not to confuse these expressions with our 'presence' ('Anwesenheit') and 'the Present' ('die Gegenwart'), etc., or with a few other verbs and adjectives which we may find it convenient to translate by 'present'.

[2] '. . . des reinen "Gegenwärtigens" von etwas'. The verb 'gegenwärtigen', which is derived from the adjective 'gegenwärtig', is not a normal German verb, but was used by Husserl and is used extensively by Heidegger. While we shall translate it by various forms of 'make present', it does not necessarily mean 'making physically present', but often means something like 'bringing vividly to mind'.

[3] 'Das Seiende, das sich in ihm für es zeigt und das als das eigentliche Seiende verstanden wird, erhält demnach seine Auslegung in Rücksicht auf—Gegen-wart, d.h. es ist als Anwesenheit (οὐσία) begriffen.' The hyphenation of 'Gegen-wart' calls attention to the structure of this word in a way which cannot be reproduced in English. See note 2, p. 47, H. 25 above. The pronouns 'ihm' and 'es' presumably both refer back to λέγειν, though their reference is ambiguous, as our version suggests.

phenomenon which has come down to us. Every subsequent account of time, including Bergson's, has been essentially determined by it. When we analyse the Aristotelian conception, it will likewise become clear, as we go back, that the Kantian account of time operates within the structures which Aristotle has set forth; this means that Kant's basic ontological orientation remains that of the Greeks, in spite of all the distinctions which arise in a new inquiry.

The question of Being does not achieve its true concreteness until we have carried through the process of destroying the ontological tradition. In this way we can fully prove that the question of the meaning of Being is one that we cannot avoid, and we can demonstrate what it means to talk about 'restating' this question.

In any investigation in this field, where 'the thing itself is deeply veiled'[iii] one must take pains not to overestimate the results. For in such an inquiry one is constantly compelled to face the possibility of disclosing an even more primordial and more universal horizon from which we may draw the answer to the question, "What is *'Being'*?" We can discuss such possibilities seriously and with positive results only if the question of Being has been reawakened and we have arrived at a field where we can come to terms with it in a way that can be controlled.

¶ 7. *The Phenomenological Method of Investigation*

In provisionally characterizing the object which serves as the theme of our investigation (the Being of entities, or the meaning of Being in general), it seems that we have also delineated the method to be employed. The task of ontology is to explain Being itself and to make the Being of entities stand out in full relief. And the method of ontology remains questionable in the highest degree as long as we merely consult those ontologies which have come down to us historically, or other essays of that character. Since the term "ontology" is used in this investigation in a sense which is formally broad, any attempt to clarify the method of ontology by tracing its history is automatically ruled out.

When, moreover, we use the term "ontology", we are not talking about some definite philosophical discipline standing in interconnection with the others. Here one does not have to measure up to the tasks of some discipline that has been presented beforehand; on the contrary, only in terms of the objective necessities of definite questions and the kind of treatment which the 'things themselves' require, can one develop such a discipline.

With the question of the meaning of Being, our investigation comes up against the fundamental question of philosophy. This is one that must be treated *phenomenologically*. Thus our treatise does not subscribe to a 'standpoint' or represent any special 'direction'; for phenomenology is nothing of either sort, nor can it become so as long as it understands itself. The expression 'phenomenology' signifies primarily a *methodological conception*. This expression does not characterize the w h a t of the objects of philosophical research as subject-matter, but rather the *how* of that research. The more genuinely a methodological concept is worked out and the more comprehensively it determines the principles on which a science is to be conducted, all the more primordially is it rooted in the way we come to terms with the things themselves,[1] and the farther is it removed from what we call "technical devices", though there are many such devices even in the theoretical disciplines.

Thus the term 'phenomenology' expresses a maxim which can be formulated as 'To the things themselves!' It is opposed to all free-floating constructions and accidental findings; it is opposed to taking over any conceptions which only seem to have been demonstrated; it is opposed to those pseudo-questions which parade themselves as 'problems', often for generations at a time. Yet this maxim, one may rejoin, is abundantly self-evident, and it expresses, moreover, the underlying principle of any scientific knowledge whatsoever. Why should anything so self-evident be taken up explicitly in giving a title to a branch of research? In point of fact, the issue here is a kind of 'self-evidence' which we should like to bring closer to us, so far as it is important to do so in casting light upon the procedure of our treatise. We shall expound only the preliminary conception [Vorbegriff] of phenomenology.

This expression has two components: "phenomenon" and "logos". Both of these go back to terms from the Greek: φαινόμενον and λόγος. Taken superficially, the term "phenomenology" is formed like "theology", "biology", "sociology"—names which may be translated as "science of God", "science of life", "science of society". This would make phenomenology the *science of phenomena*. We shall set forth the preliminary conception of phenomenology by characterizing what one has in mind in the term's two components, 'phenomenon' and 'logos', and by establishing the meaning of the name in which these are *put together*. The history of

---

[1] The appeal to the 'Sachen selbst', which Heidegger presents as virtually a slogan for Husserl's phenomenology, is not easy to translate without giving misleading impressions. What Husserl has in mind is the 'things' that words may be found to signify when their significations are correctly intuited by the right kind of *Anschauung*. (Cf. his *Logische Untersuchungen*, vol. 2, part 1, second edition, Halle, 1913, p. 6.) We have followed Marvin Farber in adopting 'the things themselves'. (Cf. his *The Foundation of Phenomenology*, Cambridge, Mass., 1943, pp. 202-3.) The word 'Sache' will, of course, be translated in other ways also.

the word itself, which presumably arose in the Wolffian school, is here of no significance.

A. The Concept of Phenomenon

The Greek expression φαινόμενον, to which the term 'phenomenon' goes back, is derived from the verb φαίνεσθαι, which signifies "to show itself". Thus φαινόμενον means that which shows itself, the manifest [das, was sich zeigt, das Sichzeigende, das Offenbare]. φαίνεσθαι itself is a *middle-voiced* form which comes from φαίνω—to bring to the light of day, to put in the light. Φαίνω comes from the stem φα—, like φῶς, the light, that which is bright—in other words, that wherein something can become manifest, visible in itself. Thus we must *keep in mind* that the expression '*phenomenon*' signifies *that which shows itself in itself*, the manifest. Accordingly the φαινόμενα or 'phenomena' are the totality of what lies in the light of day or can be brought to the light—what the Greeks some-times identified simply with τὰ ὄντα (entities). Now an entity can show itself from itself [von ihm selbst her] in many ways, depending in each case on the kind of access we have to it. Indeed it is even possible for an entity to show itself as something which in itself it is *not*. When it shows itself in this way, it 'looks like something or other' ["sieht" . . . "so aus wie . . ."]. This kind of showing-itself is what we call "*seeming*" [*Scheinen*]. Thus in Greek too the expression φαινόμενον ("phenomenon") signifies that which looks like something, that which is 'semblant', 'semblance' [das "Scheinbare", der "Schein"]. Φαινόμενον ἀγαθόν means some-thing good which looks like, but 'in actuality' is not, what it gives itself out to be. If we are to have any further understanding of the concept of phenomenon, everything depends on our seeing how what is designated in the first signification of φαινόμενον ('phenomenon' as that which shows itself) and what is designated in the second ('phenomenon' as semblance) are structurally interconnected. Only when the meaning of something is such that it makes a pretension of showing itself—that is, of being a phenome-non—*can* it show itself *as* something which it is *not*; only then can it 'merely look like so-and-so'. When φαινόμενον signifies 'semblance', the primordial signification (the phenomenon as the manifest) is already included as that upon which the second signification is founded. We shall allot the term 'phenomenon' to this positive and primordial signification of φαινόμενον, and distinguish "phenomenon" from "semblance", which is the privative modification of "phenomenon" as thus defined. But what *both* these terms express has proximally nothing at all to do with what is called an 'appearance', or still less a 'mere appearance'.[1]

[1] '. . . was man "Erscheinung" oder gar "blosse Erscheinung" nennt.' Though the noun 'Erscheinung' and the verb 'erscheinen' behave so much like the English 'appear-ance' and 'appear' that the ensuing discussion presents relatively few difficulties in this

This is what one is talking about when one speaks of the 'symptoms of a disease' ["Krankheitserscheinungen"]. Here one has in mind certain occurrences in the body which show themselves and which, in showing themselves a s thus showing themselves, 'indicate' ["indizieren"] something which does *not* show itself. The emergence [Auftreten] of such occurrences, their showing-themselves, goes together with the Being-present-at-hand of disturbances which do not show themselves. Thus appearance, as the appearance 'of something', does *not* mean showing-itself; it means rather the announcing-itself by [von] something which does not show itself, but which announces itself through something which does show itself. Appearing is a *not-showing-itself*. But the 'not' we find here is by no means to be confused with the privative "not" which we used in defining the structure of semblance.[1] What appears does *not* show itself; and anything which thus fails to show itself, is also something which can never s e e m.[2] All indications, presentations, symptoms, and symbols have this basic formal structure of appearing, even though they differ among themselves.

respect for the translator, the passage shows some signs of hasty construction, and a few comments may be helpful. We are told several times that 'appearance' and 'phenomenon' are to be sharply distinguished; yet we are also reminded that there is a sense in which they coincide, and even this sense seems to be twofold, though it is not clear that Heidegger is fully aware of this. The whole discussion is based upon two further distinctions: the distinction between 'showing' ('zeigen') and 'announcing' ('melden') and 'bringing forth' ('hervorbringen'), and the distinction between ('*x*') that which 'shows itself' ('das Sichzeigende') or which 'does the announcing' ('das Meldende') or which 'gets brought forth' ('das Hervorgebrachte'), and ('*y*') that which 'announces itself' ('das Sichmeldende') or which does the bringing-forth. Heidegger is thus able to introduce the following senses of 'Erscheinung' or 'appearance':

    1a. an observable event *y*, such as a symptom which announces a disease *x* by showing itself, and in or through which *x* announces itself without showing itself;

    1b. *y*'s showing-itself;

    2. *x*'s announcing-itself in or through *y*;

    3a. the 'mere appearance' *y* which *x* may *bring forth* when *x* is of such a kind that its real nature can *never* be made manifest;

    3b. the 'mere appearance' which is the *bringing-forth* of a 'mere appearance' in sense 3a.
Heidegger makes abundantly clear that sense 2 is the proper sense of 'appearance' and that senses 3a and 3b are the proper senses of 'mere appearance'. On H. 30 and 31 he concedes that sense 1b corresponds to the primordial sense of 'phenomenon'; but his discussion on H. 28 suggests that 1a corresponds to this more accurately, and he reverts to this position towards the end of H. 30.

    [1] '. . . als welches es die Struktur des Scheins bestimmt.' (The older editions omit the 'es'.)

    [2] 'Was sich in *der* Weise *nicht* zeigt, wie das Erscheinende, kann auch nie scheinen.' This passage is ambiguous, but presumably 'das Erscheinende' is to be interpreted as the *x* of our note 1, p. 51, not our *y*. The reader should notice that our standardized translation of 'scheinen' as 'seem' is one which here becomes rather misleading, even though these words correspond fairly well in ordinary usage. In distinguishing between 'scheinen' and 'erscheinen', Heidegger seems to be insisting that 'scheinen' can be done only by the *y* which 'shows itself' or 'does the announcing', not by the *x* which 'announces itself' in or through *y*, even though German usage does not differentiate these verbs quite so sharply.

In spite of the fact that 'appearing' is never a showing-itself in the sense of "phenomenon", appearing is possible only *by reason of a showing-itself* of something. But this showing-itself, which helps to make possible the appearing, is not the appearing itself. Appearing is an *announcing*-itself [das Sich-*melden*] through something that shows itself. If one then says that with the word 'appearance' we allude to something wherein something appears without being itself an appearance, one has not thereby defined the concept of phenomenon: one has rather *presupposed* it. This presupposition, however, remains concealed; for when one says this sort of thing about 'appearance', the expression 'appear' gets used in two ways. "That wherein something 'appears' " means that wherein something announces itself, and therefore does not show itself; and in the words [Rede] 'without being itself an "appearance" ', "appearance" signifies the *showing-itself*. But this showing-itself belongs essentially to the 'wherein' in which something announces itself. According to this, phenomena are *never* appearances, though on the other hand every appearance is dependent on phenomena. If one defines "phenomenon" with the aid of a conception of 'appearance' which is still unclear, then everything is stood on its head, and a 'critique' of phenomenology on this basis is surely a remarkable undertaking.

So again the expression 'appearance' itself can have a double signification: first, *appearing*, in the sense of announcing-itself, as not-showing-itself; and next, that which does the announcing [das Meldende selbst]— that which in its showing-itself indicates something which does not show itself. And finally one can use "appearing" as a term for the genuine sense of "phenomenon" as showing-itself. If one designates these three different things as 'appearance', bewilderment is unavoidable.

But this bewilderment is essentially increased by the fact that 'appearance' can take on still another signification. That which does the announcing—that which, in its showing-itself, indicates something non-manifest— may be taken as that which emerges in what is itself non-manifest, and which emanates [ausstrahlt] from it in such a way indeed that the non-manifest gets thought of as something that is essentially *never* manifest. When that which does the announcing is taken this way, "appearance" is tantamount to a "bringing forth" or "something brought forth", but something which does not make up the real Being of what brings it forth: here we have an appearance in the sense of 'mere appearance'. That which does the announcing and is brought forth does, of course, show itself, and in such a way that, as an emanation of what it announces, it keeps this very thing constantly veiled in itself. On the other hand, this not-showing which veils is not a semblance. Kant uses the term "appearance" in this twofold way. According to him "appearances" are, in the first place, the 'objects of empirical intuition': they are what shows itself in such intuition. But what thus shows itself (the "phenomenon" in the genuine primordial sense) is at the same time an 'appearance' as an emanation of something which *hides* itself in that appearance—an emanation which announces.

In so far as a phenomenon is constitutive for 'appearance' in the signi-' fication of announcing itself through something which shows itself, though such a phenomenon can privatively take the variant form of semblance, appearance too can become mere semblance. In a certain kind of lighting someone can look as if his cheeks were flushed with red; and the redness which shows itself can be taken as an announcement of the Being-present-at-hand of a fever, which in turn indicates some disturbance in the organism.

"*Phenomenon*", the showing-itself-in-itself, signifies a distinctive way in which something can be encountered.[1] "*Appearance*", on the other hand, means a reference-relationship which i s in an entity itself,[2] and which is such that what *does the referring* (or the announcing) can fulfil its possible function only if it shows itself in itself and is thus a 'phenomenon'. Both appearance and semblance are founded upon the phenomenon, though in different ways. The bewildering multiplicity of 'phenomena' designated by the words "phenomenon", "semblance", "appearance", "mere appearance", cannot be disentangled unless the concept of the phenomenon is understood from the beginning as that which shows itself in itself.

If in taking the concept of "phenomenon" this way, we leave indefinite which entities we consider as "phenomena", and leave it open whether what shows itself is an entity or rather some characteristic which an entity may have in its Being, then we have merely arrived at the *formal* conception of "phenomenon". If by "that which shows itself" we understand those entities which are accessible through the empirical "intuition" in, let us say, Kant's sense, then the formal conception of "phenomenon" will indeed be legitimately employed. In this usage "phenomenon" has the signification of the *ordinary* conception of phenomenon. But this ordinary conception is not the phenomenological conception. If we keep within the horizon of the Kantian problematic, we can give an illustration of what is conceived phenomenologically as a "phenomenon", with reservations as to other differences; for we may then say that that which already shows itself in the appearance as prior to the "phenomenon" as

---

[1] '. . . eine ausgezeichnete Begegnisart von etwas.' The noun 'Begegnis' is derived from the verb 'begegnen', which is discussed in note 2, p. 70, H. 44 below.

[2] '. . . einen seienden Verweisungsbezug im Seienden selbst . . .' The verb 'verweisen', which we shall translate as 'refer' or 'assign', depending upon the context, will receive further attention in Section 17 below. See also our note 2, p. 97, H. 68 below.

ordinarily understood and as accompanying it in every case, can, even though it thus shows itself unthematically, be brought thematically to show itself; and what thus shows itself in itself (the 'forms of the intuition') will be the "phenomena" of phenomenology. For manifestly space and time must be able to show themselves in this way—they must be able to become phenomena—if Kant is claiming to make a transcendental assertion grounded in the facts when he says that space is the *a priori* "inside-which" of an ordering.[1]

If, however, the phenomenological conception of phenomenon is to be understood at all, regardless of how much closer we may come to determining the nature of that which shows itself, this presupposes inevitably that we must have an insight into the meaning of the formal conception of phenomenon and its legitimate employment in an ordinary signification.—But before setting up our preliminary conception of phenomenology, we must also define the signification of λόγος so as to make clear in what sense phenomenology can be a 'science of' phenomena at all.

B. *The Concept of the Logos*

In Plato and Aristotle the concept of the λόγος has many competing significations, with no basic signification positively taking the lead. In fact, however, this is only a semblance, which will maintain itself as long as our Interpretation is unable to grasp the basic signification properly in its primary content. If we say that the basic signification of λόγος is "discourse",[2] then this word-for-word translation will not be validated until we have determined what is meant by "discourse" itself. The real signification of "discourse", which is obvious enough, gets constantly covered up by the later history of the word λόγος, and especially by the numerous and arbitrary Interpretations which subsequent philosophy has provided. Λόγος gets 'translated' (and this means that it is always getting interpreted) as "reason", "judgment", "concept", "definition", "ground", or "relationship".[3] But how can 'discourse' be so susceptible of modification that λόγος can signify all the things we have listed, and in good scholarly usage? Even if λόγος is understood in the sense of "assertion", but of "assertion" as 'judgment', this seemingly legitimate translation may still miss the fundamental signification, especially if "judgment" is conceived in a sense taken over from some contemporary 'theory of judgment'. Λόγος does not mean "judgment", and it certainly does not mean this

---

[1] Cf. *Critique of Pure Reason*[2], 'Transcendental Aesthetic', Section I, p. 34.

[2] On λόγος, 'Rede', etc., see note 3, p. 47, H. 25 above.

[3] '. . . Vernunft, Urteil, Begriff, Definition, Grund, Verhältnis.'

primarily—if one understands by "judgment" a way of 'binding' something with something else, or the 'taking of a stand' (whether by acceptance or by rejection).

Λόγος as "discourse" means rather the same as δηλοῦν: to make manifest what one is 'talking about' in one's discourse.[1] Aristotle has explicated this function of discourse more precisely as ἀποφαίνεσθαι.[1v] The λόγος lets something be seen (φαίνεσθαι), namely, what the discourse is about; and it does so either *for* the one who is doing the talking (the *medium*) or for persons who are talking with one another, as the case may be. Discourse 'lets something be seen' ἀπό . . .: that is, it lets us see something from the very thing which the discourse is about.[2] In discourse (ἀπόφανσις), so far as it is genuine, *what* is said [*was* geredet ist] is drawn *from* what the talk is about, so that discursive communication, in what it says [in ihrem Gesagten], makes manifest what it is talking about, and thus makes this accessible to the other party. This is the structure of the λόγος as ἀπόφανσις. This mode of making manifest in the sense of letting something be seen by pointing it out, does not go with all kinds of 'discourse'. Requesting (εὐχή), for instance, also makes manifest, but in a different way.

When fully concrete, discoursing (letting something be seen) has the character of speaking [Sprechens]—vocal proclamation in words. The λόγος is φωνή, and indeed, φωνὴ μετὰ φαντασίας—an utterance in which something is sighted in each case.

And only *because* the function of the λόγος as ἀπόφανσις lies in letting something be seen by pointing it out, can the λόγος have the structural form of σύνθεσις. Here "synthesis" does not mean a binding and linking together of representations, a manipulation of psychical occurrences where the 'problem' arises of how these bindings, as something inside, agree with something physical outside. Here the συν has a purely apophantical signification and means letting something be seen in its *togetherness* [Beisammen] with something—letting it be seen *as* something.

Furthermore, because the λόγος is a letting-something-be-seen, it can *therefore* be true or false. But here everything depends on our steering clear of any conception of truth which is construed in the sense of 'agreement'. This idea is by no means the primary one in the concept of ἀλήθεια. The 'Being-true' of the λόγος as ἀληθεύειν means that in λέγειν as ἀποφαίνεσθαι the entities *of which* one is talking must be taken out of their hiddenness; one must let them be seen as something unhidden (ἀληθές);

---

[1] '. . . offenbar machen das, wovon in der Rede "die Rede" ist.'
[2] '. . . von dem selbst her, wovon die Rede ist.'

that is, they must be *discovered*.[1] Similarly, 'Being false' (ψεύδεσθαι) amounts to deceiving in the sense of *covering up* [*verdecken*] : putting something in front of something (in such a way as to let it be seen) and thereby passing it off *as* something which it is *not*.

But because 'truth' has this meaning, and because the λόγος is a definite mode of letting something be seen, the λόγος is just *not* the kind of thing that can be considered as the primary 'locus' of truth. If, as has become quite customary nowadays, one defines "truth" as something that 'really' pertains to judgment,[2] and if one then invokes the support of Aristotle with this thesis, not only is this unjustified, but, above all, the Greek conception of truth has been misunderstood. Αἴσθησις, the sheer sensory perception of something, is 'true' in the Greek sense, and indeed more primordially than the λόγος which we have been discussing. Just as seeing aims at colours, any αἴσθησις aims at its ἴδια (those entities which are genuinely accessible only *through* it and *for* it); and to that extent this perception is always true. This means that seeing always discovers colours, and hearing always discovers sounds. Pure νοεῖν is the perception of the simplest determinate ways of Being which entities as such may possess, and it perceives them just by looking at them.[3] This νοεῖν is what is 'true' in the purest and most primordial sense; that is to say, it merely discovers, and it does so in such a way that it can never cover up. This νοεῖν can never cover up; it can never be false; it can at worst remain a *non-perceiving*, ἀγνοεῖν, not sufficing for straightforward and appropriate access.

When something no longer takes the form of just letting something be seen, but is always harking back to something else to which it points, so that it lets something be seen *as* something, it thus acquires a synthesis-structure, and with this it takes over the possibility of covering up.[4] The 'truth of judgments', however, is merely the opposite of this covering-up, a secondary phenomenon of truth, *with more than one kind of foundation*.[5] Both realism and idealism have—with equal thoroughness—missed the meaning of the Greek conception of truth, in terms of which only the

---

[1] The Greek words for 'truth' (ἡ ἀλήθεια, τὸ ἀληθές) are compounded of the privative prefix ἀ- ('not') and the verbal stem -λαθ- ('to escape notice', 'to be concealed'). The truth may thus be looked upon as that which is un-concealed, that which gets discovered or uncovered ('entdeckt').

[2] 'Wenn man ... Wahrheit als das bestimmt, was "eigentlich" dem Urteil zukommt...'

[3] '... das schlicht hinsehende Vernehmen der einfachsten Seinsbestimmungen des Seienden als solchen.'

[4] 'Was nicht mehr die Vollzugsform des reinen Sehenlassens hat, sondern je im Aufweisen auf ein anderes rekurriert und so je etwas *als* etwas sehen lässt, das übernimmt mit dieser Synthesisstruktur die Möglichkeit des Verdeckens.'

[5] '... ein *mehrfach fundiertes* Phänomen von Wahrheit.' A 'secondary' or 'founded' phenomenon is one which is based upon something else. The notion of 'Fundierung' is one which Heidegger has taken over from Husserl. See our note 1, p. 86, on H. 59 below.

possibility of something like a 'doctrine of ideas' can be understood as philosophical *knowledge*.

And because the function of the λόγος lies in merely letting something be seen, in *letting* entities be *perceived* [im *Vernehmenlassen* des Seienden], λόγος can signify the *reason* [*Vernunft*]. And because, moreover, λόγος is used not only with the signification of λέγειν but also with that of λεγόμενον (that which is exhibited, as such), and because the latter is nothing else than the ὑποκείμενον which, as present-at-hand, already lies at the *bottom* [zum *Grunde*] of any procedure of addressing oneself to it or discussing it, λόγος *qua* λεγόμενον means the ground, the *ratio*. And finally, because λόγος as λεγόμενον can also signify that which, as something to which one addresses oneself, becomes visible in its relation to something in its 'relatedness', λόγος acquires the signification of *relation* and *relationship*.[1]

This Interpretation of 'apophantical discourse' may suffice to clarify the primary function of the λόγος.

C. *The Preliminary Conception of Phenomenology*

When we envisage concretely what we have set forth in our Interpretation of 'phenomenon' and 'logos', we are struck by an inner relationship between the things meant by these terms. The expression "phenomenology" may be formulated in Greek as λέγειν τὰ φαινόμενα, where λέγειν means ἀποφαίνεσθαι. Thus "phenomenology" means ἀποφαίνεσθαι τὰ φαινόμενα—to let thatwhichshowsitselfbeseenfromitselfin thevery way in which it showsitselffrom itself. This is the formal meaning of that branch of research which calls itself "phenomenology". But here we are expressing nothing else than the maxim formulated above: 'To the things themselves!'

Thus the term "phenomenology" is quite different in its meaning from expressions such as "theology" and the like. Those terms designate the

---

[1] Heidegger is here pointing out that the word λόγος is etymologically akin to the verb λέγειν, which has among its numerous meanings those of *laying out, exhibiting, setting forth, recounting, telling a tale, making a statement*. Thus λόγος as λέγειν can be thought of as the faculty of 'reason' ('Vernunft') which makes such activities possible. But λόγος can also mean τὸ λεγόμενον (*that which* is laid out, exhibited, set forth, told); in this sense it is the underlying subject matter (τὸ ὑποκείμενον) to which one addresses oneself and which one discusses ('Ansprechen und Besprechen'); as such it lies 'at the bottom' ('zum Grunde') of what is exhibited or told, and is thus the 'ground' or 'reason' ('Grund') for telling it. But when something is exhibited or told, it is exhibited in its *relatedness* ('in seiner Bezogenheit'); and in this way λόγος as λεγόμενον comes to stand for just such a relation or relationship ('Beziehung und Verhältnis'). The three senses here distinguished correspond to three senses of the Latin '*ratio*', by which λόγος was traditionally translated, though Heidegger explicitly calls attention to only one of these. Notice that 'Beziehung' (which we translate as 'relation') can also be used in some contexts where 'Ansprechen' (our 'addressing oneself') would be equally appropriate. Notice further that 'Verhältnis' (our 'relationship'), which is ordinarily a synonym for 'Beziehung', can, like λόγος and '*ratio*', also refer to the special kind of relationship which one finds in a mathematical proportion. The etymological connection between 'Vernehmen' and 'Vernunft' should also be noted.

objects of their respective sciences according to the subject-matter which they comprise at the time [in ihrer jeweiligen Sachhaltigkeit]. 'Phenomenology' neither designates the object of its researches, nor characterizes the subject-matter thus comprised. The word merely informs us of the *"how"* with which *what* is to be treated in this science gets exhibited and handled. To have a science 'of' phenomena means to grasp its objects *in such a way* that everything about them which is up for discussion must be treated by exhibiting it directly and demonstrating it directly.[1] The expression 'descriptive phenomenology', which is at bottom tautological, has the same meaning. Here "description" does not signify such a procedure as we find, let us say, in botanical morphology; the term has rather the sense of a prohibition—the avoidance of characterizing anything without such demonstration. The character of this description itself, the specific meaning of the λόγος, can be established first of all in terms of the 'thinghood' ["Sachheit"] of what is to be 'described'—that is to say, of what is to be given scientific definiteness as we encounter it phenomenally. The signification of "phenomenon", as conceived both formally and in the ordinary manner, is such that any exhibiting of an entity as it shows itself in itself, may be called "phenomenology" with formal justification.

Now what must be taken into account if the formal conception of phenomenon is to be deformalized into the phenomenological one, and how is this latter to be distinguished from the ordinary conception? What is it that phenomenology is to 'let us see'? What is it that must be called a 'phenomenon' in a distinctive sense? What is it that by its very essence is *necessarily* the theme whenever we exhibit something *explicitly*? Manifestly, it is something that proximally and for the most part does *not* show itself at all: it is something that lies *hidden*, in contrast to that which proximally and for the most part does show itself; but at the same time it is something that belongs to what thus shows itself, and it belongs to it so essentially as to constitute its meaning and its ground.

Yet that which remains *hidden* in an egregious sense, or which relapses and gets *covered up* again, or which shows itself only '*in disguise*', is not just this entity or that, but rather the *Being* of entities, as our previous observations have shown. This Being can be covered up so extensively that it becomes forgotten and no question arises about it or about its meaning. Thus that which demands that it become a phenomenon, and which demands this in a distinctive sense and in terms of its ownmost content as a thing, is what phenomenology has taken into its grasp thematically as its object.

---

1 . . . in direkter Aufweisung und direkter Ausweisung . . .'

Phenomenology is our way of access to what is to be the theme of
ontology, and it is our way of giving it demonstrative precision. *Only as
phenomenology, is ontology possible.* In the phenomenological conception of
"phenomenon" what one has in mind as that which shows itself is the
Being of entities, its meaning, its modifications and derivatives.[1] And this
showing-itself is not just any showing-itself, nor is it some such thing as
appearing. Least of all can the Being of entities ever be anything such that
'behind it' stands something else 'which does not appear'.

'Behind' the phenomena of phenomenology there is essentially nothing
else; on the other hand, what is to become a phenomenon can be hidden.
And just because the phenomena are proximally and for the most part
not given, there is need for phenomenology. Covered-up-ness is the counter-
concept to 'phenomenon'.

There are various ways in which phenomena can be covered up. In the
first place, a phenomenon can be covered up in the sense that it is still
quite *undiscovered*. It is neither known nor unknown.[2] Moreover, a
phenomenon can be *buried over* [*verschüttet*]. This means that it has at some
time been discovered but has deteriorated [verfiel] to the point of getting
covered up again. This covering-up can become complete; or rather—and
as a rule—what has been discovered earlier may still be visible, though
only as a semblance. Yet so much semblance, so much 'Being'.[3] This covering-up as a 'disguising' is both the most frequent and the most dangerous,
for here the possibilities of deceiving and misleading are especially
stubborn. Within a 'system', perhaps, those structures of Being—and
their concepts—which are still available but veiled in their indigenous
character, may claim their rights. For when they have been bound
together constructively in a system, they present themselves as something
'clear', requiring no further justification, and thus can serve as the point
of departure for a process of deduction.

The covering-up itself, whether in the sense of hiddenness, burying-
over, or disguise, has in turn two possibilities. There are coverings-up
which are accidental; there are also some which are necessary, grounded
in what the thing discovered consists in [der Bestandart des Entdeckten].
Whenever a phenomenological concept is drawn from primordial sources,

[1] 'Der phänomenologische Begriff von Phänomen meint als das Sichzeigende das Sein
des Seienden, seinen Sinn, seine Modifikationen und Derivate.'

[2] 'Über seinen Bestand gibt es weder Kenntnis noch Unkenntnis.' The earlier editions
have 'Erkenntnis' where the latter ones have 'Unkenntnis'. The word 'Bestand' always
presents difficulties in Heidegger; here it permits either of two interpretations, which we
have deliberately steered between: 'Whether there *is* any such thing, is neither known nor
unknown', and 'What it comprises is something of which we have neither knowledge
nor ignorance.'

[3] 'Wieviel Schein jedoch, soviel "Sein".'

there is a possibility that it may degenerate if communicated in the form of an assertion. It gets understood in an empty way and is thus passed on, losing its indigenous character, and becoming a free-floating thesis. Even in the concrete work of phenomenology itself there lurks the possibility that what has been primordially 'within our grasp' may become hardened so that we can no longer grasp it. And the difficulty of this kind of research lies in making it self-critical in a positive sense.

The way in which Being and its structures are encountered in the mode of phenomenon is one which must first of all be *wrested* from the objects of phenomenology. Thus the very *point of departure* [*Ausgang*] for our analysis requires that it be secured by the proper method, just as much as does our *access* [*Zugang*] to the phenomenon, or our *passage* [*Durchgang*] through whatever is prevalently covering it up. The idea of grasping and explicating phenomena in a way which is 'original' and 'intuitive' ["originären" und "intuitiven"] is directly opposed to the *naïveté* of a haphazard, 'immediate', and unreflective 'beholding'. ["Schauen"].

Now that we have delimited our preliminary conception of phenomenology, the terms *'phenomenal'* and *phenomenological'* can also be fixed in their signification. That which is given and explicable in the way the phenomenon is encountered is called 'phenomenal'; this is what we have in mind when we talk about "phenomenal structures". Everything which belongs to the species of exhibiting and explicating and which goes to make up the way of conceiving demanded by this research, is called 'phenomenological'.

Because phenomena, as understood phenomenologically, are never anything but what goes to make up Being, while Being is in every case the Being of some entity, we must first bring forward the entities themselves if it is our aim that Being should be laid bare; and we must do this in the right way. These entities must likewise show themselves with the kind of access which genuinely belongs to them. And in this way the ordinary conception of phenomenon becomes phenomenologically relevant. If our analysis is to be authentic, its aim is such that the prior task of assuring ourselves 'phenomenologically' of that entity which is to serve as our example, has already been prescribed as our point of departure.

With regard to its subject-matter, phenomenology is the science of the Being of entities—ontology. In explaining the tasks of ontology we found it necessary that there should be a fundamental ontology taking as its theme that entity which is ontologico-ontically distinctive, Dasein, in order to confront the cardinal problem—the question of the meaning of Being in general. Our investigation itself will show that the meaning of phenomenological description as a method lies in *interpretation*. The λόγος of the phenomenology of Dasein has the character of a ἑρμηνεύειν, through which the authentic meaning of Being, and also those basic structures of Being which Dasein itself possesses, are *made known* to Dasein's understanding of Being. The phenomenology of Dasein is a *hermeneutic* in the primordial signification of this word, where it designates this business of interpreting. But to the extent that by uncovering the meaning of Being and the basic structures of Dasein in general we may exhibit the horizon for any further ontological study of those entities which do not have the character of Dasein, this hermeneutic also becomes a 'hermeneutic' in the sense of working out the conditions on which the possibility of any ontological investigation depends. And finally, to the extent that Dasein, as an entity with the possibility of existence, has ontological priority over every other entity, "hermeneutic", as an interpretation of Dasein's Being, has the third and specific sense of an analytic of the existentiality of existence; and this is the sense which is philosophically *primary*. Then so far as this hermeneutic works out Dasein's historicality ontologically as the ontical condition for the possibility of historiology, it contains the roots of what can be called 'hermeneutic' only in a derivative sense: the methodology of those humane sciences which are historiological in character.

Being, as the basic theme of philosophy, is no class or genus of entities; yet it pertains to every entity. Its 'universality' is to be sought higher up. Being and the structure of Being lie beyond every entity and every possible character which an entity may possess. *Being is the transcendens pure and simple.*[1] And the transcendence of Dasein's Being is distinctive in that it implies the possibility and the necessity of the most radical *individuation*. Every disclosure of Being as the *transcendens* is *transcendental* knowledge. *Phenomenological truth (the disclosedness of Being) is veritas transcendentalis.*

Ontology and phenomenology are not two distinct philosophical disciplines among others. These terms characterize philosophy itself with regard to its object and its way of treating that object. Philosophy is universal phenomenological ontology, and takes its departure from the hermeneutic of Dasein, which, as an analytic of *existence*, has made fast the guiding-line for all philosophical inquiry at the point where it *arises* and to which it *returns*.

The following investigation would have have been possible if the ground had not been prepared by Edmund Husserl, with whose *Logische Untersuchungen* phenomenology first emerged. Our comments on the preliminary conception of phenomenology have shown that what is essential in it

---

[1] 'Sein und Seinsstruktur liegen über jedes Seiende and jede mögliche seiende Bestimmtheit eines Seienden hinaus. *Sein ist das transcendens schlechthin.*'

does not lie in its *actuality* as a philosophical 'movement' ["Richtung"]. Higher than actuality stands *possibility*. We can understand phenomenology only by seizing upon it as a possibility.[v]

With regard to the awkwardness and 'inelegance' of expression in the analyses to come, we may remark that it is one thing to give a report in which we tell about *entities*, but another to grasp entities in their *Being*. For the latter task we lack not only most of the words but, above all, the 'grammar'. If we may allude to some earlier researchers on the analysis of Being, incomparable on their own level, we may compare the ontological sections of Plato's *Parmenides* or the fourth chapter of the seventh book of Aristotle's *Metaphysics* with a narrative section from Thucydides; we can then see the altogether unprecedented character of those formulations which were imposed upon the Greeks by their philosophers. And where our powers are essentially weaker, and where moreover the area of Being to be disclosed is ontologically far more difficult than that which was presented to the Greeks, the harshness of our expression will be enhanced, and so will the minuteness of detail with which our concepts are formed.

¶ 8. Design of the Treatise

The question of the meaning of Being is the most universal and the emptiest of questions, but at the same time it is possible to individualize it very precisely for any particular Dasein. If we are to arrive at the basic concept of 'Being' and to outline the ontological conceptions which it requires and the variations which it necessarily undergoes, we need a clue which is concrete. We shall proceed towards the concept of Being by way of an Interpretation of a certain special entity, Dasein, in which we shall arrive at the horizon for the understanding of Being and for the possibility of interpreting it; the universality of the concept of Being is not belied by the relatively 'special' character of our investigation. But this very entity, Dasein, is in itself 'historical', so that its ownmost ontological elucidation necessarily becomes an 'historiological' Interpretation.

Accordingly our treatment of the question of Being branches out into two distinct tasks, and our treatise will thus have two parts:

Part One: the Interpretation of Dasein in terms of temporality, and the explication of time as the transcendental horizon for the question of Being.

Part Two: basic features of a phenomenological destruction of the history of ontology, with the problematic of Temporality as our clue.

Part One has *three divisions*

1. the preparatory fundamental analysis of Dasein;
2. Dasein and temporality;
3. time and Being.[1]

Part Two likewise has *three divisions :*[1]

1. Kant's doctrine of schematism and time, as a preliminary stage in a problematic of Temporality;
2. the ontological foundation of Descartes' *'cogito sum'*, and how the medieval ontology has been taken over into the problematic of the *'res cogitans'* ;
3. Aristotle's essay on time, as providing a way of discriminating the phenomenal basis and the limits of ancient ontology.

[1] Part Two and the third division of Part One have never appeared.

THE INTERPRETATION OF DASEIN IN TERMS OF TEMPORALITY, AND THE EXPLICATION OF TIME AS THE TRANSCENDENTAL HORIZON FOR THE QUESTION OF BEING

DIVISION ONE

PREPARATORY FUNDAMENTAL ANALYSIS OF DASEIN

In the question about the meaning of Being, what is primarily interrogated is those entities which have the character of Dasein. The preparatory existential analytic of Dasein must, in accordance with its peculiar character, be expounded in outline, and distinguished from other kinds of investigation which seem to run parallel (Chapter 1.) Adhering to the procedure which we have fixed upon for starting our investigation, we must lay bare a fundamental structure in Dasein: Being-in-the-world (Chapter 2). In the interpretation of Dasein, this structure is something 'a priori'; it is not pieced together, but is primordially and constantly a whole. It affords us, however, various ways of looking at the items which are constitutive for it. The whole of this structure always comes first; but if we keep this constantly in view, these items, as phenomena, will be made to stand out. And thus we shall have as objects for analysis: the world in its worldhood (Chapter 3), Being-in-the-world as Being-with and Being-one's-Self (Chapter 4), and Being-in as such (Chapter 5). By analysis of this fundamental structure, the Being of Dasein can be indicated provisionally. Its existential meaning is *care* (Chapter 6).

I

EXPOSITION OF THE TASK OF A PREPARATORY ANALYSIS OF DASEIN

¶ *9. The Theme of the Analytic of Dasein*

WE are ourselves the entities to be analysed. The Being of any such entity is *in each case mine*.[1] These entities, in their Being, comport themselves towards their Being. As entities with such Being, they are delivered over to their own Being.[2] *Being* is that which is an issue for every such entity.[3] This way of characterizing Dasein has a double consequence:

1. The 'essence' ["Wesen"] of this entity lies in its "to be" [Zu-sein]. Its Being-what-it-is [Was-sein] (*essentia*) must, so far as we can speak of it at all, be conceived in terms of its Being (*existentia*). But here our ontological task is to show that when we choose to designate the Being of this entity as "existence" [Existenz], this term does not and cannot have the onto-logical signification of the traditional term "*existentia*"; ontologically, *existentia* is tantamount to *Being-present-at-hand*, a kind of Being which is essentially inappropriate to entities of Dasein's character. To avoid getting bewildered, we shall always use the Interpretative expression "*presence-at-hand*" for the term "*existentia*", while the term "existence", as a designation of Being, will be allotted solely to Dasein.

The essence of Dasein lies in its existence. Accordingly those characteristics which can be exhibited in this entity are not 'properties' present-at-hand of some entity which 'looks' so and so and is itself present-at-hand; they are in each case possible ways for it to be, and no more than that. All the Being-as-it-is [So-sein] which this entity possesses is primarily Being. So when we designate this entity with the term 'Dasein', we are expressing not its "what" (as if it were a table, house or tree) but its Being.

2. That Being which is an *issue* for this entity in its very Being, is in each case mine. Thus Dasein is never to be taken ontologically as an

---

[1] 'Das Seiende, dessen Analyse zur Aufgabe steht, sind wir je selbst. Das Sein dieses Seienden ist *je meines*.' The reader must not get the impression that there is anything solipsistic about the second of these sentences. The point is merely that the kind of Being which belongs to Dasein is of a sort which any of us may call his own.

[2] 'Als Seiendes dieses Seins ist es seinem eigenen Sein überantwortet.' The earlier editions read '. . . seinem eigenen Zu-sein . . .'

[3] See note 2, p. 28, H. 8 above.

instance or special case of some genus of entities as things that are present-at-hand.[1] To entities such as these, their Being is 'a matter of indifference';[2] or more precisely, they 'are' such that their Being can be neither a matter of indifference to them, nor the opposite. Because Dasein has *in each case mineness* [*Jemeinigkeit*], one must always use a *personal* pronoun when one addresses it: 'I am', 'you are'.

Furthermore, in each case Dasein is mine to be in one way or another. Dasein has always made some sort of decision as to the way in which it is in each case mine [je meines]. That entity which in its Being has this very Being as an issue, comports itself towards its Being as its ownmost possibility. In each case Dasein *is* its possibility, and it 'has' this possibility, but not just as a property [eigenschaftlich], as something present-at-hand would. And because Dasein is in each case essentially its own possibility, it *can*, in its very Being, 'choose' itself and win itself; it can also lose itself and never win itself; or only 'seem' to do so. But only in so far as it is essentially something which can be *authentic*—that is, something of its own[3] —can it havelostitselfand not yet won itself. As modesof Being, *authenticity* and *inauthenticity* (these expressions have been chosen terminologically in a strict sense) are both grounded in the fact that any Dasein whatsoever is characterized by mineness.[4] But the inauthenticity of Dasein doesnotsignify any 'less' Being or any 'lower' degree of Being. Rather it is the case that even in its fullest concretion Dasein can be characterized by inauthenticity —when busy, when excited, when interested, when ready for enjoyment.

The two characteristics of Dasein which we have sketched—the priority of '*existentia*' over *essentia*, and the fact that Dasein is in each case mine [die Jemeinigkeit]—have already indicated that in the analytic of this entity we are facing a peculiar phenomenal domain. Dasein does not have the kind of Being which belongs to something merely present-at-hand within the world, nor does it ever have it. So neither is it to be presented thematically as something we come across in the same way as

---

[1] '. . . als Vorhandenem'. The earlier editions have the adjective 'vorhandenem' instead of the substantive.

[2] 'gleichgültig'. This adjective must be distinguished from the German adjective 'indifferent', though they might both ordinarily be translated by the English 'indifferent', which we shall reserve exclusively for the former. In most passages, the latter is best translated by 'undifferentiated' or 'without further differentiation'; occasionally, however, it seems preferable to translate it by 'Indifferent' with an initial capital. We shall follow similar conventions with the nouns 'Gleichgültigkeit' and 'Indifferenz'.

[3] 'Und weil Dasein wesenhaft je seine Möglichkeit ist, *kann* dieses Seiende in seinem Sein sich selbst "wählen", gewinnen, es kann sich verlieren, bzw. nie und nur "scheinbar" gewinnen. Verloren habenkann es sich nur und noch nicht sich gewonnen haben kann es nur, sofern es seinem Wesen nach mögliches *eigentliches*, das heisst sich zueigen ist.' Older editions have 'je wesenhaft' and 'zueigenes'. The connection between 'eigentlich' ('authentic', 'real') and 'eigen' ('own') is lost in translation.

[4] '. . . dass Dasein überhaupt durch Jemeinigkeit bestimmt ist.'

we come across what is present-at-hand. The right way of presenting it is so far from self-evident that to determine what form it shall take is itself an essential part of the ontological analytic of this entity. Only by presenting this entity in the right way can we have any understanding of its Being. No matter how provisional our analysis may be, it always requires the assurance that we have started correctly.

In determining itself as an entity, Dasein always does so in the light of a possibility which it *is* itself and which, in its very Being, it somehow understands. This is the formal meaning of Dasein's existential constitution. But this tells us that if we are to Interpret this entity *ontologically*, the problematic of its Being must be developed from the existentiality of its existence. This cannot mean, however, that "Dasein" is to be construed in terms of some concrete possible idea of existence. At the outset of our analysis it is particularly important that Dasein should not be Interpreted with the differentiated character [Differenz] of some definite way of existing, but that it should be uncovered [aufgedeckt] in the undifferentiated character which it has proximally and for the most part. This undifferentiated character of Dasein's everydayness is *not nothing*, but a positive phenomenal characteristic of this entity. Out of this kind of Being —and back into it again—is all existing, such as it is.[1] We call this everyday undifferentiated character of Dasein *"averageness"* [*Durchschnittlichkeit*].

And because this average everydayness makes up what is ontically proximal for this entity, it has again and again been *passed over* in explicating Dasein. That which is ontically closest and well known, is ontologically the farthest and not known at all; and its ontological signification is constantly overlooked. When Augustine asks: *"Quid autem propinquius meipso mihi?"* and must answer: *"ego certe laboro hic et laboro in meipso: factus sum mihi terra difficultatis et sudoris nimii"*,[1] this applies not only to the ontical and pre-ontological opaqueness of Dasein but even more to the ontological task which lies ahead; for not only must this entity not be missed in that kind of Being in which it is phenomenally closest, but it must be made accessible by a positive characterization.

Dasein's average everydayness, however, is not to be taken as a mere 'aspect'. Here too, and even in the mode of inauthenticity, the structure of existentiality lies *a priori*. And here too Dasein's Being is an issue for it in a definite way; and Dasein comports itself towards it in the mode of average everydayness, even if this is only the mode of fleeing *in the face of it* and forgetfulness *thereof*.[2]

---

[1] 'Aus dieser Seinsart heraus und in sie zurück ist alles Existieren, wie est ist.'

[2] 'Auch in ihr geht es dem Dasein in bestimmter Weise um sein Sein, zu dem es sich im Modus der durchschnittlichen Alltäglichkeit verhält und sei es auch nur im Modus der Flucht *davor* und des Vergessens *seiner*.' For further discussion, see Section 40 below.

But the explication of Dasein in its average everydayness does not give us just average structures in the sense of a hazy indefiniteness. Anything which, taken ontically, *is* in an average way, can be very well grasped ontologically in pregnant structures which may be structurally indistinguishable from certain ontological characteristics [Bestimmungen] of an *authentic* Being of Dasein.

All *explicata* to which the analytic of Dasein gives rise are obtained by considering Dasein's existence-structure. Because Dasein's characters of Being are defined in terms of existentiality, we call them "*existentialia*". These are to be sharply distinguished from what we call "*categories*"—characteristics of Being for entities whose character is not that of Dasein.[1] Here we are taking the expression "category" in its primary ontological signification, and abiding by it. In the ontology of the ancients, the entities we encounter within the world[2] are taken as the basic examples for the interpretation of Being. Νοεῖν (or the λόγος, as the case may be) is accepted as a way of access to them.[3] Entities are encountered therein. But the Being of these entities must be something which can be grasped in a distinctive kind of λέγειν (letting something be seen), so that this Being becomes intelligible in advance as that which it is—and as that which it is already in every entity. In any discussion (λόγος) of entities, we have previously addressed ourselves to Being; this addressing is κατηγορεῖσθαι.[4] This signifies, in the first instance, making a public accusation, taking someone to task for something in the presence of everyone. When used ontologically, this term means taking an entity to task, as it were, for whatever it is as an entity—that is to say, letting everyone see it in its Being. The κατηγορίαι are what is sighted and what is visible in such a seeing.[5] They include the various ways in which the nature of those entities which can be addressed and discussed in a λόγος may be

1 'Weil sie sich aus der Existenzialität bestimmen, nennen wir die Seinscharaktere des Daseins *Existenzialien*. Sie sind scharf zu trennen von den Seinsbestimmungen des nicht daseinsmässigen Seienden, die wir *Kategorien* nennen.'

2 '. . . das innerhalb der Welt begegnende Seiende.' More literally: 'the entity that encounters within the world.' While Heidegger normally uses the verb 'begegnen' in this active intransitive sense, a similar construction with the English 'encounter' is unidiomatic and harsh. We shall as a rule use either a passive construction (as in 'entities encountered') or an active transitive construction (as in 'entities we encounter').

3 'Als Zugangsart zu ihm gilt das νοεῖν bzw. der λόγος.' Here we follow the reading of the earlier editions. In the later editions, 'Zugangsart', which is used rather often, is here replaced by 'Zugangsort', which occurs very seldom and is perhaps a misprint. This later version might be translated as follows: 'νοεῖν (or the λόγος, as the case may be) is accepted as the locus of access to such entities.' On νοεῖν and λόγος see Section 7 above, especially H. 32-34.

4 'Das je schon vorgängige Ansprechen des Seins im Besprechen (λόγος) des Seienden ist das κατηγορεῖσθαι.'

5 'Das in solchem Sehen Gesichtete und Sichtbare . . .' On 'Sehen' and 'Sicht' see H. 147.

determined *a priori*. *Existentialia* and categories are the two basic possibilities for characters of Being. The entities which correspond to them require different kinds of primary interrogation respectively: any entity is either a *"who"* (existence) or a *"what"* (presence-at-hand in the broadest sense). The connection between these two modes of the characters of Being cannot be handled until the horizon for the question of Being has been clarified.

In our introduction we have already intimated that in the existential analytic of Dasein we also make headway with a task which is hardly less pressing than that of the question of Being itself—the task of laying bare that *a priori* basis which must be visible before the question of 'what man is' can be discussed philosophically. The existential analytic of Dasein comes *before* any psychology or anthropology, and certainly before any biology. While these too are ways in which Dasein can be investigated, we can define the theme of our analytic with greater precision if we distinguish it from these. And at the same time the necessity of that analytic can thus be proved more incisively.

¶ 10. How the Analytic of Dasein is to be Distinguished from Anthropology, Psychology, and Biology

After a theme for investigation has been initially outlined in positive terms, it is always important to show what is to be ruled out, although it can easily become fruitless to discuss what is not going to happen. We must show that those investigations and formulations of the question which have been aimed at Dasein heretofore, have missed the real *philosophical* problem (notwithstanding their objective fertility), and that as long as they persist in missing it, they have no right to claim that they *can* accomplish that for which they are basically striving. In distinguishing the existential analytic from anthropology, psychology, and biology, we shall confine ourselves to what is in principle the ontological question. Our distinctions will necessarily be inadequate from the standpoint of 'scientific theory' simply because the scientific structure of the above-mentioned disciplines (not, indeed, the 'scientific attitude' of those who work to advance them) is today thoroughly questionable and needs to be attacked in new ways which must have their source in ontological problematics.

Historiologically, the aim of the existential analytic can be made plainer by considering Descartes, who is credited with providing the point of departure for modern philosophical inquiry by his discovery of the *"cogito sum"*. He investigates the *"cogitare"* of the *"ego"*, at least within certain limits. On the other hand, he leaves the *"sum"* completely undiscussed, even though it is regarded as no less primordial than the *cogito*. Our

4

analytic raises the ontological question of the Being of the "*sum*". Not until the nature of this Being has been determined can we grasp the kind of Being which belongs to *cogitationes*.

At the same time it is of course misleading to exemplify the aim of our analytic historiologically in this way. One of our first tasks will be to prove that if we posit an "I" or subject as that which is proximally given, we shall completely miss the phenomenal content [Bestand] of Dasein. *Ontologically*, every idea of a 'subject'—unless refined by a previous onto-logical determination of its basic character—still posits the *subjectum* (ὑποκείμενον) along with it, no matter how vigorous one's ontical protestations against the 'soul substance' or the 'reification of conscious-ness'. The Thinghood itself which such reification implies must have its ontological origin demonstrated if we are to be in a position to ask what we are to understand *positively* when we think of the unreified *Being* of the subject, the soul, the consciousness, the spirit, the person. All these terms refer to definite phenomenal domains which can be 'given form' ["ausformbare"]: but they are never used without a notable failure to see the need for inquiring about the Being of the entities thus designated. So we are not being terminologically arbitrary when we avoid these terms—or such expressions as 'life' and 'man'—in designating those entities which we are ourselves.

On the other hand, if we understand it rightly, in any serious and scientifically-minded 'philosophy of life' (this expression says about as much as "the botany of plants") there lies an unexpressed tendency towards an understanding of Dasein's Being. What is conspicuous in such a philosophy (and here it is defective in principle) is that here 'life' itself as a kind of Being does not become ontologically a problem.

The researches of Wilhelm Dilthey were stimulated by the perennial question of 'life'. Starting from 'life' itself as a whole, he tried to under-stand its 'Experiences'[1] in their structural and developmental inter-connec-tions. His '*geisteswissenschaftliche Psychologie*' is one which no longer seeks to be oriented towards psychical elements and atoms or to piece the life of the soul together, but aims rather at '*Gestalten*' and 'life as a whole'. Its philosophical relevance, however, is not to be sought here, but rather in the fact that in all this he was, *above all*, on his way towards the question of 'life'. To be sure, we can also see here very plainly how limited were both his problematic and the set of concepts with which it had to be put

---

[1] 'Die "Erlebnisse" dieses "Lebens" . . .' The connection between 'Leben' ('life') and 'Erlebnisse' ('Experiences') is lost in translation. An 'Erlebnis' is not just *any* 'experience' ('Erfahrung'), but one which we feel deeply and 'live through'. We shall translate 'Erlebnis' and 'erleben' by 'Experience' with a capital 'E', reserving 'experience' for 'Erfahrung' and 'erfahren'.

into words. These limitations, however, are found not only in Dilthey and Bergson but in all the 'personalitic' movements to which they have given direction and in every tendency towards a philosophical anthropology. The phenomenological Interpretation of personality is in principle more radical and more transparent; but the question of the Being of Dasein has a dimension which this too fails to enter. No matter how much Husserl[ii] and Scheler may differ in their respective inquiries, in their methods of conducting them, and in their orientations towards the world as a whole, they are fully in agreement on the negative side of their Interpretations of personality. The question of 'personal *Being*' itself is one which they no longer raise. We have chosen Scheler's Interpretation as an example, not only because it is accessible in print,[iii] but because he emphasizes personal Being explicitly as such, and tries to determine its character by defining the specific Being of acts as contrasted with anything 'psychical'. For Scheler, the person is never to be thought of as a Thing or a substance; the person 'is rather the *unity* of living-through [Er-lebens] which is immediately experienced in and with our Experiences—not a Thing merely thought of behind and outside what is immediately Experienced'.[iv] The person is no Thinglike and substantial Being. Nor can the Being of a person be entirely absorbed in being a subject of rational acts which follow certain laws.

The person is not a Thing, not a substance, not an object. Here Scheler is emphasizing what Husserl[v] suggests when he insists that the unity of the person must have a Constitution essentially different from that required for the unity of Things of Nature.[1] What Scheler says of the person, he applies to acts as well: 'But an act is never also an object; for it is essential to the Being of acts that they are Experienced only in their performance itself and given in reflection.'[vi] Acts are something non-psychical. Essentially the person exists only in the performance of intentional acts, and is therefore essentially *not* an object. Any psychical Objectification of acts, and hence any way of taking them as something psychical, is tantamount to depersonalization. A person is in any case given as a performer of intentional acts which are bound together by the unity of a meaning. Thus psychical Being has nothing to do with personal Being. Acts get performed; the person is a performer of acts. What, however, is the ontological meaning of 'performance'? How is the kind of Being which belongs to a person to be ascertained ontologically in a positive way? But the critical question cannot stop here. It must face the Being of the whole man, who is customarily taken as a unity of body,

---

[1] '... wenn er für die Einheit der Person eine wesentlich andere Konstitution fordert als für die der Naturdinge.' The second 'der' appears in the later editions only.

soul, and spirit. In their turn "body", "soul", and "spirit" may designate phenomenal domains which can be detached as themes for definite investigations; within certain limits their ontological indefiniteness may not be important. When, however, we come to the question of man's Being, this is not something we can simply compute[1] by adding together those kinds of Being which body, soul, and spirit respectively possess— kinds of Being whose nature has not as yet been determined. And even if we should attempt such an ontological procedure, some idea of the Being of the whole must be presupposed. But what stands in the way of the basic question of Dasein's Being (or leads it off the track) is an orientation thoroughly coloured by the anthropology of Christianity and the ancient world, whose inadequate ontological foundations have been overlooked both by the philosophy of life and by personalism. There are two important elements in this traditional anthropology:

1. 'Man' is here defined as a ζῷον λόγον ἔχον, and this is Interpreted to mean an *animal rationale*, something living which has reason. But the kind of Being which belongs to a ζῷον is understood in the sense of occurring and Being-present-at-hand. The λόγος is some superior endowment; the kind of Being which belongs to it, however, remains quite as obscure as that of the entire entity thus compounded.

2. The second clue for determining the nature of man's Being and essence is a *theological* one καὶ εἶπεν ὁ Θεός. ποιήσωμεν ἄνθρωπον κατ' εἰκόνα ἡμετέραν καὶ καθ' ὁμοίωσιν—'*faciamus hominem ad imaginem nostram et similitudinem*'[vii] With this as its point of departure, the anthropology of Christian theology, taking with it the ancient definition, arrives at an interpretation of that entity which we call "man". But just as the Being of God gets Interpreted ontologically by means of the ancient ontology, so does the Being of the *ens finitum*, and to an even greater extent. In modern times the Christian definition has been deprived of its theological character. But the idea of 'transcendence' —that man is something that reaches beyond himself—is rooted in Christian dogmatics, which can hardly be said to have made an ontological problem of man's Being. The idea of transcendence, according to which man is more than a mere something endowed with intelligence, has worked itself out with different variations. The following quotations will illustrate how these have originated: '*His praeclaris dotibus excelluit prima hominis conditio, ut ratio, intelligentia, prudentia, judicium non modo ad terrenae vitae gubernationem suppeterent, sed quibus t r a n s c e n d e r e t usque ad Deum et aeternam felicitatem.*'[viii] '*Denn dass der mensch sin u f s e h e n hat uf Gott und*

---

[1] Reading 'errechnet'. The earliest editions have 'verrechnet', with the correct reading provided in a list of *errata*.

sin wort, zeigt er klarlich an, dass er nach siner natur etwas Gott näher anerborn, etwas mee n a c h s c h l ä g t, etwas z u z u g s z u im hat, das alles on zwyfel darus flüsst, dass er nach dem b i l d n u s Gottes geschaffen ist'.[ix]

The two sources which are relevant for the traditional anthropology—the Greek definition and the clue which theology has provided—indicate that over and above the attempt to determine the essence of 'man' as an entity, the question of his Being has remained forgotten, and that this Being is rather conceived as something obvious or 'self-evident' in the sense of the *Being-present-at-hand* of other created Things. These two clues become intertwined in the anthropology of modern times, where the *res cogitans*, consciousness, and the interconnectedness of Experience serve as the point of departure for methodical study. But since even the *cogitationes* are either left ontologically undetermined, or get tacitly assumed as something 'self-evidently' 'given' whose 'Being' is not to be questioned, the decisive ontological foundations of anthropological problematics remain undetermined.

This is no less true of '*psychology*', whose anthropological tendencies are today unmistakable. Nor can we compensate for the absence of onto-logical foundations by taking anthropology and psychology and building them into the framework of a general *biology*. In the order which any possible comprehension and interpretation must follow, biology as a 'science of life' is founded upon the ontology of Dasein, even if not entirely. Life, in its own right, is a kind of Being; but essentially it is accessible only in Dasein. The ontology of life is accomplished by way of a privative Interpretation; it determines what must be the case if there can be anything like mere-aliveness [Nur-noch-leben]. Life is not a mere Being-present-at-hand, nor is it Dasein. In turn, Dasein is never to be defined ontologically by regarding it as life (in an ontologically indefinite manner) plus something else.

In suggesting that anthropology, psychology, and biology all fail to give an unequivocal and ontologically adequate answer to the question about the *kind of Being* which belongs to those entities which we ourselves are, we are not passing judgment on the positive work of these disciplines. We must always bear in mind, however, that these ontological foundations can never be disclosed by subsequent hypotheses derived from empirical material, but that they are always 'there' already, even when that empirical material simply gets *collected*. If positive research fails to see these foundations and holds them to be self-evident, this by no means proves that they are not basic or that they are not problematic in a more radical sense than any thesis of positive science can ever be.[x]

¶ 11. *The Existential Analytic and the Interpretation of Primitive Dasein. The Difficulties of Achieving a 'Natural Conception of the World'*

The Interpretation of Dasein in its everydayness, however, is not identical with the describing of some primitive stage of Dasein with which we can become acquainted empirically through the medium of anthropology. *Everydayness does not coincide with primitiveness*, but is rather a mode of Dasein's Being, even when that Dasein is active in a highly developed and differentiated culture—and precisely then. Moreover, even primitive Dasein has possibilities of a Being which is not of the everyday kind, and it has a specific everydayness *of its own*. To orient the analysis of Dasein towards the 'life of primitive peoples' can have positive significance [Bedeutung] as a method because 'primitive phenomena' are often less concealed and less complicated by extensive self-interpretation on the part of the Dasein in question. Primitive Dasein often speaks to us more directly in terms of a primordial absorption in 'phenomena' (taken in a pre-phenomenological sense). A way of conceiving things which seems, perhaps, rather clumsy and crude from our standpoint, can be positively helpful in bringing out the ontological structures of phenomena in a genuine way.

But heretofore our information about primitives has been provided by ethnology. And ethnology operates with definite preliminary conceptions and interpretations of human Dasein in general, even in first 'receiving' its material, and in sifting it and working it up. Whether the everyday psychology or even the scientific psychology and sociology which the ethnologist brings with him can provide any scientific assurance that we can have proper access to the phenomena we are studying, and can interpret them and transmit them in the right way, has not yet been established. Here too we are confronted with the same state of affairs as in the other disciplines we have discussed. Ethnology itself already presupposes as its clue an inadequate analytic of Dasein. But since the positive sciences neither 'can' nor should wait for the ontological labours of philosophy to be done, the further course of research will not take the form of an 'advance' but will be accomplished by *recapitulating* what has already been ontically discovered, and by purifying it in a way which is ontologically more transparent.[xi]

No matter how easy it may be to show how ontological problematics differ formally from ontical research there are still difficulties in carrying out an existential analytic, especially in *making a start*. This task includes a *desideratum* which philosophy has long found disturbing but has continually refused to achieve: *to work out the idea of a 'natural conception of the world'*. The rich store of information now available as to the most exotic and manifold cultures and forms of Dasein seems favourable to our setting about this task in a fruitful way. But this is merely a semblance. At bottom this plethora of information can seduce us into failing to recognize the real problem. We shall not get a genuine knowledge of essences simply by the syncretistic activity of universal comparison and classification. Subjecting the manifold to tabulation does not ensure any actual understanding of what lies there before us as thus set in order. If an ordering principle is genuine, it has its own content as a thing [Sachgehalt], which is never to be found by means of such ordering, but is already presupposed in it. So if one is to put various pictures of the world in order, one must have an explicit idea of the world as such. And if the 'world' itself is something constitutive for Dasein, one must have an insight into Dasein's basic structures in order to treat the world-phenomenon conceptually.

In this chapter we have characterized some things positively and taken a negative stand with regard to others; in both cases our goal has been to promote a correct understanding of the tendency which underlies the following Interpretation and the kind of questions which it poses. Ontology can contribute only indirectly towards advancing the positive disciplines as we find them today. It has a goal of its own, even if, beyond the acquiring of information about entities, the question of Being is the spur for all scientific seeking.

II

BEING-IN-THE-WORLD IN GENERAL AS THE BASIC STATE OF DASEIN

¶ *12. A Preliminary Sketch of Being-in-the-World, in terms of an Orientation towards Being-in as such*

In our preparatory discussions (Section 9) we have brought out some characteristics of Being which will provide us with a steady light for our further investigation, but which will at the same time become structurally concrete as that investigation continues. Dasein is an entity which, in its very Being, comports itself understandingly towards that Being. In saying this, we are calling attention to the formal concept of existence. Dasein exists. Furthermore, Dasein is an entity which in each case I myself am. Mineness belongs to any existent Dasein, and belongs to it as the condition which makes authenticity and inauthenticity possible. In each case Dasein exists in one or the other of these two modes, or else it is modally undifferentiated.[1]

But these are both ways in which Dasein's Being takes on a definite character, and they must be seen and understood *a priori* as grounded upon that state of Being which we have called "*Being-in-the-world*'. An interpretation of this constitutive state is needed if we are to set up our analytic of Dasein correctly.

The compound expression 'Being-in-the-world' indicates in the very way we have coined it, that it stands for a *unitary* phenomenon. This primary datum must be seen as a whole. But while Being-in-the-world cannot be broken up into contents which may be pieced together, this does not prevent it from having several constitutive items in its structure. Indeed the phenomenal datum which our expression indicates is one which may, in fact, be looked at in three ways. If we study it, keeping the whole phenomenon firmly in mind beforehand, the following items may be brought out for emphasis:

First, the '*in-the-world*'. With regard to this there arises the task of inquiring into the ontological structure of the 'world' and defining the idea of *worldhood* as such. (See the third chapter of this Division.)

---

[1] 'Zum existierenden Dasein gehört die Jemeinigkeit als Bedingung der Möglichkeit von Eigentlichkeit und Uneigentlichkeit. Dasein existiert je in einem dieser Modi, bzw. in der modalen Indifferenz ihrer.'

Second, that *entity* which in every case has Being-in-the-world as the way in which it is. Here we are seeking that which one inquires into when one asks the question 'Who?' By a phenomenological demonstration[1] we shall determine who is in the mode of Dasein's average everydayness. (See the fourth chapter of this Division.)

Third, *Being-in* [*In-sein*] as such. We must set forth the ontological Constitution of inhood [Inheit] itself. (See the fifth chapter of this Division.) Emphasis upon any one of these constitutive items signifies that the others are emphasized along with it; this means that in any such case the whole phenomenon gets seen. Of course Being-in-the-world is a state of Dasein[2] which is necessary *a priori*, but it is far from sufficient for completely determining Dasein's Being. Before making these three phenomena the themes for special analyses, we shall attempt by way of orientation to characterize the third of these factors.

What is meant by *"Being-in"*? Our proximal reaction is to round out this expression to "Being-in 'in the world' ", and we are inclined to understand this Being-in as 'Being in something' ["Sein in . . ."]. This latter term designates the kind of Being which an entity has when it is 'in' another one, as the water is 'in' the glass, or the garment is 'in' the cupboard. By this 'in' we mean the relationship of Being which two entities extended 'in' space have to each other with regard to their location in that space. Both water and glass, garment and cupboard, are 'in' space and 'at' a location, and both in the same way. This relationship of Being can be expanded: for instance, the bench is in the lecture-room, the lecture-room is in the university, the university is in the city, and so on, until we can say that the bench is 'in world-space'. All entities whose Being 'in' one another can thus be described have the same kind of Being —that of Being-present-at-hand—as Things occurring 'within' the world. Being-present-at-hand 'in' something which is likewise present-at-hand, and Being-present-at-hand-along-with [Mitvorhandensein] in the sense of a definite location-relationship with something else which has the same kind of Being, are ontological characteristics which we call *"categorial"*: they are of such a sort as to belong to entities whose kind of Being is not of the character of Dasein.

Being-in, on the other hand, is a state of Dasein's Being; it is an existentiale. So one cannot think of it as the Being-present-at-hand of some corporeal Thing (such as a human body) 'in' an entity which is present-at-hand. Nor does the term "Being-in" mean

---

[1] Here we follow the older editions in reading, 'Ausweisung'. The newer editions have 'Aufweisung' ('exhibition').

[2] '. . . Verfassung des Daseins . . .' The earliest editions read 'Wesens' instead 'Daseins'. Correction is made in a list of *errata*.

a spatial 'in-one-another-ness' of things present-at-hand, any more than the word 'in' primordially signifies a spatial relationship of this kind.[1] 'In' is derived from "*innan*"—"to reside",[1] "*habitare*", "to dwell" [sich auf halten]. '*An*' signifies "I am accustomed", "I am familiar with", "I look after something".[2] It has the signification of "*colo*" in the senses of "*habito*" and "*diligo*". The entity to which Being-in in this signification belongs is one which we have characterized as that entity which in each case I myself am [bin]. The expression '*bin*' is connected with '*bei*', and so '*ich bin*' ['I am'] means in its turn "I reside" or "dwell alongside" the world, as that which is familiar to me in such and such a way.[3] "Being" [Sein], as the infinitive of '*ich bin*' (that is to say, when it is understood as an *existentiale*), signifies "to reside alongside . . .", "to be familiar with . . .". "*Being-in*" *is thus the formal existential expression for the Being of Dasein, which has Being-in-the-world as its essential state.*

'Being alongside' the world in the sense of being absorbed in the world[4]

---

[1] Reading 'innan—wohnen'. As Heidegger points out in his footnote, this puzzling passage has its source in Grimm's *Kleinere Schriften*, Vol. VII, pp. 247 ff., where we find two short articles, the first entitled 'IN' and the second 'IN UND BEI'. The first article begins by comparing a number of archaic German words meaning '*domus*', all having a form similar to our English 'inn', which Grimm mentions. He goes on to postulate 'a strong verb "*innan*", which must have meant either "*habitare*", "*domi esse*", or "*recipere in domum*" ' (though only a weak derivative form '*innian*' is actually found), with a surviving strong preterite written either as '*an*' or as '*ann*'. Grimm goes on to argue that the preposition '*in*' is derived from the verb, rather than the verb from the preposition.

[2] '. . . "an" bedeutet: ich bin gewohnt, vertraut mit, ich pflege etwas . . .'
In Grimm's second article he adds: 'there was also an anomalous "*ann*" with the plural "*unnum*", which expressed "*amo*", "*diligo*", "*faveo*", and to which our "*gonnen*" and "*Gunst*" are immediately related, as has long been recognized. "*Ann*" really means "ich bin eingewohnt", "pflege zu bauen"; this conceptual transition may be shown with minimal complication in the Latin "*colo*", which stands for "*habito*" as well as "*diligo*".'
It is not entirely clear whether Heidegger's discussion of '*an*' is aimed to elucidate the preposition '*an*' (which corresponds in some of its usages to the English 'at', and which he has just used in remarking that the water and the glass are both *at* a location), or rather to explain the preterite '*an*' of 'innan'.
The reader should note that while the verb 'wohnen' normally means 'to reside' or 'to dwell', the expression 'ich bin gewohnt' means 'I am accustomed to', and 'ich bin einge-wohnt' means 'I have become accustomed to the place where I reside—to my surroundings'. Similarly 'ich pflege etwas' may mean either 'I am accustomed to do something' or 'I take care of something' or 'I devote myself to it'. (Grimm's 'pflege zu bauen' pre-sumably means 'I am accustomed to putting my trust in something', 'I can build on it'.) The Latin, '*colo*' has the parallel meanings of 'I take care of something' or 'cherish' it ('*diligo*') and 'I dwell' or 'I inhabit' ('*habito*').

[3] '. . . ich wohne, halte mich auf bei . . . der Welt, als dem so und so Vertrauten.' The preposition '*bei*', like '*an*', does not have quite the semantical range of any English pre-position. Our 'alongside', with which we shall translate it when other devices seem less satisfactory, especially in the phrase 'Being alongside' ('Sein bei'), is often quite mis-leading; the sense here is closer to that of 'at' in such expressions as 'at home' or 'at my father's', or that of the French '*chez*'. Here again Heidegger seems to be relying upon Grimm, who proceeds (*loc. cit.*) to connect '*bei*' with '*bauen*' ('build') and '*bin*'.

[4] '. . . in dem . . . Sinne des Aufgehens in der Welt . . .' 'Aufgehen' means literally 'to go up', or 'to rise' in the sense that the sun 'rises' or the dough 'rises'. But when followed by the preposition 'in', it takes on other meanings. Thus 5 '*geht auf*' into 30 in the sense that

(a sense which calls for still closer interpretation) is an *existentiale* founded upon Being-in. In these analyses the issue is one of *seeing* a primordial structure of Dasein's Being—a structure in accordance with whose phenomenal content the concepts of Being must be Articulated; because of this, and because this structure is in principle one which cannot be grasped by the traditional ontological categories, this 'being-alongside' must be examined still more closely. We shall again choose the method of contrasting it with a relationship of Being which is essentially different ontologically—*viz.* categorial—but which we express by the same linguistic means. Fundamental ontological distinctions are easily obliterated; and if they are to be envisaged phenomenally in this way, this must be done *explicitly*, even at the risk of discussing the 'obvious'. The status of the ontological analytic shows, however, that we have been far from interpreting these obvious matters with an adequate 'grasp', still less with regard for the meaning of their Being; and we are even farther from possessing a stable coinage for the appropriate structural concepts.

As an *existentiale*, 'Being alongside' the world never means anything like the Being-present-at-hand-together of Things that occur. There is no such thing as the 'side-by-side-ness' of an entity called 'Dasein' with another entity called 'world'. Of course when two things are present-at-hand together alongside one another,[1] we are accustomed to express this occasionally by something like 'The table stands "by" ['bei'] the door' or 'The chair "touches" ['berührt'] the wall'. Taken strictly, 'touching' is never what we are talking about in such cases, not because accurate re-examination will always eventually establish that there is a space between the chair and the wall, but because in principle the chair can never touch the wall, even if the space between them should be equal to zero. If the chair could touch the wall, this would presuppose that the wall is the sort of thing 'for' which a chair would be *encounterable*.[2] An entity present-at-hand within the world can be touched by another entity only if by its very nature the latter entity has Being-in as its own kind of Being—only if, with its Being-there [Da-sein], something like the world is already revealed to it, so that from out of that world another entity can manifest itself in touching, and thus become accessible in its Being-present-at-hand. When two entities are present-at-hand within the world, and furthermore are *worldless* in themselves, they can never 'touch' each other,

it 'goes into' 30 without remainder; a country '*geht auf*' into another country into which it is taken over or absorbed; a person '*geht auf*' in anything to which he devotes himself fully, whether an activity or another person. We shall usually translate '*aufgehen*' by some form of 'absorb'.

[1] 'Das Beisammen zweier Vorhandener . . .'

[2] 'Voraussetzung dafür wäre, dass die Wand "für" den Stuhl *begegnen* könnte.' (Cf. also H. 97 below.)

nor can either of them '*be*' '*alongside*' the other. The clause 'furthermore are worldless' must not be left out; for even entities which are not world-less—Dasein itself, for example—are present-at-hand 'in' the world, or, more exactly, *can* with some right and within certain limits be *taken* as merely present-at-hand. To do this, one must completely disregard or just not see the existential state of Being-in. But the fact that 'Dasein' can be taken as something which is present-at-hand and just present-at-hand, is not to be confused with a certain way of 'presence-at-hand' which is Dasein's *own*. This latter kind of presence-at-hand becomes accessible not by dis-regarding Dasein's specific structures but only by understanding them in advance. Dasein understands its ownmost Being in the sense of a certain 'factual Being-present-at-hand'.[ii] And yet the 'factuality' of the fact [Tatsache] of one's own Dasein is at bottom quite different ontologically from the factual occurrence of some kind of mineral, for example. When-ever Dasein is, it is as a Fact; and the factuality of such a Fact is what we shall call Dasein's "*facticity*".[1] This is a definite way of Being [Seinsbe-stimmtheit], and it has a complicated structure which cannot even be grasped *as a problem* until Dasein's basic existential states have been worked out. The concept of "facticity" implies that an entity 'within-the-world' has Being-in-the-world in such a way that it can understand itself as bound up in its 'destiny' with the Being of those entities which it encounters within its own world.

In the first instance it is enough to see the ontological difference between Being-in as an *existentiale* and the category of the 'insideness' which things present-at-hand can have with regard to one another. By thus delimiting Being-in, we are not denying every kind of 'spatiality' to Dasein. On the contrary, Dasein itself has a 'Being-in-space' of its own; but this in turn is possible only *on the basis of Being-in-the-world in general*. Hence Being-in is not to be explained ontologically by some ontical characterization, as if one were to say, for instance, that Being-in in a world is a spiritual property, and that man's 'spatiality' is a result of his bodily nature (which, at the same time, always gets 'founded' upon corporeality). Here again we are faced with the Being-present-at-hand-together of some such spiritual Thing along with a corporeal Thing, while the Being of the entity thus compounded remains more obscure

---

[1] 'Die Tatsächlichkeit des Faktums Dasein, als welches jeweilig jedes Dasein ist, nennen wir seine *Faktizität*.' We shall as a rule translate 'Tatsächlichkeit' as 'factuality', and 'Faktizität' as 'facticity', following our conventions for 'tatsächlich' and 'faktisch'. (See note 2, p. 27, H. 7 above.) The present passage suggests a comparable distinction between the nouns 'Tatsache' and 'Faktum'; so while we find many passages where these seem to be used interchangeably, we translate 'Faktum' as 'Fact' with an initial capital, using 'fact' for 'Tatsache' and various other expressions. On 'factuality' and 'facticity' see also H. 135 below.

than ever. Not until we understand Being-in-the-world as an essential
structure of Dasein can we have any insight into Dasein's *existential
spatiality*. Such an insight will keep us from failing to see this structure or
from previously cancelling it out—a procedure motivated not ontologically but rather 'metaphysically' by the naïve supposition that man is,
in the first instance, a spiritual Thing which subsequently gets misplaced
'into' a space.

Dasein's facticity is such that its Being-in-the-world has always dispersed [zerstreut] itself or even split itself up into definite ways of Being-
in. The multiplicity of these is indicated by the following examples: having
to do with something, producing something, attending to something and
looking after it, making use of something, giving something up and letting
it go, undertaking, accomplishing, evincing, interrogating, considering,
discussing, determining. . . . All these ways of Being-in have *concern*[1] as   5
their kind of Being—a kind of Being which we have yet to characterize in
detail. Leaving undone, neglecting, renouncing, taking a rest—these too
are ways of concern; but these are all *deficient* modes, in which the possibilities of concern are kept to a 'bare minimum'.[2] The term 'concern'
has, in the first instance, its colloquial [vorwissenschaftliche] signification,
and can mean to carry out something, to get it done [erledigen], to
'straighten it out'. It can also mean to 'provide oneself with something'.[3]
We use the expression with still another characteristic turn of phrase
when we say "I am concerned for the success of the undertaking."[4] Here
'concern' means something like apprehensiveness. In contrast to these
colloquial ontical significations, the expression 'concern' will be used in
this investigation as an ontological term for an *existentiale*, and will designate the Being of a possible way of Being-in-the-world. This term has
been chosen not because Dasein happens to be proximally and to a large
extent 'practical' and economic, but because the Being of Dasein itself

[1] '*Besorgen*'. As Heidegger points out, he will use this term in a special sense which is to
be distinguished from many of its customary usages. We shall, as a rule, translate it by
'concern', though this is by no means an exact equivalent. The English word 'concern' is
used in many expressions where 'Besorgen' would be inappropriate in German, such as
'This concerns you', 'That is my concern', 'He has an interest in several banking concerns'. 'Besorgen' stands rather for the kind of 'concern' in which we 'concern ourselves'
with activities which we perform or things which we procure.

[2] '. . . aile Modi des "Nur noch" in bezug auf Möglichkeiten des Besorgens.' The point
is that in these cases concern is *just barely* ('nur noch') involved.

[3] '. . . sich etwas besorgen im Sinne von "sich etwas verschaffen".'

[4] '. . . ich besorge, dass das Unternehmen misslingt.' Here it is not difficult to find a
corresponding usage of 'concern', as our version suggests. But the analogy is imperfect.
While we can say that we are 'concerned for the success of the enterprise' or 'concerned
lest the enterprise should fail,' we would hardly follow the German to the extent of
expressing 'concern that' the enterprise should fail; nor would the German express
'Besorgen' at discovering that the enterprise has failed already.

is to be made visible as *care*.[1] This expression too is to be taken as an ontological structural concept. (See Chapter 6 of this Division.) It has nothing to do with 'tribulation', 'melancholy', or the 'cares of life', though ontically one can come across these in every Dasein. These—like their opposites, 'gaiety' and 'freedom from care'—are ontically possible only because Dasein, when understood *ontologically*, is care. Because Being-in-the-world belongs essentially to Dasein, its Being towards the world [Sein zur Welt] is essentially concern.

From what we have been saying, it follows that Being-in is not a 'property' which Dasein sometimes has and sometimes does not have, and *without* which it could *be* just as well as it could with it. It is not the case that man 'is' and then has, by way of an extra, a relationship-of-Being towards the 'world'—a world with which he provides himself occasionally.[2] Dasein is never 'proximally' an entity which is, so to speak, free from Being-in, but which sometimes has the inclination to take up a 'relationship' towards the world. Taking up relationships towards the world is possible only *because* Dasein, as Being-in-the-world, is as it is. This state of Being does not arise just because some other entity is present-at-hand outside of Dasein and meets up with it. Such an entity can 'meet up with' Dasein only in so far as it can, of its own accord, show itself within a *world*.

Nowadays there is much talk about 'man's having an environment [Umwelt]'; but this says nothing ontologically as long as this 'having' is left indefinite. In its very possibility this 'having' is founded upon the existential state of Being-in. Because Dasein is essentially an entity with Being-in, it can explicitly discover those entities which it encounters environmentally, it can know them, it can avail itself of them, it can *have* the 'world'. To talk about 'having an environment' is ontically trivial, but ontologically it presents a problem. To solve it requires nothing else than defining the Being of Dasein, and doing so in a way which is ontologically adequate. Although this state of Being is one of which use has made in biology, especially since K. von Baer, one must not conclude that its philosophical use implies 'biologism'. For the environment is a structure which even biology as a positive science can never find and can never define, but must presuppose and constantly employ. Yet, even as an *a priori* condition for the objects which biology takes for its theme, this structure itself can be explained philosophically only if it has been conceived beforehand as a structure of Dasein. Only in terms of an orientation

---

[1] 'Sorge'. The important etymological connection between 'Besorgen' ('concern') and 'Sorge' ('care') is lost in our translation. On 'Sorge' see especially Sections 41 and 42 below.

[2] 'Der Mensch "ist" nicht und hat überdies noch ein Seinsverhältnis zur "Welt", die er sich gelegentlich zulegt.'

towards the ontological structure thus conceived can 'life' as a state of Being be defined *a priori*, and this must be done in a privative manner.[1] Ontically as well as ontologically, the priority belongs to Being-in-the world as concern. In the analytic of Dasein this structure undergoes a basic Interpretation.

But have we not confined ourselves to negative assertions in all our attempts to determine the nature of this state of Being? Though this Being-in is supposedly so fundamental, we always keep hearing about what it is *not*. Yes indeed. But there is nothing accidental about our characterizing it predominantly in so negative a manner. In doing so we have rather made known what is peculiar to this phenomenon, and our characterization is therefore positive in a genuine sense—a sense appropriate to the phenomenon itself. When Being-in-the-world is exhibited phenomenologically, disguises and concealments are rejected *because* this phenomenon itself always gets 'seen' in a certain way in every Dasein. And it thus gets 'seen' *because* it makes up a basic state of Dasein, and in every case is already disclosed for Dasein's understanding of Being, and disclosed along with that Being itself. But for the most part this phenomenon has been explained in a way which is basically wrong, or interpreted in an ontologically inadequate manner. On the other hand, this 'seeing in a certain way and yet for the most part wrongly explaining' is itself based upon nothing else than this very state of Dasein's Being, which is such that Dasein itself—and this means also its Being-in-the world—gets its ontological understanding of itself in the first instance from those entities which it itself is *not* but which it encounters 'within' its world, and from the Being which they possess.

Both in Dasein and for it, this state of Being is always in some way familiar [bekannt]. Now if it is also to become known [erkannt], the *knowing* which such a task explicitly implies takes *itself* (as a knowing of the world [Welterkennen]) as the chief exemplification of the 'soul's' relationship to the world. Knowing the world (νοεῖν)—or rather addressing oneself to the 'world' and discussing it (λόγος)—thus functions as the primary mode of Being-in-the-world, even though Being-in-the-world does not as such get conceived. But because this structure of Being remains ontologically inaccessible, yet is experienced ontically as a 'relationship' between one entity (the world) and another (the soul), and because one proximally understands Being by taking entities as entities within-the-world for one's ontological foothold, one tries to conceive the relationship between world and soul as grounded in these two entities

---

[1] '. . . auf dem Wege der Privation . . .' The point is that in order to understand life merely *as such*, we must make abstraction from the fuller life of Dasein. See H. 50 above.

themselves and in the meaning of their Being—namely, to conceive it as Being-present-at-hand. And even though Being-in-the-world is something of which one has pre-phenomenological experience and acquaintance [erfahren und gekannt], it becomes *invisible* if one interprets it in a way which is ontologically inappropriate. This state of Dasein's Being is now one with which one is just barely acquainted (and indeed as something obvious), with the stamp of an inappropriate interpretation. So in this way it becomes the 'evident' point of departure for problems of epistemology or the 'metaphysics of knowledge'. For what is more obvious than that a 'subject' is related to an 'Object' and *vice versa*? This 'subject-Object-relationship' must be presupposed. But while this presupposition is unimpeachable in its facticity, this makes it indeed a baleful one, if its ontological necessity and especially its ontological meaning are to be left in the dark.

Thus the phenomenon of Being-in has for the most part been represented exclusively by a single exemplar—knowing the world. This has not only been the case in epistemology; for even practical behaviour has been understood as behaviour which is '*non*-theoretical' and 'atheoretical'. Because knowing has been given this priority, our understanding of its ownmost kind of Being gets led astray, and accordingly Being-in-the-world must be exhibited even more precisely with regard to knowing the world, and must itself be made visible as an existential 'modality' of Being-in.

¶ *13. A Founded Mode in which Being-in is Exemplified.*[1] *Knowing the World.*

If Being-in-the-world is a basic state of Dasein, and one in which Dasein operates not only in general but pre-eminently in the mode of everydayness, then it must also be something which has always been experienced ontically. It would be unintelligible for Being-in-the-world to remain totally veiled from view, especially since Dasein has at its disposal an understanding of its own Being, no matter how indefinitely this understanding may function. But no sooner was the 'phenomenon of knowing the world' grasped than it got interpreted in a 'superficial',

---

[1] '*Die Exemplifizierung des In-Seins an einem fundierten Modus.*' The conception of 'founded' modes is taken from Husserl, who introduces the concept of 'founding' in his *Logische Untersuchungen*, vol. II, Part I, chapter 2 (second edition, Halle, 1913, p. 261). This passage has been closely paraphrased as follows by Marvin Farber in his *The Foundation of Phenomenology*, Cambridge, Massachusetts, 1943, p. 297; 'If in accordance with essential law an a can only exist in a comprehensive unity which connects it with a μ, then we say, an a as such needs foundation through a μ, or also, an a as such is in need of completion by means of a μ. If accordingly a_0, μ_0 are definite particular cases of the pure genera a, or μ, which stand in the cited relationship, and if they are members of one whole, then we say that a_0 is *founded* by μ_0; and it is *exclusively* founded by μ_0 if the need of the completion of a_0 is alone satisfied by μ_0. This terminology can be applied to the species themselves; the equivocation is harmless.' Thus a founded mode of Being-in is simply a mode which can subsist only when connected with something else.

formal manner. The evidence for this is the procedure (still customary today) of setting up knowing as a 'relation between subject and Object' —a procedure in which there lurks as much 'truth' as vacuity. But subject and Object do not coincide with Dasein and the world.

Even if it were feasible to give an ontological definition of "Being-in" primarily in terms of a Being-in-the-world which *knows*, it would still be our first task to show that knowing has the phenomenal character of a Being which is in and towards the world. If one reflects upon this relationship of Being, an entity called "Nature" is given proximally as that which becomes known. Knowing, as such, is not to be met in this entity. If knowing 'is' at all, it belongs solely to those entities which know. But even in those entities, human-Things, knowing is not present-at-hand. In any case, it is not externally ascertainable as, let us say, bodily properties are.[1] Now, inasmuch as knowing belongs to these entities and is not some external characteristic, it must be 'inside'. Now the more unequivocally one maintains that knowing is proximally and really 'inside' and indeed has by no means the same kind of Being as entities which are both physical and psychical, the less one presupposes when one believes that one is making headway in the question of the essence of knowledge and in the clarification of the relationship between subject and Object. For only then can the problem arise of how this knowing subject comes out of its inner 'sphere' into one which is 'other and external', of how knowing can have any object at all, and of how one must think of the object itself so that eventually the subject knows it without needing to venture a leap into another sphere. But in any of the numerous varieties which this approach may take, the question of the kind of Being which belongs to this knowing subject is left entirely unasked, though whenever its knowing gets handled, its way of Being is already included tacitly in one's theme. Of course we are sometimes assured that we are certainly not to think of the subject's "inside" [Innen] and its 'inner sphere' as a sort of 'box' or 'cabinet'. But when one asks for the positive signification of this 'inside' of immanence in which knowing is proximally enclosed, or when one inquires how this 'Being inside' ["Innenseins"] which knowing possesses has its own character of Being grounded in the kind of Being which belongs to the subject, then silence reigns. And no matter how this inner sphere may get interpreted, if one does no more than ask how knowing makes its way 'out of' it and achieves 'transcendence', it becomes evident that the knowing which presents such enigmas will remain problematical unless one has previously clarified how it is and what it is.

---

[1] 'In jedem Falle ist est nicht so äusserlich feststellbar wie etwa leibliche Eigenschaften. The older editions have '. . . nicht ist es . . .' and place a comma after 'feststellbar'.

With this kind of approach one remains blind to what is already tacitly implied even when one takes the phenomenon of knowing as one's theme in the most provisional manner: namely, that knowing is a mode of Being of Dasein as Being-in-the-world, and is founded ontically upon this state of Being. But if, as we suggest, we thus find phenomenally that *knowing is a kind of Being which belongs to Being-in-the-world*, one might object that with such an Interpretation of knowing, the problem of knowledge is nullified; for what is left to be asked if one *presupposes* that knowing is already 'alongside' its world, when it is not supposed to reach that world except in the transcending of the subject? In this question the constructivist 'standpoint', which has not been phenomenally demonstrated, again comes to the fore; but quite apart from this, what higher court is to decide *whether* and *in what sense* there is to be any problem of knowledge other than that of the phenomenon of knowing as such and the kind of Being which belongs to the knower?

If we now ask what shows itself in the phenomenal findings about knowing, we must keep in mind that knowing is grounded beforehand in a Being-already-alongside-the-world, which is essentially constitutive for Dasein's Being.[1] Proximally, this Being-already-alongside is not just a fixed staring at something that is purely present-at-hand. Being-in-the-world, as concern, is *fascinated by* the world with which it is concerned.[2] If knowing is to be possible as a way of determining the nature of the present-at-hand by observing it,[3] then there must first be a *deficiency* in our having-to-do with the world concernfully. When concern holds back [Sichenthalten] from any kind of producing, manipulating, and the like, it puts itself into what is now the sole remaining mode of Being-in, the mode of just tarrying alongside. . . . [das Nur-noch-verweilen bei . . .] This kind of Being towards the world is one which lets us encounter entities within-the-world purely in the *way they look* ($\epsilon\tilde{\iota}\delta os$), just that; *on the basis* of this kind of Being, and *as* a mode of it, looking explicitly at what we encounter is possible.[4] Looking *at* something in this way is sometimes a definite way of taking up a direction towards something—of setting our sights towards what is present-at-hand. It takes over a 'view-point' in advance from the entity which it encounters. Such looking-at enters the

---

[1] '. . . dass das Erkennen selbst vorgängig gründet in einem Schon-sein-bei-der-Welt, als welches das Sein von Dasein wesenhaft konstituiert.'

[2] 'Das In-der-Welt-sein ist als Besorgen von der besorgten Welt *benommen*.' Here we follow the older editions. The newer editions have 'das Besorgen' instead of 'als Besorgen'.

[3] 'Damit Erkennen als betrachtendes Bestimmen des Vorhandenen möglich sei . . .' Here too we follow the older editions. The newer editions again have 'das' instead of 'als'.

[4] '*Auf dem Grunde* dieser Seinsart zur Welt, die das innerweltlich begegnende Seiende nur noch in seinem puren *Aussehen* ($\epsilon\tilde{\iota}\delta os$) begegnen lässt, und *als* Modus dieser Seinsart ist ein ausdrückliches Hinsehen auf das so Begegnende möglich.'

mode of dwelling autonomously alongside entities within-the-world.[1] In this kind of *'dwelling'* as a holding-oneself-back from any manipulation or utilization, the *perception* of the present-at-hand is consummated.[2] Perception is consummated when one *addresses* oneself to something as something and *discusses* it as such.[3] This amounts to *interpretation* in the broadest sense; and on the basis of such interpretation, perception becomes an act of *making determinate*.[4] What is thus perceived and made determinate can be expressed in propositions, and can be retained and preserved as what has thus been asserted. This perceptive retention of an assertion[5] about something is itself a way of Being-in-the-world; it is not to be Interpreted as a 'procedure' by which a subject provides itself with representations [Vorstellungen] of something which remain stored up 'inside' as having been thus appropriated, and with regard to which the question of how they 'agree' with actuality can occasionally arise.

When Dasein directs itself towards something and grasps it, it does not somehow first get out of an inner sphere in which it has been proximally encapsulated, but its primary kind of Being is such that it is always 'outside' alongside entities which it encounters and which belong to a world already discovered. Nor is any inner sphere abandoned when Dasein dwells alongside the entity to be known, and determines its character; but even in this 'Being-outside' alongside the object, Dasein is still 'inside', if we understand this in the correct sense; that is to say, it is itself 'inside' as a Being-in-the-world which knows. And furthermore, the perceiving of what is known is not a process of returning with one's booty to the 'cabinet' of consciousness after one has gone out and grasped it; even in perceiving, retaining, and preserving, the Dasein which knows *remains outside*, and it does so *as Dasein*. If I 'merely 'know [Wissen] about some way in which the Being of entities is interconnected, if I 'only' represent them, if I 'do no more' than 'think' about them, I am no less

[1] 'Solches Hinsehen kommt selbst in den Modus eines eigenständigen Sichaufhaltens bei dem innerweltlichen Seienden.'

[2] 'In sogerateten *"Aufenthalt"*—als dem Sichenthalten von jeglicher Hantierung und Nutzung—vollzieht sich das *Vernehmen* des Vorhandenen.' The word 'Aufenthalt' normally means a stopping-off at some place, a sojourn, an abiding, or even an abode or dwelling. Here the author is exploiting the fact that it includes both the prefixes 'auf-' and 'ent-', which we find in the verbs 'aufhalten' and 'enthalten'. 'Aufhalten' means to hold something at a stage which it has reached, to arrest it, to stop it; when used reflexively it can mean to stay at a place, to dwell there. While 'enthalten' usually means to contain, it preserves its more literal meaning of holding back or refraining, when it is used reflexively. All these meanings are presumably packed into the word 'Aufenthalt' as used here, and are hardly suggested by our 'dwelling'.

[3] 'Das Vernehmen hat die Vollzugsart des *Ansprechens* und *Besprechens* von etwas als etwas.' On 'something as something' see Section 32 below (H. 149), where 'interpretation' is also discussed.

[4] '. . . wird das Vernehmen zum *Bestimmen*.'

[5] 'Aussage'. For further discussion see Section 33 below.

longside the entities outside in the world than when I *originally* grasp
hem.[1] Even the forgetting of something, in which every relationship of
Being towards what one formerly knew has seemingly been obliterated,
must be conceived *as a modification of the primordial Being-in*; and this holds
for every delusion and for every error.

We have now pointed out how those modes of Being-in-the-world
which are constitutive for knowing the world are interconnected in their
foundations; this makes it plain that in knowing, Dasein achieves a new
status of Being [*Seinsstand*] towards a world which has already been discovered in Dasein itself. This new possibility of Being can develop itself
autonomously; it can become a task to be accomplished, and as scientific
knowledge it can take over the guidance for Being-in-the-world. But a
'*commercium*' of the subject with a world does not get *created* for the first
time by knowing, nor does it *arise* from some way in which the world acts
upon a subject. Knowing is a mode of Dasein founded upon Being-in-the-
world. Thus Being-in-the-world, as a basic state, must be Interpreted
beforehand.

---

[1] '. . . bei einem *originären* Erfassen.'

III

THE WORLDHOOD OF THE WORLD

¶ *14. The Idea of the Worldhood of the World*[1] *in General*

BEING-IN-THE-WORLD shall first be made visible with regard to that item of its structure which is the 'world' itself. To accomplish this task seems easy and so trivial as to make one keep taking for granted that it may be dispensed with. What can be meant by describing 'the world' as a phenomenon? It means to let us see what shows itself in 'entities' within the world. Here the first step is to enumerate the things that are 'in' the world: houses, trees, people, mountains, stars. We can *depict* the way such entities 'look', and we can give an *account* of occurrences in them and with them. This, however, is obviously a pre-phenomenological 'business' which cannot be at all relevant phenomenologically. Such a description is always confined to entities. It is ontical. But what we are seeking is Being. And we have formally defined 'phenomenon' in the phenomenological sense as that which shows itself as Being and as a structure of Being.

Thus, to give a phenomenological description of the 'world' will mean to exhibit the Being of those entities which are present-at-hand within the world, and to fix it in concepts which are categorial. Now the entities within the world are Things—Things of Nature, and Things 'invested with value' ["wertbehaftete" Dinge]. Their Thinghood becomes a problem; and to the extent that the Thinghood of Things 'invested with value' is based upon the Thinghood of Nature, our primary theme is the Being of Things of Nature—Nature as such. That characteristic of Being which belongs to Things of Nature (substances), and upon which

---

1 'Welt', 'weltlich', 'Weltlichkeit', 'Weltmässigkeit'. We shall usually translate 'Welt' as 'the world' or 'a world', following English idiom, though Heidegger frequently omits the article when he wishes to refer to 'Welt' as a 'characteristic' of Dasein. In ordinary German the adjective 'weltlich' and the derivative noun 'Weltlichkeit' have much the same connotations as the English 'worldly' and 'worldliness'; but the meanings which Heidegger assigns to them (H. 65) are quite different from those of their English cognates. At the risk of obscuring the etymological connection and occasionally misleading the reader, we shall translate 'weltlich' as 'worldly', 'Weltlichkeit' as 'worldhood', and 'Weltmässigkeit' as 'worldly character'. The reader must bear in mind, however, that there is no suggestion here of the 'worldliness' of the 'man of the world'.

everything is founded, is substantiality. What is its ontological meaning? By asking this, we have given an unequivocal direction to our inquiry.

But is this a way of asking ontologically about the 'world'? The problematic which we have thus marked out is one which is undoubtedly ontological. But even if this ontology should itself succeed in explicating the Being of Nature in the very purest manner, in conformity with the basic assertions about this entity, which the mathematical natural sciences provide, it will never reach the phenomenon that is the 'world'. Nature is itself an entity which is encountered within the world and which can be discovered in various ways and at various stages.

Should we then first attach ourselves to those entities with which Dasein proximally and for the most part dwells—Things 'invested with value'? Do not these 'really' show us the world in which we live? Perhaps, in fact, they show us something like the 'world' more penetratingly. But these Things too are entities 'within' the world.

Neither the ontical depiction of entities within-the-world nor the ontological Interpretation of their Being is such as to reach the phenomenon of the 'world.' In both of these ways of access to 'Objective Being', the 'world' has already been 'presupposed', and indeed in various ways.

Is it possible that ultimately we cannot address ourselves to 'the world' as determining the nature of the entity we have mentioned? Yet we call this entity one which is "within-the-world". Is 'world' perhaps a characteristic of Dasein's Being? And in that case, does every Dasein 'proximally' have its world? Does not 'world' thus become something 'subjective'? How, then, can there be a 'common' world 'in' which, nevertheless, we *are*? And if we raise the question of the 'world', *what* world do we have in view? Neither the common world nor the subjective world, but *the worldhood of the world as such.* By what avenue do we meet this phenomenon?

'Worldhood' is an ontological concept, and stands for the structure of one of the constitutive items of Being-in-the-world. But we know Being-in-the-world as a way in which Dasein's character is defined existentially. Thus worldhood itself is an *existentiale.* If we inquire ontologically about the 'world', we by no means abandon the analytic of Dasein as a field for thematic study. Ontologically, 'world' is not a way of characterizing those entities which Dasein essentially is *not*; it is rather a characteristic of Dasein itself. This does not rule out the possibility that when we investigate the phenomenon of the 'world' we must do so by the avenue of entities within-the-world and the Being which they possess. The task of 'describing' the world phenomenologically is so far from obvious that even if we do no more than determine adequately what form it shall take, essential ontological clarifications will be needed.

This discussion of the word 'world', and our frequent use of it have made it apparent that it is used in several ways. By unravelling these we can get an indication of the different kinds of phenomena that are signified, and of the way in which they are interconnected.

1. "World" is used as an ontical concept, and signifies the totality of those entities which can be present-at-hand within the world.

2. "World" functions as an ontological term, and signifies the Being of those entities which we have just mentioned. And indeed 'world' can become a term for any realm which encompasses a multiplicity of entities: for instance, when one talks of the 'world' of a mathematician, 'world' signifies the realm of possible objects of mathematics.

3. "World" can be understood in another ontical sense—not, however, as those entities which Dasein essentially is not and which can be encountered within-the-world, but rather as that '*wherein*' a factical Dasein as such can be said to 'live'. "World" has here a pre-ontological existentiell signification. Here again there are different possibilities: "world" may stand for the 'public' we-world, or one's 'own' closest (domestic) environment.[1]

4. Finally, "world" designates the ontologico-existential concept of *worldhood*. Worldhood itself may have as its modes whatever structural wholes any special 'worlds' may have at the time; but it embraces in itself the *a priori* character of worldhood in general. We shall reserve the expression "world" as a term for our third signification. If we should sometimes use it in the first of these senses, we shall mark this with single quotation marks.

The derivative form 'worldly' will then apply terminologically to a kind of Being which belongs to Dasein, never to a kind which belongs to entities present-at-hand 'in' the world. We shall designate these latter entities as "belonging to the world" or "within-the-world" [weltzugehörig oder innerweltlich].

A glance at previous ontology shows that if one fails to see Being-in-the-world as a state of Dasein, the phenomenon of worldhood likewise gets *passed over*. One tries instead to Interpret the world in terms of the Being of those entities which are present-at-hand within-the-world but which are by no means proximally discovered—namely, in terms of Nature. If one understands Nature ontologico-categorially, one finds that

---

[1] '. . . die "eigene" und nächste (häusliche) Umwelt.' The word 'Umwelt', which is customarily translated as 'environment', means literally the 'world around' or the 'world about'. The prefix 'um-', however, not only may mean 'around' or 'about', but, as we shall see, can also be used in an expression such as 'um zu . . .', which is most easily translated as 'in order to'. Section 15 will be largely devoted to a study of several words in which this same prefix occurs, though this is by no means apparent in the words we have chosen to represent them: 'Umgang' ('dealings'); 'das Um-zu' ('the "in-order-to" '); 'Umsicht' ('circumspection').

Nature is a limiting case of the Being of possible entities within-the-world. Only in some definite mode of its own Being-in-the-world can Dasein discover entities as Nature.[1] This manner of knowing them has the character of depriving the world of its worldhood in a definite way. 'Nature', as the categorial aggregate of those structures of Being which a definite entity encountered within-the-world may possess, can never make *worldhood* intelligible. But even the phenomenon of 'Nature', as it is conceived, for instance, in romanticism, can be grasped ontologically only in terms of the concept of the world—that is to say, in terms of the analytic of Dasein.

When it comes to the problem of analysing the world's worldhood onto-logically, traditional ontology operates in a blind alley, if, indeed, it sees this problem at all. On the other hand, if we are to Interpret the world-hood of Dasein and the possible ways in which Dasein is made worldly [Verweltlichung], we must show *why* the kind of Being with which Dasein knows the world is such that it passes over the phenomenon of worldhood both ontically and ontologically. But at the same time the very Fact of this passing-over suggests that we must take special precautions to get the right phenomenal point of departure [Ausgang] for access [Zugang] to the phenomenon of worldhood, so that it will not get passed over.

Our method has already been assigned [Anweisung]. The theme of our analytic is to be Being-in-the-world, and accordingly the very world itself; and these are to be considered within the horizon of average every-dayness—the kind of Being which is *closest* to Dasein. We must make a study of everyday Being-in-the-world; with the phenomenal support which this gives us, something like the world must come into view.

That world of everyday Dasein which is closest to it, is the *environment*. From this existential character of average Being-in-the-world, our investigation will take its course [Gang] towards the idea of worldhood in general. We shall seek the worldhood of the environment (environ-mentality) by going through an ontological Interpretation of those entities within-the-*environment* which we encounter as closest to us. The expression "environment" [Umwelt] contains in the 'environ' ["um"] a suggestion of spatiality. Yet the 'around' ["Umherum"] which is constitutive for the environment does not have a primarily 'spatial' meaning. Instead, the spatial character which incontestably belongs to any environment, can be clarified only in terms of the structure of worldhood. From this point of view, Dasein's spatiality, of which we have given an indication in Section 12, becomes phenomenally visible. In ontology, however, an attempt has

---

[1] 'Das Seiende als Natur kann das Dasein nur in einem bestimmten Modus seines In-der-Welt-seins entdecken.'

been made to start with spatiality and then to Interpret the Being of the 'world' as *res extensa*. In Descartes we find the most extreme tendency towards such an ontology of the 'world', with, indeed, a counter-orientation towards the *res cogitans*—which does not coincide with Dasein either ontically or ontologically. The analysis of worldhood which we are here attempting can be made clearer if we show how it differs from such an ontological tendency. Our analysis will be completed in three stages: (*A*) the analysis of environmentality and worldhood in general; (*B*) an illustrative contrast between our analysis of worldhood and Descartes' ontology of the 'world'; (*C*) the aroundness [das Umhafte] of the environment, and the 'spatiality' of Dasein.[1]

A. Analysis of Environmentality and Worldhood in General

¶ *15. The Being of the Entities Encountered in the Environment*

The Being of those entities which we encounter as closest to us can be exhibited phenomenologically if we take as our clue our everyday Being-in-the-world, which we also call our *"dealings"*[2] in the world and *with* entities within-the-world. Such dealings have already dispersed themselves into manifold ways of concern.[3] The kind of dealing which is closest to us is as we have shown, not a bare perceptual cognition, but rather that kind of concern which manipulates things and puts them to use; and this has its own kind of 'knowledge'. The phenomenological question applies in the first instance to the Being of those entities which we encounter in such concern. To assure the kind of seeing which is here required, we must first make a remark about method.

In the disclosure and explication of Being, entities are in every case our preliminary and our accompanying theme [das Vor-und Mitthematische]; but our real theme is Being. In the domain of the present analysis, the entities we shall take as our preliminary theme are those which show themselves in our concern with the environment. Such entities are not thereby objects for knowing the 'world' theoretically; they are simply what gets used, what gets produced, and so forth. As entities so encountered, they become the preliminary theme for the purview of a 'knowing' which, as phenomenological, looks primarily towards Being, and which, in thus taking Being as its theme, takes these entities as its accompanying theme. This phenomenological interpretation is accordingly not a way of knowing

6

---

[1] *A* is considered in Sections 15-18; *B* in Sections 19-21; *C* in Sections 22-24.

[2] 'Umgang'. This word means literally a 'going around' or 'going about', in a sense not too far removed from what we have in mind when we say that someone is 'going about his business'. 'Dealings' is by no means an accurate translation, but is perhaps as convenient as any. 'Intercourse' and 'trafficking' are also possible translations.

[3] See above, H. 57, n. 1, p. 83.

those characteristics of entities which themselves a r e [seiender Beschaff-
enheiten des Seienden]; it is rather a determination of the structure of
the Being which entities possess. But as an investigation of Being, it brings
to completion, autonomously and explicitly, that understanding of Being
which belongs already to Dasein and which 'comes alive' in any of its
dealings with entities. Those entities which serve phenomenologically as
our preliminary theme—in this case, those which are used or which are
to be found in the course of production—become accessible when we put
ourselves into the position of concerning ourselves with them in some
such way. Taken strictly, this talk about "putting ourselves into such a
position" [Sichversetzen] is misleading; for the kind of Being which
belongs to such concernful dealings is not one into which we need to put
ourselves first. This is the way in which everyday Dasein always *is*: when
I open the door, for instance, I use the latch. The achieving of phenomenological access to the entities which we encounter, consists rather in
thrusting aside our interpretative tendencies, which keep thrusting themselves upon us and running along with us, and which conceal not only the
phenomenon of such 'concern', but even more those entities themselves *as*
encountered of their own accord *in* our concern with them. These entangling errors become plain if in the course of our investigation we now ask
which entities shall be taken as our preliminary theme and established as
the pre-phenomenal basis for our study.

One may answer: "Things." But with this obvious answer we have
perhaps already missed the pre-phenomenal basis we are seeking. For in
addressing these entities as 'Things' (*res*), we have tacitly anticipated
their ontological character. When analysis starts with such entities and
goes on to inquire about Being, what it meets is Thinghood and Reality.
Ontological explication discovers, as it proceeds, such characteristics of
Being as substantiality, materiality, extendedness, side-by-side-ness, and
so forth. But even pre-ontologically, in such Being as this, the entities
which we encounter in concern are proximally hidden. When one designates Things as the entities that are 'proximally given', one goes ontologically astray, even though ontically one has something else in mind.
What one really has in mind remains undetermined. But suppose one
characterizes these 'Things' as Things 'invested with value'? What does
"value" mean ontologically? How are we to categorize this 'investing'
and Being-invested? Disregarding the obscurity of this structure of
investiture with value, have we thus met that phenomenal characteristic
of Being which belongs to what we encounter in our concernful dealings?

The Greeks had an appropriate term for 'Things': πράγματα—that is
to say, that which one has to do with in one's concernful dealings

(πρᾶξις). But ontologically, the specifically 'pragmatic' character of the πράγματα is just what the Greeks left in obscurity; they thought of these 'proximally' as 'mere Things'. We shall call those entities which we encounter in concern *"equipment"*.[1] In our dealings we come across equipment for writing, sewing, working, transportation, measurement. The kind of Being which equipment possesses must be exhibited. The clue for doing this lies in our first defining what makes an item of equipment—namely, its equipmentality.

Taken strictly, there 'is' no such thing as *an* equipment. To the Being of any equipment there always belongs a totality of equipment, in which it can be this equipment that it is. Equipment is essentially 'something in-order-to . . .' ["etwas um-zu . . ."]. A totality of equipment is constituted by various ways of the 'in-order-to', such as serviceability, conduciveness, usability, manipulability.

In the 'in-order-to' as a structure there lies an *assignment* or *reference* of something to something.[2] Only in the analyses which are to follow can the phenomenon which this term 'assignment' indicates be made visible in its ontological genesis. Provisionally, it is enough to take a look phenomenally at a manifold of such assignments. Equipment—in accordance with its equipmentality—always is *in terms of* [aus] its belonging to other equipment: ink-stand, pen, ink, paper, blotting pad, table, lamp, furniture, windows, doors, room. These 'Things' never show themselves

---

[1] 'das *Zeug*'. The word 'Zeug' has no precise English equivalent. While it may mean any implement, instrument, or tool, Heidegger uses it for the most part as a collective noun which is analogous to our relatively specific 'gear' (as in 'gear for fishing') or the more elaborate 'paraphernalia', or the still more general 'equipment', which we shall employ throughout this translation. In this collective sense 'Zeug' can sometimes be used in a way which is comparable to the use of 'stuff' in such sentences as 'there is plenty of stuff lying around'. (See H. 74.) In general, however, this pejorative connotation is lacking. For the most part Heidegger uses the term as a collective noun, so that he can say that there is no such thing as '*an* equipment'; but he still uses it occasionally with an indefinite article to refer to some specific tool or instrument—some item or bit of equipment.

[2] 'In der Struktur "Um-zu" liegt eine *Verweisung* von etwas auf etwas.' There is no close English equivalent for the word 'Verweisung', which occurs many times in this chapter. The basic metaphor seems to be that of *turning* something away towards something else, or *pointing* it away, as when one 'refers' or 'commits' or 'relegates' or 'assigns' something to something else, whether one 'refers' a symbol to what it symbolizes, 'refers' a beggar to a welfare agency, 'commits' a person for trial, 'relegates' or 'banishes' him to Siberia, or even 'assigns' equipment to a purpose for which it is to be used. 'Verweisung' thus does some of the work of 'reference', 'commitment', 'assignment', 'relegation', 'banishment'; but it does not do *all* the work of any of these expressions. For a businessman to 'refer' to a letter, for a symbol to 'refer' to what it symbolizes, for a man to 'commit larceny or murder' or merely to 'commit himself' to certain partisan views, for a teacher to give a pupil a long 'assignment', or even for a journalist to receive an 'assignment' to the Vatican, we would have to find some other verb than 'verweisen'. We shall, however, use the verbs 'assign' and 'refer' and their derivatives as perhaps the least misleading substitutes, employing whichever seems the more appropriate in the context, and occasionally using a hendiadys as in the present passage. See Section 17 for further discussion. (When other words such as 'anweisen' or 'zuweisen' are translated as 'assign', we shall usually subjoin the German in brackets.)

proximally as they are for themselves, so as to add up to a sum of *realia* and fill up a room. What we encounter as closest to us (though not as something taken as a theme) is the room; and we encounter it not as something 'between four walls' in a geometrical spatial sense, but as equipment for residing. Out of this the 'arrangement' emerges, and it is in this that any 'individual' item of equipment shows itself. *Before* it does so, a totality of equipment has already been discovered.

Equipment can genuinely show itself only in dealings cut to its own measure (hammering with a hammer, for example); but in such dealings an entity of this kind is not *grasped* thematically as an occurring Thing, nor is the equipment-structure known as such even in the using. The hammering does not simply have knowledge about [um] the hammer's character as equipment, but it has appropriated this equipment in a way which could not possibly be more suitable. In dealings such as this, where something is put to use, our concern subordinates itself to the "in-order-to" which is constitutive for the equipment we are employing at the time; the less we just stare at the hammer-Thing, and the more we seize hold of it and use it, the more primordial does our relationship to it become, and the more unveiledly is it encountered as that which it is—as equipment. The hammering itself uncovers the specific 'manipulability' ["Handlichkeit"] of the hammer. The kind of Being which equipment possesses—in which it manifests itself in its own right—we call *"readiness-to-hand"* [*Zuhandenheit*].[1] Only because equipment has *this* 'Being-in-itself' and does not merely occur, is it manipulable in the broadest sense and at our disposal. No matter how sharply we just *look* [Nur-noch-hinsehen] at the 'outward appearance' ["Aussehen]" of Things in whatever form this takes, we cannot discover anything ready-to-hand. If we look at Things just 'theoretically', we can get along without understanding readiness-to-hand. But when we deal with them by using them and manipulating them, this activity is not a blind one; it has its own kind of sight, by which our manipulation is guided and from which it acquires its specific Thingly character. Dealings with equipment subordinate themselves to the manifold assignments of the 'in-order-to'. And the sight with which they thus accommodate themselves is *circumspection*.[2]

---

[1] Italics only in earlier editions.

[2] The word 'Umsicht', which we translate by 'circumspection', is here presented as standing for a special kind of 'Sicht' ('sight'). Here, as elsewhere, Heidegger is taking advantage of the fact that the prefix '*um*' may mean either 'around' or 'in order to'. '*Umsicht*' may accordingly be thought of as meaning 'looking around' or 'looking around for something' or 'looking around for a way to get something done'. In ordinary German usage, 'Umsicht' seems to have much the same connotation as our 'circumspection'—a kind of awareness in which one looks around before one decides just what one ought to do next. But Heidegger seems to be generalizing this notion as well as calling attention to

'Practical' behaviour is not 'atheoretical' in the sense of "sightlessness".[1]
The way it differs from theoretical behaviour does not lie simply in the
fact that in theoretical behaviour one observes, while in practical behaviour one *acts* [*gehandelt* wird], and that action must employ theoretical
cognition if it is not to remain blind; for the fact that observation is a kind
of concern is just as primordial as the fact that action has *its own* kind of
sight. Theoretical behaviour is just looking, without circumspection. But
the fact that this looking is non-circumspective does not mean that it
follows no rules: it constructs a canon for itself in the form of *method*.

The ready-to-hand is not grasped theoretically at all, nor is it itself
the sort of thing that circumspection takes proximally as a circumspective
theme. The peculiarity of what is proximally ready-to-hand is that, in
its readiness-to-hand, it must, as it were, withdraw [zurückzuziehen] in
order to be ready-to-hand quite authentically. That with which our everyday dealings proximally dwell is not the tools themselves [die Werkzeuge
selbst]. On the contrary, that with which we concern ourselves primarily
is the work—that which is to be produced at the time; and this is accordingly ready-to-hand too. The work bears with it that referential totality
within which the equipment is encountered.[2]

The work to be produced, as the "*towards-which*" of such things as the
hammer, the plane, and the needle, likewise has the kind of Being that
belongs to equipment. The shoe which is to be produced is for wearing
(footgear) [Schuhzeug]; the clock is manufactured for telling the time.
The work which we chiefly encounter in our concernful dealings—the
work that is to be found when one is "at work" on something [das in
Arbeit befindliche]—has a usability which belongs to it essentially; in
this usability it lets us encounter already the "towards-which" for which
it is usable. A work that someone has ordered [das bestellte Werk] i s only
by reason of its use and the assignment-context of entities which is discovered in using it.

But the work to be produced is not merely usable for something. The

the extent to which circumspection in the narrower sense occurs in our every-day living.
(The distinction between 'sight' (Sicht') and 'seeing' ('Sehen') will be developed further
in Sections 31 and 36 below.)

[1] '. . . im Sinne der Sichtlosigkeit . . .' The point of this sentence will be clear to the
reader who recalls that the Greek verb θεωρεῖν, from which the words 'theoretical' and
'atheoretical' are derived, originally meant 'to see'. Heidegger is pointing out that this is
not what we have in mind in the traditional contrast between the 'theoretical' and the
'practical'.

[2] 'Das Werk trägt die Verweisungsganzheit, innerhalb derer das Zeug begegnet.' In
this chapter the word 'Werk' ('work') usually refers to the product achieved by working
rather than to the process of working as such. We shall as a rule translate 'Verweisungsganzheit' as 'referential totality', though sometimes the clumsier 'totality of assignments'
may convey the idea more effectively. (The older editions read 'deren' rather than
'derer'.)

production itself is a using *of* something for something. In the work there is also a reference or assignment to 'materials': the work is dependent on [angewiesen auf] leather, thread, needles, and the like. Leather, moreover is produced from hides. These are taken from animals, which someone else has raised. Animals also occur within the world without having been raised at all; and, in a way, these entities still produce themselves even when they have been raised. So in the environment certain entities become accessible which are always ready-to-hand, but which, in themselves, do not need to be produced. Hammer, tongs, and needle, refer in themselves to steel, iron, metal, mineral, wood, in that they consist of these. In equipment that is used, 'Nature' is discovered along with it by that use—the 'Nature' we find in natural products.

Here, however, "Nature" is not to be understood as that which is just present-at-hand, nor as the *power of Nature*. The wood is a forest of timber, the mountain a quarry of rock; the river is water-power, the wind is wind 'in the sails'. As the 'environment' is discovered, the 'Nature' thus discovered is encountered too. If its kind of Being as ready-to-hand is disregarded, this 'Nature' itself can be discovered and defined simply in its pure presence-at-hand. But when this happens, the Nature which 'stirs and strives', which assails us and enthralls us as landscape, remains hidden. The botanist's plants are not the flowers of the hedgerow; the 'source' which the geographer establishes for a river is not the 'springhead in the dale'.

The work produced refers not only to the "towards-which" of its usability and the "whereof" of which it consists: under simple craft conditions it also has an assignment to the person who is to use it or wear it. The work is cut to his figure; he 'is' there along with it as the work emerges. Even when goods are produced by the dozen, this constitutive assignment is by no means lacking; it is merely indefinite, and points to the random, the average. Thus along with the work, we encounter not only entities ready-to-hand but also entities with Dasein's kind of Being— entities for which, in their concern, the product becomes ready-to-hand; and together with these we encounter the world in which wearers and users live, which is at the same time ours. Any work with which one concerns oneself is ready-to-hand not only in the domestic world of the workshop but also in the *public world*. Along with the public world, the *environing Nature* [*die Umweltnatur*] is discovered and is accessible to everyone. In roads, streets, bridges, buildings, our concern discovers Nature as having some definite direction. A covered railway platform takes account of bad weather; an installation for public lighting takes account of the darkness, or rather of specific changes in the presence or absence of daylight—the 'position of the sun'. In a clock, account is taken of some definite constellation in the world-system. When we look at the clock, we tacitly make use of the 'sun's position', in accordance with which the measurement of time gets regulated in the official astronomical manner. When we make use of the clock-equipment, which is proximally and inconspicuously ready-to-hand, the environing Nature is ready-to-hand along with it. Our concernful absorption in whatever work-world lies closest to us, has a function of discovering; and it is essential to this function that, depending upon the way in which we are absorbed, those entities within-the-world which are brought along [beigebrachte] in the work and with it (that is to say, in the assignments or references which are constitutive for it) remain discoverable in varying degrees of explicitness and with a varying circumspective penetration.

The kind of Being which belongs to these entities is readiness-to-hand. But this characteristic is not to be understood as merely a way of taking them, as if we were talking such 'aspects' into the 'entities' which we proximally encounter, or as if some world-stuff which is proximally present-at-hand in itself[1] were 'given subjective colouring' in this way. Such an Interpretation would overlook the fact that in this case these entities would have to be understood and discovered beforehand as something purely present-at-hand, and must have priority and take the lead in the sequence of those dealings with the 'world' in which something is discovered and made one's own. But this already runs counter to the ontological meaning of cognition, which we have exhibited as a *founded* mode of Being-in-the-world.[2] To lay bare what is just present-at-hand and no more, cognition must first penetrate *beyond* what is ready-to-hand in our concern. *Readiness-to-hand is the way in which entities as they are 'in themselves' are defined ontologico-categorially.* Yet only by reason of something present-at-hand, 'is there' anything ready-to-hand. Does it follow, however, granting this thesis for the nonce, that readiness-to-hand is ontologically founded upon presence-at-hand?

But even if, as our ontological Interpretation proceeds further, readiness-to-hand should prove itself to be the kind of Being characteristic of those entities which are proximally discovered within-the-world, and even if its primordiality as compared with pure presence-at-hand can be demonstrated, have all these explications been of the slightest help towards understanding the phenomenon of the world ontologically? In Interpreting these entities within-the-world, however, we have always

---

[1] '. . . ein zünächst an sich vorhandener Weltstoff . . .' The earlier editions have '. . . zunächst ein an sich vorhandener Weltstoff . . .'.

[2] See H. 61 above.

'presupposed' the world. Even if we join them together, we still do not get anything like the 'world' as their sum. If, then, we start with the Being of these entities, is there any avenue that will lead us to exhibiting the phenomenon of the world?[1]

¶ *16. How the Worldly Character of the Environment Announces itself in Entities Within-the-world*[1]

The world itself is not an entity within-the-world; and yet it is so determinative for such entities that only in so far as 'there is' a world can they be encountered and show themselves, in their Being, as entities which have been discovered. But in what way 'is there' a world? If Dasein is ontically constituted by Being-in-the-World, and if an understanding of the Being of its Self belongs just as essentially to its Being, no matter how indefinite that understanding may be, then does not Dasein have an understanding of the world—a pre-ontological understanding, which indeed can and does get along without explicit ontological insights? With those entities which are encountered within-the-world—that is to say, with their character as within-the-world—does not something like the world show itself for concernful Being-in-the-world? Do we not have a pre-phenomenological glimpse of this phenomenon? Do we not always have such a glimpse of it, without having to take it as a theme for ontological Interpretation? Has Dasein itself, in the range of its concernful absorption in equipment ready-to-hand, a possibility of Being in which the worldhood of those entities within-the-world with which it is concerned is, in a certain way, lit up for it, *along with* those entities themselves?

If such possibilities of Being for Dasein can be exhibited within its concernful dealings, then the way lies open for studying the phenomenon which is thus lit up, and for attempting to 'hold it at bay', as it were, and to interrogate it as to those structures which show themselves therein.

To the everydayness of Being-in-the-world there belong certain modes of concern. These permit the entities with which we concern ourselves to be encountered in such a way that the worldly character of what is within-the-world comes to the fore. When we concern ourselves with something, the entities which are most closely ready-to-hand may be met as something unusable, not properly adapted for the use we have decided upon. The tool turns out to be damaged, or the material unsuitable. In each of these cases *equipment* is here, ready-to-hand. We discover its unusability, however, not by looking at it and establishing its properties, but rather by the circumspection of the dealings in which we use it. When its unusability is thus discovered, equipment becomes conspicuous. This *conspicuousness*

---

[1] '*Die am innerweltlich Seienden sich meldende Weltmässigkeit der Umwelt.*'

presents the ready-to-hand equipment as in a certain un-readiness-to-hand. But this implies that what cannot be used just lies there; it shows itself as an equipmental Thing which looks so and so, and which, in its readiness-to-hand as looking that way, has constantly been present-at-hand too. Pure presence-at-hand announces itself in such equipment, but only to withdraw to the readiness-to-hand of something with which one concerns oneself—that is to say, of the sort of thing we find when we put it back into repair. This presence-at-hand of something that cannot be used is still not devoid of all readiness-to-hand whatsoever; equipment which is present-at-hand *in this way* is still not just a Thing which occurs somewhere. The damage to the equipment is still not a mere alteration of a Thing—not a change of properties which just occurs in something present-at-hand.

In our concernful dealings, however, we not only come up against unusable things *within* what is ready-to-hand already: we also find things which are missing—which not only are not 'handy' ["handlich"] but are not 'to hand' ["zur Hand"] at all. Again, to miss something in this way amounts to coming across something un-ready-to-hand. When we notice what is un-ready-to-hand, that which i s ready-to-hand enters the mode of *obtrusiveness* The more urgently [Je dringlicher] we need what is missing, and the more authentically it is encountered in its un-readiness-to-hand, all the more obtrusive₁[um so aufdringlicher] does that which is ready-to-hand become—so much so, indeed, that it seems to lose its character of readiness-to-hand. It reveals itself as something just present-at-hand and no more, which cannot be budged without the thing that is missing. The helpless way in which we stand before it is a deficient mode of concern, and as such it uncovers the Being-just-present-at-hand-and-no-more of something ready-to-hand.

In our dealings with the world[1] of our concern, the un-ready-to-hand can be encountered not only in the sense of that which is unusable or simply missing, but as something un-ready-to-hand which is *not* missing at all and *not* unusable, but which 'stands in the way' of our concern. That to which our concern refuses to turn, that for which it has 'no time', is something *un*-ready-to-hand in the manner of what does not belong here, of what has not as yet been attended to. Anything which is un-ready-to-hand in this way is disturbing to us, and enables us to see the *obstinacy* of that with which we must concern ourselves in the first instance before we do anything else. With this obstinacy, the presence-at-hand of the ready-to-hand makes itself known in a new

---

[1] In the earlier editions 'Welt' appears with quotation marks. These are omitted in the later editions.

way as the Being of that which still lies before us and calls for our attending to it.[1]

The modes of conspicuousness, obtrusiveness, and obstinacy all have the function of bringing to the fore the characteristic of presence-at-hand in what is ready-to-hand. But the ready-to-hand is not thereby just *observed* and stared at as something present-at-hand; the presence-at-hand which makes itself known is still bound up in the readiness-to-hand of equipment. Such equipment still does not veil itself in the guise of mere Things. It becomes 'equipment' in the sense of something which one would like to shove out of the way.[2] But in such a Tendency to shove things aside, the ready-to-hand shows itself as still ready-to-hand in its unswerving presence-at-hand.

Now that we have suggested, however, that the ready-to-hand is thus encountered under modifications in which its presence-at-hand is revealed, how far does this clarify the *phenomenon of the world*? Even in analysing these modifications we have not gone beyond the Being of what is within-the-world, and we have come no closer to the world-phenomenon than before. But though we have not as yet grasped it, we have brought ourselves to a point where we can bring it into view.

In conspicuousness, obtrusiveness, and obstinacy, that which is ready-to-hand loses its readiness-to-hand in a certain way. But in our dealings with what is ready-to-hand, this readiness-to-hand is itself understood, though not thematically. It does not vanish simply, but takes its farewell, as it were, in the conspicuousness of the unusable. Readiness-to-hand still shows itself, and it is precisely here that the worldly character of the ready-to-hand shows itself too.

[1] Heidegger's distinction between 'conspicuousness' (Auffälligkeit') 'obtrusiveness' ('Aufdringlichkeit'), and 'obstinacy' ('Aufsässigkeit') is hard to present unambiguously in translation. He seems to have in mind three rather similar situations. In each of these we are confronted by a number of articles which are ready-to-hand. In the first situation we wish to use one of these articles for some purpose, but we find that it cannot be used for that purpose. It then becomes 'conspicuous' or 'striking', and *in a way* 'un-ready-to-hand' —in that we are not able to use it. In the second situation we may have precisely the same articles before us, but we want one which is not there. In this case the missing article too is 'un-ready-to-hand', but in another way—in that it is not there to be used. This is annoying, and the articles which are still ready-to-hand before us, thrust themselves upon us in such a way that they become 'obtrusive' or even 'obnoxious'. In the third situation, some of the articles which are ready-to-hand before us are experienced as *obstacles* to the achievement of some purpose; as obstacles they are 'obstinate', 'recalcitrant', 'refractory', and we have to attend to them or dispose of them in some way before we can finish what we want to do. Here again the obstinate objects are un-ready-to-hand, but simply in the way of being obstinate.

In all three situations the articles which are ready-to-hand for us tend to lose their readiness-to-hand in one way or another and reveal their presence-at-hand; only in the second situation, however, do we encounter them as 'just present-at-hand and no more' ('nur noch Vorhandenes').

[2] Here 'Zeug' is used in the pejorative sense of 'stuff'. See our note 1, p. 97 on H. 68.

The structure of the Being of what is ready-to-hand as equipment is determined by references or assignments. In a peculiar and obvious manner, the 'Things' which are closest to us are 'in themselves' ["An-sich"]; and they are encountered as 'in themselves' in the concern which makes use of them without noticing them explicitly—the concern which can come up against something unusable. When equipment cannot be used, this implies that the constitutive assignment of the "in-order-to" to a "towards-this" has been disturbed. The assignments themselves are not observed; they are rather 'there' when we concernfully submit ourselves to them [Sichstellen unter sie]. But *when an assignment has been disturbed*—when something is unusable for some purpose—then the assignment becomes explicit. Even now, of course, it has not become explicit as an ontological structure; but it has become explicit ontically for the circumspection which comes up against the damaging of the tool. When an assignment to some particular "towards-this" has been thus circumspectively aroused, we catch sight of the "towards-this" itself, and along with it everything connected with the work—the whole 'work-shop'—as that wherein concern always dwells. The context of equipment is lit up, not as something never seen before, but as a totality constantly sighted beforehand in circumspection. With this totality, however, the world announces itself.

Similarly, when something ready-to-hand is found missing, though its everyday presence [Zugegensein] has been so obvious that we have never taken any notice of it, this makes a *break* in those referential contexts which circumspection discovers. Our circumspection comes up against emptiness, and now sees for the first time *what* the missing article was ready-to-hand *with*, and *what* it was ready-to-hand *for*. The environment announces itself afresh. What is thus lit up is not itself just one thing ready-to-hand among others; still less is it something *present-at-hand* upon which equipment ready-to-hand is somehow founded: it is in the 'there' before anyone has observed or ascertained it. It is itself inaccessible to circumspection, so far as circumspection is always directed towards entities; but in each case it has already been disclosed for circumspection. 'Disclose' and 'disclosedness' will be used as technical terms in the passages that follow, and shall signify 'to lay open' and 'the character of having been laid open.' Thus 'to disclose' never means anything like 'to obtain indirectly by inference'.[1]

---

[1] In ordinary German usage, the verb 'erschliessen' may mean not only to 'disclose' but also—in certain constructions—to 'infer' or 'conclude' in the sense in which one 'infers' a conclusion from premises. Heidegger is deliberately ruling out this latter interpretation, though on a very few occasions he may use the word in this sense. He explains his own meaning by the cognate verb 'aufschliessen', to 'lay open'. To say that something has been 'disclosed' or 'laid open' in Heidegger's sense, does not mean that one has any

That the world does not 'consist' of the ready-to-hand shows itself in the fact (among others) that whenever the world is lit up in the modes of concern which we have been Interpreting, the ready-to-hand becomes deprived of its worldhood so that Being-just-present-at-hand comes to the fore. If, in our everyday concern with the 'environment', it is to be possible for equipment ready-to-hand to be encountered in its 'Being-in-itself' [in seinem "An-sich-sein"], then those assignments and referential totalities in which our circumspection 'is absorbed' cannot become a theme for that circumspection any more than they can for grasping things 'thematically' but non-circumspectively. If it is to be possible for the ready-to-hand not to emerge from its inconspicuousness, the world *must not announce itself.* And it is in this that the Being-in-itself of entities which are ready-to-hand has its phenomenal structure constituted.

In such privative expressions as "inconspicuousness", "unobtrusiveness", and "non-obstinacy", what we have in view is a positive phenomenal character of the Being of that which is proximally ready-to-hand. With these negative prefixes we have in view the character of the ready-to-hand as "holding itself in"; this is what we have our eye upon in the "Being-in-itself" of something,[1] though 'proximally' we ascribe it to the present-at-hand—to the present-at-hand as that which can be thematically ascertained. As long as we take our orientation primarily and exclusively from the present-at-hand, the 'in-itself' can by no means be ontologically clarified. If, however, this talk about the 'in-itself' has any ontological importance, some interpretation must be called for. This "in-itself" of Being is something which gets invoked with considerable emphasis, mostly in an ontical way, and rightly so from a phenomenal standpoint. But if some *ontological* assertion is supposed to be given when this is *ontically* invoked, its claims are not fulfilled by such a procedure. As the foregoing analysis has already made clear, only on the basis of the phenomenon of the world can the Being-in-itself of entities within-the-world be grasped ontologically.

But if the world can, in a way, be lit up, it must assuredly be disclosed. And it has already been disclosed beforehand whenever what is ready-to-hand within-the-world is accessible for circumspective concern. The world is therefore something 'wherein' Dasein as an entity already *was*, and if in

detailed awareness of the contents which are thus 'disclosed', but rather that they have been 'laid open' to us as implicit in what is given, so that they may be made explicit to our awareness by further analysis or discrimination of the given, rather than by any inference from it.

[1] 'Diese "Un" meinen den Charakter des Ansichhaltens des Zuhandenen, das, was wir mit dem An-sich-sein im Auge haben . . .' The point seems to be that when we speak of something 'as it is "in itself" or "in its own right" ', we think of it as 'holding itself in' or 'holding itself back'—not 'stepping forth' or doing something 'out of character'.

any manner it explicitly comes away from anything, it can never do more than come back to the world.

Being-in-the-world, according to our Interpretation hitherto, amounts to a non-thematic circumspective absorption in references or assignments constitutive for the readiness-to-hand of a totality of equipment. Any concern is already as it is, because of some familiarity with the world. In this familiarity Dasein can lose itself in what it encounters within-the-world and be fascinated with it. What is it that Dasein is familiar with? Why can the worldly character of what is within-the-world be lit up? The presence-at-hand[1] of entities is thrust to the fore by the possible breaks in that referential totality in which circumspection 'operates'; how are we to get a closer understanding of this totality?

These questions are aimed at working out both the phenomenon and the problems of worldhood, and they call for an inquiry into the inter-connections with which certain structures are built up. To answer them we must analyse these structures more concretely.

¶ *17. Reference and Signs*

In our provisional Interpretation of that structure of Being which belongs to the ready-to-hand (to 'equipment'), the phenomenon of reference or assignment became visible; but we merely gave an indication of it, and in so sketchy a form that we at once stressed the necessity of uncovering it with regard to its ontological origin.[2] It became plain, moreover, that assignments and referential totalities could in some sense become constitutive for worldhood itself. Hitherto we have seen the world lit up only in and for certain definite ways in which we concern ourselves environmentally with the ready-to-hand, and indeed it has been lit up only *with* the readiness-to-hand of that concern. So the further we proceed in understanding the Being of entities within-the-world, the broader and firmer becomes the phenomenal basis on which the world-phenomenon may be laid bare.

We shall again take as our point of departure the Being of the ready-to-hand, but this time with the purpose of grasping the phenomenon of *reference* or *assignment* itself more precisely. We shall accordingly attempt an ontological analysis of a kind of equipment in which one may come across such 'references' in more senses than one. We come across 'equipment' in *signs*. The word "sign" designates many kinds of things: not only may it stand for different *kinds* of signs, but Being-a-sign-for can itself be

---

[1] Here the older editions have 'Zuhandenheit' where the newer ones have 'Vorhandenheit'.

[2] Cf. H. 68 above.

formalized as a *universal kind of relation*, so that the sign-structure itself provides an ontological clue for 'characterizing' any entity whatsoever.

But signs, in the first instance, are themselves items of equipment whose specific character as equipment consists in *showing* or *indicating*.[1] We find such signs in signposts, boundary-stones, the ball for the mariner's storm-warning, signals, banners, signs of mourning, and the like. Indicating can be defined as a 'kind' of referring. Referring is, if we take it as formally as possible, a *relating*. But relation does not function as a genus for 'kinds' or 'species' of references which may somehow become differentiated as sign, symbol, expression, or signification. A relation is something quite formal which may be read off directly by way of 'formalization' from any kind of context, whatever its subject-matter or its way of Being.[ii]

Every reference is a relation, but not every relation is a reference. Every 'indication' is a reference, but not every referring is an indicating. This implies at the same time that every 'indication' is a relation, but not every relation is an indicating. The formally general character of relation is thus brought to light. If we are to investigate such phenomena as references, signs, or even significations, nothing is to be gained by characterizing them as relations. Indeed we shall eventually have to show that 'relations' themselves, *because of* their formally general character, have their ontological source in a reference.

If the present analysis is to be confined to the Interpretation of the sign as distinct from the phenomenon of reference, then even within this limitation we cannot properly investigate the full multiplicity of possible signs. Among signs there are symptoms [Anzeichen], warning signals, signs of things that have happened already [Rückzeichen], signs to mark something, signs by which things are recognized; these have different ways of indicating, regardless of what may be serving as such a sign. From such 'signs' we must distinguish traces, residues, commemorative monuments, documents, testimony, symbols, expressions, appearances, significations. These phenomena can easily be formalized because of their formal relational character; we find it especially tempting nowadays to take such a 'relation' as a clue for subjecting every entity to a kind of 'Interpretation' which always 'fits' because at bottom it says nothing, no more than the facile schema of content and form.

As an example of a sign we have chosen one which we shall use again in a later analysis, though in another regard. Motor cars are sometimes fitted up with an adjustable red arrow, whose position indicates

---

[1] '. . . deren spezifischer Zeugcharakter im *Zeigen* besteht.' While we have often used 'show' and 'indicate' to translate 'zeigen' and 'anzeigen' respectively, in the remainder of this section it seems more appropriate to translate 'zeigen' by 'indicate', or to resort to hendiadys as in the present passage.

the direction the vehicle will take—at an intersection, for instance. The position of the arrow is controlled by the driver. This sign is an item of equipment which is ready-to-hand for the driver in his concern with driving, and not for him alone: those who are not travelling with him—and they in particular—also make use of it, either by giving way on the proper side or by stopping. This sign is ready-to-hand within-the-world in the whole equipment-context of vehicles and traffic regulations. It is equipment for indicating, and as equipment, it is constituted by reference or assignment. It has the character of the "in-order-to", its own definite serviceability; it is for indicating.[1] This indicating which the sign performs can be taken as a kind of 'referring'. But here we must notice that this 'referring' as indicating is not the ontological structure of the sign as equipment.

Instead, 'referring' as indicating is grounded in the Being-structure of equipment, in serviceability for. . . . But an entity may have serviceability without thereby becoming a sign. As equipment, a 'hammer' too is constituted by a serviceability, but this does not make it a sign. Indicating, as a 'reference', is a way in which the "towards-which" of a serviceability becomes ontically concrete; it determines an item of equipment as for this "towards-which" [und bestimmt ein Zeug zu diesem]. On the other hand, the kind of reference we get in 'serviceability-for', is an ontologico-categorial attribute of equipment *as* equipment. That the "towards-which" of serviceability should acquire its concreteness in indicating, is an accident of its equipment-constitution as such. In this example of a sign, the difference between the reference of serviceability and the reference of indicating becomes visible in a rough and ready fashion. These are so far from coinciding that only when they are united does the concreteness of a definite kind of equipment become possible. Now it is certain that indicating differs in principle from reference as a constitutive state of equipment; it is just as incontestable that the sign in its turn is related in a peculiar and even distinctive way to the kind of Being which belongs to whatever equipmental totality may be ready-to-hand in the environment, and to its worldly character. In our concernful

---

[1] 'Es hat den Charakter des Um-zu, seine bestimmte Dienlichkeit, es ist zum Zeigen.' The verb 'dienen', is often followed by an infinitive construction introduced by the preposition 'zu'. Similarly the English 'serve' can be followed by an infinitive in such expressions as 'it serves to indicate . . .' In Heidegger's German the 'zu' construction is carried over to the noun 'Dienlichkeit'; the corresponding noun 'serviceability', however, is not normally followed by an infinitive, but rather by an expression introduced by 'for' *e.g.* 'serviceability for indicating . . .' Since the preposition 'zu' plays an important role in this section and the next, it would be desirable to provide a uniform translation for it. We shall, however, translate it as 'for' in such expressions as 'Dienlichkeit zu', but as 'towards' in such expressions as 'Wozu' ('towards-which') and 'Dazu' ('towards-this'), retaining 'in-order-to' for 'Um-zu'.

dealings, equipment for indicating [Zeig-zeug] gets used in a *very special* way. But simply to establish this Fact is ontologically insufficient. The basis and the meaning of this special status must be clarified.

What do we mean when we say that a sign "indicates"? We can answer this only by determining what kind of dealing is appropriate with equipment for indicating. And we must do this in such a way that the readiness-to-hand of that equipment can be genuinely grasped. What is the appropriate way of having-to-do with signs? Going back to our example of the arrow, we must say that the kind of behaving (Being) which corresponds to the sign we encounter, is either to 'give way' or to 'stand still' *vis-à-vis* the car with the arrow. Giving way, as taking a direction, belongs essentially to Dasein's Being-in-the-world. Dasein is always somehow directed [ausgerichtet] and on its way; standing and waiting are only limiting cases of this directional 'on-its-way'. The sign addresses itself to a Being-in-the-world which is specifically 'spatial'. The sign is *not* authentically 'grasped' ["erfasst"] if we just stare at it and identify it as an indicator-Thing which occurs. Even if we turn our glance in the direction which the arrow indicates, and look at something present-at-hand in the region indicated, even then the sign is not authentically encountered. Such a sign addresses itself to the circumspection of our concernful dealings, and it does so in such a way that the circumspection which goes along with it, following where it points, brings into an explicit 'survey' whatever aroundness the environment may have at the time. This circumspective survey does not *grasp* the ready-to-hand; what it achieves is rather an orientation within our environment. There is also another way in which we can experience equipment: we may encounter the arrow simply as equipment which belongs to the car. We can do this without discovering what character it specifically has as equipment: what the arrow is to indicate and how it is to do so, may remain completely undetermined; yet what we are encountering is not a mere Thing. The experiencing of a Thing requires a *definiteness* of its own [ihre eigene *Bestimmtheit*], and must be contrasted with coming across a manifold of equipment, which may often be quite indefinite, even when one comes across it as especially close.

Signs of the kind we have described let what is ready-to-hand be encountered; more precisely, they let some context of it become accessible in such a way that our concernful dealings take on an orientation and hold it secure. A sign is not a Thing which stands to another Thing in the relationship of indicating; it is rather *an item of equipment which explicitly raises a totality of equipment into our circumspection so that together with it the worldly character of the ready-to-hand announces itself*. In a symptom or a warning-signal, 'what is coming' 'indicates itself', but not in the sense of something merely occurring, which comes as an addition to what is already present-at-hand; 'what is coming' is the sort of thing which we are ready for, or which we 'weren't ready for' if we have been attending to something else.[1] In signs of something that has happened already, what has come to pass and run its course becomes circumspectively accessible. A sign to mark something indicates what one is 'at' at any time. Signs always indicate primarily 'wherein' one lives, where one's concern dwells, what sort of involvement there is with something.[2]

The peculiar character of signs as equipment becomes especially clear in 'establishing a sign' ["Zeichenstiftung"]. This activity is performed in a circumspective fore-sight [Vorsicht] out of which it arises, and which requires that it be possible for one's particular environment to announce itself for circumspection at any time by means of something ready-to-hand, and that this possibility should itself be ready-to-hand. But the Being of what is most closely ready-to-hand within-the-world possesses the character of holding-itself-in and not emerging, which we have described above.[3] Accordingly our circumspective dealings in the environment require some equipment ready-to-hand which in its character as equipment takes over the 'work' of *letting* something ready-to-hand *become conspicuous.* So when such equipment (signs) gets produced, its conspicuousness must be kept in mind. But even when signs are thus conspicuous, one does not let them be present-at-hand at random; they get 'set up' ["angebracht"] in a definite way with a view towards easy accessibility.

In establishing a sign, however, one does not necessarily have to produce equipment which is not yet ready-to-hand at all. Signs also arise when one *takes as a sign* [Zum-Zeichen-nehmen] something that is ready-to-hand already. In this mode, signs "get established" in a sense which is even more primordial. In indicating, a ready-to-hand equipment totality, and even the environment in general, can be provided with an availability which is circumspectively oriented; and not only this: establishing a sign can, above all, reveal. What gets taken as a sign becomes accessible only through its readiness-to-hand. If, for instance, the south wind 'is accepted' ["gilt"] by the farmer as a sign of rain, then this 'acceptance' ["Geltung"] —or the 'value' with which the entity is 'invested'—is not a sort of bonus over and above what is already present-at-hand in itself—*viz*, the flow of air in a definite geographical direction. The south wind may be meteorologically accessible as something which just occurs; but it is *never* present-

---

[1] '... das "was kommt" ist solches, darauf wir uns gefasst machen, bzw. "nicht gefasst waren", sofern wir uns mit anderem befassten.'

[2] 'Das Merkzeichen zeigt, "woran" man jeweils ist. Die Zeichen zeigen primär immer das, "worin" man lebt, wobei das Besorgen sich aufhält, welche Bewandtnis es damit hat.' On 'Bewandtnis', see note 2, p. 115 H. 84 below.

[3] See H. 75-76 above.

at-hand *proximally* in such a way as this, only occasionally taking over the
function of a warning signal. On the contrary, only by the circumspection
with which one takes account of things in farming, is the south wind
discovered in its Being.

But, one will protest, *that which* gets taken as a sign must first have
become accessible in itself and been apprehended *before* the sign gets
established. Certainly it must in any case be such that in some way we
can come across it. The question simply remains as to *how* entities are discovered in this previous encountering, whether as mere Things which
occur, or rather as equipment which has not been understood—as something ready-to-hand with which we have hitherto not known 'how to
begin', and which has accordingly kept itself veiled from the purview of
circumspection. *And here again, when the equipmental characters of the ready-to-
hand are still circumspectively undiscovered, they are not to be Interpreted as bare
Thinghood presented for an apprehension of what is just present-at-hand and no
more.*

The Being-ready-to-hand of signs in our everyday dealings, and the
conspicuousness which belongs to signs and which may be produced for
various purposes and in various ways, do not merely serve to document
the inconspicuousness constitutive for what is most closely ready-to-hand;
the sign itself gets its conspicuousness from the inconspicuousness of the
equipmental totality, which is ready-to-hand and 'obvious' in its everydayness. The knot which one ties in a handkerchief [der bekannte "Knopf im
Taschentuch"] as a sign to mark something is an example of this. What
such a sign is to indicate is always something with which one has to
concern oneself in one's everyday circumspection. Such a sign can
indicate many things, and things of the most various kinds. The wider
the extent to which it can indicate, the narrower its intelligibility and its
usefulness. Not only is it, for the most part, ready-to-hand as a sign only
for the person who 'establishes' it, but it can even become inaccessible to
him, so that another sign is needed if the first is to be used circumspectively at all. So when the knot cannot be used as a sign, it does not lose
its sign-character, but it acquires the disturbing obtrusiveness of something
most closely ready-to-hand.

One might be tempted to cite the abundant use of 'signs' in primitive
Dasein, as in fetishism and magic, to illustrate the remarkable role
which they play in everyday concern when it comes to our understanding
of the world. Certainly the establishment of signs which underlies this
way of using them is not performed with any theoretical aim or in the
course of theoretical speculation. This way of using them always remains
completely within a Being-in-the-world which is 'immediate'. But on

closer inspection it becomes plain that to interpret fetishism and magic by taking our clue from the idea of signs in general, is not enough to enable us to grasp the kind of 'Being-ready-to-hand' which belongs to entities encountered in the primitive world. With regard to the sign-phenomenon, the following Interpretation may be given: for primitive man, the sign coincides with that which is indicated. Not only can the sign represent this in the sense of serving as a substitute for what it indicates, but it can do so in such a way that the sign itself always *is* what it indicates. This remarkable coinciding does not mean, however, that the sign-Thing has already undergone a certain 'Objectification'—that it has been experienced as a mere Thing and misplaced into the same realm of Being of the present-at-hand as what it indicates. This 'coinciding' is not an identification of things which have hitherto been isolated from each other: it consists rather in the fact that the sign has not as yet become free from that of which it is a sign. Such a use of signs is still absorbed completely in Being-towards what is indicated, so that a sign as such cannot detach itself at all. This coinciding is based not on a prior Objectification but on the fact that such Objectification is completely lacking. This means, however, that signs are not discovered as equipment at all—that ultimately what is 'ready-to-hand' within-the-world just does not have the kind of Being that belongs to equipment. Perhaps even readiness-to-hand and equipment have nothing to contribute [nichts auszurichten] as ontological clues in Interpreting the primitive world; and certainly the ontology of Thinghood does even less. But if an understanding of Being is constitutive for primitive Dasein and for the primitive world in general, then it is all the more urgent to work out the 'formal' idea of worldhood—or at least the idea of a phenomenon modifiable in such a way that all ontological assertions to the effect that in a given phenomenal context something is *not yet* such-and-such or *no longer* such-and-such, may acquire a *positive* phenomenal meaning in terms of what it is *not*.[1]

The foregoing Interpretation of the sign should merely provide phenomenal support for our characterization of references or assignments. The relation between sign and reference is threefold. 1. Indicating, as a way whereby the "towards-which" of a serviceability can become concrete, is founded upon the equipment-structure as such, upon the "in-order-to" (assignment). 2. The indicating which the sign does is an equipmental character of something ready-to-hand, and as such it belongs to a totality of equipment, to a context of assignments or references. 3. The sign is not only ready-to-hand with other equipment, but in its readiness-to-hand the environment becomes in each case explicitly

---

[1] '. . . aus dem, was es *nicht* ist.' The older editions write 'w a s' for 'was'.

accessible for circumspection. *A sign is something ontically ready-to-hand, which functions both as this definite ‚equipment and as something indicative of* [*was . . . anzeigt*] *the ontological ⸍structure of readiness-to-hand, of referential totalities, and of worldhood.* Here is rooted the special status of the sign as something ready-to-hand in that environment with which we concern ourselves circumspectively. Thus the reference or the assignment itself cannot be conceived as a sign of it is to serve ontologically as the foundation upon which signs are based. Reference is not an ontical characteristic of something ready-to-hand, when it is rather that by which readiness-to-hand itself is constituted.

In what sense, then, is reference 'presupposed' ontologically in the ready-to-hand, and to what extent is it, as such an ontological foundation, at the same time constitutive for worldhood in general?

¶ *18. Involvement and Significance; the Worldhood of the World*

The ready-to-hand is encountered within-the-world. The Being of this entity, readiness-to-hand, thus stands in some ontological relationship towards the world and towards worldhood. In anything ready-to-hand the world is always 'there'. Whenever we encounter anything, the world has already been previously discovered, though not thematically. But it can also be lit up in certain ways of dealing with our environment. The world is that in terms of which the ready-to-hand is ready-to-hand. How can the world let the ready-to-hand be encountered? Our analysis hitherto has shown that what we encounter within-the-world has, in its very Being, been freed[1] for our concernful circumspection, for taking account. What does this previous freeing amount to, and how is this to be understood as an ontologically distinctive feature of the world? What problems does the question of the worldhood of the world lay before us?

We have indicated that the state which is constitutive for the ready-to-hand as equipment is one of reference or assignment. How can entities with this kind of Being be freed by the world with regard to their Being? Why are these the first entities to be encountered? As definite kinds of references we have mentioned serviceability-for-, detrimentality [Abträglichkeit], usability, and the like. The "towards-which" [das Wozu] of a serviceability and the "for-which" [das Wofür] of a usability prescribed the ways in which such a reference or assignment can become concrete. But the 'indicating' of the sign and the 'hammering' of the hammer are not properties of entities. Indeed, they are not properties at all, if the ontological structure designated by the term 'property' is that of some

---

1 'freigegeben'. The idea seems to be that what we encounter has, as it were, been released, set free, given its freedom, or given free rein, so that our circumspection can take account of it.

definite character which it is possible for Things to possess [einer möglichen Bestimmtheit von Dingen]. Anything ready-to-hand is, at the worst, appropriate for some purposes and inappropriate for others; and its 'properties' are, as it were, still bound up in these ways in which it is appropriate or inappropriate,[1] just as presence-at-hand, as a possible kind of Being for something ready-to-hand, is bound up in readiness-to-hand. Serviceability too, however, as a constitutive state of equipment (and serviceability is a reference), is not an appropriateness of some entity; it is rather the condition (so far as Being is in question) which makes it possible for the character of such an entity to be defined by its appropriatenesses. But what, then, is "reference" or "assignment" to mean? To say that the Being of the ready-to-hand has the structure of assignment or reference means that it has in itself the character of *having been assigned or referred* [*Verwiesenheit*]. An entity is discovered when it has been assigned or referred to something, and referred as that entity which it is. *With* any such entity there is an involvement which it has *in* something.[2] The character of Being which belongs to the ready-to-hand is ust such an *involvement*. If something has an involvement, this implies etting it be involved in something. The relationship of the "with ... in ..." hall be indicated by the term "assignment" or "reference".[3]

---

[1] The words 'property' and 'appropriateness' reflect the etymological connection of Ieidegger's 'Eigenschaft' and "Geeignetheit'.

[2] 'Es hat *mit* ihm *bei* etwas sein Bewenden.' The terms 'Bewenden' and 'Bewandtnis' are mong the most difficult for the translator. Their root meaning has to do with the way >mething is already '*turning*' when one lets it 'go its own way', 'run its course', follow s 'bent' or 'tendency', or finish 'what it is about', 'what it is up to' or 'what it is ivolved in'. The German expressions, however, have no simple English equivalents, ut are restricted to a rather special group of idioms such as the following, which we ave taken from Wildhagen and Héraucourt's admirable *English-German, German-English Dictionary* (Volume II, Wiesbaden 1953): 'es dabei bewenden lassen'—'to leave it at iat, to let it go at that, to let it rest there'; 'und dabei hatte es sein Bewenden'—'and aere the matter ended'; 'dabei muss es sein Bewenden haben'—'there the matter must est'—'that must suffice'; 'die Sache hat eine ganz andere Bewandtnis'—'the case is juite different'; 'damit hat es seine besondere Bewandtnis'—'there is something peculiar .bout it; thereby hangs a tale'; 'damit hat est folgende Bewandtnis'—'the matter s as follows'.
We have tried to render both 'Bewenden' and 'Bewandtnis' by expressions including :ither 'involve' or 'involvement'. But the contexts into which these words can easily be fitted in ordinary English do not correspond very well to those which are possible for 'Bewenden' and 'Bewandtnis'. Our task is further complicated by the emphasis which Heidegger gives to the prepositions 'mit' and 'bei' in connection with 'Bewenden' and 'Bewandtnis'. In passages such as the present one, it would be more idiomatic to leave these prepositions untranslated and simply write: 'Any such entity is involved in doing something', or 'Any such entity is involved in some activity'. But 'mit' and 'bei' receive so much attention in this connection that in contexts such as this we shall sometimes translate them as 'with' and 'in', though elsewhere we shall handle 'bei' very differently. (The reader must bear in mind that the kind of 'involvement' with which we are here concerned is always an involvement in some *activity*, which one is performing, not an involvement in *circumstances* in which one is 'caught' or 'entangled'.)

[3] 'In Bewandtnis liegt: bewenden lassen mit etwas bei etwas. Der Bezug des "mit

When an entity within-the-world has already been proximally freed for its Being, that Being is its "involvement". With any such entity as entity, there is some involvement. The fact that it has such an involvement is *ontologically* definitive for the Being of such an entity, and is not an ontical assertion about it. That in which it is involved is the "towards-which" of serviceability, and the "for-which" of usability.[1] With the "towards-which" of serviceability there can again be an involvement: *with* this thing, for instance, which is ready-to-hand, and which we accordingly call a "hammer", there is an involvement in hammering; with hammering, there is an involvement in making something fast; with making something fast, there is an involvement in protection against bad weather; and this protection 'is' for the sake of [um-willen] providing shelter for Dasein—that is to say, for the sake of a possibility of Dasein's Being. Whenever something ready-to-hand has an involvement with it, *what* involvement this is, has in each case been outlined in advance in terms of the totality of such involvements. In a workshop, for example, the totality of involvements which is constitutive for the ready-to-hand in its readiness-to-hand, is 'earlier' than any single item of equipment; so too for the farmstead with all its utensils and outlying lands. But the totality of involvements itself goes back ultimately to a "towards-which" in which there is *no* further involvement: this "towards-which" is not an entity with the kind of Being that belongs to what is ready-to-hand within a world; it is rather an entity whose Being is defined as Being-in-the-world, and to whose state of Being, worldhood itself belongs. This primary "towards-which" is not just another "towards-this" as something in which an involvement is possible. The primary 'towards-which' is a "for-the-sake-of-which".[2] But the 'for-the-sake-of' always pertains to the Being of

... bei . . ." soll durch den Terminus Verweisung angezeigt werden.' Here the point seems to be that if something *has* an 'involvement' in the sense of 'Bewandtnis' (or rather, if there is such an involvement 'with' it), the thing which has this involvement has been 'assigned' or 'referred' for a certain activity or purpose 'in' which it may be said to be involved.

[1] 'Bewandtnis ist das Sein des innerweltlichen Seienden, darauf es je schon zunächst freigegeben ist. Mit ihm als Seiendem hat es je eine Bewandtnis. Dieses, dass es eine Bewandtnis hat, ist die *ontologische* Bestimmung des Seins dieses Seienden, nicht eine ontische Aussage über das Seiende. Das Wobei es die Bewandtnis hat, ist das Wozu der Dienlichkeit, das Wofür der Verwendbarkeit.' This passage and those which follow are hard to translate because Heidegger is using three carefully differentiated prepositions ('zu', 'für', and 'auf') where English idiom needs only 'for'. We can say that something is serviceable, usable, or applicable '*for*' a purpose. and that it may be freed or given free rein 'for' some kind of activity. In German, however, it will be said to have 'Dienlichkeit *zu* . . .', 'Verwendbarkeit *für* . . .'; and it will be 'freigegeben *auf* . . .'. In the remainder of this section we shall use 'for' both for 'für' and for 'auf' as they occur in these expressions; we shall, however, continue to use 'towards-which' for the 'Wozu' of 'Dienlichkeit'. See note 1, p. 109, H. 78 above.

[2] 'Dieses primäre Wozu ist kein Dazu als mögliches Wobei einer Bewandtnis. Das primäre "Wozu" ist ein Worum-willen.'

Dasein, for which, in its Being, that very Being is essentially an *issue*. We have thus indicated the interconnection by which the structure of an involvement leads to Dasein's very Being as the sole authentic "for-the-sake-of-which"; for the present, however, we shall pursue this no further. 'Letting something be involved' must first be clarified enough to give the phenomenon of worldhood the kind of definiteness which makes it possible to formulate any problems about it.

Ontically, "letting something be involved" signifies that within our factical concern we let something ready-to-hand *be* so-and-so *as* it is already and *in order that* it be such.[1] The way we take this ontical sense of 'letting be' is, in principle, ontological. And therewith we Interpret the meaning of previously freeing what is proximally ready-to-hand within-the-world. Previously letting something 'be' does not mean that we must first bring it into its Being and produce it; it means rather that something which is already an 'entity' must be discovered in its readiness-to-hand, and that we must thus let the entity which has this Being be encountered. This '*a priori*' letting-something-be-involved is the condition for the possibility of encountering anything ready-to-hand, so that Dasein, in its ontical dealings with the entity thus encountered, can thereby let it be involved in the ontical sense.[2] On the other hand, if letting something be involved is understood ontologically, what is then pertinent is the freeing of *everything* ready-to-hand as ready-to-hand, no matter whether, taken ontically, it is involved thereby, or whether it is rather an entity of precisely such a sort that ontically it is *not* involved thereby. Such entities are, proximally and for the most part, those with which we concern ourselves when we do not let them 'be' as we have discovered that they are, but work upon them, make improvements in them, or smash them to pieces.

When we speak of having already let something be involved, so that it has been freed for that involvement, we are using a *perfect* tense *a priori* which characterizes the kind of Being belonging to Dasein itself.[3] Letting an entity be involved, if we understand this ontologically, consists in previously freeing it for [auf] its readiness-to-hand within the environment. When we let something be involved, it must be involved in something; and in terms of this "in-which", the "with-which" of this involvement

---

[1] 'Bewendenlassen bedeutet ontisch; innerhalb eines faktischen Besorgens ein Zuhandenes so und so *sein* lassen, *wie* es nunmehr ist und *damit* es so ist.'

[2] '. . . es im ontischen Sinne dabei bewenden lassen kann.' While we have translated 'dabei' simply as 'thereby' in this context, it is possible that it should have been construed rather as an instance of the special use of 'bei' with 'bewenden lassen'. A similar ambiguity occurs in the following sentence.

[3] 'Das auf Bewandtnis hin freigebende Je-schon-haben-bewenden-lassen ist ein apriorisches Perfekt, das die Seinsart des Daseins selbst charakterisiert.'

is freed.[1] Our concern encounters it as this thing that is ready-to-hand. To the extent that any *entity* shows itself to concern[2]—that is, to the extent that it is discovered in its Being—it is already something ready-to-hand environmentally; it just is not 'proximally' a 'world-stuff' that is merely present-at-hand.

As the Being of something ready-to-hand, an involvement is itself discovered only on the basis of the prior discovery of a totality of involvements. So in any involvement that has been discovered (that is, in anything ready-to-hand which we encounter), what we have called the "worldly character" of the ready-to-hand has been discovered beforehand. In this totality of involvements which has been discovered beforehand, there lurks an ontological relationship to the world. In letting entities be involved so that they are freed for a totality of involvements, one must have disclosed already that for which [woraufhin] they have been freed. But that for which something environmentally ready-to-hand has thus been freed (and indeed in such a manner that it becomes accessible *as* an entity within-the-world first of all), cannot itself be conceived as an entity with this discovered kind of Being. It is essentially not discoverable, if we henceforth reserve *"discoveredness"* as a term for a possibility of Being which every entity *without* the character of Dasein may possess.

But what does it mean to say that that for which[3] entities within-the-world are proximally freed must have been previously disclosed? To Dasein's Being, an understanding of Being belongs. Any understanding [Verständnis] has its Being in an act of understanding [Verstehen]. If Being-in-the-world is a kind of Being which is essentially befitting to Dasein, then to understand Being-in-the-world belongs to the essential content of its understanding of Being. The previous disclosure of that for which what we encounter within-the-world is subsequently freed,[4] amounts to nothing else than understanding the world—that world towards which Dasein as an entity always comports itself.

Whenever we let there be an involvement with something in something beforehand, our doing so is grounded in our understanding such things as letting something be involved, and such things as the "with-which" and the "in-which" of involvements. Anything of this sort, and anything else

1 'Aus dem Wobei des Bewendenlassens her ist das Womit der Bewandtnis freigegeben.'
2 Here we follow the newer editions in reading: 'Sofern sich ihm überhaupt ein *Seiendes* zeigt . . .'. The older editions read 'Sofern sich mit ihm . . .', which is somewhat ambiguous but suggests that we should write: 'To the extent that with what is ready-to-hand any *entity* shows itself . . .'.
3 'Worauf'. The older editions have 'woraufhin'.
4 'Das vorgängige Erschliessen dessen, woraufhin die Freigabe des innerweltlichen Begegnenden erfolgt . . .'

that is basic for it, such as the "towards-this" as that in which there is an involvement, or such as the "for-the-sake-of-which" to which. every "towards-which" ultimately goes back[1]—all these must be disclosed beforehand with a certain intelligibility [Verständlichkeit]. And what is that wherein Dasein as Being-in-the-world understands itself pre-ontologically? In understanding a context of relations such as we have mentioned, Dasein has assigned itself to an "in-order-to" [Um-zu], and it has done so in terms of a potentiality-for-Being for the sake of which it itself is—one which it may have seized upon either explicitly or tacitly, and which may be either authentic or inauthentic. This "in-order-to" prescribes a "towards-this" as a possible "in-which" for letting something be involved; and the structure of letting it be involved implies that this is an involvement which something *has*—an involvement which is *with* something. Dasein always assigns itself from a "for-the-sake-of-which" to the "with-which" of an involvement; that is to say, to the extent that it is, it always lets entities be encountered as ready-to-hand.[2] *That wherein* [*Worin*] Dasein understands itself beforehand in the mode of assigning itself is *that for which* [das *Woraufhin*] it has let entities be encountered beforehand. *The "wherein" of an act of understanding which assigns or refers itself, is that for which one lets entities be encountered in the kind of Being that belongs to involvements; and this "wherein" is the phenomenon of the world.*[3] And the structure of that to which [woraufhin] Dasein assigns itself is what makes up the *worldhood* of the world.

That wherein Dasein already understands itself in this way is always something with which it is primordially familiar. This familiarity with the world does not necessarily require that the relations which are constitutive for the world as world should be theoretically transparent. However, the possibility of giving these relations an explicit ontologico-existential Interpretation, is grounded in this familiarity with the world; and this familiarity, in turn, is constitutive for Dasein, and goes to make up Dasein's understanding of Being. This possibility is one which can be seized upon explicitly in so far as Dasein has set itself the task of giving a primordial Interpretation for its own Being and for the possibilities of that Being, or indeed for the meaning of Being in general.

---

[1] '. . . wie das Dazu, als wobei es die Bewandtnis hat, das Worum-willen, darauf letztlich alles Wozu zurückgeht.' The older editions have '. . . als wobei es je die Bewandtnis hat . . .' and omit the hyphen in 'Worum-willen'.

[2] 'Dieses zeichnet ein Dazu vor, als mögliches Wobei eines Bewendenlassens, das strukturmässig *mit* etwas bewenden lässt. Dasein verweist sich je schon immer aus einem Worum-willen her an das Womit einer Bewandtnis, d. h. es lässt je immer schon, sofern es ist, Seiendes als Zuhandenes begegnen.'

[3] '*Das Worin des sichverweisenden Verstehens als Woraufhin des Begegnenlassens von Seiendem in der Seinsart der Bewandtnis ist das Phänomen der Welt.*'

But as yet our analyses have done no more than lay bare the horizon within which such things as the world and worldhood are to be sought. If we are to consider these further, we must, in the first instance, make it still more clear how the context of Dasein's assigning-itself is to be taken ontologically.

In the *act of understanding* [*Verstehen*], which we shall analyse more thoroughly later (Compare Section 31), the relations indicated above must have been previously disclosed; the act of understanding holds them in this disclosedness. It holds itself in them with familiarity; and in so doing, it holds them *before* itself, for it is in these that its assignment operates.[1] The understanding lets itself make assignments both i n these relationships themselves and o f them.[2] The relational character which these relationships of assigning possess, we take as one of *signifying*.[3] In its familiarity with these relationships, Dasein 'signifies' to itself: in a prim-ordial manner it gives itself both its Being and its potentiality-for-Being as something which it is to understand with regard to its Being-in-the-world. The "for-the-sake-of-which" signifies an "in-order-to"; this in turn, a "towards-this"; the latter, an "in-which" of letting something be involved; and that in turn, the "with-which" of an involvement. These relationships are bound up with one another as a primordial totality; they are what they are a s this signifying [Be-deuten] in which Dasein gives itself beforehand its Being-in-the-world as something to be under-stood. The relational totality of this signifying we call "*significance*". This is what makes up the structure of the world—the structure of that wherein Dasein as such already is. *Dasein, in its familiarity with significance, is the ontical condition for the possibility of discovering entities which are encountered in a world with involvement (readiness-to-hand) as their kind of Being, and which can thus make themselves known as they are in themselves* [*in seinem An-sich*]. Dasein as such is always something of this sort; along with its Being, a context of the ready-to-hand is already essentially discovered: Dasein, in so far as it

---

1 'Das . . . Verstehen . . . hält die angezeigten Bezüge in einer vorgängigen Erschlossen-heit. Im vertrauten Sich-darin-halten hält es sich diese *vor* als das, worin sich sein Ver-weisen bewegt.' The context suggests that Heidegger's 'diese' refers to the relationships (Bezüge) rather than to the disclosedness (Erschlossenheit), though the latter interpreta-tion seems a bit more plausible grammatically.

2 'Das Verstehen lässt sich in und von diesen Bezügen selbst verweisen.' It is not entirely clear whether 'von' should be translated as 'of', 'from', or 'by'.

3 '*be-deuten*'. While Heidegger ordinarily writes this word without a hyphen (even, for instance, in the next sentence), he here takes pains to hyphenate it so as to suggest that etymologically it consists of the intensive prefix 'be-' followed by the verb 'deuten'—to 'interpret', 'explain' or 'point to' something. We shall continue to follow our convention of usually translating 'bedeuten' and 'Bedeutung' by 'signify' and 'signification' respec-tively, reserving 'significance' for 'Bedeutsamkeit' (or, in a few cases, for 'Bedeutung'). But these translations obscure the underlying meanings which Heidegger is emphasizing in this passage.

is, has always submitted[1] itself already to a 'world' which it encounters, and this *submission*[1] belongs essentially to its Being.

But in significance itself, with which Dasein is always familiar, there lurks the ontological condition which makes it possible for Dasein, as something which understands and interprets, to disclose such things as 'significations'; upon these, in turn, is founded the Being of words and of language.

The significance thus disclosed is an existential state of Dasein—of its Being-in-the-world; and as such it is the ontical condition for the possibility that a totality of involvements can be discovered.

If we have thus determined that the Being of the ready-to-hand (involvement) is definable as a context of assignments or references, and that even worldhood may so be defined, then has not the 'substantial Being' of entities within-the-world been volatilized into a system of Relations? And inasmuch as Relations are always 'something thought', has not the Being of entities within-the-world been dissolved into 'pure thinking'?

Within our present field of investigation the following structures and dimensions of ontological problematics, as we have repeatedly emphasized, must be kept in principle distinct: 1. the Being of those entities within-the-world which we proximally encounter—readiness-to-hand; 2. the Being of those entities which we can come across and whose nature we can determine if we discover them in their own right by going through the entities proximally encountered—presence-at-hand; 3. the Being of that ontical condition which makes it possible for entities within-the-world to be discovered at all—the worldhood of the world. This third kind of Being gives us an *existential* way of determining the nature of Being-in-the-world, that is, of Dasein. The other two concepts of Being are *categories*, and pertain to entities whose Being is not of the kind which Dasein possesses. The context of assignments or references, which, as significance, is constitutive for worldhood, can be taken formally in the sense of a system of Relations. But one must note that in such formalizations the phenomena get levelled off so much that their real phenomenal content may be lost, especially in the case of such 'simple' relationships as those which lurk in significance. The phenomenal content of these 'Relations' and 'Relata'

---

[1] 'angewiesen'; '*Angewiesenheit*'. The verb 'anweisen', like 'verweisen', can often be translated as 'assign', particularly in the sense in which one assigns or allots a place to something, or in the sense in which one gives an 'assignment' to someone by instructing him how to proceed. The past participle 'angewiesen' can thus mean 'assigned' in either of these senses; but it often takes on the connotation of 'being dependent on' something or even 'at the mercy' of something. In this passage we have tried to compromise by using the verb 'submit'. Other passages call for other idioms, and no single standard translation seems feasible.

—the "in-order-to", the "for-the-sake-of", and the "with-which" of an involvement—is such that they resist any sort of mathematical functionalization; nor are they merely something thought, first posited in an 'act of thinking.' They are rather relationships in which concernful circumspection as such already dwells. This 'system of Relations', as something constitutive for worldhood, is so far from volatilizing the Being of the ready-to-hand within-the-world, that the worldhood of the world provides the basis on which such entities can for the first time be discovered as they are 'substantially' 'in themselves'. And only if entities within-the-world can be encountered at all, is it possible, in the field of such entities, to make accessible what is just present-at-hand and no more. By reason of their Being-just-present-at-hand-and-no-more, these latter entities can have their 'properties' defined mathematically in 'functional concepts.' Ontologically, such concepts are possible only in relation to entities whose Being has the character of pure substantiality. Functional concepts are never possible except as formalized substantial concepts.

In order to bring out the specifically ontological problematic of worldhood even more sharply, we shall carry our analysis no further until we have clarified our Interpretation of worldhood by a case at the opposite extreme.

B. *A Contrast between our Analysis of Worldhood and Descartes' Interpretation of the World*

Only step by step can the concept of worldhood and the structures which this phenomenon embraces be firmly secured in the course of our investigation. The Interpretation of the world begins, in the first instance, with some entity within-the-world, so that the phenomenon of the world in general no longer comes into view; we shall accordingly try to clarify this approach ontologically by considering what is perhaps the most extreme form in which it has been carried out. We not only shall present briefly the basic features of Descartes' ontology of the 'world', but shall inquire into its presuppositions and try to characterize these in the light of what we have hitherto achieved. The account we shall give of these matters will enable us to know upon what basically undiscussed ontological 'foundations' those Interpretations of the world which have come after Descartes—and still more those which preceded him—have operated.

Descartes sees the *extensio* as basically definitive ontologically for the world. In so far as extension is one of the constituents of spatiality (according to Descartes it is even identical with it), while in some sense spatiality remains constitutive for the world, a discussion of the Cartesian ontology of the 'world' will provide us likewise with a negative support for a positive explication of the spatiality of the environment and of Dasein itself. With regard to Descartes' ontology there are three topics which we shall treat: 1. the definition of the 'world' as *res extensa* (Section 19); 2. the foundations of this ontological definition (Section 20); 3. a hermeneutical discussion of the Cartesian ontology of the 'world' (Section 21). The considerations which follow will not have been grounded in full detail until the '*cogito sum*' has been phenomenologically destroyed. (See Part Two, Division 2.)[1]

¶ *19. The Definition of the 'World' as res extensa.*

Descartes distinguishes the '*ego cogito*' from the '*res corporea*'. This distinction will thereafter be determinative ontologically for the distinction between 'Nature' and 'spirit'. No matter with how many variations of content the opposition between 'Nature' and 'spirit' may get set up ontically, its ontological foundations, and indeed the very poles of this opposition, remain unclarified; this unclarity has its proximate [nächste] roots in Descartes' distinction. What kind of understanding of Being does he have when he defines the Being of these entities? The term for the Being of an entity that is in itself, is "*substantia*". Sometimes this expression means the *Being* of an entity as substance, *substantiality*; at other times it means the entity itself, *a substance*. That "*substantia*" is used in these two ways is not accidental; this already holds for the ancient conception of οὐσία.

To determine the nature of the *res corporea* ontologically, we must explicate the substance of this entity as a substance—that is, its substantiality. What makes up the authentic Being-in-itself [An-ihm-selbstsein] of the *res corporea*? How is it at all possible to grasp a substance as such, that is, to grasp its substantiality? "*Et quidem ex quolibet attributo substantia cognoscitur; sed una tamen est cuiusque substantiae praecipua proprietas, quae ipsius naturam essentiamque constituit, et ad quam aliae omnes referuntur.*"[iii] Substances become accessible in their 'attributes', and every substance has some distinctive property from which the essence of the substantiality of that definite substance can be read off. Which property is this in the case of the *res corporea*? "*Nempe extensio in longum, latum et profundum, substantiae corporeae naturam constituit.*"[iv] Extension—namely, in length, breadth, and thickness—makes up the real Being of that corporeal substance which we call the 'world'. What gives the *extensio* this distinctive status? "*Nam omne aliud quod corpori tribui potest, extensionem praesupponit . . .*"[v] Extension is a state-of-Being constitutive for the entity we are talking about; it is that

[1] This portion of *Being and Time* has never been published.

which must already 'be' before any other ways in which Being is determined, so that these can 'be' what they are. Extension must be 'assigned' ["zugewiesen"] primarily to the corporeal Thing. The 'world's' extension and substantiality (which itself is characterized by extension) are accordingly demonstrated by showing how all the other characteristics which this substance definitely possesses (especially *divisio, figura, motus*), can be conceived only as *modi* of *extensio*, while, on the other hand, *extensio sine figura vel motu* remains quite intelligible.

Thus a corporeal Thing that maintains its total extension can still undergo many changes in the ways in which that extension is distributed in the various dimensions, and can present itself in manifold shapes as one and the same Thing. ". . . *atque unum et idem corpus, retinendo suam eandem quantitatem, pluribus diversis modis potest extendi: nunc scilicet magis secundum longitudinem, minusque secundum latitudinem vel profunditatem, ac paulo post e contra magis secundum latitudinem, et minus secundum longitudinem.*"[vi]

Shape is a *modus* of *extensio*, and so is motion: for *motus* is grasped only "*si de nullo nisi locali cogitemus, ac de vi a qua excitatur . . . non inquiramus.*"[vii] If the motion is a property of the *res corporea*, and a property which i s, then in order for it to be experienceable in its Being, it must be conceived in terms of the Being of this entity itself, in terms of *extensio*; this means that it must be conceived as mere change of location. So nothing like 'force' counts for anything in determining what the *Being* of this entity is. Matter may have such definite characteristics as hardness, weight, and colour; (*durities, pondus, color*); but these can all be taken away from it, and it still remains what it is. These do not go to make up its real Being; and in so far as they *are*, they turn out to be modes of *extensio*. Descartes tries to show this in detail with regard to 'hardness': "*Nam, quantum ad duritiem, nihil aliud de illa sensus nobis indicat, quam partes durorum corporum resistere motui manuum nostrarum, cum in illas incurrant. Si enim, quotiescunque manus nostrae versus aliquam partem moventur, corpora omnia ibi existentia recederent eadem celeritate qua illae accedunt, nullam unquam duritiem sentiremus. Nec ullo modo potest intelligi, corpora quae sic recederent, idcirco naturam corporis esse amissura; nec proinde ipsa in duritie consistit.*"[viii] Hardness is experienced when one feels one's way by touch [Tasten]. What does the sense of touch 'tell' us about it? The parts of the hard Thing 'resist' a movement of the hand, such as an attempt to push it away. If, however, hard bodies, those which do not give way, should change their locations with the same velocity as that of the hand which 'strikes at' them, nothing would ever get touched [Berühren], and hardness would not be experienced and would accordingly never *be*. But it is quite incomprehensible that bodies which give way with such velocity should thus forfeit any of their corporeal Being. If they retain this even under a change in velocity which makes it impossible for anything like 'hardness' to be, then hardness does not belong to the Being of entities of this sort. *"Eademque ratione ostendi potest, et pondus, et colorem, et alias omnes eiusmodi qualitates, quae in materia corporea sentiuntur, ex ea tolli posse, ipsa integra remanente: unde sequitur, a nulla ex illis eius ⟨sc. extensionis⟩ naturam dependere."*[ix] Thus what makes up the Being of the *res corporea* is the *extensio*: that which is *omnimodo divisibile, figurabile et mobile* (that which can change itself by being divided, shaped, or moved in any way), that which is *capax mutationum*—that which maintains itself (*remanet*) through all these changes. In any corporeal Thing the real entity is what is suited for thus *remaining constant* [*ständigen Verbleib*], so much so, indeed that this is how the substantiality of such a substance gets characterized.

¶ *20. Foundations of the Ontological Definition of the 'World'*

Substantiality is the idea of Being to which the ontological characterization of the *res extensa* harks back. *"Per substantiam nihil aliud intelligere possumus, quam rem quae ita existit, ut nulla alia re indigeat ad existendum."* "By substance we can understand nothing else than an entity which *is* in such a way that it needs no other entity in order to *be*."[x] The Being of a 'substance' is characterized by not needing anything. That whose Being is such that it has no need at all for any other entity satisfies the idea of substance in the authentic sense; this entity is the *ens perfectissimum*. *". . . substantia quae nulla plane re indigeat, unica tantum potest intelligi, nempe Deus."*[xi] Here 'God' is a purely ontological term, if it is to be understood as *ens perfectissimum*. At the same time, the 'self-evident' connotation of the concept of God is such as to permit an ontological interpretation for the characteristic of not needing anything—a constitutive item in substantiality. *"Alias vero omnes ⟨res⟩, non nisi ope concursus Dei existere posse percipimus."*[xii] All entities other than God need to be "produced" in the widest sense and also to be sustained. 'Being' is to be understood within a horizon which ranges from the production of what is to be present-at-hand to something which has no need of being produced. Every entity which is not God is an *ens creatum*. The Being which belongs to one of these entities is 'infinitely' different from that which belongs to the other; yet we still consider creation and creator alike *as entities*. We are thus using "Being" in so wide a sense that its meaning embraces an 'infinite' difference. So even created entities can be called "substance" with some right. Relative to God, of course, these entities need to be produced and sustained; but within the realm of created entities—the 'world' in the sense of *ens creatum*—there are things which 'are in need of no other entity' relatively to the creaturely production and sustentation that we find, for instance, in man. Of these substances there are two kinds: the *res cogitans* and the *res extensa*.

The Being of that substance whose distinctive *proprietas* is presented by *extensio* thus becomes definable in principle ontologically if we clarify the *meaning* of Being which is '*common*' to the three kinds of substances, one of them infinite, the others both finite. But ". . . *nomen substantiae non convenit Deo et illis univoce ut dici solet in Scholis, hoc est . . . quae Deo et creaturis sit communis.*"xiii Here Descartes touches upon a problem with which medieval ontology was often busied—the question of how the signification of "Being" signifies any entity which one may on occasion be considering. In the assertions 'God is' and 'the world is', we assert Being. This word 'is', however, cannot be meant to apply to these entities in the same sense (συνωνύμως, *univoce*), when between them there is an *infinite* difference of Being; if the signification of 'is' were univocal, then what is created would be viewed as if it were uncreated, or the uncreated would be reduced to the status of something created. But neither does 'Being' function as a mere name which is the same in both cases: in both cases 'Being' is understood. This positive sense in which 'Being' signifies is one which the Schoolmen took as a signification 'by analogy', as distinguished from one which is univocal or merely homonymous. Taking their departure from Aristotle, in whom this problem is foreshadowed in prototypical form just as at the very outset of Greek ontology, they established various kinds of analogy, so that even the 'Schools' have different ways of taking the signification-function of "Being". In working out this problem ontologically, Descartes is always far behind the Schoolmen;xiv indeed he evades the question. ". . . *nulla eius ⟨substantiae⟩ nominis significatio potest distincte intelligi, quae Deo et creaturis sit communis.*"xv This evasion is tantamount to his failing to discuss the meaning of Being which the idea of substantiality embraces, or the character of the 'universality' which belongs to this signification. Of course even the ontology of the medievals has gone no further than that of the ancients in inquiring into what "Being" itself may mean. So it is not surprising if no headway is made with a question like that of the way in which "Being" signifies, as long as this has to be discussed on the basis of an unclarified meaning of Being which this signification 'expresses'. The meaning remains unclarified because it is held to be 'self-evident'.

Descartes not only evades the ontological question of substantiality altogether; he also emphasizes explicitly that substance as such—that is to say, its substantiality—is in and for itself inaccessible from the outset [vorgängig]. "*Verumtamen non potest substantia primum animadverti ex hoc solo, quod sit res existens, quia hoc solum per se nos non afficit . . .".*[xvi] 'Being' itself does not 'affect' us, and therefore cannot be perceived. 'Being is not a Real predicate,' says Kant,[1] who is merely repeating Descartes' principle. Thus the possibility of a pure problematic of Being gets renounced in principle, and a way is sought for arriving at those definite characteristics of substance which we have designated above. Because 'Being' is not in fact accessible *as an entity*, it is expressed through attributes—definite characteristics of the entities under consideration, characteristics which themselves a r e.[2] Being is not expressed through just a n y such characteristics, but rather through those satisfying in the purest manner that meaning of "Being" and "substantiality", which has still been tacitly presupposed. To the *substantia finita* as *res corporea*, what must primarily be 'assigned' ["Zuweisung"] is the *extensio*. *"Quin et facilius intelligimus substantiam extensam, vel substantiam cogitantem, quam substantiam solam, omisso eo quod cogitet vel sit extensa"*;[xvii] for substantiality is detachable *ratione tantum*; it is not detachable *realiter*, nor can we come across it in the way in which we come across those entities themselves which a r e substantially.

Thus the ontological grounds for defining the 'world' as *res extensa* have been made plain: they lie in the idea of substantiality, which not only remains unclarified in the meaning of its Being, but gets passed off as something incapable of clarification, and gets represented indirectly by way of whatever substantial property belongs most pre-eminently to the particular substance. Moreover, in this way of defining a substance through some substantial entity, lies the reason why the term "substance" is used in two ways. What is here intended is substantiality; and it gets understood in terms of a characteristic of substance—a characteristic which is itself an entity.[3] Because something ontical is made to underlie the ontological, the expression *"substantia"* functions sometimes with a signification which is ontological, sometimes with one which is ontical, but mostly with one which is hazily ontico-ontological. Behind this slight difference of signification, however, there lies hidden a failure to master the basic problem of Being. To treat this adequately, we must 'track down' the equivocations *in the right way*. He who attempts this sort of thing does not just 'busy himself' with 'merely verbal significations'; he must venture forward into the most primordial problematic of the 'things themselves' to get such 'nuances' straightened out.

---

[1] Immanuel Kant, *Critique of Pure Reason, Transcendental Dialectic*, Book II, chapter III, Section 4.

[2] '. . . seiende Bestimmtheiten des betreffenden Seienden . . .'

[3] '. . . aus einer seienden Beschaffenheit der Substanz.'

¶ *21. Hermeneutical Discussion of the Cartesian Ontology of the 'World'*

The critical question now arises: does this ontology of the 'world' seek the phenomenon of the world at all, and if not, does it at least define some entity within-the-world fully enough so that the worldly character of this entity can be made visible in it? *To both questions we must answer "No".* The entity which Descartes is trying to grasp ontologically and in principle with his *"extensio"*, is rather such as to become discoverable first of all by going through an entity within-the-world which is proximally ready-to-hand—Nature. Though this is the case, and though any ontological characterization of this *latter* entity within-the-world may lead us into obscurity, even if we consider both the idea of substantiality and the meaning of the *"existit"* and *"ad existendum"* which have been brought into the definition of that idea, it still remains possible that through an ontology based upon a radical separation of God, the "I", and the 'world', the ontological problem of the world will in some sense get formulated and further advanced. If, however, this is not possible, we must then demonstrate explicitly not only that Descartes' conception of the world is ontologically defective, but that his Interpretation and the foundations on which it is based have led him to *pass over* both the phenomenon of the world and the Being of those entities within-the-world which are proximally ready-to-hand.

In our exposition of the problem of worldhood (Section 14), we suggested the importance of obtaining proper access to this phenomenon. So in criticizing the Cartesian point of departure, we must ask which kind of Being that belongs to Dasein we should fix upon as giving us an appropriate way of access to those entities with whose Being as *extensio* Descartes equates the Being of the 'world'. The only genuine access to them lies in knowing [Erkennen], *intellectio*, in the sense of the kind of knowledge [Erkenntnis] we get in mathematics and physics. Mathematical knowledge is regarded by Descartes as the one manner of apprehending entities which can always give assurance that their Being has been securely grasped. If anything measures up in its own kind of Being to the Being that is accessible in mathematical knowledge, then it *is* in the authentic sense. Such entities are those *which always are what they are.* Accordingly, that which can be shown to have the character of something that *constantly remains* (as *remanens capax mutationum*), makes up the real Being of those entities of the world which get experienced. That which enduringly remains, really *is*. This is the sort of thing which mathematics knows. That which is accessible in an entity *through mathematics*, makes up its Being. Thus the Being of the 'world' is, as it were, dictated to it in terms of a definite idea of Being which lies veiled in the concept of substantiality, and in terms of the idea of a knowledge by which *such* entities are cognized. The kind of Being which belongs to entities within-the-world is something which they themselves might have been permitted to present; but Descartes does not let them do so.[1] Instead he prescribes for the world its 'real' Being, as it were, on the basis of an idea of Being whose source has not been unveiled and which has not been demonstrated in its own right—an idea in which Being is equated with constant presence-at-hand. Thus his ontology of the world is not primarily determined by his leaning towards mathematics, a science which he chances to esteem very highly, but rather by his ontological orientation in principle towards Being as constant presence-at-hand, which mathematical knowledge is exceptionally well suited to grasp. In this way Descartes explicitly switches over philosophically from the development of traditional ontology to modern mathematical physics and its transcendental foundations.

The problem of how to get appropriate access to entities within-the-world is one which Descartes feels no need to raise. Under the unbroken ascendance of the traditional ontology, the way to get a genuine grasp of what really is [des eigentlichen Seienden] has been decided in advance: it lies in νοεῖν—'beholding' in the widest sense [der "Anschauung" im weitesten Sinne]; διανοεῖν or 'thinking' is just a more fully achieved form of νοεῖν and is founded upon it. *Sensatio* (αἴσθησις), as opposed to *intellectio*, still remains possible as a way of access to entities by a beholding which is perceptual in character; but Descartes presents his 'critique' of it because he is oriented ontologically by these principles.

Descartes knows very well that entities do not proximally show themselves in their real Being. What is 'proximally' given is this waxen Thing which is coloured, flavoured, hard, and cold in definite ways, and which gives off its own special sound when struck. But this is not of any importance ontologically, nor, in general, is anything which is given through the senses. "*Satis erit, si advertamus sensuum perceptiones non referri, nisi ad istam corporis humani cum mente coniunctionem, et nobis quidem ordinarie exhibere, quid ad illam externa corpora prodesse possint aut nocere . . .*"[xviii] The senses do not enable us to cognize any entity in its Being; they merely serve to announce the ways in which 'external' Things within-the-world are useful or harmful for human creatures encumbered with bodies. "*. . . non . . . nos docere, qualia ⟨corpora⟩ in seipsis existant*";[xix] they tell us nothing about entities in their Being. "*Quod agentes, percipiemus naturam materiae, sive corporis in universum spectati, non consistere in eo quod sit res dura, vel ponderosa, vel colorata,*

---

[1] 'Descartes lässt sich nicht die Seinsart des innerweltlichen Seienden von diesem vorgeben . . .'

vel alio aliquo modo sensus afficiens : sed tantum in eo quod sit res extensa in longum, latum et profundum."xx

If we subject Descartes' Interpretation of the experience of hardness and resistance to a critical analysis, it will be plain how unable he is to let what shows itself in sensation present itself in its own kind of Being,[1] or even to determine its character (Cf. Section 19).

Hardness gets taken as resistance. But neither hardness nor resistance is understood in a phenomenal sense, as something experienced in itself whose nature can be determined in such an experience. For Descartes, resistance amounts to no more than not yielding place—that is, not undergoing any change of location. So if a Thing resists, this means that it stays in a definite location relatively to some other Thing which is changing its location, or that it is changing its own location with a velocity which permits the other Thing to 'catch up' with it. But when the experience of hardness is Interpreted this way, the kind of Being which belongs to sensory perception is obliterated, and so is any possibility that the entities encountered in such perception should be grasped in their Being. Descartes takes the kind of Being which belongs to the perception of something, and translates it into the only kind he knows: the perception of something becomes a definite way of Being-present-at-hand-side-by-side of two *res extensae* which are present-at-hand; the way in which their movements are related is itself a mode of that *extensio* by which the presence-at-hand of the corporeal Thing is primarily characterized. Of course no behaviour in which one feels one's way by touch [eines tastenden Verhaltens] can be 'completed' unless what can thus be felt [des Betastbaren] has 'closeness' of a very special kind. But this does not mean that touching [Berührung] and the hardness which makes itself known in touching consist ontologically in different velocities of two corporeal Things. Hardness and resistance do not show themselves at all unless an entity has the kind of Being which Dasein—or at least something living—possesses.

Thus Descartes' discussion of possible kinds of *access* to entities within-the-world is dominated by an idea of Being which has been gathered from a definite realm of these entities themselves.

The idea of Being as permanent presence-at-hand not only gives Descartes a motive for identifying entities within-the-world with the world in general, and for providing so extreme a definition of their Being; it also keeps him from bringing Dasein's ways of behaving into view in a manner which is ontologically appropriate. But thus the road is completely

---

[1] '. . . das in der Sinnlichkeit sich Zeigende in seiner eigenen Seinsart sich vorgeben zu lassen . . .'

blocked to seeing the founded character of all sensory and intellective
awareness, and to understanding these as possibilities of Being-in-the-
world.[1] On the contrary, he takes the Being of 'Dasein' (to whose basic
constitution Being-in-the-world belongs) in the very same way as he takes
the Being of the *res extensa*—namely, as substance.

But with these criticisms, have we not fobbed off on Descartes a task
altogether beyond his horizon, and then gone on to 'demonstrate' that
he has failed to solve it? If Descartes does not know the phenomenon of
the world, and thus knows no such thing as within-the-world-ness, how
can he identify the world itself with certain entities within-the-world and
the Being which they possess?

In controversy over principles, one must not only attach oneself to
theses which can be grasped doxographically; one must also derive one's
orientation from the objective tendency of the problematic, even if it
does not go beyond a rather ordinary way of taking things. In his doctrine
of the *res cogitans* and the *res extensa*, Descartes not only *wants to formulate*
the problem of 'the "I" and the world'; he claims to have solved it in a
radical manner. His *Meditations* make this plain. (See especially Meditations I and VI.) By taking his basic ontological orientation from traditional
sources and not subjecting it to positive criticism, he has made it impossible to lay bare any primordial ontological problematic of Dasein; this
has inevitably obstructed his view of the phenomenon of the world, and
has made it possible for the ontology of the 'world' to be compressed into
that of certain entities within-the-world. The foregoing discussion should
have proved this.

One might retort, however, that even if in point of fact both the problem
of the world and the Being of the entities encountered environmentally
as closest to us remain concealed, Descartes has still laid the basis for
characterizing ontologically that entity within-the-world upon which, in
its very Being, every other entity is founded—material Nature. This would
be the fundamental stratum upon which all the other strata of actuality
within-the-world are built up. The extended Thing as such would serve,
in the first instance, as the ground for those definite characters which
show themselves, to be sure, as qualities, but which 'at bottom' are
quantitative modifications of the modes of the *extensio* itself. These
qualities, which are themselves reducible, would provide the footing for
such specific qualities as "beautiful", "ugly", "in keeping", "not in

[1] 'Damit ist aber vollends der Weg dazu verlegt, gar auch noch den fundierten Charakter
alles sinnlichen und verstandesmässigen Vernehmens zu sehen und sie als eine Möglichkeit
des In-der-Welt-seins zu verstehen.' While we have construed the pronoun 'sie' as referring to the two kinds of awareness which have just been mentioned, it would be
grammatically more plausible to interpret it as referring either to 'Dasein's ways of
behaving' or to 'the idea of Being as permanent presence-at-hand'.

keeping," "useful", "useless". If one is oriented primarily by Thinghood, these latter qualities must be taken as non-quantifiable value-predicates by which what is in the first instance just a material Thing, gets stamped as something good. But with this stratification, we come to those entities which we have characterized ontologically as equipment ready-to-hand The Cartesian analysis of the 'world' would thus enable us for the first time to build up securely the structure of what is proximally ready-to-hand; all it takes is to round out the Thing of Nature until it becomes a full-fledged Thing of use, and this is easily done.

But quite apart from the specific problem of the world itself, can the Being of what we encounter proximally within-the-world be reached ontologically by this procedure? When we speak of material Thinghood, have we not tacitly posited a kind of Being—the constant presence-at hand of Things—which is so far from having been rounded out ontologically by subsequently endowing entities with value-predicates, that these value-characters themselves are rather just ontical characteristics of those entities which have the kind of Being possessed by Things? Adding on value-predicates cannot tell us anything at all new about the Being of goods, *but would merely presuppose again that goods have pure presence-at-hand as their kind of Being.* Values would then be determinate characteristics which a Thing possesses, and they would be *present-at-hand*. They would have their sole ultimate ontological source in our previously laying down the actuality of Things as the fundamental stratum. But even pre-phenomenological experience shows that in an entity which is supposedly a Thing, there is something that will not become fully intelligible through Thinghood alone. Thus the Being of Things has to be rounded out. What, then does the Being of values or their 'validity' ["Geltung"] (which Lotze took as a mode of 'affirmation') really amount to ontologically? And what does it signify ontologically for Things to be 'invested' with values in this way? As long as these matters remain obscure, to reconstruct the Thing of use in terms of the Thing of Nature is an ontologically questionable undertaking, even if one disregards the way in which the problematic has been perverted in principle. And if we are to reconstruct this Thing of use, which supposedly comes to us in the first instance 'with its skin off', does not this always require *that we previously take a positive look at the phenomenon whose totality such a reconstruction is to restore*? But if we have not given a proper explanation beforehand of its ownmost state of Being, are we not building our reconstruction without a plan? Inasmuch as this reconstruction and 'rounding-out' of the traditional ontology of the 'world' results in our reaching the same *entities* with which we started when we analysed the readiness-to-hand of equipment and the totality of involvements, it seems as if the *Being* of these entities has in fact been clarified or has at least become a *problem*. But by taking *extensio* as a *proprietas*, Descartes can hardly reach the Being of substance; and by taking refuge in 'value'-characteristics ["wertlichen" Beschaffenheiten] we are just as far from even catching a glimpse of Being as readiness-to-hand, let alone permitting it to become an ontological theme.

Descartes has narrowed down the question of the world to that of Things of Nature [Naturdinglichkeit] as those entities within-the-world which are proximally accessible. He has confirmed the opinion that to *know* an entity in what is supposedly the most rigorous ontical manner is our only possible access to the primary Being of the entity which such knowledge reveals. But at the same time we must have the insight to see that in principle the 'roundings-out' of the Thing-ontology also operate on the same dogmatic basis as that which Descartes has adopted.

We have already intimated in Section 14 that passing over the world and those entities which we proximally encounter is not accidental, not an oversight which it would be simple to correct, but that it is grounded in a kind of Being which belongs essentially to Dasein itself. When our analytic of Dasein has given some transparency to those main structures of Dasein which are of the most importance in the framework of this problematic, and when we have assigned [zugewiesen] to the concept of Being in general the horizon within which its intelligibility becomes possible, so that readiness-to-hand and presence-at-hand also become primordially intelligible ontologically for the first time, only then can our critique of the Cartesian ontology of the world (an ontology which, in principle, is still the usual one today) come philosophically into its own.

To do this, we must show several things. (See Part One, Division Three.)[1]

1. Why was the phenomenon of the world passed over at the beginning of the ontological tradition which has been decisive for us (explicitly in the case of Parmenides), and why has this passing-over kept constantly recurring?

2. Why is it that, instead of the phenomenon thus passed over, entities within-the-world have intervened as an ontological theme?[2]

3. Why are these entities found in the first instance in 'Nature'?

4. Why has recourse been taken to the phenomenon of value when it has seemed necessary to round out such an ontology of the world?

---

[1] This Division has never been published.

[2] 'Warum springt für das übersprungene Phänomen das innerweltlich Seiende als ontologisches Thema ein?' The verbal play on 'überspringen' ('pass over') and 'einspringen' ('intervene' or 'serve as a deputy') is lost in translation. On 'einspringen' see our note 1, p. 158, H. 122 below.

In the answers to these questions a positive understanding of the *problematic* of the world will be reached for the first time, the sources of our failure to recognize it will be exhibited, and the ground for rejecting the traditional ontology of the world will have been demonstrated.

The world and Dasein and entities within-the-world are the ontologically constitutive states which are closest to us; but we have no guarantee that we can achieve the basis for meeting up with these as phenomena by the seemingly obvious procedure of starting with the Things of the world, still less by taking our orientation from what is supposedly the most rigorous knowledge of entities. Our observations on Descartes should have brought us this insight.

But if we recall that spatiality is manifestly one of the constituents of entities within-the-world, then in the end the Cartesian analysis of the 'world' can still be 'rescued'. When Descartes was so radical as to set up the *extensio* as the *praesuppositum* for every definite characteristic of the *res corporea*, he prepared the way for the understanding of something *a priori* whose content Kant was to establish with greater penetration. Within certain limits the analysis of the *extensio* remains independent of his neglecting to provide an explicit interpretation for the Being of extended entities. There is some phenomenal justification for regarding the *extensio* as a basic characteristic of the 'world', even if by recourse to this neither the spatiality of the world nor that of the entities we encounter in our environment (a spatiality which is proximally discovered) nor even that of Dasein itself, can be conceived ontologically.

C. The Aroundness of the Environment[1] and Dasein's Spatiality

In connection with our first preliminary sketch of Being-in (See Section 12), we had to contrast Dasein with a way of Being in space which we call "insideness" [Inwendigkeit]. This expression means that an entity which is itself extended is closed round [umschlɔssen] by the extended boundaries of something that is likewise extended. The entity inside [Das inwendig Seiende] and that which closes it round are both present-at-hand in space. Yet even if we deny that Dasein has any such insideness in a spatial receptacle, this does not in principle exclude it from having any spatiality at all, but merely keeps open the way for seeing the kind of spatiality which is constitutive for Dasein. This must now be set forth. But inasmuch as any entity within-the-*world* is likewise in space, its spatiality will have an ontological connection with the world. We must therefore determine in what sense space is a constituent for that world which has in turn been characterized as an item in the structure of Being-in-the-world. In particular

---

1 '*Das Umhafte der Umwelt*'. See our note 1, p. 93, H. 65 above.

we must show how the aroundness of the environment, the specific spatiality of entities encountered in the environment, is founded upon the worldhood of the world, while contrariwise the world, on its part, is not present-at-hand in space. Our study of Dasein's spatiality and the way in which the world is spatially determined will take its departure from an analysis of what is ready-to-hand in space within-the-world. We shall consider three topics: 1. the spatiality of the ready-to-hand within-the-world (Section 22); 2. the spatiality of Being-in-the-world (Section 23); 3. space and the spatiality of Dasein (Section 24).

¶ *22. The Spatiality of the Ready-to-hand Within-the-world*

If space is constitutive for the world in a sense which we have yet to determine, then it cannot surprise us that in our foregoing ontological characterization of the Being of what is within-the-world we have had to look upon this as something that is also within space. This spatiality of the ready-to-hand is something which we have not yet grasped explicitly as a phenomenon; nor have we pointed out how it is bound up with the structure of Being which belongs to the ready-to-hand. This is now our task.

To what extent has our characterization of the ready-to-hand already come up against its spatiality? We have been talking about what is *proximally* ready-to-hand. This means not only those entities which we encounter *first* before any others, but also those which are 'close by'.[1] What is ready-to-hand in our everyday dealings has the character of *closeness*. To be exact, this closeness of equipment has already been intimated in the term 'readiness-to-hand', which expresses the Being of equipment. Every entity that is 'to hand' has a different closeness, which is not to be ascertained by measuring distances. This closeness regulates itself in terms of circumspectively 'calculative' manipulating and using. At the same time what is close in this way gets established by the circumspection of concern, with regard to the direction in which the equipment is accessible at any time. When this closeness of the equipment has been given directionality,[2] this signifies not merely that the equipment has its

---

[1] 'in der Nähe.' While the noun 'Nähe' often means the '*closeness*' or '*nearness*' of something that is close to us, it can also stand for our immediate '*vicinity*', as in the present expression, and in many passages it can be interpreted either way. We shall in general translate it as 'closeness', but we shall translate 'in der Nähe' and similar phrases as 'close by'.

[2] 'Die ausgerichtete Nähe des Zeugs . . .' The verb 'ausrichten' has many specialized meanings—to 'align' a row of troops, to 'explore' a mine, to 'make arrangements' for something, to 'carry out' a commission, etc. Heidegger, however, keeps its root meaning in mind and associates it with the word 'Richtung' ('direction', 'route to be taken', etc.). We shall accordingly translate it as a rule by some form of the verb 'direct' (which will also be used occasionally for the verb 'richten'), or by some compound expression involving the word 'directional'. For further discussion, see H. 108 ff. below.

position [Stelle] in space as present-at-hand somewhere, but also that as
equipment it has been essentially fitted up and installed, set up, and put
to rights. Equipment has its *place* [*Platz*], or else it 'lies around'; this must
be distinguished in principle from just occurring at random in some
spatial position. When equipment for something or other has its place,
this place defines itself as the place of this equipment—as one place out
of a whole totality of places directionally lined up with each other and
belonging to the context of equipment that is environmentally ready-to-
hand. Such a place and such a muliplicity of places are not to be interpreted as the "where" of some random Being-present-at-hand of Things.
In each case the place is the definite 'there' or 'yonder' ["Dort" und
"Da"] of an item of equipment which *belongs somewhere*. Its belonging-
somewhere at the time [Die jeweilige Hingehörigkeit] corresponds to the
equipmental character of what is ready-to-hand; that is, it corresponds to
the belonging-to [Zugehörigkeit] which the ready-to-hand has towards a
totality of equipment in accordance with its involvements. But in general
the "whither" to which the totality of places for a context of equipment
gets allotted, is the underlying condition which makes possible the belonging-somewhere of an equipmental totality as something that can be placed.
This "whither", which makes it possible for equipment to belong somewhere, and which we circumspectively keep in view ahead of us in our
concernful dealings, we call the *"region"*.[1]

'In the region of' means not only 'in the direction of' but also within
the range [Umkreis] of something that lies in that direction. The kind of
place which is constituted by direction and remoteness[2] (and closeness
is only a mode of the latter) is already oriented towards a region and
oriented within it. Something like a region must first be discovered if
there is to be any possibility of allotting or coming across places for a
totality of equipment that is circumspectively at one's disposal. The
regional orientation of the multiplicity of places belonging to the ready-
to-hand goes to make up the aroundness—the "round-about-us" [das
Um-uns-herum]—of those entities which we encounter as closest environmentally. A three-dimensional multiplicity of possible positions which
gets filled up with Things present-at-hand is never proximally given. This
dimensionality of space is still veiled in the spatiality of the ready-to-hand.
The 'above' is what is 'on the ceiling'; the 'below' is what is 'on the floor';

---

[1] 'Gegend'. There is no English word which quite corresponds to 'Gegend'. 'Region'
and 'whereabouts' perhaps come the closest, and we have chosen the former as the more
convenient. (Heidegger himself frequently uses the word 'Region', but he does so in
contexts where 'realm' seems to be the most appropriate translation; we have usually so
translated it, leaving the English 'region' for 'Gegend'.)

[2] 'Entferntheit'. For further discussion, see Section 23 and our note 2, p. 138, H. 105.

the 'behind' is what is 'at the door'; all "wheres" are discovered and circumspectively interpreted as we go our ways in everyday dealings; they are not ascertained and catalogued by the observational measurement of space.

Regions are not first formed by things which are. present-at-hand together; they always are ready-to-hand already in individual places. Places themselves either get allotted to the ready-to-hand in the circumspection of concern, or we come across them. Thus anything constantly ready-to-hand of which circumspective Being-in-the-world takes account beforehand, has its place. The "where" of its readiness-to-hand is put to account as a matter for concern, and oriented towards the rest of what is ready-to-hand. Thus the sun, whose light and warmth are in everyday use, has its own places—sunrise, midday, sunset, midnight; these are discovered in circumspection and treated distinctively in terms of changes in the usability of what the sun bestows. Here we have something which is ready-to-hand with uniform constancy, although it keeps changing; its places become accentuated 'indicators' of the regions which lie in them. These celestial regions, which need not have any geographical meaning as yet, provide the "whither" beforehand for every[1] special way of giving form to the regions which places can occupy. The house has its sunny side and its shady side; the way it is divided up into 'rooms' ["Räume"] is oriented towards these, and so is the 'arrangement' ["Einrichtung"] within them, according to their character as equipment. Churches and graves, for instance, are laid out according to the rising and the setting of the sun—the regions of life and death, which are determinative for Dasein itself with regard to its ownmost possibilities of Being in the world. Dasein, in its very Being, has this Being as an issue; and its concern discovers beforehand those regions in which some involvement is decisive. This discovery of regions beforehand is co-determined [mitbestimmt] by the totality of involvements for which the ready-to-hand, as something encountered, is freed.

The readiness-to-hand which belongs to any such region beforehand has the *character of inconspicuous familiarity*, and it has it in an even more primordial sense than does the Being of the ready-to-hand.[2] The region itself becomes visible in a conspicuous manner only when one discovers

---

[1] Reading 'jede' with the later editions. The earliest editions have 'je', which has been corrected in the list of *errata*.

[2] 'Die vorgängige Zuhandenheit der jeweiligen Gegend hat in einem noch ursprünglicheren Sinne als das Sein des Zuhandenen den *Charakter der unauffälligen Vertrautheit*.' Here the phrase 'als das Sein des Zuhandenen' is ambiguously placed. In the light of Section 16 above, we have interpreted 'als' as 'than' rather than 'as', and have treated 'das Sein' as a nominative rather than an accusative. But other readings are grammatically just as possible.

the ready-to-hand circumspectively and does so in the deficient modes of concern.[1] Often the region of a place does not become accessible explicitly as such a region until one fails to find something in *its* place. The space which is discovered in circumspective Being-in-the-world as the spatiality of the totality of-equipment, always belongs to entities themselves as the place of that totality. The bare space itself is still veiled over. Space has been split up into places. But this spatiality has its own unity through that totality-of-involvements in-accordance-with-the-world [weltmässige] which belongs to the spatially ready-to-hand. The 'environment' does not arrange itself in a space which has been given in advance; but its specific worldhood, in its significance, Articulates the context of involvements which belongs to some current totality of circumspectively allotted places. The world at such a time always reveals the spatiality of the space which belongs to it. To encounter the ready-to-hand in its environmental space remains ontically possible only because Dasein itself is 'spatial' with regard to its Being-in-the-world.

¶ 23. *The Spatiality of Being-in-the-world*

If we attribute spatiality to Dasein, then this 'Being in space' must manifestly be conceived in terms of the kind of Being which that entity possesses. Dasein is essentially not a Being-present-at-hand; and its "spatiality" cannot signify anything like occurrence at a position in 'world-space', nor can it signify Being-ready-to-hand at some place. Both of these are kinds of Being which belong to entities encountered within-the-world. Dasein, however, is 'in' the world in the sense that it deals with entities encountered within-the-world, and does so concernfully and with familiarity. So if spatiality belongs to it in any way, that is possible only because of this Being-in. But its spatiality shows the characters of *de-severance* and *directionality*.[2]

---

[1] 'Sie wird selbst nur sichtbar in der Weise des Auffallens bei einem umsichtigen Entdecken des Zuhandenen und zwar in den defizienten Modi des Besorgens.' This sentence too is ambiguous. The pronoun 'Sie' may refer either to the *region*, as we have suggested, or to its *readiness-to-hand*. Furthermore, while we have taken 'nur sichtbar in der Weise des Auffallens' as a unit, it is possible that 'in der Weise des Auffallens' should be construed as going with the words that follow. In this case we should read: '. . . becomes visible only when it becomes conspicuous in our circumspective discovery of the ready-to-hand, and indeed in the deficient modes of concern.'

[2] '*Ent-fernung und Ausrichtung.*' The nouns 'Entfernung' and 'Entfernheit' can usually be translated by 'removing', 'removal', 'remoteness', or even 'distance'. In this passage, however, Heidegger is calling attention to the fact that these words are derived from the stem 'fern-' ('far' or 'distant') and the privative prefix 'ent-'. Usually this prefix would be construed as merely intensifying the notion of separation or distance expressed in the 'fern-'; but Heidegger chooses to construe it as more strictly privative, so that the verb 'entfernen' will be taken to mean *abolishing* a distance or farness rather than enhancing it. It is as if by the very act of recognizing the 'remoteness' of something, we have in a sense brought it closer and made it less 'remote'.
Apparently there is no word in English with an etymological structure quite parallel

When we speak of deseverance as a kind of Being which Dasein has with
regard to its Being-in-the-world, we do not understand by it any such
thing as remoteness (or closeness) or even a distance.[1] We use the expression "deseverance"* in a signification which is both active and transitive.
It stands for a constitutive state of Dasein's Being—a state with regard
to which removing something in the sense of putting it away is only a
determinate factical mode. "De-severing"* amounts to making the farness
vanish—that is, making the remoteness of something disappear, bringing
it close.[2] Dasein is essentially de-severant: it lets any entity be encountered
close by as the entity which it is. De-severance discovers remoteness; and
remoteness, like distance, is a determinate categorial characteristic of
entities whose nature is not that of Dasein. De-severance*, however, is
an *existentiale*; this must be kept in mind. Only to the extent that entities
are revealed for Dasein in their deseveredness [Entferntheit], do 'remote-
nesses' ["Entfernungen"] and distances with regard to other things
become accessible in entities within-the-world themselves. Two points are
just as little desevered from one another as two Things, for neither of these
types of entity has the kind of Being which would make it capable of
desevering. They merely have a measurable distance between them,
which we can come across in our de-severing.

Proximally and for the most part, de-severing[3] is a circumspective

to that of 'entfernen'; perhaps 'dissever' comes the nearest, for this too is a verb of separation in which a privative prefix is used as an intensive. We have coined the similar verb
'desever' in the hope that this will suggest Heidegger's meaning when 'remove' and its
derivatives seem inappropriate. But with 'desever', one cannot slip back and forth from
one sense to another as easily as one can with 'entfernen'; so we have resorted to the
expedient of using both 'desever' and 'remove' and their derivatives, depending upon the
sense we feel is intended. Thus 'entfernen' will generally be rendered by 'remove' or
'desever', 'entfernt' by 'remote' or 'desevered'. Since Heidegger is careful to distinguish
'Entfernung' and 'Entferntheit', we shall usually translate these by 'deseverance' and
'remoteness' respectively; in the few cases where these translations do not seem appropriate, we shall subjoin the German word in brackets.

Our problem is further complicated by Heidegger's practise of occasionally putting a
hyphen after the prefix 'ent-', presumably to emphasize its privative character. In such
cases we shall write 'de-sever', 'de-severance', etc. Unfortunately, however, there are
typographical discrepancies between the earlier and later editions. Some of the earlier
hyphens occur at the ends of lines and have been either intentionally or inadvertently
omitted in resetting the type; some appear at the end of the line in the later editions, but
not in the earlier ones; others have this position in both editions. We shall indicate each
of these ambiguous cases with an asterisk, supplying a hyphen only if there seems to be a
good reason for doing so.

On 'Ausrichtung' see our note 2, p. 135, H. 102 above.

[1] 'Abstand'. Heidegger uses three words which might be translated as 'distance':
'Ferne' (our 'farness'), 'Entfernung' (our 'deseverance'), and 'Abstand' ('distance' in the
sense of a measurable interval). We shall reserve 'distance' for 'Abstand'.

[2] 'Entfernen* besagt ein Verschwindenmachen der Ferne, d. h. der Entferntheit von
etwas, Näherung.'

[3] This hyphen is found only in the later editions.

bringing-close—bringing something close by, in the sense of procuring it, putting it in readiness, having it to hand. But certain ways in which entities are discovered in a purely cognitive manner also have the character of bringing them close. *In Dasein there lies an essential tendency towards closeness.* All the ways in which we speed things up, as we are more or less compelled to do today, push us on towards the conquest of remoteness. With the 'radio', for example, Dasein has so expanded its everyday environment that it has accomplished a de-severance of the 'world'— a de-severance which, in its meaning for Dasein, cannot yet be visualized.

De-severing does not necessarily imply any explicit estimation of the farness of something ready-to-hand in relation to Dasein. Above all, remoteness* never gets taken as a distance. If farness is to be estimated, this is done relatively to deseverances in which everyday Dasein maintains itself. Though these estimates may be imprecise and variable if we try to compute them, in the everydayness of Dasein they have their *own definiteness* which is thoroughly intelligible. We say that to go over yonder is "a good walk", "a stone's throw", or 'as long as it takes to smoke a pipe'. These measures express not only that they are not intended to 'measure' anything but also that the remoteness* here estimated belongs to some entity to which one goes with concernful circumspection. But even when we avail ourselves of a fixed measure and say 'it is half an hour to the house', this measure must be taken as an estimate. 'Half an hour' is not thirty minutes, but a duration [Dauer] which has no 'length' at all in the sense of a quantitative stretch. Such a duration is always interpreted in terms of well-accustomed everyday ways in which we 'make provision' ["Besorgungen"]. Remotenesses* are estimated proximally by circumspection, even when one is quite familiar with 'officially' calculated measures. Since what is de-severed in such estimates is ready-to-hand, it retains its character as specifically within-the-world. This even implies that the pathways we take towards desevered entities in the course of our dealings will vary in their length from day to day. What is ready-to-hand in the environment is certainly not present-at-hand for an eternal observer exempt from Dasein: but it is encountered in Dasein's circumspectively concernful everydayness. As Dasein goes along its ways, it does not measure off a stretch of space as a corporeal Thing which is present-at-hand; it does not 'devour the kilometres'; bringing-close or de-severance is always a kind of concernful Being towards what is brought close and de-severed. A pathway which is long 'Objectively' can be much shorter than one which is 'Objectively' shorter still but which is perhaps 'hard going' and comes before us[1] as interminably long. *Yet only in thus 'coming before us'*[1] *is the current world authentically ready-to-hand.* The Objective distances of Things present-at-hand do not coincide with the remoteness and closeness of what is ready-to-hand within-the-world. Though we may know these distances exactly, this knowledge still remains blind; it does not have the function of discovering the environment circumspectively and bringing it close; this knowledge is used only in and for a concernful Being which does not measure stretches—a Being towards the world that 'matters' to one [. . . Sein zu der einen "angehenden" Welt].

When one is oriented beforehand towards 'Nature' and 'Objectively' measured distances of Things, one is inclined to pass off such estimates and interpretations of deseverance as 'subjective'. Yet this 'subjectivity' perhaps uncovers the 'Reality' of the world at its most Real; it has nothing to do with 'subjective' arbitrariness or subjectivistic 'ways of taking' an entity which 'in itself' is otherwise. *The circumspective de-severing of Dasein's everydayness reveals the Being-in-itself of the 'true world'—of that entity which Dasein, as something existing, is already alongside.*[2]

When one is primarily and even exclusively oriented towards remote-nesses as measured distances, the primordial spatiality of Being-in is concealed. That which is presumably 'closest' is by no means that which is at the smallest distance 'from us'. It lies in that which is desevered to an average extent when we reach for it, grasp it, or look at it. Because Dasein is essentially spatial in the way of de-severance, its dealings always keep within an 'environment' which is desevered from it with a certain leeway [Spielraum]; accordingly our seeing and hearing always go proximally beyond what is distantially 'closest'. Seeing and hearing are distance-senses [Fernsinne] not because they are far-reaching, but because it is in them that Dasein as deseverant mainly dwells. When, for instance, a man wears a pair of spectacles which are so close to him distantially that they are 'sitting on his nose', they are environmentally more remote from him than the picture on the opposite wall. Such equipment has so little closeness that often it is proximally quite impossible to find. Equipment for seeing—and likewise for hearing, such as the telephone receiver—has what we have designated as the inconspicuousness of the proximally ready-to-hand. So too, for instance, does the street, as equipment for walking. One feels the touch of it at every step as one walks; it is seemingly the closest and Realest of all that is ready-to-hand, and it slides itself, as it

[1] 'vorkommt'; ' "Vorkommen" '. In general 'vorkommen' may be translated as 'occur', and is to be thought of as applicable strictly to the present-at-hand. In this passage, however, it is applied to the ready-to-hand; and a translation which calls attention to its etymological structure seems to be called for.

[2] '*Das unsichtige Ent-fernen der Alltäglichkeit des Daseins entdeckt das An-sich-sein der "wahren Welt", des Seienden, bei dem Dasein als existierendes je schon ist.*'

were, along certain portions of one's body—the soles of one's feet. And yet it is farther remote than the acquaintance whom one encounters 'on the street' at a 'remoteness' ["Entfernung"] of twenty paces when one is taking such a walk. Circumspective concern decides as to the closeness and farness of what is proximally ready-to-hand environmentally. Whatever this concern dwells alongside beforehand is what is closest, and this is what regulates our de-severances.

If Dasein, in its concern, brings something close by, this does not signify that it fixes something at a spatial position with a minimal distance from some point of the body. When something is close by, this means that it is within the range of what is proximally ready-to-hand for circumspection. Bringing-close is not oriented towards the I-Thing encumbered with a body, but towards concernful Being-in-the-world—that is, towards whatever is proximally encountered in such Being. It follows, moreover, that Dasein's spatiality is not to be defined by citing the position at which some corporeal Thing is present-at-hand. Of course we say that even Dasein always occupies a place. But this 'occupying' must be distinguished in principle from Being-ready-to-hand at a place in some particular region. Occupying a place must be conceived as a desevering of the environmentally ready-to-hand into a region which has been circumspectively discovered in advance. Dasein understands its "here" [Hier] in terms of its environmental "yonder". The "here" does not mean the "where" of something present-at-hand, but rather the "whereat" [Wobei] of a de-severant Being-alongside, together with this de-severance. Dasein, in accordance with its spatiality, is proximally never here but yonder; from this "yonder" it comes back to its "here"; and it comes back to its "here" only in the way in which it interprets its concernful Being-towards in terms of what is ready-to-hand yonder. This becomes quite plain if we consider a certain phenomenal peculiarity of the de-severance structure of Being-in.

As Being-in-the-world, Dasein maintains itself essentially in a de-severing. This de-severance—the farness of the ready-to-hand from Dasein itself—is something that Dasein can *never cross over*. Of course the remoteness of something ready-to-hand from Dasein can show up as a distance from it,[1] if this remoteness is determined by a relation to some Thing which gets thought of as present-at-hand at the place Dasein has formerly occupied. Dasein can subsequently traverse the "between" of this distance, but only in such a way that the distance itself becomes one which has been desevered*. So little has Dasein crossed over its de-severance that it has rather taken it along with it and keeps doing so constantly; for

---

[1] '. . . kann zwar selbst von diesem als Abstand vorfindlich werden . . .'

Dasein is essentially de-severance—that is, it is spatial. It cannot wander about within the current range of its de-severances; it can never do more than change them. Dasein is spatial in that it discovers space circumspectively, so that indeed it constantly comports itself de-severantly* towards the entities thus spatially encountered.

As de-severant Being-in, Dasein has likewise the character of *directionality.* Every bringing-close [Näherung] has already taken in advance a direction towards a region out of which what is de-severed brings itself close [sich nähert], so that one can come across it with regard to its place. Circumspective concern is de-severing which gives directionality. In this concern —that is, in the Being-in-the-world of Dasein itself—a supply of 'signs' is presented. Signs, as equipment, take over the giving of directions in a way which is explicit and easily manipulable. They keep explicitly open those regions which have been used circumspectively—the particular "whithers" to which something belongs or goes, or gets brought or fetched. If Dasein *is*, it already has, as directing and desevering, its own discovered region. Both directionality and de-severance, as modes of Being-in-the-world, are guided beforehand *by the circumspection* of concern.

Out of this directionality arise the fixed directions of right and left. Dasein constantly takes these directions along with it, just as it does its de-severances. Dasein's spatialization in its 'bodily nature' is likewise marked out in accordance with these directions. (This 'bodily nature' hides a whole problematic of its own, though we shall not treat it here.) Thus things which are ready-to-hand and used for the body—like gloves, for example, which are to move with the hands—must be given directionality towards right and left. A craftsman's tools, however, which are held in the hand and are moved with it, do not share the hand's specifically 'manual' ["handliche"] movements. So although hammers are handled just as much with the hand as gloves are, there are no right- or left-handed hammers.

One must notice, however, that the directionality which belongs to de-severance is founded upon Being-in-the-world. Left and right are not something 'subjective' for which the subject has a feeling; they are directions of one's directedness into a world that is ready-to-hand already. 'By the mere feeling of a difference between my two sides'xxi I could never find my way about in a world. The subject with a 'mere feeling' of this difference is a construct posited in disregard of the state that is truly constitutive for any subject—namely, that whenever Dasein has such a 'mere feeling', it is in a world already *and must be* in it to be able to orient itself at all. This becomes plain from the example with which Kant tries to clarify the phenomenon of orientation.

Suppose I step into a room which is familiar to me but dark, and which has been rearranged [umgeräumt] during my absence so that everything which used to be at my right is now at my left. If I am to orient myself the 'mere feeling of the difference' between my two sides will be of no help at all as long as I fail to apprehend some definite object 'whose position', as Kant remarks casually, 'I have in mind'. But what does this signify except that whenever this happens I necessarily orient myself both in and from my being already alongside a world which is 'familiar'?[1] The equipment-context of a world must have been presented to Dasein. That I am already in a world is no less constitutive for the possibility of orientation than is the feeling for right and left. While this state of Dasein's Being is an obvious one, we are not thereby justified in suppressing the ontologically constitutive role which it plays. Even Kant does not suppress it, any more than any other Interpretation of Dasein. Yet the fact that this is a state of which we constantly make use, does not exempt us from providing a suitable ontological explication, but rather demands one. The psychological Interpretation according to which the "I" has something 'in the memory' ["im Gedächtnis"] is at bottom a way of alluding to the existentially constitutive state of Being-in-the-world. Since Kant fails to see this structure, he also fails to recognize all the interconnections which the Constitution of any possible orientation implies. Directedness with regard to right and left is based upon the essential directionality of Dasein in general, and this directionality in turn is essentially co-determined by Being-in-the-world. Even Kant, of course, has not taken orientation as a theme for Interpretation. He merely wants to show that every orientation requires a 'subjective principle'. Here 'subjective' is meant to signify that this principle is *a priori*.[2] Nevertheless, the *a priori* character of directedness with regard to right and left is based upon the 'subjective' *a priori* of Being-in-the-world, which has nothing to do with any determinate character restricted beforehand to a worldless subject.

De-severance and directionality, as constitutive characteristics of Being-in, are determinative for Dasein's spatiality—for its being concernfully and circumspectively in space, in a space discovered and within-the-world. Only the explication we have just given for the spatiality of the ready-to-hand within-the-world and the spatiality of Being-in-the-world, will provide the prerequisites for working out the phenomenon of the world's spatiality and formulating the ontological problem of space.

[1] '. . . in und aus einem je schon sein bei einer "bekannten" Welt.' The earlier editions have 'Sein' for 'sein'.
[2] Here we follow the later editions in reading '. . . bedeuten wollen: a priori.' The earlier editions omit the colon, making the passage ambiguous.

¶ *24. Space and Dasein's Spatiality*

As Being-in-the-world, Dasein has already discovered a 'world' at any time. This discovery, which is founded upon the worldhood of the world, is one which we have characterized as freeing entities for a totality of involvements. Freeing something and letting it be involved, is accomplished by way of referring or assigning oneself circumspectively, and this in turn is based upon one's previously understanding significance. We have now shown that circumspective Being-in-the-world is spatial. And only because Dasein is spatial in the way of de-severance and directionality can what is ready-to-hand within-the-world be encountered in its spatiality. To free a totality of involvements is, equiprimordially, to let something be involved at a region, and to do so by de-severing and giving directionality; this amounts to freeing the spatial belonging-somewhere of the ready-to-hand. In that significance with which Dasein (as concernful Being-in) is familiar, lies the essential co-disclosedness of space.[1]

The space which is thus disclosed with the worldhood of the world still lacks the pure multiplicity of the three dimensions. In this disclosedness which is closest to us, space, as the pure "wherein" in which positions are ordered by measurement and the situations of things are determined, still remains hidden. In the phenomenon of the region we have already indicated that on the basis of which space is discovered beforehand in Dasein. By a 'region" we have understood the "whither" to which an equipment-context ready-to-hand might possibly belong, when that context is of such a sort that it can be encountered as directionally desevered—that is, as having been placed.[2] This belongingness [Gehörigkeit] is determined in terms of the significance which is constitutive for the world, and it Articulates the "hither" and "thither" within the possible "whither". In general the "whither" gets prescribed by a referential totality which has been made fast in a "for-the-sake-of-which" of concern, and within which letting something be involved by freeing it, assigns itself. *With* anything encountered as ready-to-hand there is always an involvement in [bei] a region. To the totality of involvements which makes up the Being of the ready-to-hand within-the-world, there belongs a spatial involvement which has the character of a region. By reason of such an involvement, the ready-to-hand becomes something which we can come across and ascertain as having form and direction.[3] With the factical Being of

---

[1] '... die wesenhafte Miterschlossenheit des Raumes.'

[2] 'Wir verstehen sie als das Wohin der möglichen Zugehörigkeit des zuhandenen Zeugzusammenhanges, der als ausgerichtet entfernter, d. h. platzierter soll begegnen können.'

[3] 'Auf deren Grunde wird das Zuhandene nach Form und Richtung vorfindlich und bestimmbar'. The earliest editions have 'erfindlich', which has been corrected to 'vorfindlich' in a list of *errata*.

Dasein, what is ready-to-hand within-the-world is desevered* and given directionality, depending upon the degree of transparency that is possible for concernful circumspection.

When we let entities within-the-world be encountered in the way which is constitutive for Being-in-the-world, we 'give them space'. This 'giving space', which we also call '*making room*' for them,[1] consists in freeing the ready-to-hand for its spatiality. As a way of discovering and presenting a possible totality of spaces determined by involvements, this making-room is what makes possible one's factical orientation at the time. In concerning itself circumspectively with the world, Dasein can move things around or out of the way or 'make room' for them [um—, weg—, und "einräumen"] only because making-room—understood as an *existentiale*—belongs to its Being-in-the-world. But neither the region previously discovered nor in general the current spatiality is explicitly in view. In itself it is present [zugegen] for circumspection in the inconspicuousness of those ready-to-hand things in which that circumspection is concernfully absorbed. With Being-in-the-world, space is proximally discovered in this spatiality. On the basis of the spatiality thus discovered, space itself becomes accessible for cognition.

Space is not in the subject, nor is the world in space. Space is rather 'in' the world in so far as space has been disclosed by that Being-in-the-world which is constitutive for Dasein. Space is not to be found in the subject, nor does the subject observe the world 'as if' that world were in a space; but the 'subject' (Dasein), if well understood ontologically, is spatial. And because Dasein is spatial in the way we have described, space shows itself as *a priori*. This term does not mean anything like previously belonging to a subject which is proximally still worldless and which emits a space out of itself. Here "*apriority*" means the previousness with which space has been encountered (as a region) whenever the ready-to-hand is encountered environmentally.

The spatiality of what we proximally encounter in circumspection can become a theme for circumspection itself, as well as a task for calculation and measurement, as in building and surveying. Such thematization of the spatiality of the environment is still predominantly an act of circumspection by which space in itself already comes into view in a certain way. The space which thus shows itself can be studied purely by looking at it, if one gives up what was formerly the only possibility of access to it— circumspective calculation. When space is 'intuited formally', the pure

---

[1] Both 'Raum-geben' (our 'giving space') and 'Einräumen' (our 'making room') are often used in the metaphorical sense of 'yielding', 'granting', or 'making concessions'. 'Einräumen' may also be used for 'arranging' furniture, 'moving it in', or 'stowing it away'.

possibilities of spatial relations are discovered. Here one may go through a series of stages in laying bare pure homogeneous space, passing from the pure morphology of spatial shapes to *analysis situs* and finally to the purely metrical science of space. In our present study we shall not consider how all these are interconnected.[xxii] Our problematic is merely designed to establish ontologically the phenomenal basis upon which one can take the discovery of pure space as a theme for investigation, and work it out.

When space is discovered non-circumspectively by just looking at it, the environmental regions get neutralized to pure dimensions. Places—and indeed the whole circumspectively oriented totality of places belonging to equipment ready-to-hand—get reduced to a multiplicity of positions for random Things. The spatiality of what is ready-to-hand within-the-world loses its involvement-character, and so does the ready-to-hand. The world loses its specific aroundness; the environment becomes the world of Nature. The 'world', as a totality of equipment ready-to-hand, becomes spatialized [verräumlicht] to a context of extended Things which are just present-at-hand and no more. The homogeneous space of Nature shows itself only when the entities we encounter are discovered in such a way that the worldly character of the ready-to-hand gets specifically *deprived of its worldhood*.[1]

In accordance with its Being-in-the-world, Dasein always has space presented as already discovered, though not thematically. On the other hand, space in itself, so far as it embraces the mere possibilities of the pure spatial Being of something, remains proximally still concealed. The fact that space essentially *shows* itself *in a world* is not yet decisive for the kind of Being which it possesses. It need not have the kind of Being characteristic of something which is itself spatially ready-to-hand or present-at-hand. Nor does the Being of space have the kind of Being which belongs to Dasein. Though the Being of space itself cannot be conceived as the kind of Being which belongs to a *res extensa*, it does not follow that it must be defined ontologically as a 'phenomenon' of such a *res*. (In its Being, it would not be distinguished from such a *res*.) Nor does it follow that the Being of space can be equated to that of the *res cogitans* and conceived as merely 'subjective', quite apart from the questionable character of the *Being* of such a subject.

The Interpretation of the Being of space has hitherto been a matter of perplexity, not so much because we have been insufficiently acquainted with the content of space itself as a thing [des Sachgehaltes des Raumes

---

[1] '. . . die den Charakter einer spezifischen *Entweltlichung* der Weltmässigkeit des Zuhandenen hat.'

selbst], as because the possibilities of Being in general have not been in principle transparent, and an Interpretation of them in terms of ontological concepts has been lacking. If we are to understand the ontological problem of space, it is of decisive importance that the question of Being must be liberated from the narrowness of those concepts of Being which merely chance to be available and which are for the most part rather rough; and the problematic of the Being of space (with regard to that phenomenon itself and various phenomenal spatialities) must be turned in such a direction as to clarify the possibilities of Being in general.

In the phenomenon of space the primary ontological character of the Being of entities within-the-world is not to be found, either as unique or as one among others. Still less does space constitute the phenomenon of the world. Unless we go back to the world, space cannot be conceived. Space becomes accessible only if the environment is deprived of its worldhood; and spatiality is not discoverable at all except on the basis of the world. Indeed space is still *one* of the things that is constitutive for the world, just as Dasein's own spatiality is essential to its basic state of Being-in-the-world.[1]

[1] '. . . so zwar, dass der Raum die Welt doch *mit*konstituiert, entsprechend der wesenhaften Räumlichkeit des Daseins selbst hinsichtlich seiner Grundverfassung des In-der-Welt-seins.'

IV

BEING-IN-THE-WORLD AS BEING-WITH AND BEING-ONE'S-SELF. THE "THEY"

Our analysis of the worldhood of the world has constantly been bringing the whole phenomenon of Being-in-the-world into view, although its constitutive items have not all stood out with the same phenomenal distinctness as the phenomenon of the world itself. We have Interpreted the world ontologically by going through what is ready-to-hand within-the-world; and this Interpretation has been put first, because Dasein, in its everydayness (with regard to which Dasein remains a constant theme for study), not only is in a world but comports itself towards that world with one predominant kind of Being. Proximally and for the most part Dasein is fascinated with its world. Dasein is thus absorbed in the world; the kind of Being which it thus possesses, and in general the Being-in which underlies it, are essential in determining the character of a phenomenon which we are now about to study. We shall approach this phenomenon by asking *who* it is that Dasein is in its everydayness. All the structures of Being which belong to Dasein, together with the phenomenon which provides the answer to this question of the "who", are ways of its Being. To characterize these ontologically is to do so existentially. We must therefore pose the question correctly and outline the procedure for bringing into view a broader phenomenal domain of Dasein's everydayness. By directing our researches towards the phenomenon which is to provide us with an answer to the question of the "who", we shall be led to certain structures of Dasein which are equiprimordial with Being-in-the-world: *Being-with* and *Dasein-with* [*Mitsein* und *Mitdasein*]. In this kind of Being is grounded the mode of everyday Being-one's-Self [Selbstsein]; the explication of this mode will

1

---

1 'Das Man'. In German one may write 'man glaubt' where in French one would write '*on croit*', or in English 'they believe', 'one believes', or 'it is believed'. But the German 'man' and the French '*on*' are specialized for such constructions in a way in which the pronouns 'they', 'one', and 'it' are not. There is accordingly no single idiomatic translation for the German 'man' which will not sometimes lend itself to ambiguity, and in general we have chosen whichever construction seems the most appropriate in its context. But when Heidegger introduces this word with a definite article and writes 'das Man', as he does very often in this chapter, we shall translate this expression as 'the "they" ', trusting that the reader will not take this too literally.

enable us to see what we may call the 'subject' of everydayness—the *"they"*. Our chapter on the 'who' of the average Dasein will thus be divided up as follows: 1. an approach to the existential question of the "who" of Dasein (Section 25); 2. the Dasein-with of Others, and everyday Being-with (Section 26); 3. everyday Being-one's-Self and the "they" (Section 27).

¶ *25. An Approach to the Existential Question of the "Who" of Dasein*

The answer to the question of who Dasein is, is one that was seemingly given in Section 9, where we indicated formally the basic characteristics of Dasein. Dasein is an entity which is in each case I myself; its Being is in each case mine. This definition *indicates* an *ontologically* constitutive state, but it does no more than indicate it. At the same time this tells us *ontically* (though in a rough and ready fashion) that in each case an "I"—not Others—is this entity. The question of the "who" answers itself in terms of the "I" itself, the 'subject', the 'Self'.[1] The "who" is what maintains itself as something identical throughout changes in its Experiences and ways of behaviour, and which relates itself to this changing multiplicity in so doing. Ontologically we understand it as something which is in each case already constantly present-at-hand, both in and for a closed realm, and which lies at the basis, in a very special sense, as the *subjectum*. As something selfsame in manifold otherness,[2] it has the character of the *Self*. Even if one rejects the "soul substance" and the Thinghood of consciousness, or denies that a person is an object, ontologically one is still positing something whose Being retains the meaning of present-at-hand, whether it does so explicitly or not. Substantiality is the ontological clue for determining which entity is to provide the answer to the question of the "who". Dasein is tacitly conceived in advance as something present-at-hand. This meaning of Being is always implicated in any case where the Being of Dasein has been left indefinite. Yet presence-at-hand is the kind of Being which belongs to entities whose character is not that of Dasein.

The assertion that it is I who in each case Dasein is, is ontically obvious; but this must not mislead us into supposing that the route for an onto-logical Interpretation of what is 'given' in this way has thus been unmis-takably prescribed. Indeed it remains questionable whether even the mere ontical content of the above assertion does proper justice to the stock of phenomena belonging to everyday Dasein. It could be that the "who" of everyday Dasein just is *not* the "I myself".

[1] 'dem "Selbst" '. While we shall ordinarily translate the *intensive* 'selbst' by the corre-sponding English intensives 'itself', 'oneself', 'myself', etc., according to the context, we shall translate the *substantive* 'Selbst' by the substantive 'Self' with a capital.

[2] '. . . als Selbiges in der vielfältigen Andersheit . . .' While the words 'identisch' and 'selbig' are virtually synonyms in ordinary German, Heidegger seems to be intimating a distinction between them. We shall accordingly translate the former by 'identical' and the latter by 'selfsame' to show its etymological connection with 'selbst'. Cf. H. 130 below.

If, in arriving at ontico-ontological assertions, one is to exhibit the phenomena in terms of the kind of Being which the entities themselves possesses, and if this way of exhibiting them is to retain its priority over even the most usual and obvious of answers and over whatever ways of formulating problems may have been derived from those answers, then the phenomenological Interpretation of Dasein must be defended against a perversion of our problematic when we come to the question we are about to formulate.

But is it not contrary to the rules of all sound method to approach a problematic without sticking to what is given as evident in the area of our theme? And what is more indubitable than the givenness of the "I"? And does not this givenness tell us that if we aim to work this out primordially, we must disregard everything else that is 'given'—not only a 'world' that is [einer seienden "Welt"], but even the Being of other 'I's? The kind of "giving" we have here is the mere, formal, reflective awareness of the "I"; and perhaps what it gives is indeed evident.[1] This insight even affords access to a phenomenological problematic in its own right, which has in principle the signification of providing a framework as a 'formal phenomenology of consciousness'.

In this context of an existential analytic of factical Dasein, the question arises whether giving the "I" in the way we have mentioned discloses Dasein in its everydayness, if it discloses Dasein at all. Is it then obvious *a priori* that access to Dasein must be gained only by mere reflective awareness of the "I" of actions? What if this kind of 'giving-itself' on the part of Dasein should lead our existential analytic astray and do so, indeed, in a manner grounded in the Being of Dasein itself? Perhaps when Dasein addresses itself in the way which is closest to itself, it always says "I am this entity", and in the long run says this loudest when it is 'not' this entity. Dasein is in each case mine, and this is its constitution; but what if this should be the very reason why, proximally and for the most part, Dasein *is not itself*? What if the aforementioned approach, starting with the givenness of the "I" to Dasein itself, and with a rather patent self-interpretation of Dasein, should lead the existential analytic, as it were, into a pitfall? If that which is accessible by mere "giving" can be determined, there is presumably an ontological horizon for determining it; but what if this horizon should remain in principle undetermined? It may well be that it is always ontically correct to say of this entity that 'I' am it. Yet the ontological analytic which makes use of such assertions must make certain reservations about them in principle. The word 'I' is to be

[1] 'Vielleicht ist in der Tat das, was diese Art von Gebung, das schlichte, formale, reflektive Ichvernehmen gibt, evident.'

understood only in the sense of a non-committal *formal indicator*, indicating
something which may perhaps reveal itself as its 'opposite' in some particular phenomenal context of Being. In that case, the 'not-I' is by no means
tantamount to an entity which essentially lacks 'I-hood' ["Ichheit"],
but is rather a definite kind of Being which the 'I' itself possesses, such as
having lost itself [Selbstverlorenheit].

Yet even the positive Interpretation of Dasein which we have so far
given, already forbids us to start with the formal givenness of the "I", if our
purpose is to answer the question of the "who" in a way which is phenomenally adequate. In clarifying Being-in-the-world we have shown that
a bare subject without a world never 'is' proximally, nor is it ever given.
And so in the end an isolated "I" without Others is just as far from being
proximally given.[1] If, however, 'the Others' already *are there with us* [*mit
da sind*] in Being-in-the-world, and if this is ascertained phenomenally, even
this should not mislead us into supposing that the *ontological* structure of
what is thus 'given' is obvious, requiring no investigation. Our task is to
make visible phenomenally the species to which this Dasein-with in closest
everydayness belongs, and to Interpret it in a way which is ontologically
appropriate.

Just as the ontical obviousness of the Being-in-itself of entities within-
the-world misleads us into the conviction that the meaning of this Being
is obvious ontologically, and makes us overlook the phenomenon of the
world, the ontical obviousness of the fact that Dasein is in each case mine,
also hides the possibility that the ontological problematic which belongs
to it has been led astray. *Proximally* the "who" of Dasein is not only a
problem *ontologically*; even *ontically* it remains concealed.

But does this mean that there are no clues whatever for answering the
question of the "who" by way of existential analysis? Certainly not. Of
the ways in which we formally indicated the constitution of Dasein's Being
in Sections 9 and 12 above, the one we have been discussing does not, of
course, function so well as such a clue as does the one according to which
Dasein's 'Essence' is grounded in its existence.[1] *If the 'I' is an Essential
characteristic of Dasein, then it is one which must be Interpreted existentially.* In
that case the "Who?" is to be answered only by exhibiting phenomenally
a definite kind of Being which Dasein possesses. If in each case Dasein is
its Self only in *existing*, then the constancy of the Self no less than the

---

[1] 'as such a clue': here we read 'als solcher', following the later editions. The earliest
editions have 'als solche', which has been corrected in the list of *errata*.
  "Essence": while we ordinarily use 'essence' and 'essential' to translate 'Wesen' and
'wesenhaft', we shall use 'Essence' and "Essential' (with initial capitals) to translate the
presumably synonymous but far less frequent 'Essenz' and 'essentiell'.
  The two 'formal indications' to which Heidegger refers are to be found on H. 42 above.

possibility of its 'failure to stand by itself'[1] requires that we formulate the question existentially and ontologically as the sole appropriate way of access to its problematic.

But if the Self is conceived 'only' as a way of Being of this entity, this seems tantamount to volatilizing the real 'core' of Dasein. Any apprehensiveness however which one may have about this gets its nourishment from the perverse assumption that the entity in question has at bottom the kind of Being which belongs to something present-at-hand, even if one is far from attributing to it the solidity of an occurrent corporeal Thing. Yet man's *substance* is not spirit as a synthesis of soul and body; it is rather *existence*.

¶ 26. *The Dasein-with of Others and Everyday Being-with*

The answer to the question of the "who" of everyday Dasein is to be obtained by analysing that kind of Being in which Dasein maintains itself proximally and for the most part. Our investigation takes its orientation from Being-in-the-world—that basic state of Dasein by which every mode of its Being gets co-determined. If we are correct in saying that by the foregoing explication of the world, the remaining structural items of Being-in-the-world have become visible, then this must also have prepared us, in a way, for answering the question of the "who".

In our 'description' of that environment which is closest to us—the work-world of the craftsman, for example,—the outcome was that along with the equipment to be found when one is at work [in Arbeit], those Others for whom the 'work' ["Werk"] is destined are 'encountered too'.[2] If this is ready-to-hand, then there lies in the kind of Being which belongs to it (that is, in its involvement) an essential assignment or reference to possible wearers, for instance, for whom it should be 'cut to the figure'. Similarly, when material is put to use, we encounter its producer or 'supplier' as one who 'serves' well or badly. When, for example, we walk along the edge of a field but 'outside it', the field shows itself as belonging to such-and-such a person, and decently kept up by him; the book we have used was bought at So-and-so's shop and given by such-and-such

---

1 '... die Ständigkeit des Selbst ebensosehr wie seine mögliche "Unselbständigkeit" ...' The adjective 'ständig', which we have usually translated as 'constant' in the sense of 'permanent' or 'continuing', goes back to the root meaning of 'standing', as do the adjectives 'selbständig' ('independent') and 'unselbständig' ('dependent'). These concepts will be discussed more fully in Section 64 below, especially H. 322, where 'Unselbständigkeit' will be rewritten not as 'Un-selbständkeit' ('failure to stand by one's Self') but as 'Unselbst-ständigkeit' ('constancy to the Unself'). See also H. 128. (The connection with the concept of existence will perhaps be clearer if one recalls that the Latin verb 'existere' may also be derived from a verb of *standing*, as Heidegger points out in his later writings.)

2 Cf. Section 15 above, especially H. 70f.

a person, and so forth. The boat anchored at the shore is assigned in its Being-in-itself to an acquaintance who undertakes voyages with it; but even if it is a 'boat which is strange to us', it still is indicative of Others. The Others who are thus 'encountered' in a ready-to-hand, environmental context of equipment, are not somehow added on in thought to some Thing which is proximally just present-at-hand; such 'Things' are encountered from out of the world in which they are ready-to-hand for Others—a world which is always mine too in advance. In our previous analysis, the range of what is encountered within-the-world was, in the first instance, narrowed down to equipment ready-to-hand or Nature present-at-hand, and thus to entities with a character other than that of Dasein. This restriction was necessary not only for the purpose of simplifying our explication but above all because the kind of Being which belongs to the Dasein of Others, as we encounter it within-the-world, differs from readiness-to-hand and presence-at-hand. Thus Dasein's world frees entities which not only are quite distinct from equipment and Things, but which also—in accordance with their kind of Being *as Dasein* themselves— are 'in' the world in which they are at the same time encountered within-the-world, and are 'in' it by way of Being-in-the-world.[1] These entities are neither present-at-hand nor ready-to-hand; on the contrary, they are *like* the very Dasein which frees them, in that *they are there too, and there with it.* So if one should want to identify the world in general with entities within-the-world, one would have to say that Dasein too is 'world'.[2]

Thus in characterizing the encountering of *Others*, one is again still oriented by that Dasein which is in each case one's *own*. But even in this characterization does one not start by marking out and isolating the 'I' so that one must then seek some way of getting over to the Others from this isolated subject? To avoid this misunderstanding we must notice in what sense we are talking about 'the Others'. By 'Others' we do not mean everyone else but me—those over against whom the "I" stands out. They are rather those from whom, for the most part, one does *not* distinguish oneself—those among whom one is too. This Being-there-too [Auch-dasein] with them does not have the ontological character of a Being-present-at-hand-along-'with' them within a world. This 'with' is something of the character of Dasein; the 'too' means a sameness of Being as circumspectively concernful Being-in-the-world. 'With' and 'too' are to be

---

[1] '. . . sondern gemäss seiner Seinsart *als Dasein* selbst in der Weise des In-der-Weltseins "in" der Welt ist, in der es zugleich innerweltlich begegnet.'

[2] 'Dieses Seiende ist weder vorhanden noch zuhanden, sondern ist *so, wie* das freigebende Dasein selbst—es *ist auch und mit da*. Wollte man denn schon Welt überhaupt mit dem innerweltlich Seienden identifizieren, dann müsste man sagen, "Welt" ist auch Dasein.'

understood *existentially*, not categorially. By reason of this *with-like* [*mithaften*] Being-in-the-world, the world is always the one that I share with Others. The world of Dasein is a *with-world* [*Mitwelt*]. Being-in is *Being-with* Others. Their Being-in-themselves within-the-world is *Dasein-with* [*Mit-dasein*].

When Others are encountered, it is not the case that one's own subject is *proximally* present-at-hand and that the rest of the subjects, which are likewise occurrents, get discriminated beforehand and then apprehended; nor are they encountered by a primary act of looking at oneself in such a way that the opposite pole of a distinction first gets ascertained. They are encountered from out of the *world*, in which concernfully circumspective Dasein essentially dwells. Theoretically concocted 'explanations' of the Being-present-at-hand of Others urge themselves upon us all too easily; but over against such explanations we must hold fast to the phenomenal facts of the case which we have pointed out, namely, that Others are encountered *environmentally*. This elemental worldly kind of encountering, which belongs to Dasein and is closest to it, goes so far that even one's *own* Dasein becomes something that it can itself proximally 'come across' only when it *looks away* from 'Experiences' and the 'centre of its actions', or does not as yet 'see' them at all. Dasein finds 'itself' proximally in *what* it does, uses, expects, avoids—in those things environmentally ready-to-hand with which it is proximally *concerned*.

And even when Dasein explicitly addresses itself as "I here", this locative personal designation must be understood in terms of Dasein's existential spatiality. In Interpreting this (See Section 23) we have already intimated that this "I-here" does not mean a certain privileged point—that of an I-Thing—but is to be understood as Being-in in terms of the "yonder" of the world that is ready-to-hand—the "yonder" which is the dwelling-place of Dasein as *concern*.[1]

W. von Humboldt[ii] has alluded to certain languages which express the 'I' by 'here', the 'thou' by 'there', the 'he' by 'yonder', thus rendering the personal pronouns by locative adverbs, to put it grammatically. It is controversial whether indeed the primordial signification of locative expressions is adverbial or pronominal. But this dispute loses its basis if one notes that locative adverbs have a relationship to the "I" *qua* Dasein. The 'here' and the 'there' and the 'yonder' are primarily not mere ways of designating the location of entities present-at-hand within-the-world at positions in space; they are rather characteristics of Dasein's primordial

---

[1] '. . . dass dieses Ich-hier nicht einen ausgezeichneten Punkt des Ichdinges meint, sondern sich versteht als In-sein aus dem Dort der zuhandenen Welt, bei dem Dasein als *Besorgen* sich aufhält.' The older editions have 'In-Sein' for 'In-sein', and 'dabei' for 'bei dem'.

spatiality. These supposedly locative adverbs are Dasein-designations; they have a signification which is primarily existential, not categorial. But they are not pronouns either; their signification is prior to the differentiation of locative adverbs and personal pronouns: these expressions have a Dasein-signification which is authentically spatial, and which serves as evidence that when we interpret Dasein without any theoretical distortions we can see it immediately as 'Being-alongside' the world with which it concerns itself, and as Being-alongside it spatially—that is to say, as desevering* and giving directionality. In the 'here', the Dasein which is absorbed in its world speaks not towards itself but away from itself towards the 'yonder' of something circumspectively ready-to-hand; yet it still has *itself* in view in its existential spatiality.

Dasein understands itself proximally and for the most part in terms of its world; and the Dasein-with of Others is often encountered in terms of what is ready-to-hand within-the-world. But even if Others become themes for study, as it were, in their own Dasein, they are not encountered as person-Things present-at-hand: we meet them 'at work', that is, primarily in their Being-in-the-world. Even if we see the Other 'just standing around', he is never apprehended as a human-Thing present-at-hand, but his 'standing-around' is an existential mode of Being—an unconcerned, uncircumspective tarrying alongside everything and nothing [Verweilen bei Allem und Keinem]. The Other is encountered in his Dasein-with in the world.

The expression 'Dasein', however, shows plainly that 'in the first instance' this entity is unrelated to Others, and that of course it can still be 'with' Others afterwards. Yet one must not fail to notice that we use the term "Dasein-with" to designate that Being for which the Others who a r e [die seienden Anderen] are freed within-the-world. This Dasein-with of the Others is disclosed within-the-world for a Dasein, and so too for those who are Daseins with us [die Mitdaseienden], only because Dasein in itself is essentially Being-with. The phenomenological assertion that "Dasein is essentially Being-with" has an existential-ontological meaning. It does not seek to establish ontically that factically I am not present-at-hand alone, and that Others of my kind occur. If this were what is meant by the proposition that Dasein's Being-in-the-world is essentially constituted by Being-with, then Being-with would not be an existential attribute which Dasein, of its own accord, has coming to it from its own kind of Being. It would rather be something which turns up in every case by reason of the occurrence of Others. Being-with is an existential characteristic of Dasein even when factically no Other is present-at-hand or perceived. Even Dasein's Being-alone is Being-with

in the world. The Other can *be missing* only *in*[1] and *for*[1] a Being-with.
Being-alone is a deficient mode of Being-with; its very possibility is the
proof of this. On the other hand, factical Being-alone is not obviated by
the occurrence of a second example of a human being 'beside' me, or by ten
such examples. Even if these and more are present-at-hand, Dasein can
still be alone. So Being-with and the facticity of Being with one another
are not based on the occurrence together of several 'subjects'. Yet Being-
alone 'among' many does not mean that with regard to their Being they
are merely present-at-hand there alongside us. Even in our Being 'among
them' they are *there with* us; their Dasein-with is encountered in a mode
in which they are indifferent and alien. Being missing and 'Being away'
[Das Fehlen und "Fortsein"] are modes of Dasein-with, and are possible
only because Dasein as Being-with lets the Dasein of Others be encountered in its world. Being-with is in every case a characteristic of one's
own Dasein; Dasein-with characterizes the Dasein of Others to the extent
that it is freed by its world for a Being-with. Only so far as one's own
Dasein has the essential structure of Being-with, is it Dasein-with as
encounterable for Others.[2]

If Dasein-with remains existentially constitutive for Being-in-the-
world, then, like our circumspective dealings with the ready-to-hand
within-the-world (which, by way of anticipation, we have called 'concern'), it must be Interpreted in terms of the phenomenon of *care*; for as
"care" the Being of Dasein in general is to be defined.[3] (Compare Chapter
6 of this Division.) Concern is a character-of-Being which Being-with
cannot have as its own, even though Being-with, like concern, is a *Being
towards* entities encountered within-the-world. But those entities towards
which Dasein as Being-with comports itself do not have the kind of Being
which belongs to equipment ready-to-hand; they are themselves Dasein.
These entities are not objects of concern, but rather of *solicitude*.[4]

---

[1] Italics supplied in the later editions.

[2] '. . . Mitdasein charakterisiert das Dasein anderer, sofern es für ein Mitsein durch
dessen Welt freigegeben ist. Das eigene Dasein ist, sofern es die Wesensstruktur des
Mitseins hat, als für Andere begegnend Mitdasein.'

[3] '. . . als welche das Sein des Daseins überhaupt bestimmt wird.' The older editions
omit 'wird'.

[4] 'Dieses Seiende wird nicht besorgt, sondern steht in der *Fürsorge*.' There is no good
English equivalent for 'Fürsorge', which we shall usually translate by 'solicitude'. The more
literal 'caring-for' has the connotation of 'being fond of', which we do not want here;
'personal care' suggests personal hygiene; 'personal concern' suggests one's personal
business or affairs. 'Fürsorge' is rather the kind of care which we find in 'prenatal care' or
'taking care of the children', or even the kind of care which is administered by welfare
agencies. Indeed the word 'Fürsorge' is regularly used in contexts where we would speak
of 'welfare work' or 'social welfare; this is the usage which Heidegger has in mind in his
discussion of 'Fürsorge' as 'a factical social arrangement'. (The etymological connection
between 'Sorge ('care'), 'Fürsorge' ('solicitude'), and 'Besorgen ('concern'), is entirely
lost in our translation.)

Even 'concern' with food and clothing, and the nursing of the sick body, are forms of solicitude. But we understand the expression "solicitude" in a way which corresponds to our use of "concern" as a term for an *existentiale*. For example, 'welfare work' ["Fürsorge"], as a factical social arrangement, is grounded in Dasein's state of Being as Being-with. Its factical urgency gets its motivation in that Dasein maintains itself proximally and for the most part in the deficient modes of solicitude. Being for, against, or without one another, passing one another by, not "mattering" to one another—these are possible ways of solicitude. And it is precisely these last-named deficient and Indifferent modes that characterize everyday, average Being-with-one-another. These modes of Being show again the characteristics of inconspicuousness and obviousness which belong just as much to the everyday Dasein-with of Others within-the-world as to the readiness-to-hand of the equipment with which one is daily concerned. These Indifferent modes of Being-with-one-another may easily mislead ontological Interpretation into interpreting this kind of Being, in the first instance, as the mere Being-present-at-hand of several subjects. It seems as if only negligible variations of the same kind of Being lie before us; yet ontologically there is an essential distinction between the 'indifferent' way in which Things at random occur together and the way in which entities who are with one another do not "matter" to one another.

With regard to its positive modes, solicitude has two extreme possibilities. It can, as it were, take away 'care' from the Other and put itself in his position in concern: it can *leap in* for him.[1] This kind of solicitude takes over for the Other that with which he is to concern himself. The Other is thus thrown out of his own position; he steps back so that afterwards, when the matter has been attended to, he can either take it over as something finished and at his disposal,[2] or disburden himself of it completely. In such solicitude the Other can become one who is dominated and dependent, even if this domination is a tacit one and remains hidden from him. This kind of solicitude, which leaps in and takes away 'care', is to a large extent determinative for Being with one another, and pertains for the most part to our concern with the ready-to-hand.

In contrast to this, there is also the possibility of a kind of solicitude which does not so much leap in for the Other as *leap ahead* of him [ihm

---

[1] '. . . sich an seine Stelle setzen, für ihn *einspringen*.' Here, as on H. 100 (See our note 2, p. 133), it would be more idiomatic to translate 'für ihn einspringen' as 'intervene for him', 'stand in for him' or 'serve as deputy for him'; but since 'einspringen' is to be contrasted with 'vorspringen', 'vorausspringen' and perhaps even 'entspringen' in the following paragraphs, we have chosen a translation which suggests the etymological connection.

[2] '. . . um nachträglich das Besorgte als fertig Verfügbares zu übernehmen . . .'

vorausspringt] in his existentiell potentiality-for-Being, not in order to take away his 'care' but rather to give it back to him authentically as such for the first time. This kind of solicitude pertains essentially to authentic care —that is, to the existence of the Other, not to a *"what"* with which he is concerned; it helps the Other to become transparent to himself *in* his care and to become *free for* it.

Solicitude proves to be a state of Dasein's Being—one which, in accordance with its different possibilities, is bound up with its Being towards the world of its concern, and likewise with its authentic Being towards itself. Being with one another is based proximally and often exclusively upon what is a matter of common concern in such Being. A Being-with-one-another which arises [entspringt] from one's doing the same thing as someone else, not only keeps for the most part within the outer limits, but enters the mode of distance and reserve. The Being-with-one-another of those who are hired for the same affair often thrives only on mistrust. On the other hand, when they devote themselves to the same affair in common, their doing so is determined by the manner in which their Dasein, each in its own way, has been taken hold of.[1] They thus become *authentically* bound together, and this makes possible the right kind of objectivity [die rechte Sachlichkeit], which frees the Other in his freedom for himself.

Everyday Being-with-one-another maintains itself between the two extremes of positive solicitude—that which leaps in and dominates, and that which leaps forth and liberates [vorspringend-befreienden]. It brings numerous mixed forms to maturity;[2] to describe these and classify them would take us beyond the limits of this investigation.

Just as *circumspection* belongs to concern as a way of discovering what is ready-to-hand, solicitude is guided by *considerateness* and *forbearance*.[3] Like solicitude, these can range through their respective deficient and Indifferent modes up to the point of *inconsiderateness* or the perfunctoriness for which indifference leads the way.[4]

---

[1] 'Umgekehrt ist das gemeinsame Sicheinsetzen für dieselbe Sache aus dem je eigens ergriffenen Dasein bestimmt.'

[2] Reading '. . . und zeitigt mannigfache Mischformen . . .' with the older editions. The later editions have 'zeigt' ('shows') instead of 'zeitigt' ('brings to maturity'). On 'zeitigen' see H. 304 and our note ad loc.

[3] 'Wie dem Besorgen als Weise des Entdeckens des Zuhandenen die *Umsicht* zugehört, so ist die Fürsorg: g:leitet durch die *Rücksicht* und *Nachsicht*.' Heidegger is here calling attention to the etymological kinship of the three words which he italicizes, each of which stands for a special kind of *sight* or *seeing* ('Sicht').

The italicization of 'Umsicht' ('circumspection') is introduced in the newer editions.

[4] '. . . bis zur *Rücksichtslosigkeit* und dem Nachsehen, das die Gleichgültigkeit leitet.' This passage is ambiguous both syntactically and semantically. It is not clear, for instance, whether the subject of the relative clause is 'die Gleichgültigkeit' or the pronoun 'das', though we prefer the former interpretation. 'Nachsehen', which is etymologically

The world not only frees the ready-to-hand as entities encountered within-the-world; it also frees Dasein, and the Others in their Dasein-with. But Dasein's ownmost meaning of Being is such that this entity (which has been freed environmentally) is Being-in in the same world in which, as encounterable for Others, it is there with them. We have interpreted worldhood as that referential totality which constitutes significance (Section 18). In Being-familiar with this significance and previously understanding it, Dasein lets what is ready-to-hand be encountered as discovered in its involvement. In Dasein's Being, the context of references or assignments which significance implies is tied up with Dasein's ownmost Being—a Being which essentially can have no involvement, but which is rather that Being *for the sake of which* Dasein itself is as it is.

According to the analysis which we have now completed, Being with Others belongs to the Being of Dasein, which is an issue for Dasein in its very Being.[1] Thus as Being-with, Dasein 'is' essentially for the sake of Others. This must be understood as an existential statement as to its essence. Even if the particular factical Dasein does *not* turn to Others, and supposes that it has no need of them or manages to get along without them, it *is* in the way of Being-with. In Being-with, as the existential "for-the-sake-of" of Others, these have already been disclosed in their Dasein. With their Being-with, their disclosedness has been constituted beforehand; accordingly, this disclosedness also goes to make up significance—that is to say, worldhood. And, significance, as worldhood, is tied up with the existential "for-the-sake-of-which".[2] Since the worldhood of that world in which every Dasein essentially is already, is thus constituted, it accordingly lets us encounter what is environmentally ready-to-hand as something with which we are circumspectively concerned, and it does so in such a way that together with it we encounter the Dasein-with of Others. The structure of the world's worldhood is such that Others are not proximally present-at-hand as free-floating subjects along with other Things, but show themselves in the world in their special environmental Being, and do so in terms of what is ready-to-hand in that world.

Being-with is such that the disclosedness of the Dasein-with of Others

---

akin to 'Nachsicht', means to 'inspect' or 'check' something; but it often means to do this in a very perfunctory manner, and this latter sense may well be the one which Heidegger has in mind.

[1] '. . . zum Sein des Daseins, um das es ihm in seinem Sein selbst geht . . .' The older editions have 'darum' instead of 'um das'.

[2] 'Diese mit dem Mitsein vorgängig konstituierte Erschlossenheit der Anderen macht demnach auch die Bedeutsamkeit, d.h. die Weltlichkeit mit aus, als welche sie im existenzialen Worum-willen festgemacht ist.' The word 'sie' appears only in the later editions.

belongs to it; this means that because Dasein's Being is Being-with, its understanding of Being already implies the understanding of Others. This understanding, like any understanding, is not an acquaintance derived from knowledge about them, but a primordially existential kind of Being, which, more than anything else, makes such knowledge and acquaintance possible.[1] Knowing oneself [Sichkennen] is grounded in   1 Being-with, which understands primordially. It operates proximally in accordance with the kind of Being which is closest to us—Being-in-the-world as Being-with; and it does so by an acquaintance with that which Dasein, along with the Others, comes across in its environmental circumspection and concerns itself with—an acquaintance in which Dasein understands. Solicitous concern is understood in terms of what we are concerned with, and along with our understanding of it. Thus in concernful solicitude the Other is proximally disclosed.

But because solicitude dwells proximally and for the most part in the deficient or at least the Indifferent modes (in the indifference of passing one another by), the kind of knowing-oneself which is essential and closest, demands that one become acquainted with oneself.[2] And when, indeed, one's knowing-oneself gets lost in such ways as aloofness, hiding oneself away, or putting on a disguise, Being-with-one-another must follow special routes of its own in order to come close to Others, or even to 'see through them' ["hinter sie" zu kommen].

But just as opening oneself up [Sichoffenbaren] or closing oneself off is grounded in one's having Being-with-one-another as one's kind of Being at the time, and indeed *is* nothing else but this, even the explicit disclosure of the Other in solicitude grows only out of one's primarily Being with him in each case. Such a disclosure of the Other (which is indeed thematic, but not in the manner of theoretical psychology) easily becomes the phenomenon which proximally comes to view when one considers the theoretical problematic of understanding the 'psychical life of Others' ["fremden Seelenlebens"]. In this phenomenally 'proximal' manner it thus presents a way of Being with one another understandingly; but at the same time it gets taken as that which, primordially and 'in the beginning', constitutes Being towards Others and makes it possible at all.

---

[1] 'Dieses Verstehen ist, wie Verstehen überhaupt, nicht eine aus Erkennen erwachsene Kenntnis, sondern eine ursprünglich existenziale Seinsart die Erkennen und Kenntnis allererst möglich macht'. While we have here translated 'Kenntnis' as 'acquaintance' and 'Erkennen' as 'knowledge about', these terms must not be understood in the special senses exploited by Lord Russell and C. I. Lewis. The 'acquaintance' here involved is of the kind which may be acquired whenever one is well informed about something, whether one has any direct contact with it or not.

[2] '. . . bedarf das nächste und wesenhafte Sichkennen eines Sichkennenlernens.' 'Sichkennen' ('knowing oneself') is to be distinguished sharply from 'Selbsterkenntnis' ('knowledge of the Self'), which will be discussed on H. 146. See our note 1, p. 186.

This phenomenon, which is none too happily designated as '*empathy*' ["*Einfühlung*"], is then supposed, as it were, to provide the first ontological bridge from one's own subject, which is given proximally as alone, to the other subject, which is proximally quite closed off.

Of course Being towards Others is ontologically different from Being towards Things which are present-at-hand. The entity which is 'other' has itself the same kind of Being as Dasein. In Being with and towards Others, there is thus a relationship of Being [Seinsverhältnis] from Dasein to Dasein. But it might be said that this relationship is already constitutive for one's own Dasein, which, in its own right, has an understanding of Being, and which thus relates itself[1] towards Dasein. The relationship-of-Being which one has towards Others would then become a Projection[2] of one's own Being-towards-oneself 'into something else'. The Other would be a duplicate of the Self.

But while these deliberations seem obvious enough, it is easy to see that they have little ground to stand on. The presupposition which this argument demands—that Dasein's Being towards an Other is its Being towards itself—fails to hold. As long as the legitimacy of this presupposition has not turned out to be evident, one may still be puzzled as to how Dasein's relationship to itself is thus to be disclosed to the Other as Other.

Not only is Being towards Others an autonomous, irreducible relationship of Being: this relationship, as Being-with, is one which, with Dasein's Being, already is.[3] Of course it is indisputable that a lively mutual acquaintanceship on the basis of Being-with, often depends upon how far one's own Dasein has understood itself at the time; but this means that it depends only upon how far one's essential Being with Others has made itself transparent and has not disguised itself.[4] And that is possible only if Dasein, as Being-in-the-world, already is with Others. 'Empathy' does not first constitute Being-with; only on the basis of Being-with does 'empathy' become possible: it gets its motivation from the unsociability of the dominant modes of Being-with.[5]

[1] '. . . sich . . . verhält . . .' We have often translated this expression as 'comports' itself', compromising between two other possible meanings: 'relates itself' and 'behaves or 'conducts itself'. In this passage, however, and in many others where this expression is tied up with 'Verhältnis' ('relationship') rather than with 'Verhalten' ('behaviour or 'conduct'), only 'relates itself' seems appropriate.

[2] 'Projektion'. Here we are dealing with 'projection' in the familiar psychological sense, not in the sense which would be expressed by 'Entwurf'. See H. 145 ff.

[3] 'Das Sein zu Anderen ist nicht nur ein eigenständiger, irreduktibler Seinsbezug, er ist als Mitsein mit dem Sein des Daseins schon seiend.'

[4] '. . . wie weit es das wesenhafte Mitsein mit anderen sich durchsichtig gemacht und nicht verstellt hat . . .' (The older editions have '. . . sich nicht undurchsichtig gemacht und verstellt hat . . .'.)

[5] ' "Einfühlung" konstituiert nicht erst das Mitsein, sondern ist auf dessen Grunde erst möglich und durch die vorherrschenden defizienten Modi des Mitseins in ihrer Unumgänglichkeit motiviert.'

But the fact that 'empathy' is not a primordial existential phenomenon, any more than is knowing in general, does not mean that there is nothing problematical about it. The special hermeneutic of empathy will have to show how Being-with-one-another and Dasein's knowing of itself are led astray and obstructed by the various possibilities of Being which Dasein itself possesses, so that a genuine 'understanding' gets suppressed, and Dasein takes refuge in substitutes; the possibility of understanding the stranger correctly presupposes such a hermeneutic as its positive existential condition.[1] Our analysis has shown that Being-with is an existential constituent of Being-in-the-world. Dasein-with has proved to be a kind of Being which entities encountered within-the-world have as their own. So far as Dasein *is* at all, it has Being-with-one-another as its kind of Being. This cannot be conceived as a summative result of the occurrence of several 'subjects'. Even to come across a number of 'subjects' [einer Anzahl von "Subjekten"] becomes possible only if the Others who are concerned proximally in their Dasein-with are treated merely as 'numerals' ["Nummer"]. Such a number of 'subjects' gets discovered only by a definite Being-with-and-towards-one-another. This 'inconsiderate' Being-with 'reckons' ["rechnet"] with the Others without seriously 'counting on them' ["auf sie zählt"], or without even wanting to 'have anything to do' with them.

One's own Dasein, like the Dasein-with of Others, is encountered proximally and for the most part in terms of the with-world with which we are environmentally concerned. When Dasein is absorbed in the world of its concern—that is, at the same time, in its Being-with towards Others —it is not itself. *Who* is it, then, who has taken over Being as everyday Being-with-one-another?

¶ 27. *Everyday Being-one's-Self and the "They"*

The *ontologically* relevant result of our analysis of Being-with is the insight that the 'subject character' of one's own Dasein and that of Others is to be defined existentially—that is, in terms of certain ways in which one may be. In that with which we concern ourselves environmentally the Others are encountered as what they are; they *are* what they do [sie *sind* das, was sie betreiben].

In one's concern with what one has taken hold of, whether with, for, or against, the Others, there is constant care as to the way one differs from them, whether that difference is merely one that is to be evened out, whether one's own Dasein has lagged behind the Others and wants to

---

[1] '... welche positive existenziale Bedingung rechtes Fremdverstehen für seine Möglichkeit voraussetzt.' We have construed 'welche' as referring back to 'Hermeneutik', though this is not entirely clear.

catch up in relationship to them, or whether one's Dasein already has some priority over them and sets out to keep them suppressed. The care about this distance between them is disturbing to Being-with-one-another, though this disturbance is one that is hidden from it. If we may express this existentially, such Being-with-one-another has the character of *distantiality* [*Abständigkeit*]. The more inconspicuous this kind of Being is to everyday Dasein itself, all the more stubbornly and primordially does it work itself out.

But this distantiality which belongs to Being-with, is such that Dasein, as everyday Being-with-one-another, stands in *subjection* [*Botmässigkeit*] to Others. It itself *is* not;[1] its Being has been taken away by the Others. Dasein's everyday possibilities of Being are for the Others to dispose of as they please. These Others, moreover, are not *definite* Others. On the contrary, any Other can represent them. What is decisive is just that inconspicuous domination by Others which has already been taken over unawares from Dasein as Being-with. One belongs to the Others oneself and enhances their power. 'The Others' whom one thus designates in order to cover up the fact of one's belonging to them essentially oneself, are those who proximally and for the most part '*are there*' in everyday Being-with-one-another. The "who" is not this one, not that one, not oneself [man selbst], not some people [einige], and not the sum of them all. The 'who' is the neuter, the "*they*" [*das Man*].

We have shown earlier how in the environment which lies closest to us, the public 'environment' already is ready-to-hand and is also a matter of concern [mitbesorgt]. In utilizing public means of transport and in making use of information services such as the newspaper, every Other is like the next. This Being-with-one-another dissolves one's own Dasein completely into the kind of Being of 'the Others', in such a way, indeed, that the Others, as distinguishable and explicit, vanish more and more. In this inconspicuousness and unascertainability, the real dictatorship of the "they" is unfolded. We take pleasure and enjoy ourselves as *they* [*man*] take pleasure; we read, see, and judge about literature and art as *they* see and judge; likewise we shrink back from the 'great mass' as *they* shrink back; we find 'shocking' what *they* find shocking. The "they", which is nothing definite, and which all are, though not as the sum, prescribes the kind of Being of everydayness.

The "they" has its own ways in which to be. That tendency of Being-with which we have called "distantiality" is grounded in the fact that Being-with-one-another concerns itself as such with *averageness*, which is an existential characteristic of the "they". The "they", in its Being,

---

[1] 'Nicht es selbst *ist*; . . .'

essentially makes an issue of this. Thus the "they" maintains itself factically in the averageness of that which belongs to it, of that which it regards
as valid and that which it does not, and of that to which it grants success
and that to which it denies it. In this averageness with which it prescribes
what can and may be ventured, it keeps watch over everything exceptional
that thrusts itself to the fore. Every kind of priority gets noiselessly suppressed. Overnight, everything that is primordial gets glossed over as
something that has long been well known. Everything gained by a struggle
becomes just something to be manipulated. Every secret loses its force.
This care of averageness reveals in turn an essential tendency of Dasein
which we call the "levelling down" [*Einebnung*] of all possibilities of Being.

Distantiality, averageness, and levelling down, as ways of Being for the
"they", constitute what we know as 'publicness' ["die Offentlichkeit"].
Publicness proximally controls every way in which the world and Dasein
get interpreted, and it is always right—not because there is some distinctive and primary relationship-of-Being in which it is related to 'Things',
or because it avails itself of some transparency on the part of Dasein which
it has explicitly appropriated, but because it is insensitive to every difference of level and of genuineness and thus never gets to the 'heart of the
matter' ["auf die Sachen"]. By publicness everything gets obscured, and
what has thus been covered up gets passed off as something familiar and
accessible to everyone.

The "they" is there alongside everywhere [ist überall dabei], but in
such a manner that it has always stolen away whenever Dasein presses
for a decision. Yet because the "they" presents every judgment and decision as its own, it deprives the particular Dasein of its answerability. The
"they" can, as it were, manage to have 'them' constantly invoking it.[1]
It can be answerable for everything most easily, because it is not someone
who needs to vouch for anything. It 'was' always the "they" who did it,
and yet it can be said that it has been 'no one'. In Dasein's everydayness
the agency through which most things come about is one of which we
must say that "it was no one".

Thus the particular Dasein in its everydayness is *disburdened* by the
"they". Not only that; by thus disburdening it of its Being, the "they"
accommodates Dasein [kommt . . . dem Dasein entgegen] if Dasein
has any tendency to take things easily and make them easy. And because the "they" constantly accommodates the particular Dasein by disburdening it of its Being, the "they" retains and enhances its stubborn
dominion.

Everyone is the other, and no one is himself. The "*they*", which supplies

I

---

[1] 'Das Man kann es sich gleichsam leisten, dass "man" sich ständig auf es beruft.'

the answer to the question of the *"who"* of everyday Dasein, is the *"nobody"* to whom every Dasein has already surrendered itself in Being-among-one-other [Untereinandersein].

In these characters of Being which we have exhibited—everyday Being-among-one-another, distantiality, averageness, levelling down, public-ness, the disburdening of one's Being, and accommodation—lies that 'constancy' of Dasein which is closest to us. This "constancy" pertains not to the enduring Being-present-at-hand of something, but rather to Dasein's kind of Being as Being-with. Neither the Self of one's own Dasein nor the Self of the Other has as yet found itself or lost itself as long as it is [seiend] in the modes we have mentioned. In these modes one's way of Being is that of inauthenticity and failure to stand by one's Self.[1] To be in this way signifies no lessening of Dasein's facticity, just as the "they", as the "nobody", is by no means nothing at all. On the contrary, in this kind of Being, Dasein is an *ens realissimum*, if by 'Reality' we understand a Being with the character of Dasein.

Of course, the "they" is as little present-at-hand as Dasein itself. The more openly the "they" behaves, the harder it is to grasp, and the slier it is, but the less is it nothing at all. If we 'see' it ontico-ontologically with an unprejudiced eye, it reveals itself as the 'Realest subject' of everyday-ness. And even if it is not accessible like a stone that is present-at-hand, this is not in the least decisive as to its kind of Being. One may neither decree prematurely that this "they" is 'really' nothing, nor profess the opinion that one can Interpret this phenomenon ontologically by some-how 'explaining' it as what results from taking the Being-present-at-hand-together of several subjects and then fitting them together. On the contrary, in working out concepts of Being one must direct one's course by these phenomena, which cannot be pushed aside.

Furthermore, the "they" is not something like a 'universal subject' which a plurality of subjects have hovering above them. One can come to take it this way only if the Being of such 'subjects' is understood as having a character other than that of Dasein, and if these are regarded as cases of a genus of occurrents—cases which are factually present-at-hand. With this approach, the only possibility ontologically is that everything which is not a case of this sort is to be understood in the sense of genus and species. The "they" is not the genus to which the individual Dasein belongs, nor can we come across it in such entities as an abiding characteristic. That even the traditional logic fails us when confronted with these phenomena, is not surprising if we bear in mind that it has its foundation in an

---

[1] 'Man ist in der Weise der Unselbständigkeit und Uneigentlichkeit.' On 'Ständigkeit' and 'Unselbständigkeit' see our note 1, p. 153, H. 117 above.

ontology of the present-at-hand—an ontology which, moreover, is still a rough one. So no matter in how many ways this logic may be improved and expanded, it cannot in principle be made any more flexible. Such reforms of logic, oriented towards the 'humane sciences', only increase the ontological confusion.

The "they" is an existentiale; and as a primordial phenomenon, it belongs to Dasein's positive constitution. It itself has, in turn, various possibilities of becoming concrete as something characteristic of Dasein [seiner daseins-mässigen Konkretion]. The extent to which its dominion becomes com-pelling and explicit may change in the course of history.

The Self of everyday Dasein is the *they-self*,[1] which we distinguish from the *authentic Self*—that is, from the Self which has been taken hold of in its own way [eigens ergriffenen]. As they-self, the particular Dasein has been dispersed into the "they", and must first find itself. This dispersal characterizes the 'subject' of that kind of Being which we know as con-cernful absorption in the world we encounter as closest to us. If Dasein is familiar with itself as they-self, this means at the same time that the "they" itself prescribes that way of interpreting the world and Being-in-the-world which lies closest. Dasein is for the sake of the "they" in an everyday manner, and the "they" itself Articulates the referential context of significance.[2] When entities are encountered, Dasein's world frees them for a totality of involvements with which the "they" is familiar, and within the limits which have been established with the "they's" averageness. *Proxi-mally*, factical Dasein is in the with-world, which is discovered in an average way. *Proximally*, it is not 'I', in the sense of my own Self, that 'am', but rather the Others, whose way is that of the "they".[3] In terms of the "they", and as the "they", I am 'given' proximally to 'myself' [mir "selbst"]. Proximally Dasein is "they", and for the most part it remains so. If Dasein discovers the world in its own way [eigens] and brings it close, if it discloses to itself its own authentic Being, then this discovery of the 'world' and this disclosure of Dasein are always accomplished as a clearing-away of concealments and obscurities, as a breaking up of the disguises with which Dasein bars its own way.

With this Interpretation of Being-with and Being-one's-Self in the

---

[1] '. . . das Man-selbst . . .' This expression is also to be distinguished from 'das Man selbst' ('the "they" itself'), which appears elsewhere in this paragraph. In the first of these expressions 'selbst' appears as a substantive, in the second as a mere intensive.

[2] 'Das Man selbst, worum-willen das Dasein alltäglich ist, artikuliert den Verweisungs-zusammenhang der Bedeutsamkeit.' It is also possible to construe 'alltäglich' as a pre-dicate adjective after 'ist'; in that case we should read: 'Dasein is everyday for the sake of the "they".'

[3] '*Zunächst* "bin" nicht "ich" im Sinne des eigenen Selbst, sondern die Anderen in der Weise des Man.' In the earlier editions there are commas after ' "ich" ' and 'Anderen', which would suggest a somewhat different interpretation.

"they", the question of the "who" of the everydayness of Being-with-one-another is answered. These considerations have at the same time brought us a concrete understanding of the basic constitution of Dasein: Being-in-the-world, in its everydayness and its averageness, has become visible.

From the kind of Being which belongs to the "they"—the kind which is closest—everyday Dasein draws its pre-ontological way of interpreting its Being. In the first instance ontological Interpretation follows the tendency to interpret it this way: it understands Dasein in terms of the world and comes across it as an entity within-the-world. But that is not all: even that meaning of Being on the basis of which these 'subject' entities [diese seienden "Subjekte"] get understood, is one which that ontology of Dasein which is 'closest' to us lets itself present in terms of the 'world'. But because the phenomenon of the world itself gets passed over in this absorption in the world, its place gets taken [tritt an seine Stelle] by what is present-at-hand within-the-world, namely, Things. The Being of those entities which *are there with us*, gets conceived as presence-at-hand. Thus by exhibiting the positive phenomenon of the closest everyday Being-in-the-world, we have made it possible to get an insight into the reason why an ontological Interpretation of this state of Being has been missing. *This very state of Being,*[1] *in its everyday kind of Being, is what proximally misses itself and covers itself up.*

If the Being of everyday Being-with-one-another is already different in principle from pure presence-at-hand—in spite of the fact that it is seemingly close to it ontologically—still less can the Being of the authentic Self be conceived as presence-at-hand. *Authentic Being-one's-Self* does not rest upon an exceptional condition of the subject, a condition that has been detached from the "they"; *it is rather an existentiell modification of the "they"— of the "they" as an essential existentiale.*

But in that case there is ontologically a gap separating the selfsameness of the authentically existing Self from the identity of that "I" which maintains itself throughout its manifold Experiences.

[1] We interpret Heidegger's pronoun 'Sie' as referring to 'Seinsverfassung' ('state of Being'); but there are other words in the previous sentence to which it might refer with just as much grammatical plausibility, particularly 'Interpretation'.

V

BEING-IN AS SUCH

¶ *28. The Task of a Thematic Analysis of Being-in*

In the preparatory stage of the existential analytic of Dasein, we have for our leading theme this entity's basic state, Being-in-the-World. Our first aim is to bring into relief phenomenally the unitary primordial structure of Dasein's Being, in terms of which its possibilities and the ways for it 'to be' are ontologically determined. Up till now, our phenomenal characterization of Being-in-the-world has been directed towards the world, as a structural item of Being-in-the-world, and has attempted to provide an answer to the question about the "who" of this entity in its everydayness. But even in first marking out the tasks of a preparatory fundamental analysis of Dasein, we have already provided an advance orientation as to *Being-in as such*,[1] and have illustrated it in the concrete mode of knowing the world.[ii]

The fact that we foresaw this structural item which carries so much weight, arose from our aim of setting the analysis of single items, from the outset, within the frame of a steady preliminary view of the structural whole, and of guarding against any disruption or fragmentation of the unitary phenomenon. Now, keeping in mind what has been achieved in the concrete analysis of the world and the "who", we must turn our Interpretation back to the phenomenon of Being-in. By considering this more penetratingly, however, we shall not only get a new and surer phenomenological view of the structural totality of Being-in-the-world, but shall also pave the way to grasping the primordial Being of Dasein itself—namely, care.

But what more is there to point out in Being-in-the-world, beyond the essential relations of Being alongside the world (concern), Being-with (solicitude), and Being-one's-Self ("who")? If need be, there still remains the possibility of broadening out the analysis by characterizing comparatively the variations of concern and its circumspection, of solicitude and the considerateness which goes with it; there is also the possibility of contrasting Dasein with entities whose character is not that of Dasein by a more precise explication of the Being of all possible entities within-the-world. Without question, there are unfinished tasks still lying in this field. What we have hitherto set forth needs to be rounded out in many ways by working out fully the existential *a priori* of philosophical anthropology and taking a look at it. But this is not the aim of our investigation. *Its aim is one of fundamental ontology.* Consequently, if we inquire about Being-in as our theme, we cannot indeed consent to nullify the primordial character of this phenomenon by deriving it from others—that is to say, by an inappropriate analysis, in the sense of a dissolving or breaking up. But the fact that something primordial is underivable does not rule out the possibility that a multiplicity of characteristics of Being may be constitutive for it. If these show themselves, then existentially they are equiprimordial. The phenomenon of the *equiprimordiality* of constitutive items has often been disregarded in ontology, because of a methodologically unrestrained tendency to derive everything and anything from some simple 'primal ground'.

2   In which direction must we look, if we are to characterize Being-in, as such, phenomenally? We get the answer to this question by recalling what we were charged with keeping phenomenologically in view when we called attention to this phenomenon: Being-in is distinct from the present-at-hand insideness of something present-at-hand 'in' something else that is present-at-hand; Being-in is not a characteristic that is effected, or even just elicited, in a present-at-hand subject by the 'world's' Being-present-at-hand; Being-in is rather an essential kind of Being of this entity itself. But in that case, what else is presented with this phenomenon than the *commercium* which is present-at-hand *between* a subject present-at-hand and an Object present-at-hand? Such an interpretation would come closer to the phenomenal content if we were to say that *Dasein is the Being* of this 'between'. Yet to take our orientation from this 'between' would still be misleading. For with such an orientation we would also be covertly assuming the entities between which this "between", as such, 'is', and we would be doing so in a way which is ontologically vague. The "between" is already conceived as the result of the *convenientia* of two things that are present-at-hand. But to assume these beforehand always *splits* the phenomenon asunder, and there is no prospect of putting it together again from the fragments. Not only do we lack the 'cement'; even the 'schema' in accordance with which this joining-together is to be accomplished, has been split asunder, or never as yet unveiled. What is decisive for ontology is to prevent the splitting of the phenomenon—in other words, to hold its positive phenomenal content secure. To say that for this we need far-reaching and detailed study, is simply to express the fact that something which was ontically self-evident in the traditional way of treating the

'problem of knowledge' has often been ontologically disguised to the point where it has been lost sight of altogether.

The entity which is essentially constituted by Being-in-the-world *is* itself in every case its 'there'. According to the familiar signification of the word, the 'there' points to a 'here' and a 'yonder'. There 'here' of an 'I-here' is always understood in relation to a 'yonder' ready-to-hand, in the sense of a Being towards this 'yonder'—a Being which is de-severant, directional, and concernful. Dasein's existential spatiality, which thus determines its 'location', is itself grounded in Being-in-the-world. The "yonder" belongs definitely to something encountered within-the-*world*. 'Here' and 'yonder' are possible only in a 'there'—that is to say, only if there is an entity which has made a disclosure of spatiality as the Being of the 'there'. This entity carries in its ownmost Being the character of not being closed off. In the expression 'there' we have in view this essential disclosedness. By reason of this disclosedness, this entity (Dasein), together with the Being-there[1] of the world, is 'there' for itself.

When we talk in an ontically figurative way of the *lumen naturale* in man, we have in mind nothing other than the existential-ontological structure of this entity, that it *is* in such a way as to be its "there". To say that it is 'illuminated' ["erleuchtet"] means that *as* Being-in-the-world it is cleared [gelichtet] in itself, not through any other entity, but in such a way that it *is* itself the clearing.[2] Only for an entity which is existentially cleared in this way does that which is present-at-hand become accessible in the light or hidden in the dark. By its very nature, Dasein brings its "there" along with it. If it lacks its "there", it is not factically the entity which is essentially Dasein; indeed, it is not this entity at all. *Dasein is its disclosedness.*

We are to set forth the Constitution of this Being. But in so far as the essence of this entity is existence, the existential proposition, 'Dasein *is* its disclosedness', means at the same time that the Being which is an issue for this entity in its very Being is to be its 'there'. In addition to characterizing the primary Constitution of the Being of disclosedness, we will require, in conformity with the course of the analysis, an Interpretation of the kind of Being in which this entity is its "there" in an *everyday* manner.

This chapter, in which we shall undertake the explication of Being-in as such (that is to say, of the Being of the "there"), breaks up into two parts: A. the existential Constitution of the "there"; B. the everyday Being of the "there", and the falling of Dasein.

In *understanding* and *state-of-mind*, we shall see the two constitutive ways

---

[1] '*Da-sein*'. See our note I, p. 27, H. 7 above.
[2] 'Lichtung'. This word is customarily used to stand for a 'clearing' in the woods, not for a 'clarification'; the verb 'lichten' is similarly used. The force of this passage lies in the fact that these words are cognates of the noun 'Licht' ('light').

of being the "there"; and these are equiprimordial. If these are to be analysed, some phenomenal confirmation is necessary; in both cases this will be attained by Interpreting some concrete mode which is important for the subsequent problematic. State-of-mind and understanding are characterized equiprimordially by *discourse*.

Under A (the existential Constitutuon of the "there") we shall accordingly treat: Being-there as state-of-mind (Section 29); fear as a mode of state-of-mind (Section 30); Being-there as understanding (Section 31); understanding and interpretation (Section 32); assertion as a derivative mode of interpretation (Section 33); Being-there, discourse, and language (Section 34).

The analysis of the characteristics of the Being of Being-there is an existential one. This means that the characteristics are not properties of something present-at-hand, but essentially existential ways to be. We must therefore set forth their kind of Being in everydayness.

Under B (the everyday Being of the "there", and the falling of Dasein) we shall analyse idle talk (Section 35), curiosity (Section 36), and ambiguity (Section 37) as existential modes of the everyday Being of the "there"; we shall analyse them as corresponding respectively to the constitutive phenomenon of discourse, the sight which lies in understanding, and the interpretation (or explaining [Deutung]) which belongs to understanding. In these phenomenal modes a basic kind of Being of the "there" will become visible—a kind of Being which we Interpret as *falling*; and this 'falling' shows a movement [Bewegtheit] which is existentially its own.[1]

A. *The Existential Constitution of the "There"*

¶ 29. *Being there as State-of-mind*

What we indicate *ontologically* by the term "state-of-mind"[2] is *ontically* the most familiar and everyday sort of thing; our mood, our Being-attuned.[3] Prior to all psychology of moods, a field which in any case still

---

[1] While we shall ordinarily reserve the word 'falling' for 'Verfallen' (see our note 2, p. 42, H. 21 above), in this sentence it represents first 'Verfallen' and then 'Fallen', the usual German word for 'falling'. 'Fallen' and 'Verfallen' are by no means strictly synonymous; the latter generally has the further connotation of 'decay' or 'deterioration', though Heidegger will take pains to point out that in his own usage it 'does not express any negative evaluation'. See Section 38 below.

[2] 'Befindlichkeit'. More literally: 'the state in which one may be found'. (The common German expression 'Wie befinden Sie sich?' means simply 'How are you?' or 'How are you feeling?') Our translation, 'state-of-mind', comes fairly close to what is meant; but it should be made clear that the 'of-mind' belongs to English idiom, has no literal counterpart in the structure of the German word, and fails to bring out the important connotation of finding oneself.

[3] '. . . die Stimmung, das Gestimmtsein.' The noun 'Stimmung' originally means the tuning of a musical instrument, but it has taken on several other meanings and is the usual word for one's mood or humour. We shall usually translate it as 'mood', and we shall generally translate both 'Gestimmtsein' and 'Gestimmtheit' as 'having a mood', though sometimes, as in the present sentence, we prefer to call attention to the root metaphor of 'Gestimmtsein' by writing 'Being-attuned', etc.

lies fallow, it is necessary to see this phenomenon as a fundamental *existentiale*, and to outline its structure.

Both the undisturbed equanimity and the inhibited ill-humour of our everyday concern, the way we slip over from one to the other, or slip off into bad moods, are by no means nothing ontologically,[1] even if these phenomena are left unheeded as supposedly the most indifferent and fleeting in Dasein. The fact that moods can deteriorate [verdorben werden] and change over means simply that in every case Dasein always has some mood [gestimmt ist]. The pallid, evenly balanced lack of mood [Ungestimmtheit], which is often persistent and which is not to be mistaken for a bad mood, is far from nothing at all. Rather, it is in this that Dasein becomes satiated with itself. Being has become manifest as a burden. Why that should be, one does not *know*. And Dasein cannot know anything of the sort because the possibilities of disclosure which belong to cognition reach far too short a way compared with the primordial disclosure belonging to moods, in which Dasein is brought before its Being as "there". Furthermore, a mood of elation can alleviate the manifest burden of Being; that such a mood is possible also discloses the burdensome character of Dasein, even while it alleviates the burden. A mood makes manifest 'how one is, and how one is faring' ["wie einem ist und wird"]. In this 'how one is', having a mood brings Being to its "there".

In having a mood, Dasein is always disclosed moodwise as that entity to which it has been delivered over in its Being; and in this way it has been delivered over to the Being which, in existing, it has to be. "To be disclosed" does not mean "to be known as this sort of thing". And even in the most indifferent and inoffensive everydayness the Being of Dasein can burst forth as a naked 'that it is and has to be' [als nacktes "Dass es est ist und zu sein hat"]. The pure 'that it is' shows itself, but the "whence" and the "whither" remain in darkness. The fact that it is just as everyday a matter for Dasein not to 'give in' ["nachgibt"] to such moods—in other words, not to follow up [nachgeht] their disclosure and allow itself to be brought before that which is disclosed—is no evidence *against* the phenomenal facts of the case, in which the Being of the "there" is disclosed moodwise in its "that-it-is";[2] it is rather evidence for it. In an

[1] In this sentence 'equanimity' represents 'Gleichmut', 'ill-humour' represents 'Missmut', and 'bad moods' represents 'Verstimmungen'.

[2] '. . . den phänomenalen Tatbestand der stimmungsmässigen Erschlossenheit des Seins des Da in seinem Dass . . .' It would be more literal to write simply 'in its "that" '; but to avoid a very natural confusion between the conjunction 'that' and pronoun 'that', we shall translate 'das Dass' as 'the "that-it-is" ', even though we use the same expression *unhyphenated* for 'das "Dass es ist" ' in this paragraph and in that which follows. (The striking contrast between the 'Da' and the 'Dass' is of course lost in translation.)

ntico-existentiell sense, Dasein for the most part evades the Being which
s disclosed in the mood. In an *ontologico*-existential sense, this means that
:ven in that to which such a mood pays no attention, Dasein is unveiled
n its Being-delivered-over to the "there". In the evasion itself the "there"
s something disclosed.

This characteristic of Dasein's Being—this 'that it is'—is veiled in its
"whence" and "whither", yet disclosed in itself all the more unveiledly;
we call it the *"thrownness"*[1] of this entity into its "there"; indeed, it is
hrown in such a way that, as Being-in-the-world, it is the "there". The
:xpression "thrownness" is meant to suggest the *facticity of its being
delivered over.*[2] The 'that it is and has to be' which is disclosed in Dasein's
:tate-of-mind is not the same 'that-it-is' which expresses ontologico-
:ategorially the factuality belonging to presence-at-hand. This factuality
pecomes accessible only if we ascertain it by looking at it. The "that-it-is"
which is disclosed in Dasein's state-of-mind must rather be conceived as
an existential attribute of the entity which has Being-in-the-world as its
way of Being. *Facticity is not the factuality of the factum brutum of something present-at-hand, but a characteristic of Dasein's Being—one which has been
taken up into existence, even if proximally it has been thrust aside.* The "that-it-is"
of facticity never becomes something that we can come across by beholding it.

An entity of the character of Dasein is its "there" in such a way that,
whether explicitly or not, it finds itself [sich befindet] in its thrownness.
In a state-of-mind Dasein is always brought before itself, and has
always found itself, not in the sense of coming across itself by perceiving
itself, but in the sense of finding itself in the mood that it has.[3] As an entity
which has been delivered over to its Being, it remains also delivered over
to the fact that it must always have found itself—but found itself in a
way of finding which arises not so much from a direct seeking as rather
from a fleeing. The way in which the mood discloses is not one in which
we look at thrownness, but one in which we turn towards or turn away
[An- und Abkehr]. For the most part the mood does not turn towards
the burdensome character of Dasein which is manifest in it, and least of all
does it do so in the mood of elation when this burden has been alleviated.
It is always by way of a state-of-mind that this turning-away is what it is.

---

[1] *'Geworfenheit'*. This important term, which Heidegger introduces here, is further
discussed in Section 38.
[2] 'Der Ausdruck Geworfenheit soll die *Faktizität der Überantwortung andeuten.*' On the
distinction between 'facticity' and 'factuality', see H. 56 above.
[3] In this sentence there is a contrast between 'wahrnehmendes Sich-vorfinden' ('coming
across itself by perceiving') and 'gestimmtes Sichbefinden' ('finding itself in the mood
that it has'). In the next sentence, on the other hand, 'found' and 'finding' represent
gefunden' and 'Finden'.

Phenomenally, we would wholly fail to recognize both *what* mood discloses and *how* it discloses, if that which is disclosed were to be compared with what Dasein is acquainted with, knows, and believes 'at the same time' when it has such a mood. Even if Dasein is 'assured' in its belief about its 'whither', or if, in rational enlightenment, it supposes itself to know about its "whence", all this counts for nothing as against the phenomenal facts of the case: for the mood brings Dasein before the "that-it-is" of its "there", which, as such, stares it in the face with the inexorability of an enigma.[1] From the existential-ontological point of view, there is not the slightest justification for minimizing what is 'evident' in states-of-mind, by measuring it against the apodictic certainty of a theoretical cognition of something which is purely present-at-hand. However the phenomena are no less falsified when they are banished to the sanctuary of the irrational. When irrationalism, as the counterplay of rationalism, talks about the things to which rationalism is blind, it does so only with a squint.

Factically, Dasein can, should, and must, through knowledge and will, become master of its moods; in certain possible ways of existing, this may signify a priority of volition and cognition. Only we must not be misled by this into denying that ontologically mood is a primordial kind of Being for Dasein, in which Dasein is disclosed to itself *prior to* all cognition and volition, and *beyond* their range of disclosure. And furthermore, when we master a mood, we do so by way of a counter-mood; we are never free of moods. Ontologically, we thus obtain as the *first* essential characteristic of states-of-mind that *they disclose Dasein in its thrownness, and—proximally and for the most part—in the manner of an evasive turning-away.*

From what has been said we can see already that a state-of-mind is very remote from anything like coming across a psychical condition by the kind of apprehending which first turns round and then back. Indeed it is so far from this, that only because the "there" has already been disclosed in a state-of-mind can immanent reflection come across 'Experiences' at all. The 'bare mood' discloses the "there" more primordially, but correspondingly it *closes* it *off* more stubbornly than any *not*-perceiving.

This is shown by *bad moods*. In these, Dasein becomes blind to itself, the environment with which it is concerned veils itself, the circumspection of concern gets led astray. States-of-mind are so far from being reflected upon, that precisely what they do is to assail Dasein in its unreflecting devotion to the 'world' with which it is concerned and on which it expends

---

[1] '. . . so verschlägt das alles nichts gegen den phänomenalen Tatbestand, dass die Stimmung das Dasein vor das Dass seines Da bringt, als welches es ihm in unerbittlicher Rätselhaftigkeit entgegenstarrt.' The pronoun 'es' (the reference of which is not entirely unambiguous) appears only in the later editions.

itself. A mood assails us. It comes neither from 'outside' nor from 'inside', but arises out of Being-in-the-world, as a way of such Being. But with the negative distinction between state-of-mind and the reflective apprehending of something 'within', we have thus reached a positive insight into their character as disclosure. *The mood has already disclosed, in every case, Being-in-the-world as a whole, and makes it possible first of all to direct oneself towards something.* Having a mood is not related to the psychical in the first instance, and is not itself an inner condition which then reaches forth in an enigmatical way and puts its mark on Things and persons. It is in this that the *second* essential characteristic of states-of-mind shows itself. We have seen that the world, Dasein-with, and existence are *equiprimordially disclosed*; and state-of-mind is a basic existential species of their disclosedness, because this disclosedness itself is essentially Being-in-the-world.[1]

Besides these two essential characteristics of states-of-mind which have been explained—the disclosing of thrownness and the current disclosing of Being-in-the-world as a whole—we have to notice a *third*, which contributes above all towards a more penetrating understanding of the worldhood of the world. As we have said earlier,[iii] the world which has already been disclosed beforehand permits what is within-the-world to be encountered. This prior disclosedness of the world belongs to Being-in and is partly constituted by one's state-of-mind. Letting something be encountered is primarily *circumspective*; it is not just sensing something, or staring at it. It implies circumspective concern, and has the character of becoming affected in some way [Betroffenwerdens] ; we can see this more precisely from the standpoint of state-of-mind. But to be affected by the unserviceable, resistant, or threatening character [Bedrohlichkeit] of that which is ready-to-hand, becomes ontologically possible only in so far as Being-in as such has been determined existentially beforehand in such a manner that what it encounters within-the-world can *"matter"* to it in this way. The fact that this sort of thing can "matter" to it is grounded in one's state-of-mind; and as a state-of-mind it has already disclosed the world—as something by which it can be threatened, for instance.[2] Only something which is in the state-of-mind of fearing (or fearlessness) can discover that what is environmentally ready-to-hand is threatening. Dasein's openness to the world is constituted existentially by the attunement of a state-of-mind.

And only because the 'senses' [die "Sinne"] belong ontologically to an

---

[1] '. . . weil diese selbst wesenhaft In-der-Welt-sein ist.' It is not clear whether the antecedent of 'diese' is 'Existenz' ('existence') or '*Erschlossenheit*' ('*disclosedness*').

[2] 'Diese Angänglichkeit gründet in der Befindlichkeit, als welche sie die Welt zum Beispiel auf Bedrohbarkeit hin erschlossen hat.' The pronoun 'sie' appears only in the newer editions.

entity whose kind of Being is Being-in-the-world with a state-of mind,[1] can they be 'touched' by anything or 'have a sense for' ["Sinn haben für"] something in such a way that what touches them shows itself in an affect.[2] Under the strongest pressure and resistance, nothing like an affect would come about, and the resistance itself would remain essentially undiscovered, if Being-in-the-world, with its state-of-mind, had not already submitted itself [sich schon angewiesen] to having entities within-the-world "matter" to it in a way which its moods have outlined in advance. *Existentially, a state-of-mind implies a disclosive submission to the world, out of which we can encounter something that matters to us.* Indeed *from the ontological point of view* we must as a general principle leave the primary discovery of the world to 'bare mood'. Pure beholding, even if it were to penetrate to the innermost core of the Being of something present-at-hand, could never discover anything like that which is threatening.

The fact that, even though states-of-mind are primarily disclosive, everyday circumspection goes wrong and to a large extent succumbs to delusion because of them, is a μὴ ὄν [non-being] when measured against the idea of knowing the 'world' absolutely. But if we make evaluations which are so unjustified ontologically, we shall completely fail to recognize the existentially positive character of the capacity for delusion. It is precisely when we see the 'world' unsteadily and fitfully in accordance with our moods, that the ready-to-hand shows itself in its specific worldhood, which is never the same from day to day. By looking at the world theoretically, we have already dimmed it down to the uniformity of what is purely present-at-hand, though admittedly this uniformity comprises a new abundance of things which can be discovered by simply characterizing them. Yet even the purest θεωρία [theory] has not left all moods behind it; even when we look theoretically at what is just present-at-hand, it does not show itself purely as it looks unless this θεωρία lets it come towards us in a *tranquil* tarrying alongside . . . , in ῥαστώνη and διαγωγή.[iv] Any cognitive determining has its existential-ontological Constitution in the state-of-mind of Being-in-the-world; but pointing this out is not to be confused with attempting to surrender science ontically to 'feeling'.

---

[1] 'befindlichen In-der-Welt-seins'. In previous chapters we have usually translated 'befindlich' by such expressions as 'which is to be found', etc. See, for instance, H. 67, 70, 117 above, where this adjective is applied to a number of things which are hardly of the character of Dasein. In the present chapter, however, the word is tied up with the special sense of 'Befindlichkeit' as 'state-of-mind', and will be translated by expressions such as 'with a state-of-mind', 'having a state-of-mind', etc.

[2] In this sentence Heidegger has been calling attention to two ways of using the word 'Sinn' which might well be expressed by the word 'sense' but hardly by the word 'meaning': (1) 'die Sinne' as 'the five senses' or the 'senses' one has when one is 'in one's senses'; (2) 'der Sinn' as the 'sense' one has 'for' something—one's 'sense for clothes', one's 'sense of beauty', one's 'sense of the numinous', etc. Cf. the discussion of 'Sinn' on H. 151 f. below.

The different modes of state-of-mind and the ways in which they are interconnected in their foundations cannot be Interpreted within the problematic of the present investigation. The phenomena have long been well-known ontically under the terms "affects" and "feelings" and have always been under consideration in philosophy. It is not an accident that the earliest systematic Interpretation of affects that has come down to us is not treated in the framework of 'psychology'. Aristotle investigates the πάθη [affects] in the second book of his *Rhetoric*. Contrary to the traditional orientation, according to which rhetoric is conceived as the kind of thing we 'learn in school', this work of Aristotle must be taken as the first systematic hermeneutic of the everydayness of Being with one another. Publicness, as the kind of Being which belongs to the "they" (Cf. Section 27), not only has in general its own way of having a mood, but needs moods and 'makes' them for itself. It is into such a mood and out of such a mood that the orator speaks. He must understand the possibilities of moods in order to rouse them and guide them aright.

How the Interpretation of the affects was carried further in the Stoa, and how it was handed down to modern times through patristic and scholastic theology, is well known. What has escaped notice is that the basic ontological Interpretation of the affective life in general has been able to make scarcely one forward step worthy of mention since Aristotle. On the contrary, affects and feelings come under the theme of psychical phenomena, functioning as a third class of these, usually along with ideation [Vorstellen] and volition. They sink to the level of accompanying phenomena.

It has been one of the merits of phenomenological research that it has again brought these phenomena more unrestrictedly into our sight. Not only that: Scheler, accepting the challenges of Augustine and Pascal,ᵛ has guided the problematic to a consideration of how acts which 'represent' and acts which 'take an interest' are interconnected in their foundations. But even here the existential-ontological foundations of the phenomenon of the act in general are admittedly still obscure.

A state-of-mind not only discloses Dasein in its thrownness and its submission to that world which is already disclosed with its own Being; it is itself the existential kind of Being in which Dasein constantly surrenders itself to the 'world' and lets the 'world' "matter" to it in such a way that somehow Dasein evades its very self. The existential constitution of such evasion will become clear in the phenomenon of falling.

A state-of-mind is a basic existential way in which Dasein is its "there". It not only characterizes Dasein ontologically, but, because of what it discloses, it is at the same time methodologically significant in principle for the existential analytic. Like any ontological Interpretation whatsoever, this analytic can only, so to speak, "listen in" to some previously disclosed entity as regards its Being. And it will attach itself to Dasein's distinctive and most far-reaching possibilities of disclosure, in order to get information about this entity from these. Phenomenological Interpretation must make it possible for Dasein itself to disclose things primordially; it must, as it were, let Dasein interpret itself. Such Interpretation takes part in this disclosure only in order to raise to a conceptual level the phenomenal content of what has been disclosed, and to do so existentially.

Later (Cf. Section 40)[1] we shall provide an Interpretation of anxiety as such a basic state-of-mind of Dasein, and as one which is significant from the existential-ontological standpoint; with this in view, we shall now illustrate the phenomenon of state-of-mind even more concretely in its determinate mode of *fear*.

¶ 30. Fear as a Mode of State-of-Mind

There are three points of view from which the phenomenon of fear may be considered. We shall analyse: (1) that in the face of which we fear, (2) fearing, and (3) that about which we fear. These possible ways of looking at fear are not accidental; they belong together. With them the general structure of states-of-mind comes to the fore. We shall complete our analysis by alluding to the possible ways in which fear may be modified; each of these pertains to different items in the structure of fear.

That in the face of which we fear, the 'fearsome',[2] is in every case something which we encounter within-the-world and which may have either readiness-to-hand, presence-at-hand, or Dasein-with as its kind of Being. We are not going to make an ontical report on those entities which can often and for the most part be 'fearsome': we are to define the fearsome phenomenally in its fearsomeness. What do we encounter in fearing that belongs to the fearsome as such? That in the face of which we fear can be characterized as threatening. Here several points must be considered. 1. What we encounter has detrimentality as its kind of involvement. It shows itself within a context of involvements. 2. The target of this detrimentality is a definite range of what can be affected by it; thus the detrimentality is itself made definite, and comes from a definite region. 3. The region itself is well known as such, and so is that which is coming from it; but that which is coming from it has something 'queer' about it.[3] 4. That which is detrimental, as something that threatens us, is not yet within

---

[1] The earliest editions cite Section 39 rather than Section 40. This has been corrected in the list of *errata*.
[2] 'Das *Wovor* der Furcht, das Furchtbare . . .'
[3] '. . . mit dem es nicht "geheuer" ist.'

striking distance [in beherrschbarer Nähe], but it is coming close. In such a drawing-close, the detrimentality radiates out, and therein lies its threatening character. 5. This drawing-close is within what is close by. Indeed, something may be detrimental in the highest degree and may even be coming constantly closer; but if it is still far off, its fearsomeness remains veiled. If, however, that which is detrimental draws close and is close by, then it is threatening: it can reach us, and yet it may not. As it draws close, this 'it can, and yet in the end it may not' becomes aggravated. We say, "It is fearsome". 6. This implies that what is detrimental as coming-close close by carries with it the patent possibility that it may stay away and pass us by; but instead of lessening or extinguishing our fearing, this enhances it.

In *fearing as such*, what we have thus characterized as threatening is freed and allowed to matter to us. We do not first ascertain a future evil (*malum futurum*) and then fear it. But neither does fearing first take note of what is drawing close; it discovers it beforehand in its fearsomeness. And in fearing, fear can then look at the fearsome explicitly, and 'make it clear' to itself. Circumspection sees the fearsome because it has fear as its state-of-mind. Fearing, as a slumbering possibility of Being-in-the-world in a state-of-mind (we call this possibility 'fearfulness' ["Furchtsamkeit"]), has already disclosed the world, in that out of it something like the fearsome may come close. The potentiality for coming close is itself freed by the essential existential spatiality of Being-in-the-world.

That which fear fears *about* is that very entity which is afraid—Dasein.[1] Only an entity for which in its Being this very Being is an issue, can be afraid. Fearing discloses this entity as endangered and abandoned to itself. Fear always reveals Dasein in the Being of its "there", even if it does so in varying degrees of explicitness. If we fear about our house and home, this cannot be cited as an instance contrary to the above definition of what we fear about; for as Being-in-the-world, Dasein is in every case concernful Being-alongside.[2] Proximally and for the most part, Dasein *is*

---

[1] 'Das *Worum* die Furcht fürchtet, ist das sich fürchtende Seiende selbst, das Dasein.' While it is convenient to translate 'das Worum der Furcht' as 'that which one fears about', this expression must be taken in a narrower sense than one would ordinarily expect in English. What Heidegger generally has in mind is rather the person *on whose behalf* or *for whose sake* one fears. (Cf. our remarks on 'um' in note 1, p. 93, H. 65, and note 2, p. 98, H. 69 above.) Thus 'fürchten um' comes closer to the ordinary meaning of 'fear for' than it does to that of 'fear about'. We shall soon see, however, that Heidegger also uses the expression 'fürchten für', for which 'fear for' would seem to be the natural translation. Notice that what he then has in mind—namely, our fearing for Others—is only a special case of 'fearing for' in the ordinary English sense, and likewise only a special case of what we shall call 'fearing about' in this translation.

[2] 'Sein bei'. Here our usual translation, 'Being-alongside', fails to bring out the connection. A German reader would recall at once that 'bei' may mean, 'at the home of' like the French '*chez*'. See our note 3, p. 80, H. 54 above.

in terms of *what* it is concerned with. When this is endangered, Being-alongside is threatened. Fear discloses Dasein predominantly in a privative way. It bewilders us and makes us 'lose our heads'. Fear closes off our endangered Being-in, and yet at the same time lets us see it, so that when the fear has subsided, Dasein must first find its way about again.

Whether privatively or positively, fearing about something, as being-afraid in the face of something, always discloses equiprimordially entities within-the-world and Being-in—the former as threatening and the latter as threatened. Fear is a mode of state-of-mind.

One can also fear about Others, and we then speak of "fearing for" them [Fürchten für sie]. This fearing for the Other does not take away his fear. Such a possibility has been ruled out already, because the Other, *for* whom we fear, need not fear at all on his part. It is precisely when the Other is *not* afraid and charges recklessly at what is threatening him that we fear most *for* him. Fearing-for is a way of having a co-state-of-mind with Others, but not necessarily a being-afraid-with or even a fearing-with-one-another.[1] One can "fear about" without "being-afraid". Yet when viewed more strictly, fearing-about is "being-afraid-for-*oneself*".[2] Here what one "is apprehensive about" is one's Being-with with the Other, who might be torn away from one.[3] That which is fearsome is not aimed directly at him who fears with someone else. Fearing-about knows that in a certain way it is unaffected, and yet it is co-affected in so far as the Dasein-with for which it fears is affected. Fearing-about is therefore not a weaker form of being-afraid. Here the issue is one of existential modes, not of degrees of 'feeling-tones'. Fearing-about does not lose its specific genuiness even if it is not 'really' afraid.

There can be variations in the constitutive items of the full phenomenon of fear. Accordingly, different possibilities of Being emerge in fearing. Bringing-close close by, belongs to the structure of the threatening as encounterable. If something threatening breaks in suddenly upon concernful Being-in-the-world (something threatening in its 'not right away, but any moment'), fear becomes *alarm* [*Erschrecken*]. So, in what is threatening we must distinguish between the closest way in which it brings itself close, and the manner in which this bringing-close gets encountered—its suddenness. That in the face of which we are alarmed is proximally something well known and familiar. But if, on the other hand,

---

[1] 'Fürchten für . . . ist eine Weise der Mitbefindlichkeit mit den Anderen, aber nicht notwendig ein Sich-mitfürchten oder gar ein Miteinanderfürchten.'

[2] 'ein *Sich*fürchten'. We have hitherto translated 'sich fürchten' with various forms of 'be afraid', which is its usual signification in ordinary German. In this passage, however, the emphasis on the reflexive pronoun 'sich' clearly calls for 'being-afraid-for-*oneself*'.

[3] ' "Befürchtet" ist dabei das Mitsein mit dem Anderen, der einem entrissen werden könnte.'

that which threatens has the character of something altogether unfamiliar, then fear becomes *dread* [*Grauen*]. And where that which threatens is laden with dread, and is at the same time encountered with the suddenness of the alarming, then fear becomes *terror* [*Entsetzen*]. There are further variations of fear, which we know as timidity, shyness, misgiving, becoming startled. All modifications of fear, as possibilities of having a state-of-mind, point to the fact that Dasein as Being-in-the-world is 'fearful' ["furchtsam"]. This 'fearfulness' is not to be understood in an ontical sense as some factical 'individualized' disposition,[1] but as an existential possibility of the essential state-of-mind of Dasein in general, though of course it is not the only one.

¶ *31. Being-there as Understanding*

State-of-mind is *one* of the existential structures in which the Being of the 'there' maintains itself. Equiprimordial with it in constituting this Being is *understanding*. A state-of-mind always has its understanding, even if it merely keeps it suppressed. Understanding always has its mood. If we Interpret understanding as a fundamental *existentiale*, this indicates that this phenomenon is conceived as a basic mode of Dasein's *Being*. On the other hand, 'understanding' in the sense of *one* possible kind of cognizing among others (as distinguished, for instance, from 'explaining'), must, like explaining, be Interpreted as an existential derivative of that primary understanding which is one of the constituents of the Being of the "there" in general.

We have, after all, already come up against this primordial understanding in our previous investigations, though we did not allow it to be included explicitly in the theme under discussion. To say that in existing, Dasein is its "there", is equivalent to saying that the world is 'there'; its *Being-there* is Being-in. And the latter is likewise 'there', as that for the sake of which Dasein is. In the "for-the-sake-of-which", existing Being-in-the-world is disclosed as such, and this disclosedness we have called "understanding".[vii] In the understanding of the "for-the-sake-of-which", the significance which is grounded therein, is disclosed along with it. The disclosedness of understanding, as the disclosedness of the "for-the-sake-of-which" and of significance equiprimordially, pertains to the entirety of Being-in-the-world. Significance is that on the basis of which the world is disclosed as such. To say that the "for-the-sake-of-which" *and* significance are both disclosed in Dasein, means that Dasein is that entity which, as Being-in-the-world, is an issue for itself.

---

[1] '. . . im ontischen Sinne einer faktischen, "vereinzelten" Veranlagung . . .' While the verb 'vereinzeln' often means 'to isolate', Heidegger does not ordinarily use it in this sense. Indeed he contrasts it with the verb 'isolieren'. Cf. H. 188 below.

When we are talking ontically we sometimes use the expression 'under-standing something' with the signification of 'being able to manage something', 'being a match for it', 'being competent to do something'.[1] In understanding, as an *existentiale*, that which we have such competence over is not a "what", but Being as existing. The kind of Being which Dasein has, as potentiality-for-Being, lies existentially in understanding. Dasein is not something present-at-hand which possesses its competence for something by way of an extra; it is primarily Being-possible. Dasein is in every case what it can be, and in the way in which it is its possibility. The Being-possible which is essential for Dasein, pertains to the ways of its solicitude for Others and of its concern with the 'world', as we have characterized them; and in all these, and always, it pertains to Dasein's potentiality-for-Being towards itself, for the sake of itself. The Being-possible which Dasein is existentially in every case, is to be sharply distinguished both from empty logical possibility and from the contingency of something present-at-hand, so far as with the present-at-hand this or that can 'come to pass'.[2] As a modal category of presence-at-hand, possibility signifies what is *not yet* actual and what is *not at any time* necessary. It characterizes the *merely* possible. Ontologically it is on a lower level than actuality and necessity. On the other hand, possibility as an *existentiale* is the most primordial and ultimate positive way in which Dasein is characterized ontologically. As with existentiality in general, we can, in the first instance, only prepare for the problem of possibility. The phenom-enal basis for seeing it at all is provided by the understanding as a dis-closive potentiality-for-Being.

Possibility, as an *existentiale*, does not signify a free-floating potentiality-for-Being in the sense of the 'liberty of indifference' (*libertas indifferentiae*). In every case Dasein, as essentially having a state-of-mind, has already got itself into definite possibilities. As the potentiality-for-Being which is, it has let such possibilities pass by; it is constantly waiving the pos-sibilities of its Being, or else it seizes upon them and makes mistakes.[3] But this means that Dasein is Being-possible which has been delivered over to itself—*thrown possibility* through and through. Dasein is the possibility of Being-free *for* its ownmost potentiality-for-Being. Its Being-possible is transparent to itself in different possible ways and degrees.

Understanding is the Being of such potentiality-for-Being, which is

---

[1] '. . . in der Bedeutung von "einer Sache vorstehen können", "ihr gewachsen sein", "etwas können".' The expression 'vorstehen' ('to manage', 'to be in charge') is here connected with 'verstehen' ('to understand').

[2] '. . . von der Kontingenz eines Vorhandenen, sofern mit diesem das und jenes "pas-sieren" kann.'

[3] '. . . ergreift sie und vergreift sich.'

never something still outstanding as not yet present-at-hand, but which, as something which is essentially never present-at-hand, 'is' with the Being of Dasein, in the sense of existence. Dasein is such that in every case it has understood (or alternatively, not understood) that it is to be thus or thus. As such understanding it 'knows' *what* it is capable of—that is, what its potentiality-for-Being is capable of.[1] This 'knowing' does not first arise from an immanent self-perception, but belongs to the Being of the "there", which is essentially understanding. And only *because* Dasein, in understanding, is its "there", *can* it go astray and fail to recognize itself. And in so far as understanding is *accompanied by* state-of-mind and as such is existentially surrendered to thrownness, Dasein has in every case already gone astray and failed to recognize itself. In its potentiality-for-Being it is therefore delivered over to the possibility of first finding itself again in its possibilities.

Understanding is the existential Being of Dasein's own potentiality-for-Being; and it is so in such a way that this Being discloses in itself what its Being is capable of.[2] We must grasp the structure of this *existentiale* more precisely.

As a disclosure, understanding always pertains to the whole basic state of Being-in-the-world. As a potentiality-for-Being, any Being-in is a potentiality-for-Being-in-the-world. Not only is the world, *qua* world, disclosed as possible significance, but when that which is within-the-world is itself freed, this entity is freed for *its own* possibilities. That which is ready-to-hand is discovered as such in its service*ability*, its us*ability*, and its detriment*ality*. The totality of involvements is revealed as the categorial whole of a *possible* interconnection of the ready-to-hand. But even the 'unity' of the manifold present-at-hand, of Nature, can be discovered only if a *possibility* of it has been disclosed. Is it accidental that the question about the *Being* of Nature aims at the 'conditions of its *possibility*'? On what is such an inquiry based? When confronted with this inquiry, we cannot leave aside the question: *why* are entities which are not of the character of Dasein understood in their Being, if they are disclosed in accordance with the conditions of their possibility? Kant presupposes something of the sort, perhaps rightly. But this presupposition itself is something that cannot be left without demonstrating how it is justified.

Why does the understanding—whatever may be the essential dimensions of that which can be disclosed in it—always press forward into possibilities? It is because the understanding has in itself the existential

---

[1] 'Als solches Verstehen "weiss" es, *woran* es mit ihm selbst, das heisst seinem Sein-können ist.'

[2] '. . . *so zwar, dass dieses Sein an ihm selbst d as Woran des mit ihm selbst Seins erschliesst.*'

structure which we call *"projection"*.[1] With equal primordiality the understanding projects Dasein's Being both upon its "for-the-sake-of-which" and upon significance, as the worldhood of its current world. The character of understanding as projection is constitutive for Being-in-the-world with regard to the disclosedness of its existentially constitutive state-of-Being by which the factical potentiality-for-Being gets its leeway [Spielraum]. And as thrown, Dasein is thrown into the kind of Being which we call "projecting". Projecting has nothing to do with comporting oneself towards a plan that has been thought out, and in accordance with which Dasein arranges its Being. On the contrary, any Dasein has, as Dasein, already projected itself; and as long as it is, it is projecting. As long as it is, Dasein always has understood itself and always will understand itself in terms of possibilities. Furthermore, the character of understanding as projection is such that the understanding does not grasp thematically that upon which it projects—that is to say, possibilities. Grasping it in such a manner would take away from what is projected its very character as a possibility, and would reduce it to the given contents which we have in mind; whereas projection, in throwing, throws before itself the possibility as possibility, and lets it *be* as such.[2] As projecting, understanding is the kind of Being of Dasein in which it *is* its possibilities as possibilities.

Because of the kind of Being which is constituted by the *existentiale* of projection, Dasein is constantly 'more' than it factually is, supposing that one might want to make an inventory of it as something-at-hand and list the contents of its Being, and supposing that one were able to do so. But Dasein is never more than it factically is, for to its facticity its potentiality-for-Being belongs essentially. Yet as Being-possible, moreover, Dasein is never anything less; that is to say, it *is* existentially that which, in its

---

[1] *'Entwurf'*. The basic meaning of this noun and the cognate verb 'entwerfen' is that of 'throwing' something 'off' or 'away' from one; but in ordinary German usage, and often in Heidegger, they take on the sense of 'designing' or 'sketching' some 'project' which is to be carried through; and they may also be used in the more special sense of 'projection' in which a geometer is said to 'project' a curve 'upon' a plane. The words 'projection' and 'project' accordingly lend themselves rather well to translating these words in many contexts, especially since their root meanings are very similar to those of 'Entwurf' and 'entwerfen'; but while the root meaning of 'throwing off' is still very much alive in Heidegger's German, it has almost entirely died out in the ordinary English usage of 'projection' and 'project', which in turn have taken on some connotations not felt in the German. Thus when in the English translation Dasein is said to 'project' entities, or possibilities, or even its own Being 'upon' something, the reader should bear in mind that the root meaning of 'throwing' is more strongly felt in the German than in the translation.

[2] '. . . zieht es herab zu einem gegebenen, gemeinten Bestand, während der Entwurf im Werfen die Möglichkeit als Möglichkeit sich vorwirft und als solche *sein* lässt.' The expression 'einem etwas vorwerfen' means literally to 'throw something forward to someone', but often has the connotation of 'reproaching him with something', or 'throwing something in his teeth'. Heidegger may have more than one of these significations in mind.

potentiality-for-Being, it is *not yet*. Only because the Being of the "there" receives its Constitution through understanding and through the character of understanding as projection, only because it *is* what it becomes (or alternatively, does not become), can it say to itself 'Become what you are', and say this with understanding.

Projection always pertains to the full disclosedness of Being-in-the-world; as potentiality-for-Being, understanding has itself possibilities, which are sketched out beforehand within the range of what is essentially disclosable in it. Understanding *can* devote itself primarily to the disclosedness of the world; that is, Dasein can, proximally and for the most part, understand itself in terms of its world. Or else understanding throws itself primarily into the "for-the-sake-of-which"; that is, Dasein exists as itself. Understanding is either authentic, arising out of one's own Self as such, or inauthentic. The 'in-' of "inauthentic" does not mean that Dasein cuts itself off from its Self and understands 'only' the world. The world belongs to Being-one's-Self as Being-in-the-world. On the other hand, authentic understanding, no less than that which is inauthentic, *can* be either genuine or not genuine. As potentiality-for-Being, understanding is altogether permeated with possibility. When one is diverted into [Sichverlegen in] one of these basic possibilities of understanding, the other is not laid aside [legt . . . nicht ab]. *Because understanding, in every case, pertains rather to Dasein's full disclosedness as Being-in-the-world, this diversion of the understanding is an existential modification of projection as a whole.* In understanding the world, Being-in is always understood along with it, while understanding of existence as such is always an understanding of the world.

As factical Dasein, any Dasein has already diverted its potentiality-for-Being into a possibility of understanding.

In its projective character, understanding goes to make up existentially what we call Dasein's *"sight"* [*Sicht*]. With the disclosedness of the "there", this sight is existentially [existenzial seiende]; and Dasein *is* this sight equiprimordially in each of those basic ways of its Being which we have already noted: as the circumspection [Umsicht] of concern, as the considerateness [Rücksicht] of solicitude, and as that sight which is directed upon Being as such [Sicht auf das Sein als solches], for the sake of which any Dasein is as it is. The sight which is related primarily and on the whole to existence we call *"transparency"* [*Durchsichtigkeit*]. We choose this term to designate 'knowledge of the Self'[1] in a sense which is well understood,

[1] ' "Selbsterkenntnis" '. This should be carefully distinguished from the 'Sichkennen' discussed on H. 124-125. Perhaps this distinction can be expressed—though rather crudely —by pointing out that we are here concerned with a full and sophisticated knowledge of the Self in all its implications, while in the earlier passage we were concerned with the kind of 'self-knowledge' which one loses when one 'forgets oneself' or does something so out of character that one 'no longer knows oneself'.

so as to indicate that here it is not a matter of perceptually tracking down and inspecting a point called the "Self", but rather one of seizing upon the full disclosedness of Being-in-the-world *throughout all* the constitutive items which are essential to it, and doing so with understanding. In existing, entities sight 'themselves' [sichtet "sich"] only in so far as they have become transparent to themselves with equal primordiality in those items which are constitutive for their existence: their Being-alongside the world and their Being-with Others.

On the other hand, Dasein's opaqueness [Undurchsichtigkeit] is not rooted primarily and solely in 'egocentric' self-deceptions; it is rooted just as much in lack of acquaintance with the world.

We must, to be sure, guard against a misunderstanding of the expression 'sight'. It corresponds to the "clearedness" [Gelichtetheit] which we took as characterizing the disclosedness of the "there". 'Seeing' does not mean just perceiving with the bodily eyes, but neither does it mean pure non-sensory awareness of something present-at-hand in its presence-at-hand. In giving an existential signification to "sight", we have merely drawn upon the peculiar feature of seeing, that it lets entities which are accessible to it be encountered unconcealedly in themselves. Of course, every 'sense' does this within that domain of discovery which is genuinely its own. But from the beginning onwards the tradition of philosophy has been oriented primarily towards 'seeing' as a way of access to entities *and to Being*. To keep the connection with this tradition, we may formalize "sight" and "seeing" enough to obtain therewith a universal term for characterizing any access to entities or to Being, as access in general.

By showing how all sight is grounded primarily in understanding (the circumspection of concern is understanding as *common sense* [*Verständig-keit*]), we have deprived pure intuition [Anschauen] of its priority, which corresponds noetically to the priority of the present-at-hand in traditional ontology. 'Intuition' and 'thinking' are both derivatives of understanding, and already rather remote ones. Even the phenomenological 'intuition of essences' ["Wesensschau"] is grounded in existential understanding. We can decide about this kind of seeing only if we have obtained explicit conceptions of Being and of the structure of Being, such as only phenomena in the phenomenological sense can become.

The disclosedness of the "there" in understanding is itself a way of Dasein's potentiality-for-Being. In the way in which its Being is projected both upon the "for-the-sake-of-which" and upon significance (the world), there lies the disclosedness of Being in general. Understanding of Being has already been taken for granted in projecting upon possibilities. In projection, Being is understood, though not ontologically conceived. An entity whose kind of Being is the essential projection of Being-in-the-world has understanding of Being, and has this as constitutive for its Being. What was posited dogmatically at an earlier stage[viii] now gets exhibited in terms of the Constitution of the Being in which Dasein as understanding is its "there". The existential meaning of this understanding of Being cannot be satisfactorily clarified within the limits of this investigation except on the basis of the Temporal Interpretation of Being.

As *existentialia*, states-of-mind and understanding characterize the primordial disclosedness of Being-in-the-world. By way of having a mood, Dasein 'sees' possibilities, in terms of which it is. In the projective disclosure of such possibilities, it already has a mood in every case. The projection of its ownmost potentiality-for-Being has been delivered over to the Fact of its thrownness into the "there". Has not Dasein's Being become more enigmatical now that we have explicated the existential constitution of the Being of the "there" in the sense of thrown projection? It has indeed. We must first let the full enigmatical character of this Being emerge, even if all we can do is to come to a genuine breakdown over its 'solution', and to formulate anew the question about the Being of thrown projective Being-in-the-world.

But in the first instance, even if we are just to bring into view the everyday kind of Being in which there is understanding with a state-of-mind, and if we are to do so in a way which is phenomenally adequate to the full disclosedness of the "there", we must work out these *existentialia* concretely.[1]

¶ 32. *Understanding and Interpretation*[2]

As understanding, Dasein projects its Being upon possibilities. This *Being-towards-possibilities* which understands is itself a potentiality-for-Being, and it is so because of the way these possibilities, as disclosed, exert their counter-thrust [Rückschlag] upon Dasein. The projecting of the understanding has its own possibility—that of developing itself [sich auszubilden]. This development of the understanding we call "interpretation".[3] In it the understanding appropriates understandingly that which is understood by it. In interpretation, understanding does not become something different. It becomes itself. Such interpretation is grounded existentially in understanding; the latter does not arise from the former. Nor is interpretation the acquiring of information about what is

---

[1] 'konkreten'. The earlier editions have 'konkreteren' ('more concretely').

[2] '*Auslegung*'. See our note 3, p. 19, H. 1 above.

[3] 'Auslegung'. The older editions have 'A u s l e g u n g'.

understood; it is rather the working-out of possibilities projected in understanding. In accordance with the trend of these preparatory analyses of everyday Dasein, we shall pursue the phenomenon of interpretation in understanding the world—that is, in inauthentic understanding, and indeed in the mode of its genuineness.

In terms of the significance which is disclosed in understanding the world, concernful Being-alongside the ready-to-hand gives itself to understand whatever involvement that which is encountered can have.[1] To say that "circumspection discovers" means that the 'world' which has already been understood comes to be interpreted. The ready-to-hand comes *explicitly* into the sight which understands. All preparing, putting to rights, repairing, improving, rounding-out, are accomplished in the following way: we take apart[2] in its "in-order-to" that which is circumspectively ready-to-hand, and we concern ourselves with it in accordance with what becomes visible through this process. That which has been circumspectively taken apart with regard to its "in-order-to", and taken apart as such—that which is *explicitly* understood—has the structure of *something as something*. The circumspective question as to what this particular thing that is ready-to-hand may be, receives the circumspectively interpretative answer that it is for such and such a purpose [es ist zum . . .]. If we tell what it is for [des Wozu], we are not simply designating something; but that which is designated is understood *as* that *as* which we are to take the thing in question. That which is disclosed in understanding—that which is understood—is already accessible in such a way that its 'as which' can be made to stand out explicitly. The 'as' makes up the structure of the explicitness of something that is understood. It constitutes the interpretation. In dealing with what is environmentally ready-to-hand by interpreting it circumspectively, we 'see' it *as* a table, a door, a carriage, or a bridge; but what we have thus interpreted [Ausgelegte] need not necessarily be also taken apart [auseinander zu legen] by making an assertion which definitely characterizes it. Any mere pre-predicative seeing of the ready-to-hand is, in itself, something which already understands and interprets. But does not the absence of such an 'as' make up the mereness of any pure perception of something? Whenever we see with this kind of sight, we already do so understandingly and interpretatively. In the mere encountering of something, it is understood in terms of a totality of involvements; and such seeing hides in itself the explicitness of the assignment-relations (of the "in-order-to") which belong to that totality.

---

[1] '. . . gibt sich . . . zu verstehen, welche Bewandtnis es je mit dem Begegnenden haben kann.'

[2] 'auseinandergelegt'. Heidegger is contrasting the verb 'auslegen' (literally, 'lay out') with the cognate 'auseinanderlegen' ('lay asunder' or 'take apart').

That which is understood gets Articulated when the entity to be understood is brought close interpretatively by taking as our clue the 'something as something'; and this Articulation lies *before* [liegt *vor*] our making any thematic assertion about it. In such an assertion the 'as' does not turn up for the first time; it just gets expressed for the first time, and this is possible only in that it lies before us as something expressible.[1] The fact that when we look at something, the explicitness of assertion can be absent, does not justify our denying that there is any Articulative interpretation in such mere seeing, and hence that there is any as-structure in it. When we have to do with anything, the mere seeing of the Things which are closest to us bears in itself the structure of interpretation, and in so primordial a manner that just to grasp something *free*, as it were, *of the "as"*, requires a certain readjustment. When we merely stare at something, our just-having-it-before-us lies before us *as a failure to understand it any more.* This grasping which is free of the "as", is a privation of the kind of seeing in which one *merely* understands. It is not more primordial than that kind of seeing, but is derived from it. If the 'as' is ontically unexpressed, this must not seduce us into overlooking it as a constitutive state for understanding, existential and *a priori.*

But if we never perceive equipment that is ready-to-hand without already understanding and interpreting it, and if such perception lets us circumspectively encounter something as something, does this not mean that in the first instance we have experienced something purely present-at-hand, and then taken it *as* a door, *as* a house? This would be a misunderstanding of the specific way in which interpretation functions as disclosure. In interpreting, we do not, so to speak, throw a 'signification' over some naked thing which is present-at-hand, we do not stick a value on it; but when something within-the-world is encountered as such, the

---

1 '. . . was allein so möglich ist, dass es als Aussprechbares vor-liegt.' Here we follow the reading of the earlier editions. The hyphen in 'vor-liegt' comes at the end of the line in the later editions, but is undoubtedly meant to suggest (like the italicization of the 'vor' in the previous sentence) that this verb is to be interpreted with unusual literalness.

This paragraph is noteworthy for an exploitation of the prefix 'aus' ('out'), which fails to show up in our translation. Literally an 'Aussage' ('assertion') is something which is 'said out'; an 'Auslegung' ('interpretation') is a 'laying-out'; that which is 'ausdrücklich' ('explicit') is something that has been 'pressed out'; that which is 'aussprechbar' (our 'expressible') is something that can be 'spoken out'.

The verbs 'ausdrücken' and 'aussprechen' are roughly synonymous; but 'aussprechen' often has the more specific connotations of 'pronunciation', 'pronouncing oneself', 'speaking one's mind', 'finishing what one has to say', etc. While it would be possible to reserve 'express' for 'ausdrücken' and translate 'aussprechen' by some such phrase as 'speak out', it is more convenient to use 'express' for both verbs, especially since 'aussprechen' and its derivatives have occurred very seldom before the present chapter, in which 'ausdrücken' rarely appears. On the other hand, we can easily distinguish between the more frequent 'ausdrücklich' and 'ausgesprochen' by translating the latter as 'expressed' or 'expressly', and reserving 'explicit' for both 'ausdrücklich' and 'explizit'.

thing in question already has an involvement which is disclosed in our understanding of the world, and this involvement is one which gets laid out by the interpretation.[1]

The ready-to-hand is always understood in terms of a totality of involvements. This totality need not be grasped explicitly by a thematic interpretation. Even if it has undergone such an interpretation, it recedes into an understanding which does not stand out from the background. And this is the very mode in which it is the essential foundation for everyday circumspective interpretation. In every case this interpretation is grounded in *something we have in advance*—in a *fore-having*.[2] As the appropriation of understanding, the interpretation operates in Being towards a totality of involvements which is already understood—a Being which understands. When something is understood but is still veiled, it becomes unveiled by an act of appropriation, and this is always done under the guidance of a point of view, which fixes that with regard to which what is understood is to be interpreted. In every case interpretation is grounded in *something we see in advance*—in a *fore-sight*. This fore-sight 'takes the first cut' out of what has been taken into our fore-having, and it does so with a view to a definite way in which this can be interpreted.[3] Anything understood which is held in our fore-having and towards which we set our sights 'foresightedly', becomes conceptualizable through the interpretation. In such an interpretation, the way in which the entity we are interpreting is to be conceived can be drawn from the entity itself, or the interpretation can force the entity into concepts to which it is opposed in its manner of Being. In either case, the interpretation has already decided for a definite way of conceiving it, either with finality or with reservations; it is grounded in *something we grasp in advance*—in a *fore-conception*.

Whenever something is interpreted as something, the interpretation will be founded essentially upon fore-having, fore-sight, and fore-conception. An interpretation is never a presuppositionless apprehending of

---

[1] '. . . die durch die Auslegung herausgelegt wird.'

[2] In this paragraph Heidegger introduces the important words 'Vorhabe', 'Vorsicht', and 'Vorgriff'. 'Vorhabe' is perhaps best translated by some such expression as 'what we have in advance' or 'what we have before us'; but we shall usually find it more convenient to adopt the shorter term 'fore-having', occasionally resorting to hendiadys, as in the present sentence, and we shall handle the other terms in the same manner. 'Vorsicht' ('what we see in advance' or 'fore-sight') is the only one of these expressions which occurs in ordinary German usage, and often has the connotation of 'caution' or 'prudence'; Heidegger, however, uses it in a more general sense somewhat more akin to the English 'foresight', without the connotation of a shrewd and accurate prediction. 'Vorgriff' ('what we grasp in advance' or 'fore-conception') is related to the verb 'vorgreifen' ('to anticipate') as well as to the noun "Begriff".

[3] 'Die Auslegung gründet jeweils in einer *Vorsicht*, die das in Vorhabe Genommene auf eine bestimmte Auslegbarkeit hin "anschneidet".' The idea seems to be that just as the person who cuts off the first slice of a loaf of bread gets the loaf 'started', the fore-sight makes a start' on what we have in advance—the fore-having.

something presented to us.[1] If, when one is engaged in a particular concrete kind of interpretation, in the sense of exact textual Interpretation,
one likes to appeal [beruft] to what 'stands there', then one finds that
what 'stands there' in the first instance is nothing other than the obvious
undiscussed assumption [Vormeinung] of the person who does the
interpreting. In an interpretative approach there lies such an assumption,
as that which has been 'taken for granted' ["gesetzt"] with the interpretation as such—that is to say, as that which has been presented in our
fore-having, our fore-sight, and our fore-conception.

How are we to conceive the character of this 'fore'? Have we done so if
we say formally that this is something '*a priori*'? Why does understanding,
which we have designated as a fundamental *existentiale* of Dasein, have
this structure as its own? Anything interpreted, as something interpreted,
has the 'as'-structure as its own; and how is this related to the 'fore'
structure? The phenomenon of the 'as'-structure is manifestly not to be
dissolved or broken up 'into pieces'. But is a primordial analytic for it
thus ruled out? Are we to concede that such phenomena are 'ultimates'?
Then there would still remain the question, "why?" Or do the fore-
structure of understanding and the as-structure of interpretation show an
existential-ontological connection with the phenomenon of projection?
And does this phenomenon point back to a primordial state of Dasein's
Being?

Before we answer these questions, for which the preparation up till now
has been far from sufficient, we must investigate whether what has become
visible as the fore-structure of understanding and the as-structure of
interpretation, does not itself already present us with a unitary phenomenon—one of which copious use is made in philosophical problematics,
though what is used so universally falls short of the primordiality of
ontological explication.

In the projecting of the understanding, entities are disclosed in their
possibility. The character of the possibility corresponds, on each occasion,
with the kind of Being of the entity which is understood. Entities within-
the-world generally are projected upon the world—that is, upon a whole
of significance, to whose reference-relations concern, as Being-in-the-
world, has been tied up in advance. When entities within-the-world are
discovered along with the Being of Dasein—that is, when they have come
to be understood—we say that they have *meaning* [*Sinn*]. But that which
is understood, taken strictly is not the meaning but the entity, or

---

[1] '. . . eines Vorgegebenen.' Here, as in many other passages, we have translated
'vorgeben' by various forms of the verb 'to present'; but it would perhaps be more in line
with Heidegger's discussion of the prefix 'vor-' to write '. . . of something fore-given'.

alternatively, Being. Meaning is that wherein the intelligibility [Verständ-lichkeit] of something maintains itself. That which can be Articulated in a disclosure by which we understand, we call "meaning". The *concept of meaning* embraces the formal existential framework of what necessarily belongs to that which an understanding interpretation Articulates. *Meaning is the "upon-which" of a projection in terms of which something becomes intelligible as something; it gets its structure from a fore-having, a fore-sight, and a fore-conception.*[1] In so far as understanding and interpretation make up the existential state of Being of the "there", "meaning" must be conceived as the formal-existential framework of the disclosedness which belongs to understanding. Meaning is an *existentiale* of Dasein, not a property attaching to entities, lying 'behind' them, or floating somewhere as an 'intermediate domain'. Dasein only 'has' meaning, so far as the disclosedness of Being-in-the-world can be 'filled in' by the entities dis-coverable in that disclosedness.[2] *Hence only Dasein can be meaningful [sinn-voll] or meaningless [sinnlos].* That is to say, its own Being and the entities disclosed with its Being can be appropriated in understanding, or can remain relegated to non-understanding.

This Interpretation of the concept of 'meaning' is one which is onto-logico-existential in principle; if we adhere to it, then all entities whose kind of Being is of a character other than Dasein's must be conceived as *unmeaning* [*unsinniges*], essentially devoid of any meaning at all. Here 'unmeaning' does not signify that we are saying anything about the value of such entities, but it gives expression to an ontological characteristic. *And only that which is unmeaning can be absurd [widersinnig].* The present-at-hand, as Dasein encounters it, can, as it were, assault Dasein's Being; natural events, for instance, can break in upon us and destroy us.

And if we are inquiring about the meaning of Being, our investigation does not then become a "deep" one [tiefsinnig], nor does it puzzle out what stands behind Being. It asks about Being itself in so far as Being enters into the intelligibility of Dasein. The meaning of Being can never be

---

[1] '*Sinn ist das durch Vorhabe, Vorsicht und Vorgriff strukturierte Woraufhin des Entwurfs, aus dem her etwas als etwas verständlich wird.*' (Notice that our usual translation of 'verständlich, and 'Verständlichkeit' as 'intelligible' and 'intelligibility', fails to show the connection of the words with 'Verständnis', etc. This connection could have been brought out effectively by writing 'understandable,' 'understandability', etc., but only at the cost of awkwardness.)

[2] 'Sinn "hat" nur das Dasein, sofern die Erschlossenheit des In-der-Welt-seins durch das in ihr entdeckbare Seiende "erfüllbar" ist.' The point of this puzzling and ambiguous sentence may become somewhat clearer if the reader recalls that here as elsewhere (see H. 75 above) the verb 'erschliessen' ('disclose') is used in the sense of 'opening something up' so that its contents can be 'discovered'. What thus gets 'opened up' will then be 'filled in' as more and more of its contents get discovered.

G

contrasted with entities, or with Being as the 'ground' which gives entities support; for a 'ground' becomes accessible only as meaning, even if it is itself the abyss of meaninglessness.[1]

As the disclosedness of the "there", understanding always pertains to the whole of Being-in-the-world. In every understanding of the world, existence is understood with it, and *vice versa*. All interpretation, moreover, operates in the fore-structure, which we have already characterized. Any interpretation which is to contribute understanding, must already have understood what is to be interpreted. This is a fact that has always been remarked, even if only in the area of derivative ways of understanding and interpretation, such as philological Interpretation. The latter belongs within the range of scientific knowledge. Such knowledge demands the rigour of a demonstration to provide grounds for it. In a scientific proof, we may not presuppose what it is our task to provide grounds for. But if interpretation must in any case already operate in that which is understood, and if it must draw its nurture from this, how is it to bring any scientific results to maturity without moving in a circle, especially if, moreover, the understanding which is presupposed still operates within our common information about man and the world? Yet according to the most elementary rules of logic, this *circle* is a *circulus vitiosus*. If that be so, however, the business of historiological interpretation is excluded *a priori* from the domain of rigorous knowledge. In so far as the Fact of this circle in understanding is not eliminated, historiology must then be resigned to less rigorous possibilities of knowing. Historiology is permitted to compensate for this defect to some extent through the 'spiritual signification' of its 'objects'. But even in the opinion of the historian himself, it would admittedly be more ideal if the circle could be avoided and if there remained the hope of creating some time a historiology which would be as independent of the standpoint of the observer as our knowledge of Nature is supposed to be.

But if we see this circle as a vicious one and look out for ways of avoiding it, even if we just 'sense' it as an inevitable imperfection, then the act of understanding has been misunderstood from the ground up. The assimilation of understanding and interpretation to a definite ideal of knowledge is not the issue here. Such an ideal is itself only a subspecies of understanding—a subspecies which has strayed into the legitimate task of grasping the present-at-hand in its essential unintelligibility [Unverständlichkeit]. If the basic conditions which make interpretation possible are to be fulfilled, this must

[1] 'Der Sinn von Sein kann nie in Gegensatz gebracht werden zum Seienden oder zum Sein als tragenden "Grund" des Seienden, weil "Grund" nur als Sinn zugänglich wird, und sei er selbst der Abgrund der Sinnlosigkeit.' Notice the etymological kinship between 'Grund' ('ground') and 'Abgrund' ('abyss').

rather be done by not failing to recognize beforehand the essential conditions under which it can be performed. What is decisive is not to get out of the circle but to come into it in the right way. This circle of understanding is not an orbit in which any random kind of knowledge may move; it is the expression of the existential *fore-structure* of Dasein itself. It is not to be reduced to the level of a vicious circle, or even of a circle which is merely tolerated. In the circle is hidden a positive possibility of the most primordial kind of knowing. To be sure, we genuinely take hold of this possibility only when, in our interpretation, we have understood that our first, last, and constant task is never to allow our fore-having, fore-sight, and fore-conception to be presented to us by fancies and popular conceptions, but rather to make the scientific theme secure by working out these fore-structures in terms of the things themselves. Because understanding, in accordance with its existential meaning, is Dasein's own potentiality-for-Being, the ontological presuppositions of historiological knowledge transcend in principle the idea of rigour held in the most exact sciences. Mathematics is not more rigorous than historiology, but only narrower, because the existential foundations relevant for it lie within a narrower range.

The 'circle' in understanding belongs to the structure of meaning, and the latter phenomenon is rooted in the existential constitution of Dasein— that is, in the understanding which interprets. An entity for which, as Being-in-the-world, its Being is itself an issue, has, ontologically, a circular structure. If, however, we note that 'circularity' belongs ontologically to a kind of Being which is present-at-hand (namely, to subsistence [Bestand]), we must altogether avoid using this phenomenon to characterize anything like Dasein ontologically.

¶ *33. Assertion as a Derivative Mode of Interpretation*

All interpretation is grounded on understanding. That which has been articulated[1] as such in interpretation and sketched out beforehand in the understanding in general as something articulable, is the meaning. In so far as assertion ('judgment')[2] is grounded on understanding and presents us with a derivative form in which an interpretation has been carried out, it *too* 'has' a meaning. Yet this meaning cannot be defined as something which occurs 'in' ["an"] a judgment along with the judging itself. In our

---

[1] 'Gegliederte'. The verbs 'artikulieren' and 'gliedern' can both be translated by 'articulate' in English; even in German they are nearly synonymous, but in the former the emphasis is presumably on the 'joints' at which something gets divided, while in the latter the emphasis is presumably on the 'parts' or 'members'. We have distinguished between them by translating 'artikulieren' by 'Articulate' (with a capital 'A'), and 'gliedern' by 'articulate' (with a lower-case initial).

[2] '... die Aussage (das "Urteil") ...'

present context, we shall give an explicit analysis of assertion, and this analysis will serve several purposes.

For one thing, it can be demonstrated, by considering assertion, in what ways the structure of the 'as', which is constitutive for understanding and interpretation, can be modified. When this has been done, both understanding and interpretation will be brought more sharply into view. For another thing, the analysis of assertion has a special position in the problematic of fundamental ontology, because in the decisive period when ancient ontology was beginning, the λόγος functioned as the only clue for obtaining access to that which authentically i s [zum eigentlich Seienden], and for defining the Being of such entities. Finally assertion has been accepted from ancient times as the primary and authentic 'locus' of *truth*. The phenomenon of truth is so thoroughly coupled with the problem of Being that our investigation, as it proceeds further, will necessarily come up against the problem of truth; and it already lies within the dimensions of that problem, though not explicitly. The analysis of assertion will at the same time prepare the way for this latter problematic.

In what follows, we give three significations to the term "*assertion*". These are drawn from the phenomenon which is thus designated, they are connected among themselves, and in their unity they encompass the full structure of assertion.

1. The primary signification of "assertion" is "*pointing out*" [*Aufzeigen*]. In this we adhere to the primordial meaning of λόγος as ἀπόφανσις—letting an entity be seen from itself. In the assertion 'The hammer is too heavy', what is discovered for sight is not a 'meaning', but an entity in the way that it is ready-to-hand. Even if this entity is not close enough to be grasped and 'seen', the pointing-out has in view the entity itself and not, let us say, a mere "representation" [Vorstellung] of it—neither something 'merely represented' nor the psychical condition in which the person who makes the assertion "represents" it.

2. "Assertion" means no less than "*predication*". We 'assert' a 'predicate' of a 'subject', and the 'subject' is *given a definite character* [*bestimmt*] by the 'predicate'. In this signification of "assertion", that which is put forward in the assertion [Das Ausgesagte] is not the predicate, but 'the hammer itself'. On the other hand, that which does the asserting [Das Aussagende] (in other words, that which gives something a definite character) lies in the 'too heavy'. That which is put forward in the assertion in the second signification of "assertion" (that which is given a definite character, as such) has undergone a narrowing of content as compared with what is put forward in the assertion in the first signification

of this term. Every predication is what it is, only as a pointing-out. The second signification of "assertion" has its foundation in the first. Within this pointing-out, the elements which are Articulated in predication—the subject and predicate—arise. It is not by giving something a definite character that we first discover that which shows itself—the hammer—as such; but when we give it such a character, our seeing gets *restricted* to it in the first instance, so that by this explicit *restriction*[1] of our view, that which is already manifest may be made *explicitly* manifest in its definite character. In giving something a definite character, we must, in the first instance, take a step back when confronted with that which is already manifest—the hammer that is too heavy. In 'setting down the subject', we dim entities down to focus in 'that hammer there', so that by thus dimming them down we may let that which is manifest be seen *in* its own definite character as a character that can be determined.[2] Setting down the subject, setting down the predicate, and setting down the two together, are thoroughly 'apophantical' in the strict sense of the word.

3. "Assertion" means *"communication"* [*Mitteilung*], speaking forth [Heraussage]. As communication, it is directly related to "assertion" in the first and second significations. It is letting someone see with us what we have pointed out by way of giving it a definite character. Letting someone see with us shares with [teilt . . . mit] the Other that entity which has been pointed out in its definite character. That which is 'shared' is our *Being towards* what has been pointed out—a Being in which we see it in common. One must keep in mind that this Being-towards is Being-in-the-world, and that from out of this very world what has been pointed out gets encountered. Any assertion, as a communication understood in this existential manner, must have been expressed.[3] As something communicated, that which has been put forward in the assertion is something that Others can 'share' with the person making the assertion, even though the entity which he has pointed out and to which he has given a definite character is not close enough for them to grasp and see it. That which is put forward in the assertion is something which can be passed along in 'further retelling'. There is a widening of the range of that mutual sharing which sees. But at the same time, what has been pointed out may become veiled again in this further retelling, although even the kind of knowing which arises in such hearsay (whether knowledge that

---

[1] '*Einschränkung*'. The older editions have 'Entschränkung'.

[2] '. . . die "Subjektsetzung" blendet das Seiende ab auf"der Hammer da", um durch den Vollzug der Entblendung das Offenbare *in* seiner bestimmbaren Bestimmtheit sehen zu lassen.'

[3] 'Zur Aussage als der so existenzial verstandenen Mit-teilung gehört die Ausgesprochenheit.'

something is the case [Wissen] or merely an acquaintance with something [Kennen]) always has the entity itself in view and does not 'give assent' to some 'valid meaning' which has been passed around. Even hearsay is a Being-in-the-world, and a Being towards what is heard.

There is prevalent today a theory of 'judgment' which is oriented to the phenomenon of 'validity'.[1] We shall not give an extensive discussion of it here. It will be sufficient to allude to the very questionable character of this phenomenon of 'validity', though since the time of Lotze people have been fond of passing this off as a 'primal phenomenon' which cannot be traced back any further. The fact that it can play this role is due only to its ontologically unclarified character. The 'problematic' which has established itself round this idolized word is no less opaque. In the first place, validity is viewed as the *'form' of actuality* which goes with the content of the judgment, in so far as that content remains unchanged as opposed to the changeable 'psychical' process of judgment. Considering how the status of the question of Being in general has been characterized in the introduction to this treatise, we would scarcely venture to expect that 'validity' as 'ideal Being' is distinguished by special ontological clarity. In the second place, "validity" means at the same time the validity of the meaning of the judgment, which is valid of the 'Object' it has in view; and thus it attains the signification of an *'Objectively valid character'* and of Objectivity in general. In the third place, the meaning which is thus 'valid' *of* an entity, and which is valid 'timelessly' in itself, is said to be 'valid' also in the sense of being valid *for* everyone who judges rationally. "Validity" now means a *bindingness*, or 'universally valid' character.[2] Even if one were to advocate a 'critical' epistemological theory, according to which the subject does not 'really' 'come out' to the Object, then this valid character, as the validity of an Object (Objectivity), is grounded upon that stock of true (!) meaning which is itself valid. The three significations of 'being valid' which we have set forth—the way of Being of the ideal, Objectivity, and bindingness—not only are opaque in themselves but constantly get confused with one another. Methodological fore-sight

[1] Heidegger uses three words which might conveniently be translated as 'validity': 'Geltung' (our 'validity'), 'Gültigkeit' (our 'valid character'), and 'Gelten' (our 'being valid', etc.). The reader who has studied logic in English and who accordingly thinks of 'validity' as merely a property of arguments in which the premises imply the conclusion, must remember that in German the verb 'gelten' and its derivatives are used much more broadly, so as to apply to almost anything that is commonly (or even privately) accepted, so that one can speak of the 'validity' of legal tender, the 'validity' of a ticket for so many weeks or months, the 'validity' of that which 'holds' for me or for you, the 'validity' of anything that is the case. While Heidegger's discussion does not cover as many of these meanings as will be listed in any good German dictionary, he goes well beyond the narrower usage of the English-speaking logician. Of course, we shall often translate 'gelten' in other ways.

[2] '. . . *Verbindlichkeit*, "Allgemeingültigkeit".'

demands that we do not choose such unstable concepts as a clue to Interpretation. We make no advance restriction upon the concept of "meaning" which would confine it to signifying the 'content of judgment', but we understand it as the existential phenomenon already characterized, in which the formal framework of what can be disclosed in understanding and Articulated in interpretation becomes visible.

If we bring together the three significations of 'assertion' which we have analysed, and get a unitary view of the full phenomenon, then we may define *"assertion"* as *"a pointing-out which gives something a definite character and which communicates"*. It remains to ask with what justification we have taken assertion as a mode of interpretation at all. If it is something of this sort, then the essential structures of interpretation must recur in it. The pointing-out which assertion does is performed on the basis of what has already been disclosed in understanding or discovered circumspectively. Assertion is not a free-floating kind of behaviour which, in its own right, might be capable of disclosing entities in general in a primary way: on the contrary it always maintains itself on the basis of Being-in-the-world. What we have shown earlier[ix] in relation to knowing the world, holds just as well as assertion. Any assertion requires a fore-having of whatever has been disclosed; and this is what it points out by way of giving something a definite character. Furthermore, in any approach when one gives something a definite character, one is already taking a look directionally at what is to be put forward in the assertion. When an entity which has been presented is given a definite character, the function of giving it such a character is taken over by that with regard to which we set our sights towards the entity.[1] Thus any assertion requires a fore-sight; in this the predicate which we are to assign [zuzuweisende] and make stand out, gets loosened, so to speak, from its unexpressed inclusion in the entity itself. To any assertion as a communication which gives something a definite character there belongs, moreover, an Articulation of what is pointed out, and this Articulation is in accordance with significations. Such an assertion will operate with a definite way of conceiving: "The hammer is heavy", "Heaviness belongs to the hammer", "The hammer has the property of heaviness". When an assertion is made, some fore-conception is always implied; but it remains for the most part inconspicuous, because the language already hides in itself a developed way of conceiving. Like any interpretation whatever, assertion necessarily has a fore-having, a fore-sight, and a fore-conception as its existential foundations.

[1] 'Woraufhin das vorgegebene Seiende anvisiert wird, das übernimmt im Bestimmungsvollzug die Funktion des Bestimmenden.'

But to what extent does it become a *derivative* mode of interpretation? What has been modified in it? We can point out the modification if we stick to certain limiting cases of assertion which function in logic as normal cases and as examples of the 'simplest' assertion-phenomena. Prior to all analysis, logic has already understood 'logically' what it takes as a theme under the heading of the "categorical statement"—for instance, 'The hammer is heavy'. The unexplained presupposition is that the 'meaning' of this sentence is to be taken as: "This Thing—a hammer—has the property of heaviness". In concernful circumspection there are no such assertions 'at first'. But such circumspection has of course its specific ways of interpreting, and these, as compared with the 'theoretical judgment' just mentioned, may take some such form as 'The hammer is too heavy', or rather just 'Too heavy!', 'Hand me the other hammer!' Interpretation is carried out primordially not in a theoretical statement but in an action of circumspective concern—laying aside the unsuitable tool, or exchanging it, 'without wasting words'. From the fact that words are absent, it may not be concluded that interpretation is absent. On the other hand, the kind of interpretation which is circumspectively *expressed* is not necessarily already an assertion in the sense we have defined. *By what existential-ontological modifications does assertion arise from circumspective interpretation?*

The entity which is held in our fore-having—for instance, the hammer—is proximally ready-to-hand as equipment. If this entity becomes the 'object' of an assertion, then as soon as we begin this assertion, there is already a change-over in the fore-having. Something *ready-to-hand with which* we have to do or perform something, turns into something '*about which*' the assertion that points it out is made. Our fore-sight is aimed at something present-at-hand in what is ready-to-hand. Both *by* and *for* this way of looking at it [Hin-sicht], the ready-to-hand becomes veiled as ready-to-hand. Within this discovering of presence-at-hand, which is at the same time a covering-up of readiness-to-hand, something present-at-hand which we encounter is given a definite character in its Being-present-at-hand-in-such-and-such-a-manner. Only now are we given any access to *properties* or the like. When an assertion has given a definite character to something present-at-hand, it says something about it *as* a "what"; and this "what" is drawn *from that* which is present-at-hand as such. The as-structure of interpretation has undergone a modification. In its function of appropriating what is understood, the 'as' no longer reaches out into a totality of involvements. As regards its possibilities for Articulating reference-relations, it has been cut off from that significance which, as such, constitutes environmentality. The 'as' gets pushed back into the uniform plane of that which is merely present-at-hand. It dwindles to the structure of just letting one see what is present-at-hand, and letting one see it in a definite way. This levelling of the primordial 'as' of circum-spective interpretation to the "as" with which presence-at-hand is given a definite character is the specialty of assertion. Only so does it obtain the possibility of exhibiting something in such a way that we just look at it.

Thus assertion cannot disown its ontological origin from an interpreta-tion which understands. The primordial 'as' of an interpretation (ἑρμηνεία) which understands circumspectively we call the "existential-*hermeneutical* 'as' " in distinction from the "*apophantical* 'as' " of the assertion.

Between the kind of interpretation which is still wholly wrapped up in concernful understanding and the extreme opposite case of a theoretical assertion about something present-at-hand, there are many intermediate gradations: assertions about the happenings in the environment, accounts of the ready-to-hand, 'reports on the Situation', the recording and fixing of the 'facts of the case', the description of a state of affairs, the narration of something that has befallen. We cannot trace back these 'sentences' to theoretical statements without essentially perverting their meaning. Like the theoretical statements themselves, they have their 'source' in circum-spective interpretation.

With the progress of knowledge about the structure of the λόγος, it was inevitable that this phenomenon of the apophantical 'as' should come into view in some form or other. The manner in which it was proximally seen was not accidental, and did not fail to work itself out in the subsequent history of logic.

When considered philosophically, the λόγος itself is an entity, and, according to the orientation of ancient ontology, it is something present-at-hand. Words are proximally present-at-hand; that is to say, we come across them just as we come across Things; and this holds for any sequence of words, as that in which the λόγος expresses itself. In this first search for the structure of the λόγος as thus present-at-hand, what was found was the *Being-present-at-hand-together* of several words. What establishes the unity of this "together"? As Plato knew, this unity lies in the fact that the λόγος is always λόγος τινός. In the λόγος an entity is manifest, and with a view to this entity, the words are put together in *one* verbal whole. Aristotle saw this more radically: every λόγος is both σύνθεσις and διαίρεσις, not just the one (call it 'affirmative judgment') or the other (call it 'negative judgment'). Rather, every assertion, whether it affirms or denies, whether it is true or false, is σύνθεσις *and* διαίρεσις equiprim-ordially. To exhibit anything is to take it together and take it apart. It is true, of course, that Aristotle did not pursue the analytical question as far as the problem of which phenomenon within the structure of the λόγος is the one that permits and indeed obliges us to characterize every statement as synthesis and diaeresis.

Along with the formal structures of 'binding' and 'separating'—or, more precisely, along with the unity of these—we should meet the phenomenon of the 'something as something', and we should meet this as a phenomenon. In accordance with this structure, something is understood with regard to something: it is taken together with it, yet in such a way that this confrontation which *understands* will at the same time take apart what has been taken together, and will do so by Articulating it *interpretatively*. If the phenomenon of the 'as' remains covered up, and, above all, if its existential source in the hermeneutical 'as' is veiled, then Aristotle's phenomenological approach to the analysis of the λόγος collapses to a superficial 'theory of judgment', in which judgment becomes the binding or separating of representations and concepts.

Binding and separating may be formalized still further to a 'relating'. The judgment gets dissolved logistically into a system in which things are 'co-ordinated' with one another; it becomes the object of a 'calculus'; but it does not become a theme for ontological Interpretation. The possibility and impossibility of getting an analytical understanding of σύνθεσις and διαίρεσις—of the 'relation' in judgment generally—is tightly linked up with whatever the current status of the ontological problematic and its principles may be.

How far this problematic has worked its way into the Interpretation of the λόγος, and how far on the other hand the concept of 'judgment' has (by a remarkable counter-thrust) worked its way into the ontological problematic, is shown by the phenomenon of the *copula*. When we consider this 'bond', it becomes clear that proximally the synthesis-structure is regarded as self-evident, and that it has also retained the function of serving as a standard for Interpretation. But if the formal characteristics of 'relating' and 'binding' can contribute nothing phenomenally towards the structural analysis of the λόγος as subject-matter, then in the long run the phenomenon to which we allude by the term "copula" has nothing to do with a bond or binding. The Interpretation of the 'is', whether it be expressed in its own right in the language or indicated in the verbal ending, leads us therefore into the context of problems belonging to the existential analytic, if assertion and the understanding of Being are existential possibilities for the Being of Dasein itself. When we come to work out the question of Being (cf. Part I, Division 3),[1] we shall thus

[1] This Division has never appeared.

encounter again this peculiar phenomenon of Being which we meet within the λόγος.

By demonstrating that assertion is derived from interpretation and understanding, we have made it plain that the 'logic' of the λόγος is rooted in the existential analytic of Dasein; and provisionally this has been sufficient. At the same time, by knowing that the λόγος has been Interpreted in a way which is ontologically inadequate, we have gained a sharper insight into the fact that the methodological basis on which ancient ontology arose was not a primordial one. The λόγος gets experienced as something present-at-hand and Interpreted as such, while at the same time the entities which it points out have the meaning of presence-at-hand. This meaning of Being is left undifferentiated and uncontrasted with other possibilities of Being, so that Being in the sense of a formal Being-something becomes fused with it simultaneously, and we are unable even to obtain a clear-cut division between these two realms.

¶ *34. Being-there and Discourse. Language*

The fundamental *existentialia* which constitute the Being of the "there", the disclosedness of Being-in-the-world, are states-of-mind and understanding. In understanding, there lurks the possibility of interpretation— that is, of appropriating what is understood. In so far as a state-of-mind is equiprimordial with an act of understanding, it maintains itself in a certain understanding. Thus there corresponds to it a certain capacity for getting interpreted. We have seen that assertion is derived from interpretation, and is an extreme case of it. In clarifying the third significa-tion of assertion as communication (speaking forth), we were led to the concepts of "saying" and "speaking", to which we had purposely given no attention up to that point. The fact that language *now* becomes our theme *for the first time* will indicate that this phenomenon has its roots in the existential constitution of Dasein's disclosedness. *The existential-ontological foundation of language is discourse or talk.*[1] This phenomenon is one of which we have been making constant use already in our foregoing Interpretation of state-of-mind, understanding, interpretation, and asser-tion; but we have, as it were, kept it suppressed in our thematic analysis.

Discourse is existentially equiprimordial with state-of-mind and understanding. The intelligibility of something has always been articulated, even before there is any appropriative interpretation of it. Discourse is the Articulation

[1] '*Rede*'. As we have pointed out earlier (see our note 3, p. 47, H. 25 above), we have translated this word either as 'discourse' or 'talk', as the context seems to demand, some-times compromising with the hendiadys 'discourse or talk'. But in some contexts 'dis-course' is too formal while 'talk' is too colloquial; the reader must remember that there is no good English equivalent for 'Rede'. For a previous discussion see Section 7 B above (H. 32-34).

of intelligibility. Therefore it underlies both interpretation and assertion. That which can be Articulated in interpretation, and thus even
more primordially in discourse, is what we have called "meaning". That
which gets articulated as such in discursive Articulation, we call the
"totality-of-significations" [Bedeutungsganze]. This can be dissolved or
broken up into significations. Significations, as what has been Articulated
from that which can be Articulated, always carry meaning [. . . sind . . .
sinnhaft]. If discourse, as the Articulation of the intelligibility of the
"there", is a primordial *existentiale* of disclosedness, and if disclosedness is
primarily constituted by Being-in-the-world, then discourse too must have
essentially a kind of Being which is specifically *worldly*. The intelligibility
of Being-in-the-world—an intelligibility which goes with a state-of-mind
—*expresses itself as discourse*. The totality-of-significations of intelligibility
is *put into words*. To significations, words accrue. But word-Things do not
get supplied with significations.

The way in which discourse gets expressed is language.[1] Language is a
totality of words—a totality in which discourse has a 'worldly' Being of
its own; and as an entity within-the-world, this totality thus becomes
something which we may come across as ready-to-hand. Language can
be broken up into word-Things which are present-at-hand. Discourse is
existentially language, because that entity whose disclosedness it Articulates according to significations, has, as its kind of Being, Being-in-the-
world—a Being which has been thrown and submitted to the 'world'.

As an existential state in which Dasein is disclosed, discourse is constitutive for Dasein's existence. *Hearing* and *keeping silent* [Schweigen] are
possibilities belonging to discursive speech. In these phenomena the constitutive function of discourse for the existentiality of existence becomes
entirely plain for the first time. But in the first instance the issue is one of
working out the structure of discourse as such.

Discoursing or talking is the way in which we articulate 'significantly'
the intelligibility of Being-in-the-world. Being-with belongs to Being-
in-the-world, which in every case maintains itself in some definite way
of concernful Being-with-one-another. Such Being-with-one-another is
discursive as assenting or refusing, as demanding or warning, as pronouncing, consulting, or interceding, as 'making assertions', and as
talking in the way of 'giving a talk'.[2] Talking is talk about something.
That which the discourse is *about* [das *Worüber* der Rede] does not necessarily or even for the most part serve as the theme for an assertion in

[1] 'Die Hinausgesprochenheit der Rede ist die Sprache.'
[2] 'Dieses ist redend als zu- und absagen, auffordern, warnen, als Aussprache, Rücksprache, Fürsprache, ferner als "Aussagen machen" und als reden in der Weise des
"Redenhaltens".'

which one gives something a definite character. Even a command is given about something; a wish is about something. And so is intercession. What the discourse is about is a structural item that it necessarily possesses; for discourse helps to constitute the disclosedness of Being-in-the-world, and in its own structure it is modelled upon this basic state of Dasein. What is talked about [das Beredete] in talk is always 'talked to' ["angeredet"] in a definite regard and within certain limits. In any talk or discourse, there is *something said-in-the-talk* as such [ein *Geredetes* as solches]—something said as such [das . . . Gesagte als solches] whenever one wishes, asks, or expresses oneself about something. In this "something said", discourse communicates.

As we have already indicated in our analysis of assertion,[1] the phenomenon of *communication* must be understood in a sense which is ontologically broad. 'Communication' in which one makes assertions—giving information, for instance—is a special case of that communication which is grasped in principle existentially. In this more general kind of communication, the Articulation of Being with one another understandingly is constituted. Through it a co-state-of-mind [Mitbefindlichkeit] gets 'shared', and so does the understanding of Being-with. Communication is never anything like a conveying of experiences, such as opinions or wishes, from the interior of one subject into the interior of another. Dasein-with is already essentially manifest in a co-state-of-mind and a co-understanding. In discourse Being-with becomes 'explicitly' *shared*; that is to say, it *is* already, but it is unshared as something that has not been taken hold of and appropriated.[2]

Whenever something is communicated in what is said-in-the-talk, all talk about anything has at the same time the character of *expressing itself* [*Sichaussprechens*]. In talking, Dasein expresses itself [spricht sich . . . *aus*] not because it has, in the first instance, been encapsulated as something 'internal' over against something outside, but because as Being-in-the-world it is already 'outside' when it understands. What is expressed is precisely this Being-outside—that is to say, the way in which one currently has a state-of-mind (mood), which we have shown to pertain to the full disclosedness of Being-in. Being-in and its state-of-mind are made known in discourse and indicated in language by intonation, modulation, the tempo of talk, 'the way of speaking'. In 'poetical' discourse, the communication of the existential possibilities of one's state-of-mind can become an aim in itself, and this amounts to a disclosing of existence.

---

[1] Reading '. . . bei der Analyse der Aussage . . .' with the older editions. The words 'der Aussage' have been omitted in the newer editions.

[2] 'Das Mitsein wird in der Rede "ausdrücklich" *geteilt*, das heisst es *ist* schon, nur ungeteilt als nicht ergriffenes und zugeeignetes.'

In discourse the intelligibility of Being-in-the-world (an intelligibility which goes with a state-of-mind) is articulated according to significations; and discourse is this articulation. The items constitutive for discourse are: what the discourse is about (what is talked about); what is said-in-the-talk, as such; the communication; and the making-known. These are not properties which can just be raked up empirically from language. They are existential characteristics rooted in the state of Dasein's Being, and it is they that first make anything like language ontologically possible. In the factical linguistic form of any definite case of discourse, some of these items may be lacking, or may remain unnoticed. The fact that they often do *not* receive 'verbal' expression, is merely an index of some definite kind of discourse which, in so far as it is discourse, must in every case lie within the totality of the structures we have mentioned.

Attempts to grasp the 'essence of language' have always taken their orientation from one or another of these items; and the clues to their conceptions of language have been the ideas of 'expression', of 'symbolic form', of communication as 'assertion',[1] of the 'making-known' of experiences, of the 'patterning' of life. Even if one were to put these various fragmentary definitions together in syncretistic fashion, nothing would be achieved in the way of a fully adequate definition of "language". We would still have to do what is decisive here—to work out in advance the ontologico-existential whole of the structure of discourse on the basis of the analytic of Dasein.

We can make clear the connection of discourse with understanding and intelligibility by considering an existential possibility which belongs to talking itself—hearing. If we have not heard 'aright', it is not by accident that we say we have not 'understood'. Hearing is constitutive for discourse. And just as linguistic utterance is based on discourse, so is acoustic perception on hearing. Listening to . . . is Dasein's existential way of Being-open as Being-with for Others. Indeed, hearing constitutes the primary and authentic way in which Dasein is open for its ownmost potentiality-for-Being—as in hearing the voice of the friend whom every Dasein carries with it. Dasein hears, because it understands. As a Being-in-the-world with Others, a Being which understands, Dasein is 'in thrall' to Dasein-with and to itself; and in this thraldom it "belongs" to these.[2] Being-with develops in listening to one another [Aufeinander-hören], which can be done in several possible ways: following,[3] going along with,

1 '. . . der Mitteilung als "Aussage" . . .' The quotation marks around 'Aussage' appear only in the newer editions.
2 'Als verstehendes In-der-Welt-sein mit den Anderen ist es dem Mitdasein und ihm selbst "hörig" und in dieser Hörigkeit zugehörig.' In this sentence Heidegger uses some cognates of 'hören' ('hearing') whose interrelations disappear in our version.
3 '. . . des Folgens . . .' In the earlier editions there are quotation marks around 'Folgens'.

and the privative modes of not-hearing, resisting, defying, and turning away.

It is on the basis of this potentiality for hearing, which is existentially primary, that anything like *hearkening* [*Horchen*] becomes possible. Hearkening is phenomenally still more primordial than what is defined 'in the first instance' as "hearing" in psychology—the sensing of tones and the perception of sounds. Hearkening too has the kind of Being of the hearing which understands. What we 'first' hear is never noises or complexes of sounds, but the creaking waggon, the motor-cycle. We hear the column on the march, the north wind, the woodpecker tapping, the fire crackling.

It requires a very artificial and complicated frame of mind to 'hear' a 'pure noise'. The fact that motor-cycles and waggons are what we proximally hear is the phenomenal evidence that in every case Dasein, as Being-in-the-world, already dwells *alongside* what is ready-to-hand within-the-world; it certainly does not dwell proximally alongside 'sensations'; nor would it first have to give shape to the swirl of sensations to provide the springboard from which the subject leaps off and finally arrives at a 'world'. Dasein, as essentially understanding, is proximally alongside what is understood.

Likewise, when we are explicitly hearing the discourse of another, we proximally understand what is said, or—to put it more exactly—we are already with him, in advance, alongside the entity which the discourse is about. On the other hand, what we proximally hear is *not* what is expressed in the utterance. Even in cases where the speech is indistinct or in a foreign language, what we proximally hear is *unintelligible* words, and not a multiplicity of tone-data.[1]

Admittedly, when what the discourse is about is heard 'naturally', we can at the same time hear the 'diction', the way in which it is said [die Weise des Gesagtseins], but only if there is some co-understanding beforehand of what is said-in-the-talk; for only so is there a possibility of estimating whether the way in which it is said is appropriate to what the discourse is about thematically.

In the same way, any answering counter-discourse arises proximally and directly from understanding what the discourse is about, which is already 'shared' in Being-with.

Only where talking and hearing are existentially possible, can anyone hearken. The person who 'cannot hear' and 'must feel'[2] may perhaps be one who is able to hearken very well, and precisely because of this. Just

---

[1] Here we follow the reading of the newer editions: '. . . nicht eine Mannigfaltigkeit von Tondaten.' The older editions have 'reine' instead of 'eine'.

[2] The author is here alluding to the German proverb, 'Wer nicht hören kann, muss fühlen.' (I.e. he who cannot heed, must suffer.)

hearing something "all around" [Das Nur-herum-hören] is a privation of the hearing which understands. Both talking and hearing are based upon understanding. And understanding arises neither through talking at length [vieles Reden] nor through busily hearing something "all around". Only he who already understands can listen [zuhören].

Keeping silent is another essential possibility of discourse, and it has the same existential foundation. In talking with one another, the person who keeps silent can 'make one understand' (that is, he can develop an understanding), and he can do so more authentically than the person who is never short of words. Speaking at length [Viel-sprechen] about something does not offer the slightest guarantee that thereby understanding is advanced. On the contrary, talking extensively about something, covers it up and brings what is understood to a sham clarity—the unintelligibility of the trivial. But to keep silent does not mean to be dumb. On the contrary, if a man is dumb, he still has a tendency to 'speak'. Such a person has not proved that he can keep silence; indeed, he entirely lacks the possibility of proving anything of the sort. And the person who is accustomed by Nature to speak little is no better able to show that he is keeping silent or that he is the sort of person who can do so. He who never says anything cannot keep silent at any given moment. Keeping silent authentically is possible only in genuine discoursing. To be able to keep silent, Dasein must have something to say—that is, it must have at its disposal an authentic and rich disclosedness of itself. In that case one's reticence [Verschwiegenheit] makes something manifest, and does away with 'idle talk' ["Gerede"]. As a mode of discoursing, reticence Articulates the intelligibility of Dasein in so primordial a manner that it gives rise to a potentiality-for-hearing which is genuine, and to a Being-with-one-another which is transparent.

Because discourse is constititutive for the Being of the "there" (that is, for states-of-mind and understanding), while "Dasein" means Being-in-the-world, Dasein as discursive Being-in, has already expressed itself. Dasein has language. Among the Greeks, their everyday existing was largely diverted into talking with one another, but at the same time they 'had eyes' to see. Is it an accident that in both their pre-philosophical and their philosophical ways of interpreting Dasein, they defined the essence of man as ζῷον λόγον ἔχον? The later way of interpreting this definition of man in the sense of the *animal rationale*, 'something living which has reason', is not indeed 'false', but it covers up the phenomenal basis for this definition of "Dasein". Man shows himself as the entity which talks. This does not signify that the possibility of vocal utterance is peculiar to him, but rather that he is the entity which is such as to discover the world and

Dasein itself. The Greeks had no word for "language"; they understood
this phenomenon 'in the first instance' as discourse. But because the λόγος
came into their philosophical ken primarily as assertion, *this* was the
kind of *logos* which they took as their clue for working out the basic
structures of the forms of discourse and its components. Grammar sought
its foundations in the 'logic' of this *logos*. But this logic was based upon the
ontology of the present-at-hand. The basic stock of 'categories of signification', which passed over into the subsequent science of language, and
which in principle is still accepted as the standard today, is oriented
towards discourse as assertion. But if on the contrary we take this phenomenon to have in principle the primordiality and breadth of an
existentiale, then there emerges the necessity of re-establishing the science
of language on foundations which are ontologically more primordial.
The task of *liberating* grammar from logic requires *beforehand* a *positive*
understanding of the basic *a priori* structure of discourse in general as an
existentiale. It is not a task that can be carried through later on by im-   1(
proving and rounding out what has been handed down. Bearing this in
mind, we must inquire into the basic forms in which it is possible to
articulate anything understandable, and to do so in accordance with
significations; and this articulation must not be confined to entities
within-the-world which we cognize by considering them theoretically,
and which we express in sentences. A doctrine of signification will not
emerge automatically even if we make a comprehensive comparison of as
many languages as possible, and those which are most exotic. To accept,
let us say, the philosophical horizon within which W. von Humboldt
made language a problem, would be no less inadequate. The doctrine of
signification is rooted in the ontology of Dasein. Whether it prospers or
decays depends on the fate of this ontology.[x]

In the last resort, philosophical research must resolve to ask what kind
of Being goes with language in general. Is it a kind of equipment ready-
to-hand within-the-world, or has it Dasein's kind of Being, or is it neither
of these? What kind of Being does language have, if there can be such a
thing as a 'dead' language? What do the "rise" and "decline" of a
language mean ontologically? We possess a science of language, and the
Being of the entities which it has for its theme is obscure. Even the horizon
for any investigative question about it is veiled. Is it an accident that
proximally and for the most part significations are 'worldly', sketched out
beforehand by the significance of the world, that they are indeed often
predominantly 'spatial'? Or does this 'fact' have existential-ontological
necessity? and if it is necessary, why should it be so? Philosophical research
will have to dispense with the 'philosophy of language' if it is to inquire

into 'the 'things themselves' and attain the status of a problematic which has been cleared up conceptually.

Our Interpretation of language has been designed merely to point out the ontological 'locus' of this phenomenon in Dasein's state of Being, and especially to prepare the way for the following analysis, in which, taking as our clue a fundamental kind of Being belonging to discourse, in connection with other phenomena, we shall try to bring Dasein's everydayness into view in a manner which is ontologically more primordial.

B. *The Everyday Being of the "There", and the Falling of Dasein*

In going back to the existential structures of the disclosedness of Being-in-the-world, our Interpretation has, in a way, lost sight of Dasein's everydayness. In our analysis, we must now regain this phenomenal horizon which was our thematical starting-point. The question now arises: what are the existential characteristics of the disclosedness of Being-in-the-world, so far as the latter, as something which is everyday, maintains itself in the kind of Being of the "they"? Does the "they" have a state-of-mind which is specific to it, a special way of understanding, talking, and interpreting? It becomes all the more urgent to answer these questions when we remember that proximally and for the most part Dasein is absorbed in the "they" and is mastered by it. Is' not Dasein, as thrown Being-in-the-world, thrown proximally right into the publicness of the "they"? And what does this publicness mean, other than the specific disclosedness of the "they"?

If understanding must be conceived primarily as Dasein's potentiality-for-Being, then it is from an analysis of the way of understanding and interpreting which belongs to the "they" that we must gather which possibilities of its Being have been disclosed and appropriated by Dasein as "they". In that case, however, these possibilities themselves make manifest an essential tendency of Being—one which belongs to everydayness. And finally, when this tendency has been explicated in an ontologically adequate manner, it must unveil a primordial kind of Being of Dasein, in such a way, indeed, that from this kind of Being[1] the phenomenon of thrownness, to which we have called attention, can be exhibited in its existential concreteness.

In the first instance what is required is that the disclosedness of the "they"—that is, the everyday kind of Being of discourse, sight, and interpretation—should be made visible in certain definite phenomena. In

---

[1] Reading '. . . von ihr aus . . .'. The earliest editions omit 'aus'; correction is made in a list of errata.

relation to these phenomena, it may not be superfluous to remark that our own Interpretation is purely ontological in its aims, and is far removed from any moralizing critique of everyday Dasein, and from the aspirations of a 'philosophy of culture'.

¶ *35. Idle Talk*

The expression 'idle talk' ["Gerede"] is not to be used here in a 'disparaging'[1] signification. Terminologically, it signifies a positive phenomenon which constitutes the kind of Being of everyday Dasein's understanding and interpreting. For the most part, discourse is expressed by being spoken out, and has always been so expressed; it is language.[2] But in that case understanding and interpretation already lie in what has thus been expressed. In language, as a way things have been expressed or spoken out [Ausgesprochenheit], there is hidden a way in which the understanding of Dasein has been interpreted. This way of interpreting it is no more just present-at-hand than language is; on the contrary, its Being is itself of the character of Dasein. Proximally, and with certain limits, Dasein is constantly delivered over to this interpretedness, which controls and distributes the possibilities of average understanding and of the state-of-mind belonging to it. The way things have been expressed or spoken out is such that in the totality of contexts of signification into which it has been articulated, it preserves an understanding of the disclosed world and therewith, equiprimordially, an understanding of the Dasein-with of Others and of one's own Being-in. The understanding which has thus already been "deposited" in the way things have been expressed, pertains just as much to any traditional discoveredness of entities which may have been reached, as it does to one's current understanding of Being and to whatever possibilities and horizons for fresh interpretation and conceptual Articulation may be available. But now we must go beyond a bare allusion to the Fact of this interpretedness of Dasein, and must inquire about the existential kind of Being of that discourse which is expressed and which expresses itself. If this cannot be conceived as something present-at-hand, what is its Being, and what does this tell us in principle about Dasein's everyday kind of Being?

Discourse which expresses itself is communication. Its tendency of

[1] These quotation marks are supplied only in the older editions. (It is not easy to translate 'Gerede' in a way which does not carry disparaging connotations. Fortunately Heidegger makes his meaning quite clear.)

[2] 'Die Rede spricht sich zumeist aus und hat sich schon immer ausgesprochen. Sie ist Sprache.' As we have pointed out earlier (see our note 1, p. 190 H. 149 above), it is often sufficient to translate 'aussprechen' as 'express'. In the present passage, however, the connotation of 'speaking out' or 'uttering' seems especially important; we shall occasionally make it explicit in our translation by hendiadys or other devices.

Being is aimed at bringing the hearer to participate in disclosed Being towards what is talked about in the discourse.

In the language which is spoken when one expresses oneself, there lies an average intelligibility; and in accordance with this intelligibility the discourse which is communicated can be understood to a considerable extent, even if the hearer does not bring himself into such a kind of Being towards what the discourse is about as to have a primordial understanding of it. We do not so much understand the entities which are talked about; we already are listening only to what is said-in-the-talk as such. What is said-in-the-talk gets understood; but what the talk is about is understood only approximately and superficially. We have *the same thing* in view, because it is in *the same* averageness that we have a common understanding of what is said.

Hearing and understanding have attached themselves beforehand to what is said-in-the-talk as such. The primary relationship-of-Being towards the entity talked about is not 'imparted' by communication;[1] but Being-with-one-another takes place in talking with one another and in concern with what is said-in-the-talk. To this Being-with-one-another, the fact that talking is going on is a matter of consequence.[2] The Being-said, the *dictum*, the pronouncement [Ausspruch]—all these now stand surety for the genuineness of the discourse and of the understanding which belongs to it, and for its appropriateness to the facts. And because this discoursing has lost its primary relationship-of-Being towards the entity talked about, or else has never achieved such a relationship, it does not communicate in such a way as to let this entity be appropriated in a primordial manner, but communicates rather by following the route of *gossiping* and *passing the word along*.[3] What is said-in-the-talk as such, spreads in wider circles and takes on an authoritative character. Things are so because one says so. Idle talk is constituted by just such gossiping and passing the word along —a process by which its initial lack of grounds to stand on [Bodenständigkeit] becomes aggravated to complete groundlessness [Bodenlosigkeit]. And indeed this idle talk is not confined to vocal gossip, but even spreads to what we write, where it takes the form of 'scribbling' [das "Geschreibe"]. In this latter case the gossip is not based so much upon hearsay. It feeds upon superficial reading [dem Angelesenen]. The average understanding of the reader will *never be able* to decide what has been drawn from primordial sources with a struggle and how much is just gossip. The average understanding, moreover, will not want any such distinction, and does not need it, because, of course, it understands everything.

---

[1] 'Die Mitteilung "teilt" nicht den primären Seinsbezug zum beredeten Seienden . . .'
[2] 'Ihm liegt daran, dass geredet wird.' We have interpreted 'Ihm' as referring to 'das Miteinandersein', but other interpretations are grammatically possible.
[3] '. . . sondern auf dem Wege des *Weiter*- und *Nachredens*.'

The groundlessness of idle talk is no obstacle to its becoming public; instead it encourages this. Idle talk is the possibility of understanding everything without previously making the thing one's own. If this were done, idle talk would founder; and it already guards against such a danger. Idle talk is something which anyone can rake up; it not only releases one from the task of genuinely understanding, but develops an undifferentiated kind of intelligibility, for which nothing is closed off any longer.

Discourse, which belongs to the essential state of Dasein's Being and has a share in constituting Dasein's disclosedness, has the possibility of becoming idle talk. And when it does so, it serves not so much to keep Being-in-the-world open for us in an articulated understanding, as rather to close it off, and cover up the entities within-the-world. To do this, one need not aim to deceive. Idle talk does not have the kind of Being which belongs to *consciously passing off* something as something else. The fact that something has been said groundlessly, and then gets passed along in further retelling, amounts to perverting the act of disclosing [Erchliessen] into an act of closing off [Verschliessen]. For what is said is always understood proximally as 'saying' something—that is, an uncovering something. Thus, by its very nature, idle talk is a closing-off, since to go back to the ground of what is talked about is something which it *leaves undone*.

This closing-off is aggravated afresh by the fact that an understanding of what is talked about is supposedly reached in idle talk. Because of this, idle talk discourages any new inquiry and any disputation, and in a peculiar way suppresses them and holds them back.

This way in which things have been interpreted in idle talk has already established itself in Dasein. There are many things with which we first become acquainted in this way, and there is not a little which never gets beyond such an average understanding. This everyday way in which things have been interpreted is one into which Dasein has grown in the first instance, with never a possibility of extrication. In it, out of it, and against it, all genuine understanding, interpreting, and communicating, all re-discovering and appropriating anew, are performed. In no case is a Dasein, untouched and unseduced by this way in which things have been interpreted, set before the open country of a 'world-in-itself, so that it just beholds what it encounters. The dominance of the public way in which things have been interpreted has already been decisive even for the possibilities of having a mood—that is, for the basic way in which Dasein lets the world "matter" to it.[1] The "they" prescribes one's state-of-mind, and determines what and how one 'sees'.

[1] '. . . über die Möglichkeiten des Gestimmtseins entschieden, das heisst über die Grundart, in der sich das Dasein von der Welt angehen lässt.' The second 'über' is found only in the later editions.

Idle talk, which closes things off in the way we have designated, is the kind of Being which belongs to Dasein's understanding when that understanding has been uprooted. But idle talk does not occur as a condition which is present-at-hand in something present-at-hand: idle talk has been uprooted existentially, and this uprooting is constant. Ontologically this means that when Dasein maintains itself in idle talk, it is—as Being-in-the-world—cut off from its primary and primordially genuine relationships-of-Being towards the world, towards Dasein-with, and towards its very Being-in. Such a Dasein keeps floating unattached [in einer Schwebe]; yet in so doing, it is always alongside the world, with Others, and towards itself. To be uprooted in this manner is a possibility-of-Being only for an entity whose disclosedness is constituted by discourse as characterized by understanding and states-of-mind—that is to say, for an entity whose disclosedness, in such an ontologically constitutive state, *is* its "there", its 'in-the-world'. Far from amounting to a "not-Being" of Dasein, this uprooting is rather Dasein's most everyday and most stubborn 'Reality'.

Yet the obviousness and self-assurance of the average ways in which things have been interpreted, are such that while the particular Dasein drifts along towards an ever-increasing groundlessness as it floats, the uncanniness of this floating remains hidden from it under their protecting shelter.

¶ 36. Curiosity

In our analysis of understanding and of the disclosedness of the "there" in general, we have alluded to the *lumen naturale*, and designated the disclosedness of Being-in as Dasein's *"clearing"*, in which it first becomes possible to have something like sight.[1] Our conception of "sight" has been gained by looking at the basic kind of disclosure which is characteristic of Dasein—namely, understanding, in the sense of the genuine appropriation of those entities towards which Dasein can comport itself in accordance with its essential possibilities of Being.

The basic state of sight shows itself in a peculiar tendency-of-Being which belongs to everydayness—the tendency towards 'seeing'. We designate this tendency by the term *"curiosity"* [*Neugier*], which characteristically is not confined to seeing, but expresses the tendency towards a peculiar way of letting the world be encountered by us in perception. Our aim in Interpreting this phenomenon is in principle one which is existential-ontological. We do not restrict ourselves to an orientation towards cognition. Even at an early date (and in Greek philosophy this

[1] See H. 133 above.

was no accident) cognition was conceived in terms of the 'desire to see'.[1] The treatise which stands first in the collection of Aristotle's treatises on ontology begins with the sentence: πάντες ἄνθρωποι τοῦ εἰδέναι ὀρέγονται φύσει.[xi] The care for seeing is essential to man's Being.[2] This remark introduces an investigation in which Aristotle seeks to uncover the source of all learned exploration of entities and their Being, by deriving it from that species of Dasein's Being which we have just mentioned. This Greek Interpretation of the existential genesis of science is not accidental. It brings to explicit understanding what has already been sketched out beforehand in the principle of Parmenides: τὸ γὰρ αὐτὸ νοεῖν ἐστίν τε καὶ εἶναι.[3] Being is that which shows itself in the pure perception which belongs to beholding, and only by such seeing does Being get discovered. Primordial and genuine truth lies in pure beholding. This thesis has remained the foundation of western philosophy ever since. The Hegelian dialectic found in it its motivating conception, and is possible only on the basis of it.

The remarkable priority of 'seeing' was noticed particularly by Augustine, in connection with his Interpretation of *concupiscentia*.[xii] "*Ad oculos enim videre proprie pertinet.*" ("Seeing belongs properly to the eyes.") "*Utimur autem hoc verbo etiam in ceteris sensibus cum eos ad cognoscendum intendimus.*" ("But we even use this word 'seeing' for the other senses when we devote them to cognizing.") "*Neque enim dicimus: audi quid rutilet; aut, olfac quam niteat; aut, gusta quam splendeat; aut, palpa quam fulgeat: videri enim dicuntur haec omnia.*" ("For we do not say 'Hear how it glows', or 'Smell how it glistens', or 'Taste how it shines', or 'Feel how it flashes'; but we say of each, '*See*'; we say that all this is seen.") "*Dicimus autem non solum, vide quid luceat, quod soli oculi sentire possunt.*" ("We not only say, 'See how that shines', when the eyes alone can perceive it;") "*sed etiam, vide quid sonet; vide quid oleat; vide quid sapiat; vide quam durum sit;*" ("but we even say, 'See how that sounds', 'See how that is scented', 'See how that tastes', 'See how hard that is'.") "*Ideoque generalis experientia sensuum concupiscentia sicut dictum est oculorum vocatur, quia videndi officium in quo primatum oculi tenent, etiam ceteri sensus sibi de similitudine usurpant, cum aliquid cognitionis explorant.*" ("Therefore the experience of the senses in general is designated

---

[1] '. . . nicht in der verengten Orientierung am Erkennen, das schon früh und in der griechischen Philosophie nicht zufällig aus der "Lust zu sehen" begriffen wird.' The earlier editions have '. . . am Erkennen, als welches schon früh . . .'

[2] While the sentence from Aristotle is usually translated, 'All men by nature desire to know', Heidegger takes εἰδέναι in its root meaning, 'to see', and connects ὀρέγονται (literally: 'reach out for') with 'Sorge' ('care').

[3] This sentence has been variously interpreted. The most usual version is: 'For thinking and being are the same.' Heidegger, however, goes back to the original meaning of νοεῖν as 'to perceive with the eyes'.

as he 'lust of the eyes'; for when the issue is one of knowing something, the other senses, by a certain resemblance, take to themselves the function of seeing—a function in which the eyes have priority.")

What is to be said about this tendency just to perceive? Which existential state of Dasein will become intelligible in the phenomenon of curiosity?

Being-in-the-world is proximally absorbed in the world of concern. This concern is guided by circumspection, which discovers the ready-to-hand and preserves it as thus discovered. Whenever we have something to contribute or perform, circumspection gives us the route for proceeding with it, the means of carrying it out, the right opportunity, the appropriate moment. Concern may come to rest in the sense of one's interrupting the performance and taking a rest, or it can do so by getting it finished. In rest, concern does not disappear; circumspection, however, becomes free and is no longer bound to the world of work. When we take a rest, care subsides into circumspection which has been set free. In the world of work, circumspective discovering has de-severing as the character of its Being. When circumspection has been set free, there is no longer anything ready-to-hand which we must concern ourselves with bringing close. But, as essentially de-severant, this circumspection provides itself with new possibilities of de-severing. This means that it tends away from what is most closely ready-to-hand, and into a far and alien world. Care becomes concern with the possibilities of seeing the 'world' merely as it *looks* while one tarries and takes a rest. Dasein seeks what is far away simply in order to bring it close to itself in the way it looks. Dasein lets itself be carried along [mitnehmen] solely by the looks of the world; in this kind of Being, it concerns itself with becoming rid of itself as Being-in-the-world and rid of its Being alongside that which, in the closest everyday manner, is ready-to-hand.

When curiosity has become free, however, it concerns itself with seeing, not in order to understand what is seen (that is, to come into a Being towards it) but *just* in order to see. It seeks novelty only in order to leap from it anew to another novelty. In this kind of seeing, that which is an issue for care does not lie in grasping something and being knowingly in the truth; it lies rather in its possibilities of abandoning itself to the world. Therefore curiosity is characterized by a specific way of *not tarrying* alongside what is closest. Consequently it does not seek the leisure of tarrying observantly, but rather seeks restlessness and the excitement of continual novelty and changing encounters. In not tarrying, curiosity is concerned with the constant possibility of *distraction*. Curiosity has nothing to do with observing entities and marvelling at them—θαυμάζειν. To be amazed to the point of not understanding is something in which it has no interest.

Rather it concerns itself with a kind of knowing, but just in order to have known. Both this *not tarrying* in the environment with which one concerns oneself, and this *distraction by* new possibilities, are constitutive items for curiosity; and upon these is founded the third essential characteristic of this phenomenon, which we call the character of *"never dwelling anywhere"* [*Aufenthaltslosigkeit*]. Curiosity is everywhere and nowhere. This mode of Being-in-the-world reveals a new kind of Being of everyday Dasein—a kind in which Dasein is constantly uprooting itself.

Idle talk controls even the ways in which one may be curious. It says what one "must" have read and seen. In being everywhere and nowhere, curiosity is delivered over to idle talk. These two everyday modes of Being for discourse and sight are not just present-at-hand side by side in their tendency to uproot, but *either* of these ways-to-be drags the *other* one with it. Curiosity, for which nothing is closed off, and idle talk, for which there is nothing that is not understood, provide themselves (that is, the Dasein which is in this manner [dem so seienden Dasein]) with the guarantee of a 'life' which, supposedly, is genuinely 'lively'. But with this supposition a third phenomenon now shows itself, by which the disclosedness of everyday Dasein is characterized.

¶ 37. Ambiguity

When, in our everyday Being-with-one-another, we encounter the sort of thing which is accessible to everyone, and about which anyone can say anything, it soon becomes impossible to decide what is disclosed in a genuine understanding, and what is not. This ambiguity [Zweideutigkeit] extends not only to the world, but just as much to Being-with-one-another as such, and even to Dasein's Being towards itself.

Everything looks as if it were genuinely understood, genuinely taken hold of, genuinely spoken, though at bottom it is not; or else it does not look so, and yet at bottom it is. Ambiguity not only affects the way we avail ourselves of what is accessible for use and enjoyment, and the way we manage it; ambiguity has already established itself in the understanding as a potentiality-for-Being, and in the way Dasein projects itself and presents itself with possibilities.[1] Everyone is acquainted with what is up for discussion and what occurs,[2] and everyone discusses it; but everyone also knows already how to talk about what has to happen first— about what is not yet up for discussion but 'really' must be done. Already everyone has surmised and scented out in advance what Others have also surmised and scented out. This Being-on-the scent is of course based upon

[1] '... sondern sie hat sich schon im Verstehen als Seinkönnen, in der Art des Entwurfs und der Vorgabe von Möglichkeiten des Daseins festgesetzt.'
[2] '... was vorliegt und vorkommt ...'

hearsay, for if anyone is genuinely 'on the scent' of anything, he does not speak about it; and this is the most entangling way in which ambiguity presents Dasein's possibilities so that they will already be stifled in their power.[1]

Even supposing that what *"they"* have surmised and scented out should some day be actually translated into deeds, ambiguity has already taken care that interest in what has been Realised will promptly die away. Indeed this interest persists, in a kind of curiosity and idle talk, only so long as there is a possibility of a non-committal just-surmising-with-someone-else. Being "in on it" with someone [das Mit-dabei-sein] when one is on the scent, and so long as one is on it, precludes one's allegiance when what has been surmised gets carried out. For in such a case Dasein is in every case forced back on itself. Idle talk and curiosity lose their power, and are already exacting their penalty.[2] When confronted with the carrying-through of what "they" have surmised together, idle talk readily establishes that "they" "could have done that too"—for "they" have indeed surmised it together. In the end, idle talk is even indignant that what it has surmised and constantly demanded now *actually* happens. In that case, indeed, the opportunity to keep on surmising has been snatched away.

But when Dasein goes in for something in the reticence of carrying it through or even of genuinely breaking down on it, its time is a different time and, as seen by the public, an essentially slower time than that of idle talk, which 'lives at a faster rate'. Idle talk will thus long since have gone on to something else which is currently the very newest thing. That which was earlier surmise and has now been carried through, has come too late if one looks at that which is newest. Idle talk and curiosity take care in their ambiguity to ensure that what is genuinely and newly created is out of date as soon as it emerges before the public. Such a new creation can become free in its positive possibilities only if the idle talk which covers it up has become ineffective, and if the 'common' interest has died away.

In the ambiguity of the way things have been publicly interpreted, talking about things ahead of the game and making surmises about them curiously, gets passed off as what is really happening, while taking action and carrying something through get stamped as something merely subsequent and unimportant. Thus Dasein's understanding in the "they" is constantly *going wrong* [*versieht sich*] in its projects, as regards the genuine possibilities of Being. Dasein is always ambiguously 'there'—that is to say, in that public disclosedness of Being-with-one-another where the loudest

---

[1] '. . . ist die verfänglichste Weise, in der die Zweideutigkeit Möglichkeiten des Daseins vorgibt, um sie auch schon in ihrer Kraft zu ersticken.' (Notice that 'ihrer' may refer to 'Zweideutigkeit' or to 'Möglichkeiten'.)
[2] 'Und sie rächen sich auch schon.'

idle talk and the most ingenious curiosity keep 'things moving', where, in an everyday manner, everything (and at bottom nothing) is happening.

This ambiguity is always tossing to curiosity that which it seeks; and it gives idle talk the semblance of having everything decided in it.

But this kind of Being of the disclosedness of Being-in-the-world dominates also Being-with-one-another as such. The Other is proximally 'there' in terms of what "they" have heard about him, what "they" say in their talk about him, and what "they" know about him. Into primordial Being-with-one-another, idle talk first slips itself in between. Everyone keeps his eye on the Other first and next, watching how he will comport himself and what he will say in reply. Being-with-one-another in the "they" is by no means an indifferent side-by-side-ness in which everything has been settled, but rather an intent, ambiguous watching of one another, a secret and reciprocal listening-in. Under the mask of "for-one-another", an "against-one-another" is in play.

In this connection, we must notice that ambiguity does not first arise from aiming explicitly at disguise or distortion, and that it is not something which the individual Dasein first conjures up. It is already implied in Being with one another, as *thrown* Being-with-one-another in a world. Publicly, however, it is quite hidden; and *"they"* will always defend themselves against this Interpretation of the kind of Being which belongs to the way things have been interpreted by the "they", lest it should prove correct. It would be a misunderstanding if we were to seek to have the explication of these phenomena confirmed by looking to the "they" for agreement.

The phenomena of idle talk, curiosity, and ambiguity have been set forth in such a manner as to indicate that they are already interconnected in their Being. We must now grasp in an existential-ontological manner the kind of Being which belongs to this interconnection. The basic kind of Being which belongs to everydayness is to be understood within the horizon of those structures of Dasein's Being which have been hitherto obtained.

¶ 38. Falling and Throwness

Idle talk, curiosity and ambiguity characterize the way in which, in an everyday manner, Dasein is its 'there'—the disclosedness of Being-in-the-world. As definite existential characteristics, these are not present-at-hand in Dasein, but help to make up its Being. In these, and in the way they are interconnected in their Being, there is revealed a basic kind of Being which belongs to everydayness; we call this the *"falling"*[1] of Dasein.

[1] '*Verfallen*'. See our note 2, p. 42, H. 21 above, and note 1, p. 172, H. 134 above.

This term does not express any negative evaluation, but is used to signify that Dasein is proximally and for the most part *alongside* the 'world' of its concern. This "absorption in . . ." [Aufgehen bei . . .] has mostly the character of Being-lost in the publicness of the "they". Dasein has, in the first instance, fallen away [abgefallen] from itself as an authentic potentiality for Being its Self, and has fallen into the 'world'.[1] "Fallenness" into the 'world' means an absorption in Being-with-one-another, in so far as the latter is guided by idle talk, curiosity, and ambiguity. Through the Interpretation of falling, what we have called the "inauthenticity" of Dasein[xiii] may now be defined more precisely. On no account, however, do the terms "inauthentic" and "non-authentic" signify 'really not',[2] as if in this mode of Being, Dasein were altogether to lose its Being. "Inauthenticity" does not mean anything like Being-no-longer-in-the-world, but amounts rather to a quite distinctive kind of Being-in-the-world—the kind which is completely fascinated by the 'world' and by the Dasein-with of Others in the "they". Not-Being-its-self [Das Nicht-es-selbst-sein] functions as a *positive* possibility of that entity which, in its essential concern, is absorbed in a world. This kind of *not-Being* has to be conceived as that kind of Being which is closest to Dasein and in which Dasein maintains itself for the most part.

So neither must we take the fallenness of Dasein as a 'fall' from a purer and higher 'primal status'. Not only do we lack any experience of this ontically, but ontologically we lack any possibilities or clues for Interpreting it.

In falling, Dasein *itself* as factical Being-in-the-world, is something *from* which it has already fallen away. And it has not fallen into some entity which it comes upon for the first time in the course of its Being, or even one which it has not come upon at all; it has fallen into the *world*, which itself belongs to its Being. Falling is a definite existential characteristic of Dasein itself. It makes no assertion about Dasein as something present-at-hand, or about present-at-hand relations to entities from which Dasein 'is descended' or with which Dasein has subsequently wound up in some sort of *commercium*.

We would also misunderstand the ontologico-existential structure of falling[3] if we were to ascribe to it the sense of a bad and deplorable ontical property of which, perhaps, more advanced stages of human culture might be able to rid themselves.

---

[1] '. . . und an die "Welt" verfallen.' While we shall follow English idioms by translating 'an die "Welt" ' as 'into the "world" ' in contexts such as this, the preposition 'into' is hardly the correct one. The idea is rather that of falling *at* the world or collapsing *against* it.

[2] 'Un- und nichteigentlich, bedeutet aber keineswegs "eigentlich nicht" . . .'

[3] 'Die ontologisch-existenziale Struktur des Verfallens . . .' The words 'des Verfallens' do not appear in the earlier editions.

Neither in our first allusion to Being-in-the-world as Dasein's basic state, nor in our characterization of its constitutive structural items, did we go beyond an analysis of the *constitution* of this kind of Being and take note of its character as a phenomenon. We have indeed described concern and solicitude, as the possible basic kinds of Being-in. But we did not discuss the question of the everyday kind of Being of these ways in which one may be. We also showed that Being-in is something quite different from a mere confrontation, whether by way of observation or by way of action; that is, it is not the Being-present-at-hand-together of a subject and an Object. Nevertheless, it must still have seemed that Being-in-the-world has the function of a rigid framework, within which Dasein's possible ways of comporting itself towards its world run their course without touching the 'framework' itself as regards its Being. But this supposed 'framework' itself helps make up the kind of Being which is Dasein's. An *existential mode* of Being-in-the-world is documented in the phenomenon of falling.

Idle talk discloses to Dasein a Being towards its world, towards Others, and towards itself—a Being in which these are understood, but in a mode of groundless floating. Curiosity discloses everything and anything, yet in such a way that Being-in is everywhere and nowhere. Ambiguity hides nothing from Dasein's understanding, but only in order that Being-in-the-world should be suppressed in this uprooted "everywhere and nowhere".

By elucidating ontologically the kind of Being belonging to everyday Being-in-the-world as it shows through in these phenomena, we first arrive at an existentially adequate determination of Dasein's basic state. Which is the structure that shows us the 'movement' of falling?

Idle talk and the way things have been publicly interpreted (which idle talk includes) constitute themselves in Being-with-one-another. Idle talk is not something present-at-hand for itself within the world, as a product detached from Being-with-one-another. And it is just as far from letting itself be volatilized to something 'universal' which, because it belongs essentially to nobody, is 'really' nothing and occurs as 'Real' only in the individual Dasein which speaks. Idle talk is the kind of Being that belongs to Being-with-one-another itself; it does not first arise through certain circumstances which have effects upon Dasein 'from outside'. But if Dasein itself, in idle talk and in the way things have been publicly interpreted, presents to itself the possibility of losing itself in the "they" and falling into groundlessness, this tells us that Dasein prepares for itself a constant temptation towards falling. Being-in-the-world is in itself *tempting* [*versucherisch*].

Since the way in which things have been publicly interpreted has already become a temptation to itself in this manner, it holds Dasein fast in its fallenness. Idle talk and ambiguity, having seen everything, having understood everything, develop the supposition that Dasein's disclosedness, which is so available and so prevalent, can guarantee to Dasein that all the possibilities of its Being will be secure, genuine, and full. Through the self-certainty and decidedness of the "they", it gets spread abroad increasingly that there is no need of authentic understanding or the state-of-mind that goes with it. The supposition of the "they" that one is leading and sustaining a full and genuine 'life', brings Dasein a *tranquillity*, for which everything is 'in the best of order' and all doors are open. Falling Being-in-the-world, which tempts itself, is at the same time *tranquillizing* [*beruhigend*].

However, this tranquillity in inauthentic Being does not seduce one into stagnation and inactivity, but drives one into uninhibited 'hustle' ["Betriebs"]. Being-fallen into the 'world' does not now somehow come to rest. The tempting tranquillization *aggravates* the falling. With special regard to the interpretation of Dasein, the opinion may now arise that understanding the most alien cultures and 'synthesizing' them with one's own may lead to Dasein's becoming for the first time thoroughly and genuinely enlightened about itself. Versatile curiosity and restlessly "knowing it all" masquerade as a universal understanding of Dasein. But at bottom it remains indefinite *what* is really to be understood, and the question has not even been asked. Nor has it been understood that understanding itself is a potentiality-for-Being which must be made free in one's *ownmost* Dasein alone. When Dasein, tranquillized, and 'understanding' everything, thus compares itself with everything, it drifts along towards an alienation [Entfremdung] in which its ownmost potentiality-for-Being is hidden from it. Falling Being-in-the-world is not only tempting and tranquillizing; it is at the same time *alienating*.

Yet this alienation cannot mean that Dasein gets factically torn away from itself. On the contrary, this alienation drives it into a kind of Being which borders on the most exaggerated 'self-dissection', tempting itself with all possibilities of explanation, so that the very 'characterologies' and 'typologies' which it has brought about[1] are themselves already becoming something that cannot be surveyed at a glance. This alienation *closes off* from Dasein its authenticity and possibility, even if only the possibility of genuinely foundering. It does not, however, surrender Dasein to an entity which Dasein itself is not, but forces it into its

---

[1] '. . . die von ihr gezeitigten . . .' We follow the *difficilior lectio* of the earlier editions. The newer editions have '. . . die von ihr gezeigten . . .' ('. . . which it has shown . . .'). See H. 304 below, and our note ad loc.

inauthenticity—into a possible kind of Being *of itself*. The alienation of falling—at once tempting and tranquillizing—leads by its own movement, to Dasein's getting *entangled* [*verfängt*] in itself.

The phenomena we have pointed out—temptation, tranquillizing, alienation and self-entangling (entanglement)—characterize the specific kind of Being which belongs to falling. This 'movement' of Dasein in its own Being, we call its *"downward plunge"* [*Absturz*]. Dasein plunges out of itself into itself, into the groundlessness and nullity of inauthentic everydayness. But this plunge remains hidden from Dasein by the way things have been publicly interpreted, so much so, indeed, that it gets interpreted as a way of 'ascending' and 'living concretely'.

This downward plunge into and within the groundlessness of the in-authentic Being of the "they", has a kind of motion which constantly tears the understanding away from the projecting of authentic possibil-ities, and into the tranquillized supposition that it possesses everything, or that everything is within its reach. Since the understanding is thus constantly torn away from authenticity and into the "they" (though always with a sham of authenticity), the movement of falling is charac-terized by *turbulence* [Wirbel].

Falling is not only existentially determinative for Being-in-the-world. At the same time turbulence makes manifest that the thrownness which can obtrude itself upon Dasein in its state-of-mind, has the character of throwing and of movement. Thrownness is neither a 'fact that is finished' nor a Fact that is settled.[1] Dasein's facticity is such that *as long as* it is what it is, Dasein remains in the throw, and is sucked into the turbulence of the "they's" inauthenticity. Thrownness, in which facticity lets itself be seen phenomenally, belongs to Dasein, for which, in its Being, that very Being is an issue. Dasein exists factically.

But now that falling has been exhibited, have we not set forth a phe-nomenon which speaks directly *against* the definition we have used in indicating the formal idea of existence? Can Dasein be conceived as an entity for which, in its Being, its potentiality-for-Being is an *issue*, if this entity, in its very everydayness, *has lost itself*, and, in falling, 'lives' *away from itself*? But falling into the world would be phenomenal 'evidence' *against* the existentiality of Dasein only if Dasein were regarded as an isolated "I" or subject, as a self-point from which it moves away. In that case, the world would be an Object. Falling into the world would then have to be re-Interpreted ontologically as Being-present-at-hand in the manner of an entity within-the-world. If, however, we keep in mind

---

[1] 'Die Geworfenheit ist nicht nur nicht eine "fertige Tatsache", sondern auch nicht ein abgeschlossenes Faktum.'

that Dasein's Being is in the state of *Being-in-the-world*, as we have already pointed out, then it becomes manifest that falling, as a *kind of Being of this Being-in*, affords us rather the most elemental evidence *for* Dasein's existentiality. In falling, nothing other than our potentiality-for-Being-in world is the issue, even if in the mode of inauthenticity. Dasein *can* fall only *because* Being-in-the-world understandingly with a state-of-mind is an issue for it. On the other hand, *authentic* existence is not something which floats above falling everydayness; existentially, it is only a modified way in which such everydayness is seized upon.

The phenomenon of falling does not give us something like a 'night view' of Dasein, a property which occurs ontically and may serve to round out the innocuous aspects of this entity. Falling reveals an *essential* ontological structure of Dasein itself. Far from determining its nocturnal side, it constitutes all Dasein's days in their everydayness.

It follows that our existential-ontological Interpretation makes no ontical assertion about the 'corruption of human Nature', not because the necessary evidence is lacking, but because the problematic of this Interpretation is *prior* to any assertion about corruption or incorruption. Falling is conceived ontologically as a kind of motion. Ontically, we have not decided whether man is 'drunk with sin' and in the *status corruptionis*, whether he walks in the *status integritatis*, or whether he finds himself in an intermediate stage, the *status gratiae*. But in so far as any faith or 'world view', makes any such assertions, and if it asserts anything about Dasein as Being-in-the-world, it must come back to the existential structures which we have set forth, provided that its assertions are to make a claim to *conceptual* understanding.

The leading question of this chapter has been about the Being of the "there". Our theme has been the ontological Constitution of the disclosedness which essentially belongs to Dasein. The Being of that disclosedness is constituted by states-of-mind, understanding, and discourse. Its everyday kind of Being is characterized by idle talk, curiosity, and ambiguity. These show us the movement of falling, with temptation, tranquillizing, alienation, and entanglement as its essential characteristics.

But with this analysis, the whole existential constitution of Dasein has been laid bare in its principal features, and we have obtained the phenomenal ground for a 'comprehensive' Interpretation of Dasein's Being as care.

VI

CARE AS THE BEING OF DASEIN

¶ *39. The Question of the Primordial Totality of Dasein's Structural Whole*

BEING-IN-THE-WORLD is a structure which is primordially and constantly *whole*. In the preceding chapters (Division One, Chapters 2-5) this structure has been elucidated phenomenally as a whole, and also in its constitutive items, though always on this basis. The preliminary glance which we gave to the whole of this phenomenon in the beginning[1] has now lost the emptiness of our first general sketch of it. To be sure, the constitution of the structural whole and its everyday kind of Being, is phenomenally so *manifold* that it can easily obstruct our looking at the whole as such phenomenologically in a way which is *unified*. But we may look at it more freely and our unified view of it may be held in readiness more securely if we now raise the question towards which we have been working in our preparatory fundamental analysis of Dasein in general: *"how is the totality of that structural whole which we have pointed out to be defined in an existential-ontological manner?"*

Dasein exists factically. We shall inquire whether existentiality and facticity have an ontological unity, or whether facticity belongs essentially to existentiality. Because Dasein essentially has a state-of-mind belonging to it, Dasein has a kind of Being in which it is brought before itself and becomes disclosed to itself in its thrownness. But thrownness, as a kind of Being, belongs to an entity which in each case *is* its possibilities, and is them in such a way that it understands itself in these possibilities and in terms of them, projecting itself upon them. Being alongside the ready-to-hand, belongs just as primordially to Being-in-the-world as does Being-with Others; and Being-in-the-world is in each case for the sake of itself. The Self, however, is proximally and for the most part inauthentic, the they-self. Being-in-the-world is always fallen. Accordingly *Dasein's* "*average everydayness*" can be defined as "*Being-in-the-world which is falling and disclosed, thrown and projecting, and for which its ownmost potentiality-for-Being is an issue, both in its Being alongside the 'world' and in its Being-with Others*".

H

Can we succeed in grasping this structural whole of Dasein's every-dayness in its totality? Can Dasein's Being be brought out in such a unitary manner that in terms of it the essential equiprimordiality of the structures we have pointed out, as well as their existential possibilities of modification, will become intelligible? Does our present approach *via* the existential analytic provide us an avenue for arriving at this Being phenomenally?

To put it negatively, it is beyond question that the totality of the structural whole is not to be reached by building it up out of elements. For this we would need an architect's plan. The Being of Dasein, upon which the structural whole as such is ontologically supported, becomes accessible to us when we look all the way *through* this whole *to a single* primordially unitary phenomenon which is already in this whole in such a way that it provides the ontological foundation for each structural item in its structural possibility. Thus we cannot Interpret this 'comprehensively' by a process of gathering up what we have hitherto gained and taking it all together. The question of Dasein's basic existential character is essentially different from that of the Being of something present-at-hand. Our everyday environmental experiencing [Erfahren], which remains directed both ontically and ontologically towards entities within-the-world, is not the sort of thing which can present Dasein in an ontically primordial manner for ontological analysis. Similarly our immanent per-ception of Experiences [Erlebnissen] fails to provide a clue which is ontologically adequate. On the other hand, Dasein's Being is not be to deduced from an idea of man. Does the Interpretation of Dasein which we have hitherto given permit us to infer what Dasein, *from its own standpoint*, demands as the only appropriate ontico-ontological way of access to itself?

An understanding of Being belongs to Dasein's ontological structure. As something that is [Seiend], it is disclosed to itself in its Being. The kind of Being which belongs to this disclosedness is constituted by state-of-mind and understanding. Is there in Dasein an understanding state-of-mind in which Dasein has been disclosed to itself in some distinctive way?

If the existential analytic of Dasein is to retain clarity in principle as to its function in fundamental ontology, then in order to master its provis-ional task of exhibiting Dasein's Being, it must seek for one of the *most far-reaching* and *most primordial* possibilities of disclosure—one that lies in Dasein itself. The way of disclosure in which Dasein brings itself before itself must be such that in it Dasein becomes accessible as *simplified* in a certain manner. With what is thus disclosed, the structural totality of the Being we seek must then come to light in an elemental way.

As a state-of-mind which will satisfy these methodological requirements, the phenemonon of *anxiety*[1] will be made basic for our analysis. In working out this basic state-of-mind and characterizing ontologically what is disclosed in it as such, we shall take the phenomenon of falling as our point of departure, and distinguish anxiety from the kindred phenomenon of fear, which we have analysed earlier. As one of Dasein's possibilities of Being, anxiety—together with Dasein itself as disclosed in it—provides the phenomenal basis for explicitly grasping Dasein's primordial totality of Being. Dasein's Being reveals itself as *care*. If we are to work out this basic existential phenomenon, we must distinguish it from phenomena which might be proximally identified with care, such as will, wish, addiction, and urge.[2] Care cannot be derived from these, since they themselves are founded upon it.

Like every ontological analysis, the ontological Interpretation of Dasein as care, with whatever we may gain from such an Interpretation, lies far from what is accessible to the pre-ontological understanding of Being or even to our ontical acquaintance with entities. It is not surprising that when the common understanding has regard to that with which it has only ontical familiarity, that which is known ontologically seems rather strange to it. In spite of this, even the ontical approach with which we have tried to Interpret Dasein ontologically as care, may appear farfetched and theoretically contrived, to say nothing of the act of violence one might discern in our setting aside the confirmed traditional definition of "man". Accordingly our existential Interpretation of Dasein as care requires pre-ontological confirmation. This lies in demonstrating that no sooner has Dasein expressed anything about itself to itself, than it has already interpreted itself as *care* (*cura*), even though it has done so only pre-ontologically.

The analytic of Dasein, which is proceeding towards the phenomenon of care, is to prepare the way for the problematic of fundamental ontology— *the question of the meaning of Being in general.* In order that we may turn our glance explicitly upon this in the light of what we have gained, and go beyond the special task of an existentially *a priori* anthropology, we must look back and get a more penetrating grasp of the phenomena which are most intimately connected with our leading question—the question of Being. These phenomena are those very ways of Being which we have been hitherto explaining: readiness-to-hand and presence-at-hand, as attributes

---

[1] 'Angst'. While this word has generally been translated as 'anxiety' in the post-Freudian psychological literature, it appears as 'dread' in the translations of Kierkegaard and in a number of discussions of Heidegger. In some ways 'uneasiness' or '*malaise*' would be more appropriate still.

[2] '... Wille, Wunsch, Hang und Drang.' For further discussion see H. 194 ff. below.

of entities within-the-world whose character is not that of Dasein. Because the ontological problematic of Being has heretofore been understood primarily in the sense of presence-at-hand ('Reality', 'world-actuality'), while the nature of Dasein's Being has remained ontologically undetermined, we need to discuss the ontological interconnections of care, worldhood, readiness-to-hand, and presence-at-hand (Reality). This will lead to a more precise characterization of the concept of *Reality* in the context of a discussion of the epistemological questions oriented by this idea which have been raised in realism and idealism.

Entities *are*, quite independently of the experience by which they are disclosed, the acquaintance in which they are discovered, and the grasping in which their nature is ascertained. But Being 'is' only in the understanding of those entities to whose Being something like an understanding of Being belongs. Hence Being can be something unconceptualized, but it never completely fails to be understood. In ontological problematics *Being and truth* have, from time immemorial, been brought together if not entirely identified. This is evidence that there is a necessary connecton between Being and understanding, even if it may perhaps be hidden in its primordial grounds. If we are to give an adequate preparation for the question of Being, the phenomenon of *truth* must be ontologically clarified. This will be accomplished in the first instance on the basis of what we have gained in our foregoing Interpretation, in connection with the phenomena of disclosedness and discoveredness, interpretation and assertion.

Thus our preparatory fundamental analysis of Dasein will conclude with the following themes: the basic state-of-mind of anxiety as a distinctive way in which Dasein is disclosed (Section 40); Dasein's Being as care (Section 41); the confirmation of the existential Interpretation of Dasein as care in terms of Dasein's pre-ontological way of interpreting itself (Section 42); Dasein, worldhood, and Reality (Section 43); Dasein, disclosedness, and truth (Section 44).

¶ *40. The Basic State-of-mind of Anxiety as a Distinctive Way in which Dasein is Disclosed*

One of Dasein's possibilities of Being is to give us ontical 'information' about Dasein itself as an entity. Such information is possible only in that disclosedness which belongs to Dasein and which is grounded in state-of-mind and understanding. How far is anxiety a state-of-mind which is distinctive? How is it that in anxiety Dasein gets brought before itself through its own Being, so that we can define phenomenologically the character of the entity disclosed in anxiety, and define it as such in its Being, or make adequate preparations for doing so?

Since our aim is to proceed towards the Being of the totality of the structural whole, we shall take as our point of departure the concrete analyses of falling which we have just carried through. Dasein's absorption in the "they" and its absorption in the 'world' of its concern, make manifest something like a *fleeing* of Dasein in the face of itself—of itself as an authentic potentiality-for-Being-its-Self.[1] This phenomenon of Dasein's fleeing *in the face of itself* and in the face of its authenticity, seems at least a suitable phenomenal basis for the following investigation. But to bring itself face to face with itself, is precisely what Dasein does *not* do when it thus flees. It turns *away from* itself in accordance with its ownmost inertia [Zug] of falling. In investigating such phenomena, however, we must be careful not to confuse ontico-existentiell characterization with ontologico-existential Interpretation nor may we overlook the positive phenomenal bases provided for this Interpretation by such a characterization.

From an existentiell point of view, the authenticity of Being-one's-Self has of course been closed off and thrust aside in falling; but to be thus closed off is merely the *privation* of a disclosedness which manifests itself phenomenally in the fact that Dasein's fleeing is a fleeing *in the face of* itself. That in the face of which Dasein flees, is precisely what Dasein comes up 'behind'.[2] Only to the extent that Dasein has been brought before itself in an ontologically essential manner through whatever disclosedness belongs to it, *can* it flee *in the face of* that in the face of which it flees. To be sure, that in the face of which it flees is *not grasped* in thus turning away [Abkehr] in falling; nor is it experienced even in turning thither [Hinkehr]. Rather, in turning away *from* it, it is disclosed 'there'. This existentiell-ontical turning-away, by reason of its character as a disclosure, makes it phenomenally possible to grasp existential-ontologically that in the face of which Dasein flees, and to grasp it as such. Within the ontical 'away-from' which such turning-away implies, that in the face of which Dasein flees can be understood and conceptualized by 'turning thither' in a way which is phenomenologically Interpretative.

So in orienting our analysis by the phenomenon of falling, we are not in principle condemned to be without any prospect of learning something ontologically about the Dasein disclosed in that phenomenon. On the contrary, here, least of all, has our Interpretation been surrendered to an artificial way in which Dasein grasps itself; it merely carries out the

---

[1] '. . . offenbart so etwas wie eine *Flucht* des Daseins vor ihm selbst als eigentlichem Selbst-sein-können.' The point of this paragraph is that if we are to study the totality of Dasein, Dasein must be brought '*before* itself' or 'face to face with itself' ('*vor es selbst*'); and the fact that Dasein flees '*from* itself' or 'in the face of itself' ('*vor ihm selbst*'), which may seem at first to lead us off the track, is actually very germane to our inquiry.

[2] 'Im Wovor der Flucht kommt das Dasein gerade "hinter" ihm her.'

explication of what Dasein itself ontically discloses. The possibility of proceeding towards Dasein's Being by going along with it and following it up [Mit- und Nachgehen] Interpretatively with an understanding and the state-of-mind that goes with it, is the greater, the more primordial is that phenomenon which functions methodologically as a disclosive state-of-mind. It might be contended that anxiety performs some such function.

We are not entirely unprepared for the analysis of anxiety. Of course it still remains obscure how this is connected ontologically with fear. Obviously these are kindred phenomena. This is betokened by the fact that for the most part they have not been distinguished from one another: that which is fear, gets designated as "anxiety", while that which has the character of anxiety, gets called "fear". We shall try to proceed towards the phenomenon of anxiety step by step.

Dasein's falling into the "they" and the 'world' of its concern, is what we have called a 'fleeing' in the face of itself. But one is not necessarily fleeing whenever one shrinks back in the face of something or turns away from it. Shrinking back in the face of what fear discloses—in the face of something threatening—is founded upon fear; and this shrinking back has the character of fleeing. Our Interpretation of fear as a state-of-mind has shown that in each case that in the face of which we fear is a detrimental entity within-the-world which comes from some definite region but is close by and is bringing itself close, and yet might stay away. In falling, Dasein turns away from itself. That in the face of which it thus shrinks back must, in any case, be an entity with the character of threatening; yet this entity has the same kind of Being as the one that shrinks back: it is Dasein itself. That in the face of which it thus shrinks back cannot be taken as something 'fearsome', for anything 'fearsome' is always encountered as an entity within-the-world. The only threatening which can be 'fearsome' and which gets discovered in fear, always comes from entities within-the-world.

Thus the turning-away of falling is not a fleeing that is founded upon a fear of entities within-the-world. Fleeing that is so grounded is still less a character of this turning-away, when what this turning-away does is precisely to *turn thither* towards entities within-the-world by absorbing itself in them. *The turning-away of falling is grounded rather in anxiety, which in turn is what first makes fear possible.*

To understand this talk about Dasein's fleeing in the face of itself in falling, we must recall that Being-in-the-world is a basic state of Dasein. *That in the face of which one has anxiety* [*das Wovor der Angst*] *is Being-in-the-world as such.* What is the difference phenomenally between that in the face of which anxiety is anxious [sich ängstet] and that in the face of which fear is afraid? That in the face of which one has anxiety is not an entity within-the-world. Thus it is essentially incapable of having an involvement. This threatening does not have the character of a definite detrimentality which reaches what is threatened, and which reaches it with definite regard to a special factical potentiality-for-Being. That in the face of which one is anxious is completely indefinite. Not only does this indefiniteness leave factically undecided which entity within-the-world is threatening us, but it also tells us that entities within-the-world are not 'relevant' at all. Nothing which is ready-to-hand or present-at-hand within the world functions as that in the face of which anxiety is anxious. Here the totality of involvements of the ready-to-hand and the present-at-hand discovered within-the-world, is, as such, of no consequence; it collapses into itself; the world has the character of completely lacking significance. In anxiety one does not encounter this thing or that thing which, as something threatening, must have an involvement.

Accordingly, when something threatening brings itself close, anxiety does not 'see' any definite 'here' or 'yonder' from which it comes. That in the face of which one has anxiety is characterized by the fact that what threatens is *nowhere*. Anxiety 'does not know' what that in the face of which it is anxious is. 'Nowhere', however, does not signify nothing: this is where any region lies, and there too lies any disclosedness of the world for essentially spatial Being-in. Therefore that which threatens cannot bring itself close from a definite direction within what is close by; it is already 'there', and yet nowhere; it is so close that it is oppressive and stifles one's breath, and yet it is nowhere.

In that in the face of which one has anxiety, the 'It is nothing and nowhere' becomes manifest. The obstinacy of the "nothing and nowhere within-the-world" means as a phenomenon that *the world as such is that in the face of which one has anxiety*. The utter insignificance which makes itself known in the "nothing and nowhere", does not signify that the world is absent, but tells us that entities within-the-world are of so little importance in themselves that on the basis of this *insignificance* of what is within-the-world, the world in its worldhood is all that still obtrudes itself.

What oppresses us is not this or that, nor is it the summation of everything present-at-hand; it is rather the *possibility* of the ready-to-hand in general; that is to say, it is the world itself. When anxiety has subsided, then in our everyday way of talking we are accustomed to say that 'it was really nothing'. And *what* it was, indeed, does get reached ontically by such a way of talking. Everyday discourse tends towards concerning itself with the ready-to-hand and talking about it. That in the face of which anxiety is anxious is nothing ready-to-hand within-the-world. But this "nothing ready-to-hand", which only our everyday circumspective discourse understands, is not totally nothing.[1] The "nothing" of readiness-to-hand is grounded in the most primordial 'something'—in the *world*. Ontologically, however, the world belongs essentially to Dasein's Being as Being-in-the-world. So if the "nothing"—that is, the world as such—exhibits itself as that in the face of which one has anxiety, this means that *Being-in-the-world itself is that in the face of which anxiety is anxious.*

Being-anxious discloses, primordially and directly, the world as world. It is not the case, say, that the world first gets thought of by deliberating about it, just by itself, without regard for the entities within-the-world, and that, in the face of this world, anxiety then arises; what is rather the case is that the *world as world* is disclosed first and foremost by anxiety, as a mode of state-of-mind. This does not signify, however, that in anxiety the worldhood of the world gets conceptualized.

Anxiety is not only anxiety in the face of something, but, as a state-of-mind, it is also *anxiety about* something. That which anxiety is profoundly anxious [sich abängstet] about is not a *definite* kind of Being for Dasein or a *definite* possibility for it. Indeed the threat itself is indefinite, and therefore cannot penetrate threateningly to this or that factically concrete potentiality-for-Being. That which anxiety is anxious about is Being-in-the world itself. In anxiety what is environmentally ready-to-hand sinks away, and so, in general, do entities within-the-world. The 'world' can offer nothing more, and neither can the Dasein-with of Others. Anxiety thus takes away from Dasein the possibility of understanding itself, as it falls, in terms of the 'world' and the way things have been publicly interpreted. Anxiety throws Dasein back upon that which it is anxious about —its authentic potentiality-for-Being-in-the-world. Anxiety individualizes Dasein for its ownmost Being-in-the-world, which as something that understands, projects itself essentially upon possibilities. Therefore, with that which it is anxious about, anxiety discloses Dasein *as Being-possible*, and indeed as the only kind of thing which it can be of its own accord as something individualized in individualization [vereinzeltes in der Vereinzelung].

Anxiety makes manifest in Dasein its *Being towards* its ownmost potentiality-for-Being—that is, its *Being-free for* the freedom of choosing itself and taking hold of itself. Anxiety brings Dasein face to face with its *Being-free for (propensio in . . .)* the authenticity of its Being, and for this authenticity as a possibility which it always is.[2] But at the same time, this is the

---

[1] 'Allein dieses Nichts von Zuhandenem, das die alltägliche umsichtige Rede einzig versteht, ist kein totales Nichts.' This sentence is grammatically ambiguous.

[2] 'Die Angst bringt das Dasein vor sein *Freisein für* . . . (*propensio in* . . .) die Eigentlichkeit seines Seins als Möglichkeit, die es immer schon ist.'

Being to which Dasein as Being-in-the-world has been delivered over. That *about which* anxiety is anxious reveals itself as that *in the face of which* it is anxious—namely, Being-in-the-world. The selfsameness of that in the face of which and that about which one has anxiety, extends even to anxiousness [Sichängsten] itself. For, as a state-of-mind, anxiousness is a basic kind of Being-in-the-world. *Here the disclosure and the disclosed are existentially selfsame in such a way that in the latter the world has been disclosed as world, and Being-in has been disclosed as a potentiality-for-Being which is individualized, pure, and thrown; this makes it plain that with the phenomenon of anxiety a distinctive state-of-mind has become a theme for Interpretation.* Anxiety individualizes Dasein and thus discloses it as '*solus ipse*'. But this existential 'solipsism' is so far from the displacement of putting an isolated subject-Thing into the innocuous emptiness of a worldless occurring, that in an extreme sense what it does is precisely to bring Dasein face to face with its world as world, and thus bring it face to face with itself as Being-in-the-world.

Again everyday discourse and the everyday interpretation of Dasein furnish our most unbiased evidence that anxiety as a basic state-of-mind is disclosive in the manner we have shown. As we have said earlier, a state-of-mind makes manifest 'how one is'. In anxiety one feels '*uncanny*'.[1] Here the peculiar indefiniteness of that which Dasein finds itself alongside in anxiety, comes proximally to expression: the "nothing and nowhere". But here "uncanniness" also means "not-being-at-home" [das Nicht-zuhause-sein]. In our first indication of the phenomenal character of Dasein's basic state and in our clarification of the existential meaning of "Being-in" as distinguished from the categorial signification of 'insideness', Being-in was defined as "residing alongside . . .", "Being-familiar with . . ."[11] This character of Being-in was then brought to view more concretely through the everyday publicness of the "they", which brings tranquillized self-assurance—'Being-at-home', with all its obviousness—into the average everydayness of Dasein.[111] On the other hand, as Dasein falls, anxiety brings it back from its absorption in the 'world'. Everyday familiarity collapses. Dasein has been individualized, but individualized *as* Being-in-the-world. Being-in enters into the existential 'mode' of the "*not-at-home*". Nothing else is meant by our talk about 'uncanniness'.

By this time we can see phenomenally what falling, as fleeing, flees in the face of. It does not flee *in the face of* entities within-the-world; these are precisely what it flees *towards*—as entities alongside which our concern,

[1] 'Befindlichkeit, so wurde früher gesagt, macht offenbar, "wie einem ist". In der Angst ist einem "*unheimlich*".' The reference is presumably to H. 134 above. While 'unheimlich' is here translated as 'uncanny', it means more literally 'unhomelike', as the author proceeds to point out.

lost in the "they", can dwell in tranquillized familiarity. When in falling we flee *into* the "at-home" of publicness, we flee *in the face of* the "not-at-home"; that is, we flee in the face of the uncanniness which lies in Dasein —in Dasein as thrown Being-in-the-world, which has been delivered over to itself in its Being. This uncanniness pursues Dasein constantly, and is a threat to its everyday lostness in the "they", though not explicitly. This threat can go together factically with complete assurance and self-sufficiency in one's everyday concern. Anxiety can arise in the most innocuous Situations. Nor does it have any need for darkness, in which it is commonly easier for one to feel uncanny. In the dark there is emphatically 'nothing' to see, though the very world itself is *still* 'there', and 'there' *more obtrusively.*

If we Interpret Dasein's uncanniness from an existential-ontological point of view as a threat which reaches Dasein itself and which comes from Dasein itself, we are not contending that in factical anxiety too it has always been understood in this sense. When Dasein "understands" uncanniness in the everyday manner, it does so by turning away from it in falling; in this turning-away, the "not-at-home" gets 'dimmed down'. Yet the everydayness of this fleeing shows phenomenally that anxiety, as a basic state-of-mind, belongs to Dasein's essential state of Being-in-the-world, which, as one that is existential, is never present-at-hand but *is* itself always in a mode of factical Being-there[1]—that is, in the mode of a state-of-mind. That kind of Being-in-the-world which is tranquillized and familiar is a mode of Dasein's uncanniness, not the reverse. *From an existential-ontological point of view, the "not-at-home" must be conceived as the more primordial phenomenon.*

And only because anxiety is always latent in Being-in-the-world, can such Being-in-the-world, as Being which is alongside the 'world' and which is concernful in its state-of-mind, ever be afraid. Fear is anxiety, fallen into the 'world', inauthentic, and, as such, hidden from itself.

After all, the mood of uncanniness remains, factically, something for which we mostly have no existentiell understanding. Moreover, under the ascendancy of falling and publicness, 'real' anxiety is rare. Anxiety is often conditioned by 'physiological' factors. This fact, in its facticity, is a problem *ontologically*, not merely with regard to its ontical causation and course of development. Only because Dasein is anxious in the very depths of its Being, does it become possible for anxiety to be elicited physiologically.

Even rarer than the existentiell Fact of "real" anxiety are attempts to

---

[1] Here we follow the earlier editions in reading 'Da-seins'. In the later editions the hyphen appears ambiguously at the end of a line.

Interpret this phenomenon according to the principles of its existential-ontological Constitution and function. The reasons for this lie partly in the general neglect of the existential analytic of Dasein, but more particularly in a failure to recognize the phenomenon of state-of-mind[iv]. Yet the factical rarity of anxiety as a phenomenon cannot deprive it of its fitness to take over a methodological function *in principle* for the existential analytic. On the contrary, the rarity of the phenomenon is an index that Dasein, which for the most part remains concealed from itself in its authenticity because of the way in which things have been publicly interpreted by the "they", becomes disclosable in a primordial sense in this basic state-of-mind.

Of course it is essential to every state-of-mind that in each case Being-in-the-world should be fully disclosed in all those items which are constitutive for it—world, Being-in, Self. But in anxiety there lies the possibility of a disclosure which is quite distinctive; for anxiety individualizes. This individualization brings Dasein back from its falling, and makes manifest to it that authenticity and inauthenticity are possibilities of its Being. These basic possibilities of Dasein (and Dasein is in each case mine) show themselves in anxiety as they are in themselves—undisguised by entities within-the-world, to which, proximally and for the most part, Dasein clings.

How far has this existential Interpretation of anxiety arrived at a phenomenal basis for answering the guiding question of the Being of the totality of Dasein's structural whole?

¶ 41. Dasein's Being as Care

Since our aim is to grasp the totality of this structural whole ontologically, we must first ask whether the phenomenon of anxiety and that which is disclosed in it, can give us the whole of Dasein in a way which is phenomenally equiprimordial, and whether they can do so in such a manner that if we look searchingly at this totality, our view of it will be filled in by what has thus been given us. The entire stock of what lies therein may be counted up formally and recorded: anxiousness as a state-of-mind is a way of Being-in-the-world; that in the face of which we have anxiety is thrown Being-in-the-world; that which we have anxiety about is our potentiality-for-Being-in-the-world. Thus the entire phenomenon of anxiety shows Dasein as factically existing Being-in-the-world. The fundamental ontological characteristics of this entity are existentiality, facticity, and Being-fallen. These existential characteristics are not pieces belonging to something composite, one of which might sometimes be missing; but there is woven together in them a primordial context which makes up that totality of the structural whole which we are seeking. In the unity of those characteristics of Dasein's Being which we have mentioned, this Being becomes something which it is possible for us to grasp as such ontologically. How is this unity itself to be characterized?

Dasein is an entity for which, in its Being, that Being is an issue. The phrase 'is an issue' has been made plain in the state-of-Being of understanding—of understanding as self-projective Being towards its ownmost potentiality-for-Being. This potentiality is that for the sake of which any Dasein is as it is. In each case Dasein has already compared itself, in its Being, with a possibility of itself. Being-free *for* one's ownmost potentiality-for-Being, and therewith for the possibility of authenticity and inauthenticity, is shown, with a primordial, elemental concreteness, in anxiety. But ontologically, Being towards one's ownmost potentiality-for-Being means that in each case Dasein is already *ahead* of itself [ihm selbst . . . *vorweg*] in its Being. Dasein is always 'beyond itself' ["über sich hinaus"], not as a way of behaving towards other entities which it is *not*, but as Being towards the potentiality-for-Being which it is itself. This structure of Being, which belongs to the essential 'is an issue', we shall denote as Dasein's "*Being-ahead-of-itself*".

But this structure pertains to the whole of Dasein's constitution. "Being-ahead-of-itself" does not signify anything like an isolated tendency in a worldless 'subject', but characterizes Being-in-the-world. To Being-in-the-world, however, belongs the fact that it has been delivered over to itself—that it has in each case already been thrown *into a world*. The abandonment of Dasein to itself is shown with primordial concreteness in anxiety. "Being-ahead-of-itself" means, if we grasp it more fully, "*ahead-of-itself-in-already-being-in-a-world*". As soon as this essentially unitary structure is seen as a phenomenon, what we have set forth earlier in our analysis of worldhood also becomes plain. The upshot of that analysis was that the referential totality of significance (which as such is constitutive for worldhood) has been 'tied up' with a "for-the-sake-of-which". The fact that this referential totality of the manifold relations of the 'in-order-to' has been bound up with that which is an issue for Dasein, does not signify that a 'world' of Objects which is present-at-hand has been welded together with a subject. It is rather the phenomenal expression of the fact that the constitution of Dasein, whose totality is now brought out explicitly as ahead-of-itself-in-Being-already-in . . ., is primordially a whole. To put it otherwise, existing is always factical. Existentiality is essentially determined by facticity.

Furthermore, Dasein's factical existing is not only generally and without further differentiation a thrown potentiality-for-Being-in-the-world; it is always also absorbed in the world of its concern. In this falling Being-alongside . . ., fleeing in the face of uncanniness (which for the most part remains concealed with latent anxiety, since the publicness of the "they" suppresses everything unfamiliar), announces itself, whether it does so explicitly or not, and whether it is understood or not. Ahead-of-itself-Being-already-in-a-world essentially includes one's falling and one's *Being alongside* those things ready-to-hand within-the-world with which one concerns oneself.

The formally existential totality of Dasein's ontological structural whole must therefore be grasped in the following structure: the Being of Dasein means ahead-of-itself-Being-already-in-(the-world) as Being-alongside (entities encountered within-the-world). This Being fills in the significa-tion of the term *"care"* [*Sorge*], which is used in a purely ontologico-existential manner. From this signification every tendency of Being which one might have in mind ontically, such as worry [Besorgnis] or carefreeness [Sorglosigkeit], is ruled out.

Because Being-in-the-world is essentially care, Being-alongside the ready-to-hand could be taken in our previous analyses as *concern*, and being with the Dasein-with of Others as we encounter it within-the-world could be taken as *solicitude*.[1] Being-alongside something is concern, because it is defined as a way of Being-in by its basic structure—care. Care does not characterize just existentiality, let us say, as detached from facticity and falling; on the contrary, it embraces the unity of these ways in which Being may be characterized. So neither does "care" stand primarily and exclusively for an isolated attitude of the "I" towards itself. If one were to construct the expression 'care for oneself' ["Selbst-sorge"], following the analogy of "concern" [Besorgen] and "solicitude" [Fürsorge], this would be a tautology. "Care" cannot stand for some special attitude towards the Self; for the Self has already been character-ized ontologically by "Being-ahead-of-itself", a characteristic in which the other two items in the structure of care—Being-already-in . . . and Being-alongside . . .—have been *jointly posited* [*mitgesetzt*].

In Being-ahead-of-oneself as Being towards one's ownmost potentiality-for-Being, lies the existential-ontological condition for the possibility of *Being-free* for authentic existentiell possibilities. For the sake of its potenti-ality-for-Being, any Dasein is as it factically is. But to the extent that this Being towards its potentiality-for-Being is itself characterized by freedom, Dasein *can* comport itself towards its possibilities, even *unwillingly*; it *can* be inauthentically; and factically it is inauthentically, proximally and for the most part. The authentic "for-the-sake-of-which" has not been taken

[1] Cf. H. 121 and 131 above.

hold of; the projection of one's own potentiality-for-Being has been abandoned to the disposal of the "they". Thus when we speak of "Being-ahead-of-itself", the 'itself' which we have in mind is in each case the Self in the sense of the they-self. Even in inauthenticity Dasein remains essentially ahead of itself, just as Dasein's fleeing in the face of itself as it falls, still shows that it has the state-of-Being of an entity *for which its Being is an issue.*

Care, as a primordial structural totality, lies 'before' ["vor"] every factical 'attitude' and 'situation' of Dasein, and it does so existentially *a priori*; this means that it always lies *in* them. So this phenomenon by no means expresses a priority of the 'practical' attitude over the theoretical. When we ascertain something present-at-hand by merely beholding it, this activity has the character of care just as much as does a 'political action' or taking a rest and enjoying oneself. 'Theory' and 'practice' are possibilities of Being for an entity whose Being must be defined as "care".

The phenomenon of care in its totality is essentially something that cannot be torn asunder; so any attempts to trace it back to special acts or drives like willing and wishing or urge and addiction,[1] or to construct it out of these, will be unsuccessful.

Willing and wishing are rooted with ontological necessity in Dasein as care; they are not just ontologically undifferentiated Experiences occurring in a 'stream' which is completely indefinite with regard to the meaning of its Being. This is no less the case with urge and addiction. These too are grounded in care so far as they can be exhibited in Dasein at all. This does not prevent them from being ontologically constitutive even for entities that merely 'live'. But the basic ontological state of 'living' is a problem in its own right and can be tackled only reductively and privatively in terms of the ontology of Dasein.

Care is ontologically 'earlier' than the phenomena we have just mentioned, which admittedly can, within certain limits, always be 'described' appropriately without our needing to have the full ontological horizon visible, or even to be familiar with it at all. From the standpoint of our present investigation in fundamental ontology, which aspires neither to a thematically complete ontology of Dasein nor even to a concrete anthropology, it must suffice to suggest how these phenomena are grounded existentially in care.

That very potentiality-for-Being for the sake of which Dasein is, has Being-in-the-world as its kind of Being. Thus it implies ontologically a relation to entities within-the-world. Care is always concern and solicitude,

---

[1] '... besondere Akte oder Triebe wie Wollen und Wünschen oder Drang und Hang...' Cf. H. 182.

even if only privatively. In willing, an entity which is understood—that is, one which has been projected upon its possibility—gets seized upon, either as something with which one may concern oneself, or as something which is to be brought into its Being through solicitude. *Hence*, to any willing there belongs something willed, which has already made itself definite in terms of a "for-the-sake-of-which". If willing is to be possible ontologically, the following items are constitutive for it: (1) the prior disclosedness of the "for-the-sake-of-which" in general (Being-ahead-of-itself); (2) the disclosedness of something with which one can concern oneself (the world as the "wherein" of Being-already);[1] (3) Dasein's projection of itself understandingly upon a potentiality-for-Being towards a possibility of the entity 'willed'. In the phenomenon of willing, the underlying totality of care shows through.

As something factical, Dasein's projection of itself understandingly is in each case already alongside a world that has been discovered. From this world it takes its possibilities, and it does so first in accordance with the way things have been interpreted by the "they". This interpretation has already restricted the possible options of choice to what lies within the range of the familiar, the attainable, the respectable—that which is fitting and proper. This levelling off of Dasein's possibilities to what is proximally at its everyday disposal also results in a dimming down of the possible as such. The average everydayness of concern becomes blind to its possibilities, and tranquillizes itself with that which is merely 'actual'. This tranquillizing does not rule out a high degree of diligence in one's concern, but arouses it. In this case no positive new possibilities are willed, but that which is at one's disposal becomes 'tactically' altered in such a way that there is a semblance of something happening.

All the same, this tranquillized 'willing' under the guidance of the "they", does not signify that one's Being towards one's potentiality-for-Being has been extinguished, but only that it has been modified. In such a case, one's Being towards possibilities shows itself for the most part as mere *wishing*. In the wish Dasein projects its Being upon possibilities which not only have not been taken hold of in concern, but whose fulfilment has not even been pondered over and expected. On the contrary, in the mode of mere wishing, the ascendancy of Being-ahead-of-oneself brings with it a lack of understanding for the factical possibilities. When the world has been primarily projected as a wish-world, Being-in-the-world has lost itself inertly in what is at its disposal; but it has done so in such a way that, in the light of what is wished for, that which is at its disposal (and this is all that is ready-to-hand) is never enough. Wishing is an existential

---

[1] '. . . (Welt als das Worin des Schon-seins) . . .'

modification of projecting oneself understandingly, when such self-projection has fallen forfeit to thrownness and just keeps *hankering* after possibilities.[1] Such hankering *closes off* the possibilities; what is 'there' in wishful hankering turns into the 'actual world'. Ontologically, wishing presupposes care.

In hankering, Being-already-alongside . . . takes priority. The "ahead-of-itself-in-Being-already-in . . ." is correspondingly modified. Dasein's hankering as it falls makes manifest its *addiction* to becoming 'lived' by whatever world it is in. This addiction shows the character of Being out for something [Ausseins auf . . .]. Being-ahead-of-oneself has lost itself in a 'just-always-already-alongside'.[2] What one is addicted 'towards' [Das "Hin-zu" des Hanges] is to let oneself be drawn by the sort of thing for which the addiction hankers. If Dasein, as it were, sinks into an addiction then there is not merely an addiction present-at-hand, but the entire structure of care has been modified. Dasein has become blind, and puts all possibilities into the service of the addiction.

On the other hand, the *urge* 'to live' is something 'towards' which one is impelled, and it brings the impulsion along with it of its own accord.[3] It is 'towards this at any price'. The urge seeks to crowd out [verdrängen] other possibilities. Here too the Being-ahead-of-oneself is one that is inauthentic, even if one is assailed by an urge coming from the very thing that is urging one on. The urge can outrun one's current state-of-mind and one's understanding. But then Dasein is not—and never is—a 'mere urge' to which other kinds of controlling or guiding behaviour are added from time to time; rather, as a modification of the entirety of Being-in-the-world, it is always care already.

In pure urge, care has not yet become free, though care first makes it ontologically possible for Dasein to be urged on by itself.[4] In addiction, however, care has always been bound. Addiction and urge are possibilities rooted in the thrownness of Dasein. The urge 'to live' is not to be annihilated; the addiction to becoming 'lived' by the world is not to be rooted out. But because these are both grounded ontologically in care, and only because of this, they are both to be modified in an ontical and existentiell manner by care—by care as something authentic.

With the expression 'care' we have in mind a basic existential-ontological phenomenon, which all the same is *not simple* in its structure. The

---

[1] '. . . das, der Geworfenheit verfallen, den Möglichkeiten lediglich noch *nachhängt*.'
[2] '. . . in ein "Nur-immer-schon-bei . . .".' Here we follow the reading of the later editions. The earlier editions have ' "Nur-immer-schon-sein-bei . . ." ' ('just-always-Being-already-alongside').
[3] 'Dagegen ist der *Drang* "zu leben" ein "Hin-zu", das von ihm selbst her den Antrieb mitbringt.' The italicization of '*Drang*' appears only in the later editions.
[4] '. . . das Bedrängtsein des Daseins aus ihm selbst her . . .'

ontologically elemental totality of the care-structure cannot be traced back to some ontical 'primal element', just as Being certainly cannot be 'explained' in terms of entities. In the end it will be shown that the idea of Being in general is just as far from being 'simple' as is the Being of Dasein. In defining "care" as "Being-ahead-of-oneself—in-Being-already-in . . .—as Being-alongside . . .", we have made it plain that even this phenomenon is, in itself, still structurally *articulated*. But is this not a phenomenal symptom that we must pursue the ontological question even further until we can exhibit a *still more primordial* phenomenon which provides the ontological support for the unity and the totality of the structural manifoldness of care? Before we follow up this question, we must look back and appropriate with greater precision what we have hitherto Interpreted in aiming at the question of fundamental ontology as to the meaning of Being in general. First, however, we must show that what is ontologically 'new' in this Interpretation is ontically quite old. In explicating Dasein's Being as care, we are not forcing it under an idea of our own contriving, but we are conceptualizing existentially what has already been disclosed in an ontico-existentiell manner.

¶ *42. Confirmation of the Existential Interpretation of Dasein as Care in terms of Dasein's Pre-ontological Way of Interpreting Itself*[1]

In our foregoing Interpretations, which have finally led to exhibiting care as the Being of Dasein, everything depended on our arriving at the right *ontological* foundations for that entity which in each case we ourselves are, and which we call 'man'. To do this it was necessary from the outset to change the direction of our analysis from the approach presented by the traditional definition of "man"—an approach which has not been clarified ontologically and is in principle questionable. In comparison with this definition, the existential-ontological Interpretation may seem strange, especially if 'care' is understood just ontically as 'worry' or 'grief' [als "Besorgnis" und "Bekümmernis"]. Accordingly we shall now cite a document which is pre-ontological in character, even though its demonstrative force is 'merely historical'.

We must bear in mind, however, that in this document Dasein is expressing itself 'primordially', unaffected by any theoretical Interpretation and without aiming to propose any. We must also note that Dasein's Being is characterized by historicality, though this must first be demonstrated ontologically. If Dasein is 'historical' in the very depths of its Being, then a deposition [Aussage] which comes from its history and goes back to it,

---

[1] '*Die Bewährung der existenzialen Interpretation des Daseins als Sorge aus der vorontologischen Selbstauslegung des Daseins.*'

and which, moreover, is *prior* to any scientific knowledge, will have especial weight, even though its importance is never purely ontological. That understanding of Being which lies in Dasein itself, expresses itself pre-ontologically. The document which we are about to cite should make plain that our existential Interpretation is not a mere fabrication, but that as an ontological 'construction' it is well grounded and has been sketched out beforehand in elemental ways.

There is an ancient fable in which Dasein's interpretation of itself as 'care' has been embedded: v

> *Cura cum fluvium transiret, vidit cretosum lutum*
> *sustulitque cogitabunda atque coepit fingere.*
> *dum deliberat quid iam fecisset, Jovis intervenit.*
> *rogat eum Cura ut det illi spiritum, et facile impetrat.*
> *cui cum vellet Cura nomen ex sese ipsa imponere,*
> *Jovis prohibuit suumque nomen ei dandum esse dictitat.*
> *dum Cura et Jovis disceptant, Tellus surrexit simul*
> *suumque nomen esse volt cui corpus praebuerit suum.*
> *sumpserunt Saturnum iudicem, is sic aecus iudicat:*
> *'tu Jovis quia spiritum dedisti, in morte spiritum,*
> *tuque Tellus, quia dedisti corpus, corpus recipito,*
> *Cura eum quia prima finxit, teneat quamdiu vixerit.*
> *sed quae nunc de nomine eius vobis controversia est,*
> *homo vocetur, quia videtur esse factus ex humo.'*

'Once when 'Care' was crossing a river, she saw some clay; she thoughtfully took up a piece and began to shape it. While she was meditating on what she had made, Jupiter came by. 'Care' asked him to give it spirit, and this he gladly granted. But when she wanted her name to be bestowed upon it, he forbade this, and demanded that it be given his name instead. While 'Care' and Jupiter were disputing, Earth arose and desired that her own name be conferred on the creature, since she had furnished it with part of her body. They asked Saturn to be their arbiter, and he made the following decision, which seemed a just one: 'Since you, Jupiter, have given its spirit, you shall receive that spirit at its death; and since you, Earth, have given its body, you shall receive its body. But since 'Care' first shaped this creature, she shall possess it as long as it lives. And because there is now a dispute among you as to its name, let it be called '*homo*', for it is made out of *humus* (earth).'[1]

[1] In both the earlier and later editions Heidegger has 'videt' in the first line of the Latin version of the fable, where Bücheler, from whom the text has been taken, has 'vidit'; in the 12th line Heidegger has 'enim' where Bücheler has 'eum'. The punctuation of the Latin version is as Bücheler gives it. The single quotation marks in the English translation

This pre-ontological document becomes especially significant not only in that 'care' is here seen as that to which human Dasein belongs 'for its lifetime', but also because this priority of 'care' emerges in connection with the familiar way of taking man as compounded of body (earth) and spirit. *"Cura prima finxit"*: in care this entity has the 'source' of its Being. *"Cura teneat, quamdiu vixerit"*; the entity is not released from this source but is held fast, dominated by it through and through as long as this entity 'is in the world'. 'Being-in-the-world' has the stamp of 'care', which accords with its Being. It gets the name *"homo"* not in consideration of its Being but in relation to that of which it consists (*humus*). The decision as to wherein the 'primordial' Being of this creature is to be seen, is left to Saturn, 'Time'.[vi] Thus the pre-ontological characterization of man's essence expressed in this fable, has brought to view in advance the kind of Being which dominates his *temporal sojourn in the world*, and does so through and through.

The history of the signification of the ontical concept of 'care' permits us to see still further basic structures of Dasein. Burdach [vii] calls attention to a double meaning of the term *'cura'* according to which it signifies not only 'anxious exertion' but also 'carefulness' and 'devotedness' ["Sorgfalt", "Hingabe"]. Thus Seneca writes in his last epistle (*Ep.* 124): 'Among the four existent Natures (trees, beasts, man, and God), the latter two, which alone are endowed with reason, are distinguished in that God is immortal while man is mortal. Now when it comes to these, the good of the one, namely God, is fulfilled by his Nature; but that of the other, man, is fulfilled by *care* (*cura*): *"unius bonum natura perficit, dei scilicet, alterius cura, hominis."*'

Man's *perfectio*—his transformation into that which he can be in Being-free for his ownmost possibilities (projection)—is 'accomplished' by 'care'. But with equal primordiality 'care' determines what is basically specific in this entity, according to which it has been surrendered to the world of its concern (thrownness). In the 'double meaning' of 'care', what we have in view is a *single* basic state in its essentially twofold structure of thrown projection.

As compared with this ontical interpretation, the existential-ontological Interpretation is not, let us say, merely an ontical generalization which is theoretical in character. That would just mean that ontically all man's ways of behaving are 'full of care' and are guided by his 'devotedness' to

correspond strictly to the double quotation marks in Heidegger's version; some of these are not found in Burdach's translation, which, except for two entirely trivial changes, Heidegger has otherwise reproduced very accurately. (On Bücheler and Burdach, see Heidegger's note v, ad loc.) Our translation is a compromise between Burdach and the original Latin.

something. The 'generalization' is rather one that is *ontological and a priori*. What it has in view is not a set of ontical properties which constantly keep emerging, but a state of Being which is already underlying in every case, and which first makes it ontologically possible for this entity to be addressed ontically as *"cura"*. The existential condition for the possibility of 'the cares of life' and 'devotedness', must be conceived as care, in a sense which is primordial—that is ontological.

The transcendental 'generality' of the phenomenon of care and of all fundamental *existentialia* is, on the other hand, broad enough to present a basis on which *every* interpretation of Dasein which is ontical and belongs to a world-view must move, whether Dasein is understood as affliction [Not] and the 'cares of life' or in an opposite manner.

The very 'emptiness' and 'generality' which obtrude themselves ontically in existential structures, have an ontological definiteness and fulness of their *own*. Thus Dasein's whole constitution itself is not simple in its unity, but shows a structural articulation; in the existential conception of care, this articulation becomes expressed.

Thus, by our ontological Interpretation of Dasein, we have been brought to the *existential conception* of care from Dasein's pre-ontological interpretation of itself as 'care'. Yet the analytic of Dasein is not aimed at laying an ontological basis for anthropology; its purpose is one of fundamental ontology. This is the purpose that has tacitly determined the course of our considerations hitherto, our selection of phenomena, and the limits to which our analysis may proceed. Now, however, with regard to our leading question of the meaning of Being and our way of working this out, our investigation must give us *explicit* assurance as to what we have so far achieved. But this sort of thing is not to be reached by superficially taking together what we have discussed. Rather, with the help of what we have achieved, that which could be indicated only crudely at the beginning of the existential analytic, must now be concentrated into a more penetrating understanding of the problem.

¶ 43. *Dasein, Worldhood, and Reality*

The question of the meaning of Being becomes possible at all only if there *is* something like an understanding of Being. Understanding of Being belongs to the kind of Being which the entity called "Dasein" possesses. The more appropriately and primordially we have succeeded in explicating this entity, the surer we are to attain our goal in the further course of working out the problem of fundamental ontology.

In our pursuit of the tasks of a preparatory existential analytic of Dasein, there emerged an Interpretation of understanding, meaning, and interpretation. Our analysis of Dasein's disclosedness showed further that, with this disclosedness, Dasein, in its basic state of Being-in-the-world, has been revealed equiprimordially with regard to the world, Being-in, and the Self. Furthermore, in the factical disclosedness of the world, entities within-the-world are discovered too. This implies that the Being of these entities is always understood in a certain manner, even if it is not conceived in a way which is appropriately ontological. To be sure, the pre-onto- logical understanding of Being embraces all entities which are essentially disclosed in Dasein; but the understanding of Being has not yet Articulated itself in a way which corresponds to the various modes of Being.

At the same time our interpretation of understanding has shown that, in accordance with its falling kind of Being, it has, proximally and for the most part, diverted itself [sich . . . verlegt] into an understanding of the 'world'. Even where the issue is not only one of ontical experience but also one of ontological understanding, the interpretation of Being takes its orientation in the first instance from the Being of entities within-the- world. Thereby the Being of what is proximally ready-to-hand gets passed over, and entities are first conceived as a context of Things (*res*) which are present-at-hand. "*Being*" acquires the meaning of "*Reality*".[viii] Substantiality becomes the basic characteristic of Being. Corresponding to this way in which the understanding of Being has been diverted, even the ontological understanding of Dasein moves into the horizon of this conception of Being. Like any other entity, *Dasein* too is *present-at-hand as Real*. In this way "*Being in general*" acquires the meaning of "*Reality*". Accordingly the concept of Reality has a peculiar priority in the ontological problematic. By this priority the route to a genuine existential analytic of Dasein gets diverted, and so too does our very view of the Being of what is proximally ready-to-hand within-the-world. It finally forces the general problematic of Being into a direction that lies off the course. The other modes of Being become defined negatively and privatively with regard to Reality.

Thus not only the analytic of Dasein but the working-out of the question of the meaning of Being in general must be turned away from a one-sided orientation with regard to Being in the sense of Reality. We must demonstrate that Reality is not only *one* kind of Being *among* others, but that ontologically it has a definite connection in its foundations with Dasein, the world, and readiness-to-hand. To demonstrate this we must discuss in principle the *problem of Reality*, its conditions and its limits.

Under the heading 'problem of Reality' various questions are clustered: (1) whether any entities which supposedly 'transcend our consciousness' *are* at all; (2) whether this Reality of the 'external world' can be adequately *proved*; (3) how·far this entity, if it is Real, is to be known in its Being-in-itself; (4) what the meaning of this entity, Reality, signifies in general. The following discussion of the problem of Reality will treat three topics with regard to the question of fundamental ontology: (*a*) Reality as a problem of Being, and whether the 'external world' can be proved; (*b*) Reality as an ontological problem; (*c*) Reality and care.

(*a*) *Reality as a problem of Being, and whether the 'External World' can be Proved*

Of these questions about Reality, the one which comes first in order is the ontological question of what "Reality" signifies in general. But as long as a pure ontological problematic and methodology was lacking, this question (if it was explicitly formulated at all) was necessarily confounded with a discussion of the 'problem of the external world'; for the analysis of Reality is possible only on the basis of our having appropriate access to the Real. But it has long been held that the way to grasp the Real is by that kind of knowing which is characterized by beholding [das anschauende Erkennen]. Such knowing 'is' as a way in which the soul— or consciousness—behaves. In so far as Reality has the character of something independent and "in itself", the question of the meaning of "Reality" becomes linked with that of whether the Real can be independent 'of consciousness' or whether there can be a transcendence of consciousness into the 'sphere' of the Real. The possibility of an adequate ontological analysis of Reality depends upon how far *that of which* the Real is to be thus independent—how far *that which* is to be transcended[1]—has *itself* been clarified with regard to its *Being*. Only thus can even the kind of Being which belongs to transcendence be ontologically grasped. And finally we must make sure what kind of primary access we have to the Real, by deciding the question of whether knowing can take over this function at all.

These investigations, which *take precedence over* any possible ontological question about Reality, have been carried out in the foregoing existential analytic. According to this analytic, knowing is a *founded* mode of access to the Real. The Real is essentially accessible only as entities within-the-world. All access to such entities is founded ontologically upon the basic state of Dasein, Being-in-the-world; and this in turn has care as its even more primordial state of Being (ahead of itself—Being already in a world —as Being alongside entities within-the-world).

The question of whether there is a world at all and whether its Being

[1] '. . . das, *wovon* Unabhängigkeit bestehen soll, *was* transzendiert werden soll . . .'

can be proved, makes no sense if it is raised by *Dasein* as Being-in-the-world; and who else would raise it? Furthermore, it is encumbered with a double signification. The world as the "wherein" [das Worin] of Being-in, and the 'world' as entities within-the-world (that in which [das Wobei] one is concernfully absorbed) either have been confused or are not distinguished at all. But the world is disclosed essentially *along with the* Being of Dasein; with the disclosedness of the world, the 'world' has in each case been discovered too. Of course entities within-the-world in the sense of the Real as merely present-at-hand, are the very things that can remain concealed. But even the Real can be discovered only on the basis of a world which has already been disclosed. And only on this basis can anything Real still remain *hidden*. The question of the 'Reality' of the 'external world' gets raised without any previous clarification of the *phenomenon of the world* as such. Factically, the 'problem of the external *world*' is constantly oriented with regard to entities within-the-world (Things and Objects). So these discussions drift along into a problematic which it is almost impossible to disentangle ontologically.

Kant's 'Refutation of Idealism'[ix] shows how intricate these questions are and how what one wants to prove gets muddled with what one does prove and with the means whereby the proof is carried out. Kant calls it 'a scandal of philosophy and of human reason in general'[x] that there is still no cogent proof for the 'Dasein of Things outside of us' which will do away with any scepticism. He proposes such a proof himself, and indeed he does so to provide grounds for his 'theorem' that 'The mere consciousness of my own Dasein—a consciousness which, however, is empirical in character—proves the Dasein of objects in the space outside of me.'[xi]

We must in the first instance note explicitly that Kant uses the term 'Dasein' to designate that kind of Being which in the present investigation we have called 'presence-at-hand'. 'Consciousness of my Dasein' means for Kant a consciousness of my Being-present-at-hand in the sense of Descartes. When Kant uses the term 'Dasein' he has in mind the Being-present-at-hand of consciousness just as much as the Being-present-at-hand of Things.

The proof for the 'Dasein of Things outside of me' is supported by the fact that both change and performance belong, with equal primordiaity, to the essence of time. My own Being-present-at-hand—that is, the Being-present-at-hand of a multiplicity of representations, which has been given in the inner sense—is a process of change which is present-at-hand. To have a determinate temporal character [Zeitbestimmtheit], however, presupposes something present-at-hand which is permanent. But this cannot be 'in us', 'for only through what is thus permanent can my

Dasein in time be determined'.[xii] Thus if changes which are present-at-
hand have been posited empirically 'in me', it is necessary that along with
these something permanent which is present-at-hand should be posited
empirically 'outside of me'. What is thus permanent is the condition which
makes it possible for the changes 'in me' to be present-at-hand. The
experience of the Being-in-time of representations posits something
changing 'in me' and something permanent 'outside of me', and it posits
both with equal primordiality.

Of course this proof is not a causal inference and is therefore not
encumbered with the disadvantages which that would imply. Kant gives,
as it were, an 'ontological proof' in terms of the idea of a temporal entity.
It seems at first as if Kant has given up the Cartesian approach of positing
a subject one can come across in isolation. But only in semblance. That
Kant demands any proof at all for the 'Dasein of Things outside of me'
shows already that he takes the subject—the 'in me'—as the starting-
point for this problematic. Moreover, his proof itself is then carried
through by starting with the empirically given changes '*in me*'. For only
'in me' is 'time' experienced, and time carries the burden of the proof.
Time provides the basis for leaping off into what is 'outside of me' in the
course of the proof. Furthermore, Kant emphasizes that "The problematical kind [of idealism], which merely alleges our inability to prove by
immediate experience that there is a Dasein outside of our own, is reasonable and accords with a sound kind of philosophical thinking: namely, to
permit no decisive judgment until an adequate proof has been found."[xiii]

But even if the ontical priority of the isolated subject and inner experience should be given up, Descartes' position would still be retained
ontologically. What Kant proves—if we may suppose that his proof is
correct and correctly based—is that entities which are changing and
entities which are permanent are necessarily present-at-hand together.
But when two things which are present-at-hand are thus put on the same
level, this does not as yet mean that subject and Object are present-at-
hand together. And even if this were proved, what is ontologically decisive
would still be covered up—namely, the basic state of the 'subject', Dasein,
as Being-in-the-world. *The Being-present-at-hand-together of the physical and
the psychical is completely different ontically and ontologically from the phenomenon
of Being-in-the-world.*

Kant presupposes both the distinction between the 'in me' and the
'outside of me', *and also the connection* between these; factically he is correct
in doing so, but he is incorrect from the standpoint of the tendency of his
proof. It has not been demonstrated that the sort of thing which gets
established about the Being-present-at-hand-together of the changing and

the permanent when one takes time as one's clue, will also apply to the connection between the 'in me' and the 'outside of me'. But if one were to see the whole distinction between the 'inside' and the 'outside' and the whole connection between them which Kant's proof presupposes, and if one were to have an ontological conception of what has been presupposed in this presupposition, then the possibility of holding that a proof of the 'Dasein of Things outside of me' is a necessary one which has yet to be given [noch ausstehend], would collapse.

The 'scandal of philosophy' is not that this proof has yet to be given, but that *such proofs are expected and attempted again and again*. Such expectations, aims, and demands arise from an ontologically inadequate way of starting with *something* of such a character that independently *of it* and 'outside' *of it* a 'world' is to be proved as present-at-hand. It is not that the proofs are inadequate, but that the kind of Being of the entity which does the proving and makes requests for proofs has *not been made definite enough*. This is why a demonstration that two things which are present-at-hand are necessarily present-at-hand together, can give rise to the illusion that something has been proved, or even can be proved, about Dasein as Being-in-the-world. If Dasein is understood correctly, it defies such proofs, because, in its Being, it already *is* what subsequent proofs deem necessary to demonstrate for it.

If one were to conclude that since the Being-present-at-hand of Things outside of us is impossible to prove, it must therefore 'be taken merely on *faith*',[xiv] one would still fail to surmount this perversion of the problem. The assumption would remain that at bottom and ideally it must still be possible to carry out such a proof. This inappropriate way of approaching the problem is still endorsed when one restricts oneself to a 'faith in the Reality of the external world', even if such a faith is explicitly 'acknowledged' as such. Although one is not offering a stringent proof, one is still in principle demanding a proof and trying to satisfy that demand.

Even if one should invoke the doctrine that the subject must presuppose and indeed always does unconsciously presuppose the presence-at-hand of the 'external world', one would still be starting with the construct of an isolated subject. The phenomenon of Being-in-the-world is something that one would no more meet in this way than one would by demonstrating that the physical and the psychical are present-at-hand together. With such presuppositions, Dasein always comes 'too late'; for in so far as it does this presupposing as an entity (and otherwise this would be impossible), it is, *as an entity*, already in a world. 'Earlier' than any presupposition which Dasein makes, or any of its ways of behaving, is the '*a priori*' character of its state of Being as one whose kind of Being is care.

To *have faith* in the Reality of the 'external world', whether rightly or wrongly; to *"prove"* this Reality for it, whether adequately or inadequately; to *presuppose* it, whether explicitly or not—attempts such as these which have not mastered their own basis with full transparency, presuppose a subject which is proximally *worldless* or unsure of its world, and which must, at bottom, first assure itself of a world. Thus from the very beginning, Being-in-a-world is disposed to "take things" in some way [Auffassen], to suppose, to be certain, to have faith—a way of behaving which itself is always a founded mode of Being-in-the-world.

The 'problem of Reality' in the sense of the question whether an external world is present-at-hand and whether such a world can be proved, turns out to be an impossible one, not because its consequences lead to inextricable impasses, but because the very entity which serves as its theme, is one which, as it were, repudiates any such formulation of the question. Our task is not to prove that an 'external world' is present-at-hand or to show how it is present-at-hand, but to point out why Dasein, as Being-in-the-world, has the tendency to bury the 'external world' in nullity 'epistemologically' before going on to prove it.[1] The reason for this lies in Dasein's falling and in the way in which the primary understanding of Being has been diverted to Being as presence-at-hand—a diversion which is motivated by that falling itself. If one formulates the question 'critically' with such an ontological orientation, then what one finds present-at-hand as proximally and solely certain, is something merely 'inner'. After the primordial phenomenon of Being-in-the-world has been shattered, the isolated subject is all that remains, and this becomes the basis on which it gets joined together with a 'world'.

In this investigation we cannot discuss at length the many attempts to solve the 'problem of Reality' which have been developed in various kinds of realism and idealism and in positions which mediate between them. Certainly a grain of genuine inquiry is to be found in each of these; but certain as this is, it would be just as perverse if one should want to achieve a tenable solution of the problem by reckoning up how much has been correct in each case. What is needed rather is the basic insight that while the different epistemological directions which have been pursued have not gone so very far off epistemologically, their neglect of any existential analytic of Dasein has kept them from obtaining any basis for a well secured phenomenal problematic. Nor is such a *basis* to be obtained by subsequently making phenomenological corrections on the concepts of subject and consciousness. Such a procedure would give no guarantee

[1] '. . . warum das Dasein als In-der-Welt-sein die Tendenz hat, die "Aussenwelt" zunächst "erkenntnistheoretisch" in Nichtigkeit zu begraben um sie dann erst zu beweisen.'

that the inappropriate *formulation of the question* would not continue to stand.

Along with Dasein as Being-in-the-world, entities within-the-world have in each case already been disclosed. This existential-ontological assertion seems to accord with the thesis of *realism* that the external world is Really present-at-hand. In so far as this existential assertion does not deny that entities within-the-world are present-at-hand, it agrees—doxographically, as it were—with the thesis of realism in its results. But it differs in principle from every kind of realism; for realism holds that the Reality of the 'world' not only needs to be proved but also is capable of proof. In the existential assertion both of these positions are directly negated. But what distinguishes this assertion from realism altogether, is the fact that in realism there is a lack of ontological understanding. Indeed realism tries to explain Reality ontically by Real connections of interaction between things that are Real.

As compared with realism, *idealism*, no matter how contrary and untenable it may be in its results, has an advantage in principle, provided that it does not misunderstand itself as 'psychological' idealism. If idealism emphasizes that Being and Reality are only 'in the consciousness', this expresses an understanding of the fact that Being cannot be explained through entities. But as long as idealism fails to clarify what this very understanding of Being means ontologically, or how this understanding is possible, or that it belongs to Dasein's state of Being, the Interpretation of Reality which idealism constructs is an empty one. Yet the fact that Being cannot be explained through entities and that Reality is possible only in the understanding of Being, does not absolve us from inquiring into the Being of consciousness, of the *res cogitans* itself. If the idealist thesis is to be followed consistently, the ontological analysis of consciousness itself is prescribed as an inevitable prior task. Only because Being is 'in the consciousness'—that is to say, only because it is understandable in Dasein—can Dasein also understand and conceptualize such characteristics of Being as independence, the 'in-itself', and Reality in general. Only because of this are 'independent' entities, as encountered within-the-world, accessible to circumspection.

If what the term "idealism" says, amounts to the understanding that Being can never be explained by entities but is already that which is 'transcendental' for every entity, then idealism affords the only correct possibility for a philosophical problematic. If so, Aristotle was no less an idealist than Kant. But if "idealism" signifies tracing back every entity to a subject or consciousness whose sole distinguishing features are that it remains *indefinite* in its Being and is best characterized negatively as 'un-Thing-like', then this idealism is no less naïve in its method than the most grossly militant realism.

It is still possible that one may give the problematic of Reality *priority* over any orientation in terms of 'standpoints' by maintaining the thesis that every subject is what it is only for an Object, and *vice versa*. But in this formal approach the terms thus correlated—like the correlation itself —remain ontologically indefinite. At the bottom, however, the whole correlation necessarily gets thought of as 'somehow' *being*, and must therefore be thought of with regard to some definite idea of Being. Of course, if the existential-ontological basis has been made secure beforehand by exhibiting Being-in-the-world, then this correlation is one that we can know later as a formalized relation, ontologically undifferentiated.

Our discussion of the unexpressed presuppositions of attempts to solve the problem of Reality in ways which are just 'epistemological', shows that this problem must be taken back, as an ontological one, into the existential analytic of Dasein.[xvi]

(b) Reality as an Ontological Problem

If the term "Reality" is meant to stand for the Being of entities present-at-hand within-the-world (*res*) (and nothing else is understood thereby), then when it comes to analysing this mode of Being, this signifies that entities *within-the-world* are ontologically conceivable only if the pheno-menon of within-the-world-ness has been clarified. But within-the-world-ness is based upon the phenomenon of the *world*, which, for its part, as an essential item in the structure of Being-in-the-world, belongs to the basic constitution of Dasein. Being-in-the-world, in turn, is bound up onto-logically in the structural totality of Dasein's Being, and we have charac-terized care as such a totality. But in this way we have marked out the foundations and the horizons which must be clarified if an analysis of Reality is to be possible. Only in this connection, moreover, does the character of the "in-itself" become ontologically intelligible. By taking our orientation from this context of problems, we have in our earlier analyses Interpreted the Being of entities within-the-world.[xvii]

To be sure, the Reality of the Real can be characterized phenomen-ologically within certain limits without any explicit existential-ontological basis. This is what Dilthey has attempted in the article mentioned above. He holds that the Real gets experienced in impulse and will, and that Reality is *resistance*, or, more exactly, the character of resisting.[1] He then works out the phenomenon of resistance analytically. This is the positive contribution of his article, and provides the best concrete substantiation

---

[1] 'Realität ist *Widerstand*, genauer Widerständigkeit.'

for his idea of a 'psychology which both describes and dissects'. But he is kept from working out the analysis of this phenomenon correctly by the epistemological problematic of Reality. The 'principle of phenomenality' does not enable him to come to an ontological Interpretation of the Being of consciousness. 'Within the same consciousness,' he writes, 'the will and its inhibition emerge.'[xviii] What kind of Being belongs to this 'emerging'? What is the meaning of the Being of the 'within'? What relationship-of-Being does consciousness bear to the Real itself? All this must be determined ontologically. That this has not been done, depends ultimately on the fact that Dilthey has left 'life' standing in such a manner that it is ontologically undifferentiated; and of course 'life' is something which one cannot go back 'behind'. But to Interpret Dasein ontologically does not signify that we must go back ontically to some other entity. The fact that Dilthey has been refuted epistemologically cannot prevent us from making fruitful use of what is positive in his analyses—the very thing that has not been understood in such refutations.

Thus Scheler has recently taken up Dilthey's Interpretation of Reality.[xix] He stands for a 'voluntative theory of Dasein'. Here "Dasein" is understood in the Kantian sense as Being-present-at-hand. The 'Being of objects is given immediately only in the way it is related to drive and will'. Scheler not only emphasizes, as does Dilthey, that Reality is never primarily given in thinking and apprehending; he also points out particularly that cognition [Erkennen] itself is not judgment, and that knowing [Wissen] is a 'relationship of Being'.

What we have already said about the ontological indefiniteness of Dilthey's foundations holds in principle for this theory too. Nor can the fundamental ontological analysis of 'life' be slipped in afterwards as a substructure. Such a fundamental analysis provides the supporting conditions for the analysis of Reality—for the entire explication of the character of resisting and its phenomenal presuppositions. Resistance is encountered in a not-coming-through, and it is encountered as a hindrance to willing to come through. With such willing, however, something must already have been disclosed which one's drive and one's will *are out for*. But what they are out for is ontically indefinite, and this indefiniteness must not be overlooked ontologically or taken as if it were nothing. When Being-out-for-something comes up against resistance, and can do nothing but 'come up against it', it is itself already *alongside* a totality of involvements. But the fact that this totality has been discovered is grounded in the disclosedness of the referential totality of significance. *The experiencing of resistance—that is, the discovery of what is resistant to one's endeavours—is possible ontologically only by reason of the disclosedness of the world.* The character of resisting is one that belongs to entities with-the-world. Factically, experiences of resistance determine only the extent and the direction in which entities encountered within-the-world are discovered. The summation of such experiences does not introduce the disclosure of the world for the first time, but presupposes it. The 'against' and the 'counter to' as ontological possibilities, are supported by disclosed Being-in-the-world.

Nor is resistance experienced in a drive or will which 'emerges' in its own right. These both turn out to be modifications of care. Only entities with this kind of Being can come up against something resistant as something within-the-world. So if "Reality" gets defined as "the character of resisting", we must notice two things: first, that this is only *one* character of Reality among others; second, that the character of resisting presupposes necessarily a world which has already been disclosed. Resistance characterizes the 'external world' in the sense of entities within-the-world, but never in the sense of the world itself. *'Consciousness of Reality' is itself a way of Being-in-the-world.* Every 'problematic of the external world' comes back necessarily to this basic existential phenomenon.

If the *'cogito sum'* is to serve as the point of departure for the existential analytic of Dasein, then it needs to be turned around, and furthermore its content needs new ontologico-phenomenal confirmation. The *'sum'* is then asserted first, and indeed in the sense that "I am in a world". As such an entity, 'I am' in the possibility of Being towards various ways of comporting myself—namely, *cogitationes*—as ways of Being alongside entities within-the-world. Descartes, on the contrary, says that *cogitationes* are present-at-hand, and that in these an *ego* is present-at-hand too as a worldless *res cogitans*.

(c) Reality and Care

"Reality", as an ontological term, is one which we have related to entities within-the-world. If it serves to designate this kind of Being in general, then readiness-to-hand and presence-at-hand function as modes of Reality. If, however, one lets this world have its traditional signification, then it stands for Being in the sense of the pure presence-at-hand of Things. But not all presence-at-hand is the presence-at-hand of Things. The 'Nature' by which we are 'surrounded' is, of course, an entity within-the-world; but the kind of Being which it shows belongs neither to the ready-to-hand nor to what is present-at-hand as 'Things of Nature'. No matter how this Being of 'Nature' may be Interpreted, *all* the modes of Being of entities within-the-world are founded ontologically upon the worldhood of the world, and accordingly upon the phenomenon of Being-in-the world. From this there arises the insight that among the modes of

Being of entities within-the-world, Reality has no priority, and that Reality is a kind of Being which cannot even characterize anything like the world or Dasein in a way which is ontologically appropriate.

In the order of the ways in which things are connected in their onto-logical foundations and in the order of any possible categorial and existential demonstration, *Reality is referred back to the phenomenon of care.* But the fact that Reality is ontologically grounded in the Being of Dasein, does not signify that only when Dasein exists and as long as Dasein exists, can the Real be as that which in itself it is.

Of course only as long as Dasein *is* (that is, only as long as an under-standing of Being is ontically possible), 'is there' Being.[1] When Dasein does not exist, 'independence' 'is' not either, nor 'is' the 'in-itself'. In such a case this sort of thing can be neither understood nor not under-stood. In such a case even entities within-the-world can neither be dis-covered nor lie hidden. *In such a case* it cannot be said that entities are, nor can it be said that they are not. But *now*, as long as there is an under-standing of Being and therefore an understanding of presence-at-hand, it can indeed be said that *in this case* entities will still continue to be.

As we have noted, Being (not entities) is dependent upon the under-standing of Being; that is to say, Reality (not the Real) is dependent upon care. By this dependency our further analytic of Dasein is held secure in the face of an uncritical Interpretation which nevertheless keeps urging itself upon us—an Interpretation in which the idea of Reality is taken as the clue to Dasein. Only if we take our orientation from existentiality as Interpreted in an ontologically *positive* manner, can we have any guar-antee that in the factical course of the analysis of 'consciousness' or of 'life', some sense of "Reality" does not get made basic, even if it is one which has not been further differentiated.

Entities with Dasein's kind of Being cannot be conceived in terms of Reality and substantiality; we have expressed this by the thesis that *the substance of man is existence.* Yet if we have Interpreted existentiality as care, and distinguished this from Reality, this does not signify that our exist-ential analytic is at an end; we have merely allowed the intricate problems of the question of Being and its possible modes, and the question of the meaning of such modifications, to emerge more sharply: only if the under-standing of Being *is*, do entities as entities become accessible; only if

[1] '. . . "gibt es" Sein.' In his letter *Über den Humanismus* (Klostermann, Frankfurt A.M., n.d., p. 22, reprinted from *Platons Lehre von der Wahrheit*, Francke A.G., Bern, 1947), Heidegger insists that the expression 'es gibt' is here used deliberately, and should be taken literally as 'it gives'. He writes: 'For the "it" which here "gives" is Being itself. The "gives", however, designates the essence of Being, which gives and which confers its truth.' He adds that the 'es gibt' is used to avoid writing that 'Being is', for the verb 'is' is appropriate to entities but not to Being itself.

entities are of Dasein's kind of Being is the understanding of Being possible as an entity.

¶ 44. Dasein, Disclosedness, and Truth

From time immemorial, philosophy has associated truth and Being. Parmenides was the first to discover the Being of entities, and he 'identified' Being with the perceptive understanding of Being: τὸ γὰρ αὐτὸ νοεῖν ἐστίν τε καὶ εἶναι.[xx] Aristotle, in outlining the history of how the ἀρχαί have been uncovered,[xxi] emphasizes that the philosophers before him, under the guidance of 'the things themselves' have been compelled to inquire further: αὐτὸ τὸ πρᾶγμα ὡδοποίησεν αὐτοῖς καὶ συνηνάγκασε ζητεῖν.[xxii] He is describing the same fact when he says that ἀναγκαζόμενος δ'ἀκολουθεῖν τοῖς φαινομένοις[xxiii]—that he (Parmenides) was compelled to follow that which showed itself in itself. In another passage he remarks that these thinkers carried on their researches ὑπ' αὐτῆς τῆς ἀληθείας ἀναγκαζόμενοι[xxiv]—"compelled by the 'truth' itself". Aristotle describes these researches as φιλοσοφεῖν περὶ τῆς ἀληθείας[xxv]—" 'philosophizing' about the 'truth' "—or even as ἀποφαίνεσθαι περὶ τῆς ἀληθείας[xxvi]—as exhibiting something and letting it be seen with regard to the 'truth' and within the range of the 'truth'. Philosophy itself is defined as ἐπιστήμη τῆς ἀληθείας[xxvii]—"the science of the 'truth' ". But it is also characterized as ἐπιστήμη, ἣ θεωρεῖ τὸ ὄν ἧ ὄν[xxviii]—as "a science which contemplates entities as entities"—that is, with regard to their Being.

What is signified here by 'carrying on researches into the "truth" ', by "science of the 'truth' "? In such researches is 'truth' made a theme as it would be in a theory of knowledge or of judgment? Manifestly not, for 'truth' signifies the same as 'thing' ["Sache"], 'something that shows itself'. But what then does the expression 'truth' signify if it can be used as a term for 'entity' and 'Being'?

If, however, *truth* rightfully has a primordial connection with *Being*, then the phenomenon of truth comes within the range of the problematic of fundamental ontology. In that case, must not this phenomenon have been encountered already within our preparatory fundamental analysis, the analytic of Dasein? What ontico-ontological connection does 'truth' have with Dasein and with that ontical characteristic of Dasein which we call the "understanding of Being"? Can the reason why Being necessarily goes together with truth and *vice versa* be pointed out in terms of such understanding?

These questions are not to be evaded. Because Being does indeed 'go together' with truth, the phenomenon of truth has already been one of the themes of our earlier analyses, though not explicitly under this title. In giving precision to the problem of Being, it is now time to delimit the phenomenon of truth explicitly and to fix the problems which it comprises. In doing this, we should not just take together what we have previously taken apart. Our investigation requires a new approach.

Our analysis takes its departure from the *traditional conception of truth*, and attempts to lay bare the ontological foundations of that conception (*a*). In terms of these foundations the *primordial* phenomenon of truth becomes visible. We can then exhibit the way in which the traditional conception of truth has been *derived* from this *phenomenon* (*b*). Our investigation will make it plain that to the question of the 'essence' of truth, there belongs necessarily the question of the *kind of Being* which truth possesses. Together with this we must clarify the ontological meaning of the kind of talk in which we say that 'there is truth', and we must also clarify the kind of necessity with which 'we must presuppose' that 'there is' truth (*c*).

(*a*) *The Traditional Conception of Truth, and its Ontological Foundations*

There are three theses which characterize the way in which the essence of truth has been traditionally taken and the way it is supposed to have been first defined: (1) that the 'locus' of truth is assertion (judgment); (2) that the essence of truth lies in the 'agreement' of the judgment with its object; (3) that Aristotle, the father of logic, not only has assigned truth to the judgment as its primordial locus but has set going the definition of "truth" as 'agreement'.[1]

Here it is not our aim to provide a history of the concept of truth, which could be presented only on the basis of a history of ontology. We shall introduce our analytical discussions by alluding to some familiar matters.

Aristotle says that the παθήματα τῆς ψυχῆς are τῶν πραγμάτων ὁμοιώματα[xxix]—that the soul's 'Experiences', its νοήματα ('representations'), are likenings of Things. This assertion, which is by no means proposed as an explicit definition of the essence of truth, has also given occasion for developing the later formulation of the essence of truth as *adaequatio intellectus et rei*.[2] Thomas Aquinas,[xxx] who refers this definition to Avicenna (who, in turn, has taken it over from Isaac Israeli's tenth-century '*Book of Definitions*') also uses for "*adaequatio*" (likening) the terms "*correspondentia*" ("correspondence") and "*convenientia*" (" coming together").

---

[1] Here we follow the older editions in reading '. . . hat sowohl die Wahrheit dem Urteil als ihrem ursprünglichen Ort zugewiesen als auch die Definition der Wahrheit als "Übereinstimmung" in Gang gebracht.' The newer editions read '. . . hat sowohl . . . zugewiesen, er hat auch . . .'

[2] This is usually translated as 'adequation of the intellect and the thing'. Heidegger makes the connection seem closer by translating both the Latin *adaequatio* and the Greek ὁμοίωμα by the word 'Angleichung', which we have somewhat arbitrarily translated as 'likening'.

The neo-Kantian epistemology of the nineteenth century often characterized this definition of "truth" as an expression of a methodologically retarded naïve realism, and declared it to be irreconcilable with any formulation of this question which has undergone Kant's 'Copernican revolution'. But Kant too adhered to this conception of truth, so much so that he did not even bring it up for discussion; this has been overlooked, though Brentano has already called our attention to it. 'The old and celebrated question with which it was supposed that one might drive the logicians into a corner is this: *"what is truth?"* The explanation of the name of truth—namely, that it is the agreement of knowledge with its object—will here be granted and presupposed . . .'ˣˣˣⁱ.

'If truth consists in the agreement of knowledge with its object, then this object must thus be distinguished from others; for knowledge is false if it does not agree with the object to which it is related, even if it should contain something which might well be valid for other objects.'ˣˣˣⁱⁱ And in the introduction to the "Transcendental Dialectic" Kant states: 'Truth and illusion are not in the object so far as it is intuited, but in the judgment about it so far as it is thought.'ˣˣˣⁱⁱⁱ

Of course this characterization of truth as 'agreement', *adaequatio*, ὁμοίωσις, is very general and empty. Yet it will still have some justification if it can hold its own without prejudice to any of the most various Interpretations which that distinctive predicate "knowledge" will support. We are now inquiring into the foundations of this 'relation'. *What else is tacitly posited in this relational totality of the adaequatio intellectus et rei? And what ontological character does that which is thus posited have itself?*

What in general does one have in view when one uses the term 'agreement'? The agreement of something with something has the formal character of a relation of something to something. Every agreement, and therefore 'truth' as well, is a relation. But not every relation is an agreement. A sign points *at* what is indicated.[1] Such indicating is a relation, but not an agreement of the sign with what is indicated. Yet manifestly not every agreement is a *convenientia* of the kind that is fixed upon in the definition of "truth". The number "6" agrees with "16 minus 10". These numbers agree; they are equal with regard to the question of "how much?" Equality is *one* way of agreeing. Its structure is such that something like a 'with-regard-to' belongs to it. In the *adaequatio* something gets related; what is that with regard to which it agrees? In clarifying the 'truth-relation' we must notice also what is peculiar to the terms of this relation. With regard to what do *intellectus* and *res* agree? In their kind of Being and their essential content do they give us anything at all with

---

[1] 'Ein Zeichen zeigt *auf* das Gezeigte.'

regard to which they can agree? If it is impossible for *intellectus* and *res* to be equal because they are not of the same species, are they then perhaps similar? But knowledge is still supposed to 'give' the thing *just as* it is. This 'agreement' has the Relational character of the 'just as' ["So— Wie"]. In what way is this relation possible as a relation between *intellectus* and *res*? From these questions it becomes plain that to clarify the structure of truth it is not enough simply to presuppose this relational totality, but we must go back and inquire into the context of Being which provides the support for this totality as such.

Must we, however, bring up here the 'epistemological' problematic as regards the subject-Object relation, or can our analysis restrict itself to Interpreting the 'immanent consciousness of truth', and thus remain 'within the sphere' of the subject? According to the general opinion, what is true is knowledge. But knowledge is judging. In judgment one must distinguish between the judging as a *Real* psychical process, and that which is judged, as an *ideal* content. It will be said of the latter that it is 'true'. The Real psychical process, however, is either present-at-hand or not. According to this opinion, the ideal content of judgment stands in a relationship of agreement. This relationship thus pertains to a connection between an ideal content of judgment and the Real Thing as that which is judged *about*. Is this agreement Real or ideal in its kind of Being, or neither of these? *How are we to take ontologically the relation between an ideal entity and something that is Real and present-at-hand?* Such a relation indeed subsists [besteht]; and in factical judgments it subsists not only as a relation between the content of judgment and the Real Object, but likewise as a relation between the ideal content and the Real act of judgment. And does it manifestly subsist 'more inwardly' in this latter case?

Or is the ontological meaning of the relation between Real and ideal (μέθεξις) something about which we must not inquire? Yet the relation is to be one which *subsists*. What does such "subsisting" [Bestand] mean ontologically?

Why should this not be a legitimate question? Is it accidental that no headway has been made with this problem in over two thousand years? Has the question already been perverted in the very way it has been approached —in the ontologically unclarified separation of the Real and the ideal?

And with regard to the 'actual' judging of what is judged, is the separation of the Real act of judgment from the ideal content altogether unjustified? Does not the actuality of knowing and judging get broken asunder into two ways of Being—two 'levels' which can never be pieced together in such a manner as to reach the kind of Being that belongs to knowing? Is not psychologism correct in holding out against this separation, even if it neither clarifies ontologically the kind of Being which belongs to the thinking of that which is thought, nor is even so much as acquainted with it as a problem?

If we go back to the distinction between the act of judgment and its content, we shall not advance our discussion of the question of the kind of Being which belongs to the *adaequatio*; we shall only make plain the indispensability of clarifying the kind of Being which belongs to knowledge itself. In the analysis which this necessitates we must at the same time try to bring into view a phenomenon which is characteristic of knowledge— the phenomenon of truth. When does truth become phenomenally explicit in knowledge itself? It does so when such knowing demonstrates itself *as true*. By demonstrating itself it is assured of its truth. Thus in the phenomenal context of demonstration, the relationship of agreement must become visible.

Let us suppose that someone with his back turned to the wall makes the true assertion that 'the picture on the wall is hanging askew.' This assertion demonstrates itself when the man who makes it, turns round and perceives the picture hanging askew on the wall. What gets demonstrated in this demonstration? What is the meaning of "confirming" [Bewährung] such an assertion? Do we, let us say, ascertain some agreement between our 'knowledge' or 'what is known' and the Thing on the wall? Yes and no, depending upon whether our Interpretation of the expression 'what is known' is phenomenally appropriate. If he who makes the assertion judges without perceiving the picture, but 'merely represents' it to himself, to what is he related? To 'representations', shall we say? Certainly not, if "representation" is here supposed to signify representing, as a psychical process. Nor is he related to "representations" in the sense of what is thus "represented," if what we have in mind here is a 'picture' of that Real Thing which is on the wall.[1] The asserting which 'merely represents' is related rather, in that sense which is most its own, to the Real picture on the wall. What one has in mind is the Real picture, and nothing else. Any Interpretation in which something else is here slipped in as what one supposedly has in mind in an assertion that merely represents, belies the phenomenal facts of the case as to that about which the assertion gets made. Asserting is a way of Being towards the Thing itself that is.[2] And what does one's perceiving of it demonstrate? Nothing

1 'Er ist auch nicht auf Vorstellungen bezogen im Sinne des Vorgestellten, sofern damit gemeint wird ein "Bild" von dem realen Ding an der Wand.' While we follow tradition in translating 'Vorstellung' as 'representation', the literal meaning is somewhat closer to 'putting before us'. In this sense our 'picture' or 'image' ('Bild') of the actual picture ('Bild') on the wall, is itself something which we have 'put before us' and which is thus 'vorgestellt', though in English we would hardly call it 'that which we represent'.

2 'Das Aussagen ist ein Sein zum seienden Ding selbst.'

else than *that* this Thing *is* the very entity which one has in mind in one's assertion. What comes up for confirmation is that this entity is pointed out by the Being in which the assertion is made—which is Being towards what is put forward in the assertion; thus what is to be confirmed is *that* such Being *uncovers* the entity towards which it is. What gets demonstrated is the Being-uncovering of the assertion.[1] In carrying out such a demonstration, the knowing remains related solely to the entity itself. In this entity the confirmation, as it were, gets enacted. The entity itself which one has in mind shows itself *just as* it is in itself; that is to say, it shows that it, in its selfsameness, is just as *it* gets pointed out in the assertion as being—just as *it* gets uncovered as being. Representations do not get compared, either among themselves or in *relation* to the Real Thing. What is to be demonstrated is not an agreement of knowing with its object, still less of the psychical with the physical; but neither is it an agreement between 'contents of consciousness' among themselves. What is to be demonstrated is solely the Being-uncovered [Entdeckt-sein] of the entity itself—*that entity* in the "how" of its uncoveredness. This uncoveredness is confirmed when that which is put forward in the assertion (namely the entity itself) shows itself *as that very same thing.* *"Confirmation"* signifies *the entity's showing itself in its selfsameness.*[xxxiv] The confirmation is accomplished on the basis of the entity's showing itself. This is possible only in such a way that the knowing which asserts and which gets confirmed is, in its ontological meaning, itself a *Being towards* Real entities, and a Being that *uncovers.*

To say that an assertion *"is true"* signifies that it uncovers the entity as it is in itself. Such an assertion asserts, points out, 'lets' the entity 'be seen' (ἀπόφανσις) in its uncoveredness. The *Being-true* (*truth*) of the assertion must be understood as *Being-uncovering**. Thus truth has by no means the structure of an agreement between knowing and the object in the sense of a likening of one entity (the subject) to another (the Object).

Being-true as Being-uncovering*, is in turn ontologically possible only on the basis of Being-in-the-world. This latter phenomenon, which we have known as a basic state of Dasein, is the *foundation* for the primordial phenomenon of truth. We shall now follow this up more penetratingly.

---

[1] 'Ausgewiesen wird das Entdeckend-sein der Aussage.' Here and in the following pages we find the expression 'Entdeckend-sein' consistently printed with a hyphen in the more recent editions. In the older editions it is written sometimes as one word, sometimes as two, and it is hyphenated only at the ends of lines. In both editions we sometimes find this word printed with a lower-case initial. We have marked such cases with an asterisk; for while we prefer the translation 'Being-uncovering' in such cases, the lower-case initial suggests that 'to-be-uncovering' may be a better reading.

(b) *The Primordial Phenomenon of Truth and the Derivative Character of the Traditional Conception of Truth*

"Being-true" ("truth") means Being-uncovering*. But is not this a highly arbitrary way to define "truth"? By such drastic ways of defining this concept we may succeed in eliminating the idea of agreement from the conception of truth. Must we not pay for this dubious gain by plunging the 'good' old tradition into nullity? But while our definition is seemingly *arbitrary*, it contains only the *necessary* Interpretation of what was primordially surmised in the *oldest* tradition of ancient philosophy and even understood in a pre-phenomenological manner. If a λόγος as ἀπόφανσις is to be true, its Being-true is ἀληθεύειν in the manner of ἀποφαίνεσθαι —of taking entities out of their hiddenness and letting them be seen in their unhiddenness (their uncoveredness). The ἀλήθεια which Aristotle equates with πρᾶγμα and φαινόμενα in the passages cited above, signifies the 'things themselves'; it signifies what shows itself—*entities in the "how"* *of their uncoveredness.* And is it accidental that in one of the fragments of Heracleitusxxxv—the oldest fragments of philosophical doctrine in which the λόγος is *explicitly* handled—the phenomenon of truth in the sense of uncoveredness (unhiddenness), as we have set it forth, shows through? Those who are lacking in understanding are contrasted with the λόγος, and also with him who speaks that λόγος, and understands it. The λόγος is φράζων ὅπως ἔχει: it tells how entities comport themselves. But to those who are lacking in understanding, what they do remains hidden —λανθάνει. They forget it (ἐπιλανθάνονται); that is, for them it sinks back into hiddenness. Thus to the λόγος belongs unhiddenness— ἀ-λήθεια. To translate this word as 'truth', and, above all, to define this expression conceptually in theoretical ways, is to cover up the meaning of what the Greeks made 'self-evidently' basic for the terminological use of ἀλήθεια as a pre-philosophical way of understanding it.

In citing such evidence we must avoid uninhibited word-mysticism. Nevertheless, the ultimate business of philosophy is to preserve the *force of the most elemental words* in which Dasein expresses itself, and to keep the common understanding from levelling them off to that unintelligibility which functions in turn as a source of pseudo-problems.

We have now given a phenomenal demonstration of what we set forth earlierxxxvi as to λόγος and ἀλήθεια in, so to speak, a dogmatic Interpretation. In proposing our 'definition' of "truth" we have not *shaken off* the tradition, but we have *appropriated* it primordially; and we shall have done so all the more if we succeed in demonstrating that the idea of agreement is one to which theory had to come on the basis of the primordial phenomenon of truth, and if we can show how this came about.

Moreover, the 'definition' of "truth" as "uncoveredness" and as "Being-uncovering", it not a mere explanation of a word. Among those ways in which Dasein comports itself there are some which we are accustomed in the first instance to call 'true'; from the analysis of these our definition emerges.

Being-true as Being-uncovering*, is a way of Being for Dasein. What makes this very uncovering possible must necessarily be called 'true' in a still more primordial sense. *The most primordial phenomenon of truth is first shown by the existential-ontological foundations of uncovering.*

Uncovering is a way of Being for Being-in-the-world. Circumspective concern, or even that concern in which we tarry and look at something, uncovers entities within-the-world. These entities become that which has been uncovered. They are 'true' in a second sense. What is primarily 'true'—that is, uncovering—is Dasein. "Truth" in the second sense does not mean Being-uncovering* (uncovering), but Being-uncovered (uncoveredness).

Our earlier analysis of the worldhood of the world and of entities within-the-world has shown, however, that the uncoveredness of entities within-the-world is *grounded* in the world's disclosedness. But disclosedness is that basic character of Dasein according to which it *is* its "there". Disclosedness is constituted by state-of-mind, understanding, and discourse, and pertains equiprimordially to the world, to Being-in, and to the Self. In its very structure, care is *ahead of itself*—Being already in a world—as Being alongside entities within-the-world; and in this structure the disclosedness of Dasein lies hidden. *With* and *through* it is uncoveredness;[1] hence only with Dasein's *disclosedness* is the *most primordial* phenomenon of truth attained. What we have pointed out earlier with regard to the existential Constitution of the "there"[xxxvii] and in relation to the everyday Being of the "there",[xxxviii] pertains to the most primordial phenomenon of truth, nothing less. In so far as Dasein *is* its disclosedness essentially, and discloses and uncovers as something disclosed to this extent it is essentially 'true'. *Dasein is 'in the truth'*. This assertion has meaning ontologically. It does not purport to say that ontically Dasein is introduced 'to all the truth' either always or just in every case, but rather that the disclosedness of its ownmost Being belongs to its existential constitution.

If we accept the results we have obtained earlier, the full existential meaning of the principle that 'Dasein is in the truth' can be restored by the following considerations:

2'

---

[1] '*Mit* und *durch* sie ist Entdecktheit . . .' Our version reflects the ambiguity of the German, which leaves the grammatical function of the pronoun 'sie' obscure and permits it to refer either to 'the disclosedness of Dasein', to 'care', or—perhaps most likely—to 'the structure of care'.

(1) To Dasein's state of Being, *disclosedness in general* essentially belongs. It embraces the whole of that structure-of-Being which has become explicit through the phenomenon of care. To care belongs not only Being-in-the-world but also Being alongside entities within-the-world. The uncoveredness of such entities is equiprimordial with the Being of Dasein and its disclosedness.

(2) To Dasein's state of Being belongs *thrownness*; indeed it is constitutive for Dasein's disclosedness. In thrownness is revealed that in each case Dasein, as my Dasein and this Dasein, is already in a definite world and alongside a definite range of definite entities within-the-world.[1] Disclosedness is essentially factical.

(3) To Dasein's state of Being belongs *projection*—disclosive Being towards its potentiality-for-Being. As something that understands, Dasein *can* understand *itself* in terms of the 'world' and Others or in terms of its ownmost potentiality-for-Being.[2] The possibility just mentioned means that Dasein discloses itself to itself in and as its ownmost potentiality-for-Being. This *authentic* disclosedness shows the phenomenon of the most primordial truth in the mode of authenticity. The most primordial, and indeed the most authentic, disclosedness in which Dasein, as a potentiality-for-Being, can be, is the *truth of existence*. This becomes existentially and ontologically definite only in connection with the analysis of Dasein's authenticity.

(4) To Dasein's state of Being belongs *falling*. Proximally and for the most part Dasein is lost in its 'world'. Its understanding, as a projection upon possibilities of Being, has diverted itself thither. Its absorption in the "they" signifies that it is dominated by the way things are publicly interpreted. That which has been uncovered and disclosed stands in a mode in which it has been disguised and closed off by idle talk, curiosity, and ambiguity. Being towards entities has not been extinguished, but it has been uprooted. Entities have not been completely hidden; they are precisely the sort of thing that has been uncovered, but at the same time they have been disguised. They show themselves, but in the mode of semblance. Likewise what has formerly been uncovered sinks back again, hidden and disguised. *Because Dasein is essentially falling, its state of Being is such that it is in 'untruth'.* This term, like the expression 'falling', is here used ontologically. If we are to use it in existential analysis, we must

---

[1] 'In ihr enthüllt sich, dass Dasein je schon als meines und dieses in einer bestimmten Welt und bei einem bestimmten Umkreis von bestimmten innerweltlichen Seienden ist.'

[2] '. . . der Entwurf: das erschliessende Sein zu seinem Seinkönnen. Dasein *kann sich* als verstehendes aus der "Welt" und den Anderen her verstehen oder aus seinem eigensten Seinkönnen.' The earlier editions have a full stop after '*Entwurf*' rather than a colon, and introduce 'das' with a capital. The grammatical function of 'als verstehendes' seems ambiguous.

avoid giving it any ontically negative 'evaluation'. To be closed off and covered up belongs to Dasein's *facticity*. In its full existential-ontological meaning, the proposition that 'Dasein is in the truth' states equiprimordially that 'Dasein is in untruth'. But only in so far as Dasein has been disclosed has it also been closed off; and only in so far as entities within-the-world have been uncovered along with Dasein, have such entities, as possibly encounterable within-the-world, been covered up (hidden) or disguised.

It is therefore essential that Dasein should explicitly appropriate what has already been uncovered, defend it *against* semblance and disguise, and assure itself of its uncoveredness again and again. The uncovering of anything new is never done on the basis of having something completely hidden, but takes its departure rather from uncoveredness in the mode of semblance. Entities look as if . . . That is, they have, in a certain way, been uncovered already, and yet they are still disguised.

Truth (uncoveredness) is something that must always first be wrested from entities. Entities get snatched out of their hiddenness. The factical uncoveredness of anything is always, as it were, a kind of *robbery*. Is it accidental that when the Greeks express themselves as to the essence of truth, they use a *privative* expression—ἀ-λήθεια? When Dasein so expresses itself, does not a primordial understanding of its own Being thus make itself known—the understanding (even if it is only pre-ontological) that Being-in-untruth makes up an essential characteristic of Being-in-the-world?

The goddess of Truth who guides Parmenides, puts two pathways before him, one of uncovering, one of hiding; but this signifies nothing else than that Dasein is already both in the truth and in untruth. The way of uncovering is achieved only in κρίνειν λόγῳ—in distinguishing between these understandingly, and making one's decision for the one rather than the other.xxxix

The existential-ontological condition for the fact that Being-in-the-world is characterized by 'truth' and 'untruth', lies in that state of Dasein's Being which we have designated as *thrown projection*. This is something that is constitutive for the structure of care.

The upshot of our existential-ontological Interpretation of the phenomenon of truth is (1) that truth, in the most primordial sense, is Dasein's disclosedness, to which the uncoveredness of entities within-the-world belongs; and (2) that Dasein is equiprimordially both in the truth and in untruth.

Within the horizon of the traditional Interpretation of the phenomenon of truth, our insight into these principles will not be complete until it can

be shown: (1) that truth, understood as agreement, originates from disclosedness by way of definite modification; (2) that the kind of Being
which belongs to disclosedness itself is such that its derivative modification
first comes into view and leads the way for the theoretical explication of
the structure of truth.

Assertion and its structure (namely, the apophantical "as") are founded
upon interpretation and its structure (viz, the hermeneutical "as") and
also upon understanding—upon Dasein's disclosedness. Truth, however,
is regarded as a distinctive character of assertion as so derived. Thus the
roots of the truth of assertion reach back to the disclosedness of the understanding.[xi] But over and above these indications of how the truth of
assertion has originated, the phenomenon of *agreement* must not be
exhibited *explicitly* in its derivative character.

Our Being alongside entities within-the-world is concern, and this is
Being which uncovers. To Dasein's disclosedness, however, discourse
belongs essentially.[xii] Dasein expresses itself [spricht sich aus] : it expresses
itself as a Being-towards entities—a Being-towards which uncovers. And
in assertion it expresses itself as such about entities which have been
uncovered. Assertion communicates entities in the "how" of their uncoveredness. When Dasein is aware of the communication, it brings itself
in its awareness into an uncovering Being-towards the entities discussed.
The assertion which is expressed is about something, and in what it is
about [in ihrem Worüber] it contains the uncoveredness of these entities.
This uncoveredness is preserved in what is expressed. What is expressed
becomes, as it were, something ready-to-hand within-the-world which can
be taken up and spoken again.[1] Because the uncoveredness has been
preserved, that which is expressed (which thus is ready-to-hand) has in
itself a relation to any entities about which it is, an assertion. Any uncoveredness is an uncoveredness of something. Even when Dasein speaks
over again what someone else has said, it comes into a Being-towards the
very entities which have been discussed.[2] But it has been exempted from
having to uncover them again, primordially, and it holds that it has
been thus exempted.

Dasein need not bring itself face to face with entities themselves in an
'original' experience; but it nevertheless remains in a Being-towards these
entities. In a large measure uncoveredness gets appropriated not by one's
own uncovering, but rather by hearsay of something that has been said.

1 'Das Ausgesprochene wird gleichsam zu einem innerweltlich Zuhandenen, das
aufgenommen und weitergesprochen werden kann.' While we have followed our usual
policy in translating 'das Ausgesprochene' as 'what is expressed', it might perhaps be
translated as 'that which is spoken out', 'the utterance', or even 'the pronouncement'.

2 "Auch im Nachsprechen kommt das nachsprechende Dasein in ein Sein zum be-
sprochenen Seienden selbst.'

Absorption in something that has been said belongs to the kind of Being which the "they" possesses. That which has been expressed as such takes over Being-towards those entities which have been uncovered in the assertion. If, however, these entities are to be appropriated explicitly with regard to their uncoveredness, this amounts to saying that the assertion is to be demonstrated as one that uncovers. But the assertion expressed is something ready-to-hand, and indeed in such a way that, as something by which uncoveredness is preserved, it has in itself a relation to the entities uncovered. Now to demonstrate that it is something which uncovers [ihres Entdeckend-seins] means to demonstrate how the assertion by which the uncoveredness is preserved is related *to* these entities. The assertion is something ready-to-hand. The entities to which it is related as something that uncovers, are either ready-to-hand or present-at-hand within-the-world. The relation itself presents itself thus, as one that is present-at-hand. But this relation lies in the fact that the uncoveredness preserved in the assertion is in each case an uncoveredness o f something. The judgment 'contains something which holds for the objects' (Kant). But the relation itself now acquires the character of presence-at-hand by getting switched over to a relationship between things which are present-at-hand. The uncoveredness of something becomes the present-at-hand conformity of one thing which is present-at-hand—the assertion expressed—*to* something else which is present-at-hand—the entity under discussion. And if this conformity is seen only as a relationship between things which are present-at-hand—that is, if the kind of Being which belongs to the terms of this relationship has not been discriminated and is understood as something merely present-at-hand—then the relation shows itself as an agreement of two things which are present-at-hand, an agreement which is present-at-hand itself.

When the assertion has been expressed, the uncoveredness of the entity moves into [2] *the kind of Being of that which is ready-to-hand within-the-world.*[1] *But now to the extent that in this uncoveredness, as an uncoveredness o f something, a relationship to something present-at-hand persists, the uncoveredness* (*truth*) *becomes, for its part, a relationship between things which are present-at-hand* intellectus *and* res)—*a relationship that is present-at-hand itself.*

Though it is founded upon Dasein's disclosedness, the existential phenomenon of uncoveredness becomes a property which is present-at-hand but in which there still lurks a relational character; and as such a property, it gets broken asunder into a relationship which is present-at-hand. Truth as disclosedness and as a Being-towards uncovered entities—a

---

[1] '*Die Entdecktheit des Seienden rückt mit der Ausgesprochenheit der Aussage in die Seinsart des innerweltlich Zuhandenen.*'

Being which itself uncovers—has become truth as agreement between things which are present-at-hand within-the-world. And thus we have pointed out the ontologically derivative character of the traditional conception of truth.

Yet that which is last in the order of the way things are connected in their foundations existentially and ontologically, is regarded ontically and factically as that which is first and closest to us. The necessity of this Fact, however, is based in turn upon the kind of Being which Dasein itself possesses. Dasein, in its concernful absorption, understands itself in terms of what it encounters within-the-world. The uncoveredness which belongs to uncovering, is something that we come across proximally within-the-world in that which has been *ex*pressed [im *Aus*gesprochenen]. Not only truth, however, is encountered as present-at-hand: in general our understanding of Being is such that every entity is understood in the first instance as present-at-hand. If the 'truth' which we encounter proximally in an ontical manner is considered ontologically in the way that is closest to us, then the λόγος (the assertion) gets understood as λόγος τινός— as an assertion about something, an uncoveredness of something; but the phenomenon gets Interpreted as something present-at-hand with regard to its possible presence-at-hand.[1] Yet because presence-at-hand has been equated with the meaning of Being in general, the question of whether this kind of Being of truth is a primordial one, and whether there is anything primordial in that structure of it which we encounter as closest to us, can not come alive at all. *The primordial phenomenon of truth has been covered up by Dasein's very understanding of Being—that understanding which is proximally the one that prevails, and which even today has not been surmounted* explicitly *and in principle.*

At the same time, however, we must not overlook the fact that while this way of understanding Being (the way which is closest to us) is one which the Greeks were the first to develop as a branch of knowledge and to master, the primordial understanding of truth was simultaneously alive among them, even if pre-ontologically, and it even held its own against the concealment implicit in their ontology—at least in Aristotle.[xlii]

Aristotle never defends the thesis that the primordial 'locus' of truth is in the judgment. He says rather that the λόγος is that way of Being in which Dasein can *either* uncover *or* cover up. This *double possibility* is what is distinctive in the Being-true of the λόγος: the λόγος is that way of comporting oneself which can *also cover things up*. And because Aristotle never upheld the thesis we have mentioned, he was also never in a

---

[1] '. . . interpretiert aber das Phänomen als Vorhandenes auf seine mögliche Vorhandenheit.'

situation to 'broaden' the conception of truth in the λόγος to include pure νοεῖν. The truth of αἴσθησις and of the seeing of 'ideas' is the primordial kind of uncovering. And only because νόησις primarily uncovers, can the λόγος as διανοεῖν also have uncovering as its function.

Not only is it wrong to invoke Aristotle for the thesis that the genuine 'locus' of truth lies in the judgment; even in its content this thesis fails to recognize the structure of truth. Assertion is not the primary 'locus' of truth. *On the contrary,* whether as a mode in which uncoveredness is appropriated or as a way of Being-in-the-world, assertion is grounded in Dasein's uncovering, or rather in its *disclosedness.* The most primordial 'truth' is the 'locus' of assertion; it is the ontological condition for the possibility that assertions can be either true or false—that they may uncover or cover things up.

Truth, understood in the most primordial sense, belongs to the basic constitution of Dasein. The term signifies an *existentiale.* But herewith we have already sketched out our answers to the question of what kind of Being truth possesses, and to the question of in what sense it is necessary to presuppose that 'there is truth'.

(c) *The Kind of Being which Truth Possesses, and the Presupposition of Truth*

Dasein, as constituted by disclosedness, is essentially in the truth. Disclosedness is a kind of Being which is essential to Dasein. '*There is*' *truth only in so far as Dasein i s and so long as Dasein i s.* Entities are uncovered only *when* Dasein *is*; and only as long as Dasein *is*, are they disclosed. Newton's laws, the principle of contradiction, any truth whatever —these are true only as long as Dasein *is*. Before there was any Dasein, there was no truth; nor will there be any after Dasein is no more. For in such a case truth as disclosedness, uncovering, and uncoveredness, *cannot* be. Before Newton's laws were discovered, they were not 'true'; it does not follow that they were false, or even that they would become false if ontically no discoveredness were any longer possible. Just as little does this 'restriction' imply that the Being-true of 'truths' has in any way been diminished.

To say that before Newton his laws were neither true nor false, cannot signify that before him there were no such entities as have been uncovered and pointed out by those laws. Through Newton the laws became true; and with them, entities became accessible in themselves to Dasein. Once entities have been uncovered, they show themselves precisely as entities which beforehand already were. Such uncovering is the kind of Being which belongs to 'truth'.

That there are 'eternal truths' will not be adequately proved until someone has succeeded in demonstrating that Dasein has been and will be for all eternity. As long as such a proof is still outstanding, this principle remains a fanciful contention which does not gain in legitimacy from having philosophers commonly 'believe' it.

Because the kind of Being that is essential to truth is of the character of Dasein, all truth is relative to Dasein's Being. Does this relativity signify that all truth is 'subjective'? If one Interprets 'subjective' as 'left to the subject's discretion', then it certainly does not. For uncovering, in the sense which is most its own, takes asserting out of the province of 'subjective' discretion, and brings the uncovering Dasein face to face with the entities themselves. And only *because* 'truth', as uncovering, *is a kind of Being which belongs to Dasein*, can it be taken out of the province of *Dasein's* discretion. Even the 'universal validity' of truth is rooted solely in the fact that Dasein can uncover entities in themselves and free them. Only so can these entities in themselves be binding for every possible assertion—that is, for every way of pointing them out.[1] If truth has been correctly understood, is it in the least impaired by the fact that it is ontically possible only in the 'subject' and that it stands and falls with the Being of that 'subject'?

Now that we have an existential conception of the kind of Being that belongs to truth, the meaning of "presupposing the truth" also becomes intelligible. *Why must we presuppose that there is truth?* What is 'presupposing'? What do we have in mind with the 'must' and the 'we'? What does it mean to say 'there is truth'? 'We' presuppose truth because 'we', being in the kind of Being which Dasein possesses, *are* 'in the truth'. We do not presuppose it as something 'outside' us and 'above' us, towards which, along with other 'values', we comport ourselves. It is not we who presuppose 'truth'; but it is *'truth'* that makes it at all possible ontologically for us to be able to *be* such that we 'presuppose' anything at all. Truth is what first *makes possible* anything like presupposing.

What does it mean to 'presuppose'? It is to understand something as the ground for the Being of some other entity. Such understanding of an entity in its interconnections of Being, is possible only on the ground of disclosedness—that is, on the ground of Dasein's Being something which uncovers. Thus to presuppose 'truth' means to understand it as something for the sake of which Dasein i s. But Dasein is already ahead of itself in each case; this is implied in its state-of-Being as care. It is an entity for which, in its Being, its ownmost potentiality-for-Being is an issue. To Dasein's Being and its potentiality-for-Being as Being-in-the-world,

[1] 'Auch die "Allgemeingültigkeit" der Wahrheit ist lediglich verwurzelt, dass das Dasein Seiendes an ihm selbst entdecken und freigeben kann. Nur so vermag dieses Seiende an ihm selbst jede mögliche Aussage, das heisst Aufzeigung seiner, zu binden.'

disclosedness and uncovering belong essentially. To Dasein its potentiality-for-Being-in-the-world is an issue, and this includes[1] concerning itself with entities within-the-world and uncovering them circumspectively. In Dasein's state-of-Being as care, in Being-ahead-of-itself, lies the most primordial 'presupposing'. *Because this presupposing of itself belongs to Dasein's Being, 'we' must also presuppose 'ourselves' as having the attribute of disclosedness.* There are also entities with a character other than that of Dasein, but the 'presupposing' which lies in Dasein's Being does not relate itself to these; it relates itself solely to Dasein itself. The truth which has been pre-supposed, or the 'there is' by which its Being is to be defined, has that kind of Being—or meaning of Being—which belongs to Dasein itself. We must 'make' the presupposition of truth because it *is* one that has been 'made' already with the Being of the 'we'.

We *must* presuppose truth. Dasein itself, as in each case m y Dasein and this Dasein, *must* be; and in the same way the truth, as Dasein's dis-closedness, *must be*. This belongs to Dasein's essential thrownness into the world. *Has Dasein as itself ever decided freely whether it wants to come into 'Dasein' or not, and will it ever be able to make such a decision?* 'In itself' it is quite incomprehensible why entities are to be *uncovered*, why *truth* and *Dasein* must be. The usual refutation of that scepticism which denies either the Being of 'truth' or its cognizability, stops half way. What it shows, as a formal argument, is simply that if anything gets judged, truth has been presupposed. This suggests that 'truth' belongs to assertion—that pointing something out is, by its very meaning, an uncovering. But when one says this, *one has to clarify why* that in which there lies the onto-logical ground for this necessary connection between assertion and truth as regards their Being, must be as it is. The kind of Being which belongs to truth is likewise left completely obscure, and so is the meaning of presupposing, and that of its ontological foundation in Dasein itself. Moreover, one here fails to recognize that even when nobody *judges*, truth already gets presupposed in so far as Dasein i s at all.

A sceptic can no more be refuted than the Being of truth can be 'proved'. And if any sceptic of the kind who denies the truth, factically *is*, he does *not* even *need* to be refuted. In so far as he *is*, and has understood himself in this Being, he has obliterated Dasein in the desperation of suicide; and in doing so, he has also obliterated truth. Because Dasein, for its own part, cannot first be subjected to proof, the necessity of truth cannot be proved either. It has no more been demonstrated that there ever has 'been' an 'actual' sceptic[2] (though this is what has at bottom

---

[1] Reading 'und darin' with the newer editions. The older editions have 'd.h. u.a.'

[2] '. . . dass es je . . . einen "wirklichen" Skeptiker "gegeben" hat.' The older editions have 'nie' ('never') instead of 'je' ('ever').

been believed in the refutations of scepticism, in spite of what these undertake to do) than it has been demonstrated that there are any 'eternal
truths'. But perhaps such sceptics have been more frequent than one
would innocently like to have true when one tries to bowl over 'scepticism'
by formal dialectics.

Thus with the question of the Being of truth and the necessity of presupposing it, just as with the question of the essence of knowledge, an
'ideal subject' has generally been posited. The motive for this, whether
explicit or tacit, lies in the requirement that philosophy should have the
'*a priori*' as its theme, rather than 'empirical facts' as such. There is some
justification for this requirement, though it still needs to be grounded
ontologically. Yet is this requirement satisfied by positing an 'ideal
subject'? Is not such a subject *a fanciful idealization*? With such a conception have we not missed precisely the *a priori* character of that merely
'factual' subject, Dasein? Is it not an attribute of the *a priori* character of
the factical subject (that is, an attribute of Dasein's facticity) that it is in
the truth and in untruth equiprimordially?

The ideas of a 'pure "I"' and of a 'consciousness in general' are so far
from including the *a priori* character of 'actual' subjectivity that the ontological characters of Dasein's facticity and its state of Being are either
passed over or not seen at all. Rejection of a 'consciousness in general'
does not signify that the *a priori* is negated, any more than the positing
of an idealized subject guarantees that Dasein has an *a priori* character
grounded upon fact.

Both the contention that there are 'eternal truths' and the jumbling
together of Dasein's phenomenally grounded 'ideality' with an idealized
absolute subject, belong to those residues of Christian theology within
philosophical problematics which have not as yet been radically
extruded.

The Being of truth is connected primordially with Dasein. And only
because Dasein i s as constituted by disclosedness (that is, by understanding), can anything like Being be understood; only so is it possible
to understand Being.

Being (not entities) is something which 'there is' only in so far as truth
is. And truth *is* only in so far as and as long as Dasein is. Being and truth
'are' equiprimordially. What does it signify that Being 'is', where Being
is to be distinguished from every entity? One can ask this concretely only
if the meaning of Being and the full scope of the understanding of Being
have in general been clarified. Only then can one also analyse primordially
what belongs to the concept of a science *of Being as such*, and to its possibilities and its variations. And in demarcating this research and its

truth, the kind of research in which *entities* are uncovered, and its accompanying truth, must be defined ontologically.

The answer to the question of the meaning of Being has yet to be given [steht . . . aus]. What has our fundamental analysis of Dasein, as we have carried it out so far, contributed to working out this question? By laying bare the phenomenon of care, we have clarified the state of Being of that entity to whose Being something like an understanding of Being belongs. At the same time the Being of Dasein has thus been distinguished from modes of Being (readiness-to-hand, presence-at-hand, Reality) which characterize entities with a character other than that of Dasein. Understanding has itself been elucidated; and at the same time the methodological transparency of the procedure of Interpreting Being by understanding it and interpreting it, has thus been guaranteed.

If in care we have arrived at Dasein's primordial state of Being, then this must also be the basis for conceptualizing that understanding of Being which lies in care; that is to say, it must be possible to define the meaning of Being. But *is* the phenomenon of care one in which the most primordial existential-ontological state of Dasein is disclosed? And has the structural manifoldness which lies in this phenomenon, presented us with the most primordial totality of factical Dasein's Being? Has our investigation up to this point ever brought Dasein into view *as a whole*?

¶ 45. *The Outcome of the Preparatory Fundamental Analysis of Dasein, and the Task of a Primordial Existential Interpretation of this Entity*

WHAT have we gained by our preparatory analysis of Dasein, and what are we seeking? In Being-in-the-world, whose essential structures centre in disclosedness, we have *found* the basic state of the entity we have taken as our theme. The totality of Being-in-the-world as a structural whole has revealed itself as care. In care the Being of Dasein is included. When we came to analyse this Being, we took as our clue existence[i], which, in anticipation, we had designated as the essence of Dasein. This term "existence" formally indicates that Dasein *is* as an understanding potentiality-for-Being, which, in its Being, makes an issue of that Being itself. In every case, I myself am the entity which is in such a manner [dergestalt seiend]. By working out the phenomenon of care, we have given ourselves an insight into the concrete constitution of existence—that is, an insight into its equiprimordial connection with Dasein's facticity and its falling.

What we are *seeking* is the answer to the question about the meaning of Being in general, and, prior to that, the possibility of working out in a radical manner this basic question of all ontology. But to lay bare the horizon within which something like Being in general becomes intelligible, is tantamount to clarifying the possibility of having any understanding of Being at all—an understanding which itself belongs to the constitution of the entity called Dasein.[ii] The understanding of Being, however, cannot be *radically* clarified as an essential element in Dasein's Being, unless the entity to whose Being it belongs, has been Interpreted *primordially* in itself with regard to its Being.

Are we entitled to the claim that in characterizing Dasein ontologically *qua* care we have given a *primordial* Interpretation of this entity? By what criterion is the existential analytic of Dasein to be assessed as regards its

---

[1] 'Dasein und Zeitlichkeit'. In this heading and in others which follow in this Division, we have capitalized such words as 'temporal' and 'constitution' in accordance with normal practice in titles, even when this violates the orthographic conventions of our translation.

primordiality, or the lack of it? What, indeed, do we mean by the "*primordiality*" of an ontological Interpretation?

Ontological investigation is a possible kind of interpreting, which we have described as the working-out and appropriation of an understanding.[111] Every interpretation has its fore-having, its fore-sight, and its fore-conception. If such an interpretation, as Interpretation, becomes an explicit task for research, then the totality of these 'presuppositions' (which we call the "*hermeneutical Situation*") needs to be clarified and made secure beforehand, both in a basic experience of the 'object' to be disclosed, and in terms of such an experience. In ontological Interpretation an entity is to be laid bare with regard to its own state of Being; such an Interpretation obliges us first to give a phenomenal characterization of the entity we have taken as our theme, and thus to bring it into the scope of our fore-having, with which all the subsequent steps of our analysis are to conform. But at the same time these steps need to be guided by whatever fore-sight is possible as to the kind of Being which the entity may possess. Our fore-having and our fore-sight will then give us at the same time a sketch of that way of conceiving (or fore-conception) to the level of which all structures of Being are to be raised.

If, however, the ontological Interpretation is to be a *primordial* one, this not only demands that in general the hermeneutical Situation shall be one which has been made secure in conformity with the phenomena; it also requires explicit assurance that the *whole* of the entity which it has taken as its theme has been brought into the fore-having. Similarly, it is not enough just to make a first sketch of the Being of this entity, even if our sketch is grounded in the phenomena. If we are to have a fore-sight of Being, we must see it in such a way as not to miss the *unity* of those structural items which belong to it and are possible. Only then can the question of the meaning of the unity which belongs to the whole entity's totality of Being, be formulated and answered with any phenomenal assurance.

Has the existential analysis of Dasein which we have carried out, arisen from such a hermeneutical Situation as will guarantee the primordiality which fundamental ontology demands? Can we progress from the result we have obtained—that the being of Dasein is care—to the question of the primordial unity of this structural whole?

What is the status of the fore-sight by which our ontological procedure has hitherto been guided? We have defined the idea of existence as a potentiality-for-Being—a potentiality which understands, and for which its own Being is an issue. But this *potentiality-for-Being*, as one which is in each case *mine*, is free either for authenticity or for inauthenticity or for a mode in which neither of these has been differentiated.[iv] In starting with

average everydayness, our Interpretation has heretofore been confined to
the analysis of such existing as is either undifferentiated or inauthentic.
Of course even along this path, it was possible and indeed necessary to
reach a concrete determination of the existentiality of existence. Nevertheless, our ontological characterization of the constitution of existence
still lacked something essential. "Existence" means a potentiality-for-Being
—but also one which is authentic. As long as the existential structure
of an authentic potentiality-for-Being has not been brought into the
idea of existence, the fore-sight by which an *existential* Interpretation is
guided will lack primordiality.

And how about what we have had in advance in our hermeneutical
Situation hitherto? How about its fore-having? When and how has our
existential analysis received any assurance that by starting with everydayness, it has forced the *whole* of Dasein—this entity from its 'beginning' to
its 'end'—into the phenomenological view which gives us our theme?
We have indeed contended that care is the totality of the structural whole
of Dasein's constitution.ᵛ But have we not at the very outset of our Interpretation renounced the possibility of bringing Dasein into view as a whole?
Everydayness is precisely that Being which is 'between' birth and death.
And if existence is definitive for Dasein's Being and if its essence is constituted in part by potentiality-for-Being, then, as long as Dasein exists,
it must in each case, as such a potentiality, *not yet be* something. Any entity
whose Essence is made up of existence, is essentially opposed to the
possibility of our getting it in our grasp as an entity which is a
whole. Not only has the hermeneutical Situation hitherto given us no
assurance of 'having' the whole entity: one may even question whether
"having" the whole entity is attainable at all, and whether a primordial
ontological Interpretation of Dasein will not founder on the kind of Being
which belongs to the very entity we have taken as our theme.

One thing has become unmistakable: *our existential analysis of Dasein up
till now cannot lay claim to primordiality.* Its fore-having never included more
than the *inauthentic* Being of Dasein, and of Dasein as *less* than a *whole*
[*als unganzes*]. If the Interpretation of Dasein's Being is to become primordial, as a foundation for working out the basic question of ontology,
then it must first have brought to light existentially the Being of Dasein
in its possibilities of *authenticity* and *totality*.

Thus arises the task of putting Dasein as a whole into our fore-having.
This signifies, however, that we must first of all raise the question of this
entity's potentiality-for-Being-a-whole. As long as Dasein is, there is in
every case something still outstanding, which Dasein can be and will be.
But to that which is thus outstanding, the 'end' itself belongs. The 'end'

of Being-in-the-world is death. This end, which belongs to the poten†
iality-for-Being—that is to say, to existence—limits and determines i
every case whatever totality is possible for Dasein. If, however, Dasein'
Being-at-an-end[1] in death, and therewith its Being-a-whole, are to b
included in the discussion of its possibly *Being-a-whole*, and if this is to b
done in a way which is appropriate to the phenomena, then we must hav
obtained an ontologically adequate conception of death—that is to say
an *existential* conception of it. But as something of the character of Dasein
death *is* only in an existentiell *Being towards death* [*Sein zum Tode*]. Th
existential structure of such Being proves to be the ontologically constitu
tive state of Dasein's potentiality-for-Being-a-whole. Thus the whol
existing Dasein allows itself to be brought into our existential fore-having
But can Dasein also exist *authentically* as a whole? How is the authenticity
of existence to be determined at all, if not with regard to authenti
existing? Where do we get our criterion for this? Manifestly, Dasein
itself must, in its Being, present us with the possibility and the manner o
its authentic existence, unless such existence is something that can b
imposed upon it ontically, or ontologically fabricated. But an authentic
potentiality-for-Being is attested by the conscience. And conscience, as a
phenomenon of Dasein, demands, like death, a genuinely existentia
Interpretation. Such an Interpretation leads to the insight that Dasein has
an authentic potentiality-for-Being in that it *wants to have a conscience*. But
this is an existentiell possibility which tends, from the very meaning of its
Being, to be made definite in an existentiell way by Being-towards-death.

By pointing out that Dasein has an *authentic potentiality-for-Being-a-whole,*
the existential analytic acquires assurance as to the constitution of Dasein's
primordial Being. But at the same time the authentic potentiality-for-Being-
a-whole becomes visible as a mode of care. And therewith the phenomenally adequate ground for a primordial Interpretation of the meaning
of Dasein's Being has also been assured.

But the primordial ontological basis for Dasein's existentiality is *temporality*. In terms of temporality, the articulated structural totality of
Dasein's Being as care first becomes existentially intelligible. The Interpretation of the meaning of Dasein's Being cannot stop with this demonstration. The existential-temporal analysis of this entity needs to be
confirmed concretely. We must go back and lay bare in their temporal
meaning the ontological structures of Dasein which we have previously
obtained. Everydayness reveals itself as a mode of temporality. But by
thus recapitulating our preparatory fundamental analysis of Dasein, we

---

[1] 'Zu-Ende-sein'. This expression is to be distinguished from 'Sein-zum-Ende', which
we shall translate as 'Being-towards-the-end'.

will at the same time make the phenomenon of temporality itself more transparent. In terms of temporality, it then becomes intelligible why Dasein is, and can be, historical in the basis of its Being, and why, *as historical*, it can develop historiology.

If temporality makes up the primordial meaning of Dasein's Being, and if moreover this entity is one for which, in its Being, *this very Being* is an *issue*, then care must use 'time' and therefore must reckon with 'time'. 'Time-reckoning' is developed by Dasein's temporality. The 'time' which is experienced in such reckoning is that phenomenal aspect of temporality which is closest to us. Out of it arises the ordinary everyday understanding of time. And this understanding evolves into the traditional conception of time.

By casting light on the source of the 'time' 'in which' entities within-the-world are encountered—time as "within-time-ness"—we shall make manifest an essential possibility of the temporalizing of temporality.[1] Therewith the understanding prepares itself for an even more primordial temporalizing of temporality. In this[2] is grounded that understanding of Being which is constitutive for the Being of Dasein. Within the horizon of time the projection of a meaning of Being in general can be accomplished.

Thus the investigation comprised in the division which lies before us will now traverse the following stages: Dasein's possibility of Being-a-whole, and Being-towards-death (Chapter 1); Dasein's attestation of an authentic potentiality-for-Being, and resoluteness (Chapter 2); Dasein's authentic potentiality-for-Being-a-whole, and temporality as the ontological meaning of care (Chapter 3); temporality and everydayness (Chapter 4); temporality and historicality (Chapter 5); temporality and within-time-ness as the source of the ordinary conception of time (Chapter 6).[vi]

---

[1] 'Die Aufhellung des Ursprungs der "Zeit", "in der" innerweltliches Seiendes begegnet, der Zeit als Innerzeitigkeit, offenbart eine wesenhafte Zeitigungsmöglichkeit der Zeitlichkeit.' On 'zeitigen' see H. 304 below.

[2] 'In ihr . . .' It is not clear whether the pronoun 'ihr' refers to 'Zeitigung' ('temporalizing') or 'Zeitlichkeit' ('temporality').

I

DASEIN'S POSSIBILITY OF BEING-A-WHOLE, AND BEING-TOWARDS-DEATH

¶ *46. The Seeming Impossibility of Getting Dasein's Being-a-whole into our Grasp Ontologically and Determining its Character*

THE inadequacy of the hermeneutical Situation from which the preceding analysis of Dasein has arisen, must be surmounted. It is necessary for us to bring the whole Dasein into our fore-having. We must accordingly ask whether this entity, as something existing, can ever become accessible in its Being-a-whole. In Dasein's very state of Being, there are important reasons which seem to speak against the possibility of having it presented [Vorgabe] in the manner required.

The possibility of this entity's Being-a-whole is manifestly inconsistent with the ontological meaning of care, and care is that which forms the totality of Dasein's structural whole. Yet the primary item in care is the 'ahead-of-itself', and this means that in every case Dasein exists for the sake of itself. 'As long as it is', right to its end, it comports itself towards its potentiality-for-Being. Even when it still exists but has nothing more 'before it' and has 'settled [abgeschlossen] its account', its Being is still determined by the 'ahead-of-itself'. Hopelessness, for instance, does not tear Dasein away from its possibilities, but is only one of its own modes of *Being towards* these possibilities. Even when one is without Illusions and 'is ready *for* anything' ["Gefasstsein *auf* Alles"], here too the 'ahead-of-itself' lies hidden. The 'ahead-of-itself', as an item in the structure of care, tells us unambiguously that in Dasein there is always something *still outstanding*,[1] which, as a potentiality-for-Being for Dasein itself, has not yet become 'actual'. It is essential to the basic constitution of Dasein that there is *constantly something still to be settled* [*eine ständige Unabgeschlossenheit*]. Such a lack of totality signifies that there is something still outstanding in one's potentiality-for-Being.

[1] '. . . im Dasein immer noch etwas *aussteht* . . .' The verb 'ausstehen' and the noun 'Ausstand' (which we usually translate as 'something still outstanding', etc.), are ordinarily used in German to apply to a debt or a bank deposit which, from the point of view of the lender or depositor, has yet to be repaid to him, liquidated, or withdrawn.

But as soon as Dasein 'exists' in such a way that absolutely nothing more is still outstanding in it, then it has already for this very reason become "no-longer-Being-there" [Nicht-mehr-da-sein]. Its Being is annihilated when what is still outstanding in its Being has been liquidated. As long as Dasein *is* as an entity, it has never reached its 'wholeness'.[1] But if it gains such 'wholeness', this gain becomes the utter loss of Being-in-the-world. In such a case, it can never again be experienced *as an entity*.

The reason for the impossibility of experiencing Dasein ontically as a whole which is [als seiendes Ganzes], and therefore of determining its character ontologically in its Being-a-whole, does not lie in any imperfection of our *cognitive powers*. The hindrance lies rather in the *Being* of this entity. That which cannot ever *be such as* any experience which pretends to get Dasein in its grasp would claim, eludes in principle any possibility of getting experienced at all.[2] But in that case is it not a hopeless undertaking to try to discern in Dasein its ontological totality of Being?

We cannot cross out the 'ahead-of-itself' as an essential item in the structure of care. But how sound are the conclusions which we have drawn from this? Has not the impossibility of getting the whole of Dasein into our grasp been inferred by an argument which is merely formal? Or have we not at bottom inadvertently posited that Dasein is something present-at-hand, ahead of which something that is not yet present-at-hand is constantly shoving itself? Have we, in our argument, taken "Being-not-yet" and the 'ahead' in a sense that is genuinely *existential*? Has our talk of the 'end' and 'totality' been phenomenally appropriate to Dasein? Has the expression 'death' had a biological signification or one that is existential-ontological, or indeed any signification that has been adequately and surely delimited? Have we indeed exhausted all the possibilities for making Dasein accessible in its wholeness?

We must answer these questions before the problem of Dasein's totality can be dismissed as nugatory [nichtiges]. This question—both the existentiell question of whether a potentiality-for-Being-a-whole is possible, and the existential question of the state-of-Being of 'end' and 'totality'— is one in which there lurks the task of giving a positive analysis for some phenomena of existence which up till now have been left aside. In the centre of these considerations we have the task of characterizing ontologically Dasein's Being-at-an-end and of achieving an existential conception

---

[1] 'Die Behebung des Seinsausstandes besagt Vernichtung seines Seins. Solange das Dasein als Seiendes *ist*, hat es seine "Gänze" nie erreicht.' The verb 'beheben' is used in the sense of closing one's account or liquidating it by withdrawing money from the bank. The noun 'Gänze', which we shall translate as 'wholeness', is to be distinguished from 'Ganze' ('whole', or occasionally 'totality') and 'Ganzheit' ('totality').

[2] 'Was *so* gar nicht erst *sein* kann, *wie* ein Erfahren das Dasein zu erfassen prätendiert, entzieht sich grundsätzlich einer Erfahrbarkeit.'

of death. The investigations relating to these topics are divided up as follows: the possibility of experiencing the death of Others, and the possibility of getting a whole Dasein into our grasp (Section 47); that which is still outstanding, the end, and totality (Section 48); how the existential analysis of death is distinguished from other possible Interpretations of this phenomenon (Section 49); a preliminary sketch of the existential-ontological structure of death (Section 50); Being-towards-death and the everydayness of Dasein (Section 51); everyday Being-towards-death, and the full existential conception of death (Section 52); an existential projection of an authentic Being-towards-death (Section 53).

¶ *47. The Possibility of Experiencing the Death of Others, and the Possibility of Getting a Whole Dasein into our Grasp*

When Dasein reaches its wholeness in death, it simultaneously loses the Being of its "there". By its transition to no-longer-Dasein [Nichtmehr-dasein], it gets lifted right out of the possibility of experiencing this transition and of understanding it as something experienced. Surely this sort of thing is denied to any particular Dasein in relation to itself. But this makes the death of Others more impressive. In this way a termination [Beendigung] of Dasein becomes 'Objectively' accessible. Dasein can thus gain an experience of death, all the more so because Dasein is essentially Being with Others. In that case, the fact that death has been thus 'Objectively' given must make possible an ontological delimitation of Dasein's totality.

Thus from the kind of Being which Dasein possesses as Being with one another, we might draw the fairly obvious information that when the Dasein of Others has come to an end, it might be chosen as a substitute theme for our analysis of Dasein's totality. But does this lead us to our appointed goal?

Even the Dasein of Others, when it has reached its wholeness in death, is no-longer-Dasein, in the sense of Being-no-longer-in-the-world. Does not dying mean going-out-of-the-world, and losing one's Being-in-the-world? Yet when someone has died, his Being-no-longer-in-the-world (if we understand it in an extreme way) is still a Being, but in the sense of the Being-just-present-at-hand-and-no-more of a corporeal Thing which we encounter. In the dying of the Other we can experience that remarkable phenomenon of Being which may be defined as the change-over of an entity from Dasein's kind of Being (or life) to no-longer-Dasein. The *end* of the entity *qua* Dasein is the *beginning* of the same entity *qua* something present-at-hand.

However, in this way of Interpreting the change-over from Dasein to

Being-just-present-at-hand-and-no-more, the phenomenal content is missed, inasmuch as in the entity which still remains we are not presented with a mere corporeal Thing. From a theoretical point of view, even the corpse which is present-at-hand is still a possible object for the student of pathological anatomy, whose understanding tends to be oriented to the idea of life. This something which is just-present-at-hand-and-no-more is 'more' than a *lifeless* material Thing. In it we encounter something *unalive*, which has lost its life.[1]

But even this way of characterizing that which still remains [des Noch-verbleibenden] does not exhaust the full phenomenal findings with regard to Dasein.

The 'deceased' [Der "Verstorbene"] as distinct from the dead person [dem Gestorbenen], has been torn away from those who have 'remained behind' [den "Hinterbliebenen"], and is an object of 'concern' in the ways of funeral rites, interment, and the cult of graves. And that is so because the deceased, in his kind of Being, is 'still more' than just an item of equipment, environmentally ready-to-hand, about which one can be concerned. In tarrying alongside him in their mourning and commemoration, those who have remained behind *are with him*, in a mode of respectful solicitude. Thus the relationship-of-Being which one has towards the dead is not to be taken as a *concernful* Being-alongside something ready-to-hand.

In such Being-with the dead [dem Toten], the deceased *himself* is no longer factically 'there'. However, when we speak of "Being-with", we always have in view Being with one another in the same world. The deceased has abandoned our *'world'* and left it behind. But *in terms of that world* [Aus ihr her] those who remain can still *be with him*.

The greater the phenomenal appropriateness with which we take the no-longer-Dasein of the deceased, the more plainly is it shown that in such Being-with the dead, the authentic Being-come-to-an-end [Zuen-degekommensein] of the deceased is precisely the sort of thing which we do *not* experience. Death does indeed reveal itself as a loss, but a loss such as is experienced by those who remain. In suffering this loss, however, we have no way of access to the loss-of-Being as such which the dying man 'suffers'. The dying of Others is not something which we experience in a genuine sense; at most we are always just 'there alongside'.[2]

And even if, by thus Being there alongside, it were possible and feasible

---

[1] 'Das Nur-noch-Vorhandene ist "mehr" als ein *lebloses* materielles Ding. Mit ihm begegnet ein des Lebens verlustig gegangenes *Unlebendiges*.'

[2] '... sind ... "dabei".' Literally the verb 'dabeisein' means simply 'to be at that place', 'to be there alongside'; but it also has other connotations which give an ironical touch to this passage, for it may also mean, 'to be engaged in' some activity, 'to be at it', 'to be in the swim', 'to be ready to be "counted in"'.

for us to make plain to ourselves 'psychologically' the dying of Others
this would by no means let us grasp the way-to-be which we would ther
have in mind—namely, coming-to-an-end. We are asking about the
ontological meaning of the dying of the person who dies, as a possibility·
of-Being which belongs to *his* Being. We are not asking about the way in
which the deceased has Dasein-with or is still-a-Dasein [Nochdaseins]
with those who are left behind. If death as experienced in Others is what
we are enjoined to take as the theme for our analysis of Dasein's end and
totality, this cannot give us, either ontically or ontologically, what it
presumes to give.

But above all, the suggestion that the dying of Others is a substitute
theme for the ontological analysis of Dasein's totality and the settling of
its account, rests on a presupposition which demonstrably fails altogether¹
to recognize Dasein's kind of Being. This is what one presupposes when
one is of the opinion that any Dasein may be substituted for another at
random, so that what cannot be experienced in one's own Dasein is
accessible in that of a stranger. But is this presupposition actually so
baseless?

Indisputably, the fact that one Dasein *can be represented*² by another
belongs to its possibilities of Being in Being-with-one-another in the world.
In everyday concern, constant and manifold use is made of such representability. Whenever we go anywhere or have anything to contribute, we can
be represented by someone within the range of that 'environment' with
which we are most closely concerned. The great multiplicity of ways of
Being-in-the-world in which one person can be represented by another,
not only extends to the more refined modes of publicly being with one
another, but is likewise germane to those possibilities of concern which
are restricted within definite ranges, and which are cut to the measure of
one's occupation, one's social status, or one's age. But the very meaning
of such representation is such that it is always a representation 'in' ["in"
und "bei"] something—that is to say, in concerning oneself with something.
But proximally and for the most part everyday Dasein understands itself
in terms of that with *which* it is customarily concerned. 'One *is*' what one
does. In relation to this sort of Being (the everyday manner in which we
join with one another in absorption in the 'world' of our concern)
representability is not only quite possible but is even constitutive for our

---

¹ '. . . eine völlige Verkennung . . .' The older editions have 'totale' rather than
'völlige'.

² 'Vertretbarkeit'. The verb 'vertreten' means 'to represent' in the sense of 'deputizing'
for someone. It should be noted that the verb 'vorstellen' is also sometimes translated as
'to represent', but in the quite different sense of 'affording a "representation" or "idea"'
of something'.

being with one another. *Here* one Dasein can and must, within certain limits, '*be*' another Dasein.

However, this possibility of representing breaks down completely if the issue is one of representing that possibility-of-Being which makes up Dasein's coming to an end, and which, as such, gives to it its wholeness. *No one can take the Other's dying away from him.* Of course someone can 'go to his death for another'. But that always means to sacrifice oneself for the Other '*in some definite affair*'. Such "dying for" can never signify that the Other has thus had his death taken away in even the slightest degree. Dying is something that every Dasein itself must take upon itself at the time. By its very essence, death is in every case mine, in so far as it 'is' at all. And indeed death signifies a peculiar possibility-of-Being in which the very Being of one's own Dasein is an issue. In dying, it is shown that mineness and existence are ontologically constitutive for death.[1] Dying is not an event; it is a phenomenon to be understood existentially; and it is to be understood in a distinctive sense which must be still more closely delimited.

But if 'ending', as dying, is constitutive for Dasein's totality, then the Being of this wholeness itself must be conceived as an existential phenomenon of a Dasein which is in each case one's own. In 'ending', and in Dasein's Being-a-whole, for which such ending is constitutive, there is, by its very essence, no representing. These are the facts of the case existentially; one fails to recognize this when one interposes the expedient of making the dying of Others a substitute theme for the analysis of totality.

So once again the attempt to make Dasein's Being-a-whole accessible in a way that is appropriate to the phenomena, has broken down. But our deliberations have not been negative in their outcome; they have been oriented by the phenomena, even if only rather roughly. We have indicated that death is an existential phenomenon. Our investigation is thus forced into a purely existential orientation to the Dasein which is in every case one's own. The only remaining possibility for the analysis of death as dying, is either to form a purely *existential* conception of this phenomenon, or else to forgo any ontological understanding of it.

When we characterized the transition from Dasein to no-longer-Dasein as Being-no-longer-in-the-world, we showed further that *Dasein's* going-out-of-the-world in the sense of dying must be distinguished from the going-out-of-the-world of that which merely has life [des Nur-leben-den]. In our terminology the ending of anything that is alive, is denoted as "perishing" [Verenden]. We can see the difference only if the kind of ending which Dasein can have is distinguished from the end of a life.[11] Of course "dying" may also be taken physiologically and biologically.

But the medical concept of the *'exitus'* does not coincide with that of "perishing".

From the foregoing discussion of the ontological possibility of getting death into our grasp, it becomes clear at the same time that substructures of entities with another kind of Being (presence-at-hand or life) thrust themselves to the fore unnoticed, and threaten to bring confusion to the Interpretation of this phenomenon—even to the *first* suitable *way of presenting* it. We can encounter this phenomenon only by seeking, for our further analysis, an ontologically adequate way of defining the phenomena which are constitutive for it, such as "end" and "totality".

¶ *48. That which is Still Outstanding; the End; Totality*

Within the framework of this investigation, our ontological characterization of the end and totality can be only provisional. To perform this task adequately, we must not only set forth the *formal* structure of end in general and of totality in general; we must likewise disentangle the structural variations which are possible for them in different realms—that is to say, deformalized variations which have been put into relationship respectively with definite kinds of entities as 'subject-matter', and which have had their character Determined in terms of the Being of these entities. This task, in turn, presupposes that a sufficiently unequivocal and positive Interpretation shall have been given for the kinds of Being which require that the aggregate of entities be divided into such realms. But if we are to understand these ways of Being, we need a clarified idea of Being in general. The task of carrying out in an appropriate way the ontological analysis of end and totality breaks down not only because the theme is so far-reaching, but because there is a difficulty in principle: to master this task successfully, we must presuppose that precisely what we are seeking in this investigation—the meaning of Being in general—is something which we have found already and with which we are quite familiar.

In the following considerations, the 'variations' in which we are chiefly interested are those of end and totality; these are ways in which Dasein gets a definite character ontologically, and as such they should lead to a primordial Interpretation of this entity. Keeping constantly in view the existential constitution of Dasein already set forth, we must try to decide how inappropriate to Dasein ontologically are those conceptions of end and totality which first thrust themselves to the fore, no matter how   2 categorially indefinite they may remain. The rejection [Zurückweisung] of such concepts must be developed into a positive *assignment* [*Zuweisung*] of them to their specific realms. In this way our understanding of end and totality in their variant forms as *existentialia* will be strengthened, and this will guarantee the possibility of an ontological Interpretation of death. But even if the analysis of Dasein's end and totality takes on so broad an orientation, this cannot mean that the existential concepts of end and totality are to be obtained by way of a deduction. On the contrary, the existential meaning of Dasein's coming-to-an-end must be taken from Dasein itself, and we must show how such 'ending' can constitute *Being-a-whole* for the entity which *exists*.

We may formulate in three theses the discussion of death up to this point: 1. there belongs to Dasein, as long as it is, a "not-yet" which it will be—that which is constantly still outstanding; 2. the coming-to-its-end of what-is-not-yet-at-an-end (in which what is still outstanding is liquidated as regards its Being) has the character of no-longer-Dasein; 3. coming-to-an-end implies a mode of Being in which the particular Dasein simply cannot be represented by someone else.

In Dasein there is undeniably a constant 'lack of totality' which finds an end with death. This "not-yet" 'belongs' to Dasein as long as it is; this is how things stand phenomenally. Is this to be Interpreted as *still outstanding*?[1] With relation to what entities do we talk about that which is still outstanding? When we use this expression we have in view that which indeed 'belongs' to an entity, but is still missing. Outstanding, as a way of being missing, is grounded upon a belonging-to.[2] For instance, the remainder yet to be received when a debt is to be balanced off, is still outstanding. That which is still outstanding is not yet at one's disposal. When the 'debt' gets paid off, that which is still outstanding gets liquidated; this signifies that the money 'comes in', or, in other words, that the remainder comes successively along. By this procedure the "not-yet" gets filled up, as it were, until the sum that is owed is "all together".[3] Therefore, to be still outstanding means that what belongs together is not yet all together. Ontologically, this implies the un-readiness-to-hand of those portions which have yet to be contributed. These portions have the same kind of Being as those which are ready-to-hand already; and the latter, for their part, do not have their kind of Being modified by having the remainder come in. Whatever "lack-of-togetherness" remains [Das bestehende Unzusammen] gets "paid off" by a cumulative piecing-together. *Entities for which anything is still outstanding have the kind of Being of something*

---

[1] 'Aber darf der phänomenale Tatbestand, dass zum Dasein, solange es ist, dieses Noch-nicht "gehört", als *Ausstand* interpretiert werden?' The contrast between 'Tatbestand' and 'Ausstand' is perhaps intentional.

[2] Ausstehen als Fehlen gründet in einer Zugehörigkeit.'

[3] 'Tilgung der "Schuld" als Behebung des Ausstandes bedeutet das "Eingehen", das ist Nacheinanderankommen des Restes, wodurch das Noch-nicht gleichsam aufgefüllt wird, bis die geschuldete Summe "beisammen" ist.' On 'Schuld' see note 1, p. 325, H. 280.

ready-to-hand. The togetherness [Das Zusammen] is characterized as a "*sum*", and so is that lack-of-togetherness which is founded upon it.

But this lack-of-togetherness which belongs to such a mode of together-   2
ness—this being-missing as still-outstanding—cannot by any means define ontologically that "not-yet" which belongs to Dasein as its possible death. Dasein does not have at all the kind of Being of something ready-to-hand-within-the-world. The togetherness of an entity of the kind which Dasein is 'in running its course' until that 'course' has been completed, is not constituted by a 'continuing' piecing-on of entities which, somehow and somewhere, are ready-to-hand already in their own right.[1]

That Dasein should *be* together only when its "not-yet" has been filled up is so far from the case that it is precisely then that Dasein is no longer. Any Dasein always exists in just such a manner that its "not-yet" *belongs* to it. But are there not entities which are as they are and to which a "not-yet" can belong, but which do not necessarily have Dasein's kind of Being?

For instance, we can say, "The last quarter is still outstanding until the moon gets full". The "not-yet" diminishes as the concealing shadow disappears. But here the moon is always present-at-hand as a whole already. Leaving aside the fact that we can never get the moon *wholly* in our grasp even when it is full, this "not-yet" does not in any way signify a not-yet-*Being*-together of the parts which belongs to the moon, but pertains only to the way we *get it in our grasp* perceptually. The "not-yet" which belongs to Dasein, however, is not just something which is provisionally and occasionally inaccessible to one's own experience or even to that of a stranger; it 'is' not yet 'actual' at all. Our problem does not pertain to *getting into our grasp* the "not-yet' which is of the character of Dasein; it pertains to the possible *Being* or *not-Being* of this "not-yet". Dasein must, as itself, *become*—that is to say, *be*—what it is not yet. Thus if we are to be able, by comparison, to define that *Being of the "not-yet"* *which is of the character of Dasein*, we must take into consideration entities to whose kind of Being becoming belongs.

When, for instance, a fruit is unripe, it "goes towards" its ripeness. In this process of ripening, that which the fruit is not yet, is by no means pieced on as something not yet present-at-hand. The fruit brings itself to ripeness, and such a bringing of itself is a characteristic of its Being as a fruit. Nothing imaginable which one might contribute to it, would eliminate the unripeness of the fruit, if this entity did not come to ripeness *of its*

---

[1] Throughout this sentence Heidegger uses words derived from the verb 'laufen', 'to run'. Thus, 'in running its course' represents 'in seinem Verlauf', ' "its course" has been completed' represents 'es "seinem Lauf" vollendet hat'; 'continuing' represents 'fort-laufende'.

own accord. When we speak of the "not-yet" of the unripeness, we do not have in view something else which stands outside [aussenstehendes], and which—with utter indifference to the fruit—might be present-at-hand in it and with it. What we have in view is the fruit itself in its specific kind of Being. The sum which is not yet complete is, as something ready-to-hand, 'a matter of indifference' as regards the remainder which is lacking and un-ready-to-hand, though, taken strictly, it can neither be indifferent to that remainder nor not be indifferent to it.[1] The ripening fruit, however, not only is not indifferent to its unripeness as something other than itself, but it is that unripeness as it ripens. The "not-yet" has already been included in the very Being of the fruit, not as some random characteristic, but as something constitutive. Correspondingly, as long as any Dasein is, it too *is already its "not-yet"*.[iii]

That which makes up the 'lack of totality' in Dasein, the constant "ahead-of-itself", is neither something still outstanding in a summative togetherness, nor something which has not yet become accessible. It is a "not-yet" which any Dasein, as the entity which it is, has to be. Nevertheless, the comparison with the unripeness of the fruit shows essential differences, although there is a certain agreement. If we take note of these differences, we shall recognize how indefinite our talk about the end and ending has hitherto been.

Ripening is the specific Being of the fruit. It is also a kind of Being of the "not-yet" (of unripeness); and, as such a kind of Being, it is formally analogous to Dasein, in that the latter, like the former, *is* in every case already its "not-yet" in a sense still to be defined. But even then, this does not signify that ripeness as an 'end' and death as an 'end' coincide with regard to their ontological structure as ends. With ripeness, the fruit *fulfils* itself.[2] But is the death at which Dasein arrives, a fulfilment in this sense? With its death, Dasein has indeed 'fulfilled its course'. But in doing so, has it necessarily exhausted its specific possibilities? Rather, are not these precisely what gets taken away from Dasein? Even 'unfulfilled' Dasein ends. On the other hand, so little is it the case that Dasein comes to its ripeness only with death, that Dasein may well have passed its ripeness before the end.[3] For the most part, Dasein ends in unfulfilment, or else by having disintegrated and been used up.

---

[1] 'Die noch nicht volle Summe ist als Zuhandenes gegen den fehlenden unzuhand'enen Rest "gleichgültig". Streng genommen kann sie weder ungleichgültig, noch gleichgültig dagegen sein.'

[2] 'Mit der Reife *vollendet* sich die Frucht.' Notice that the verb 'vollenden', which we here translate as 'fulfil', involves the verb 'enden' ('to end'). While 'vollenden' may mean 'to bring fully to an end' or 'to terminate', it may also mean 'to complete' or 'to perfect'.

[3] While we have translated 'Reife' by its cognate 'ripeness', this word applies generally to almost any kind of maturity, even that of Dasein—not merely the maturity of fruits and vegetables.

Ending does not necessarily mean fulfilling oneself. It thus becomes more urgent to ask *in what sense, if any, death must be conceived as the ending of Dasein.*

In the first instance, "ending" signifies *"stopping"*, and it signifies this in senses which are ontologically different. The rain stops. It is no longer present-at-hand. The road stops. Such an ending does not make the road disappear, but such a stopping is determinative for the road as this one, which is present-at-hand. Hence ending, as stopping, can signify either "passing over into non-presence-at-hand" or else "Being-present-at-hand only when the end comes". The latter kind of ending, in turn, may either be determinative for something which is present-at-hand *in an unfinished way*, as a road breaks off when one finds it under construction; or it may rather constitute the 'finishedness" of something present-at-hand, as the painting is finished with the last stroke of the brush.

But ending as "getting finished" does not include fulfilling. On the other hand, whatever has got to be fulfilled must indeed reach the finishedness that is possible for it. Fulfilling is a mode of 'finishedness', and is founded upon it. Finishedness is itself possible only as a determinate form of something present-at-hand or ready-to-hand.

Even ending in the sense of "disappearing" can still have its modifications according to the kind of Being which an entity may have. The rain is at an end—that is to say it has disappeared. The bread is at an end— that is to say, it has been used up and is no longer available as something ready-to-hand.

By none of these modes of ending can death be suitably characterized as the "end" of Dasein. If dying, as Being-at-an-end, were understood in the sense of an ending of the kind we have discussed, then Dasein would thereby be treated as something present-at-hand or ready-to-hand. In death, Dasein has not been fulfilled nor has it simply disappeared; it has not become finished nor is it wholly at one's disposal as something ready-to-hand.

On the contrary, just as Dasein *is* already its "not-yet", and is its "not-yet" constantly as long as it is, it *is* already its end too. The "ending" which we have in view when we speak of death, does not signify Dasein's Being-at-an-end [Zu-Ende-sein], but a *Being-towards-the-end* [Sein zum Ende] of this entity. Death is a way to be, which Dasein takes over as soon as it is. "As soon as man comes to life, he is at once old enough to die.'[iv]

Ending, as Being-towards-the-end, must be clarified ontologically in terms of Dasein's kind of Being. And presumably the possibility of an existent Being of that "not-yet" which lies 'before' the 'end',[1] will become

---

[1] '. . . die Möglichkeit eines existierenden Seins des Noch-nicht, das "vor" dem "Ende" liegt . . .' The earlier editions have '. . . das ja "vor" dem "Ende" . . .'

intelligible only if the character of ending has been determined existentially. The existential clarification of Being-towards-the-end will also give us for the first time an adequate basis for defining what can possibly be the meaning of our talk about a totality of Dasein, if indeed this totality is to be constituted by death as the 'end'.

Our attempt to understand Dasein's totality by taking as our point of departure a clarification of the "not-yet" and going on to a characterization of "ending", has not led us to our goal. It has shown only *in a negative way* that the "not-yet" which Dasein in every case *is*, resists Interpretation as something still outstanding. The end *towards* which Dasein *is* as existing, remains inappropriately defined by the notion of a "Being-at-an-end". These considerations, however, should at the same time make it plain that they must be turned back in their course. A positive characterization of the phenomena in question (Being-not-yet, ending, totality) succeeds only when it is unequivocally oriented to Dasein's state of Being. But if we have any insight into the realms where those end-structures and totality-structures which are to be construed ontologically with Dasein belong, this will, in a negative way, make this unequivocal character secure against wrong turnings.

If we are to carry out a positive Interpretation of death and its character as an end, by way of existential analysis, we must take as our clue the basic state of Dasein at which we have already arrived—the phenomenon of care.

¶ *49. How the Existential Analysis of Death is Distinguished from Other Possible Interpretations of this Phenomenon*

The unequivocal character of our ontological Interpretation of death must first be strengthened by our bringing explicitly to mind what such an Interpretation can *not* inquire about, and what it would be vain to expect it to give us any information or instructions about.[1]

Death, in the widest sense, is a phenomenon of life. Life must be understood as a kind of Being to which there belongs a Being-in-the-world. Only if this kind of Being is oriented in a privative way to Dasein, can we fix its character ontologically. Even Dasein may be considered purely as life. When the question is formulated from the viewpoint of biology and physiology, Dasein moves into that domain of Being which we know as the world of animals and plants. In this field, we can obtain data and statistics about the longevity of plants, animals and men, and we do this by ascertaining them ontically. Connections between longevity, propagation, and

---

[1] '. . . wonach diese *nicht* fragen, und worüber eine Auskunft und Anweisung von ihr vergeblich erwartet werden kann.' The older editions have 'kann' after 'fragen', and 'muss' where the newer editions have 'kann'.

growth may be recognized. The 'kinds' of death, the causes, 'contrivances' and ways in which it makes its entry, can be explored.ᵛ

Underlying this biological-ontical exploration of death is a problematic that is ontological. We still have to ask how the ontological essence of death is defined in terms of that of life. In a certain way, this has always been decided already in the ontical investigation of death. Such investigations operate with preliminary conceptions of life and death, which have been more or less clarified. These preliminary conceptions need to be sketched out by the ontology of Dasein. Within the ontology of Dasein, which is *superordinate* to an ontology of life, the existential analysis of death is, in turn, *subordinate* to a characterization of Dasein's basic state. The ending of that which lives we have called 'perishing'. Dasein too 'has' its death, of the kind appropriate to anything that lives; and it has it, not in ontical isolation, but as codetermined by its primordial kind of Being. In so far as this is the case, Dasein too can end without authentically dying, though on the other hand, *qua* Dasein, it does not simply perish. We designate this intermediate phenomenon as its *"demise"*.[1] Let the term *"dying"* stand for that *way of Being* in which Dasein *is towards* its death.[2] Accordingly we must say that Dasein never perishes. Dasein, however, can demise only as long as it is dying. Medical and biological investigation into "demising" can obtain results which may even become significant ontologically if the basic orientation for an existential Interpretation of death has been made secure. Or must sickness and death in general—even from a medical point of view—be primarily conceived as existential phenomena?

The existential Interpretation of death takes precedence over any biology and ontology of life. But it is also the foundation for any investigation of death which is biographical or historiological, ethnological or psychological. In any 'typology' of 'dying', as a characterization of the conditions under which a demise is 'Experienced' and of the ways in which it is 'Experienced', the concept of death is already presupposed. Moreover, a psychology of 'dying' gives information about the 'living' of the person who is 'dying', rather than about dying itself. This simply reflects the fact that when Dasein dies—and even when it dies authentically —it does not have to do so with an Experience of its factical demising, or in such an Experience. Likewise the ways in which death is taken among

---

[1] *'Ableben'*. This term, which literally means something like 'living out' one's life, is used in ordinary German as a rather legalistic term for a person's death. We shall translate it as 'demise' (both as a noun and as a verb), which also has legalistic connotations. But this translation is an arbitrary one, and does not adequately express the meaning which Heidegger is explaining.

[2] '. . . *Seinsweise*, in der das Dasein *zu* seinem Tode *ist*.'

primitive peoples, and their ways of comporting themselves towards it in magic and cult, illuminate primarily the understanding of *Dasein*; but the Interpretation of this understanding already requires an existential analytic and a corresponding conception of death.

On the other hand, in the ontological analysis of Being-towards-the-end there is no anticipation of our taking any existential stand towards death. If "death" is defined as the 'end' of Dasein—that is to say, of Being-in-the-world—this does not imply any ontical decision whether 'after death' still another Being is possible, either higher or lower, or whether Dasein 'lives on' or even 'outlasts' itself and is 'immortal'. Nor is anything decided ontically about the 'other-worldly' and its possibility, any more than about the 'this-worldly';[1] it is not as if norms and rules for comporting oneself towards death were to be proposed for 'edification'. But our analysis of death remains purely 'this-worldly' in so far as it Interprets that phenomenon merely in the way in which it *enters into* any particular Dasein as a possibility of its Being. Only when death is conceived in its full ontological essence can we have any methodological assurance in even *asking* what *may be after death*; only then can we do so with meaning and justification. Whether such a question is a possible *theoretical* question at all will not be decided here. The this-worldly ontological Interpretation of death takes precedence over any ontical other-worldly speculation.

Finally, what might be discussed under the topic of a 'metaphysic of death' lies outside the domain of an existential analysis of death. Questions of how and when death 'came into the world', what 'meaning' it can have and is to have as an evil and affliction in the aggregate of entities—these are questions which necessarily presuppose an understanding not only of the character of Being which belongs to death, but of the ontology of the aggregate of entities as a whole, and especially of the ontological clarification of evil and negativity in general.

Methodologically, the existential analysis is superordinate to the questions of a biology, psychology, theodicy, or theology of death. Taken ontically, the results of the analysis show the peculiar *formality* and emptiness of any ontological characterization. However, that must not blind us to the rich and complicated structure of the phenomenon. If Dasein in general never becomes accessible as something present-at-hand, because Being-possible belongs in its own way to Dasein's kind of Being, even less may we expect that we can simply read off the ontological structure of death, if death is indeed a distinctive possibility of Dasein.

On the other hand, the analysis cannot keep clinging to an idea of death

[1] 'Über das "Jenseits" und seine Möglichkeit wird ebensowenig ontisch entschieden wie über das "Diesseits" . . .' The quotation marks around "Diesseits" appear only in the later editions.

which has been devised accidentally and at random. We can restrain this arbitrariness only by giving beforehand an ontological characterization of the kind of Being in which the 'end' enters into Dasein's average everydayness. To do so, we must fully envisage those structures of everydayness which we have earlier set forth. The fact that in an existential analysis of death, existentiell possibilities of Being-towards-death are consonant with it, is implied by the essence of all ontological investigation. All the more explicitly must the existential definition of concepts be unaccompanied by any existentiell commitments,[1] especially with relation to death, in which Dasein's character as possibility lets itself be revealed most precisely. The existential problematic aims only at setting forth the ontological structure of Dasein's Being-*towards*-the-end.[vi]

¶ *50. Preliminary Sketch of the Existential-ontological Structure of Death*

From our considerations of totality, end, and that which is still outstanding, there has emerged the necessity of Interpreting the phenomenon of death as Being-towards-the-end, and of doing so in terms of Dasein's basic state. Only so can it be made plain to what extent Being-a-whole, as constituted by Being towards-the-end, is possible in Dasein itself in conformity with the structure of its Being. We have seen that care is the basic state of Dasein. The ontological signification of the expression "care" has been expressed in the 'definition': "ahead-of-itself-Being-already-in (the world) as Being-alongside entities which we encounter (within-the-world)".[vii] In this are expressed the fundamental characteristics of Dasein's Being: existence, in the "ahead-of-itself"; facticity, in the "Being-already-in"; falling, in the "Being-alongside". If indeed death belongs in a distinctive sense to the Being of Dasein, then death (or Being-towards-the-end) must be defined in terms of these characteristics.

We must, in the first instance, make plain in a preliminary sketch how Dasein's existence, facticity, and falling reveal themselves in the phenomenon of death.

The Interpretation in which the "not-yet—and with it even the uttermost "not-yet", the end of Dasein—was taken in the sense of something still outstanding, has been rejected as inappropriate in that it included the ontological perversion of making Dasein something present-at-hand. Being-at-an-end implies existentially Being-towards-the-end. The uttermost "not-yet" has the character of something *towards which* Dasein *comports itself*. The end is impending [steht . . . bevor] for Dasein. Death is not something not yet present-at-hand, nor is it that which is ultimately

---

[1] 'Um so ausdrücklicher muss mit der existenzialen Begriffsbestimmung die existenzielle Unverbindlichkeit zusammengehen . . .'

still outstanding but which has been reduced to a minimum. *Death is something that stands before us—something impending.*[1]

However, there is much that can impend for Dasein as Being-in-the-world. The character of impendence is not distinctive of death. On the contrary, this Interpretation could even lead us to suppose that death must be understood in the sense of some impending event encountered environmentally. For instance, a storm, the remodelling of the house, or the arrival of a friend, may be impending; and these are entities which are respectively present-at-hand, ready-to-hand, and there-with-us. The death which impends does not have this kind of Being.

But there may also be impending for Dasein a journey, for instance, or a disputation with Others, or the forgoing of something of a kind which Dasein itself can be—its own possibilities of Being, which are based on its Being with Others.

Death is a possibility-of-Being which Dasein itself has to take over in every case. With death, Dasein stands before itself in its ownmost potentiality-for-Being. This is a possibility in which the issue is nothing less than Dasein's Being-in-the-world. Its death is the possibility of no-longer being-able-to-be-there.[2] If Dasein stands before itself as this possibility, it has been *fully* assigned to its ownmost potentiality-for-Being. When it stands before itself in this way, all its relations to any other Dasein have been undone.[3] This ownmost non-relational[4] possibility is at the same time the uttermost one.

As potentiality-for-Being, Dasein cannot outstrip the possibility of death. Death is the possibility of the absolute impossibility of Dasein. Thus death reveals itself as that *possibility which is one's ownmost, which is non-relational, and which is not to be outstripped* [*unüberholbare*]. As such, death is something *distinctively* impending. Its existential possibility is based on the fact that Dasein is essentially disclosed to itself, and disclosed, indeed, as ahead-of-itself. This item in the structure of care has its most primordial concretion in Being-towards-death. As a phenomonon, Being-towards-the-end

---

[1] '. . . sondern eher ein *Bevorstand.*' While we shall ordinarily use various forms of 'impend' to translate 'Bevorstand', 'bevorstehen', etc., one must bear in mind that the literal meaning of these expressions is one of 'standing before', so that they may be quite plausibly contrasted with 'Ausstehen', etc. ('standing out'). Thus we shall occasionally use forms of 'stand before' when this connotation seems to be dominant.

[2] 'Nicht-mehr-dasein-können.' Notice that the expressions 'Seinkönnen' (our 'potentiality-for-Being') and 'Nichtmehrdasein' (our 'no-longer-Dasein') are here fused. Cf. H. 237-242.

[3] 'So sich bevorstehend sind in ihm alle Bezüge zu anderem Dasein gelöst.'

[4] 'unbezügliche'. This term appears frequently throughout the chapter, and, as the present passage makes clear, indicates that in death Dasein is cut off from relations with others. The term has accordingly been translated as 'non-relational', in the sense of 'devoid of relationships'.

becomes plainer as Being towards that distinctive possibility of Dasein which we have characterized.

This ownmost possibility, however, non-relational and not to be outstripped, is not one which Dasein procures for itself subsequently and occasionally in the course of its Being. On the contrary, if Dasein exists, it has already been *thrown* into this possibility. Dasein does not, proximally and for the most part, have any explicit or even any theoretical knowledge of the fact that it has been delivered over to its death, and that death thus belongs to Being-in-the-world. Thrownness into death reveals itself to Dasein in a more primordial and impressive manner in that state-of-mind which we have called "anxiety".[viii] Anxiety in the face of death is anxiety 'in the face of' that potentiality-for-Being which is one's ownmost, non-relational, and not to be outstripped. That in the face of which one has anxiety is Being-in-the-world itself. That about which one has this anxiety is simply Dasein's potentiality-for-Being. Anxiety in the face of death must not be confused with fear in the face of one's demise. This anxiety is not an accidental or random mood of 'weakness' in some individual; but, as a basic state-of-mind of Dasein, it amounts to the disclosedness of the fact that Dasein exists as thrown Being *towards* its end. Thus the existential conception of "dying" is made clear as thrown Being towards its ownmost potentiality-for-Being, which is non-relational and not to be outstripped. Precision is gained by distinguishing this from pure disappearance, and also from merely perishing, and finally from the 'Experiencing' of a demise.[1]

Being-towards-the-end does not first arise through some attitude which occasionally emerges, nor does it arise as such an attitude; it belongs essentially to Dasein's thrownness, which reveals itself in a state-of-mind (mood) in one way or another. The factical 'knowledge' or 'ignorance' which prevails in any Dasein as to its ownmost Being-towards-the-end, is only the expression of the existentiell possibility that there are different ways of maintaining oneself in this Being. Factically, there are many who, proximally and for the most part, do not know about death; but this must not be passed off as a ground for proving that Being-towards-death does not belong to Dasein 'universally'. It only proves that proximally and for the most part Dasein covers up its ownmost Being-towards-death, fleeing *in the face* of it. Factically, Dasein is dying as long as it exists, but proximally and for the most part, it does so by way of *falling*. For factical existing is not only generally and without further differentiation a thrown potentiality-for-Being-in-the-world, but it has always likewise been absorbed in the 'world' of its concern. In this falling Being-alongside, fleeing from

[1] '. . . gegen ein "Erleben" des Ablebens.' (Cf. Section 49 above.)

uncanniness announces itself; and this means now, a fleeing in the face of one's ownmost Being-towards-death. Existence, facticity, and falling characterize Being-towards-the-end, and are therefore constitutive for the existential conception of death. *As regards its ontological possibility, dying is grounded in care.*

But if Being-towards-death belongs primordially and essentially to Dasein's Being, then it must also be exhibitable in everydayness, even if proximally in a way which is inauthentic.[1] And if Being-towards-the-end should afford the existential possibility of an existentiell Being-a-whole for Dasein, then this would give phenomenal confirmation for the thesis that "care" is the ontological term for the totality of Dasein's structural whole. If, however, we are to provide a full phenomenal justification for this principle, a *preliminary sketch* of the connection between Being-towards-death and care is not sufficient. We must be able to see this connection above all in that *concretion* which lies closest to Dasein—its everydayness.

¶ 51. *Being-towards-death and the Everydayness of Dasein*

In setting forth average everyday Being-towards-death, we must take our orientation from those structures of everydayness at which we have earlier arrived. In Being-towards-death, Dasein comports itself *towards itself* as a distinctive potentiality-for-Being. But the Self of everydayness is the "they".[ix] The "they" is constituted by the way things have been publicly interpreted, which expresses itself in idle talk.[2] Idle talk must accordingly make manifest the way in which everyday Dasein interprets for itself its Being-towards-death. The foundation of any interpretation is an act of understanding, which is always accompanied by a state-of-mind, or, in other words, which has a mood. So we must ask how Being-towards-death is disclosed by the kind of understanding which, with its state-of-mind, lurks in the idle talk of the "they". How does the "they" comport itself understandingly towards that ownmost possibility of Dasein, which is non-relational and is not to be outstripped? What state-of-mind discloses to the "they" that it has been delivered over to death, and in what way?

In the publicness with which we are with one another in our everyday manner, death is 'known' as a mishap which is constantly occurring—as a 'case of death'.[3] Someone or other 'dies', be he neighbour or stranger

---

[1] '. . . dann muss es auch—wenngleich zunächst uneigentlich—in der Alltäglichkeit aufweisbar sein.' The earlier editions have another 'auch' just before 'in der Alltäglichkeit'.

[2] '. . . das sich in der öffentlichen Ausgelegtheit konstituiert, die sich im Gerede ausspricht.' The earlier editions have '. . . konstituiert. Sie spricht sich aus im Gerede.'

[3] 'Die Öffentlichkeit des alltäglichen Miteinander "kennt" den Tod als ständig vorkommendes Begegnis, als "Todesfall".'

[Nächste oder Fernerstehende]. People who are no acquaintances of ours are 'dying' daily and hourly. 'Death' is encountered as a well-known event occurring within-the-world. As such it remains in the inconspicuousness[x] characteristic of what is encountered in an everyday fashion. The "they" has already stowed away [gesichert] an interpretation for this event. It talks of it in a 'fugitive' manner, either expressly or else in a way which is mostly inhibited, as if to say, "One of these days one will die too, in the end; but right now it has nothing to do with us."[1]

The analysis of the phrase 'one dies' reveals unambiguously the kind of Being which belongs to everyday Being-towards-death. In such a way of talking, death is understood as an indefinite something which, above all, must duly arrive from somewhere or other, but which is proximally *not yet present-at-hand* for oneself, and is therefore no threat. The expression 'one dies' spreads abroad the opinion that what gets reached, as it were, by death, is the "they". In Dasein's public way of interpreting, it is said that 'one dies', because everyone else and oneself can talk himself into saying that "in no case is it I myself", for this "one" is *the "nobody"*.[2] 'Dying' is levelled off to an occurrence which reaches Dasein, to be sure, but belongs to nobody in particular. If idle talk is always ambiguous, so is this manner of talking about death. Dying, which is essentially mine in such a way that no one can be my representative, is perverted into an event of public occurrence which the "they" encounters. In the way of talking which we have characterized, death is spoken of as a 'case' which is constantly occurring. Death gets passed off as always something 'actual'; its character as a possibility gets concealed, and so are the other two items that belong to it—the fact that it is non-relational and that it is not to be outstripped. By such ambiguity, Dasein puts itself in the position of losing itself in the "they" as regards a distinctive potentiality-for-Being which belongs to Dasein's ownmost Self. The "they" gives its approval, and aggravates the *temptation* to cover up from oneself one's ownmost Being-towards-death.[xi] This evasive concealment in the face of death dominates everydayness so stubbornly that, in Being with one another, the 'neighbours' often still keep talking the 'dying person' into the belief that he will escape death and soon return to the tranquillized everydayness of the world of his concern. Such 'solicitude' is meant to 'console' him. It insists upon bringing him back into Dasein, while in addition it helps him

---

[1] '. . . man stirbt am Ende auch einmal, aber zunächst bleibt man selbst unbetroffen.'

[2] 'Die öffentliche Daseinsauslegung sagt: "man stirbt", weil damit jeder andere und man selbst sich einreden kann: je nicht gerade ich; denn dieses Man ist das *Niemand*.' While we have usually followed the convention of translating the indefinite pronoun 'man' as 'one' and the expression 'das Man' as 'the "they" ', to do so here would obscure the point.

to keep his ownmost non-relational possibility-of-Being completely concealed. In this manner the "they" provides [besorgt] a *constant tranquilliza-*
tion about death. At bottom, however, this is a tranquillization not only for
him who is 'dying' but just as much for those who 'console' him. And even
in the case of a demise, the public is still not to have its own tranquillity
upset by such an event, or be disturbed in the carefreeness with which it
concerns itself.[1] Indeed the dying of Others is seen often enough as a
social inconvenience, if not even a downright tactlessness, against which
the public is to be guarded.[xii]

But along with this tranquillization, which forces Dasein away from its
death, the "they" at the same time puts itself in the right and makes
itself respectable by tacitly regulating the way in which *one* has to comport
oneself towards death. It is already a matter of public acceptance that
'thinking about death' is a cowardly fear, a sign of insecurity on the part
of Dasein, and a sombre way of fleeing from the world. *The "they" does*
not permit us the courage for anxiety in the face of death. The dominance of the
manner in which things have been publicly interpreted by the "they",
has already decided what state-of-mind is to determine our attitude
towards death. In anxiety in the face of death, Dasein is brought face to
face with itself as delivered over to that possibility which is not to be
outstripped. The "they" concerns itself with transforming this anxiety into
fear in the face of an oncoming event. In addition, the anxiety which has
been made ambiguous as fear, is passed off as a weakness with which no
self-assured Dasein may have any acquaintance. What is 'fitting' [Was
sich . . . "gehört"] according to the unuttered decree of the "they", is
indifferent tranquillity as to the 'fact' that one dies. The cultivation of
such a 'superior' indifference *alienates* Dasein from its ownmost non-
relational potentiality-for-Being.

But temptation, tranquillization, and alienation are distinguishing
marks of the kind of Being called "*falling*". As falling, everyday Being-
towards-death is a constant *fleeing in the face of death.* Being-*towards*-the-end
has the mode of *evasion in the face of it*—giving new explanations for it,
understanding it inauthentically, and concealing it. Factically one's own
Dasein is always dying already; that is to say, it is in a Being-towards-
its-end. And it hides this Fact from itself by recoining "death" as just a
"case of death" in Others—an everyday occurrence which, if need be,
gives us the assurance still more plainly that 'oneself' is still 'living'. But
in thus falling and fleeing *in the face of* death, Dasein's everydayness
attests that the very "they" itself already has the definite character of

---

[1] 'Und selbst im Falle des Ablebens noch soll die Öffentlichkeit durch das Ereignis
nicht in ihrer besorgten Sorglosigkeit gestört und beunruhigt werden.'

Being-towards-death, even when it is not explicitly engaged in 'thinking about death'. *Even in average everydayness, this ownmost potentiality-for-Being, which is non-relational and not to be outstripped, is constantly an issue for Dasein. This is the case when its concern is merely in the mode of an untroubled indifference* **towards** *the uttermost possibility of existence.*[1]

In setting forth everyday Being-towards-death, however, we are at the same time enjoined to try to secure a full existential conception of Being-towards-the-end, by a more penetrating Interpretation in which falling Being-towards-death is taken as an evasion *in the face of death. That in the face of which one flees* has been made visible in a way which is phenomenally adequate. Against this it must be possible to project phenomenologically the way in which evasive Dasein itself understands its death.[xiii]

¶ *52. Everyday Being-towards-the-end, and the Full Existential Conception of Death*

In our preliminary existential sketch, Being-towards-the-end has been defined as Being towards one's ownmost potentiality-for-Being, which is non-relational and is not to be outstripped. Being towards this possibility, as a Being which exists, is brought face to face with the absolute impossibility of existence. Beyond this seemingly empty characterization of Being-towards-death, there has been revealed the concretion of this Being in the mode of everydayness. In accordance with the tendency to falling, which is essential to everydayness, Being-towards-death has turned out to be an evasion in the face of death—an evasion which conceals. While our investigation has hitherto passed from a formal sketch of the ontological structure of death to the concrete analysis of everyday Being-towards-the-end, the direction is now to be reversed, and we shall arrive at the full existential conception of death by rounding out our Interpretation of everyday Being-towards-the-end.

In explicating everyday Being-towards-death we have clung to the idle talk of the "they" to the effect that "one dies too, sometime, but not right away."[2] All that we have Interpreted thus far is the 'one dies' as such. In the 'sometime, but not right away', everydayness concedes something like a *certainty* of death. Nobody doubts that one dies. On the other hand, this 'not doubting' need not imply that kind of Being-certain which corresponds to the way death—in the sense of the distinctive possibility characterized above—enters into Dasein. Everydayness confines itself to

---

[1] '. . . *wenn auch nur im Modus des Besorgens einer unbehelligten Gleichgültigkeit* **gegen** *die äusserste Möglichkeit seiner Existenz.*' Ordinarily the expression 'Gleichgültigkeit gegen' means simply 'indifference towards'. But Heidegger's use of boldface type suggests that here he also has in mind that 'gegen' may mean 'against' or 'in opposition to'.

[2] '. . . *man stirbt auch einmal, aber vorläufig noch nicht.*'

conceding the 'certainty' of death in this ambiguous manner just in order to weaken that certainty by covering up dying still more and to alleviate its own thrownness into death.

By its very meaning, this evasive concealment in the face of death can *not* be *authentically* 'certain' of death, and yet it *is* certain of it. What are we to say about the 'certainty of death'?

To be certain of an entity means to *hold* it for true as something true.[1] But "truth" signifies the uncoveredness of some entity, and all uncoveredness is grounded ontologically in the most primordial truth, the disclosedness of Dasein.[xiv] As an entity which is both disclosed and disclosing, and one which uncovers, Dasein is essentially 'in the truth'. *But certainty is grounded in the truth, or belongs to it equiprimordially.* The expression 'certainty', like the term 'truth', has a double signification. Primordially "truth" means the same as "Being-disclosive", as a way in which Dasein behaves. From this comes the derivative signification: "the uncoveredness of entities". Correspondingly, "certainty", in its primordial signification, is tantamount to "Being-certain", as a kind of Being which belongs to Dasein. However, in a derivative signification, any entity of which Dasein can be certain will also get called something 'certain'.

One mode of certainty is *conviction*. In conviction, Dasein lets the testimony of the thing itself which has been uncovered (the true thing itself) be the sole determinant for its Being towards that thing understandingly.[2] Holding something for true is adequate as a way of maintaining oneself in the truth, if it is grounded in the uncovered entity itself, and if, as Being towards the entity so uncovered, it has become transparent to itself as regards its appropriateness to that entity. In any arbitrary fiction or in merely having some 'view' ["Ansicht"] about an entity, this sort of thing is lacking.

The adequacy of holding-for-true is measured according to the truth-claim to which it belongs. Such a claim gets its justification from the kind of Being of the entity to be disclosed, and from the direction of the disclosure. The kind of truth, and along with it, the certainty, varies with the way entities differ, and accords with the guiding tendency and extent of the disclosure. Our present considerations will be restricted to an

---

[1] 'Eines Seienden gewiss-sein besagt: es als wahres für wahr *halten.*' The earlier editions have 'Gewisssein' instead of 'gewiss-sein'. Our literal but rather unidiomatic translation of the phrase 'für wahr halten' seems desirable in view of Heidegger's extensive use of the verb 'halten' ('hold') in subsequent passages where this phrase occurs, though this is obscured by our translating 'halten sich in . . .' as 'maintain itself in . . .' and 'halten sich an . . .' as 'cling to . . .' or 'stick to . . .'.

[2] 'In ihr lässt sich das Dasein einzig durch das Zeugnis der entdeckten (wahre) Sache selbst sein verstehendes Sein zu dieser bestimmen.' The connection between 'Überzeugung' ('conviction') and 'Zeugnis' (testimony) is obscured in our translation.

analysis of Being-certain with regard to death; and this Being-certain will in the end present us with a distinctive *certainty of Dasein*.

For the most part, everyday Dasein covers up the ownmost possibility of its Being—that possibility which is non-relational and not to be outstripped. This factical tendency to cover up confirms our thesis that Dasein, as factical, is in the 'untruth'.^{xv} Therefore the certainty which belongs to such a covering-up of Being-towards-death must be an inappropriate way of holding-for-true, and not, for instance, an uncertainty in the sense of a doubting. In inappropriate certainty, that of which one is certain is held covered up. If 'one' understands death as an event which one encounters in one's environment, then the certainty which is related to such events does not pertain to Being-towards-the-end.

They say, "It is certain that 'Death' is coming."[1] *They* say it, and the "they" overlooks the fact that in order to be able to be certain of death, Dasein itself must in every case be certain of its ownmost non-relational potentiality-for-Being. They say, "Death is certain"; and in saying so, they implant in Dasein the illusion that it is *itself* certain of its death. And what is the ground of everyday Being-certain? Manifestly, it is not just mutual persuasion. Yet the 'dying' of Others is something that one experiences daily. Death is an undeniable 'fact of experience'.

The way in which everyday Being-towards-death understands the certainty which is thus grounded, betrays itself when it tries to 'think' about death, even when it does so with critical foresight—that is to say, in an appropriate manner. So far as one knows, all men 'die'. Death is probable in the highest degree for everyman, yet it is not 'unconditionally' certain. Taken strictly, a certainty which is 'only' *empirical* may be attributed to death. Such certainty necessarily falls short of the highest certainty, the apodictic, which we reach in certain domains of theoretical knowledge.

In this 'critical' determination of the certainty of death, and of its impendence, what is manifested in the first instance is, once again, a failure to recognize Dasein's kind of Being and the Being-towards-death which belongs to Dasein—a failure that is characteristic of everydayness. *The fact that demise, as an event which occurs, is 'only' empirically certain, is in no way decisive as to the certainty of death.* Cases of death may be the factical occasion for Dasein's first paying attention to death at all. So long, however, as Dasein remains in the empirical certainty which we have mentioned, death, in the way that it 'is', is something of which Dasein can by no means become certain. Even though, in the publicness of the "they", Dasein

---

[1] 'Man sagt: es ist gewiss, dass "der" Tod kommt.'

seems to 'talk' only of this 'empirical' certainty of death, *neverthaess at bottom* Dasein does *not* exclusively or primarily stick to those cases of death which merely occur. *In evading its death,* even everyday Being-towards-the-end is indeed certain of its death in another way than it might itself like to have true on purely theoretical considerations. This 'other way' is what everydayness for the most part veils from itself. Everydayness does not dare to let itself become transparent in such a manner. We have already characterized the every-day state-of-mind which consists in an air of superiority with regard to the certain 'fact' of death—a superiority which is 'anxiously' concerned while seemingly free from anxiety. In this state-of-mind, everydayness acknowledges a 'higher' certainty than one which is only empirical. One *knows* about the certainty of death, and yet 'is' not authentically certain of one's own. The falling everydayness of Dasein is acquainted with death's certainty, and yet evades *Being*-certain. But in the light of what it evades, this very evasion attests phenomenally that death must be conceived as one's ownmost possibility, non-relational, not to be outstripped, and—above all—*certain.*

One says, "Death certainly comes, but not right away". With this 'but . . .', the "they" denies that death is certain. 'Not right away' is not a purely negative assertion, but a way in which the "they" interprets itself. With this interpretation, the "they" refers itself to that which is proximally accessible to Dasein and amenable to its concern. Everydayness forces its way into the urgency of concern, and divests itself of the fetters of a weary 'inactive thinking about death'. Death is deferred to 'sometime later', and this is done by invoking the so-called 'general opinion' ["allgemeine Ermessen"]. Thus the "they" covers up what is peculiar in death's certainty—*that it is possible at any moment.* Along with the certainty of death goes the *indefiniteness* of its "when". Everyday Being-towards-death evades this indefiniteness by conferring definiteness upon it. But such a procedure cannot signify calculating when the demise is due to arrive. In the face of definiteness such as this, Dasein would sooner flee. Everyday concern makes definite for itself the indefiniteness of certain death by interposing before it those urgencies and possibilities which can be taken in at a glance, and which belong to the everyday matters that are closest to us.

But when this indefiniteness has been covered up, the certainty has been covered up too. Thus death's ownmost character as a possibility gets veiled—a possibility which is certain and at the same time indefinite—that is to say, possible at any moment.

Now that we have completed our Interpretation of the everyday manner in which the "they" talks about death and the way death enters into Dasein, we have been led to the characters of certainty and indefinite-ness. The full existential-ontological conception of death may now be defined as follows: *death, as the end of Dasein, is Dasein's ownmost possibility—non-relational, certain and as such indefinite, not to be outstripped. Death is,* as *Dasein's* end, in the Being of this entity *towards* its end.

Defining the existential structure of Being-towards-the-end helps us to work out a kind of Being of Dasein in which Dasein, *as Dasein,* can be a *whole.* The fact that even everyday Dasein already *is towards* its end—that is to say, is constantly coming to grips with its death, though in a 'fugitive' manner—shows that this end, conclusive [abschliessende] and determina-tive for Being-a-whole, is not something to which Dasein ultimately comes only in its demise. In Dasein, as being towards its death, its own utter-most "not-yet" has already been included—that "not-yet" which all others lie ahead of.[1] So if one has given an ontologically inappropriate Interpretation of Dasein's "not-yet" as something still outstanding, any formal inference from this to Dasein's lack of totality will not be correct. *The phenomenon of the "not-yet" has been taken over from the "ahead-of-itself"; no more than the care-structure in general, can it serve as a higher court which would rule against the possibility of an existent Being-a-whole; indeed this "ahead-of-itself" is what first of all makes such a Being-towards-the-end possible.* The problem of the possible Being-a-whole of that entity which each of us is, is a correct one if care, as Dasein's basic state, is 'connected' with death —the uttermost possibility for that entity.

Meanwhile, it remains questionable whether this problem has been as yet adequately worked out. Being-towards-death is grounded in care. Dasein, as thrown Being-in-the-world, has in every case already been delivered over to its death. In being towards its death, Dasein is dying factically and indeed constantly, as long as it has not yet come to its demise. When we say that Dasein is factically dying, we are saying at the same time that in its Being-towards-death Dasein has always decided itself in one way or another. Our everyday falling evasion *in the face of* death is an *inauthentic* Being-*towards*-death. But inauthenticity is based on the pos-sibility of authenticity.[xvi] Inauthenticity characterizes a kind of Being into which Dasein can divert itself and has for the most part always diverted itself; but Dasein does not necessarily and constantly have to divert itself into this kind of Being. Because Dasein exists, it determines its

---

[1] '. . . dem alle anderen vorgelagert sind . . .' This clause is ambiguous, both in the German and in our translation, though the point is fairly clear. The ultimate 'not-yet' is not one which all others 'lie ahead of' in the sense that they lie beyond it or come after it; for nothing can 'lie ahead of it' in this sense. But they *can* 'lie ahead of it' in the sense that they might be actualized *before* the ultimate 'not-yet' has been actualized. (Contrast this passage with H. 302, where the same participle 'vorgelagert' is apparently applied in the *former* sense to death itself.)

own character as the kind of entity it is, and it does so in every case in terms of a possibility which it itself *is* and which it understands.[1]

Can Dasein also *understand authentically* its ownmost possibility, which is non-relational and not to be outstripped, which is certain and, as such, indefinite? That is, can Dasein maintain itself in an authentic Being-towards-its-end? As long as this authentic Being-towards-death has not been set forth and ontologically defined, there is something essentially lacking in our existential Interpretation of Being-towards-the-end.

Authentic Being-towards-death signifies an existentiell possibility of Dasein. This ontical potentiality-for-Being must, in turn, be ontologically possible. What are the existential conditions of this possibility? How are they themselves to become accessible?

¶ *53. Existential Projection of an Authentic Being-towards-death*

Factically, Dasein maintains itself proximally and for the most part in an inauthentic Being-towards-death. How is the ontological possibility of an *authentic* Being-towards-death to be characterized 'Objectively', if, in the end, Dasein never comports itself authentically towards its end, or if, in accordance with its very meaning, this authentic Being must remain hidden from the Others? Is it not a fanciful undertaking, to project the existential possibility of so questionable an existentiell potentiality-for-Being? What is needed, if such a projection is to go beyond a merely fictitious arbitrary construction? Does Dasein itself give us any instructions for carrying it out? And can any grounds for its phenomenal legitimacy be taken from Dasein itself? Can our analysis of Dasein up to this point give us any prescriptions for the ontological task we have now set ourselves, so that what we have before us may be kept on a road of which we can be sure?

The existential conception of death has been established; and therewith we have also established what it is that an authentic Being-towards-the-end should be able to comport itself towards. We have also characterized inauthentic Being-towards-death, and thus we have prescribed in a negative way [prohibitiv] how it is possible for authentic Being-towards-death *not* to be. It is with these positive and prohibitive instructions that the existential edifice of an authentic Being-towards-death must let itself be projected.

Dasein is constituted by disclosedness—that is, by an understanding with a state-of-mind. *Authentic* Being-towards-death can *not evade* its ownmost non-relational possibility, or *cover up* this possibility by thus fleeing

---

[1] 'Weil das Dasein existiert, bestimmt es sich als Seiendes, wie es ist, je aus einer Möglichkeit, die es selbst *ist* und versteht.'

from it, or *give a new explanation* for it to accord with the common sense of the "they". In our existential projection of an authentic Being-towards-death, therefore, we must set forth those items in such a Being which are constitutive for it as an understanding of death—and as such an understanding in the sense of Being towards this possibility without either fleeing it or covering it up.

In the first instance, we must characterize Being-towards-death as a *Being towards a possibility*—indeed, towards a distinctive possibility of Dasein itself. "Being towards" a possibility—that is to say, towards something possible—may signify "Being out for" something possible, as in concerning ourselves with its actualization. Such possibilities are constantly encountered in the field of what is ready-to-hand and present-at-hand—what is attainable, controllable, practicable, and the like. In concernfully Being out for something possible, there is a tendency to *annihilate the possibility* of the possible by making it available to us. But the concernful actualization of equipment which is ready-to-hand (as in producing it, getting it ready, readjusting it, and so on) is always merely relative, since even that which has been actualized is still characterized in terms of some involvements—indeed this is precisely what characterizes its Being. Even though actualized, it remains, as actual, something possible for doing something; it is characterized by an "in-order-to". What our analysis is to make plain is simply how Being out for something concernfully, comports itself towards the possible: it does so not by the theoretico-thematical consideration of the possible as possible, and by having regard for its possibility as such, but rather by looking *circum*-spectively *away* from the possible and looking at that for which it is possible [das Wofür-möglich].

Manifestly Being-towards-death, which is now in question, cannot have the character of concernfully Being out to get itself actualized. For one thing, death as possible is not something possible which is ready-to-hand or present-at-hand, but a possibility of *Dasein's* Being. So to concern oneself with actualizing what is thus possible would have to signify, "bringing about one's demise". But if this were done, Dasein would deprive itself of the very ground for an existing Being-towards-death.

Thus, if by "Being towards death" we do not have in view an 'actualizing' of death, neither can we mean "dwelling upon the end in its possibility". This is the way one comports oneself when one 'thinks about death', pondering over when and how this possibility may perhaps be actualized. Of course such brooding over death does not fully take away from it its character as a possibility. Indeed, it always gets brooded over as something that is coming; but in such brooding we weaken it by calculating how we are to have it at our disposal. As something possible, it is to show as little as possible of its possibility. On the other hand, if Being-towards-death has to disclose understandingly the possibility which we have characterized, and if it is to disclose it *as a possibility*, then in such Being-towards-death this possibility must not be weakened: it must be understood *as a possibility*, it must be cultivated *as a possibility*, and we must *put up with* it *as a possibility*, in the way we comport ourselves towards it.

However, Dasein comports itself towards something possible in its possibility by *expecting* it [im *Erwarten*]. Anyone who is intent on something possible, may encounter it unimpeded and undiminished in its 'whether it comes or does not, or whether it comes after all'.[1] But with this pheno-menon of expecting, has not our analysis reached the same kind of Being towards the possible to which we have already called attention in our description of "Being out for something" concernfully? To expect some-thing possible is always to understand it and to 'have' it with regard to whether and when and how it will be actually present-at-hand. Expecting is not just an occasional looking-away from the possible to its possible actualization, but is essentially a *waiting for that actualization* [ein *Warten auf diese*]. Even in expecting, one leaps away from the possible and gets a foothold in the actual. It is for its actuality that what is expected is expected. By the very nature of expecting, the possible is drawn into the actual, arising out of the actual and returning to it.[2]

But Being towards this possibility, as Being-towards-death, is so to comport ourselves towards *death* that in this Being, and for it, death reveals itself *as a possibility*. Our terminology for such Being towards this possibility is *"anticipation"* of *this possibility*.[3] But in this way of behaving does there not lurk a coming-close to the possible, and when one is close to the possible, does not its actualization emerge? In this kind of coming close, however, one does not tend towards concernfully making available something actual; but as one comes closer understandingly, the pos-sibility of the possible just becomes 'greater'. *The closest closeness which one may have in Being towards death as a possibility, is as far as possible from anything*

---

[1] 'Für ein Gespanntsein auf es vermag ein Mögliches in seinem "ob oder nicht oder schliesslich doch" ungehindert und ungeschmälert zu begegnen.'

[2] 'Auch im Erwarten liegt ein Abspringen vom Möglichen und Fussfassen im Wirk-lichen, dafür das Erwartete erwartet ist. Vom Wirklichen aus und auf es zu wird das Mögliche in das Wirkliche erwartungsmässig hereingezogen.'

[3] '. . . *Vorlaufen in die Möglichkeit*.' While we have used 'anticipate' to translate 'vor-greifen', which occurs rather seldom, we shall also use it—less literally—to translate 'vorlaufen', which appears very often in the following pages, and which has the special connotation of 'running ahead'. But as Heidegger's remarks have indicated, the kind of 'anticipation' which is involved in Being-towards-death, does not consist in 'waiting for' death or 'dwelling upon it' or 'actualizing' it before it normally comes; nor does 'running ahead into it' in this sense mean that we 'rush headlong into it'.

actual. The more unveiledly this possibility gets understood, the more purely does the understanding penetrate into it *as the possibility of the impossibility of any existence at all.* Death, as possibility, gives Dasein nothing to be 'actualized', nothing which Dasein, as actual, could itself *be.* It is the possibility of the impossibility of every way of comporting oneself towards anything, of every way of existing. In the anticipation of this possibility it becomes 'greater and greater'; that is to say, the possibility reveals itself to be such that it knows no measure at all, no more or less, but signifies the possibility of the measureless impossibility of existence. In accordance with its essence, this possibility offers no support for becoming intent on something, 'picturing' to oneself the actuality which is possible, and so forgetting its possibility. Being-towards-death, as anticipation of possibility, is what first *makes* this possibility *possible,* and sets it free as possibility.

Being-towards-death is the anticipation of a potentiality-for-Being of that entity whose kind of Being is anticipation itself.[1] In the anticipatory revealing of this potentiality-for-Being, Dasein discloses itself to itself as regards its uttermost possibility. But to project itself on its ownmost potentiality-for-Being means to be able to understand itself in the Being of the entity so revealed—namely, to exist. Anticipation turns out to be the possibility of understanding one's *ownmost* and uttermost potentiality-for-Being—that is to say, the possibility of *authentic existence.* The ontological constitution of such existence must be made visible by setting forth the concrete structure of anticipation of death. How are we to delimit this structure phenomenally? Manifestly, we must do so by determining those characteristics which must belong to an anticipatory disclosure so that it can become the pure understanding of that ownmost possibility which is non-relational and not to be outstripped—which is certain and, as such, indefinite. It must be noted that understanding does not primarily mean just gazing at a meaning, but rather understanding oneself in that potentiality-for-Being which reveals itself in projection.[xvii]

Death is Dasein's *ownmost* possibility. Being towards this possibility discloses to Dasein its *ownmost* potentiality-for-Being, in which its very Being is the issue. Here it can become manifest to Dasein that in this distinctive possibility of its own self, it has been wrenched away from the "they". This means that in anticipation any Dasein can have wrenched itself away from the "they" already. But when one understands that this is something which Dasein 'can' have done, this only reveals its factical lostness in the everydayness of the they-self.

---

[1] '. . . dessen Seinsart das Vorlaufen selbst ist.' The earlier editions have 'hat' instead of 'ist'.

The ownmost possibility is *non-relational*. Anticipation allows Dasein to understand that that potentiality-for-being in which its ownmost Being is an issue, must be taken over by Dasein alone. Death does not just 'belong' to one's own Dasein in an undifferentiated way; death *lays claim* to it as an *individual* Dasein. The non-relational character of death, as understood in anticipation, individualizes Dasein down to itself. This individualizing is a way in which the 'there' is disclosed for existence. It makes manifest that all Being-alongside the things with which we concern ourselves, and all Being-with Others, will fail us when our ownmost potentiality-for-Being is the issue. Dasein can be *authentically itself* only if it makes this possible for itself of its own accord. But if concern and solicitude fail us, this does not signify at all that these ways of Dasein have been cut off from its authentically Being-its-Self. As structures essential to Dasein's constitution, these have a share in conditioning the possibility of any existence whatsoever. Dasein is authentically itself only to the extent that, *as* concernful Being-alongside and solicitous Being-with, it projects itself upon its ownmost potentiality-for-Being rather than upon the possibility of the they-self. The entity which anticipates its non-relational possibility, is thus forced by that very anticipation into the possibility of taking over from itself its ownmost Being, and doing so of its own accord.

The ownmost, non-relational possibility is *not to be outstripped*. Being towards this possibility enables Dasein to understand that giving itself up impends for it as the uttermost possibility of its existence. Anticipation, however, unlike inauthentic Being-towards-death, does not evade the fact that death is not to be outstripped; instead, anticipation frees itself *for* accepting this. When, by anticipation, one becomes free *for* one's own death, one is liberated from one's lostness in those possibilities which may accidentally thrust themselves upon one; and one is liberated in such a way that for the first time one can authentically understand and choose among the factical possibilities lying ahead of that possibility which is not to be outstripped.[1] Anticipation discloses to existence that its uttermost possibility lies in giving itself up, and thus it shatters all one's tenaciousness to whatever existence one has reached. In anticipation, Dasein guards itself against falling back behind itself, or behind the potentiality-for-Being which it has understood. It guards itself against 'becoming too old for its victories' (Nietzsche). Free for its ownmost possibilities, which are determined by the *end* and so are understood as *finite* [*endliche*], Dasein dispels the danger that it may, by its own finite understanding of existence, fail to recognize that it is getting outstripped by the existence-possibilities of Others, or rather that it may explain these possibilities wrongly and

---

[1] '. . . die der unüberholbaren vorgelagert sind.' See note 1, p. 303, H. 259 above.

force them back upon its own, so that it may divest itself of its ownmost factical existence. As the non-relational possibility, death individualizes —but only in such a manner that, as the possibility which is not to be out-stripped, it makes Dasein, as Being-with, have some understanding of the potentiality-for-Being of Others. Since anticipation of the possibility which is not to be outstripped discloses also all the possibilities which lie ahead of that possibility, this anticipation includes the possibility of taking the *whole* of Dasein in advance [Vorwegnehmens] in an existentiell manner; that is to say, it includes the possibility of existing as a *whole potentiality-for-Being*.

The ownmost, non-relational possibility, which is not to be outstripped, is *certain*. The way *to be* certain of it is determined by the kind of truth which corresponds to it (disclosedness). The certain possibility of death, however, discloses Dasein as a possibility, but does so only in such a way that, in anticipating this possibility, Dasein *makes* this possibility *possible* for itself as its ownmost potentiality-for-Being.[1] The possibility is disclosed because it is made possible in anticipation. To maintain oneself in this truth—that is, to be certain of what has been disclosed—demands all the more that one should anticipate. We cannot compute the certainty of death by ascertaining how many cases of death we encounter. This certainty is by no means of the kind which maintains itself in the truth of the present-at-hand. When something present-at-hand has been un-covered, it is encountered most purely if we just look at the entity and let it be encountered in itself. Dasein must first have lost itself in the factual circumstances [Sachverhalte] (this can be one of care's own tasks and possibilities) if it is to obtain the pure objectivity—that is to say, the indifference—of apodictic evidence. If Being-certain in relation to death does not have this character, this does not mean that it is of a lower grade, but that *it does not belong at all to the graded order of the kinds of evidence we can have about the present-at-hand.*

Holding death for true (death *is* just one's own) shows another kind of certainty, and is more primordial than any certainty which relates to entities encountered within-the-world, or to formal objects; for it is certain of Being-in-the-world. As such, holding death for true does not demand just *one* definite kind of behaviour in Dasein, but demands Dasein

---

[1] 'Die gewisse Möglichkeit des Todes erschliesst das Dasein aber als Möglichkeit nur so, dass es vorlaufend zu ihr diese Möglichkeit als eigenstes Seinkönnen für sich *ermög-licht*.' While we have taken 'Die gewisse Möglichkeit des Todes' as the subject of this puzzling sentence, 'das Dasein' *may* be the subject instead. The use of the preposition 'zu' instead of the usual 'in' after 'vorlaufend' suggests that in 'anticipating' the possibility of death, Dasein is here thought of as 'running ahead' *towards* it or *up to* it rather than *into* it. When this construction occurs in later passages, we shall indicate it by subjoining 'zu' in brackets.

itself in the full authenticity of its existence.ˣᵛⁱⁱⁱ In anticipation Dasein can first make certain of its ownmost Being in its totality—a totality which is not to be outstripped. Therefore the evidential character which belongs to the immediate givenness of Experiences, of the "I", or of consciousness, must necessarily lag behind the certainty which anticipation includes. Yet this is not because the way in which these are grasped would not be a rigorous one, but because in principle such a way of grasping them cannot hold *for true* (disclosed) something which at bottom it insists upon 'having there' as true: namely, Dasein itself, which I myself *am*, and which, as a potentiality-for-Being, I can be authentically only by anticipation.

The ownmost possibility, which is non-relational, not to be outstripped, and certain, is *indefinite* as regards its certainty. How does anticipation disclose this characteristic of Dasein's distinctive possibility? How does the anticipatory understanding project itself upon a potentiality-for-Being which is certain and which is constantly possible in such a way that the "when" in which the utter impossibility of existence becomes possible remains constantly indefinite? In anticipating [zum] the indefinite certainty of death, Dasein opens itself to a constant *threat* arising out of its own "there". In this very threat Being-towards-the-end must maintain itself. So little can it tone this down that it must rather cultivate the indefiniteness of the certainty. How is it existentially possible for this constant threat to be genuinely disclosed? All understanding is accompanied by a state-of-mind. Dasein's mood brings it face to face with the thrownness of its 'that it is there'.ˣˡˣ *But the state-of-mind which can hold open the utter and constant threat to itself arising from Dasein's ownmost individualized Being, is anxiety.*ˣˣ ¹ In this state-of-mind, Dasein finds itself *face to face* with the "nothing" of the possible impossibility of its existence. Anxiety is anxious *about* the potentiality-for-Being of the entity so destined [des so bestimmten Seienden], and in this way it discloses the uttermost possibility. Anticipation utterly individualizes Dasein, and allows it, in this individualization of itself, to become certain of the totality of its potentiality-for-Being. For this reason, anxiety as a basic state-of-mind belongs to such a self-understanding of Dasein on the basis of Dasein itself.² Being-towards-death is essentially anxiety. This is attested unmistakably, though 'only' indirectly, by Being-towards-death as we have described it,

¹ '*Die Befindlichkeit aber, welche die ständige und schlechthinnige, aus dem eigensten vereinzelten Sein des Daseins aufsteigende Bedrohung seiner selbst offen zu halten vermag, ist die Angst.*' Notice that '*welche*' may be construed either as the subject or as the direct object of the relative clause.

² '. . . gehört zu diesem Sichverstehen des Daseins aus seinem Grunde die Grund-. befindlichkeit der Angst.' It is not grammatically clear whether 'seinem' refers to 'Sichverstehen' or to 'Daseins'.

when it perverts anxiety into cowardly fear and, in surmounting this fear, only makes known its own cowardliness in the face of anxiety.

We may now summarize our characterization of authentic Being-towards-death as we have projected it existentially: *anticipation reveals to Dasein its lostness in the they-self, and brings it face to face with the possibility of being itself, primarily unsupported by concernful solicitude, but of being itself, rather, in an impassioned* **freedom towards death**—*a freedom which has been released from the Illusions of the "they", and which is factical, certain of itself, and anxious.*

All the relationships which belong to Being-towards-death, up to the full content of Dasein's uttermost possibility, as we have characterized it, constitute an anticipation which they combine in revealing, unfolding, and holding fast, as that which makes this possibility possible. The existential projection in which anticipation has been delimited, has made visible the *ontological* possibility of an existentiell Being-towards-death which is authentic. Therewith, however, the possibility of Dasein's having an authentic potentiality-for-Being-a-whole emerges, *but only as an ontological possibility.* In our existential projection of anticipation, we have of course clung to those structures of Dasein which we have arrived at earlier, and we have, as it were, let Dasein itself project itself upon this possibility, without holding up to Dasein an ideal of existence with any special 'content', or forcing any such ideal upon it 'from outside'. Nevertheless, this existentially 'possible' Being-towards-death remains, from the existentiell point of view, a fantastical exaction. The fact that an authentic potentiality-for-Being-a-whole is ontologically possible for Dasein, signifies nothing, so long as a corresponding ontical potentiality-for-Being has not been demonstrated in Dasein itself. Does Dasein ever factically throw itself into such a Being-towards-death? Does Dasein *demand*, even by reason of its ownmost Being, an authentic potentiality-for-Being determined by anticipation?

Before answering these questions, we must investigate whether to *any* extent and in any way Dasein *gives testimony*, from its ownmost potentiality-for-Being, as to a possible *authenticity* of its existence, so that it not only makes known that in an existentiell manner such authenticity is possible, but *demands* this of itself. 2

The question of Dasein's authentic Being-a-whole and of its existential constitution still hangs in mid-air. It can be put on a phenomenal basis which will stand the test only if it can cling to a possible authenticity of its Being which is attested by Dasein itself. If we succeed in uncovering that attestation phenomenologically, together with what it attests, then the problem will arise anew as to *whether the anticipation of [zum] death, which we have hitherto projected only in its* **ontological** *possibility, has an essential connection with that authentic potentiality-for-Being which has been* **attested**.

II

DASEIN'S ATTESTATION OF AN AUTHENTIC POTENTIALITY-FOR-BEING, AND RESOLUTENESS

¶ *54. The Problem of How an Authentic Existentiell Possibility is Attested.*

WHAT we are seeking is an authentic potentiality-for-Being of Dasein, which will be attested in its existentiell possibility by Dasein itself. But this very attestation must first be such that we can find it. If in this attestation, Dasein itself, as something for which authentic existence is possible, is to be 'given' to Dasein 'to understand',[1] this attestation will have its roots in Dasein's Being. So in exhibiting it phenomenologically, we include a demonstration that in Dasein's state of Being it has its source.

In this attestation an authentic *potentiality-for-Being-one's-Self* is to be given us to understand. The question of the *"who"* of Dasein has been answered with the expression 'Self'.[1] Dasein's Selfhood has been defined formally as a *way of existing*, and therefore not as an entity present-at-hand. For the most part *I myself* am not the "who" of Dasein; the they-self is its "who". Authentic Being-one's-Self takes the definite form of an existentiell modification of the "they"; and this modification must be defined existentially.[ii] What does this modification imply, and what are the ontological conditions for its possibility?

With Dasein's lostness in the "they", that factical potentiality-for-Being which is closest to it (the tasks, rules, and standards, the urgency and extent, of concernful and solicitous Being-in-the-world) has already been decided upon. The "they" has always kept Dasein from taking hold of these possibilities of Being. The "they" even hides the manner in which it has tacitly relieved Dasein of the burden of explicitly *choosing* these possibilities. It remains indefinite who has 'really' done the choosing. So Dasein make no choices, gets carried along by the nobody, and thus ensnares itself in inauthenticity. This process can be reversed only if Dasein specifically brings itself back to itself from its lostness in the "they". But this bringing-back must have that kind of Being *by the neglect of which*

---

[1] '. . . wenn sie dem Dasein es selbst in seiner möglichen eigentlichen Existenz "zu verstehen geben" . . .'

Dasein has lost itself in inauthenticity. When Dasein thus brings itself back [Das Sichzurückholen] from the "they", the they-self is modified in an existentiell manner so that it becomes *authentic* Being-one's-Self. This must be accomplished by *making up for not choosing* [*Nachholen einer Wahl*]. But "making up" for not choosing signifies *choosing to make this choice—* deciding for a potentiality-for-Being, and making this decision from one's own Self. In choosing to make this choice, Dasein *makes possible*, first and foremost, its authentic potentiality-for-Being.

But because Dasein is *lost* in the "they", it must first *find* itself. In order to find *itself* at all, it must be 'shown' to itself in its possible authenticity. In terms of its *possibility*, Dasein *is* already a potentiality-for-Being-its-Self, but it needs to have this potentiality attested.

In the following Interpretation we shall claim that this potentiality is attested by that which, in Dasein's everyday interpretation of itself, is familiar to us as the "*voice of conscience*" [*Stimme des Gewissens*].[111] That the very 'fact' of conscience has been disputed, that its function as a higher court for Dasein's existence has been variously assessed, and that 'what conscience says' has been interpreted in manifold ways—all this might only mislead us into dismissing this phenomenon if the very 'doubtfulness' of this Fact—or of the way in which it has been interpreted—did not *prove* that here a *primordial* phenomenon of Dasein lies before us. In the following analysis conscience will be taken as something which we have in advance theoretically, and it will be investigated in a purely existential mannner, with fundamental ontology as our aim.

We shall first trace conscience back to its existential foundations and structures and make it visible *as* a phenomenon of Dasein, holding fast to what we have hitherto arrived at as that entity's state of Being. The, ontological analysis of conscience on which we are thus embarking, is prior to any description and classification of Experiences of conscience, and likewise lies outside of any biological 'explanation' of this phenomenon (which would mean its dissolution). But it is no less distant from a theological exegesis of conscience or any employment of this phenomenon for proofs of God or for establishing an 'immediate' consciousness of God.

Nevertheless, even when our investigation of conscience is thus restricted, we must neither exaggerate its outcome nor make perverse claims about it and lessen its worth. As a phenomenon of Dasein, conscience is not just a fact which occurs and is occasionally present-at-hand. It '*is*' only in Dasein's kind of Being, and it makes itself known as a Fact only with factical existence and i n it. The demand that an 'inductive empirical proof' should be given for the 'factuality' of conscience and for the legitimacy of its 'voice', rests upon an ontological perversion of the phenomenon. This perversion, however, is one that is shared by every "superior" criticism in which conscience is taken as something just occurring from time to time rather than as a 'universally established and ascertainable fact'. Among such proofs and counterproofs, the Fact of conscience cannot present itself at all. This is no lack in it, but merely a sign by which we can recognize it as ontologically of a different kind from what is environmentally present-at-hand.

Conscience gives us 'something' to understand; it *discloses*. By characterizing this phenomenon formally in this way, we find ourselves enjoined to take it back into the *disclosedness* of Dasein. This disclosedness, as a basic state of that entity which we ourselves are, is constituted by state-of-mind, understanding, falling, and discourse. If we analyse conscience more penetratingly, it is revealed as a call [*Ruf*]. Calling is a mode of *discourse*. The call of conscience has the character of an *appeal* to Dasein by calling it to its ownmost potentiality-for-Being-its-Self; and this is done by way of *summoning* it to its ownmost Being-guilty.[1]

This existential Interpretation is necessarily a far cry from everyday ontical common sense, though it sets forth the ontological foundations of what the ordinary way of interpreting conscience has always understood within certain limits and has conceptualized as a 'theory' of conscience. Accordingly our existential Interpretation needs to be confirmed by a critique of the way in which conscience is ordinarily interpreted. When this phenomenon has been exhibited, we can bring out the extent to which it attests an authentic potentiality-for-Being of Dasein. To the call of conscience there corresponds a possible hearing. Our understanding of the appeal unveils itself as our *wanting to have a conscience* [*Gewissenhaben-wollen*]. But in this phenomenon lies that existentiell choosing which we seek—the choosing to choose a kind of Being-one's-Self which, in accordance with its existential structure, we call "*resoluteness*".[2] Thus we can see how the analyses of this chapter are divided up: the existential-onto-

---

[1] 'Der Gewissensruf hat den Charakter des *Anrufs* des Daseins auf sein eigenstes Selbstseinkönnen und das in der Weise des *Aufrufs* zum eigensten Schuldigsein.' Our translation of 'Anruf' as 'appeal' and of 'Aufruf' as 'summoning' conceals the etymological connection of these expressions with 'Ruf', which we here translate as 'call'—a word which we have already used in translating expressions such as 'nennen', 'heissen', and a number of others. The verb '*anrufen*' ('appeal') means literally 'to call *to*'; 'einen *auf* etwas anrufen' means 'to call to someone and call him *to* something'. Similarly '*aufrufen*' ('summon') means 'to call *up*'; 'einen *zu* etwas *aufrufen*' means 'to call someone *up to* something which he is to do', in the sense of challenging him or 'calling' him to a higher level of performance.

[2] '. . . das gesuchte existenzielle Wählen der Wahl eines Selbstseins, das wir, seiner existenzialen Struktur entsprechend, die *Entschlossenheit* nennen.' While our version preserves the grammatical ambiguity of the German, it seems clear from H. 298 that the antecedent of the second relative clause is 'Selbstsein' ('a kind of Being-one's-self'), not 'Wählen' ('choosing').

logical foundations of conscience (Section 55); the character of conscience as a call (Section 56); conscience as the call of care (Section 57); understanding the appeal, and guilt (Section 58); the existential Interpretation of conscience and the way conscience is ordinarily interpreted (Section 59); the existential structure of the authentic potentiality-for-Being which is attested in the conscience (Section 60).

¶ *55. The Existential-ontological Foundations of Conscience*

In the phenomenon of conscience we find, without further differentiation, that in some way it gives us something to understand. Our analysis of it takes its departure from this finding. Conscience discloses, and thus belongs within the range of those existential phenomena which constitute the *Being of the "there"* as disclosedness.[iv] We have analysed the most universal structures of state-of-mind, understanding, discourse and falling. If we now bring conscience into this phenomenal context, this is not a matter of applying these structures schematically to a special 'case' of Dasein's disclosure. On the contrary, our Interpretation of conscience not only will carry further our earlier analysis of the disclosedness of the "there", but it will also grasp it more primordially with regard to Dasein's authentic Being.

Through disclosedness, that entity which we call "Dasein" is in the possibility of *being* its "there". With its world, it is there for itself, and indeed—proximally and for the most part—in such a way that it has disclosed to itself its potentiality-for-Being in terms of the 'world' of its concern. Dasein exists as a potentiality-for-Being which has, in each case, already abandoned itself to definite possibilities.[1] And it has abandoned itself to these possibilities because it is an entity which has been thrown, and an entity whose thrownness gets disclosed more or less plainly and impressively by its having a mood. To any state-of-mind or mood, understanding belongs equiprimordially. In this way Dasein 'knows' what it is itself capable of [woran es mit ihm selbst ist], inasmuch as it has either projected itself upon possibilities of its own or has been so absorbed in the "they" that it has let such possibilities be presented to it by the way in which the "they" has publicly interpreted things. The presenting of these possibilities, however, is made possible existentially through the fact that Dasein, as a Being-with which understands, can *listen* to Others. Losing itself in the publicness and the idle talk of the "they", it *fails to hear* [*überhört*] its own Self in listening to the they-self. If Dasein is to be able to get brought back from this lostness of failing to hear itself, and if this is to be done through itself, then it must first be able to find itself—to find

---

[1] 'Das Seinkönnen, als welches das Dasein existiert, hat sich je schon bestimmten Möglichkeiten überlassen.'

itself as something which has failed to hear itself, and which fails to hear in that it *listens away* to the "they".[1] This listening-away must get broken off; in other words, the possibility of another kind of hearing which will interrupt it, must be given by Dasein itself.[2] The possibility of its thus getting broken off lies in its being appealed to without mediation. Dasein fails to hear itself, and listens away to the "they"; and this listening-away gets broken by the call if that call, in accordance with its character as such, arouses another kind of hearing, which, in relationship to the hearing that is lost,[3] has a character in every way opposite. If in this lost hearing, one has been fascinated with the 'hubbub' of the manifold ambiguity which idle talk possesses in its everyday 'newness', then the call must do its calling without any hubbub and unambiguously, leaving no foothold for curiosity. *That which, by calling in this manner, gives us to understand, is the conscience.*

We take calling as a mode of discourse. Discourse articulates intelligibility. Characterizing conscience as a call is not just giving a 'picture', like the Kantian representation of the conscience as a court of justice. Vocal utterance, however, is not essential for discourse, and therefore not for the call either; this must not be overlooked. Discourse is already presupposed in any expressing or 'proclaiming' ["Ausrufen"]. If the everyday interpretation knows a 'voice' of conscience, then one is not so much thinking of an utterance (for this is something which factically one never comes across); the 'voice' is taken rather as a giving-to-understand. In the tendency to disclosure which belongs to the call, lies the momentum of a push—of an abrupt arousal. The call is from afar unto afar. It reaches him who wants to be brought back.

But by this characterization of the conscience we have only traced the phenomenal horizon for analysing its existential structure. We are not

---

[1] '. . . sich selbst, das sich überhört hat und überhört im *Hinhören* auf das Man.' In this passage, Heidegger has been exploiting three variations on the verb 'hören': 'hören auf . . .' (our 'listen to . . .'), 'überhören' ('fail to hear'), and 'hinhören' ('listen away'). The verb 'überhören' has two quite distinct uses. It may mean the 'hearing' which a teacher does when he 'hears' a pupil recite his lesson; but it may also mean to 'fail to hear', even to 'ignore' what one hears. This is the meaning which Heidegger seems to have uppermost in mind; but perhaps he is also suggesting that when one is lost in the "they", one 'hears' one's own Self only in the manner of a perfunctory teacher who 'hears' a recitation without 'really listening to it'. In ordinary German the verb 'hinhören' means hardly more than to 'listen'; but Heidegger is emphasizing the prefix 'hin-', which suggests that one is listening *to* something other than oneself—listening *away*, in this case listening to the "they". On other verbs of hearing and listening, see Section 34 above, especially H. 163 ff.

[2] 'Dieses Hinhören muss gebrochen, das heisst es muss vom Dasein selbst die Möglichkeit eines Hörens gegeben werden, das jenes unterbricht.'

[3] '. . . zum verlorenen Hören . . .' One might suspect that the 'lost hearing' is the hearing which one 'loses' by 'failing to hear'; but Heidegger may mean rather the kind of hearing one does when one is lost in the "they"—'Überhören' of one's own Self and 'Hinhören' to the 'they'.

comparing this phenomenon with a call; we are understanding it as a kind of discourse—in terms of the disclosedness that is constitutive for Dasein. In considering this we have from the beginning avoided the first route which offers itself for an Interpretation of conscience —that of tracing it back to some psychical faculty such as understanding, will, or feeling, or of explaining it as some sort of mixture of these. When one is confronted with such a phenomenon as conscience, one is struck by the ontologico-anthropological inadequacy of a free-floating framework of psychical faculties or personal actions all duly classified.ᵛⁱ

¶ 56. *The Character of Conscience as a Call*

To any discourse there belongs that which is talked about in it. Discourse gives information about something, and does so in some definite regard. From what is thus talked about, it draws whatever it is saying as this particular discourse—what is said in the talk as such. In discourse as communication, this becomes accessible to the Dasein-with of Others, for the most part by way of uttering it in language.

In the call of conscience, what is it that is talked about—in other words, to what is the appeal made? Manifestly Dasein itself. This answer is as incontestable as it is indefinite. If the call has so vague a target, then it might at most remain an occasion for Dasein to pay attention to itself. But it is essential to Dasein that along with the disclosedness of its world it has been disclosed to itself, so that it always *understands itself*. The call reaches Dasein in this understanding of itself which it always has, and which is concernful in an everyday, average manner. The call reaches the they-self of concernful Being with Others.

And to what is one called when one is thus appealed to?[1] To one's *own Self*. Not to what Dasein counts-for, can do, or concerns itself with in being with one another publicly, nor to what it has taken hold of, set about, or let itself be carried along with. The sort of Dasein which is understood after the manner of the world both for Others and for itself, gets *passed over* in this appeal; this is something of which the call to the Self takes not the slightest cognizance. And because only the *Self* of the they-self gets appealed to and brought to hear, the "*they*" collapses. But the fact that the call *passes over* both the "they" and the manner in which Dasein has been publicly interpreted, does not by any means signify that the "they" is not *reached too*. Precisely *in passing over* the "they" (keen as it is for public repute) the call pushes it into insignificance [Bedeutungslosigkeit]. But the Self, which the appeal has robbed of this lodgement and hiding-place, gets brought to itself by the call.

[1] 'Und woraufhin wird es angerufen?'

When the they-self is appealed to, it gets called to the Self.[1] But it does not get called to that Self which can become for itself an 'object' on which to pass judgment, nor to that Self which inertly dissects its 'inner life' with fussy curiosity, nor to that Self which one has in mind when one gazes 'analytically' at psychical conditions and what lies behind them. The appeal to the Self in the they-self does not force it inwards upon itself, so that it can close itself off from the 'external world'. The call passes over everything like this and disperses it, so as to appeal solely to that Self which, notwithstanding, is in no other way than Being-in-the-world.

But how are we to determine *what is said in the talk* that belongs to this kind of discourse? *What* does the conscience call to him to whom it appeals? Taken strictly, nothing. The call asserts nothing, gives no information about world-events, has nothing to tell. Least of all does it try to set going a 'soliloquy' in the Self to which it has appealed. 'Nothing' gets called *to* [*zu*-gerufen] this Self, but it has been *summoned* [*aufgerufen*] to itself—that is, to its ownmost potentiality-for-Being. The tendency of the call is not such as to put up for 'trial' the Self to which the appeal is made; but it calls Dasein forth (and 'forward') into its ownmost possibilities, as a summons to its ownmost *potentiality*-for-Being-its-Self.[2]

The call dispenses with any kind of utterance. It does not put itself into words at all; yet it remains nothing less than obscure and indefinite. *Conscience discourses solely and constantly in the mode of keeping silent.* In this way it not only loses none of its perceptibility, but forces the Dasein which has been appealed to and summoned, into the reticence of itself. The fact that what is called in the call has not been formulated in words, does not give this phenomenon the indefiniteness of a mysterious voice, but merely indicates that our understanding of what is 'called' is not to be tied up with an expectation of anything like a communication.

Yet what the call discloses is unequivocal, even though it may undergo a different interpretation in the individual Dasein in accordance with its own possibilities of understanding. While the content of the call is seemingly indefinite, the *direction it takes* is a sure one and is not to be overlooked. The call does not require us to search gropingly for him to whom it appeals, nor does it require any sign by which we can recognize that he is or is not the one who is meant. When 'delusions' arise in the conscience, they do so not because the call has committed some oversight (has miscalled),[3] but only because the call gets *heard* in such a way that instead of

---

[1] 'Auf das Selbst wird das Man-selbst angerufen.'

[2] 'Der Ruf stellt, seiner Ruftendenz entsprechend, das angerufene Selbst nicht zu einer "Verhandlung", sondern als Aufruf zum eigensten Selbstsein*können* ist er ein Vor-(nach-"vorne"-)Rufen des Daseins in seine eigensten Möglichkeiten.' The verbs 'anrufen', 'aufrufen', and 'vorrufen' can all be used in the legal sense of a 'summons'.

[3] '. . . ein Sichversehen (Sichver-rufen) des Rufes . . .'

becoming authentically understood, it gets drawn by the they-self into a soliloquy in which causes get pleaded, and it becomes perverted in its tendency to disclose.

One must keep in mind that when we designate the conscience as a "call", this call is an appeal to the they-self in its Self; as such an appeal, it summons the Self to its potentiality-for-Being-its-Self, and thus calls Dasein forth to its possibilities.

But we shall not obtain an ontologically adequate Interpretation of the conscience until it can be made plain not only *who* is called by the call but also *who does the calling*, how the one to whom the appeal is made is related to the one who calls, and how this 'relationship' must be taken ontologically as a way in which these are interconnected in their Being.

¶ 57. *Conscience as the Call of Care*

Conscience summons Dasein's Self from its lostness in the "they". The Self to which the appeal is made remains indefinite and empty in its "what". When Dasein interprets itself in terms of that with which it concerns itself, the call passes over *what* Dasein, proximally and for the most part, understands itself a s. And yet the Self has been reached, unequivocally and unmistakably. Not only is the call meant for him to whom the appeal is made 'without regard for persons', but even the caller maintains itself in conspicuous indefiniteness. If the caller is asked about its name, status, origin, or repute, it not only refuses to answer, but does not even leave the slightest possibility of one's making it into something with which one can be familiar when one's understanding of Dasein has a 'worldly' orientation. On the other hand, it by no means disguises itself in the call. That which calls the call, simply holds itself aloof from any way of becoming well-known, and this belongs to its phenomenal character. To let itself be drawn into getting considered and talked about, goes against its kind of Being.[1] The peculiar indefiniteness of the caller and the impossibility of making more definite what this caller is, are not just nothing; they are distinctive for it in a *positive* way. They make known to us that the caller is solely absorbed in summoning us to something, that it is *heard only as such*, and furthermore that it will not let itself be coaxed. But if so, is it not quite appropriate to the phenomenon to leave unasked the question of what the caller is? Yes indeed, when it comes to listening to the factical call of conscience in an existentiell way, but not when it comes to analysing existentially the facticity of the calling and the existentiality of the hearing.

[1] 'Es geht wider die Art seines Seins, sich in ein Betrachten und Bereden ziehen zu lassen.'

But is it at all necessary to keep raising explicitly the question of *who* does the calling? Is this not answered for Dasein just as unequivocally as the question of to whom the call makes its appeal? *In conscience Dasein calls itself.* This understanding of the caller may be more or less awake in the factical hearing of the call. Ontologically, however, it is not enough to answer that Dasein is *at the same time* both the caller and the one to whom the appeal is made. When Dasein is appealed to, *is* it not 'there' in a different way from that in which it does the calling? Shall we say that its ownmost potentiality-for-Being-its-Self functions as the caller?

Indeed the call is precisely something which *we ourselves* have neither planned nor prepared for nor voluntarily performed, nor have we ever done so. 'It' calls,[1] against our expectations and even against our will. On the other hand, the call undoubtedly does not come from someone else who is with me in the world. The call comes *from* me and yet *from beyond me.*[2]

These phenomenal findings are not to be explained away. After all, they have been taken as a starting-point for explaining the voice of conscience as an alien power by which Dasein is dominated. If the interpretation continues in this direction, one supplies a possessor for the power thus posited,[3] or one takes the power itself as a person who makes himself known—namely God. On the other hand one may try to reject this explanation in which the caller is taken as an alien manifestation of such a power, and to explain away the conscience 'biologically' at the same time. Both these explanations pass over the phenomenal findings too hastily. Such procedures are facilitated by the unexpressed but ontologically dogmatic guiding thesis that what *is* (in other words, anything so factual as the call) must be *present-at-hand*, and that what does not let itself be Objectively demonstrated as *present-at-hand*, just *is not* at all.

But methodologically this is too precipitate. We must instead hold fast not only to the phenomenal finding that I receive the call as coming both from me and from beyond me, but also to the implication that this phenomenon is here delineated ontologically as a phenomenon of *Dasein*. Only the existential constitution of *this* entity can afford us a clue for Interpreting the kind of Being of the 'it' which does the calling.

Does our previous analysis of Dasein's state of Being show us a way of making ontologically intelligible the kind of Being which belongs to the caller, and, along with it, that which belongs to the calling? The fact that the call is not something which is explicitly performed *by me*, but that

---

[1] ' "Es" ruft . . .' Here the pronoun 'es' is used quite impersonally, and does not refer back to 'the call' itself ('Der Ruf').
[2] 'Der Ruf kommt *aus* mir und doch *über* mich.'
[3] '. . . unterlegt man der festgelegten Macht einen Besitzer . . .'

rather 'it' does the calling, does not justify seeking the caller in some entity with a character other than that of Dasein. Yet every Dasein always exists factically. It is not a free-floating self-projection; but its character is determined by thrownness as a Fact of the entity which it is; and, as so determined, it has in each case already been delivered over to existence, and it constantly so remains. Dasein's facticity, however, is essentially distinct from the factuality of something present-at-hand. Existent Dasein does not encounter itself as something present-at-hand within-the-world. But neither does thrownness adhere to Dasein as an inaccessible characteristic which is of no importance for its existence. As something thrown, Dasein has been thrown *into existence*. It exists as an entity which has to be as it is and as it can be.

That it is factically, may be obscure and hidden as regards the *"why"* of it; but the *"that-it-is"* has *itself* been disclosed to Dasein.[1] The thrownness of this entity belongs to the disclosedness of the 'there' and reveals itself constantly in its current state-of-mind. This state-of-mind brings Dasein, more or less explicitly and authentically, face to face with the fact 'that it is, and that it has to be something with a potentiality-for-Being as the entity which it is'.[2] For the most part, however, its mood is such that its thrownness gets *closed off*. In the face of its thrownness Dasein flees to the relief which comes with the supposed freedom of the they-self. This fleeing has been described as a fleeing in the face of the uncanniness which is basically determinative for individualized Being-in-the-world. Uncanniness reveals itself authentically in the basic state-of-mind of anxiety; and, as the most elemental way in which thrown Dasein is disclosed, it puts Dasein's Being-in-the-world face to face with the "nothing" of the world; in the face of this "nothing", Dasein is anxious with anxiety about its ownmost potentiality-for-Being. *What if this Dasein, which finds itself* [*sich befindet*] *in the very depths of its uncanniness, should be the caller of the call of conscience?*

Nothing speaks against this; but all those phenomena which we have hitherto set forth in characterizing the caller and its calling speak f o r it.

In its "who", the caller is definable in a 'worldly' way by *nothing* at all. The caller is Dasein in its uncanniness: primordial, thrown Being-in-the-world as the "not-at-home"—the bare 'that-it-is' in the "nothing" of the world. The caller is unfamiliar to the everyday they-self; it is something like an *alien* voice. What could be more alien to the "they", lost in the

---

[1] '*Dass* es faktisch ist, mag hinsichtlich des *Warum* verborgen sein, das *'Dass'* selbst jedoch ist dem Dasein erschlossen.' (Cf. H. 135 above.)

[2] 'Diese bringt das Dasein mehr oder minder ausdrücklich und eigentlich vor sein "dass es ist und als das Seiende, das es ist, seinkönnend zu sein hat".'

L

manifold 'world' of its concern, than the Self which has been individualized down to itself in uncanniness and been thrown into the "nothing"? 'It' calls, even though it gives the concernfully curious ear nothing to hear which might be passed along in further retelling and talked about in public. But what is Dasein even to report from the uncanniness of its thrown Being? *What* else remains for it than its own potentiality-for-Being as revealed in anxiety? How else is "it" to call than by summoning Dasein towards this potentiality-for-Being, which alone is the issue?

The call does not report events; it calls without uttering anything. The call discourses in the uncanny mode of *keeping silent*. And it does this only because, in calling the one to whom the appeal is made, it does not call him into the public idle talk of the "they", but *calls* him *back* from this *into the reticence of his existent* potentiality-for-Being. When the caller reaches him to whom the appeal is made, it does so with a cold assurance which is uncanny but by no means obvious. Wherein lies the basis for this assurance if not in the fact that when Dasein has been individualized down to itself in its uncanniness, it is for itself something that simply cannot be mistaken for anything else? What is it that so radically deprives Dasein of the possibility of misunderstanding itself by any sort of alibi and failing to recognize itself, if not the forsakenness [Verlassenheit] with which it has been abandoned [Überlassenheit] to itself?

Uncanniness is the basic kind of Being-in-the-world, even though in an everyday way it has been covered up. Out of the depths of this kind of Being, Dasein itself, as conscience, calls. The 'it calls me' ["es ruft mich"] is a distinctive kind of discourse for Dasein. The call whose mood has been attuned by anxiety is what makes it possible first and foremost for Dasein to project itself upon its ownmost *potentiality-for-Being*. The call of conscience, existentially understood, makes known for the first time what we have hitherto merely contended:[vii] that uncanniness pursues Dasein and is a threat to the lostness in which it has forgotten itself.

The proposition that Dasein is at the same time both the caller and the one to whom the appeal is made, has now lost its empty formal character and its obviousness. *Conscience manifests itself as the call of care*: the caller is Dasein, which, in its thrownness (in its Being-already-in), is anxious[1] about its potentiality-for-Being. The one to whom the appeal is made is this very same Dasein, summoned to its ownmost potentiality-for-Being (ahead of itself . . .). Dasein is falling into the "they" (in Being-already-alongside the world of its concern), and it is summoned out of this falling by the appeal. The call of conscience—that is, conscience itself—has its

---

1 '. . . sich ängstigend . . .' The older editions have 'sich ängstend', which has virtually the same meaning, and is more characteristic of Heidegger's style.

ontological possibility in the fact that Dasein, in the very basis of its Being, is care.

So we need not resort to powers with a character other than that of Dasein; indeed, recourse to these is so far from clarifying the uncanniness of the call that instead it annihilates it. In the end, does not the reason why 'explanations' of the conscience have gone off the track, lie in the fact that we have not looked *long enough* to establish our phenomenal findings as to the call, and that Dasein has been presupposed as having some kind of ontological definiteness or indefiniteness, whichever it may chance? Why should we look to alien powers for information before we have made sure that in starting our analysis we have not given *too low* an assessment of Dasein's Being, regarding it as an innocuous subject endowed with personal consciousness, somehow or other occurring?

And yet, if the caller—who is 'nobody', when seen after the manner of the world—is interpreted as a power, this seems to be a dispassionate recognition of something that one can 'come across Objectively'. When seen correctly, however, this interpretation is only a fleeing in the face of the conscience—a way for Dasein to escape by slinking away from that thin wall by which the "they" is separated, as it were, from the uncanniness of its Being. This interpretation of the conscience passes itself off as recognizing the call in the sense of a voice which is 'universally' binding, and which speaks in a way that is 'not just subjective'. Furthermore, the 'universal' conscience becomes exalted to a 'world-conscience', which still has the phenomenal character of an 'it' and 'nobody', yet which speaks—there in the individual 'subject'—as this indefinite something.

But this 'public conscience'—what else is it than the voice of the "they"? A 'world-conscience' is a dubious fabrication, and Dasein can come to this only *because* conscience, in its basis and its essence, is *in each case mine*—not only in the sense that in each case the appeal is to one's ownmost potentiality-for-Being, but because the call comes from that entity which in each case I myself am.

With this Interpretation of the caller, which is purely in accord with the phenomenal character of the calling, the 'power' of conscience is not diminished and rendered 'merely subjective'. On the contrary, only in this way do the inexorability and unequivocal character of the call become free. This Interpretation does justice to the 'Objectivity' of the appeal for the first time by leaving it its 'subjectivity', which of course denies the they-self its dominion.

Nevertheless, this Interpretation of the conscience as the call of care will be countered by the question of whether any interpretation of the conscience can stand up if it removes itself so far from 'natural experience'. How is the conscience to function as that which *summons* us to our ownmost potentiality-for-Being, when proximally and for the most part it merely *warns* and *reproves*? Does the conscience speak in so indefinite and empty a manner about our potentiality-for-Being? Does it not rather speak definitely and concretely in relation to failures and omissions which have already befallen or which we still have before us? Does the alleged appeal stem from a '*bad*' conscience or from a '*good*' one? Does the conscience give us anything positive at all? Does it not function rather in just a critical fashion?

Such considerations are indisputably within their rights. We can, however, demand that in any Interpretation of conscience 'one' should recognize in it the phenomenon in question as it is experienced in an everyday manner. But satisfying this requirement does not mean in turn that the ordinary ontical way of understanding conscience must be recognized as the first court of appeal [erste Instanz] for an ontological Interpretation. On the other hand, the considerations which we have just marshalled remain premature as long as the analysis of conscience to which they pertain falls short of its goal. Hitherto we have merely tried to trace back conscience *as a phenomenon of Dasein* to the ontological constitution of that entity. This has served to prepare us for the task of making the conscience intelligible as *an attestation of Dasein's ownmost potentiality-for-Being*—an attestation which lies in Dasein itself.

But what the conscience attests becomes completely definite only when we have delimited plainly enough the character of the *hearing* which genuinely corresponds to the calling. The *authentic* understanding which 'follows' the call is not a mere addition which attaches itself to the phenomenon of conscience by a process which may or may not be forthcoming. Only *from* an understanding of the appeal and together *with* such an understanding does the *full* Experience of conscience let itself be grasped. If in each case the caller and he to whom the appeal is made are *at the same time* one's own Dasein *themselves*, then in any failure to hear the call or any incorrect hearing of *oneself*, there lies a *definite kind* of Dasein's *Being*. A free-floating call from which 'nothing ensues' is an impossible fiction when seen existentially. With regard to Dasein, 'that *nothing* ensues' signifies something *positive*.

So then, only by analysing the way the appeal is understood can one be led to discuss explicitly *what the call gives one to understand*. But only with our foregoing general ontological characterization of the conscience does it become possible to conceive existentially the conscience's call of

'Guilty!'[1] All experiences and interpretations of the conscience are a
one in that they make the 'voice' of conscience speak somehow of 'guilt'

¶ 58. *Understanding the Appeal, and Guilt*

To grasp phenomenally what one hears in understanding the appeal
we must go back to the appeal anew. The appeal to the they-self signifie
summoning one's ownmost Self to its potentiality-for-Being, and of cours
as Dasein—that is, as concernful Being-in-the-world and Being witl
Others. Thus in Interpreting existentially that towards which the cal
summons us, we cannot seek to delimit any concrete single possibility o
existence as long as we correctly understand the methodological possibili
ties and tasks which such an Interpretation implies. That which can b
established, and which seeks to be established, is not what gets called in
and to each particular Dasein from an existentiell standpoint, but i
rather what *belongs* to the *existential condition for the possibility* of its factical
existentiell potentiality-for-Being.[2]

When the call is understood with an existentiell kind of hearing, sucl
understanding is more authentic the more non-relationally Dasein hear
and understands *its* own Being-appealed-to, and the less the meaning o
the call gets perverted by what one says or by what is fitting and accepted
[was sich gehört und gilt]. But what is it that is essentially implied wher
the appeal is understood authentically? What is it that has been essentiall
given us to understand in the call at any particular time, even if factically
it has not always been understood?

We have already answered this question, however, in our thesis tha
the call 'says' *nothing* which might be talked about, gives no informatior
about events. The call points *forward to* Dasein's potentiality-for-Being
and it does this as a call which comes *from* uncanniness.[3] The caller is
to be sure, indefinite; but the "whence" from which it calls does no
remain a matter of indifference for the calling. This "whence"—the
uncanniness of thrown individualization—gets called too [mitgerufen] ir
the calling; that is, it too gets disclosed [miterschlossen]. In calling fortl

---

[1] '... das im Gewissen gerufene "schuldig" existenzial zu begreifen.' As Heidegger wil
point out, the words 'schuldig', 'Schuld' and their derivatives have many differen
meanings, corresponding not only to 'indebtedness', as we have seen on H. 242 above, bu
also to 'guilt' and 'responsibility'. In the present chapter we shall translate them b
'guilty' and 'guilt' whenever possible, even though these expressions will not always b
entirely appropriate.

[2] 'Nicht das je existenziell im jeweiligen Dasein in dieses Gerufene kann und wil
fixiert werden, sondern das, was zur *existenzialen Bedingung der Möglichkeit* des je faktisch
existenziellen Seinkönnens *gehört*.' In the older editions we find 'an dieses' rather than 'i
dieses', and 'zur' appears in spaced type.

[3] 'Der Ruf weist das Dasein *vor auf* sein Seinkönnen und das als Ruf *aus* der Unheim
lichkeit.'

to something, the "whence" of the calling is the "whither" to which we are called back. When the call gives us a potentiality-for-Being to understand, it does not give us one which is ideal and universal; it discloses it as that which has been currently individualized and which belongs to that particular Dasein. We have not fully determined the character of the call as disclosure until we understand it as one which calls us back in calling us forth [als vorrufender Rückruf]. If we take the call this way and orient ourselves by it, we must first ask *what* it gives us to understand.

But is not the question of what the call says answered more easily and surely if we 'simply' allude to what we generally hear or fail to hear in any experience of conscience: namely, that the call either addresses Dasein as 'Guilty!', or, as in the case when the conscience gives warning, refers to a possible 'Guilty!', or affirms, as a 'good' conscience, that one is 'conscious of no guilt'? Whatever the ways in which conscience is experienced or interpreted, all our experiences 'agree' on this 'Guilty!'. If only it were not defined in such wholly different ways! And even if the meaning of this 'Guilty!' should let itself be taken in a way upon which everyone is agreed, the *existential conception* of this Being-guilty would still remain obscure. Yet if Dasein addresses itself as 'Guilty!', whence could it draw its idea of guilt except from the Interpretation of its own Being? All the same, the question arises anew: *who says how we are guilty and what "guilt" signifies?* On the other hand, the idea of guilt is not one which could be thought up arbitrarily and forced upon Dasein. If any understanding of the essence of guilt is possible at all, then this possibility must have been sketched out in Dasein beforehand. How are we to find the trail which can lead to revealing this phenomenon? All ontological investigations of such phenomena as guilt, conscience, and death, must start with what the everyday interpretation of Dasein 'says' about them. Because Dasein has falling as its kind of Being, the way Dasein gets interpreted is for the most part *inauthentically* 'oriented' and does not reach the 'essence'; for to Dasein the primordially appropriate ontological way of formulating questions remains alien. But whenever we see something wrongly, some injunction as to the primordial 'idea' of the phenomenon is revealed along with it. Where, however, shall we get our criterion for the primordial existential meaning of the 'Guilty!'? From the fact that this 'Guilty!' turns up as a predicate for the 'I am'. Is it possible that what is understood as 'guilt' in our inauthentic interpretation lies in Dasein's Being as such, and that it does so in such a way that so far as any Dasein factically exists, it *is* also guilty?

Thus by invoking the 'Guilty!' which everyone agrees that he hears, one has not yet answered the question of the existential meaning of what

has been called in the call. What has been called must first be conceptualized if we are to understand what the call of 'Guilty!' means, and why
and how it becomes perverted in its signification by the everyday way of
interpreting it.

Everyday common sense first takes 'Being-guilty' in the sense of 'owing',
of 'having something due on account'.[1] One is to give back to the Other
something to which the latter has a claim. This 'Being-guilty' as *'having
debts'* [*"Schulden haben"*] is a way of Being with Others in the field of
concern, as in providing something or bringing it along. Other modes of
such concern are: depriving, borrowing, withholding, taking, stealing—
failing to satisfy, in some way or other, the claims which Others have
made as to their possessions. This kind of Being-guilty is related to
that with which one can concern oneself.

"Being-guilty" also has the signification of *'being responsible for'* [*"schuld
sein an"*]—that is, being the cause or author of something, or even 'being
the occasion' for something. In this sense of 'having responsibility' for
something, one can 'be guilty' of something without 'owing' anything to
someone else or coming to 'owe' him. On the other hand, one can owe
something to another without being responsible for it oneself. Another
person can 'incur debts' with Others 'for me'.[2]

These ordinary significations of "Being-guilty" as 'having debts to
someone' and 'having responsibility for something' can go together and
define a kind of behaviour which we call *'making oneself responsible'*; that is,
by having the responsibility for having a debt, one may break a law and
make oneself punishable.[3] Yet the requirement which one fails to satisfy
need not necessarily be related to anyone's possessions; it can regulate
the very manner in which we are with one other publicly. 'Making oneself
responsible' by breaking a law, as we have thus defined it, can indeed also
have the character of *'coming to owe something to Others'*.[4] This does not
happen merely through law-breaking as such, but rather through my
having the responsibility for the Other's becoming endangered in his
existence, led astray, or even ruined. This way of coming to owe something

---

[1] 'Die alltägliche Verständigkeit nimmt das "Schuldigsein" zunächst im Sinne von
"schulden", "bei einem etwas an Brett haben".' While this represents a very familiar
usage of the German 'Schuldigsein', it of course does not represent a 'common-sense' usage
of the English 'Being-guilty', which comes from an entirely different stem.

[2] 'Im Sinne dieses "Schuld habens" an etwas kann man "schuldig sein", ohne einem
Andern etwas zu "schulden" oder "schuldig" zu werden. Umgekehrt kann man einem
Andern etwas schulden, ohne selbst schuld daran zu sein. Ein Anderer kann bei Anderen
"für mich" "Schulden machen".' On ' "schuldig" zu werden', Cf. our note 1, p. 334,
H. 287 below.

[3] '. . . das wir nennen *"sich schuldig machen"*, das heisst durch das Schuldhaben an einem
Schuldenhaben ein Recht verletzen und sich strafbar machen.'

[4] '. . . eines *"Schuldigwerdens an Anderen"*.'

to Others is possible without breaking the 'public' law. Thus the formal conception of "Being-guilty" in the sense of having come to owe something to an Other, may be defined as follows: *"Being-the-basis* for a lack of something in the Dasein of an Other, and in such a manner that this very Being-the-basis determines itself as 'lacking in some way' in terms of that for which it is the basis."[1] This kind of lacking is a failure to satisfy some requirement which applies to one's existent Being with Others.

We need not consider how such requirements arise and in what way their character as requirements and laws must be conceived by reason of their having such a source. In any case, *"Being-guilty"* in the sense last mentioned, the breach of a 'moral requirement', is a *kind of Being which belongs to Dasein.* Of course this holds good also for "Being-guilty" as 'making oneself punishable' and as 'having debts', and for any 'having responsibility for . . .'. These too are ways in which Dasein behaves. If one takes 'laden with moral guilt' as a 'quality' of Dasein, one has said very little. On the contrary, this only makes it manifest that such a characterization does not suffice for distinguishing ontologically between this kind of 'attribute of Being' for Dasein and those other ways of behaving which we have just listed. After all, the concept of moral guilt has been so little clarified ontologically that when the idea of deserving punishment, or even of having debts to someone, has also been included in this concept, or when these ideas have been employed in the very defining of it, such interpretations of this phenomenon could become prevalent and have remained so. But therewith the 'Guilty!' gets thrust aside into the domain of concern in the sense of reckoning up claims and balancing them off.

The phenomenon of guilt, which is not necessarily related to 'having debts' and law-breaking, can be clarified only if we first inquire in principle into Dasein's *Being*-guilty—in other words, if we conceive the idea of 'Guilty!' in terms of Dasein's kind of Being.

If this is our goal, the idea of 'Guilty!' must be sufficiently *formalized* so that those ordinary phenomena of "guilt" which are related to our concernful Being with Others, will *drop out.* The idea of guilt must not only be raised above the domain of that concern in which we reckon things up, but it must also be detached from relationship to any law or "ought" such that by failing to comply with it one loads himself with guilt. For here too "guilt" is still necessarily defined as a *lack*—when something which ought to be and which can be is missing.[2] To be missing,

---

[1] '. . . *Grundsein* für einen Mangel im Dasein eines Andern, so zwar, dass dieses Grundsein selbst sich aus seinem Wofür als "mangelhaft" bestimmt.'

[2] '. . . auf ein Sollen und Gesetz, wogegen sich verfehlend jemand Schuld auf sich lädt. Denn auch hier wird die Schuld notwendig noch als *Mangel* bestimmt, als Fehlen von etwas, was sein soll und kann.'

however, means not-Being-present-at-hand. A lack, as the not-Being-present-at-hand of something which ought to be, is a definite sort of Being which goes with the present-at-hand. In this sense it is essential that in existence there can be nothing lacking, not because it would then be perfect, but because its character of Being remains distinct from any presence-at-hand.

Nevertheless, in the idea of 'Guilty!' there lies the character of the *"not"*. If the 'Guilty!' is something that can definitely apply to existence, then this raises the ontological problem of clarifying existentially the *character* of this "not" *as a "not"*. Moreover, to the idea of 'Guilty!' belongs what is expressed without further differentiation in the conception of guilt as 'having responsibility for'—that is, as Being-the basis for . . . Hence we define the formally existential idea of the 'Guilty!' as "Being-the-basis for a Being which has been defined by a 'not' "—that is to say, as *"Being-the-basis of a nullity"*.[1] The idea of the "not" which lies in the concept of guilt as understood existentially, excludes relatedness to anything present-at-hand which is possible or which may have been required; furthermore, Dasein is altogether incommensurable with anything present-at-hand or generally accepted [Geltenden] which is not it itself, or which is not *in the way Dasein is*—namely, *existing*; so any possibility that, with regard to Being-the-basis for a lack, the entity which is itself such a basis might be reckoned up as 'lacking in some manner', is a possibility which drops out. If a lack, such as failure to fulfil some requirement, has been 'caused' in a manner characteristic of Dasein, we cannot simply reckon back to there being something lacking [Mangelhaftigkeit] in the 'cause'. Being-the-basis-for-something need not have the same "not"-character as the *privativum* which is based upon it and which arises from it. The basis need not acquire a nullity of its own from that for which it is the basis [seinem Begründeten]. This implies, however, that *Being-guilty does not first result from an indebtedness* [*Verschuldung*], *but that, on the contrary, indebtedness becomes possible only 'on the basis' of a primordial Being-guilty*. Can something like this be exhibited in Dasein's Being, and how is it at all possible existentially?

Dasein's Being is care. It comprises in itself facticity (thrownness), existence (projection), and falling. As being, Dasein is something that has been thrown; it has been brought into its "there", but *not* of its own accord. As being, it has taken the definite form of a potentiality-for-Being which

----

[1] '. . . Grundsein für ein durch ein Nicht bestimmtes Sein—das heisst *Grundsein einer Nichtigkeit*'. The noun 'Nichtigkeit' which might well be translated here as 'notness', may be used in legal contexts where something has been declared 'null and void', and can be used more generally to apply to almost anything that is vacuous, trifling, ephemeral, or 'nil'. Heidegger will rule out some of these connotations on H. 285.

has heard itself and has devoted itself to itself, but *not* as itself. [1]As existent, it never comes back behind its thrownness in such a way that it might first release this 'that-it-is-and-has-to-be' from *its Being-its-*Self and lead it into the "there". Thrownness, however, does not lie behind it as some event which has happened to Dasein, which has factually befallen and fallen loose from Dasein again;[2] on the contrary, as long as Dasein is, *Dasein*, as care, *is* constantly its 'that-it-is'. To this entity it has been delivered over, and as such it can exist solely as the entity which it is; and *as this entity* to which it has been thus delivered over, it *is*, *in its existing*, the basis of its potentiality-for-Being. Although it has *not* laid that basis *itself*, it reposes in the weight of it, which is made manifest to it as a burden by Dasein's mood.

And how *is* Dasein this thrown basis? Only in that it projects itself upon possibilities into which it has been thrown. The Self, which as such has to lay the basis for itself, can *never* get that basis into its power; and yet, as existing, it must take over Being-a-basis. To be its own thrown basis is that potentiality-for-Being which is the issue for care.

In being a basis—that is, in existing as thrown—Dasein constantly lags behind its possibilities. It is never existent *before* its basis, but only *from it* and *as this basis*. Thus "Being-a-basis" means *never* to have power over one's ownmost Being from the ground up. This "*not*" belongs to the existential meaning of "thrownness". It itself, being a basis, *is* a nullity of itself.[3] "Nullity" does not signify anything like not-Being-present-at-hand or not-subsisting; what one has in view here is rather a "not" which is constitutive for this *Being* of Dasein—its thrownness. The character of this "not" as a "not" may be defined existentially: in being its *Self*, Dasein is, *as* a Self, the entity that has been thrown. It has been *released* from its basis, *not through* itself but *to* itself, so as to be *as this basis*. Dasein is not itself the basis of its Being, inasmuch as this basis first arises from its own projection; rather, as Being-its-Self, it is the *Being* of its basis.[4] This basis

---

[1] 'Seiend ist es als Seinkönnen bestimmt, das sich selbst gehört und doch *nicht* als es selbst sich zu eigen gegeben hat.' It is perhaps tempting to interpret 'gehört' as coming from the verb 'gehören' ('belong') rather than 'hören' ('hear'); we could then read 'belongs to itself' rather than 'has heard itself'. Our version, however, seems to be favoured by the grammar of this passage.

[2] 'Die Geworfenheit aber liegt nicht hinter ihm als ein tatsächlich vorgefallenes und vom Dasein wieder losgefallenes Ereignis, das mit ihm geschah . . '

[3] 'Es ist nie existent *vor* seinem Grunde, sondern je nur *aus ihm* und *als dieser*. Grundsein besagt demnach, des eigensten Seins von Grund auf *nie* mächtig sein. Dieses *Nicht* gehört zum existenzialen Sinn der Geworfenheit. Grund-seiend *ist* es selbst eine Nichtigkeit seiner selbst.' Presumably the 'not' to which Heidegger refers in this puzzling passage, is implied in the 'never' of the preceding sentence.

[4] '. . . *Selbst* seiend ist das Dasein das geworfene Seiende *als* Selbst. *Nicht durch* es selbst, sondern *an* es selbst *entlassen* aus dem Grunde, um *als dieser* zu sein. Das Dasein ist nicht insofern selbst der Grund seines Seins, als dieser aus eigenem Entwurf erst entspringt, wohl aber ist es als Selbstsein das *Sein* des Grundes.'

is never anything but the basis for an entity whose Being has to take over Being-a-basis.

Dasein is its basis existently—that is, in such a manner that it understands itself in terms of possibilities, and, as so understanding itself, is that entity which has been thrown. But this implies that in having a potentiality-for-Being it always stands in one possibility or another: it constantly is *not* other possibilities, and it has waived these in its existentiell projection. Not only is the projection, as one that has been thrown, determined by the nullity of Being-a-basis; *as projection* it is itself essentially *null.* This does not mean that it has the ontical property of 'inconsequentiality' or 'worthlessness'; what we have here is rather something existentially constitutive for the structure of the Being of projection. The nullity we have in mind belongs to Dasein's Being-free for its existentiell possibilities. Freedom, however, *is* only in the choice of o n e possibility— that is, in tolerating one's not having chosen the others and one's not being able to choose them.

In the structure of thrownness, as in that of projection, there lies essentially a nullity. This nullity is the basis for the possibility of *in*authentic Dasein in its falling; and as falling, every inauthentic Dasein factically is. *Care itself, in its very essence, is permeated with nullity through and through.* Thus "care"—Dasein's Being—means, as thrown projection, Being-the-basis of a nullity (and this Being-the-basis is itself null). This means that *Dasein as such is guilty,* if our formally existential definition of "guilt" as "Being-the-basis of a nullity" is indeed correct.

Existential nullity has by no means the character of a privation, where something is lacking in comparison with an ideal which has been set up but does not get attained in Dasein; rather, the Being of this entity is already null *as projection*; and it is null *in advance of* [*vor*] any of the things which it can project and which it mostly attains.[1] This nullity, moreover, is thus not something which emerges in Dasein occasionally, attaching itself to it as an obscure quality which Dasein might eliminate if it made sufficient progress.

In spite of this, the *ontological meaning of the notness* [*Nichtheit*] of this existential nullity is still obscure. But this holds also for the *ontological essence of the "not" in general.* Ontology and logic, to be sure, have exacted a great deal from the "not", and have thus made its possibilities visible in a piecemeal fashion; but it itself has not been unveiled ontologically. Ontology came across the "not" and made use of it. But is it so obvious

---

[1] The negative character to which Heidegger here calls attention is not brought out as clearly by the word 'projection' (etymologically, 'throwing forward') as it is by the German 'entwerfen' ('throwing off' or 'throwing away'), where the prefix 'ent-' indicates separation.

that every "not" signifies something negative in the sense of a lack? Is its
positivity exhausted by the fact that it constitutes 'passing over' something?
Why does all dialectic take refuge in negation, though it cannot provide
dialectical grounds for this sort of thing *itself*, or even just establish it *as a
problem*? Has anyone ever made a problem of the *ontological source* of
notness, or, *prior to that*, even sought the mere *conditions* on the basis of
which the problem of the "not" and its notness and the possibility of that
notness can be raised? And how else are these conditions to be found
except by taking the meaning of Being in general as a theme and clarifying it?

The concepts of privation and lack—which, moreover, are not very
transparent—are already insufficient for the ontological Interpretation
of the phenomenon of guilt, though if we take them formally enough, we
can put them to considerable use. Least of all can we come any closer to
the existential phenomenon of guilt by taking our orientation from the
idea of evil, the *malum* as *privatio boni*. Just as the *bonum* and its *privatio*
have the same ontological origin in the ontology of the *present-at-hand*,
this ontology also applies to the idea of 'value', which has been 'abstracted'
from these.

Not only can entities whose Being is care load themselves with factical
guilt, but they *are* guilty in the very basis of their Being; and this Being-
guilty is what provides, above all, the ontological condition for Dasein's
ability to come to o w e anything in factically existing. This essential Being-
guilty is, equiprimordially, the existential condition for the possibility of
the 'morally' good and for that of the 'morally' evil—that is, for morality
in general and for the possible forms which this may take factically. The
primordial "Being-guilty" cannot be defined by morality, since morality
already presupposes it for itself.

But what kind of experience speaks for this primordial Being-guilty
which belongs to Dasein? Nor may we forget the counter-question: 'is'
guilt 'there' only if a consciousness of guilt gets awakened, or does not the
primordial Being-guilty[1] make itself known rather in the very fact that
guilt is 'asleep'? That this primordial Being-guilty remains proximally
and for the most part undisclosed, that it is kept closed off by Dasein's
falling Being, *reveals* only the aforesaid nullity. *Being*-guilty is more
primordial than any *knowledge* about it. And only because Dasein is
guilty in the basis of its Being, and closes itself off from itself as something
thrown and falling, is conscience possible, if indeed the call gives us *this*
Being-guilty as something which at bottom we are to understand.

The call is the call of care. Being-guilty constitutes the Being to which

---

[1] 'Schuldigsein'. In the earlier editions the 'sein' is emphasized by having the type
spaced out.

we give the name of "care". In uncanniness Dasein stands together with itself primordially. Uncanniness brings this entity face to face with its undisguised nullity, which belongs to the possibility of its ownmost potentiality-for-Being. To the extent that for Dasein, as care, its Being is an issue, it summons itself as a "they" which is factically falling, and summons itself from its uncanniness towards its potentiality-for-Being.[1] The appeal calls back by calling forth:[2] it calls Dasein *forth* to the possibility of taking over, in existing, even that thrown entity which it is; it calls Dasein *back* to its thrownness so as to understand this thrownness as the null basis which it has to take up into existence. This calling-back in which conscience calls forth, gives Dasein to understand that Dasein itself—the null basis for its null projection, standing in the possibility of its Being—is to bring itself back to itself from its lostness in the "they"; and this means that it *is guilty*.

But in that case the sort of thing which Dasein gives itself to understand would be information about itself. And the hearing which corresponds to such a call would be a *taking cognizance* of the Fact that one is 'guilty'. If, however, the call is to have the character of a summons, does not this way of interpreting the conscience lead to a complete perversion of its function? Does not a "summons to Being-guilty" mean a summons to evil?

One would not want to impose upon the conscience such a meaning for the "call", even in the most violent of Interpretations. But if not, what does it mean to 'summon one to Being-guilty'?

The meaning of the "call" becomes plain if, in our understanding of it, we stick to the existential sense of "Being-guilty", instead of making basic the derivative conception of guilt in the sense of an indebtedness which has 'arisen' through some deed done or left undone. Such a demand is not arbitrary, if the call of conscience, coming from Dasein itself, is directed towards that entity alone. But if so, the "summons to Being-guilty" signifies a calling-forth to that potentiality-for-Being which in each case I as Dasein am already. Dasein need not first load a 'guilt' upon itself through its failures or omissions; it must only *be* 'guilty' *authentically*—'guilty' in the way in which it is.[3]

Hearing the appeal correctly is thus tantamount to having an understanding of oneself in one's ownmost potentiality-for-Being—that is, to projecting oneself upon one's *ownmost* authentic potentiality for becoming

---

[1] We follow the newer editions in reading: '. . . ruft es aus der Unheimlichkeit sich selbst als faktisch-verfallendes Man auf zu seinem Seinkönnen.' This is apparently a correction of the older version, where one finds 'Man selbst' instead of 'Man', and might be tempted to construe this as a misprint for 'Man-selbst' ('they-self').

[2] 'Der Anruf ist vorrufender Rückruf.'

[3] '. . . es soll nur das "schuldig"—als welches es ist—*eigentlich sein*.'

guilty.[1] When Dasein understandingly lets itself be called forth to this possibility, this includes its *becoming free* for the call—its readiness for the potentiality of getting appealed to. In understanding the call, Dasein is *in thrall to* [*hörig*] *its ownmost possibility of existence*. It has chosen itself.

In so choosing, Dasein makes possible its ownmost Being-guilty, which remains closed off from the they-self. The common sense of the "they" knows only the satisfying of manipulable rules and public norms and the failure to satisfy them. It reckons up infractions of them and tries to balance them off. It has slunk away from its ownmost Being-guilty so as to be able to talk more loudly about making "mistakes". But in the appeal, the they-self gets called to [angerufen] the ownmost Being-guilty of the Self. Understanding the call is choosing; but it is not a choosing of conscience, which as such cannot be chosen. What is chosen is *having-a-conscience* as Being-free for one's ownmost Being-guilty. "*Understanding the appeal*" means "*wanting to have a conscience*".

This does not mean that one wants to have a 'good conscience', still less that one cultivates the call voluntarily; it means solely that one is ready to be appealed to. Wanting to have a conscience is just as far from seeking out one's factical indebtednesses as it is from the tendency to *liberation* from guilt in the sense of the essential 'guilty'.

Wanting to have a conscience is rather the most primordial existentiell presupposition for the possibility of factically coming to owe something. In understanding the call, Dasein lets its ownmost Self *take action in itself* [*in sich handeln*] in terms of that potentiality-for-Being which it has chosen. Only so can it *be* answerable [verantwortlich]. Factically, however, any taking-action is necessarily 'conscienceless', not only because it may fail to avoid some factical moral indebtedness, but because, on the null basis of its null projection, it has, in Being with Others, already become guilty towards them. Thus one's wanting-to-have-a-conscience becomes the taking-over of that essential conscienceless within which alone the existentiell possibility of *being* 'good' subsists.

Though the call gives no information, it is not merely critical; it is *positive*, in that it discloses Dasein's most primordial potentiality-for-Being as Being-guilty. Thus conscience manifests itself as an *attestation* which belongs to Dasein's Being—an attestation in which conscience calls Dasein itself face to face with its ownmost potentiality-for-Being. Is there an existentially more concrete way of determining the character of the

---

[1] 'Schuldigwerdenkönnen'. This '*ownmost* authentic' sense of 'schuldig werden' is presumably to be contrasted with the sense to which we have called attention in notes 2 and 4, p. 327, H. 282 above, and which we have expressed by the phrase 'come to owe'. When it seems to us that Heidegger has the authentic sense in mind, we shall express it by the phrase 'become guilty', though this device exaggerates a contrast which would not be felt so sharply by the German reader.

authentic potentiality-for-Being which has thus been attested? But now that we have exhibited a potentiality-for-Being which is attested in Dasein itself, a preliminary question arises: can we claim sufficient evidential weight for the way we have exhibited this, as long as the embarrassment of our Interpreting the conscience in a one-sided manner by tracing it back to Dasein's constitution while hastily passing over all the familiar findings of the ordinary interpretation of conscience, is one that is still undiminished? Is, then, the phenomenon of conscience, as it 'actually' is, still recognizable at all in the Interpretation we have given? Have we not been all too sure of ourselves in the ingenuousness with which we have deduced an idea of the conscience from Dasien's state of Being?

The final step of our Interpretation of the conscience is the existential delimitation of the authentic potentiality-for-Being which conscience attests. If we are to assure ourselves of a way of access which will make such a step possible even for the ordinary understanding of the conscience, we must explicitly demonstrate the connection between the results of our ontological analysis and the everyday ways in which the conscience is experienced.

¶ *59. The Existential Interpretation of the Conscience, and the Way Conscience is Ordinarily Interpreted*[1]

Conscience is the call of care from the uncanniness of Being-in-the-world—the call which summons Dasein to its ownmost potentiality-for-Being-guilty. And corresponding to this call, wanting-to-have-a-conscience has emerged as the way in which the appeal is understood. These two definitions cannot be brought into harmony at once with the ordinary interpretation of conscience. Indeed they seem to be in direct conflict with it. We call this interpretation of conscience the "ordinary" one [Vulgär] because in characterizing this phenomenon and describing its 'function', it sticks to what "*they*" know as the conscience, and how "they" follow it or fail to follow it.

But *must* the ontological Interpretation agree with the ordinary interpretation at all? Should not the latter be, in principle, ontologically suspect? If indeed Dasein understands itself proximally and for the most part in terms of that with which it concerns itself, and if it interprets all its ways of behaving as concern, then will not there be falling and concealment in its interpretation of that very way of its Being which, as a call, seeks to bring it back from its lostness in the concerns of the "they"?[2]

---

[1] '*Die existenziale Interpretation des Gewissens und die vulgäre Gewissensauslegung*'.

[2] '... wird es dann nicht gerade *die* Weise seines Seins verfallend-verdeckend auslegen, die es als Ruf aus der Verlorenheit in die Besorgnisse des Man zurückholen will.' While we feel that the meaning of this sentence is probably as we have represented it, the grammar is quite ambiguous.

Everydayness takes Dasein as something ready-to-hand to be concerned with—that is, something that gets managed and reckoned up. 'Life' is a 'business', whether or not it covers its costs.

And so with regard to the ordinary kind of Being of Dasein itself, there is no guarantee that the way of interpreting conscience which springs from it or the theories of conscience which are thus oriented, have arrived at the right ontological horizon for its Interpretation. In spite of this, even the ordinary experience of conscience must somehow—pre-ontologically— reach this phenomenon. Two things follow from this: on the one hand, the everyday way of interpreting conscience cannot be accepted as the final criterion for the 'Objectivity' of an ontological analysis. On the other hand, such an analysis has no right to disregard the everyday under- standing of conscience and to pass over the anthropological, psychological, and theological theories of conscience which have been based upon it. *If* existential analysis has laid bare the phenomenon of conscience in its ontological roots, then precisely in terms of this analysis the ordinary interpretations must become intelligible; and they must become intellig- ible not least in the ways in which they miss the phenomenon and in the reasons why they conceal it. But since in the context of the problems of this treatise the analysis of conscience is merely ancillary to what is ontologically the fundamental question, we must be satisfied with alluding to the essential problems when we characterize the connection between the existential Interpretation of conscience and the way it is ordinarily interpreted.

In this ordinary interpretation there are four objections which might be brought up against our Interpretation of conscience as the summons of care to Being-guilty: (1) that the function of conscience is essentially critical; (2) that conscience always speaks in a way that is relative to some definite deed which has been performed or willed; (3) that when the 'voice' is experienced, it is never so radically related to Dasein's Being; (4) that our Interpretation takes no account of the basic forms of the phenomenon—'evil' conscience and 'good', that which 'reproves' and that which 'warns'.

Let us begin our discussion with the last of these considerations. In all interpretations of conscience, the 'evil' or 'bad' conscience gets the priority: conscience is primarily 'evil'; such a conscience makes known to us that in every experience of conscience something like a 'Guilty!' gets experienced first. But in the idea of bad conscience, how is this making- known of Being-evil understood? The 'Experience of conscience' turns up *after* the deed has been done or left undone. The voice follows the trans- gression and points back to that event which has befallen and by which

Dasein has loaded itself with guilt. If conscience makes known a 'Being-guilty', then it cannot do this by summoning us to something, but it does so by remembering the guilt which has been incurred, and referring to it. But does the 'fact' that the voice comes afterwards, prevent the call from being basically a calling-forth? That the voice gets taken as a stirring of conscience which *follows after* is not enough to prove that we understand the phenomenon of conscience primordially. What if factical indebtedness were only the occasion for the factical calling of conscience? What if that Interpretation of the 'evil' conscience which we have described goes only half way? That such is the case is evident from the ontological fore-having within whose scope the phenomenon has been brought by this Interpretation. The voice is something that turns up; it has its position in the sequence of Experiences which are present-at-hand, and it follows after the Experience of the deed. But neither the call, nor the deed which has happened, nor the guilt with which one is laden, is an occurrence with the character of something present-at-hand which runs its course. The call has the kind of Being which belongs to care. In the call Dasein 'is' ahead of itself in such a way that at the same time it directs itself back to its thrownness. Only by first positing that Dasein is an interconnected sequence of successive Experiences, is it possible to take the voice as something which comes afterwards, something later, which therefore necessarily refers back. The voice does call back, but it calls beyond the deed which has happened, and back to the Being-guilty into which one has been thrown, which is 'earlier' than any indebtedness. But at the same time, this calling-back calls forth to *Being*-guilty, as something to be seized upon in one's own existence, so that authentic existentiell *Being*-guilty only 'follows after' the call, not *vice versa*. Bad conscience is basically so far from just reproving and pointing back that it rather points forward[1] as it calls one back into one's thrownness. *The order of the sequence in which Experiences run their course does not give us the phenomenal structure of existing.*

If we cannot reach the primordial phenomenon by a characterization of 'bad' conscience, still less can we do so by a characterization of 'good' conscience, whether we take this as a self-subsistent[2] form of conscience or as one which is essentially founded upon 'bad' conscience. Just as Dasein's 'Being-evil' would be made known to us in the 'bad' conscience, the 'good' conscience must have made known its 'Being-good'. It is easy to see that the conscience which used to be an 'effluence of the divine power' now becomes a slave of Pharisaism. Such a conscience would let a man say of

---

[1] 'vorweisend'. We have followed English idiom in translating 'vorweisen' as 'point forward' and 'vorrufen' as 'call forth'; but the prefix 'vor-' is the same in both cases, and means 'forward' as opposed to 'backward'.

[2] 'selbständige'. See note 1, p. 153, H. 1 17 and note 1, p. 351, H. 303.

himself 'I am good'; who else can say this than the good man himself, and who would be less willing to affirm it? But if this impossible conclusion is drawn from the idea of the good conscience, the fact that 'Being-guilty" is what the conscience calls, only comes to the fore.

To escape this conclusion, the "good' conscience has been Interpreted as a privation of the 'bad' one, and defined as 'an Experienced lack of bad conscience'.viii This would make it an experience of not having the call turn up—that is, of my having nothing with which to reproach myself. But how is such a 'lack' *'Experienced'*? This supposed Experience is by no means the experiencing of a call; it is rather a making-certain[1] that a deed attributed to Dasein has not been perpetrated by it and that Dasein is *therefore* not guilty. Becoming certain that one has not done something, has *by no means* the character of a conscience-phenomenon. It can, however, signify rather that one is forgetting one's conscience—in other words, that one is emerging from the possibility of being able to be appealed to. In the 'certainty' here mentioned lurks the tranquillizing suppression of one's wanting to have a conscience—that is, of understanding one's ownmost and constant Being-guilty. The 'good' conscience is neither a self-subsistent form of conscience, nor a founded form of conscience; in short, it is not a conscience-phenomenon at all.

In so far as talk about a 'good' conscience arises from everyday Dasein's way of experiencing the conscience, everyday Dasein merely betrays thereby that even when it speaks of the 'bad' conscience it basically fails to reach the phenomenon. For the idea of the 'bad' conscience is oriented factically by that of the 'good' conscience. The everyday interpretation keeps within the dimension of concernfully reckoning up 'guilt' and 'innocence' ["Unschuld"] and balancing them off. This, then, is the horizon within which the voice of conscience gets 'Experienced'.

In characterizing what is primordial in the ideas of 'bad' and 'good' conscience, we have also decided as to the distinction between a conscience which points forward and warns and one which points back and reproves. The idea of the warning conscience seems, of course, to come closest to the phenomenon of the summons. It shares with this the character of pointing forward. But this agreement is just an illusion. When we experience a warning conscience, the voice is regarded in turn as merely oriented towards the deed which has been willed, from which it seeks to preserve us. But the warning, as a check on what we have willed, is possible only because the 'warning' call is aimed at Dasein's potentiality-for-Being—that is, at its understanding of itself in Being-guilty; not until we have such

[1] In this paragraph Heidegger takes pains to disassociate 'Gewissen' ('conscience') from the adjective 'gewiss' ('certain') and its derivatives—'Sichvergewissern' ('making-certain'), 'Gewisswerden' ('becoming certain'), and 'Gewissheit' ('certainty').

understanding does 'what we have willed' get shattered. The conscience which warns us has the function of regulating from moment to moment our remaining free from indebtednesses.[1] In the experience of a 'warning' conscience the tendency of its call is seen only to the extent that it remains accessible to the common sense of the "they".

The third consideration which we have mentioned invokes the fact that the everyday experience of the conscience *has no acquaintance* with anything like getting summoned to Being-guilty. This must be conceded. But does this everyday experience thus give us any guarantee that the full possible content of the call of the voice of conscience has been heard therein? Does it follow from this that theories of conscience which are based on the ordinary way of experiencing it have made certain that their ontological horizon for analysing this phenomenon is an appropriate one? Does not falling, which is an essential kind of Being for Dasein, show us rather that ontically this entity understands itself proximally and for the most part in terms of the horizon of concern, but that ontologically, it defines "Being" in the sense of presence-at-hand? This, however, leads to covering up the phenomenon in two ways: what one sees in this theory is a sequence of Experiences or 'psychical processes'—a sequence whose kind of Being is for the most part wholly indefinite. In such experience the conscience is encountered as an arbiter and admonisher, with whom Dasein reckons and pleads its cause.

When Kant represented the conscience as a 'court of justice' and made this the basic guiding idea in his Interpretation of it, he did not do so by accident; this was suggested by the idea of moral *law*—although his conception of morality was far removed from utilitarianism and eudae-monism. Even the theory of value, whether it is regarded formally or materially, has as its unexpressed ontological presupposition a 'metaphysic of morals'—that is, an ontology of Dasein and existence. Dasein is regarded as an entity with which one might concern oneself, whether this "concern" has the sense of 'actualizing values' or of satisfying a norm.

If one is to invoke the full range of what the everyday experience of conscience—as the only higher court for the Interpretation of conscience—is acquainted with, this cannot be justified unless one has considered beforehand whether the conscience can ever become authentically accessible here at all.

Thus the further objection that the existential Interpretation overlooks the fact that the call of conscience always relates itself to some definite deed which has been either 'actualized' or willed, also loses its force.

---

[1] 'Das warnende Gewissen hat die Funktion der momentweisen Regelung eines Freibleibens von Verschuldungen.' The earlier editions contradict this by writing '. . . hat nicht die Funktion . . .'

It cannot be denied that the call is often experienced as having such a tendency. It remains questionable only whether this experience of the call permits it to 'proclaim' itself fully. In the common-sense interpretation, one may suppose that one is sticking to the 'facts'; but in the end, by its very common sense, this interpretation has restricted the call's disclosive range. As little as the 'good' conscience lets itself be put in the service of a 'Pharisaism', just as little may the function of the 'bad' conscience be reduced to indicating indebtednesses which are present-at-hand or thrusting aside those which are possible. This would be as if Dasein were a 'household' whose indebtednesses simply need to be balanced off in an orderly manner so that the Self may stand 'by' as a disinterested spectator while these Experiences run their course.

If, however, that which is primary in the call is not a relatedness to a guilt which is factically 'present-at-hand', or to some guilt-charged deed which has been factically willed, and if accordingly the 'reproving' and 'warning' types of conscience express no primordial call-functions, then we have also undermined the consideration we mentioned first, that the existential Interpretation fails to recognize the 'essentially' *critical* character of what the conscience does. This consideration too is one that springs from catching sight of the phenomenon in a manner which, within certain limits, is genuine; for in the content of the call, one can indeed point to nothing which the voice 'positively' recommends and imposes. But how are we to understand this positivity which is missing in what the conscience does? Does it follow from this that conscience has a 'negative' character?

We miss a 'positive' content in that which is called, *because we expect to be told something currently useful about assured possibilities of 'taking action' which are available and calculable.* This expectation has its basis within the horizon of that way of interpreting which belongs to common-sense concern—a way of interpreting which forces Dasein's existence to be subsumed under the idea of a business procedure that can be regulated. Such expectations (and in part these tacitly underlie even the demand for a *material* ethic of value as contrasted with one that is 'merely' formal) are of course disappointed by the conscience. The call of conscience fails to give any such 'practical' injunctions, *solely because* it summons Dasein to existence, to its ownmost potentiality-for-Being-its-Self. With the maxims which one might be led to expect—maxims which could be reckoned up unequivocally—the conscience would deny to existence nothing less than the very *possibility of taking action.* But because the conscience manifestly cannot be 'positive' in this manner, neither does it function 'just negatively' in this same manner. The call discloses nothing which could be either positive or negative as something with which we *can concern ourselves*; for what it has in view is a Being which is ontologically quite different—namely, *existence*. On the other hand, when the call is rightly understood, it gives us that which in the existential sense is the 'most positive' of all—namely, the ownmost possibility which Dasein can present to itself, as a calling-back which calls it forth into its factical potentiality-for-being-its-Self at the time. To hear the call authentically, signifies bringing oneself into a factical taking-action. But only by setting forth the existential structure implied in our understanding of the appeal when we *hear it authentically*, shall we obtain a fully adequate Interpretation of what is called in the call.

We must first show how the only phenomena with which the ordinary interpretation has any familiarity point back to the primordial meaning of the call of conscience when they are understood in a way that is ontologically appropriate; we must then show that the ordinary interpretation springs from the limitations of the way Dasein interprets itself in falling; and, since falling belongs to care itself, we must also show that this interpretation, *in spite of all its obviousness, is by no means accidental.*

In criticizing the ordinary interpretation of the conscience ontologically, one might be subject to the misunderstanding of supposing that if one demonstrates that the everyday way of experiencing the conscience is not *existentially* primordial, one will have made some judgment as to the *existentiell* 'moral quality' of any Dasein which maintains itself in that kind of experience. Just as little as existence is necessarily and directly impaired by an ontologically inadequate way of understanding the conscience, so little does an existentially appropriate Interpretation of the conscience guarantee that one has understood the call in an existentiell manner. It is no less possible to be serious when one experiences the conscience in the ordinary way than not to be serious when one's understanding of it is more primordial. Nevertheless, the Interpretation which is more primordial existentially, also discloses *possibilities* for a more primordial existentiell understanding, as long as our ontological conceptualization does not let itself get cut off from our ontical experience.

¶ *60. The Existential Structure of the Authentic Potentiality-for-Being which is Attested in the Conscience*

The existential Interpretation of conscience is to exhibit an attestation of Dasein's ownmost potentiality-for-Being—an attestation which *is* [*seiende*] in Dasein itself. Conscience attests not by making something known in an undifferentiated manner, but by calling forth and summoning us to Being-guilty. That which is so attested becomes 'grasped'

in the hearing which understands the call undisguisedly in the sense it
has itself intended. The understanding of the appeal is a mode of Dasein's
Being, and only as such does it give us the phenomenal content of what the
call of conscience attests. The authentic understanding of the call has been
characterized as "wanting to have a conscience". This is a way of letting
one's ownmost Self take action in itself of its own accord in its Being-
guilty, and represents phenomenally that authentic potentiality-for-Being
which Dasein itself attests. The existential structure of this must now be
laid bare. Only so can we proceed to the basic constitution of the *authenticity* of Dasein's existence as disclosed in Dasein itself.

Wanting to have a conscience is, as an understanding of oneself in
one's ownmost potentiality-for-Being, a way in which Dasein has been
disclosed. This disclosedness is constituted by discourse and state-of-mind,
as well as by understanding. To understand in an existentiell manner
implies projecting oneself in each case upon one's ownmost factical possibility of having the potentiality-for-Being-in-the-world. But the *potentiality*-for-Being is understood only by existing in this possibility.

What kind of mood corresponds to such understanding? Understanding
the call discloses one's own Dasein in the uncanniness of its individualization. The uncanniness which is revealed in understanding and revealed
along with it, becomes genuinely disclosed by the state-of-mind of anxiety
which belongs to that understanding. The fact of the *anxiety of conscience*,
gives us phenomenal confirmation that in understanding the call Dasein
is brought face to face with its own uncanniness. Wanting-to-have-a-
conscience becomes a readiness for anxiety.

The third essential item in disclosedness is *discourse*. The call itself is a
primordial kind of discourse for Dasein; but there is no corresponding
counter-discourse in which, let us say, one talks about what the conscience has said, and pleads one's cause. In hearing the call understandingly, one denies oneself any counter-discourse, not because one has been
assailed by some 'obscure power', which suppresses one's hearing, but
because this hearing has appropriated the content of the call unconcealedly. In the call one's constant Being-guilty is represented, and in this
way the Self is brought back from the loud idle talk which goes with the
common sense of the "they". Thus the mode of Articulative discourse
which belongs to wanting to have a conscience, is one of *reticence*. Keeping
silent has been characterized as an essential possibility of discourse.[ix]
Anyone who keeps silent when he wants to give us to understand something, must 'have something to say'. In the appeal Dasein gives itself to
understand its ownmost potentiality-for-Being. This calling is therefore a
keeping-silent. The discourse of the conscience never comes to utterance.

Only in keeping silent does the conscience call; that is to say, the call comes from the soundlessness of uncanniness, and the Dasein which it summons is called back into the stillness of itself, and called back as something that is to become still. Only in reticence, therefore, is this silent discourse understood appropriately in wanting to have a conscience. It takes the words away from the common-sense idle talk of the "they".

The common-sense way of interpreting the conscience, which 'sticks rigorously to the facts', takes the silent discourse of the conscience as an occasion for passing it off as something which is not at all ascertainable or present-at-hand. The fact that *"they"*, who hear and understand nothing but loud idle talk, cannot 'report' any call, is held against the conscience on the subterfuge that it is 'dumb' and manifestly not present-at-hand. With this kind of interpretation the "they" merely covers up its own failure to hear the call and the fact that its 'hearing' does not reach very far.

The disclosedness of Dasein in wanting to have a conscience, is thus constituted by anxiety as state-of-mind, by understanding as a projection of oneself upon one's ownmost Being-guilty, and by discourse as reticence. This distinctive and authentic disclosedness, which is attested in Dasein itself by its conscience—*this reticent self-projection upon one's ownmost Being-guilty, in which one is ready for anxiety*—we call *"resoluteness"*.

Resoluteness is a distinctive mode of Dasein's disclosedness.[1] In an earlier passage, however, we have Interpreted disclosedness existentially as the *primordial truth*,[x] Such truth is primarily not a quality of 'judgment' nor of any definite way of behaving, but something essentially constitutive for Being-in-the-world as such. Truth must be conceived as a fundamental *existentiale*. In our ontological clarification of the proposition that 'Dasein is in the truth' we have called attention to the primordial disclosedness of this entity as the *truth of existence*; and for the delimitation of its character we have referred to the analysis of Dasein's authenticity.[xi]

In resoluteness we have now arrived at that truth of Dasein which is most primordial because it is *authentic*. Whenever a "there" is disclosed, its whole Being-in-the-world—that is to say, the world, Being-in, and the Self which, as an 'I am', this entity is—is disclosed with equal primordiality.[2] Whenever the world is disclosed, entities within-the-world have

---

[1] The etymological connection between 'Entschlossenheit' ('resoluteness') and 'Erschlossenheit' ('disclosedness') is not to be overlooked.

[2] 'Die Erschlossenheit des Da erschliesst gleichursprünglich das je ganze In-der-Welt-sein, das heisst die Welt, das In-Sein und das Selbst, das als "ich bin" dieses Seiende ist.' It is not clear grammatically whether 'dieses Seiende' or the pronoun 'das' is the subject of the final clause, or whether 'this entity' is 'Dasein' or 'Being-in'. The grammatical function of the 'als "ich bin" ' is also doubtful. In support of our interpretation, consult H. 54, 114, 117, 267.

been discovered already. The discoveredness of the ready-to-hand and the present-at-hand is based on the disclosedness of the world xⁱⁱ for if the current totality of involvements is to be freed, this requires that significance be understood beforehand. In understanding significance, concernful Dasein submits itself circumspectively to what it encounters as ready-to-hand. Any discovering of a totality of involvements goes back to a "for-the-sake-of-which"; and on the understanding of such a "for-the-sake-of-which" is based in turn the understanding of significance as the disclosedness of the current world. In seeking shelter, sustenance, livelihood, we do so "for the sake of" constant possibilities of Dasein which are very close to it;[1] upon these the entity for which its own Being is an issue, has already projected itself. Thrown into its 'there', every Dasein has been factically submitted to a definite 'world'—its 'world'. At the same time those factical projections which are closest to it, have been guided by its concernful *lostness* in the "they". To this lostness, one's own Dasein can appeal, and this appeal can be understood in the way of resoluteness. But in that case this *authentic* disclosedness modifies with equal primordiality both the way in which the 'world' is discovered (and this is founded upon that disclosedness) and the way in which the Dasein-with of Others is disclosed. The 'world' which is ready-to-hand does not become another one 'in its content', nor does the circle of Others get exchanged for a new one; but both one's Being towards the ready-to-hand understandingly and concernfully, and one's solicitous Being with Others, are now given a definite character in terms of their ownmost potentiality-for-Being-their-Selves.

Resoluteness, as *authentic Being-one's-Self*, does not detach Dasein from its world, nor does it isolate it so that it becomes a free-floating "I". And how should it, when resoluteness as authentic disclosedness, is *authentically* nothing else than *Being-in-the-world*? Resoluteness brings the Self right into its current concernful Being-alongside what is ready-to-hand, and pushes it into solicitous Being with Others.

In the light of the "for-the-sake-of-which" of one's self-chosen potentiality-for-Being, resolute Dasein frees itself for its world. Dasein's resoluteness towards itself is what first makes it possible to let the Others who are with it 'be' in their ownmost potentiality-for-Being, and to co-disclose this potentiality in the solicitude which leaps forth and liberates. When Dasein is resolute, it can become the 'conscience' of Others. Only by authentically Being-their-Selves in resoluteness can people authentically be with one another—not by ambiguous and jealous stipulations and

---

[1] 'Das Umwillen des Unterkommens, des Unterhalts, des Fortkommens sind nächste und ständige Möglichkeiten des Daseins . . .'

talkative fraternizing in the "they" and in what "they" want to undertake.

Resoluteness, by its ontological essence, is always the resoluteness of some factical Dasein at a particular time. The essence of Dasein as an entity is its existence. Resoluteness 'exists' only as a resolution [Entschluss] which understandingly projects itself. But on what basis does Dasein disclose itself in resoluteness? On what is it to resolve?[1] *Only* the resolution itself can give the answer. One would completely misunderstand the phenomenon of resoluteness if one should want to suppose that this consists simply in taking up possibilities which have been proposed and recommended, and seizing hold of them. *The resolution is precisely the disclosive projection and determination of what is factically possible at the time.* To resoluteness, the *indefiniteness* characteristic of every potentiality-for-Being into which Dasein has been factically thrown, is something that necessarily *belongs*. Only in a resolution is resoluteness sure of itself. The *existentiell indefiniteness* of resoluteness never makes itself definite except in a resolution; yet it has, all the same, its *existential definiteness*.

What one resolves upon in resoluteness has been prescribed ontologically in the existentiality of Dasein in general as a potentiality-for-Being in the manner of concernful solicitude. As care, however, Dasein has been Determined by facticity and falling. Disclosed in its 'there', it maintains itself both in truth and in untruth with equal primordiality.[xlii] This 'really' holds in particular for resoluteness as authentic truth. Resoluteness appropriates untruth authentically. Dasein is already in irresoluteness [Unentschlossenheit], and soon, perhaps, will be in it again. The term "irresoluteness' merely expresses that phenomenon which we have Interpreted as a Being-surrendered to the way in which things have been prevalently interpreted by the "they". Dasein, as a they-self, gets 'lived' by the common-sense ambiguity of that publicness in which nobody resolves upon anything but which has always made its decision.[2] "Resoluteness" signifies letting oneself be summoned out of one's lostness in the "they". The irresoluteness of the "they" remains dominant notwithstanding, but it cannot impugn resolute existence. In the counter-concept to irresoluteness, as resoluteness as existentially understood, we do not have in mind any ontico-psychical characteristic in the sense of Being-burdened with inhibitions. Even resolutions remain dependent upon

[1] 'Aber woraufhin erschliesst sich das Dasein in der Entschlossenheit? Wozu soll es sich entschliessen?' (For similar constructions with 'woraufhin' etc. and 'erschliessen', see H. 141, 143, 145 above.)

[2] 'Das Dasein wird als Man-selbst von der verständigen Zweideutigkeit der Öffentlichkeit "gelebt", in der sich niemand entschliesst, und die doch schon immer beschlossen hat.' The etymological connection between 'entschliesst' and 'beschlossen' is lost in our translation.

the "they" and its world. The understanding of this is one of the things that a resolution discloses, inasmuch as resoluteness is what first gives authentic transparency to Dasein. In resoluteness the issue for Dasein is its ownmost potentiality-for-Being, which, as something thrown, can project itself only upon definite factical possibilities. Resolution does not withdraw itself from 'actuality', but discovers first what is factically possible; and it does so by seizing upon it in whatever way is possible for it as its ownmost potentiality-for-Being in the "they". The existential attributes of any possible resolute Dasein include the items constitutive for an existential phenomenon which we call a *"Situation"* and which we have hitherto passed over.

In the term "Situation" ("situation"—'to be in a situation') there is an overtone of a signification that is spatial.[1] We shall not try to eliminate this from the existential conception for such an overtone is also implied in the 'there' of Dasein. Being-in-the-world has a spatiality of its own, characterized by the phenomena of de-severance and directionality. Dasein 'makes room' in so far as it factically exists.[xiv] But spatiality of the kind which belongs to Dasein, and on the basis of which existence always determines its 'location', is grounded in the state of Being-in-the-world, for which disclosedness is primarily constitutive. Just as the spatiality of the "there" is grounded in disclosedness, the Situation has its foundations in resoluteness. The Situation is the "there" which is disclosed in resoluteness—the "there" as which the existent entity is there. It is not a framework present-at-hand in which Dasein occurs, or into which it might even just bring itself. Far removed from any present-at-hand mixture of circumstances and accidents which we encounter, the Situation *is* only through resoluteness and in it. The current factical involvement-character of the circumstances discloses itself to the Self only when that involvement-character is such that one has resolved upon the "there" as which that Self, in existing, has to be.[2] When what we call "accidents" befall from the with-world and the environment, they can be-*fall* only resoluteness.[3]

For the "they", however, the Situation is essentially something that has been closed off.[4] The "they" knows only the '*general situation*', loses itself in those '*opportunities*' which are closest to it, and pays Dasein's way by a reckoning

[1] The German words 'Situation' and 'Lage' will be translated by 'Situation' and 'situation' respectively.

[2] 'Entschlossen für das Da, als welches das Selbst existierend zu sein hat, erschliesst sich ihm erst der jeweilige faktische Bewandtnischarakter der Umstände.'

[3] 'Nur der Ent-schlossenheit kann das aus der Mit- und Umwelt *zu-fallen*, was wir Zufälle nennen.' Literally a 'Zufall' ('accident') is something that 'falls to' something, or 'befalls' it. (Compare the Latin '*accidens*', which has basically the same meaning).

[4] 'verschlossen'. Contrast 'erschlossen' ('disclosed') and 'entschlossen' ('resolved').

up of 'accidents' which it fails to recognize, deems its own achievement, and passes off as such.[1]

Resoluteness brings the Being of the "there" into the existence of its Situation. Indeed it delimits the existential structure of that authentic potentiality-for-Being which the conscience attests—wanting to have a conscience. In this potentiality we have recognized the appropriate way of understanding the appeal. This makes it entirely plain that when the call of conscience summons us to our potentiality-for-Being, it does not hold before us some empty ideal of existence, but *calls us forth into the Situation.* This existential positivity which the call of conscience possesses when rightly understood, gives us at the same time an insight: it makes us see to what extent we fail to recognize the disclosive character of the conscience if the tendency of the call is restricted to indebtednesses which have already occurred or which we have before us; it also makes us see to what extent the concrete understanding of the voice of conscience is only seemingly transmitted to us if this restriction is made. When our understanding of the appeal is Interpreted existentially as resoluteness, the conscience is revealed as that kind of Being—included in the very basis of Dasein[2]—in which Dasein makes possible for itself its factical existence, thus attesting its ownmost potentiality-for-Being.

This phenomenon which we have exhibited as "resoluteness' can hardly be confused with an empty '*habitus*' or an indefinite 'velleity'. Resoluteness does not first take cognizance of a Situation and put that Situation before itself; it has put itself into that Situation already.[3] As resolute, Dasein is already *taking action.* The term 'take action'[4] is one which we are purposely avoiding. For in the first place this term must be taken so broadly that "activity" [Aktivität] will also embrace the passivity of resistance. In the second place, it suggests a misunderstanding in the ontology of Dasein, as if resoluteness were a special way of behaviour belonging to the practical faculty as contrasted with one that is theoretical. Care, however, as

---

[1] 'Es kennt nur die "*allgemeine Lage*", verliert sich an die nächsten "*Gelegenheiten*" und bestreitet das Dasein aus der Verrechnung der "Zufälle", die es, sie verkennend, für die eigene Leistung hält und ausgibt.' We have preserved the grammatical ambiguity of the pronouns 'die' and '*es*'.

[2] '. . . als die im Grunde des Daseins beschlossene Seinsart . . .' The participle 'beschlossene', which is etymologically akin to 'erschlossen', etc., may mean either 'included' or 'decided upon', as we have seen on H. 299. Very likely both meanings are here intended.

[3] 'Die Entschlossenheit stellt sich nicht erst, kenntnisnehmend, eine Situation vor, sondern hat sich schon in sie gestellt.' Our rather literal translation brings out the contrast between 'sich stellen in . . .' ('put itself in . . .') and 'sich stellen . . . vor . . .' ('put before itself . . .'), but fails to bring out the important sense of the latter expression: 'to represent' or 'to form an idea of'.

[4] ' "Handeln" '. Far from avoiding this term, Heidegger has used it quite frequently. But he *is* avoiding it as a possible substitute for the term 'Entschlossenheit'.

concernful solicitude, so primordially and wholly envelops Dasein's Being
that it must already be presupposed as a whole when we distinguish
between theoretical and practical behaviour; it cannot first be built up
out of these faculties by a dialectic which, because it is existentially
ungrounded, is necessarily quite baseless. *Resoluteness, however, is only that*
authenticity which, in care, is the object of care [in der Sorge gesorgte], and which
is possible as care—the authenticity of care itself.

To present the factical existentiell possibilities in their chief features
and interconnections, and to Interpret them according to their existential
structure, falls among the tasks of a thematic existential anthropology.[xv]
For the purposes of the present investigation as a study of fundamental
ontology, it is enough if that authentic potentiality-for-Being which
conscience attests for Dasein itself in terms of Dasein itself, is defined
existentially.

Now that resoluteness has been worked out as Being-guilty, a self-
projection in which one is reticent and ready for anxiety,[1] our investigation has been put in a position for defining the ontological meaning of
that potentiality which we have been seeking—Dasein's *authentic* potentiality-for-Being-a-whole. By now the authenticity of Dasein is neither an
empty term nor an idea which someone has fabricated. But even so, as
an authentic potentiality-for-Being-a-whole, the authentic Being-towards-
death which we have deduced existentially still remains a purely existential project for which Dasein's attestation is missing. Only when such
attestation has been found will our investigation suffice to exhibit (as its
problematic requires) an authentic potentiality-for-Being-a-whole, existentially confirmed and clarified—a potentiality which belongs to Dasein.
For only when this entity has become phenomenally accessible in its
authenticity and its totality, will the question of the meaning of the
Being of *this* entity, to whose existence there belongs in general an understanding of Being, be based upon something which will stand any test.

---

1 'Mit der Herausarbeitung der Entschlossenheit als des verschwiegenen, angstbereiten
Sichentwerfens auf das eigenste Schuldigsein . . .' The earlier editions have '. . . dem
verschwiegenen, angstbereiten Sichentwerfen auf . . .'

III

DASEIN'S AUTHENTIC POTENTIALITY-FOR-BEING-A-WHOLE, AND TEMPORALITY AS THE ONTOLOGICAL MEANING OF CARE

¶ *61. A Preliminary Sketch of the Methodological Step from the Definition of Dasein's Authentic Being-a-whole to the Laying-bare of Temporality as a Phenomenon*

AN authentic potentiality-for-Being-a-whole on the part of Dasein has been projected existentially. By analysing this phenomenon, we have revealed that authentic Being-towards-death is *anticipation.*[1] Dasein's authentic potentiality-for-Being, in its existentiell attestation, has been exhibited, and at the same time existentially Interpreted, as *resoluteness.*[1] How are these two phenomena of anticipation and resoluteness to be brought together? Has not our ontological projection of the authentic potentiality-for-Being-a-whole led us into a dimension of Dasein which lies far from the phenomenon of resoluteness? What can death and the 'concrete Situation' of taking action have in common? In attempting to bring resoluteness and anticipation forcibly together, are we not seduced into an intolerable and quite unphenomenological construction, for which we can no longer claim that it has the character of an ontological projection, based upon the phenomena?

Any superficial binding together of the two phenomena is excluded. There still remains one way out, and this is the only possible method: namely, to take as our point of departure the phenomenon of resoluteness, as attested in its existentiell possibility, and to ask: *"Does resoluteness, in its ownmost existentiell tendency of Being, point forward to anticipatory resoluteness as its ownmost authentic possibility?"* What if resoluteness, in accordance with its own meaning, should bring itself into its authenticity only when it projects itself not upon any random possibilities which just lie closest, but upon that uttermost possibility which lies ahead of every factical potentiality-for-Being of Dasein,[2] and, as such, enters more or less

---

[1] 'In seiner existenziellen Bezeugung wurde das eigentliche Seinkönnen des Daseins als *Entschlossenheit* aufgezeigt und zugleich existenzial interpretiert.' In the earlier editions the words 'aufgezeigt und zugleich existenzial interpretiert' are inserted between 'Bezeugung' and 'wurde', not in their present position.

[2] '... die allem faktischen Seinkönnen des Daseins vorgelagert ist ...' Cf. note 1, p. 303, H. 259 above.

undisguisedly into every potentiality-for-Being of which Dasein factically takes hold? What if it is only in the anticipation of [zum] death that resoluteness, as Dasein's *authentic* truth, has reached the *authentic certainty* which *belongs* to it? What if it is only in the *anticipation* if death that all the factical *'anticipatoriness'* of resolving would be authentically understood— in other words, that it would be *caught up with* in an existentiell way?[1]

In our existential Interpretation, the entity which has been presented to us as our theme has *Dasein's* kind of Being, and cannot be pieced together into something present-at-hand out of pieces which are present-at-hand. So long as we do not forget this, every step in our Interpretation must be guided by the idea of *existence*. What this signifies for the question of the possible connection between anticipation and resoluteness, is nothing less than the demand that we should project these existential phenomena upon the existentiell possibilities which have been delineated in them, and 'think these possibilities through to the end' in an existential manner. If we do this, the working-out of anticipatory resoluteness as a potentiality-for-Being-a-whole such that this potentiality is authentic and is possible in an existentiell way, will lose the character of an arbitrary construction. It will have become a way of Interpreting whereby Dasein is liberated *for* its uttermost possibility of existence.

In taking this step, the existential Interpretation makes known at the same time its ownmost methodological character. Up till now, except for some remarks which were occasionally necessary, we have deferred explicit discussions of method. Our first task was to 'go forth' towards the phenomena. But, *before* laying bare the meaning of the Being of an entity which has been revealed in its basic phenomenal content, we must stop for a while in the course of our investigation, not for the purpose of 'resting', but so that we may be impelled the more keenly.

Any genuine method is based on viewing in advance in an appropriate way the basic constitution of the 'object' to be disclosed, or of the domain within which the object lies. Thus any genuinely methodical consideration— which is to be distinguished from empty discussions of technique—must likewise give information about the kind of Being of the entity which has been taken as our theme. The clarification of the methodological possibilities, requirements, and limitations of the existential analytic in general, can alone secure the transparency which is necessary if we are to

---

[1] 'Wenn im *Vorlaufen* zum Tode erst alle faktische *"Vorläufigkeit"* des Entschliessens eigentlich verstanden, das heisst existenziell *eingeholt* wäre?' Our translation of 'Vorlaufen' as 'anticipation' again fails to bring out the metaphor of 'running ahead', with which the notion of 'catching up' is here clearly connected. (Cf. our note 3, p. 306, H. 262 above.) Similarly our translation of'Vorläufigkeit' as 'anticipatoriness', which brings out the connection with 'vorlaufen', is out of line with our usual translation of the adjective 'vorläufig' as 'provisional'.

take the basic step of unveiling the meaning of the Being of care. *But the Interpretation of the ontological meaning of care must be performed on the basis of envisaging phenomenologically in a full and constant manner Dasein's existential constitution as we have exhibited it up till now.* Ontologically, Dasein is in principle different from everything that is present-at-hand or Real. Its 'subsistence' is not based on the substantiality of a substance but on the '*Self-subsistence*' of the existing Self, whose Being has been conceived as care.[1] The phenomenon of the *Self*—a phenomenon which is included in care—needs to be defined existentially in a way which is primordial and authentic, in contrast to our preparatory exhibition of the inauthentic they-self. Along with this, we must establish what possible ontological questions are to be directed towards the 'Self', if indeed it is neither substance nor subject.

In this way, the phenomenon of care will be adequately clarified for the first time, and we shall then interrogate it as to its ontological meaning. When this meaning has been determined, temporality will have been laid bare. In exhibiting this, we are not led into out-of-the-way and sequestered domains of Dasein; we merely get a conception of the entire phenomenal content of Dasein's basic existential constitution in the ultimate foundations of its own ontological intelligibility. *Temporality gets experienced in a phenomenally primordial way in Dasein's authentic Being-a-whole, in the phenomenon of anticipatory resoluteness.* If temporality makes itself known primordially in this, then we may suppose that the temporality of anticipatory resoluteness is a distinctive mode of temporality. Temporality has different possibilities and different ways of *temporalizing* itself.[2] The basic possibilities

---

[1] 'Sein "Bestand" gründet nicht in der Substanzialität einer Substanz, sondern in der "*Selbständigkeit*" des existierenden Selbst, dessen Sein als Sorge begriffen wurde.'

In this sentence Heidegger has used no less than five words derived from the Indo-European base 'stā-' (Cf. English 'stand', Latin '*stare*', German 'stehen'): 'Bestand', 'Substanz', 'Substantialität', 'Selbständigkeit', 'existierenden'. In each case we have used an English equivalent derived from the same base.

The important word 'Bestand', which we have here translated somewhat arbitrarily as 'subsistence', and have often handled elsewhere in other ways, corresponds to the verb 'bestehen' ('to subsist', 'to remain', 'to consist in', even 'to exist' in a broader sense than Heidegger's). It thus may stand for 'subsistence' in the broadest sense, or more particularly for 'continued subsistence'; and it may also stand for that of which something 'consists'— its 'content', the whole 'stock' of things of which it consists. This is the sense in which Heidegger most frequently uses it, especially in such phrases as 'der phänomenale Bestand' ('the phenomenal content', 'the stock of phenomena').

We have also somewhat arbitrarily translated 'Selbständigkeit' as 'Self-subsistence', in accordance with our translation of the adjective 'selbständig' on H. 291-292. But as we shall see later (H. 322), 'Self-constancy' would perhaps be more appropriate.

[2] 'Zeitlichkeit kann sich in verschiedenen Möglichkeiten und in verschiedener Weise *zeitigen*.' In ordinary German the verb 'zeitigen' means 'to bring about' or more strictly, 'to bring to maturity'; this is how we have translated it in the earlier portions of this work. In the present section, however, and in those which follow, Heidegger is exploiting the etymological connection of 'zeitigen' with such words as 'Zeit' ('time') and 'Zeitlichkeit' ('temporality'); we have accordingly ventured to translate it as 'to temporalize.' We have

of existence, the authenticity and inauthenticity of Dasein, are grounded ontologically on possible temporalizations of temporality.

If the ascendancy of the falling understanding of Being (of Being as presence-at-hand)[1] keeps Dasein far from the ontological character of its own Being, it keeps it still farther from the primordial foundations of that Being. So one must not be surprised if, at first glance, temporality does not correspond to that which is accessible to the ordinary understanding as 'time'. Thus neither the way time is conceived in our ordinary experience of it, nor the problematic which arises from this experience, can function without examination as a criterion for the appropriateness of an Interpretation of time. Rather, we must, in our investigation, make ourselves familiar *beforehand* with the primordial phenomenon of temporality, so that *in terms of this* we may cast light on the necessity, the source, and the reason for the dominion of the way it is ordinarily understood.

The primordial phenomenon of temporality will be held secure by demonstrating that if we have regard for the possible totality, unity, and development of those fundamental structures of Dasein which we have hitherto exhibited, these structures are all to be conceived as at bottom 'temporal' and as modes of the temporalizing of temporality. Thus, when temporality has been laid bare, there arises for the existential analytic the task of *repeating* our analysis of Dasein in the sense of Interpreting its essential structures with regard to their temporality. The basic directions of the analyses thus required are prescribed by temporality itself. Accordingly the chapter will be divided as follows: anticipatory resoluteness as the way in which Dasein's potentiality-for-Being-a-whole has existentiell authenticity[2] (Section 62); the hermeneutical Situation at which we have arrived for Interpreting the meaning of the Being of care, and the methodological character of the existential analytic in general (Section 63); care and Selfhood (Section 64); temporality as the ontological meaning of care (Section 65); Dasein's temporality and the tasks arising therefrom of repeating the existential analysis in a primordial manner (Section 66).

¶ 62. *Anticipatory Resoluteness as the Way in which Dasein's Potentiality-for-Being-a-whole has Existentiell Authenticity*

When resoluteness has been 'thought through to the end' in a way corresponding to its ownmost tendency of Being, to what extent does it

already called attention to earlier passages (H. 122, 178) where 'zeitigen' has been changed to 'zeigen' in the later editions. If these changes are not simple misprints, they may indicate a deliberate intention to avoid the use of this verb in any sense but the special one here introduced. (Contrast H. 152, where no such correction has been made.)

  1 '. . . (Sein als Vorhandenheit) . . .' The 'als' of the later editions replaces an equality-sign which we find in the earlier editions.

  2 'Das existenziell eigentliche Ganzseinkönnen· des Daseins als vorlaufende Entschlossenheit.'

lead us to authentic Being-towards-death? How are we to conceive the connection between wanting to have a conscience and Dasein's existentially projected, authentic potentiality-for-Being-a-whole? Does welding these two together yield a new phenomenon? Or are we left with the resoluteness which is attested in its existentiell possibility, and can this resoluteness undergo an *existentiell modalization* through Being-towards-death? What does it mean 'to think through to the end' existentially the phenomenon of resoluteness?

We have characterized resoluteness as a way of reticently projecting oneself upon one's ownmost Being-guilty, and exacting anxiety of oneself. Being-guilty belongs to Dasein's Being, and signifies the null *Being*-the-basis of a nullity. The 'Guilty!' which belongs to the Being of Dasein is something that can be neither augmented nor diminished. It comes *before* any quantification, if the latter has any meaning at all. Moreover, Dasein is essentially guilty—not just guilty *on some occasions*, and *on other occasions not*. Wanting-to-have-a-conscience resolves upon this Being-guilty. To project oneself upon this Being-guilty, which Dasein is *as long as it is*, belongs to the very meaning of resoluteness. The existentiell way of taking over this 'guilt' in resoluteness, is therefore authentically accomplished only when that resoluteness, in its disclosure of Dasein, has become *so* transparent that Being-guilty is understood *as something constant*. But this understanding is made possible only in so far as Dasein discloses to itself its potentiality-for-Being, and discloses it 'right to its end'. Existentially, however, Dasein's *"Being-at-an-end"* implies Being-*towards*-the-end. As *Being-towards-the-end which understands*—that is to say, as anticipation of death—resoluteness becomes authentically what it can be. Resoluteness does not just 'have' a connection with anticipation, as with something other than itself. *It harbours in itself authentic Being-towards-death, as the possible existentiell modality of its own authenticity.* This 'connection' must be elucidated phenomenally.

By "resoluteness" we mean "letting onself be called forth to one's ownmost *Being*-guilty". Being-*guilty* belongs to the Being of Dasein itself, and we have determined that this is primarily a potentiality-for-Being. To say that Dasein 'is' constantly guilty can only mean that in every case Dasein maintains itself in this Being and does so as either authentic or inauthentic existing. *Being*-guilty is not just an abiding property of something constantly present-at-hand, but the *existentiell possibility* of being authentically or inauthentically guilty. In every case, the 'guilty' *is* only in the current factical potentiality-for-Being. Thus because Being-guilty belongs to the *Being* of Dasein, it must be conceived as a potentiality-for-Being-guilty. Resoluteness projects itself upon this potentiality-for-Being

M

—that is to say, it understands itself in it. This understanding maintains itself, therefore, in a primordial possibility of Dasein. It maintains itself *authentically in it* if the resoluteness is primordially that which it tends to be. But we have revealed that Dasein's primordial Being towards its potentiality-for-Being is Being-towards-death—that is to say, towards that distinctive possibility of Dasein which we have already characterized. Anticipation discloses this possibility as possibility. Thus only *as anticipating* does resoluteness become a primordial Being towards Dasein's ownmost potentiality-for-Being. Only when it 'qualifies' itself as Being-towards-death does resoluteness understand the 'can' of its potentiality-for-Being guilty.[1]

When Dasein is resolute, it takes over authentically in its existence the fact that it *is* the null basis of its own nullity. We have conceived death existentially as what we have characterized as the possibility of the *impossibility* of existence—that is to say, as the utter nullity of Dasein. Death is not "added on" to Dasein at its 'end'; but Dasein, as care, is the thrown (that is, null) basis for its death. The nullity by which Dasein's Being is dominated primordially through and through, is revealed to Dasein itself in authentic Being-towards-death. Only on the basis of Dasein's *whole* Being does anticipation make Being-guilty manifest. Care harbours in itself both death and guilt equiprimordially. Only anticipatory resoluteness understands the potentiality-for-Being-guilty *authentically and wholly*—that is to say, *primordially*.[ii]

When the call of conscience is understood, lostness in the "they" is revealed. Resoluteness brings Dasein back to its ownmost potentiality-for-Being-its-Self. When one has an understanding Being-towards-death—towards death as one's *ownmost* possibility—one's potentiality-for-Being becomes authentic and wholly transparent.

The call of conscience passes over in its appeal all Dasein's 'worldly' prestige and potentialities. Relentlessly it individualizes Dasein down to its potentiality-for-Being-guilty, and exacts of it that it should be this potentiality authentically. The unwavering precision with which Dasein is thus essentially individualized down to its ownmost potentiality-for-Being, discloses the anticipation of [zum] death as the possibility which is *non-relational*. Anticipatory resoluteness lets the potentiality-for-Being-guilty, as one's ownmost non-relational possibility, be struck wholly into the conscience.

Any factical Dasein has been determined by its ownmost Being-guilty both *before* any factical indebtedness has been incurred and *after* any such

[1] 'Das "kann" des Schuldigseinkönnens versteht die Entschlossenheit erst, wenn sie sich als Sein zum Tode "qualifiziert".'

indebtedness has been paid off; and wanting-to-have-a-conscience signifies that one is ready for the appeal to this ownmost Being-guilty. This prior Being-guilty, which is constantly with us, does not show itself unconcealedly in its character as prior until this very priority has been enlisted in [hineingestellt] that possibility which is simply *not to be outstripped*. When, in anticipation, resoluteness has *caught up* [*eingeholt*] the possibility of death into its potentiality-for-Being, Dasein's authentic existence can no longer be *outstripped* [*überholt*] by anything.

The phenomenon of resoluteness has brought us before the primordial *truth* of existence. As resolute, Dasein is revealed to itself in its current factical potentiality-for-Being, and in such a way that Dasein itself *is* this revealing and Being-revealed. To any truth, there belongs a corresponding holding-for-true. The explicit appropriating of what has been disclosed or discovered is *Being*-certain. The primordial truth of existence demands an equiprimordial Being-certain, in which one maintains oneself in what resoluteness discloses. It[1] *gives* itself the current factical Situation, and *brings* itself into that Situation. The Situation cannot be calculated in advance or presented like something present-at-hand which is waiting for someone to grasp it. It merely gets disclosed in a free resolving which has not been determined beforehand but is open to the possibility of such determination. *What, then, does the certainty which belongs to such resoluteness signify*? Such certainty must maintain itself in what is disclosed by the resolution. But this means that it simply cannot *become rigid* as regards the Situation, but must understand that the resolution, in accordance with its own meaning as a disclosure, must be *held open* and free for the current factical possibility. The certainty of the resolution signifies that one *holds oneself free for* the possibility of *taking it back*—a possibility which is factically necessary.[2] However, such holding-for-true in resoluteness (as the truth of existence) by no means lets us fall back into irresoluteness. On the contrary, this holding-for-true, as a resolute holding-oneself-free for taking back, is *authentic resoluteness which resolves to keep repeating itself*.[3] Thus, in

---

[1] Heidegger's ambiguous pronoun refers to 'resoluteness', as is clear from H. 326 below.

[2] 'Die Gewissheit des Entschlusses bedeutet: *Sichfreihalten für* seine mögliche und je faktisch notwendige *Zurücknahme*.' It is not grammatically clear whether the possessive adjective 'seine' refers back to 'Entschlusses' ('resolution') or to the '*Sich-*' of '*Sichfreihalten*' ('oneself'). We have chosen the former interpretation as somewhat more natural. But it is tempting to construe this and the following sentence as preparing the way for Heidegger's remark a few lines below that 'In seinem Tod muss sich das Dasein schlechthin "zurücknehmen" '—which might be translated as 'In its death, Dasein must 'withdraw' itself utterly.' In that case it would be attractive to translate the present sentence by writing '. . . *holds oneself free* for one's own *withdrawal* . . .'

[3] '. . . *eigentliche Entschlossenheit zur Wiederholung ihrer selbst*.' The idea seems to be that authentic resoluteness keeps reiterating itself in the face of a constant awareness that it may have to be retracted or taken back at any time.

an existentiell manner, one's very lostness in irresoluteness gets under-mined. The holding-for-true which belongs to resoluteness, tends, in accordance with its meaning, to hold itself free *constantly*—that is, to hold itself free for Dasein's *whole* potentiality-for-Being. This constant certainty is guaranteed to resoluteness only so that it will relate itself to that pos-sibility of which it can *be* utterly certain. In its death, Dasein must simply 'take back' everything. Since resoluteness is constantly certain of death—in other words, since it *anticipates* it—resoluteness thus attains a certainty which is authentic and whole.

But Dasein is equiprimordially in the untruth. Anticipatory resoluteness gives Dasein at the same time the primordial certainty that it has been closed off. In anticipatory resoluteness, Dasein *holds* itself open for its constant lostness in the irresoluteness of the "they"—a lostness which is possible from the very basis of its own Being. As a constant possibility of Dasein, irresoluteness is *co-certain*. When resoluteness is transparent to itself, it understands that the *indefiniteness* of one's potentiality-for-Being is made definite only in a resolution as regards the current Situation. It knows about the indefiniteness by which an entity that exists is dominated through and through. But if this knowing is to correspond to authentic resoluteness, it must itself arise from an authentic disclosure. The *in-definiteness* of one's own potentiality-for-Being, even when this potentiality has become certain in a resolution, is first made *wholly* manifest in Being-towards-death. Anticipation brings Dasein face to face with a possibility which is constantly certain but which at any moment remains indefinite as to when that possibility will become an impossibility. Anticipation makes it manifest that this entity has been thrown into the indefiniteness of its 'limit-Situation'; when resolved upon the latter, Dasein gains its authentic potentiality-for-Being-a-whole. The indefiniteness of death is primordially disclosed in anxiety. But this primordial anxiety strives to exact resoluteness of itself. It moves out of the way everything which conceals the fact that Dasein has been abandoned to itself. The "nothing" with which anxiety brings us face to face, unveils the nullity by which Dasein, in its very *basis*, is defined; and this basis itself i s as thrownness into death.

Our analysis has revealed *seriatim* those *items of modalization* towards which resoluteness tends of itself and which arise from authentic Being towards death as that possibility which is one's ownmost, non-relational, not to be outstripped, certain, and yet indefinite. Resoluteness is authentic-ally and wholly what it can be, only as *anticipatory resoluteness*.

But on the other hand, in our Interpretation of the 'connection' between resoluteness and anticipation, we have first reached a full existential understanding of anticipation itself. Hitherto this could amount to no more than an ontological projection. We have now shown that anticipation is not just a fictitious possibility which we have forced upon Dasein; it is a *mode* of an existentiell potentiality-for-Being that is attested in Dasein—a mode which Dasein exacts of itself, if indeed it authentically understands itself as resolute. Anticipation 'is' not some kind of free-floating behaviour, but must be conceived as *the possibility of the authenticity of that resoluteness which has been attested in an existentiell way—a possibility hidden in such resoluteness, and thus attested therewith.* Authentic 'thinking about death' is a wanting-to-have-a-conscience, which has become transparent to itself in an existentiell manner. If resoluteness, as authentic, tends towards the mode delimited by anticipation, and if anticipation goes to make up Dasein's authentic potentiality-for-Being-a-whole, then in the resoluteness which is attested in an existentiell manner, there is attested with it an authentic potentiality-for-Being-a-whole which belongs to Dasein. *The question of the potentiality-for-Being-a-whole is one which is factical and existentiell. It is answered by Dasein as resolute.* The question of Dasein's potentiality-for-Being-a-whole has now fully sloughed off the character indicated at the beginning,[iii] when we treated it as it if were just a theoretical or methodological question of the analytic of Dasein, arising from the endeavour to have the whole of Dasein completely 'given'. The question of Dasein's totality, which at the beginning we discussed only with regard to ontological method, has its justification, but only because the ground for that justification goes back to an ontical possibility of Dasein.

By thus casting light upon the 'connection' between anticipation and resoluteness in the sense of the possible modalization of the latter by the former, we have exhibited as a phenomenon an authentic potentiality-for-Being-a-whole which belongs to Dasein. If with this phenomenon we have reached a way of Being of Dasein in which it brings itself to itself and face to face with itself, then this phenomenon must, both ontically and ontologically, remain unintelligible to the everyday common-sense manner in which Dasein has been interpreted by the "they". It would be a misunderstanding to shove this existentiell possibility aside as 'unproved' or to want to 'prove' it theoretically. Yet the phenomenon needs to be protected against the grossest perversions.

Anticipatory resoluteness is not a way of escape, fabricated for the 'overcoming' of death; it is rather that understanding which follows the call of conscience and which frees for death the possibility of acquiring *power* over Dasein's *existence* and of basically dispersing all fugitive Self-concealments. Nor does wanting-to-have-a-conscience, which has been made determinate as Being-towards-death, signify a kind of seclusion in which one flees the world; rather, it brings one without Illusions into the resoluteness of 'taking action'. Neither does anticipatory resoluteness stem from 'idealistic' exactions soaring above existence and its possibilities; it springs from a sober understanding of what are factically the basic possibilities for Dasein. Along with the sober anxiety which brings us face to face with our individualized potentiality-for-Being, there goes an unshakable joy in this possibility. In it Dasein becomes free from the entertaining 'incidentals' with which busy curiosity keeps providing itself—primarily from the events of the world.[1] But the analysis of these basic moods would transgress the limits which we have drawn for the present Interpretation by aiming towards fundamental ontology.

Is there not, however, a definite ontical way of taking authentic existence, a factical ideal of Dasein, underlying our ontological Interpretation of Dasein's existence? That is so indeed. But not only is this Fact one which must not be denied and which we are forced to grant; it must also be conceived in its *positive necessity*, in terms of the object which we have taken as the theme of our investigation. Philosophy will never seek to deny its 'presuppositions', but neither may it simply admit them. It conceives them, and it unfolds with more and more penetration both the presuppositions themselves and that for which they are presuppositions. The methodological considerations now demanded of us will have this very function.

¶ 63. *The Hermeneutical Situation at which we have Arrived for Interpreting the Meaning of the Being of Care; and the Methodological Character of the Existential Analytic in General*[2]

In its anticipatory resoluteness, Dasein has now been made phenomenally visible with regard to its possible authenticity and totality. The hermeneutical Situation[iv] which was previously inadequate for interpreting the meaning of the Being of care, now has the required primordiality. Dasein has been put into that which we have in advance, and this has been done primordially—that is to say, this has been done with regard to its authentic potentiality-for-Being-a-whole; the idea of existence, which guides us as that which we see in advance, has been made definite by the clarification of our ownmost potentiality-for-Being; and, now that we have concretely worked out the structure of Dasein's Being, its peculiar ontological character has become so plain as compared with everything present-at-hand, that Dasein's existentiality has been grasped in advance

---

[1] 'In ihr wird das Dasein frei von den "Zufälligkeiten" des Unterhaltenwerdens die sich die geschäftige Neugier primär aus den Weltbegebenheiten verschafft.'

[2] 'Die für eine Interpretation des Seinssinnes der Sorge gewonnene hermeneutische Situation und der methodische Charakter der existenzialen Analytik überhaupt.'

with sufficient Articulation to give sure guidance for working out the *existentialia* conceptually.

The way which we have so far pursued in the analytic of Dasein has led us to a concrete demonstration of the thesis[v] which was put forward just casually at the beginning—that *the entity which in every case we ourselves are, is ontologically that which is farthest*. The reason for this lies in care itself. Our Being alongside the things with which we concern ourselves most closely in the 'world'—a Being which is falling—guides the everyday way in which Dasein is interpreted, and covers up ontically Dasein's authentic Being, so that the ontology which is directed towards this entity is denied an appropriate basis. Therefore the primordial way in which this entity is presented as a phenomenon is anything but obvious, if even ontology proximally follows the course of the everyday interpretation of Dasein. The laying-bare of Dasein's primordial Being must rather be *wrested* from Dasein by following the *opposite course* from that taken by the falling ontico-ontological tendency of interpretation.

Not only in exhibiting the most elemental structures of Being-in-the-world, in delimiting the concept of the world, in clarifying the average "who" of this entity (the "who" which is closest to us—the they-self), in Interpreting the 'there', but also, above all, in analysing care, death, conscience, and guilt—in all these ways we have shown *how* in Dasein itself concernful common sense has taken control of Dasein's potentiality-for-Being and the disclosure of that potentiality—that is to say, the closing of it off.

Dasein's *kind of Being* thus *demands* that any ontological Interpretation which sets itself the goal of exhibiting the phenomena in their primordiality, *should capture the Being of this entity, in spite of this entity's own tendency to cover things up*. Existential analysis, therefore, constantly has the character of *doing violence* [*Gewaltsamkeit*], whether to the claims of the everyday interpretation, or to its complacency and its tranquillized obviousness. While indeed this characteristic is specially distinctive of the ontology of Dasein, it belongs properly to any Interpretation, because the understanding which develops in Interpretation has the structure of a projection. But is not anything of this sort *guided* and *regulated* in a way of its own? Where are ontological projects to get the evidence that their 'findings' are phenomenally appropriate? Ontological Interpretation projects the entity presented to it upon the Being which is that entity's own, so as to conceptualize it with regard to its structure. Where are the signposts to direct the projection, so that Being will be reached at all? And what if the entity which becomes the theme of the existential analytic, hides the Being that belongs to it, and does so *in* its very way of being? To answer these questions we must first restrict ourselves to clarifying the analytic of Dasein, as the questions themselves demand.

The interpretation of the Self belongs to Dasein's Being. In the circumspective-concernful discovering of the 'world', concern gets sighted too. Dasein always understands itself factically in definite existentiell possibilities, even if its projects stem only from the common sense of the "they". Whether explicitly or not, whether appropriately or not, existence is somehow understood too. There are some things which every ontical understanding 'includes', even if these are only *pre*-ontological—that is to say, not conceived theoretically or thematically. Every ontologically explicit question about Dasein's Being has had the way already prepared for it by the kind of Being which Dasein has.

Yet where are we to find out what makes up the 'authentic' existence of Dasein? Unless we have an existentiell understanding, all analysis of existentiality will remain groundless. Is it not the case that underlying our Interpretation of the authenticity and totality of Dasein, there is an ontical way of taking existence which may be possible but need not be binding for everyone? Existential Interpretation will never seek to take over any authoritarian pronouncement as to those things which, from an existentiell point of view, are possible or binding. But must it not justify itself in regard to those existentiell possibilities with which it gives ontological Interpretation its ontical basis? If the Being of Dasein is essentially potentiality-for-Being, if it is Being-free for its ownmost possibilities, and if, in every case, it exists only in freedom for these possibilities or in lack of freedom for them, can ontological Interpretation do anything else than base itself on *ontical possibilities*—ways of potentiality-for-Being—and project these possibilities upon *their ontological possibility*? And if, for the most part, Dasein interprets itself in terms of its lostness in concerning itself with the 'world', does not the appropriate way of disclosure for such an entity lie in determining the ontico-existentiell possibilities (and doing so in the manner which we have achieved by following the opposite course) and then providing an existential analysis grounded upon these possibilities? *In that case, will not the violence of this projection amount to freeing Dasein's undisguised phenomenal content?*

It may be that our method demands this 'violent' presentation of possibilities of existence, but can such a presentation be taken out of the province of our free discretion? If the analyic makes anticipatory resoluteness basic as a potentiality-for-Being which, in an existentiell manner, is authentic—a possibility to which Dasein itself summons us from the very basis of its existence—then is this possibility just one which is *left to our discretion*? Has that way-of-Being in accordance with which Dasein's potentiality-for-Being comports itself towards its distinctive possibility—death—been just accidentally pounced upon? *Does Being-in-the-world have a higher instance for its potentiality-for-Being than its own death?*[1] Even if the ontico-ontological projection of Dasein upon an authentic potentiality-for-Being-a-whole may not be just something that is left to our discretion, does this already justify the existential Interpretation we have given for this phenomenon? Where does this Interpretation get its clue, if not from an idea of existence in general which has been 'presupposed'? How have the steps in the analysis of inauthentic everydayness been regulated, if not by the concept of existence which we have posited? And if we say that Dasein 'falls', and that therefore the authenticity of its potentiality-for-Being must be wrested from Dasein in spite of this tendency of its Being,[2] from what point of view is this spoken? Is not everything already illumined by the light of the 'presupposed' idea of existence, even if rather dimly? Where does this idea get its justification? Has our initial projection, in which we called attention to it, led us nowhere? By no means.

In indicating the formal aspects of the idea of existence we have been guided by the understanding-of-Being which lies in Dasein itself. Without any ontological transparency, it has nevertheless been revealed that in every case I am myself the entity which we call Dasein, and that I am so as a potentiality-for-Being for which to be this entity is an issue. Dasein understands itself as Being-in-the-world, even if it does so without adequate ontological definiteness. Being thus, it encounters entities which have the kind of Being of what is ready-to-hand and present-at-hand. No matter how far removed from an ontological concept the distinction between existence and Reality may be, no matter even if Dasein proximally understands existence as Reality, Dasein is not just present-at-hand but has already *understood itself*, however mythical or magical the interpretation which it gives may be. For otherwise, Dasein would never 'live' in a myth and would not be concerned with magic in ritual and cult. The idea of existence which we have posited gives us an outline of the formal structure of the understanding of Dasein and does so in a way which is not binding from an existentiell point of view.

Under the guidance of this idea the preparatory analysis of the everydayness that lies closest to us has been carried out as far as the first conceptual

---

[1] '*Hat das In-der-Welt-sein eine höhere Instanz seines Seinkönnens als seinen Tod?*'

[2] '... und deshalb sei ihm die Eigentlichkeit des Seinkönnens gegen diese Seinstendenz abzuringen ...' This of course does not mean that this authenticity is to be taken away from Dasein; it means that because such authenticity runs counter to Dasein's tendency to fall, Dasein must make a very real effort to achieve it, or perhaps rather that our Interpretation calls for a similar effort if this authenticity is to be properly discerned.

definition of "care". This latter phenomenon has enabled us to get a more precise grasp of existence and of its relations to facticity and falling. And defining the structure of care has given us a basis on which to distinguish ontologically between existence and Reality for the first time.[vi] This has led us to the thesis that the substance of man is existence.[vii]

Yet even in this formal idea of existence, which is not binding upon us in an existentiell way, there already lurks a definite though unpretentious ontological 'content', which—like the idea of Reality, which has been distinguished from this—'presupposes' an idea of Being in general. Only within the horizon of *this* idea of Being can the distinction between existence and Reality be accomplished. Surely, in both of them what we have in view is *Being*.

But if we are to obtain an ontologically clarified idea of Being in general, must we not do so by first working out that understanding-of-Being which belongs to Dasein? This understanding, however, is to be grasped primordially only on the basis of a primordial Interpretation of Dasein, in which we take the idea of existence as our clue. Does it not then become altogether patent in the end that this problem of fundamental ontology which we have broached, is one which moves in a 'circle'?

We have indeed already shown, in analysing the structure of understanding in general, that what gets censured inappropriately as a 'circle', belongs to the essence and to the distinctive character of understanding as such.[viii] In spite of this, if the problematic of fundamental ontology is to have its hermeneutical Situation clarified, our investigation must now come back explicitly to this 'circular argument'. When it is objected that the existential Interpretation is 'circular', it is said that we have 'presupposed' the idea of existence and of Being in general, and that Dasein gets Interpreted 'accordingly', so that the idea of Being may be obtained from it. But what does 'presupposition' signify? In positing the idea of existence, do we also posit some proposition from which we deduce further propositions about the Being of Dasein, in accordance with formal rules of consistency? Or does this pre-supposing have the character of an understanding projection, in such a manner indeed that the Interpretation by which such an understanding gets developed, will let that which is to be interpreted *put itself into words for the very first time, so that it may decide of its own accord whether, as the entity which it is, it has that state of Being for which it has been disclosed in the projection with regard to its formal aspects*?[1] Is

---

[1] 'Oder hat dieses Voraus-setzen den Charakter des verstehenden Entwerfens, so zwar, dass die solches Verstehen ausbildende Interpretation das Auszulegende *gerade erst selbst zu Wort kommen lässt, damit es von sich aus entscheide, ob es als dieses Seiende die Seinsverfassung hergibt, auf welche es im Entwurf formalanzeigend erschlossen wurde*?' Here, however, Heidegger may be using the verb 'erschliessen' in the sense of 'infer', in spite of his remarks on H. 75 above (see our note 1, p. 105 ad loc.) and 'Entwurf' in the sense of 'sketch'.

there any other way at all by which an entity can put itself into words with regard to its Being? We cannot ever 'avoid' a 'circular' proof in the existential analytic, because such an analytic does not do *any* proving at *all* by the rules of the 'logic of consistency'. What common sense wishes to eliminate in avoiding the 'circle', on the supposition that it is measuring up to the loftiest rigour of scientific investigation, is nothing less than the basic structure of care. Because it is primordially constituted by care, any Dasein is already ahead of itself. As being, it has in every case already projected itself upon definite possibilities of its existence; and in such existentiell projections it has, in a pre-ontological manner, also projected something like existence and Being. *Like all research*, the research which wants to develop and conceptualize that kind of Being which belongs to existence, *is itself a kind of Being which disclosive Dasein possesses;* can such research be denied this projecting which is essential to Dasein?

Yet the 'charge of circularity' itself comes from a kind of Being which belongs to Dasein. Something like a projection, even an ontological one, still remains for the common sense of our concernful absorption in the "they"; but it necessarily seems strange to us, because common sense barricades itself against it 'on principle'. Common sense concerns itself, whether 'theoretically' or 'practically', only with entities which can be surveyed at a glance circumspectively. What is distinctive in common sense is that it has in view only the experiencing of 'factual' entities, in order that it may be able to rid itself of an understanding of Being. It fails to recognize that entities can be experienced 'factually' only when Being is already understood, even if it has not been conceptualized. Common sense misunderstands understanding. And *therefore* common sense must necessarily pass off as 'violent' anything that lies beyond the reach of its understanding, or any attempt to go out so far.

When one talks of the 'circle' in understanding, one expresses a failure to recognize two things: (1) that understanding as such makes up a basic kind of Dasein's Being, and (2) that this Being is constituted as care. To deny the circle, to make a secret of it, or even to want to overcome it, means finally to reinforce this failure. We must rather endeavour to leap into the 'circle', primordially and wholly, so that even at the start of the analysis of Dasein we make sure that we have a full view of Dasein's circular Being. If, in the ontology of Dasein, we 'take our departure' from a worldless "I" in order to provide this "I" with an Object and an ontologically baseless relation to that Object, then we have 'presupposed' not too much, but *too little*. If we make a problem of 'life', *and then just occasionally* have regard for death *too, our view is too short-sighted*. The object we have taken as our theme is *artificially and dogmatically curtailed* if 'in the first instance' we restrict ourselves to a 'theoretical subject', in order that we may then round it out 'on the practical side' by tacking on an 'ethic'.

This may suffice to clarify the existential meaning of the hermeneutical Situation of a primordial analytic of Dasein. By exhibiting anticipatory resoluteness, we have brought Dasein before us with regard to its authentic totality, so that we now have it in advance. The authenticity of the potentiality-for-Being-one's-Self guarantees that primordial existentiality is something we see in advance, and this assures us that we are coining the appropriate existential concepts.[1]

At the same time our analysis of anticipatory resoluteness has led us to the phenomenon of primordial and authentic truth. We have shown earlier how that understanding-of-Being which prevails proximally and for the most part, conceives Being in the sense of presence-at-hand, and so covers up the primordial phenomenon of truth.[ix] If, however, 'there is' Being only in so far as truth 'is', and if the understanding of Being varies according to the kind of truth, then truth which is primordial and authentic must guarantee the understanding of the Being of Dasein and of Being in general. The ontological 'truth' of the existential analysis is developed on the ground of the primordial existentiell truth. However, the latter does not necessarily need the former. The most primordial and basic existential truth, for which the problematic of fundamental ontology strives in preparing for the question of Being in general, is the *disclosedness of the meaning of the Being of care*. In order to lay bare this meaning, we need to hold in readiness, undiminished, the full structural content of care.

¶ 64. Care and Selfhood

Through the unity of the items which are constitutive for care—existentiality, facticity, and fallenness—it has become possible to give the first ontological definition for the totality of Dasein's structural whole. We have given an existential formula for the structure of care as "ahead-of-itself—Being-already-in (a world) as Being-alongside (entities encountered within-the-world)".[2] We have seen that the care-structure does not first arise from a coupling together, but is *articulated* all the same.[x] In assessing this ontological result, we have had to estimate how well it

---

[1] 'Die Eigentlichkeit des Selbstseinkönnens verbürgt die Vor-sicht auf die ursprüngliche Existenzialität, und diese sichert die Prägung der angemessenen existenzialen Begrifflichkeit.' The ambiguity of our 'this' reflects a similar ambiguity in Heidegger's 'diese', which may refer either to 'die Vor-sicht' or to 'die ursprüngliche Existenzialität'.

[2] 'Sich-vorweg—schon-sein-in (einer Welt) als Sein-bei (innerweltlich begegnenden Seienden)'. Here we follow the earlier editions. In the later editions there is a hyphen instead of a dash between 'vorweg' and 'schon'.

satisfies the requirements for a *primordial* Interpretation of Dasein.ˣⁱ The
upshot of these considerations has been that neither the *whole* of Dasein
nor its *authentic* potentiality-for-Being has ever been made a theme. The
structure of care, however, seems to be precisely where the attempt to
grasp the whole of Dasein as a phenomenon has foundered. The "ahead-of-
itself" presented itself as a "not-yet". But when the "ahead-of-itself" which
had been characterized as something still outstanding, was considered in a
genuinely existential manner, it revealed itself as *Being-towards-the-end*—
something which, in the depths of its Being, every Dasein is. We made it plain
at the same time that in the call of conscience care summons Dasein towards
its ownmost potentiality-for-Being. When we came to understand in a primordial manner how this appeal is understood, we saw that the understanding of it manifests itself as anticipatory resoluteness, which includes an
authentic potentiality-for-Being-a-whole—a potentiality of Dasein. Thus
the care-structure does not speak *against* the possibility of Being-a-whole
but is the *condition for the possibility* of such an existentiell potentiality-for-
Being. In the course of these analyses, it became plain that the existential
phenomena of death, conscience, and guilt are anchored in the phenomenon of care. *The totality of the structural whole has become even more richly
articulated; and because of this, the existential question of the unity of this totality
has become still more urgent.*

How are we to conceive this unity? How can Dasein exist as a unity in
the ways and possibilities of its Being which we have mentioned? Manifestly, it can so exist only in such a way that it *is itself* this Being in its
essential possibilities—that in each case *I* am this entity. The 'I' seems to
'hold together' the totality of the structural whole. In the 'ontology' of
this entity, the 'I' and the 'Self' have been conceived from the earliest
times as the supporting ground (as substance or subject). Even in its
preparatory characterization of everydayness, our analytic has already
come up against the question of Dasein's "who". It has been shown that
proximally and for the most part Dasein is *not* itself but is lost in the they-
self, which is an existentiell modification of the authentic Self. The
question of the ontological constitution of Selfhood has remained un-
answered. In principle, of course, we have already fixed upon a clue for
this problem;ˣⁱⁱ for if the Self belongs to the essential [wesenhaften] attri-   3
butes of Dasein, while Dasein's 'Essence' ["Essenz"] lies in *existence*, then
"I"-hood and Selfhood must be conceived *existentially*. On the negative
side, it has also been shown that our ontological characterization of the
"they" prohibits us from making any use of categories of presence-at-
hand (such as substance). It has become clear, in principle, that ontologically care is not to be derived from Reality or to be built up with the

categories of Reality.[xiii] Care already harbours in itself the phenomenon of the Self, if indeed the thesis is correct that the expression 'care for oneself' ["Selbstsorge"], would be *tautological* if it were proposed in conformity with the term "solicitude" [Fürsorge] as care for Others.[xiv] But in that case the problem of defining ontologically the Selfhood of Dasein gets sharpened to the question of the existential 'connection' between care and Selfhood.

To clarify the existentiality of the Self, we take as our 'natural' point of departure Dasein's everyday interpretation of the Self. In *saying* "*I*", Dasein expresses itself about 'itself'. It is not necessary that in doing so Dasein should make any utterance. With the 'I', this entity has itself in view. The content of this expression is regarded as something utterly simple. In each case, it just stands for me and nothing further. Also, this 'I', as something simple, is not an attribute of other Things; it is not *itself* a predicate, but the absolute 'subject'. What is expressed and what is addressed in saying "I", is always met as the same persisting something. The characteristics of 'simplicity', 'substantiality', and 'personality', which Kant, for instance, made the basis for his doctrine 'of the paralogisms of pure reason',[xv] arise from a genuine pre-phenomenological experience. The question remains whether that which we have experienced ontically in this way may be Interpreted ontologically with the help of the 'categories' mentioned.

Kant, indeed, in strict conformity with the phenomenal content given in saying "I", shows that the ontical theses about the soul-substance which have been inferred [erschlossenen] from these characteristics, are without justification. But in so doing, he merely rejects a wrong *ontical* explanation of the "I"; he has by no means achieved an *ontological* Interpretation of Selfhood, nor has he even obtained some assurance of it and made positive preparation for it. Kant makes a more rigorous attempt than his predecessors to keep hold of the phenomenal content of saying "I"; yet even though in theory he has denied that the ontical foundations of the ontology of the substantial apply to the "I", he still slips back into *this same* inappropriate ontology. This will be shown more exactly, in order that we may establish what it means ontologically to take saying "I" as the starting-point for the analysis of Selfhood. The Kantian analysis of the 'I think' is now to be adduced as an illustration, but only so far as is demanded for clarifying these problems.[xvi]

The 'I' is a bare consciousness, accompanying all concepts. In the 'I', 'nothing more is represented than a transcendental subject of thoughts'. 'Consciousness in itself (is) not so much a representation . . . as it is a form of representation in general.'[xvii] The 'I think' is 'the form of apperception, which clings to every experience and precedes it'.[xviii]

Kant grasps the phenomenal content of the 'I' correctly in the expression 'I think', or—if one also pays heed to including the 'practical person' when one speaks of 'intelligence'—in the expression 'I take action'. In Kant's sense we must take saying "I" as saying "I think". Kant tries to establish the phenomenal content of the "I" as *res cogitans*. If in doing so he calls this "I" a 'logical subject', that does not mean that the "I" in general is a concept obtained merely by way of logic. The "I" is rather the subject of logical behaviour, of binding together. 'I think' means 'I bind together'. All binding together is an '*I* bind together'. In any taking-together or relating, the "I" always underlies—the ὑποκείμενον. The *subjectum* is therefore 'consciousness in itself', not a representation but rather the 'form' of representation. That is to say, the "I think" is not something represented, but the formal structure of representing as such, and this formal structure alone makes it possible for anything to have been represented. When we speak of the "form" of representation, we have in view neither a framework nor a universal concept, but that which, as εἶδος, makes every representing and everything represented be what it is. If the "I" is understood as the form of representation, this amounts to saying that it is the 'logical subject'.

Kant's analysis has two positive aspects. For one thing, he sees the impossibility of ontically reducing the "I" to a substance; for another thing, he holds fast to the "I" as 'I think'. Nevertheless, he takes this "I" as subject again, and he does so in a sense which is ontologically inappropriate. For the ontological concept of the subject *characterizes not the Self-hood of the "I" qua Self, but the selfsameness and steadiness of something that is always present-at-hand*. To define the "I" ontologically as "*subject*" means to regard it as something always present-at-hand. The-Being of the "I" is understood as the Reality of the *res cogitans*.[xix]

But how does it come about that while the 'I think' gives Kant a genuine phenomenal starting-point, he cannot exploit it ontologically, and has to fall back on the 'subject'—that is to say, something *substantial*? The "I" is not just an 'I think', but an 'I think something'. And does not Kant himself keep on stressing that the "I" remains related to its representations, and would be nothing without them?

For Kant, however, these representations are the 'empirical', which is 'accompanied' by the "I"—the appearances to which the "I" 'clings'. Kant nowhere shows the kind of Being of this 'clinging' and 'accompanying'. At bottom, however, their kind of Being is understood as the constant Being-present-at-hand of the "I" along with its representations. Kant has indeed avoided cutting the "I" adrift from thinking; but he has done so without starting with the 'I think' itself in its full essential content as an

'I think something', and above all, without seeing what is ontologically 'presupposed' in taking the 'I think something' as a basic characteristic of the Self. For even the 'I think something' is not definite enough ontologically as a starting-point, because the 'something' remains indefinite. If by this "something" we understand an entity *within-the-world*, then it tacitly implies that the *world* has been presupposed; and this very phenomenon of the world co-determines the state of Being of the "I", if indeed it is to be possible for the "I" to be something like an 'I think something'. In saying "I", I have in view the entity which in each case I am as an 'I-am-in-a-world'. Kant did not see the phenomenon of the world, and was consistent enough to keep the 'representations' apart from the *a priori* content of the 'I think'. But as a consequence the "I" was again forced back to an *isolated* subject, accompanying representations in a way which is ontologically quite indefinite.ˣˣ

In saying "I", Dasein expresses itself as Being-in-the-world. But does saying "I" in the everyday manner have *itself* in view *as* being-in-the-world [in-der-Welt-seiend]? Here we must make a distinction. When saying "I", Dasein surely has in view the entity which, in every case, it is itself. The everyday interpretation of the Self, however, has a tendency to understand itself in terms of the 'world' with which it is concerned. When Dasein has itself in view ontically, it *fails to see* itself in relation to the kind of Being of that entity which it is itself. And this holds especially for the basic state of Dasein, Being-in-the-world.ˣˣⁱ

What is the motive for this 'fugitive' way of saying "I"? It is motivated by Dasein's falling; for as falling, it *flees* in the face of itself into the "they".[1] When the "I" talks in the 'natural' manner, this is performed by the they-self.[2] What expresses itself in the 'I' is that Self which, proximally and for the most part, I am *not* authentically. When one is absorbed in the everyday multiplicity and the rapid succession [Sich-jagen] of that with which one is concerned, the Self of the self-forgetful "I am concerned" shows itself as something simple which is constantly selfsame but indefinite and empty. Yet one *is* that with which one concerns oneself. In the 'natural' ontical way in which the "I" talks, the phenomenal content of the Dasein which one has in view in the "I" gets overlooked; but this gives *no justification for our joining in this overlooking of it*, or for forcing upon the problematic of the Self an inappropriate 'categorial' horizon when we Interpret the "I" ontologically.

Of course by thus refusing to follow the everyday way in which the "I"

---

[1] 'Durch das Verfallen des Daseins, als welches es vor sich selbst *flieht* in das Man.' The 'es' appears only in the later editions.

[2] 'Die "natürliche" Ich-Rede vollzieht das Man-selbst.'

talks, our ontological Interpretation of the 'I' has by no means *solved* the problem; but it has indeed *prescribed the direction* for any further inquiries. In the "I", we have in view that entity which one is in 'being-in-the-world'.

Being-already-in-a-world, however, as Being-alongside-the-ready-to-hand-within-the-world, means equiprimordially that one is ahead of oneself. With the 'I', what we have in view is that entity for which the *issue* is the Being of the entity that it is. With the 'I', care expresses itself, though proximally and for the most part in the 'fugitive' way in which the "I" talks when it concerns itself with something. The they-self keeps on saying "I" most loudly and most frequently because at bottom it *is not authentically* itself, and evades its authentic potentiality-for-Being. If the ontological constitution of the Self is not to be traced back either to an "I"-substance or to a 'subject', but if, on the contrary, the everyday fugitive way in which we keep on saying "I" must be understood in terms of our *authentic* potentiality-for-Being, then the proposition that the Self is the basis of care and constantly present-at-hand, is one that still does not follow. Selfhood is to be discerned existentially only in one's authentic potentiality-for-Being-one's-Self—that is to say, in the authenticity of Dasein's Being *as care*. In terms of care the *constancy of the Self*, as the supposed persistence of the *subjectum*, gets clarified. But the phenomenon of this authentic potentiality-for-Being also opens our eyes for the *constancy of the Self* in the sense of its having achieved some sort of position.[1] *The constancy of the Self*, in the double sense of steadiness and steadfastness, is the *authentic* counter-possibility to the non-Self-constancy which is characteristic of irresolute falling.[2] Existentially, *"Self-constancy"* signifies nothing other than anticipatory resoluteness. The ontological structure of such resoluteness reveals the existentiality of the Self's Selfhood.

Dasein *is authentically itself* in the primordial individualization of the reticent resoluteness which exacts anxiety of itself. *As something that keeps*

---

[1] '. . . für die *Ständigkeit des Selbst* in dem Sinn des Standgewonnenhabens.' Here our usual translation of 'Ständigkeit' as 'constancy' seems inadequate; possibly 'stability' would be closer to what is meant.

[2] '*Die Ständigkeit des Selbst* im Doppelsinne der beständigen Standfestigkeit ist die *eigentliche* Gegenmöglichkeit zur Unselbst-ständigkeit des unentschlossenen Verfallens.' The italicization of the opening words of this sentence appears only in the later editions.

Here, as on H. 117 and 303, Heidegger exploits various meanings of the adjective 'ständig' and other words derived from the base 'stä-', with the root-meaning of 'standing'. The noun 'Unselbständigkeit' ordinarily stands for inability to stand on one's own feet or to make up one's mind independently. But Heidegger expands it to 'Unselbst-ständigkeit', which not only suggests instability and a failure to stand by oneself, but also the constancy or stability of that which is other than the Self—the non-Self, or more specifically, the they-self. In the following sentence the noun 'Selbständigkeit', which ordinarily stands for autonomy, independence, or self-subsistence, is similarly expanded to 'Selbst-ständigkeit'—'Self-constancy'.

silent, authentic *Being*-one's-Self is just the sort of thing that does not keep on saying 'I'; but in its reticence it '*is*' that thrown entity as which it can authentically be. The Self which the reticence of resolute existence unveils is the primordial phenomenal basis for the question as to the Being of the 'I'. Only if we are oriented phenomenally by the meaning of the Being of the authentic potentiality-for-Being-one's-Self are we put in a position to discuss what ontological justification there is for treating substantiality, simplicity, and personality as characteristics of Selfhood. In the prevalent way of saying "I", it is constantly suggested that what we have in advance is a Self-Thing, persistently present-at-hand; the ontological question of the Being of the Self must turn away from any such suggestion.

Care does not need to be founded in a Self. But existentiality, as constitutive for care, provides the ontological constitution of Dasein's Self-constancy, to which there belongs, in accordance with the full structural content of care, its Being-fallen factically into non-Self-constancy. When fully conceived, the care-structure includes the phenomenon of Selfhood. This phenomenon is clarified by Interpreting the meaning of care; and it is as care that Dasein's totality of Being has been defined.

¶ *65. Temporality as the Ontological Meaning of Care*

In characterizing the 'connection' between care and Selfhood, our aim was not only to clarify the special problem of "I"-hood, but also to help in the final preparation for getting into our grasp phenomenally the totality of Dasein's structural whole. We need the *unwavering discipline* of the existential way of putting the question, if, for our ontological point of view, Dasein's kind of Being is not to be finally perverted into a mode of presence-at-hand, even one which is wholly undifferentiated. Dasein becomes 'essentially' Dasein in that authentic existence which constitutes itself as anticipatory resoluteness.[1] Such resoluteness, as a mode of the authenticity of care, contains Dasein's primordial Self-constancy and totality. We must take an undistracted look at these and understand them existentially if we are to lay bare the ontological meaning of Dasein's Being.

What are we seeking ontologically with the meaning of care? What does "*meaning*" signify? In our investigation, we have encountered this phenomenon in connection with the analysis of understanding and interpretation.[xxii] According to that analysis, meaning is that wherein the understandability [Verstehbarkeit] of something maintains itself—even

---

[1] 'Das Dasein wird "wesentlich" in der eigentlichen Existenz, die sich als vorlaufende Entschlossenheit konstituiert.'

that of something which does not come into view explicitly and thematically. "Meaning" signifies the "upon-which" [das Woraufhin] of a primary projection in terms of which something can be conceived in its possibility as that which it is. Projecting discloses possibilities—that is to say, it discloses the sort of thing that makes possible.

To lay bare the "upon-which" of a projection, amounts to disclosing that which makes possible what has been projected.[1] To lay it bare in this way requires methodologically that we study the projection (usually a tacit one) which underlies an interpretation, and that we do so in such a way that what has been projected in the projecting can be disclosed and grasped with regard to its "upon-which". To set forth the meaning of care means, then, to follow up the projection which guides and underlies the primordial existential Interpretation of Dasein, and to follow it up in such a way that in what is here projected, its "upon-which" may be seen. What has been projected is the Being of Dasein, and it is disclosed in what constitutes that Being as an authentic potentiality-for-Being-a-whole.[2] That upon which the Being which has been disclosed and is thus constituted has been projected, is that which itself makes possible this Constitution of Being as care. When we inquire about the meaning of care, we are asking *what makes possible the totality of the articulated structural whole of care, in the unity of its articulation as we have unfolded it.*

Taken strictly, "meaning" signifies the "upon-which" of the primary projection of the understanding of Being. When Being-in-the-world has been disclosed to itself and understands the Being of that entity which it itself is, it understands equiprimordially the Being of entities discovered within-the-world, even if such Being has not been made a theme, and has not yet even been differentiated into its primary modes of existence and Reality. All ontical experience of entities—both circumspective calculation of the ready-to-hand, and positive scientific cognition of the present-at-hand—is based upon projections of the Being of the corresponding entities—projections which in every case are more or less transparent. But in these projections there lies hidden the "upon-which" of the projection; and on this, as it were, the understanding of Being nourishes itself.

If we say that entities 'have meaning', this signifies that they have become accessible *in their Being*; and this Being, as projected upon its

---

[1] 'Das Woraufhin eines Entwurfs freilegen, besagt, das erschliessen, was das Entworfene ermöglicht.' This sentence is ambiguous in that 'das Entworfene' ('what is projected') may be either the subject or the direct object of 'ermöglicht' ('makes possible').

[2] 'Das Entworfene ist das Sein des Daseins und zwar erschlossen in dem, was es als eigentliches Ganzseinkönnen konstituiert.' This sentence too is ambiguous in its structure; we have chosen the interpretation which seems most plausible in the light of the following sentence.

"upon-which", is what 'really' 'has meaning' first of all. Entities 'have' meaning only because, as Being which has been disclosed beforehand, they become intelligible in the projection of that Being—that is to say, in terms of the "upon-which" of that projection. The primary projection of the understanding of Being 'gives' the meaning. The question about the meaning of the Being of an entity takes as its theme the "upon-which" of that understanding of Being which underlies all *Being* of entities.[1]

Dasein is either authentically or inauthentically disclosed to itself as regards its existence. In existing, Dasein understands itself, and in such a way, indeed, that this understandin gdoes not merely get something in its grasp, but makes up the existentiell Being of its factical potentiality-for-Being. The Being which is disclosed is that of an entity for which this Being is an issue. The meaning of this Being—that is, of care—is what makes care possible in its Constitution; and it is what makes up primordially the Being of this potentiality-for-Being. The meaning of Dasein's Being is not something free-floating which is other than and 'outside of' itself, but is the self-understanding Dasein itself. What makes possible the Being of Dasein, and therewith its factical existence?

That which was projected in the primordial existential projection of existence has revealed itself as anticipatory resoluteness. What makes this authentic Being-a-whole of Dasein possible with regard to the unity of its articulated structural whole?[2] Anticipatory resoluteness, when taken formally and existentially, without our constantly designating its full structural content, is *Being towards* one's ownmost, distinctive potentiality-for-Being. This sort of thing is possible only in that Dasein *can*, *indeed*, come towards itself in its ownmost possibility, and that it can put up with this possibility as a possibility in thus letting itself come towards itself—in other words, that it exists. This letting-itself-*come-towards*-itself in that distinctive possibility which it puts up with, is the primordial phenomenon of the *future as coming towards.*[3] If either authentic or

---

[1] 'Die Frage nach dem Sinn des Seins eines Seienden macht das Woraufhin des allem *Sein* von Seiendem zugrundeliegenden Seinsverstehens zum Thema.' The earlier editions read '. . . des allem ontischen S e i n z u Seiendem . . .' ('. . . all ontical *Being towards* entities . . .')

[2] 'Was ermöglicht dieses eigentliche Ganzsein des Daseins hinsichtlich der Einheit seines gegliederten Strukturganzen?'

[3] 'Das die ausgezeichnete Möglichkeit aushaltende, in ihr sich auf sich *Zukommen-lassen* ist das ursprüngliche Phänomen der *Zu-kunft.*' While the hyphen in '*Zukommen-lassen*' appears only in the later editions, the more important hyphen in '*Zu-kunft*' appears in both later and earlier editions. In the later editions, however, it comes at the end of the line, so that the force which was presumably intended is lost.

Without the hyphen, 'Zukunft' is the ordinary word for 'the future'; with the hyphen, Heidegger evidently wishes to call attention to its kinship with the expression 'zukommen

inauthentic *Being-towards-death* belongs to Dasein's Being, then such Being-towards-death is possible only as something *futural* [als *zukünftiges*], in the sense which we have now indicated, and which we have still to define more closely. By the term 'futural', we do not here have in view a "now" which has *not yet* become 'actual' and which sometime *will be* for the first time. We have in view the coming [Kunft] in which Dasein, in its ownmost potentiality-for-Being, comes towards itself. Anticipation makes Dasein *authentically* futural, and in such a way that the anticipation itself is possible only in so far as Dasein, *as being*, is always coming towards itself—that is to say, in so far as it is futural in its Being in general.

Anticipatory resoluteness understands Dasein in its own essential Being-guilty. This understanding means that in existing one takes over Being-guilty; it means *being* the thrown basis of nullity. But taking over thrownness signifies *being* Dasein authentically *as it already was*.[1] Taking over thrownness, however, is possible only in such a way that the futural Dasein can *be* its ownmost 'as-it-already-was'—that is to say, its 'been' [sein "Gewesen"]. Only in so far as Dasein *is* as an "I-*am*-as-having-been", can Dasein come towards itself futurally in such a way that it comes *back*.[2] As authentically futural, Dasein *is* authentically as *"having been"*.[3] Anticipation of one's uttermost and ownmost possibility is coming back understandingly to one's ownmost "been". Only so far as it is futural can Dasein *be* authentically as having been. The character of "having been" arises, in a certain way, from the future.[4]

Anticipatory resoluteness discloses the current Situation of the "there" in such a way that existence, in taking action, is circumspectively concerned with what is factically ready-to-hand environmentally. Resolute

---

auf . . .' ('to come towards . . .' or 'to come up to . . .') and its derivation from 'zu' ('to' or 'towards') and 'kommen' ('come'). Hence our hendiadys. (The use of 'zukommen' with the preposition 'auf' is to be distinguished from a use of this same verb with the dative which we have met in earlier chapters in the sense of 'belongs to . . .', 'is becoming to . . .', or 'has coming to . . .'.)

[1] 'Übernahme der Geworfenheit aber bedeutet, das Dasein in dem, *wie es je schon war*, eigentlich *sein*.'

[2] 'Nur sofern Dasein überhaupt *ist* als ich *bin*-gewesen, kann es zukünftig auf sich selbst so zukommen, dass es zurück-kommt.' Many German verbs form their perfect tense with the help of the auxiliary 'sein' ('to be') in place of the somewhat more usual 'haben' ('have'), just as we sometimes say in English 'he is gone' instead of 'he has gone'. Among such verbs is 'sein' itself. This 'I have been' is expressed by 'ich bin gewesen'; this might be translated as 'I am been', but in this context we have ventured to translate it as 'I am as having been'.

[3] 'Eigentlich zukünftig *ist* das Dasein eigentlich *gewesen*.'

[4] 'Die Gewesenheit entspringt in gewisser Weise der Zukunft.' Here 'The character of having been' represents 'Die Gewesenheit' (literally, 'beenhood'). Heidegger distinguishes this sharply from 'die Vergangenheit' ('pastness'). We shall frequently translate 'Gewesenheit' simply as 'having been'.

Being-alongside what is ready-to-hand in the Situation—that is to say, taking action in such a way as to let one encounter what *has presence* environmentally—is possible only by *making* such an entity *present*. Only as the *Present* [*Gegenwart*][1] in the sense of making present, can resoluteness be what it is: namely, letting itself be encountered undisguisedly by that which it seizes upon in taking action.

Coming back to itself futurally, resoluteness brings itself into the Situation by making present. The character of "having been" arises from the future, and in such a way that the future which "has been" (or better, which "is in the process of having been") releases from itself the Present.[2] This phenomenon has the unity of a future which makes present in the process of having been; we designate it as *"temporality"*.[3] Only in so far as Dasein has the definite character of temporality, is the authentic potentiality-for-Being-a-whole of anticipatory resoluteness, as we have described it, made possible for Dasein itself. *Temporality reveals itself as the meaning of authentic care.*

The phenomenal content of this meaning, drawn from the state of Being of anticipatory resoluteness, fills in the signification of the term "temporality". In our terminological use of this expression, we must hold ourselves aloof from all those significations of 'future', 'past', and 'Present' which thrust themselves upon us from the ordinary conception of time. This holds also for conceptions of a 'time' which is 'subjective' or 'Objective', 'immanent' or 'transcendent'. Inasmuch as Dasein understands itself in a way which, proximally and for the most part, is inauthentic, we may suppose that 'time' as ordinarily understood does indeed represent a genuine phenomenon, but one which is derivative [ein abkünftiges]. It arises from inauthentic temporality, which has a source of its own. The conceptions of 'future', 'past' and 'Present' have first arisen in terms of the inauthentic way of understanding time. In terminologically delimiting the primordial and authentic phenomena which correspond to these, we have to struggle against the same difficulty which keeps all ontological terminology in its grip. When violences are done in this field of investigation, they are not arbitrary but have a necessity grounded in the facts. If, however, we are to point out without gaps in the argument, how inauthentic temporality has its source in temporality which is

---

[1] On our expressions 'having presence', 'making present', and 'the Present', see our notes 1 and 2, p. 47, and 2, p. 48 on H. 25 above.

[2] 'Die Gewesenheit entspringt der Zukunft, so zwar, dass die gewesene (besser gewesende) Zukunft die Gegenwart aus sich entlässt.' Heidegger has coined the form 'gewesend' by fusing the past participle 'gewesen' with the suffix of the present participle '-end', as if in English one were to write 'beening'.

[3] 'Dies dergestalt als gewesend-gegenwärtigende Zukunft einheitliche Phänomen nennen wir die *Zeitlichkeit*.'

primordial and authentic, the primordial phenomenon, which we have described only in a rough and ready fashion, must first be worked out correctly.

If resoluteness makes up the mode of authentic care, and if this itself is possible only through temporality, then the phenomenon at which we have arrived by taking a look at resoluteness, must present us with only a modality of temporality, by which, after all, care as such is made possible. Dasein's totality of Being as care means: ahead-of-itself-already-being-in (a world) as Being-alongside (entities encountered within-the-world). When we first fixed upon this articulated structure, we suggested that with regard to this articulation the ontological question must be pursued still further back until the unity of the totality of this structural manifoldness has been laid bare.ˣˣⁱⁱⁱ *The primordial unity of the structure of care lies in temporality.*

The "ahead-of-itself" is grounded in the future. In the "Being-already-in . . .", the character of "having been" is made known. "Being-alongside . . ." becomes possible in making present. While the "ahead" includes the notion of a "before",[1] neither the 'before' in the 'ahead' nor the 'already' is to be taken in terms of the way time is ordinarily understood; this has been automatically ruled out by what has been said above. With this 'before' we do not have in mind 'in advance of something' [das "Vorher"] in the sense of 'not yet now—but later'; the 'already' is just as far from signifying 'no longer now—but earlier'. If the expressions 'before' and 'already' were to have a time-oriented [zeithafte] signification such as this (and they can have this signification too), then to say that care has temporality would be to say that it is something which is 'earlier' and 'later', 'not yet' and 'no longer'. Care would then be conceived as an entity which occurs and runs its course 'in time'. The *Being* of an entity having the character of Dasein would become something *present-at-hand*. If this sort of thing is impossible, then any time-oriented signification which the expressions we have mentioned may have, must be different from this. The 'before' and the 'ahead' indicate the future as of a sort which would make it possible for Dasein to be such that its potentiality-for-Being is an issue.[2] Self-projection upon the 'for-the-sake-of-oneself' is grounded in

---

[1] We have interpolated this clause in our translation to give point to Heidegger's remark about 'the "before" in the "ahead"' ('das "Vor" im "Vorweg"'), which is obvious enough in German but would otherwise seem very far-fetched in English. We have of course met the expression 'vor' in many contexts—in 'Vorhabe', 'Vorsicht', and 'Vorgriff' as 'fore-structures' of understanding (H. 150), and in such expressions as 'that in the face of which' ('das "Wovor"') one fears or flees or has anxiety (H. 140, 184, 251, etc.). Here, however, the translation 'before' seems more appropriate.

[2] 'Das "vor" und "vorweg" zeigt die Zukunft an, als welche sie überhaupt erst ermöglicht, dass Dasein so sein kann, dass es ihm *um* sein Seinkönnen geht.' The pronoun 'sie' appears only in the later editions.

the future and is an essential characteristic of *existentiality*. *The primary meaning of existentiality is the future.*

Likewise, with the 'already' we have in view the existential temporal meaning of the Being of that entity which, in so far as it *is*, is already something that has been thrown. Only because care is based on the character of "having been", can Dasein exist as the thrown entity which it is. 'As long as' Dasein factically exists, it is never past [vergangen], but it always is indeed as already having *been*, in the sense of the "I *am*-as-having-been". And only as long as Dasein is, *can* it *be* as having been. On the other hand, we call an entity "past", when it is no longer present-at-hand. Therefore Dasein, in existing, can never establish itself as a fact which is present-at-hand, arising and passing away 'in the course of time', with a bit of it past already. Dasein never 'finds itself' except as a thrown Fact. In the *state-of-mind in which it finds itself*, Dasein is assailed by itself as the entity which it still is and already was—that is to say, which it constantly *is* as having been.[1] The primary existential meaning of facticity lies in the character of "having been". In our formulation of the structure of care, the temporal meaning of existentiality and facticity is indicated by the expressions 'before' and 'already'.

On the other hand, we lack such an indication for the third item which is constitutive for care—the Being-alongside which falls. This should not signify that falling is not also grounded in temporality; it should instead give us a hint that *making-present*, as the *primary* basis for *falling* into the ready-to-hand and present-at-hand with which we concern ourselves, remains *included* in the future and in having been, and is included in these in the mode of primordial temporality. When resolute, Dasein has brought itself back from falling, and has done so precisely in order to be more authentically 'there' in the 'moment of *vision*' as regards the Situation which has been disclosed.[2]

Temporality makes possible the unity of existence, facticity, and falling, and in this way constitutes primordially the totality of the structure of care. The items of care have not been pieced together cumulatively any more than temporality itself has been put together 'in the course of time' ["mit der Zeit"] out of the future, the having been, and the Present.

---

[1] 'In der *Befindlichkeit* wird das Dasein von ihm selbst überfallen als das Seiende, das es, noch seiend, schon war, das heisst gewesen ständig *ist*.' We have expanded our usual translation of 'Befindlichkeit' to bring out better the connection with the previous sentence.

[2] 'Entschlossen hat sich das Dasein gerade zurückgeholt aus dem Verfallen, um desto eigentlicher im "Augen*blick*" auf die erschlossene Situation "da" zu sein.' The German word 'Augenblick' has hitherto been translated simply as 'moment'; but here, and in many later passages, Heidegger has in mind its more literal meaning—'a glance of the eye'. In such passages it seems more appropriate to translate it as 'moment of vision'. See Section 68 below, especially H. 338.

Temporality 'is' not an *entity* at all. It is not, but it *temporalizes* itself. Nevertheless, we cannot avoid saying, 'Temporality "is" . . . the meaning of care', 'Temporality "is" . . . defined in such and such a way'; the reason for this can be made intelligible only when we have clarified the idea of Being and that of the 'is' in general. Temporality temporalizes, and indeed it temporalizes possible ways of itself. These make possible the multiplicity of Dasein's modes of Being, and especially the basic possibility of authentic or inauthentic existence.

The future, the character of having been, and the Present, show the phenomenal characteristics of the 'towards-oneself', the 'back-to', and the 'letting-oneself-be-encountered-*by*'.[1] The phenomena of the "towards . . .", the "to . . .", and the "alongside . . .", make temporality manifest as the ἐκστατικόν pure and simple. *Temporality is the primordial 'outside-of-itself' in and for itself.* We therefore call the phenomena of the future, the character of having been, and the Present, the "*ecstases*" of temporality.[2] Temporality is not, prior to this, an entity which first emerges from *itself*; its essence is a process of temporalizing in the unity of the ecstases. What is characteristic of the 'time' which is accessible to the ordinary understanding, consists, among other things, precisely in the fact that it is a pure sequence of "nows", without beginning and without end, in which the ecstatical character of primordial temporality has been levelled off. But this very levelling off, in accordance with its existential meaning, is grounded in the possibility of a definite kind of temporalizing, in conformity with which temporality temporalizes as inauthentic the kind of 'time' we have just mentioned. If, therefore, we demonstrate that the 'time' which is accessible to Dasein's common sense is *not* primordial, but arises rather from authentic temporality, then, in accordance with the principle, "*a potiori fit denominatio*", we are justified in designating as "*primordial time*" the *temporality* which we have now laid bare.

[1] 'Zukunft, Gewesenheit, Gegenwart zeigen die phänomenalen Charaktere des "Auf-sich-zu", des "Zurück auf", des "Begegnenlassens *von*".' On these expressions cf. H. 326 above.

[2] 'Die Phänomene des zu . . ., auf . . ., bei . . . offenbaren die Zeitlichkeit als das ἐκστατικόν schlechthin. *Zeitlichkeit ist das ursprüngliche "Ausser-sich" an und für sich selbst.* Wir nennen daher die charakterisierten Phänomene Zukunft, Gewesenheit, Gegenwart die Ekstasen der Zeitlichkeit.'

The connection of the words 'zu', 'auf', and 'bei' with the expressions listed in the preceding sentence, is somewhat obscure even in the German, and is best clarified by a study of the preceding pages. Briefly the correlation seems to be as follows:

zu:	Zukunft; auf sich zukommen; Auf-sich-zu;	Sich-vorweg.
auf:	Gewesenheit; zurückkommen auf; Zurück auf;	Schon-sein-in.
bei:	Gegenwart;	Begegnenlassen von; Sein-bei.

The root-meaning of the word 'ecstasis' (Greek ἔκστασις; German, 'Ekstase') is 'standing outside'. Used generally in Greek for the 'removal' or 'displacement' of something, it came to be applied to states-of-mind which we would now call 'ecstatic'. Heidegger usually keeps the basic root-meaning in mind, but he also is keenly aware of its close connection with the root-meaning of the word 'existence'.

In enumerating the ecstases, we have always mentioned the future first. We have done this to indicate that the future has a priority in the ecstatical unity of primordial and authentic temporality. This is so, even though temporality does not first arise through a cumulative sequence of the ecstases, but in each case temporalizes itself in their equiprimordiality. But within this equiprimordiality, the modes of temporalizing are different. The difference lies in the fact that the nature of the temporalizing can be determined primarily in terms of the different ecstases. Primordial and authentic temporality temporalizes itself in terms of the authentic future and in such a way that in having been futurally, it first of all awakens the Present.[1] *The primary phenomenon of primordial and authentic temporality is the future.* The priority of the future will vary according to the ways in which the temporalizing of inauthentic temporality itself is modified, but it will still come to the fore even in the derivative kind of 'time'.[2]

Care is Being-towards-death. We have defined "anticipatory resoluteness" as authentic Being towards the possibility which we have characterized as Dasein's utter impossibility. In such Being-towards-its-end, Dasein exists in a way which is authentically whole as that entity which it can be when 'thrown into death'. This entity does not have an end at which it just stops, but it *exists finitely.*[3] The authentic future is temporalized primarily by that temporality which makes up the meaning of anticipatory resoluteness; it thus reveals itself *as finite.*[4] But 'does not time go on' in spite of my own no-longer-Dasein?[5] And can there not be an unlimited number of things which still lie 'in the future' and come along out of it?

We must answer these questions affirmatively. In spite of this, they do not contain any objections to the finitude of primordial temporality— because this is something which is no longer handled by these at all. The question is not about everything that still can happen 'in a time that goes on', or about what kind of letting-come-towards-oneself we can encounter 'out of this time', but about how "coming-towards-oneself" is, *as such,* to be primordially defined. Its finitude does not amount primarily to a stopping, but is a characterisitic of temporalization itself. The primordial and authentic future is the "towards-oneself" (to *oneself*!),[6] existing

---

[1] '... dass sie zukünftig gewesen allererst die Gegenwart weckt.'

[2] '... noch in der abkünftigen "Zeit".' Here Heidegger is contrasting the authentic kind of time in which Dasein 'comes towards' itself futurally ['auf sich zukommt zukünftig'] with the inauthentic kind of time which 'comes off' from this or is 'derived' from it ['abkommt'], and which is thus of a 'derivative' ['abkünftig'] character.

[3] '.. sondern *existiert endlich.*'

[4] 'Die eigentliche Zukunft, die primär *die* Zeitlichkeit zeitigt, die den Sinn der vorlaufenden Entschlossenheit ausmacht, enthüllt sich damit selbst *als endliche.*'

[5] 'Allein "geht" trotz des Nichtmehrdaseins meiner selbst "die Zeit nicht weiter"?'

[6] '... das Auf-sich-zu, auf *sich* ...'

as the possibility of nullity, the possibility which is not to be outstripped. The ecstatical character of the primordial future lies precisely in the fact that the future closes one's potentiality-for-Being; that is to say, the future itself is closed to one,[1] and as such it makes possible the resolute existentiell understanding of nullity. Primordial and authentic coming-towards-oneself is the meaning of existing in one's ownmost nullity. In our thesis that temporality is primordially finite, we are not disputing that 'time goes on'; we are simply holding fast to the phenomenal character of primordial temporality—a character which shows itself in what is projected in Dasein's primordial existential projecting.

The temptation to overlook the finitude of the primordial and authentic future and therefore the finitude of temporality, or alternatively, to hold '*a priori*' that such finitude is impossible, arises from the way in which the ordinary understanding of time is constantly thrusting itself to the fore. If the ordinary understanding is right in knowing a time which is endless, and in knowing only this, it has not yet been demonstrated that it also understands this time and its 'infinity'. What does it mean to say, 'Time goes on' or 'Time keep passing away?' What is the signification of 'in time' in general, and of the expressions 'in the future' and 'out of the future' in particular? In what sense is 'time' endless? Such points need to be cleared up, if the ordinary objections to the finitude of primordial time are not to remain groundless. But we can clear them up effectively only if we have obtained an appropriate way of formulating the question as regards finitude and in-finitude.[2] Such a formulation, however, arises only if we view the primordial phenomenon of time understandingly. The problem is not one of how[3] the '*derived*' ["*abgeleitete*"] infinite time, 'in which, the ready-to-hand arises and passes away, becomes *primordial* finite temporality; the problem is rather that of how *in*authentic temporality arises out of finite authentic temporality, and how inauthentic temporality, *as in*authentic, temporalizes an *in*-finite time out of the finite. Only because primordial time is *finite* can the 'derived' time temporalize itself as *infinite*. In the order in which we get things into our grasp through the understanding, the finitude of time does not become fully visible until we have exhibited 'endless time' so that these may be contrasted.

---

[1] '. . . dass sie das Seinkönnen achliesst, das heisst selbst geschlossen ist . . .' The verb 'schliessen', as here used, may mean either to close or shut, or to conclude or bring to an end. Presumably the author has both senses in mind.

[2] '. . . hinsichtlich der Endlichkeit und Un-endlichkeit . . .' We have tried to preserve Heidegger's orthographic distinction between 'Unendlichkeit' and 'Un-endlichkeit' by translating the former as 'infinity', the latter as 'in-finitude'. We shall similarly use 'infinite' and 'in-finite' for 'unendlich' and 'un-endlich' respectively.

[3] This word ('*wie*') is italicized only in the later editions.

Our analysis of primordial temporality up to this point may be summarized in the following theses. Time is primordial as the temporalizing of temporality, and as such it makes possible the Constitution of the structure of care. Temporality is essentially ecstatical. Temporality temporalizes itself primordially out of the future. Primordial time is finite.

However, the Interpretation of care as temporality cannot remain restricted to the narrow basis obtained so far, even if it has taken us the first steps along our way in viewing Dasein's primordial and authentic Being-a-whole. The thesis that the meaning of Dasein is temporality must be confirmed in the concrete content of this entity's basic state, as it has been set forth.

¶ *66. Dasein's Temporality and the Tasks Arising Therefrom of Repeating the Existential Analysis in a more Primordial Manner*

Not only does the phenomenon of temporality which we have laid bare demand a more widely-ranging confirmation of its constitutive power, but only through such confirmation will it itself come into view as regards the basic possibilities of temporalizing. The demonstration of the possibility of Dasein's state of Being on the basis of temporality will be designated in brief—though only provisionally—as "the 'temporal' Interpretation".

Our next task is to go beyond the temporal analysis of Dasein's authentic potentiality-for-Being-a-whole and a general characterization of the temporality of care so that Dasein's *inauthenticity* may be made visible in its own specific temporality. Temporality first showed itself in anticipatory resoluteness. This is the authentic mode of disclosedness, though disclosedness maintains itself for the most part in the inauthenticity with which the "they" fallingly interprets itself. In characterizing the temporality of disclosedness in general, we are led to the temporal understanding of that concernful Being-in-the-world which lies closest to us, and therefore of the average undifferentiatedness of Dasein from which the existential analytic first took its start.[xxiv] We have called Dasein's average kind of Being, in which it maintains itself proximally and for the most part, "everydayness". By repeating the earlier analysis, we must reveal *everydayness* in its *temporal* meaning, so that the problematic included in temporality may come to light, and the seemingly 'obvious' character of the preparatory analyses may completely disappear. Indeed, confirmation is to be found for temporality in all the essential structures of Dasein's basic constitution. Yet this will not lead to running through our analyses again superficially and schematically in the same sequence of presentation. The course of our temporal analysis is directed otherwise: it is to make plainer the interconnection of our earlier considerations and to do away with whatever is accidental and seemingly arbitrary. Beyond these necessities of method, however, the phenomenon itself gives us motives which compel us to articulate our analysis in a different way when we repeat it.

The ontological structure of that entity which, in each case, I *myself* am, centres in the Self-subsistence [Selbständigkeit] of existence. Because the Self cannot be conceived either as substance or as subject but is grounded in existence, our analysis of the inauthentic Self, the "they", has been left wholly in tow of the preparatory Interpretation of Dasein.[xxv] Now that Selfhood has been *explicitly* taken back into the structure of care, and therefore of temporality, the temporal Interpretation of Self-constancy and non-Self-constancy[1] acquires an importance of its own. This Interpretation needs to be carried through separately and thematically. However, it not only gives us the right kind of insurance against the paralogisms and against ontologically inappropriate questions about the Being of the "I" in general, but it provides at the same time, in accordance with its central function, a more primordial insight into the *temporalization-structure* of temporality, which reveals itself as the historicality of Dasein. The proposition, "Dasein is historical", is confirmed as a fundamental existential ontological assertion. This assertion is far removed from the mere ontical establishment of the fact that Dasein occurs in a 'world-history'. But the historicality of Dasein is the basis for a possible kind of historiological understanding which in turn carries with it the possibility of getting a special grasp of the development of historiology as a science.

By Interpreting everydayness and historicality temporally we shall get a steady enough view of primordial time to expose it as the condition which makes the everyday experience of time both possible and necessary. As an entity for which its Being is an issue, Dasein *utilizes itself* primarily *for itself* [*verwendet sich . . . für sich selbst*], whether it does so explicitly or not. Proximally and for the most part, care is circumspective concern. In utilizing itself for the sake of itself, Dasein 'uses itself up'. In using itself up, Dasein uses itself—that is to say, its time.[2] In using time, Dasein reckons with it. Time is first discovered in the concern which reckons

---

[1] '. . . Selbst-ständigkeit und Unselbst-ständigkeit . . .' Cf. note 2, p. 369, H. 322.

[2] 'Umwillen seiner selbst verwendend, "verbraucht" sich das Dasein. Sichverbrauchend braucht das Dasein sich selbst, dass heisst seine Zeit.' Here three verbs, all of which might sometimes be translated as 'use', are contrasted rather subtly. 'Verwenden' means literally to 'turn something away', but is often used in the sense of 'turning something to account', 'utilizing it'; in a reflexive construction such as we have here, it often takes on the more special meaning of 'applying oneself' on someone's behalf. (In previous passages we have generally translated 'verwenden' as 'use'.) 'Verbrauchen' means to 'consume' or 'use up'. 'Brauchen' too means to 'use'; but it also means to 'need', and it is hard to tell which of these senses Heidegger here has in mind.

circumspectively, and this concern leads to the development of a time-reckoning. Reckoning with time is constitutive for Being-in-the-world. Concernful circumspective discovering, in reckoning with its time, permits those things which we have discovered, and which are ready-to-hand or present-at-hand, to be encountered in time. Thus entities within-the-world become accessible as 'being in time'. We call the temporal attribute of entities within-the-world "*within-time-ness*" [die *Innerzeitkeit*]. The kind of 'time' which is first found ontically in within-time-ness, becomes the basis on which the ordinary traditional conception of time takes form. But time, as within-time-ness, arises from an essential kind of temporalizing of primordial temporality. The fact that this is its source, tells us that the time 'in which' what is present-at-hand arises and passes away, is a genuine phenomenon of time; it is not an externalization of a 'qualitative time' into space, as Bergson's Interpretation of time—which is ontologically quite indefinite and inadequate—would have us believe.

In working out the temporality of Dasein as everydayness, historicality, and within-time-ness, we shall be getting for the first time a relentless insight into the *complications* of a primordial ontology of Dasein. As Being-in-the-world, Dasein exists factically with and alongside entities which it encounters within-the-world. Thus Dasein's Being becomes ontologically transparent in a comprehensive way only within the horizon[1] in which the Being of entities other than Dasein—and this means even of those which are neither ready-to-hand nor present-at-hand but just 'subsist'—has been clarified. But if the variations of Being are to be Interpreted for everything of which we say, "It *is*", we need an idea of Being in general, and this idea needs to have been adequately illumined in advance. So long as this idea is one at which we have not yet arrived, then the temporal analysis of Dasein, even if we *repeat* it, will remain incomplete and fraught with obscurities; we shall not go on to talk about the objective difficulties. The existential-temporal analysis of Dasein demands, for its part, that it be repeated anew within a framework in which the concept of Being is discussed in principle.

[1] 'Das Sein des Daseins empfängt daher seine umfassende ontologische Durchsichtigkeit erst im Horizont . . .' In the older editions 'erst' appears after 'daher' rather than after 'Durchsichtigkeit'.

IV

TEMPORALITY AND EVERYDAYNESS

¶ 67. *The Basic Content of Dasein's Existential Constitution, and a Preliminary Sketch of the Temporal Interpretation of it*

OUR preparatory analysis[1] has made accessible a multiplicity of phenomena; and no matter how much we may concentrate on the foundational structural totality of care, these must not be allowed to vanish from our phenomenological purview. Far from excluding such a multiplicity, the *primordial* totality of Dasein's constitution *as articulated* demands it. The primordiality of a state of Being does not coincide with the simplicity and uniqueness of an ultimate structural element. The ontological source of Dasein's Being is not 'inferior' to what springs from it, but towers above it in power from the outset; in the field of ontology, any 'springing-from' is degeneration. If we penetrate to the 'source' ontologically, we do not come to things which are ontically obvious for the 'common understanding'; but the questionable character of everything obvious opens up for us.

If we are to bring back into our phenomenological purview the phenomena at which we have arrived in our preparatory analysis, an allusion to the stages through which we have passed must be sufficient. Our definition of "care" emerged from our analysis of the disclosedness which constitutes the Being of the 'there'. The clarification of this phenomenon signified that we must give a provisional Interpretation of Being-in-the-world—the basic state of Dasein. Our investigation set out to describe Being-in-the-world, so that from the beginning we could secure an adequate phenomenological horizon as opposed to those inappropriate and mostly inexplicit ways in which the nature of Dasein has been determined beforehand ontologically. Being-in-the-world was first characterized with regard to the phenomenon of the world. And in our explication this was done by characterizing ontico-ontologically what is ready-to-hand and present-at-hand '*in*' the environment, and then bringing within-the-world-ness into relief, so that by this the phenomenon of worldhood in general could be made visible. But understanding belongs essentially to disclosedness; and the structure of worldhood, significance, turned out to be bound up with that upon which understanding projects itself—namely that potentiality-for-Being *for the sake of which* Dasein exists.

The temporal Interpretation of everyday Dasein must start with those structures in which disclosedness constitutes itself: understanding, state-of-mind, falling, and discourse. The modes in which temporality temporalizes are to be laid bare with regard to these phenomena, and will give us a basis for defining the temporality of Being-in-the-world. This leads us back to the phenomenon of the world, and permits us to delimit the specifically temporal problematic of worldhood. This must be confirmed by characterizing that kind of Being-in-the-world which in an everyday manner is closest to us—circumspective, falling concern. The temporality of this concern makes it possible for circumspection to be modified into a perceiving which looks at things, and the theoretical cognition which is grounded in such perceiving. The temporality of Being-in-the-world thus emerges, and it turns out, at the same time, to be the foundation for that spatiality which is specific for Dasein. We must also show the temporal Constitution of deseverance and directionality. Taken as a whole, these analyses will reveal a possibility for the temporalizing of temporality in which Dasein's inauthenticity is ontologically grounded; and they will lead us face to face with the question of how the temporal character of everydayness—the temporal meaning of the phrase 'proximally and for the most part', which we have been using constantly hitherto—is to be understood. By fixing upon this problem we shall have made it plain that the clarification of this phenomenon which we have so far attained is insufficient, and we shall have shown the extent of this insufficiency.

The present chapter is thus divided up as follows: the temporality of disclosedness in general (Section 68); the temporality of Being-in-the-world and the problem of transcendence (Section 69); the temporality of the spatiality characteristic of Dasein (Section 70); the temporal meaning of Dasein's everydayness (Section 71).

¶ *68. The Temporality of Disclosedness in General*

Resoluteness, which we have characterized with regard to its temporal meaning, represents an authentic disclosedness of Dasein—a disclosedness which constitutes an entity of such a kind that in existing, it can be its very 'there'. Care has been characterized with regard to its temporal meaning, but only in its basic features. To exhibit its concrete temporal Constitution, means to give a temporal Interpretation of the items of its structure, taking them each singly: understanding, state-of-mind, falling, and discourse. Every understanding has its mood. Every state-of-mind is one in which one understands. The understanding which one has in such a state-of-mind has the character of falling. The understanding which has its mood attuned in falling, Articulates itself with relation to its intelligibility in discourse. The current temporal Constitution of these phenomena leads back in each case to that *one* kind of temporality which serves as such to guarantee the possibility that understanding, state-of-mind, falling, and discourse, are united in their structure.[1]

(a) *The Temporality of Understanding*[11]

With the term "understanding" we have in mind a fundamental *existentiale*, which is neither a definite *species of cognition* distinguished, let us say, from explaining and conceiving, nor any cognition at all in the sense of grasping something thematically. Understanding constitutes rather the Being of the "there" in such a way that, on the basis of such understanding, a Dasein can, in existing, develop the different possibilities of sight, of looking around [Sichumsehens], and of just looking. In all explanation one uncovers understandingly that which one cannot understand; and all explanation is thus rooted in Dasein's primary understanding.

If the term "understanding" is taken in a way which is primordially existential, it means *to be projecting*[2] *towards a potentiality-for-Being for the sake of which any Dasein exists*. In understanding, one's own potentiality-for-Being is disclosed in such a way that one's Dasein always knows understandingly what it is capable of. It 'knows' this, however, not by having discovered some fact, but by maintaining itself in an existentiell possibility. The kind of ignorance which corresponds to this, does not consist in an absence or cessation of understanding, but must be regarded as a deficient mode of the projectedness of one's potentiality-for-Being. Existence can be questionable. If it is to be possible for something 'to be in question' [das "In-Frage-stehen"], a disclosedness is needed. When one understands oneself projectively in an existentiell possibility, the future underlies this understanding, and it does so as a coming-towards-oneself out of that current possibility as which one's Dasein exists. The future makes ontologically possible an entity which is in such a way that it exists understandingly in its potentiality-for-Being. Projection is basically futural; it does not primarily grasp the projected possibility thematically

---

[1] 'Die jeweilige zeitliche Konstitution der genannten Phänomene führt je auf die *eine* Zeitlichkeit zurück, als welche sie die mögliche Struktureinheit von Verstehen, Befindlichkeit, Verfallen und Rede verbürgt.' The older editions omit the pronoun 'sie'.
[2] '... entwerfend-sein ...' The older editions have '... e n t w e r f e n d S e i n ...'

N

just by having it in view, but it throws itself into it as a possibility. In each case Dasein *is* understandingly in the way that it can be.[1] Resoluteness has turned out to be a kind of existing which is primordial and authentic. Proximally and for the most part, to be sure, Dasein remains irresolute; that is to say, it remains closed off in its ownmost potentiality-for-Being, to which it brings itself only when it has been individualized. This implies that temporality does not temporalize itself constantly out of the authentic future. This inconstancy, however, does not mean that temporality sometimes lacks a future, but rather that the temporalizing of the future takes various forms.

To designate the authentic future terminologically we have reserved the expression *"anticipation"*. This indicates that Dasein, existing authentically, lets itself come towards itself as its ownmost potentiality-for-Being— that the future itself must first win itself, not from a Present, but from the inauthentic future. If we are to provide a formally undifferentiated term for the future, we may use the one with which we have designated the first structural item of care—the *"ahead-of-itself"*. Factically, Dasein is constantly ahead of itself, but inconstantly anticipatory with regard to its existentiell possibility.

How is the inauthentic future to be contrasted with this? Just as the authentic future is revealed in resoluteness, the inauthentic future, as an ecstatical mode, can reveal itself only if we go back ontologically from the inauthentic understanding of everyday concern to its existential-temporal meaning. As care, Dasein is essentially ahead of itself. Proximally and for the most part, concernful Being-in-the-world understands itself in terms of that with *which* it is concerned. Inauthentic *understanding*[2] projects itself upon that with which one can concern oneself, or upon what is feasible, urgent, or indispensable in our everyday business. But that with which we concern ourselves is as it is for the sake of that potentiality-for-Being which cares. This potentiality lets Dasein come towards itself in its concernful Being-alongside that with which it is concerned. Dasein does not come towards itself primarily in its ownmost non-relational potentiality-for-Being, but it *awaits this* concernfully *in terms of that which yields or denies the object of its concern*.[3] Dasein comes towards itself from that with which it concerns itself. The inauthentic future has the character of *awaiting*.[4] One's concernful understanding of oneself as they-self in terms

---

[1] 'Verstehend *ist* das Dasein je, wie es sein kann.'
[2] 'Das uneigentliche *Verstehen* . . .' Italics only in the later editions.
[3] '. . . sondern es ist besorgend *seiner gewärtig aus dem, was das Besorgte ergibt oder versagt.'* It is not clear whether 'das Besorgte' or 'was' is the subject of its clause.
[4] ' . . . des *Gewärtigens.'* While the verb 'await' has many advantages as an approximation to 'gewärtigen', it is a bit too colourless and fails to bring out the important idea of *being prepared to reckon with* that which one awaits.

of what one does, has its possibility 'based' upon this ecstatical mode of the future. And *only because* factical Dasein *is* thus *awaiting* its potentiality-for-Being, and *is awaiting* this potentiality in terms of that with which it concerns itself, can it *expect* anything and wait for it [*erwarten* und warten auf . . .]. In each case some sort of awaiting must have disclosed the horizon and the range from which something can be expected. *Expecting is founded upon awaiting, and is a mode of that future which temporalizes itself authentically as anticipation.* Hence there lies in anticipation a more primordial Being-towards-death than in the concernful expecting of it.

Understanding, as existing in the potentiality-for-Being, however it may have been projected, is *primarily* futural. But it would not temporalize itself if it were not temporal—that is, determined with equal primordiality by having been and by the Present. The way in which the latter ecstasis helps constitute inauthentic understanding, has already been made plain in a rough and ready fashion. Everyday concern understands itself in terms of that potentiality-for-Being which confronts it as coming from its possible success or failure with regard to whatever its object of concern may be. Corresponding to the inauthentic future (awaiting), there is a special way of Being-*alongside* the things with which one concerns oneself. This way of Being-alongside is the Present—the "waiting-towards";[1] this ecstatical mode reveals itself if we adduce for comparison this very same ecstasis, but in the mode of authentic temporality. To the anticipation which goes with resoluteness, there belongs a Present in accordance with which a resolution discloses the Situation. In resoluteness, the Present is not only brought back from distraction with the objects of one's closest concern, but it gets held in the future and in having been. That *Present* which is held in authentic temporality and which thus is *authentic* itself, we call the *"moment of vision"*.[2] This term must be understood in the active sense as an ecstasis. It means the resolute rapture with which Dasein is carried away to whatever possibilities and circumstances are encountered in the Situation as possible objects of concern, but a rapture which is *held* in resoluteness.[3] The moment of vision is a phenomenon which *in principle*

---

[1] 'Gegen-wart'. In this context it seems well to translate this expression by a hendiadys which, like Heidegger's hyphenation, calls attention to the root-meaning of the noun 'Gegenwart'. See our notes 2, p. 47, (H. 25) and 2, p. 48 (H. 26) above.

[2] Cf. note 2, p. 376, H. 328 above.

[3] 'Er meint die entschlossene, aber in der Erschlossenheit *gehaltene* Entrückung des Daseins an das, was in der Situation an besorgbaren Möglichkeiten, Umständen begegnet.' The verb 'entrücken' means literally 'to move away' or 'to carry away', but it has also taken on the meaning of the 'rapture' in which one is 'carried away' in a more figurative sense. While the words 'Entrückung' and 'Ekstase' can thus be used in many contexts as synonyms, for Heidegger the former seems the more general. (See H. 365 below.) We shall translate 'entrücken' by 'rapture' or 'carry away', or, as in this case, by a combination of these expressions.

can *not* be clarified in terms of the "*now*" [dem *Jetzt*]. The "now" is a temporal phenomenon which belongs to time as within-time-ness: the "now" 'in which' something arises, passes away, or is present-at-hand. 'In the moment of vision' nothing can occur; but as an authentic Present or waiting-towards, the moment of vision permits us *to encounter for the first time* what can be 'in a time' as ready-to-hand or present-at-hand.[iii]

In contradistinction to the moment of vision as the authentic Present, we call the inauthentic Present "*making present*". Formally understood, every Present is one which makes present, but not every Present has the character of a 'moment of vision'. When we use the expression "making present" without adding anything further, we always have in mind the inauthentic kind, which is irresolute and does not have the character of a moment of vision. Making-present will become clear only in the light of the temporal Interpretation of falling into the 'world' of one's concern; such falling has its existential meaning in making present. But in so far as the potentiality-for-Being which is projected by inauthentic understanding is projected in terms of things with which one can be concerned, this means that such understanding temporalizes itself in terms of making present. The moment of vision, however, temporalizes itself in quite the opposite manner—in terms of the authentic future.

Inauthentic understanding temporalizes itself as an awaiting which makes present [gegenwärtigendes Gewartigen]—an awaiting to whose ecstatical unity there must belong a corresponding "*having been*". The authentic coming-towards-itself of anticipatory resoluteness is at the same time a coming-back to one's ownmost Self, which has been thrown into its individualization. This ecstasis makes it possible for Dasein to be able to take over resolutely that entity which it already is. In anticipating, Dasein *brings itself again forth* into its ownmost potentiality-for-Being. If *Being*-as-having-been is authentic, we call it "*repetition*".[1] But when one projects oneself inauthentically towards those possibilities which have been drawn from the object of concern in making it present, this is possible only because Dasein has *forgotten* itself in its ownmost *thrown* potentiality-for-Being. This forgetting is not nothing, nor is it just a failure to remember; it is rather a 'positive' ecstatical mode of one's having been—a mode with a character of its own. The ecstasis (rapture) of forgetting has the character of backing away *in the face of* one's ownmost "been", and of doing so in a manner which is closed off from itself—in such a manner, indeed, that this backing-away closes off ecstatically that in the face of which one is

---

[1] 'Im Vorlaufen *holt* sich das Dasein *wieder* in das eigenste Seinkönnen *vor*. Das eigentliche Gewesen-*sein* nennen wir die *Wiederholung*.' On 'Wiederholung', see H. 385 and our note ad loc.

backing away, and thereby closes itself off too.[1] *Having forgotten* [*Vergessenheit*] as an inauthentic way of having been, is thus related to that thrown *Being* which is one's own; it is the temporal meaning of that Being in accordance with which I *am* proximally and for the most part as-having-been. Only on the basis of such forgetting can anything be *retained* [*behalten*] by the concernful making-present which awaits; and what are thus retained are entities encountered within-the-world with a character other than that of Dasein. To such retaining there corresponds a non-retaining which presents us with a kind of 'forgetting' in a derivative sense.

Just as expecting is possible only on the basis of awaiting, *remembering* is possible only on that of forgetting, *and not vice versa*; for in the mode of having-forgotten, one's having been 'discloses' primarily the horizon into which a Dasein lost in the 'superficiality' of its object of concern, can bring itself by remembering.[2] The *awaiting which forgets and makes present* is an ecstatical unity in its own right, in accordance with which inauthentic understanding temporalizes itself with regard to its temporality. The unity of these ecstases closes off one's authentic potentiality-for-Being, and is thus the existential condition for the possibility of irresoluteness. Though inauthentic concernful understanding determines itself in the light of making present the object of concern, the temporalizing of the understanding is performed primarily in the future.

(b) *The Temporality of State-of-mind*[iv]

Understanding is never free-floating, but always goes with some state-of-mind. The "there" gets equiprimordially disclosed by one's mood in every case—or gets closed off by it. Having a mood brings Dasein *face to face* with its thrownness in such a manner that this thrownness is not known as such but disclosed far more primordially in 'how one is'. Existentially, "*Being*-thrown" means finding oneself in some state-of-mind or other. One's state-of-mind is therefore based upon thrownness. My mood represents whatever may be the way in which I am primarily the entity

---

[1] 'Die Ekstase (Entrückung) des Vergessens hat den Charakter des sich selbst verschlossenen Ausrückens *vor* dem eigensten Gewesen, so zwar, dass dieses Ausrücken vor... ekstatisch das Wover verschliesst und in eins damit sich selbst.' Heidegger is here connecting the word 'Entrückung' (our 'rapture') with the cognate verb 'ausrücken' ('back away'), which may be used intransitively in the military sense of 'decamping', but may also be used transitively in the sense of 'disconnecting'. Both 'entrücken' and 'ausrücken' mean originally 'to move away', but they have taken on very different connotations in ordinary German usage.

[2] '... denn im Modus der Vergessenheit "erschliesst" die Gewesenheit primär den Horizont, in den hinein das an die "Äusserlichkeit" des Besorgten verlorene Dasein sich erinnern kann.' Here there is presumably a deliberate contrast between the idea of *externality* in the root meaning of 'Äusserlichkeit' ('superficiality') and the idea of putting oneself *into* something, which is the original sense of 'sich erinnern' ('to remember'). We have tried to bring this out by our rather free translation of '... in den hinein ... sich erinnern ...'.

hat has been thrown. How does the temporal Constitution of having-a-mood let itself be made visible? How will the ecstatical unity of one's current temporality give any insight into the existential connection between one's state-of-mind and one's understanding?

One's mood discloses in the manner of turning thither or turning away from one's own Dasein. *Bringing* Dasein *face to face* with the "that-it-is" of its own thrownness—whether authentically revealing it or inauthentically covering it up—becomes existentially possible only if Dasein's Being, by its very meaning, constantly *is* as having been. The "been" is not what first brings one face to face with the thrown entity which one is oneself; but the ecstasis of the "been" is what first makes it possible to find oneself in the way of having a state-of-mind.[1]

Understanding is grounded primarily in the future; one's *state-of-mind*, however, temporalizes itself *primarily* in *having been*.[2] Moods temporalize themselves—that is, their specific ecstasis belongs to a future and a Present in such a way, indeed, that these equiprimordial ecstases are modified by having been.

We have emphasized that while moods, of course, are ontically well-known to us [bekannt], they are not recognized [erkannt] in their primordial existential function. They are regarded as fleeting Experiences which 'colour' one's whole 'psychical condition'. Anything which is observed to have the character of turning up and disappearing in a fleeting manner, belongs to the primordial constancy of existence. But all the same, what should moods have in common with 'time'? That these 'Experiences' come and go, that they run their course 'in time', is a trivial thing to establish. Certainly. And indeed this can be established in an ontico-psychological manner. Our task, however, is to exhibit the onto-logical structure of having-a-mood in its existential-temporal Constitution. And of course this is proximally just a matter of first making the temporality of moods visible. The thesis that 'one's state-of-mind is grounded primarily in having been' means that the existentially basic character of moods lies in *bringing* one *back to* something. This bringing-back does not first produce a having been; but in any state-of-mind some mode of having been is made manifest for existential analysis.[3] So if we are to Interpret

---

[1] 'Das Bringen vor das geworfene Seiende, das man selbst ist, schafft nicht erst das Gewesen, sondern dessen Ekstase ermöglicht erst das Sich-finden in der Weise des Sich-befindens.' We have construed 'das Gewesen' and 'dessen Ekstase' as the subjects of their respective clauses, but other interpretations are not impossible.

[2] In our italicization we follow the older editions. In the newer editions 'Gewesenheit' ('having been') is not italicized.

[3] 'Dieses stellt die Gewesenheit nicht erst her, sondern die Befindlichkeit offenbart für die existenziale Analyse je einen Modus der Gewesenheit.' The grammar of the first clause is ambiguous.

states-of-mind temporally, our aim is not one of deducing moods from temporality and dissolving them into pure phenomena of temporalizing. All we have to do is to demonstrate that *except on the basis of temporality*, moods *are not possible* in what they 'signify' in an existentiell way or in how they 'signify' it. Our temporal Interpretation will restrict itself to the phenomena of fear and anxiety, which we have already analysed in a preparatory manner.

We shall begin our analysis by exhibiting the temporality of *fear*.ᵛ Fear has been characterized as an inauthentic state-of-mind. To what extent does the existential meaning which makes such a state-of-mind possible lie in what has been? Which mode of this ecstasis designates the specific temporality of fear? Fear is a fearing *in the face of* something threatening— of something which is detrimental to Dasein's factical potentiality-for-Being, and which brings itself close in the way we have described, within the range of the ready-to-hand and the present-at-hand with which we concern ourselves. Fearing discloses something threatening, and it does so by way of everyday circumspection. A subject which merely beholds would never be able to discover anything of the sort. But if something is disclosed when one fears in the face of it, is not this disclosure a letting-something-come-towards-oneself [ein Auf-sich-zukommenlassen]? Has not "fear" been rightly defined as "the expectation of some oncoming evil" [eines ankommenden Übels] ("*malum futurum*")? Is not the primary meaning of fear the future, and least of all, one's having been? Not only does fearing 'relate' itself to 'something future' in the signification of something which first comes on 'in time'; but this self-relating is itself futural in the primordially temporal sense. All this is incontestable. Manifestly an *awaiting* is *one* of the things that belong to the existential-temporal Constitution of fear. But proximally this just means that the temporality of fear is one that is *inauthentic*. Is fearing in the face of something merely an expecting of something threatening which is coming on? Such an expectation need not be fear already, and it is so far from being fear that the specific character which fear as a mood possesses is missing. This character lies in the fact that in fear the awaiting lets what is threatening *come back* [*zurückkommen*] to one's factically concernful potentiality-for-Being. Only if that to which this comes back is already ecstatically open, can that which threatens be awaited *right back to* the entity which I myself am; only so can my Dasein be threatened.[1] The awaiting which fears is one which is afraid 'for itself'; that is to say, fearing in the face of something, is in each case a fearing *about*;

[1] '*Zurück auf* das Seiende, das ich bin, kann das Bedrohliche nur gewärtigt, und so das Dasein bedroht werden, wenn das Worauf des Zurück auf . . . schon überhaupt ekstatisch offen ist.'

therein lies the character of fear as mood and as *affect*. When one's Being-in-the-world has been threatened and it concerns itself with the ready-to-hand, it does so as a factical potentiality-for-Being of its own. In the face of this potentiality one backs away in bewilderment, and this kind of forgetting oneself is what constitutes the existential-temporal meaning of fear.[1] Aristotle rightly defines "fear" as λύπη τις ἢ ταραχή—as "a kind of depression or bewilderment".[vi] This depression forces Dasein back to its thrownness, but in such a way that this thrownness gets quite closed off. The bewilderment is based upon a forgetting. When one forgets and backs away in the face of a factical potentiality-for-Being which is resolute, one clings to those possibilities of self-preservation and evasion which one has already discovered circumspectively beforehand. When concern is afraid, it leaps from next to next, because it forgets itself and therefore does not *take hold of* any *definite* possibility. Every 'possible' possibility offers itself, and this means that the impossible ones do so too. The man who fears, does not stop with any of these; his 'environment' does not disappear, but it is encountered without his knowing his way about in *it* any longer.[2] This *bewildered making-present* of the first thing that comes into one's head, is something that belongs with forgetting oneself in fear. It is well known, for instance, that the inhabitants of a burning house will often 'save' the most indifferent things that are most closely ready-to-hand. When one has forgotten oneself and makes present a jumble of hovering possibilities, one thus makes possible that bewilderment which goes to make up the mood-character of fear.[3] The having forgotten which goes with such bewilderment modifies the awaiting too and gives it the character of a depressed or bewildered awaiting which is distinct from any pure expectation.

The specific ecstatical unity which makes it existentially possible to be afraid, temporalizes itself primarily out of the kind of forgetting characterized above, which, as a mode of having been, modifies its Present and its future in their own temporalizing. The temporality of fear is a forgetting which awaits and makes present. The common-sense interpretation of fear, taking its orientation from what we encounter within-the-world, seeks in the first instance to designate the 'oncoming evil' as that in the face of which we fear, and, correspondingly, to define our relation to this evil as one of "expecting". Anything else which

---

[1] 'Deren existenzial-zeitlicher Sinn wird konstituiert durch ein Sichvergessen: das verwirrte Ausrücken vor dem eigenen faktischen Seinkönnen, als welches das bedrohte In-der-Welt-sein das Zuhandene besorgt.'

[2] 'Bei keiner hält der Fürchtende, die "Umwelt" verschwindet nicht, sondern begegnet in einem Sich-nicht-mehr-auskennen in *ihr*.'

[3] 'Das selbstvergessene Gegenwärtigen eines Gewirrs von schwebenden Möglichkeiten ermöglicht die Verwirrung, als welche sie den Stimmungscharakter der Furcht ausmacht.' The pronoun 'sie' does not appear in the older editions.

belongs to the phenomenon remains a 'feeling of pleasure or displeasure'. How is the temporality of *anxiety* related to that of fear? We have called the phenomenon of anxiety a basic state-of-mind.[vii] Anxiety brings Dasein face to face with its ownmost Being-thrown and reveals the uncanniness of everyday familiar Being-in-the-world. Anxiety, like fear, has its character formally determined by something *in the face of which* one is anxious and something *about* which one is anxious. But our analysis has shown that these two phenomena coincide. This does not mean that their structural characters are melted away into one another, as if anxiety were anxious neither in the face of anything nor about anything. Their coinciding means rather that the entity by which both these structures are filled in [das sie erfüllende Seiende] is the same—namely Dasein. In particular, that in the face of which one has anxiety is not encountered as something definite with which one can concern oneself; the threatening does not come from what is ready-to-hand or present-at-hand, but rather from the fact that neither of these 'says' anything any longer. Environmental entities no longer have any involvement. The world in which I exist has sunk into insignificance; and the world which is thus disclosed is one in which entities can be freed only in the character of having no involvement. Anxiety is anxious in the face of the "nothing" of the world; but this does not mean that in anxiety we experience something like the absence of what is present-at-hand within-the-world. The present-at-hand must be encountered in just *such* a way that it does *not* have *any* involvement *whatsoever*, but can show itself in an empty mercilessness. This implies, however, that our concernful awaiting finds nothing in terms of which it might be able to understand itself; it clutches at the "nothing" of the world; but when our understanding has come up against the world, it is brought to Being-in-the-world as such through anxiety. Being-in-the-world, however, is both what anxiety is anxious in-the-face-of and what it is anxious about. To be anxious in-the-face-of . . . does not have the character of an expecting or of any kind of awaiting. That in-the-face-of which one has anxiety is indeed already 'there'—namely, Dasein itself. In that case, does not anxiety get constituted by a future? Certainly; but not by the inauthentic future of awaiting.

Anxiety discloses an insignificance of the world; and this insignificance reveals the nullity of that with which one can concern oneself—or, in other words, the impossibility of projecting oneself upon a potentiality-for-Being which belongs to existence and which is founded primarily upon one's objects of concern. The revealing of this impossibility, however, signifies that one is letting the possibility of an authentic potentiality-for-Being be lit up. What is the temporal meaning of this revealing? Anxiety is anxious about naked Dasein as something that has been thrown into uncanniness. It brings one back to the pure "that-it-is" of one's ownmost individualized thrownness. This bringing-back has neither the character of an evasive forgetting nor that of a remembering. But just as little does anxiety imply that one has already taken over one's existence into one's resolution and done so by a repeating. On the contrary, anxiety brings one back to one's thrownness as something *possible* which *can be repeated*. And in this way it *also* reveals the possibility of an authentic potentiality-for-Being—a potentiality which must, in repeating, come back to its thrown "there", but come back as something future which comes towards [zukünftiges]. *The character of having been is constitutive for the state-of-mind of anxiety; and bringing one face to face with repeatability is the specific ecstatical mode of this character.*

4   The forgetting which is constitutive for fear, bewilders Dasein and lets it drift back and forth between 'worldly' possibilities which it has not seized upon. In contrast to this making-present which is not held on to, the Present of anxiety is *held on to* when one brings oneself back to one's ownmost thrownness. The existential meaning of anxiety is such that it cannot lose itself in something with which it might be concerned. If anything like this happens in a similar state-of-mind, this is fear, which the everyday understanding confuses with anxiety. But even though the Present of anxiety is *held on to*, it does not as yet have the character of the moment of vision, which temporalizes itself in a resolution. Anxiety merely brings one into the mood for a *possible* resolution. The Present of anxiety holds the moment of vision *at the ready* [*auf dem Sprung*]; as such a moment it itself, and only itself, is possible.

The temporality of anxiety is peculiar; for anxiety is grounded primordially in having been, and only out of this do the future and the Present temporalize themselves; in this peculiar temporality is demonstrated the possibility of that power which is distinctive for the mood of anxiety. In this, Dasein is taken all the way back to its naked uncanniness, and becomes fascinated by it.[1] This fascination, however, not only *takes* Dasein back from its '*worldly*' possibilities, but at the same time *gives* it the possibility of an *authentic* potentiality-for-Being.

[1] 'An der eigentümlichen Zeitlichkeit der Angst, dass sie ursprünglich in der Gewesenheit gründet und aus ihr erst Zukunft und Gegenwart sich zeitigen, erweist sich die Möglichkeit der Mächtigkeit, durch die sich die Stimmung der Angst auszeichnet. In ihr ist das Dasein völlig auf seine nackte Unheimlichkeit zurückgenommen und von ihr benommen.' In these two sentences there are no less than six feminine nouns which might serve as the antecedents of the pronouns 'sie' and 'ihr' in their several appearances. We have chosen the interpretation which seems most plausible to us, but others are perhaps no less defensible. The etymological connection between 'zurückgenommen' ('taken . . . back') and 'benommen' ('fascinated') does not show up in the English version; it is obviously deliberate, and it gets followed up in the next sentence.

Yet neither of these moods, fear and anxiety, ever 'occurs' just isolated in the 'stream of Experiences'; each of them determines an understanding or determines itself in terms of one.[1] Fear is occasioned by entities with which we concern ourselves environmentally. Anxiety, however, springs from Dasein itself. When fear assails us, it does so from what is within-the-world. Anxiety arises out of Being-in-the-world as thrown Being-towards-death. When understood temporally, this 'mounting' of anxiety out of Dasein, means that the future and the Present of anxiety temporalize themselves out of a primordial Being-as-having-been in the sense of bringing us back to repeatability. But anxiety can mount authentically only in a Dasein which is resolute. He who is resolute knows no fear; but he understands the possibility of anxiety as the possibility of the very mood which neither inhibits nor bewilders him. Anxiety liberates him *from* possibilities which 'count for nothing' ["nichtigen"], and lets him become free *for* those which are authentic.

Although both fear and anxiety, as modes of state-of-mind, are grounded primarily in *having been*, they each have different sources with regard to their own temporalization in the temporality of care. Anxiety springs from the *future* of resoluteness, while fear springs from the lost Present, of which fear is fearfully apprehensive, so that it falls prey to it more than ever.[2]

But may not the thesis of the temporality of moods hold only for those phenomena which we have selected for our analysis? How is a temporal meaning to be found in the pallid lack of mood which dominates the 'grey everyday' through and through? And how about the temporality of such moods and affects as hope, joy, enthusiasm, gaiety? Not only fear and anxiety, but other moods, are founded existentially upon one's having been; this becomes plain if we merely mention such phenomena as satiety, sadness, melancholy, and desperation. Of course these must be Interpreted on the broader basis of an existential analytic of Dasein that has been well worked out. But even a phenomenon like hope, which seems to be founded wholly upon the future, must be analysed in much the same way as fear. Hope has sometimes been characterized as the expectation of a *bonum futurum*, to distinguish it from fear, which relates itself to a *malum futurum*. But what is decisive for the structure of hope as a phenomenon, is not so much the 'futural' character of that *to which* it relates itself

---

[1] 'Beide Stimmungen, Furcht und Angst, "kommen" jedoch nie nur isoliert "vor" im "Erlebnisstrom", sondern be-stimmen je ein Verstehen, bzw. sich aus einem solchen.' Heidegger writes 'be-stimmen' with a hyphen to call attention to the fact that the words 'bestimmen' ('determine') and 'Stimmung' ('mood') have a common stem.
[2] 'Die Angst entspringt aus der *Zukunft* der Entschlossenheit, die Furcht aus der verlorenen Gegenwart, die furchtsam die Furcht befürchtet, um ihr so erst recht zu verfallen.' The grammar of this passage is ambiguous, and would also permit us to write: '. . . the lost Present, which is fearfully apprehensive of fear, so that . . .'

but rather the existential meaning of *hoping itself*. Even here its character as a mood lies primarily in hoping as *hoping for something for oneself* [*Für-sich-erhoffen*]. He who hopes takes himself *with* him into his hope, as it were, and brings himself up against what he hopes for. But this presupposes that he has somehow arrived at himself. To say that hope *brings alleviation* [*erleichtert*] from depressing misgivings, means merely that even hope, as a state-of-mind, is still related to our burdens, and related in the mode of *Being*-as-having been. Such a mood of elation—or better, one which elates—is ontologically possible only if Dasein has an ecstatico-temporal relation to the thrown ground of itself.

Furthermore, the pallid lack of mood—indifference—which is addicted to nothing and has no urge for anything, and which abandons itself to whatever the day may bring, yet in so doing takes everything along with it in a certain manner, demonstrates *most penetratingly* the power of forgetting in the everyday mode of that concern which is closest to us. Just living along [Das Dahinleben] in a way which 'lets' everything 'be' as it is, is based on forgetting and abandoning oneself to one's thrownness. It has the ecstatical meaning of an inauthentic way of having been. Indifference, which can go along with busying oneself head over heels, must be sharply distinguished from equanimity. This latter mood springs from resoluteness, which, in a moment of *vision*, *looks* at[1] those Situations which are possible in one's potentiality-for-Being-a-whole as disclosed in our anticipation of [zum] death.

Only an entity which, in accordance with the meaning of its Being, finds itself in a state-of-mind [sich befindet]—that is to say, an entity, which in existing, is as already having been, and which exists in a constant mode of what has been—can become affected. Ontologically such affection presupposes making-present, and indeed in such a manner that in this making-present Dasein can be brought back to itself as something that has been. It remains a problem in itself to define ontologically the way in which the senses can be *stimulated* or *touched* in something that merely has life, and how and where[2] the Being of animals, for instance, is constituted by some kind of 'time'.

(c) The Temporality of Falling[viii]

In our temporal Interpretation of understanding and state-of-mind, we not only have come up against a *primary* ecstasis for each of these phenomena, but at the same time we have always come up against temporality as a *whole*. Just as understanding is made possible primarily by

---

[1] '. . . die augen*blicklich* ist auf . . .'

[2] '. . . wie und wo . . .' The earlier editions have '. . . wie und ob . . .' ('. . . how and whether . . .').

the future, and moods are made possible by having been, the third constitutive item in the structure of care—namely, *falling*—has its existential meaning in the *Present*. Our preparatory analysis of falling began with an Interpretation of idle talk, curiosity, and ambiguity.[ix] In the temporal analysis of falling we shall take the same course. But we shall restrict our investigation to a consideration of *curiosity*, for here the specific temporality of falling is most easily seen. Our analysis of idle talk and ambiguity, however, presupposes our having already clarified the temporal Constitution of discourse and of explanation (interpretation).

Curiosity is a distinctive tendency of Dasein's Being, in accordance with which Dasein concerns itself with a potentiality-for-seeing.[x] Like the concept of sight, 'seeing' will not be restricted to awareness through 'the eyes of the body'. Awareness in the broader sense lets what is ready-to-hand and what is present-at-hand be encountered 'bodily' in themselves with regard to the way they look. Letting them be thus encountered is grounded in a Present. This Present gives us in general the ecstatical horizon within which entities can have bodily *presence*. Curiosity, however, does not make present the present-at-hand in order to tarry alongside it and *understand* it; it seeks to see *only* in order to see and to have seen. As this making-present which gets entangled in itself, curiosity has an ecstatical unity with a corresponding future and a corresponding having been. The craving for the new[1] is of course a way of proceeding towards something not yet seen, but in such a manner that the making-present seeks to extricate itself from awaiting. Curiosity is futural in a way which is altogether inauthentic, and in such a manner, moreover, that it does not await a *possibility*, but, in its craving, just desires such a possibility as something that is actual. Curiosity gets constituted by a making-present which is not held on to, but which, in merely making present, thereby seeks constantly to run away from the awaiting in which it is nevertheless 'held', though not held on to.[2] The Present 'arises or leaps away' from the awaiting which belongs to it, and it does so in the sense

---

[1] 'Die Gier nach dem Neuen . . .' Here Heidegger calls attention to the etymological structure of the word 'Neugier' ('curiosity').

[2] 'Die Neugier wird konstituiert durch ein ungehaltenes Gegenwärtigen, das, nur gegenwärtigend, damit ständig dem Gewärtigen, darin es doch ungehalten "gehalten" ist, zu entlaufen sucht.' This sentence involves a play on the words 'Gewärtigen' and 'Gegenwärtigen', 'gehalten' and 'ungehalten', which is not easily reproduced. While 'ungehalten' can mean 'not held on to' (as we have often translated it), it can also mean that one can no longer 'contain' oneself, and becomes 'indignant' or 'angry'. In the present passage, Heidegger may well have more than one meaning in mind. The point would be that in curiosity we are kept (or 'held') awaiting something which we 'make present' to ourselves so vividly that we try to go beyond the mere awaiting of it and become irritated or indignant because we are unable to do so. So while we are 'held' in our awaiting, we do not 'hold on to it'.

of running away from it, as we have just emphasized.[1] But the making-present which 'leaps away' in curiosity is so little devoted to the 'thing' it is curious about, that when it obtains sight of anything it already looks away to what is coming next. The making-present which 'arises or leaps away' from the awaiting of a definite possibility which one has taken hold of, makes possible ontologically that *not-tarrying* which is distinctive of curiosity. The making-present does not 'leap away' from the awaiting in such a manner, as it were, that it detaches itself from that awaiting and abandons it to itself (if we understand this ontically). This 'leaping-away' is rather an ecstatical modification of awaiting, and of such a kind that the awaiting *leaps after* the making-present.[2] The awaiting gives itself up, as it were; nor does it any longer let any inauthentic possibilities of concern come towards it from that with which it concerns itself, unless these are possibilities only for a making-present which is not held on to. When the awaiting is ecstatically modified by the making-present which leaps away, so that it becomes an awaiting which leaps after, this modification is the existential-temporal condition for the possibility of *distraction*.

Through the awaiting which leaps after, on the other hand, the making-present is abandoned more and more to itself. It makes present for the sake of the Present. It thus entangles itself in itself, so that the distracted not-tarrying becomes *never-dwelling-anywhere*. This latter mode of the Present is the counter-phenomenon at the opposite extreme from the *moment of vision*. In never dwelling anywhere, Being-there is everywhere and nowhere. The moment *of vision*, however, brings existence into the Situation and discloses the authentic 'there'.

The more inauthentically the Present is—that is, the more making-present comes towards 'itself'—the more it flees in the face of a definite potentiality-for-Being and closes it off; but in that case, all the less can the future come back to the entity which has been thrown. In the 'leaping-away' of the Present, one also forgets increasingly. The fact that curiosity always holds by what is coming next, and has forgotten what has gone

---

[1] 'Die Gegenwart "entspringt" dem zugehörigen Gewärtigen in dem betonten Sinne des Entlaufens.' While the verb 'entspringen' can mean 'arise from' or 'spring from', as it usually does in this work, it can also mean 'run away from' or 'escape from', as Heidegger says it does here. We shall accordingly translate it in this context by the more literal 'leap away' or occasionally by 'arise or leap away'. The point of this passage will perhaps be somewhat plainer if one keeps in mind that when Heidegger speaks of the 'Present' ('Gegenwart') or 'making-present' ('Gegenwärtigen') as 'leaping away', he is using these nouns in the more literal sense of 'waiting towards'. Thus in one's 'present' curiosity, one 'leaps away' from what one has been 'awaiting', and does so by 'waiting for' something different.

[2] '. . . dass dieses dem Gegenwärtigen *nachspringt*.' The idea seems to be that when curiosity 'makes present' new possibilities, the current awaiting is re-directed towards these instead of towards the possibilities which have been awaited hitherto.

before,[1] is not a result that ensues only *from* curiosity, but is the ontological condition for curiosity itself.

As regards their temporal meaning, the characteristics of falling which we have pointed out—temptation, tranquillization, alienation, self-entanglement—mean that the making-present which 'leaps away' has an ecstatical tendency such that it seeks to temporalize itself out of itself. When Dasein entangles itself, this has an ecstatical meaning. Of course when one speaks of the rapture with which one's existence is carried away in making present, this does not signify that Dasein detaches itself from its Self and its "I". Even when it makes present in the most extreme manner, it remains temporal—that is, awaiting and forgetful. In making present, moreover, Dasein still understands itself, though it has been alienated from its ownmost potentiality-for-Being, which is based primarily on the authentic future and on authentically having been. But in so far as making-present is always offering something 'new', it does not let Dasein come back to itself and is constantly tranquillizing it anew. This tranquillizing, however, strengthens in turn the tendency towards leaping away. Curiosity is 'activated' not by the endless immensity of what we have not yet seen, but rather by the falling kind of temporalizing which belongs to the Present as it leaps away.[2] Even if one has seen everything, this is precisely when curiosity *fabricates* something new.

As a mode of temporalizing, the 'leaping-away' of the Present is grounded in the essence of temporality, which is *finite*. Having been thrown into Being-towards-death, Dasein flees—proximally and for the most part—in the face of this thrownness, which has been more or less explicitly revealed. The Present leaps away from its authentic future and from its authentic having been, so that it lets Dasein come to its authentic existence only by taking a detour through that Present. The 'leaping-away' of the Present—that is, the falling into lostness—has its source in that primordial authentic temporality itself which makes possible thrown Being-towards-death.[3]

While Dasein can indeed be brought *authentically face to face* with its thrownness, so as to understand itself in that thrownness authentically, nevertheless, this thrownness remains closed off from Dasein as regards the ontical "whence" and "how" of it. But the fact that it is thus closed

---

[1] '. . . beim Nächsten hält und das Vordem vergessen hat . . .'

[2] 'Nicht die endlose Unübersehbarkeit dessen, was noch nicht gesehen ist, "bewirkt" die Neugier, sondern die verfallende Zeitigungsart der entspringenden Gegenwart.' This sentence is grammatically ambiguous.

[3] 'Der Ursprung des "Entspringens" der Gegenwart, das heisst des Verfallens in die Verlorenheilt, ist die ursprüngliche, eigentliche Zeitlichkeit selbst, die das geworfene Sein zum Tode ermöglicht.' Our conventions for translating 'Ursprung' as 'source', 'ursprünglich' as 'primordial', and 'entspringen' as 'leap away', conceal Heidegger's exploitation of the root 'spring-' in this passage.

off is by no means just a kind of ignorance factually subsisting; it is constitutive for Dasein's facticity. It is also determinative for the *ecstatical* character of the way existence has been abandoned to its own null basis.

Proximally, the "throw" of Dasein's Being-thrown into the world is one that does not authentically get "caught". The 'movement' which such a "throw" implies does not come to 'a stop' because Dasein now 'is there'. Dasein gets dragged along in thrownness; that is to say, as something which has been thrown into the world, it loses itself in the 'world' in its factical submission to that with which it is to concern itself. The Present, which makes up the existential meaning of "getting taken along", never arrives at any other ecstatical horizon of its own accord, unless it gets brought back from its lostness by a resolution, so that both the current Situation and therewith the primordial 'limit-Situation' of Being-towards-death, will be disclosed as a moment of vision which has been held on to.

(d) The Temporality of Discourse[xi]

When the "there" has been completely disclosed, its disclosedness is constituted by understanding state-of-mind, and falling; and this disclosedness becomes Articulated by discourse. Thus discourse does not temporalize itself primarily in any definite ecstasis. Factically, however, discourse expresses itself for the most part in language, and speaks proximally in the way of addressing itself to the 'environment' by talking about things concernfully; because of this, *making-present* has, of course, a *privileged* constitutive function.

Tenses, like the other temporal phenomena of language—'aspects' and 'temporal stages' ["Zeitstufen"]—do not spring from the fact that discourse expresses itself 'also' about 'temporal' processes, processes encountered 'in time'. Nor does their basis lie in the fact that speaking runs its course 'in a psychical time'. Discourse *in itself* is temporal, since all talking about . . ., of . . ., or to . . ., is grounded in the ecstatical unity of temporality. *Aspects* have their roots in the primordial temporality of concern, whether or not this concern relates itself to that which is within time. The problem of their existential-temporal structure *cannot even be formulated* with the help of the ordinary traditional conception of time, to which the science of language needs must have recourse.[xii] But because in any discourse one is talking about entities, even if not primarily and predominantly in the sense of theoretical assertion, the analysis of the temporal Constitution of discourse and the explication of the temporal characteristics of language-patterns can be tackled only if the problem of how Being and truth are connected in principle, is broached in the light of the problematic of temporality. We can then define even the ontological meaning of the 'is', which a superficial theory of propositions and judgments has deformed to a mere 'copula'. Only in terms of the temporality of discourse—that is, of Dasein in general—can we clarify how 'signification' 'arises' and make the possibility of concept-formation ontologically intelligible.[xiii]

Understanding is grounded primarily in the future (whether in anticipation or in awaiting). States-of-mind temporalize themselves primarily in having been (whether in repetition or in having forgotten). Falling has its temporal roots primarily in the Present (whether in making-present or in the moment of vision). All the same, understanding is in every case a Present which 'is in the process of having been'. All the same, one's state-of-mind temporalizes itself as a future which is 'making present'. And all the same, the Present 'leaps away' from a future that is in the process of having been, or else it is held on to by such a future. Thus we can see that *in every ecstasis, temporality temporalizes itself as a whole; and this means that in the ecstatical unity with which temporality has fully temporalized itself currently, is grounded the totality of the structural whole of existence, facticity, and falling—that is, the unity of the care-structure.*

Temporalizing does not signify that ecstases come in a 'succession'. The future is *not later* than having been, and having been is *not earlier* than the Present. Temporality temporalizes itself as a future which makes present in the process of having been.

Both the disclosedness of the "there" and Dasein's basic existentiell possibilities, authenticity and inauthenticity, are founded upon temporality. But disclosedness always pertains with equal primordiality to the entirety of *Being-in-the-world*—to Being-in as well as to the world. So if we orient ourselves by the temporal Constitution of disclosedness, the ontological condition for the possibility that there can be entities which exist as Being-in-the-world, must be something that may also be exhibited.

¶ 69. *The Temporality of Being-in-the-world and the Problem of the Transcendence of the World*

The ecstatical unity of temporality—that is, the unity of the 'outside-of-itself' in the raptures of the future, of what has been, and of the Present—is the condition for the possibility that there can be an entity which exists as its "there". The entity which bears the title "Being-there" is one that has been '*cleared*'.[xiv] The light which constitutes this clearedness [Gelichtetheit] of Dasein, is not something ontically present-at-hand as a power or source for a radiant brightness occurring in the entity on occasion. That by which this entity is essentially cleared—in other words, that which makes it both 'open' for itself and 'bright' for itself—is what we have defined as "care", in advance of any 'temporal' Interpretation. In care is grounded the full disclosedness of the "there". Only by this clearedness is any illuminating or illumining, any awareness, 'seeing', or having of something, made possible. We understand the light of this clearedness only if we are not seeking some power implanted in us and present-at-hand, but are interrogating the whole constitution of Dasein's-Being—namely, care—and are interrogating it as to the unitary basis for its existential possibility. *Ecstatical temporality clears the "there" primordially.* It is what primarily regulates the possible unity of all Dasein's existential structures.

Only through the fact that Being-there is rooted in temporality can we get an insight into the existential *possibility* of that phenomenon which, at the beginning of our analytic of Dasein, we have designated as its basic state: *Being-in-the-world*. We had to assure ourselves in the beginning that the structural unity of this phenomenon cannot be torn apart. The question of the *basis* which makes the *unity* of this *articulated* structure *possible*, remained in the background. With the aim of protecting this phenomenon from those tendencies to split it up which were the most obvious and therefore the most baleful, we gave a rather thorough Interpretation of that everyday mode of Being-in-the-world which is closest to us—*concernful* Being alongside the ready-to-hand within-the-world. Now that *care* itself has been defined ontologically and traced back to temporality as its existential ground, *concern* can in turn be conceived *explicitly* in terms of either care or temporality.

In the first instance our analysis of the temporality of concern sticks to the mode of having to do with the ready-to-hand circumspectively. Our analysis then pursues the existential-temporal possibility that circumspective concern may be modified into a discovering of entities within-the-world in the sense of certain possibilities of scientific research, and discovering them 'merely' by looking at them. Our Interpretation of the temporality of Being alongside what is ready-to-hand and present-at-hand *within-the-world*—Being alongside circumspectively as well as with theoretical concern—shows us at the same time how this temporality is already the advance condition for that possibility of Being-in-the-world in which Being alongside entities within-the-world is grounded. If we take the temporal Constitution of Being-in-the-world as a theme for analysis, we are led to the following questions: in what way is anything like a world possible at all? in what sense *is* the world? what does the world transcend, and how does it do so? how are 'independent' ["unabhängige"] entities within-the-world 'connected' ["hängt" . . . "zusammen"] with the transcending world? To *expound* these questions *ontologically* is not to answer them. On the contrary, what such an exposition accomplishes is the clarification of those structures with regard to which the problem of transcendence must be raised—a clarification which is necessary beforehand. In the existential-temporal Interpretation of Being-in-the-world, three things will be considered: (a) the temporality of circumspective concern; (b) the temporal meaning of the way in which circumspective concern becomes modified into theoretical knowledge of what is present-at-hand within-the-world; (c) the temporal problem of the transcendence of the world.

(a) The Temporality of Circumspective Concern

How are we to obtain the right point of view for analysing the temporality of concern? We have called concernful Being alongside the 'world' our "dealings in and with the environment".[xv] As phenomena which are examples of Being alongside, we have chosen the using, manipulation, and producing of the ready-to-hand, and the deficient and undifferentiated modes of these; that is, we have chosen ways of Being alongside what belongs to one's everyday needs.[xvi] In this kind of concern Dasein's authentic existence too maintains itself, even when for such existence this concern is 'a matter of indifference'. The ready-to-hand things with which we concern ourselves are not the causes of our concern, as if this were to arise only by the effects of entities within-the-world. Being alongside the ready-to-hand cannot be explained ontically in terms of the ready-to-hand itself, nor can the ready-to-hand be derived contrariwise from this kind of Being. But neither are concern, as a kind of Being which belongs to Dasein, and that with which we concern ourselves, as something ready-to-hand within-the-world, just *present-at-hand together*. All the same, a 'connection' subsists between them. That which is dealt with, if rightly understood, sheds light upon concernful dealings themselves. And furthermore, if we miss the phenomenal structure of what is dealt with, then we fail to recognize the existential constitution of dealing. Of course we have already made an essential gain for the analysis of those entities which we encounter as closest to us, if their specific character as equipment does not get passed over. But we must understand further that concernful dealings never dwell with any individual item of equipment. Our using and manipulating of any definite item of equipment still remains oriented towards some equipmental context. If, for instance, we are searching for some equipment which we have 'misplaced', then what we have in mind is not merely what we are searching for, or even primarily this; nor do we have it in mind in an isolated 'act'; but the range of the equipmental totality has already been discovered beforehand. Whenever we 'go to work' and seize hold of something, we do not push out from the "nothing" and come upon some item of equipment which has been presented to us in isolation; in laying hold of an item of equipment, we come back to it from whatever work-world has already been disclosed.

The upshot of this is that if in our analysis of dealings we aim at that which is dealt with, then one's existent Being alongside the entities with which one concerns oneself must be given an orientation not towards some isolated item of equipment which is ready-to-hand, but towards the equipmental totality. This way of taking what is dealt with, is forced upon us also if we consider that character of Being which belongs distinctively to equipment that is ready-to-hand—namely, *involvement*.[xvii] We understand the term "involvement" ontologically. The kind of talk in which we say that something has *with* it an involvement *in* something, is not meant to establish a fact ontically, but rather to indicate the kind of Being that belongs to what is ready-to-hand. The relational character of involvement—of its 'with . . . in . . .'—suggests that *"an"* equipment is ontologically impossible. Of course just a solitary item of equipment may be ready-to-hand while another is *missing*. But this makes known to us that the very thing that is ready-to-hand belongs *to* something else. Our concernful dealings can let what is ready-to-hand be encountered circumspectively only if in these dealings we already understand something like the involvement which something has in something. The Being-alongside which discovers circumspectively in concern, amounts to letting something be involved—that is, to projecting an involvement understandingly. *Letting things be involved makes up the existential structure of concern. But concern, as Being alongside something, belongs to the essential constitution of care; and care, in turn, is grounded in temporality. If all this is so, then the existential condition of the possibility of letting things be involved must be sought in a mode of the temporalizing of temporality.*

Letting something be involved is implied in the simplest handling of an item of equipment. That which we let it be involved i n [Das Wobei desselben] has the character of a "towards-which"; with regard to this, the equipment is either usable or in use. The understanding of the "towards-which"—that is, the understanding of what the equipment is involved in—has the temporal structure of awaiting. In awaiting the "towards-which", concern can at the same time come back by itself to the sort of thing in which it is involved. The *awaiting* of what it is involved in, and—together with this awaiting—the *retaining* of that which is thus involved, make possible in its ecstatical unity the specifically manipulative way in which equipment is made present.[1]

---

1 'Das *Gewärtigen* des Wobei in eins mit dem *Behalten* des Womit der Bewandtnis ermöglicht in seiner ekstatischen Einheit das spezifisch hantierende Gegenwärtigen des Zeugs.'

The awaiting of the "towards-which" is neither a considering of the 'goal' nor an expectation of the impendent finishing of the work to be produced. It has by no means the character of getting something thematically into one's grasp. Neither does the retaining of that which has an involvement signify holding it fast thematically. Manipulative dealings no more relate themselves merely to that in which we let something be involved, than they do to what is involved itself. Letting something be involved is constituted rather in the unity of a retention which awaits, and it is constituted in such a manner, indeed, that the making-present which arises from this, makes possible the characteristic absorption of concern in its equipmental world. When one is wholly devoted to something and 'really' busies oneself with it, one does not do so just alongside the work itself, or alongside the tool, or alongside both of them 'together'. The unity of the relations in which concern circumspectively 'operates', has been established already by letting-things-be-involved—which is based upon temporality.

A specific kind of *forgetting* is essential for the temporality that is constitutive for letting something be involved. The Self must forget itself if, lost in the world of equipment, it is to be able 'actually' to go to work and manipulate something. But all the same, inasmuch as an *awaiting* always leads the way in the unity of the temporalizing of concern, concernful Dasein's own potentiality-for-Being has, as we shall show, been given a position in care.[1]

The making-present which awaits and retains, is constitutive for that familiarity in accordance with which Dasein, as Being-with-one-another, 'knows its way about' [sich "auskennt"] in its public environment. Letting things be involved is something which we understand existentially as a letting-them-'be' [ein "Sein"-lassen]. On such a basis circumspection can encounter the ready-to-hand *as that entity* which it is. Hence we can further elucidate the temporality of concern by giving heed to those modes of circumspectively letting something be encountered which we have characterized above[xviii] as "conspicuousness", "obtrusiveness", and "obstinacy". Thematical perception of Things is precisely not the way equipment ready-to-hand is encountered in its 'true "in-itself"'; it is encountered rather in the inconspicuousness of what we can come across 'obviously' and 'Objectively'. But if there is something conspicuous in the totality of such entities, this implies that the equipmental totality as such is obtruding itself along with it. What sort of existential structure must belong to letting things be involved, if such a procedure can let something be encountered as conspicuous? This question is now aimed

[1] '. . . in die Sorge gestellt.'

not at those factical occasions which turn our attention to something already presented, but rather at the ontological meaning of the fact that it can thus be turned.

When something cannot be used—when, for instance, a tool definitely refuses to work—it can be conspicuous only in and for dealings in which something is manipulated. Even by the sharpest and most persevering[1] 'perception' and 'representation' of Things, one can never discover anything like the damaging of a tool. If we are to encounter anything unmanageable, the handling must be of such a sort that it can be disturbed. But what does this signify *ontologically*? The making-present which awaits and retains, gets held up with regard to its absorption in relationships of involvement, and it gets held up by what will exhibit itself afterwards as damage. The making-present, which awaits the "towards-which" with equal primordiality, is held fast alongside the equipment which has been used, and it is held fast in such a manner, indeed, that the "towards-which" and the "in-order-to" are now encountered explicitly for the first time. On the other hand, the only way in which the making-present itself can meet up with anything unsuitable, is by already operating in such a way as to retain awaitingly that which has an involvement in something. To say that making-present gets 'held up' is to say that in its unity with the awaiting which retains, it diverts itself into itself more and more, and is thus constitutive for the 'inspecting' ["Nachsehen"], testing, and eliminating of the disturbance. If concernful dealings were merely a sequence of 'Experiences' running their course 'in time', however intimately these might be 'associated', it would still be ontologically impossible to let any conspicuous unusable equipment be encountered. Letting something be involved must, as such, be grounded in the ecstatical unity of the making-present which awaits and retains, whatever we have made accessible in dealing with contexts of equipment.[2]

And how is it possible to 'ascertain' what is missing [Fehlendem]—that is to say, un-ready-to-hand, not just ready-to-hand in an unmanageable way? That which is un-ready-to-hand is discovered circumspectively when we *miss* it [im *Vermissen*]. The 'affirmation' that something is not present-at-hand, is founded upon our missing it; and both our missing it and our affirmation have their own existential presuppositions. Such missing is by no means a not-making-present [Nichtgegenwärtigen]; it is

---

[1] 'anhaltendste'. This is the first of several compounds of the verb 'halten' ('to hold') which appear in this and the following paragraphs. Others are 'behalten' ('retain' in the sense of holding in one's memory), 'aufhalten' ('hold up' in the sense of delaying or bringing to a halt), 'festhalten' ('hold fast').

[2] 'Das Bewendenlassen muss als solches, was immer es auch an Zeugzusammenhängen umgänglich zugänglich macht, in der ekstatischen Einheit des gewärtigen-behaltenden Gegenwärtigens gründen.'

rather a deficient mode of the Present in the sense of the making-unpresent [Ungegenwärtigens] of something which one has expected or which one has always had at one's disposal. If, when one circumspectively lets something be involved, one were not 'from the outset' *awaiting* the object of one's concern, and if such awaiting did not temporalize itself in a *unity with* a making-present, then Dasein could never 'find' that something is missing [fehlt].

On the other hand, when one is making present something ready-to-hand by *awaiting*, the possibility of one's *getting surprised* by something is based upon one's *not awaiting* something else which stands in a possible context of involvement with what one awaits. In the not awaiting of the making-present which is lost, the 'horizonal' leeway within which one's Dasein can be assailed by something surprising is first disclosed.

That with which one's concernful dealings fail to cope, either by producing or procuring something, or even by turning away, holding aloof, or protecting oneself from something, reveals itself in its insurmountability. Concern resigns itself to it.[1] But resigning oneself to something is a mode peculiar to circumspectively letting it be encountered. On the basis of this kind of discovery concern can come across that which is inconvenient, disturbing, hindering, endangering, or in general resistant in some way. The temporal structure of resigning oneself to something, lies in a *non-retaining* which awaitingly makes present. In awaitingly making present, one does not, for instance, reckon 'on' that which is unsuitable but none the less available. "Not reckoning with" something, is a mode of "taking into one's reckoning" that which one can*not* cling to. That which one has "not reckoned with" does not get forgotten; it gets retained, so that *in its very unsuitability* it remains ready-to-hand.[2] That which is ready-to-hand in this manner belongs to the everyday stock or content of the factically disclosed environment.

Only in so far as something resistant has been discovered on the basis of the ecstatical temporality of concern, can factical Dasein understand itself in its abandonment to a 'world' of which it never becomes master. Even if concern remains restricted to the urgency of everyday needs, it is never a pure making-present, but arises from a retention which awaits; on the basis of such a retention, or as such a 'basis', Dasein exists in a world. Thus in a certain manner, factically existent Dasein always knows its way about, even in a 'world' which is alien.

---

[1] 'Das Besorgen findet sich damit ab.'
[2] 'Die zeitliche Struktur des Sichabfindens liegt in einem gewärtigend-gegenwärtigen-den *Unbehalten*. Das gewärtigende Gegenwärtigen rechnet zum Beispiel nicht "auf" das Ungeeignete, aber gleichwohl Verfügbare. Das Nichtrechnen mit . . . ist ein Modus des Rechnungtragens dem gegenüber, woran man sich *nicht* halten kann. Es wird nicht vergessen, sondern behalten, so dass es gerade *in seiner Ungeeignetheit* zuhanden bleibt.'

When, in one's concern, one lets something be involved, one's doing so is founded on temporality, and amounts to an altogether pre-ontological and non-thematic way of understanding involvement and readiness-to-hand. In what follows, it will be shown to what extent the understanding of these types of Being as such is, in the end, also founded on temporality. We must first give a more concrete demonstration of the temporality of Being-in-the-world. With this as our aim, we shall trace how the theoretical attitude towards the 'world' 'arises' out of circumspective concern with the ready-to-hand. Not only the circumspective discovering of entities within-the-world but also the theoretical discovering of them is founded upon Being-in-the-world. The existential-temporal Interpretation of these ways of discovering is preparatory to the temporal characterization of this basic state of Dasein.

(b) The Temporal Meaning of the Way in which Circumspective Concern becomes Modified into the Theoretical Discovery of the Present-at-hand Within-the-world

When in the course of *existential ontological* analysis we ask how *theoretical* discovery 'arises' out of *circumspective* concern, this implies already that we are not making a problem of the *ontical* history and development of science, or of the factical occasions for it, or of its proximate goals. In seeking the *ontological genesis* of the theoretical attitude, we are asking which of those conditions implied in Dasein's state of Being are existentially necessary for the possibility of Dasein's existing in the way of scientific research. This formulation of the question is aimed at an *existential conception of science*. This must be distinguished from the 'logical' conception which understands science with regard to its results and defines it as 'something established on an interconnection of true propositions—that is, propositions counted as valid'. The existential conception understands science as a way of existence and thus as a mode of Being-in-the-world, which discovers or discloses either entities or Being. Yet a fully adequate existential Interpretation of science cannot be carried out until the *meaning of Being and the 'connection' between Being and truth*[xix] have been *clarified* in terms of the temporality of existence.[1] The following deliberations are preparatory to the understanding of *this central problematic*, within which, moreover, the idea of phenomenology, as distinguished from the preliminary conception of it which we indicated by way of introduction[xx] will be developed for the first time.

Corresponding to the stage of our study at which we have now arrived, a further restriction will be imposed upon our Interpretation of the theoretical attitude. We shall investigate only the way in which circumspective

[1] The italics in this and the following sentence appear only in the later editions.

concern with the ready-to-hand changes over into an exploration of what we come across as present-at-hand within-the-world; and we shall be guided by the aim of penetrating to the temporal Constitution of Being-in-the-world in general.

In characterizing the change-over from the manipulating and using and so forth which are circumspective in a 'practical' way, to 'theoretical' exploration, it would be easy to suggest that merely looking at entities is something which emerges when concern *holds back* from any kind of manipulation. What is decisive in the 'emergence' of the theoretical attitude would then lie in the *disappearance* of *praxis*. So if one posits 'practical' concern as the primary and predominant kind of Being which factical Dasein possesses, the ontological possibility of 'theory' will be due to the *absence* of *praxis*—that is, to a *privation*. But the discontinuance of a specific manipulation in our concernful dealings does not simply leave the guiding circumspection behind as a remainder. Rather, our concern then diverts itself specifically into a just-looking-around [ein Nur-sich-umsehen]. But this is by no means the way in which the 'theoretical' attitude of science is reached. On the contrary, the tarrying which is discontinued when one manipulates, can take on the character of a more precise kind of circumspection, such as 'inspecting', checking up on what has been attained, or looking over the 'operations' ["Betrieb"] which are now 'at a standstill'. Holding back from the use of equipment is so far from sheer 'theory' that the kind of circumspection which tarries and 'considers', remains wholly in the grip of the ready-to-hand equipment with which one is concerned. 'Practical' dealings have their *own* ways of tarrying. And just as *praxis* has its own specific kind of sight ('theory'), theoretical research is not without a *praxis* of its own. Reading off the measurements which result from an experiment often requires a complicated 'technical' set-up for the experimental design. Observation with a microscope is dependent upon the production of 'preparations'. Archaeological excavation, which precedes any Interpretation of the 'findings', demands manipulations of the grossest kind. But even in the 'most abstract' way of working out problems and establishing what has been obtained, one manipulates equipment for writing, for example. However 'uninteresting' and 'obvious' such components of scientific research may be, they are by no means a matter of indifference ontologically. The explicit suggestion that scientific behaviour as a way of Being-in-the-world, is not just a 'purely intellectual activity', may seem petty and superfluous. If only it were not plain from this triviality that it is by no means patent where the ontological boundary between 'theoretical' and 'atheoretical' behaviour really runs!

Someone will hold that all manipulation in the sciences is merely in the service of pure observation—the investigative discovery and disclosure of the 'things themselves'. 'Seeing', taken in the widest sense, regulates all 'procedures' and retains its priority. 'To whatever kind of objects one's knowledge may relate itself, and by whatever means it may do so, still that through which it relates itself to them immediately, *and which all thinking as a means has as its goal* (author's italics) is *intuition*.'[xxi] The idea of the *intuitus* has guided all Interpretation of knowledge from the beginnings of Greek ontology until today, whether or not that *intuitus* can be factically reached. If we are to exhibit the existential genesis of science in accordance with the priority of 'seeing', we must set out by characterizing the *circumspection* which is the guide for 'practical' concern.

Circumspection operates in the involvement-relationships of the context of equipment which is ready-to-hand. Moreover, it is subordinate to the guidance of a more or less explicit survey of the equipmental totality of the current equipment-world and of the public environment which belongs to it. This survey is not just one in which things that are present-at-hand are subsequently scraped together. What is essential to it is that one should have a primary understanding of the totality of involvements within which factical concern always takes its start. Such a survey illumines one's concern, and receives its 'light' from that potentiality-for-Being on the part of Dasein *for the sake of which* concern exists as care. In one's current using and manipulating, the concernful circumspection which does this 'surveying', *brings* the ready-to-hand *closer* to Dasein, and does so by interpreting what has been sighted. This specific way of bringing the object of concern close by interpreting it circumspectively, we call *"deliberating"* [*Überlegung*]. The scheme peculiar to this is the 'if—then'; if this or that, for instance, is to be produced, put to use, or averted, then some ways and means, circumstances, or opportunities will be needed. Circumspective deliberation illumines Dasein's current factical situation in the environment with which it concerns itself. Accordingly, such deliberation never merely 'affirms' that some entity is present-at-hand or has such and such properties. Moreover, deliberation can be performed even when that which is brought close in it circumspectively is not palpably ready-to-hand and does not have presence within the closest range. Bringing the environment closer in circumspective deliberation has the existential meaning of a *making present*; for *envisaging*[1] is only a mode of this. In envisaging, one's deliberation catches sight directly of that which is needed but which is un-ready-to-hand. Circumspection which envisages does not relate itself to 'mere representations'.

[1] Here the familiar noun 'Vergegenwärtigung' ('envisaging') is printed with the first syllable in italics to draw attention to its connection with the special phenomenological verb 'Gegenwärtigen' ('making present').

Circumspective making-present, however, is a phenomenon with more than one kind of foundation. In the first instance, it always belongs to a full ecstatical unity of temporality. It is grounded in a *retention* of that context of equipment with which Dasein concerns itself in *awaiting* a possibility. That which has already been laid open in awaiting and retaining is brought closer by one's deliberative making-present or envisaging.[1] But if deliberation is to be able to operate in the scheme of the 'if—then', concern must already have 'surveyed' a context of involvements and have an understanding of it. That which is considered with an 'if' must already be understood *as something or other*. This does not require that the understanding of equipment be expressed in a predication. The schema 'something as something' has already been sketched out beforehand in the structure of one's pre-predicative understanding. The as-structure is grounded ontologically in the temporality of understanding. But *on the other hand*, only to the extent that Dasein, in awaiting some possibility (here this means a "towards-which"), has come back to a "towards-this" (that is to say that it retains something ready-to-hand)—only to this extent can the making-present which belongs to this awaiting and retaining, start with what is thus retained, and *bring* it, in its character of having been assigned or referred to its "towards-which", *explicitly closer*. The deliberation which brings it close must, in the schema of making present, be in conformity with the kind of Being that belongs to what is to be brought close. The involvement-character of the ready-to-hand does not first get discovered by deliberation, but only gets brought close by it in such a manner as to let that *in which* something *has* an involvement, be seen circumspectively *as* this very thing.

The way the Present is rooted in the future and in having been, is the existential-temporal condition for the possibility that what has been projected in circumspective understanding can be brought closer in a making-present, and in such a way that the Present can thus conform itself to what is encountered within the horizon of awaiting and retaining; this means that it must interpret itself in the schema of the as-structure. We have thus answered the question we formulated earlier—the question of whether the as-structure has some existential-ontological connection with the phenomenon of projection.[xxii] *Like understanding and interpretation in general, the 'as' is grounded in the ecstatico-horizonal unity of temporality.* In our fundamental analysis of Being, and of course in connection with the Interpretation of the 'is' (which, as a copula, gives 'expression' to the addressing of something *as* something), we must again make the

---

[1] 'Das im gewärtigenden Behalten schon Aufgeschlossene bringt die überlegende Gegenwärtigung bzw. Vergegenwärtigung näher.'

phenomenon of the "as" a theme and delimit the conception of this 'schema' existentially.

The question of the genesis of theoretical behaviour is one which we have left hanging. What can a temporal characterization of circumspective deliberation and its schemata contribute to the answering of it? Only that this elucidates the Situation in which circumspective concern changes over into theoretical discovering—a Situation of the kind which belongs to Dasein. We may then try to analyse this change-over itself by taking as our clue an elementary assertion which is circumspectively deliberative in character and the modifications which are possible for it.

When we are using a tool circumspectively, we can say, for instance, that the hammer is too heavy or too light. Even the proposition that the hammer is heavy can give expression to a concernful deliberation, and signify that the hammer is not an easy one—in other words, that it takes force to handle it, or that it will be hard to manipulate.[1] But this proposition *can* also mean that the entity before us, which we already know circumspectively as a hammer, has a weight—that is to say, it has the 'property' of heaviness: it exerts a pressure on what lies beneath it, and it falls if this is removed. When this kind of talk is so understood, it is no longer spoken within the horizon of awaiting and retaining an equipmental totality and its involvement-relationships. What is said has been drawn from looking at what is suitable for an entity with 'mass'. We have now sighted something that is suitable for the hammer, not as a tool, but as a corporeal Thing subject to the law of gravity. To talk circumspectively of 'too heavy' or 'too light' no longer has any 'meaning'; that is to say, the entity in itself, as we now encounter it, gives us nothing with relation to which it could be 'found' too heavy or too light.

Why is it that what we are talking about—the heavy hammer—shows itself differently when our way of talking is thus modified? Not because we are keeping our distance from manipulation, nor because we are just looking *away* [*ab*sehen] from the equipmental character of this entity, but rather because we are looking *at* [*an*sehen] the ready-to-hand thing which we encounter, and looking at it 'in a new way' as something present-at-hand. *The understanding of Being* by which our concernful dealings with entities within-the-world have been guided *has changed over*. But if, instead of deliberating circumspectively about something ready-to-hand, we 'take' it as something present-at-hand, has a scientific attitude thus constituted

---

[1] 'Auch der Satz: der Hammer ist schwer, kann einer besorgenden Überlegung Ausdruck geben und bedeuten: er ist nicht leicht, das heisst, er fordert zur Handhabung Kraft, bzw. er wird die Hantierung erschweren.' Here Heidegger is exploiting the double meaning of the German pair of adjectives, 'schwer' and 'leicht', which may correspond either to the English pair 'heavy' and 'light', or to the pair 'difficult' and 'easy'.

itself? Moreover, even that which is ready-to-hand can be made a theme for scientific investigation and determination, for instance when one studies someone's environment—his *milieu*—in the context of a historiological biography. The context of equipment that is ready-to-hand in an everyday manner, its historical emergence and utilization, and its factical role in Dasein—all these are objects for the science of economics. The ready-to-hand can become the 'Object' of a science without having to lose its character as equipment. A modification of our understanding of Being does not seem to be necessarily constitutive for the genesis of the theoretical attitude 'towards Things'. Certainly not, if this "modification" is to imply a change in the kind of Being which, in understanding the entity before us, we understand it to possess.

In our first description of the genesis of the theoretical attitude out of circumspection, we have made basic a way of theoretically grasping entities within-the-world—physical Nature—in which the modification of our understanding of Being is tantamount to a change-over. In the 'physical' assertion that 'the hammer is heavy' we *overlook* not only the tool-character of the entity we encounter, but also something that belongs to any ready-to-hand equipment: its place. Its place becomes a matter of indifference. This does not mean that what is present-at-hand loses its 'location' alto-   3 gether. But its place becomes a spatio-temporal position, a 'world-point', which is in no way distinguished from any other. This implies not only that the multiplicity of places of equipment ready-to-hand within the confines of the environment becomes modified to a pure multiplicity of positions, but that the entities of the environment are altogether *released from such confinement* [*entschränkt*]. The aggregate of the present-at-hand becomes the theme.

In the case before us, the releasing from such environmental confinement belongs to the way one's understanding of Being has been modified; and it becomes at the same time a delimitation of the 'realm' of the present-at-hand, if one now takes as one's guiding clue the understanding of Being in the sense of presence-at-hand. The more appropriately the Being of the entities to be explored is understood under the guidance of an understanding of Being, and the more the totality of entities has been Articulated in its basic attributes as a possible area of subject-matter for a science, all the more secure will be the perspective for one's methodical inquiry.

The classical example for the historical development of a science and even for its ontological genesis, is the rise of mathematical physics. What is decisive for its development does not lie in its rather high esteem for the observation of 'facts', nor in its 'application' of mathematics in determining the character of natural processes; it lies rather in *the way in which Nature herself is mathematically projected.* In this projection something constantly present-at-hand (matter) is uncovered beforehand, and the horizon is opened so that one may be guided by looking at those constitutive items in it which are quantitatively determinable (motion, force, location, and time). Only 'in the light' of a Nature which has been projected in this fashion can anything like a 'fact' be found and set up for an experiment regulated and delimited in terms of this projection. The 'grounding' of 'factual science' was possible only because the researchers understood that in principle there are no 'bare facts'. In the mathematical projection of Nature, moreover, what is decisive is not primarily the mathematical as such; what is decisive is that this projection *discloses something that is a priori.* Thus the paradigmatic character of mathematical natural science does not lie in its exactitude or in the fact that it is binding for 'Every-man'; it consists rather in the fact that the entities which it takes as its theme are discovered in it in the only way in which entities can be discovered—by the prior projection of their state of Being. When the basic concepts of that understanding of Being by which we are guided have been worked out, the clues of its methods, the structure of its way of conceiving things, the possibility of truth and certainty which belongs to it, the ways in which things get grounded or proved, the mode in which it is binding for us, and the way it is communicated—all these will be Determined. The totality of these items constitutes the full existential conception of science.

The scientific projection of any entities which we have somehow encountered already lets their kind of Being be understood explicitly and in such a manner that it thus becomes manifest what ways are possible for the pure discovery of entities within-the-world. The Articulation of the understanding of Being, the delimitation of an area of subject-matter (a delimitation guided by this understanding), and the sketching-out of the way of conceiving which is appropriate to such entities—all these belong to the totality of this projecting; and this totality is what we call *"thematizing".* Its aim is to free the entities we encounter within-the-world, and to free them in such a way that they can 'throw themselves against'[1] a pure discovering—that is, that they can become "Objects". Thematizing Objectifies. It does not first 'posit' the entities, but frees them so that one can interrogate them and determine their character 'Objectively'. Being which Objectifies and which is alongside the present-at-hand within-the-world, is characterized by a *distinctive kind of making-present.*[xxiii] This making-present is distinguished from the Present of circumspection in that

1 ' "entgegenwerfen" '. Heidegger is here calling attention to the fact that the word 'object' literally means 'something thrown against'.

—above all—the kind of discovering which belongs to the science in question awaits solely the discoveredness of the present-at-hand. This awaiting of discoveredness has its existentiell basis in a resoluteness by which Dasein projects itself towards its potentiality-for-Being in the 'truth'. This projection is possible because Being-in-the-truth makes up a definite way in which Dasein may exist. We shall not trace further how science has its source in authentic existence. It is enough now if we understand that the thematizing of entities within-the-world presupposes Being-in-the-world as the basic state of Dasein, and if we understand how it does so.

If the thematizing of the present-at-hand—the scientific projection of Nature—is to become possible, *Dasein must transcend* the entities thematized. Transcendence does not consist in Objectifying, but is presupposed by it. If, however, the thematizing of the present-at-hand within-the-world is a change-over from the concern which discovers by circumspection, then one's 'practical' Being alongside the ready-to-hand is something which a transcendence of Dasein must already underlie.

If, moreover, thematizing modifies and Articulates the understanding of Being, then, in so far as Dasein, the entity which thematizes, exists, it must already understand something like Being. Such understanding of Being can remain neutral. In that case readiness-to-hand and presence-at-hand have not yet been distinguished; still less have they been conceived ontologically. But if Dasein is to be able to have any dealings with a context of equipment, it must understand something like an involvement, even if it does not do so thematically: *a world must have been disclosed to it.* With Dasein's factical existence, this world has been disclosed, if Dasein indeed exists essentially as Being-in-the-world.[1] And if Dasein's Being is completely grounded in temporality, then temporality must make possible Being-in-the-world and therewith Dasein's transcendence; this transcendence in turn provides the support for concernful Being alongside entities within-the-world, whether this Being is theoretical or practical.

(c) The Temporal Problem of the Transcendence of the World

Circumspective concern includes the understanding of a totality of involvements, and this understanding is based upon a prior understanding of the relationships of the "in-order-to", the "towards-which", the "towards-this", and the "for-the-sake-of". The interconnection of these relationships has been exhibited earlier[xxiv] as "significance". Their unity makes up what we call the "world". The question arises of how anything like the world in its unity with Dasein is ontologically possible. In what way must the world *be*, if Dasein is to be able to exist as Being-in-the-World?

---

[1] In the older editions this sentence is introduced by 'Und' ('And').

Dasein exists for the sake of a potentiality-for-Being of itself. In existing, it has been thrown; and as something thrown, it has been delivered over to entities which it needs *in order to* be able to be as it is—namely, *for the sake of* itself. In so far as Dasein exists factically, it understands itself in the way its "for-the-sake-of-itself" is thus connected with some current "in-order-to". *That inside which* existing Dasein understands *itself*, *is* 'there' along with its factical existence. That inside which one primarily understands oneself has Dasein's kind of Being. Dasein *is* its world existingly.

We have defined Dasein's Being as "care". The ontological meaning of "care" is temporality. We have shown that temporality constitutes the disclosedness of the "there", and we have shown how it does so. In the disclosedness of the "there" the world is disclosed along with it. The unity of significance—that is, the ontological constitution of the world—must then likewise be grounded in temporality. *The existential-temporal condition for the possibility of the world lies in the fact that temporality, as an ecstatical unity, has something like a horizon.* Ecstases are not simply raptures in which one gets carried away. Rather, there belongs to each ecstasis a 'whither' to which one is carried away.[1] This "whither" of the ecstasis we call the "horizonal schema". In each of the three ecstases the ecstatical horizon is different. The schema in which Dasein comes towards itself *futurally*, whether authentically or inauthentically, is the *"for-the-sake-of-itself"*. The schema in which Dasein is disclosed to itself in a state-of-mind as thrown, is to be taken as that *in the face of which* it has been thrown and that *to which* it has been abandoned. This characterizes the horizonal schema of *what has been*. In existing for the sake of itself in abandonment to itself as something that has been thrown, Dasein, as Being-alongside, is at the same time making present. The horizonal schema for the *Present* is defined by the *"in-order-to"*.

The unity of the horizonal schemata of future, Present, and having been, is grounded in the ecstatical unity of temporality. The horizon of temporality as a whole determines that *whereupon* [*woraufhin*] factically existing entities are essentially *disclosed*. With one's factical Being-there, a potentiality-for-Being is in each case projected in the horizon of the future, one's 'Being-already' is disclosed in the horizon of having been, and that with which one concerns oneself is discovered in the horizon of the Present. The horizonal unity of the schemata of these ecstases makes possible the primordial way in which the relationships of the "in-order-to" are connected with the "for-the-sake-of". This implies that on the basis of the horizonal constitution of the ecstatical unity of temporality,

[1] 'Die Ekstasen sind nicht einfach Entrückungen zu . . . Vielmehr gehört zur Ekstase ein "Wohin" der Entrückung.'

there belongs to that entity which is in each case its own "there", something like a world that has been disclosed.

Just as the Present arises in the unity of the temporalizing of temporality out of the future and having been, the horizon of a Present temporalizes itself equiprimordially with those of the future and of having been. In so far as Dasein temporalizes itself, a world *is* too. In temporalizing itself with regard to its Being as temporality, Dasein *is*[1] essentially 'in a world', by reason of the ecstatico-horizonal constitution of that temporality. The world is neither present-at-hand nor ready-to-hand, but temporalizes itself in temporality. It 'is', with the "outside-of-itself" of the ecstases, 'there'. If no *Dasein* exists, no world is 'there' either.

The world is already presupposed in one's Being alongside the ready-to-hand concernfully and factically, in one's thematizing of the present-at-hand, and in one's discovering of this latter entity by Objectification; that is to say, all these are possible only as ways of Being-in-the-world. Having its ground [gründend] in the horizonal unity of ecstatical temporality, the world is transcendent. It must already have been ecstatically disclosed so that in terms of it entities within-the-world can be encountered. Temporality already maintains itself ecstatically within the horizons of its ecstases; and in temporalizing itself, it comes back to those entities which are encountered in the "there". With Dasein's factical existence, entities within-the-world are already encountered too. The fact that such entities are discovered along with Dasein's own "there" of existence, is not left to Dasein's discretion. Only *what* it discovers and discloses on occasion, in *what* direction it does so, *how* and *how far* it does so—only these are matters for Dasein's freedom, even if always within the limitations of its thrownness.

Thus the significance-relationships which determine the structure of the world are not a network of forms which a worldless subject has laid over some kind of material. What is rather the case is that factical Dasein, understanding itself and its world ecstatically in the unity of the "there", comes back from these horizons to the entities encountered within them. Coming back to these entities understandingly is the existential meaning of letting them be encountered by making them present; that is why we call them entities "within-the-world". The world is, as it were, already 'further outside' than any Object can ever be. The 'problem of transcendence' cannot be brought round to the question of how a subject comes out to an Object, where the aggregate of Objects is identified with the idea of the world. Rather we must ask: what makes it ontologically possible for entities to be encountered within-the-world and Objectified as so

[1] Italics supplied in later editions only.

o

encountered? This can be answered by recourse to the transcendence of the world—a transcendence with an ecstatico-horizonal foundation.

If the 'subject' gets conceived ontologically as an existing Dasein whose Being is grounded in temporality, then one must say that the world is 'subjective'. But in that case, this 'subjective' world, as one that is temporally transcendent, is 'more Objective' than any possible 'Object'.

When Being-in-the-world is traced back to the ecstatico-horizonal unity of temporality, the existential-ontological possibility of this basic state of Dasein is made intelligible. At the same time it becomes plain that a concrete working-out of the world-structure in general and its possible variations can be tackled only if the ontology of possible entities within-the-world is oriented securely enough by clarifying the idea of Being in general. If an Interpretation of this idea is to be possible, the temporality of Dasein must be exhibited beforehand; here our characterization of Being-in-the-world will be of service.

¶ *70. The Temporality of the Spatiality that is Characteristic of Dasein*

Though the expression 'temporality' does not signify what one understands by "time" when one talks about 'space and time', nevertheless spatiality seems to make up another basic attribute of Dasein corresponding to temporality. Thus with Dasein's spatiality, existential-temporal analysis seems to come to a limit, so that this entity which we call "Dasein", must be considered as 'temporal' 'and also' as spatial coordinately. Has our existential-temporal analysis of Dasein thus been brought to a halt by that phenomenon with which we have become acquainted as the spatiality that is characteristic of Dasein, and which we have pointed out as belonging to Being-in-the-world?[xxv]

If in the course of our existential Interpretation we were to talk about Dasein's having a 'spatio-temporal' character, we could not mean that this entity is present-at-hand 'in space and also in time'; this needs no further discussion. Temporality is the meaning of the Being of care. Dasein's constitution and its ways to be are possible ontologically only on the basis of temporality, regardless of whether this entity occurs 'in time' or not. Hence Dasein's specific spatiality must be grounded in temporality. On the other hand, the demonstration that this spatiality is existentially possible only through temporality, cannot aim either at deducing space from time or at dissolving it into pure time. If Dasein's spatiality is 'embraced' by temporality in the sense of being existentially founded upon it, then this connection between them (which is to be clarified in what follows) is also different from the priority of time over space in Kant's sense. To say that our empirical representations of what is present-at-hand 'in space' run their course 'in time' as psychical occurrences, so that the 'physical' occurs mediately 'in time' also, is not to give an existential-ontological Interpretation of space as a form of intuition, but rather to establish ontically that what is psychically present-at-hand runs its course 'in time'.

We must now make an existential-analytical inquiry as to the temporal conditions, for the possibility of the spatiality that is characteristic of Dasein—the spatiality upon which in turn is founded the uncovering of space within-the-world. We must first remember in what way Dasein is spatial. Dasein can *be* spatial only as care, in the sense of existing as factically falling. Negatively this means that Dasein is never present-at-hand in space, not even proximally. Dasein does not fill up a bit of space as a Real Thing or item of equipment would, so that the boundaries dividing it from the surrounding space would themselves just define that space spatially. Dasein takes space in; this is to be understood literally.[1] It is by no means just present-at-hand in a bit of space which its body fills up. In existing, it has already made room for its own leeway. It determines its own location in such a manner that it comes back from the space it has made room for to the 'place' which it has reserved.[2] To be able to say that Dasein is present-at-hand at a position in space, we must first *take* [*auffassen*] this entity in a way which is ontologically inappropriate. Nor does the distinction between the 'spatiality' of an extended Thing and that of Dasein lie in the fact that Dasein *knows* about space; for taking space in [das Raum-einnehmen] is so far from identical with a 'representing' of the spatial, that it is presupposed by it instead. Neither may Dasein's spatiality be interpreted as an imperfection which adheres to existence by reason of the fatal 'linkage of the spirit to a body'. On the contrary, because Dasein is 'spiritual', *and only because of this*, it can be spatial in a way which remains essentially impossible for any extended corporeal Thing.

Dasein's making room for itself is constituted by directionality and de-severance. How is anything of this sort existentially possible on the

---

[1] 'Das Dasein nimmt—im wörtlichen Verstande—Raum ein.' The expression 'nimmt Raum ein' would ordinarily be translatable as 'occupies space' or even 'takes up space'. But Heidegger is here interpreting it in a way which is closer to the root meaning.

[2] 'Existierend hat es sich je schon einen Spielraum eingeräumt. Es bestimmt je seinen eigenen Ort so, dass es aus dem eingeräumten Raum auf den "Platz" zurückkommt, den es belegt hat.' This passage can be read in several ways. 'Spielraum' (our 'leeway') means literally a 'space—or room—for playing'. The expression 'belegen einen Platz' ordinarily means to book or reserve a seat at a theatre or some other place of entertainment; but in a more general and basic sense, 'belegen' (which is a word of many meanings) can also mean to spread something over something else so as to 'occupy' it completely—as one spreads a slice of bread with butter or covers a wall with plaster. On 'einräumen' see our note 1, p. 146, H. 111 above.

basis of Dasein's temporality? The function of temporality as the foundation for Dasein's spatiality will be indicated briefly, but no more than is
necessary for our later discussions of the ontological meaning of the
'coupling together' of space and time. To Dasein's making room for itself
belongs the self-directive discovery of something like a *region*. By this
expression what we have in mind in the first instance is the "whither" for
the possible belonging-somewhere of equipment which is ready-to-hand
environmentally and which can be placed. Whenever one comes across
equipment, handles it, or moves it around or out of the way, some region
has already been discovered. Concernful Being-in-the-world is directional
—self-directive. Belonging-somewhere has an essential relationship to
involvement. It always Determines itself factically in terms of the
involvement-context of the equipment with which one concerns oneself.
Relationships of involvement are intelligible only within the horizon of
a world that has been disclosed. Their horizonal character, moreover,
is what first makes possible the specific horizon of the "whither" of
belonging-somewhere regionally. The self-directive discovery of a region is
grounded in an ecstatically retentive awaiting of the "hither" and
"thither" that are possible. Making room for oneself is a directional
awaiting of a region, and as such it is equiprimordially a bringing-close
(de-severing*) of the ready-to-hand and present-at-hand. Out of the
region that has been discovered beforehand, concern comes back de-
severantly to that which is closest. Both bringing-close and the estimating
and measurement of distances within that which has been de-severed and
is present-at-hand within-the-world, are grounded in a making-present
belonging to the unity of that temporality in which directionality too
becomes possible.

Because Dasein as temporality is ecstatico-horizonal in its Being, it can
take along with it a space for which it has made room, and it can do so
factically and constantly. With regard to that space which it has ecstatically taken in, the "here" of its current factical situation [Lage bzw.
Situation] never signifies a position in space, but signifies rather the
leeway of the range of that equipmental totality with which it is most
closely concerned—a leeway which has been opened up for it in directionality and de-severance.

Bringing-close makes possible the kind of handling and Being-busy
which is 'absorbed in the thing one is handling' ["in der Sache aufge-
hende"]; and in such bringing-close, the essential structure of care—
falling—makes itself known. In falling, and therefore also in the bringing-
close which is founded 'in the present', the forgetting which awaits, leaps
after the Present; this is what is distinctive in the existential-temporal

Constitution of falling.[1] When we make something present by bringing it close from its "thence" [seinem Dorther], the making-present forgets the "yonder" [das Dort] and loses itself in itself. Thus it comes about that if 'observation' of entities within-the-world commences in such a making-present, the illusion arises that 'at first' only a Thing is present-at-hand, here of course, but indefinitely—in a space in general.

Only on the basis of its ecstatico-horizonal temporality is it possible for Dasein to break into space. The world is not present-at-hand in space; yet only within a world does space let itself be discovered. The ecstatical temporality of the spatiality that is characteristic of Dasein, makes it intelligible that space is independent of time; but on the other hand, this same temporality also makes intelligible Dasein's 'dependence' on space—a 'dependence' which manifests itself in the well-known phenomenon that both Dasein's interpretation of itself and the whole stock of significations which belong to language in general are dominated through and through by 'spatial representations'. This priority of the spatial in the Articulation of concepts and significations has its basis not in some specific power which space possesses, but in Dasein's kind of Being. Temporality is essentially falling, and it loses itself in making present; not only does it understand itself circumspectively in terms of objects of concern which are ready-at-hand, but from those spatial relationships which making-present is constantly meeting in the ready-to-hand as having presence, it takes its clues for Articulating that which has been understood and can be interpreted in the understanding in general.

¶ *71. The Temporal Meaning of Dasein's Everydayness*

We have given an Interpretation of some structures which are essential to Dasein's state-of-Being, and we have done so *before* exhibiting temporality, but with the aim of leading up to this. Our analysis of the temporality of concern has shown that these structures must be *taken back into temporality* existentially. At the very start of our analytic we did not choose as our theme any definite and distinctive possibility of Dasein's existence; our analytic was oriented rather by the average way of existing, which has nothing conspicuous about it. We called that kind of Being in which Dasein maintains itself proximally and for the most part "*everdayness*".[xxvi]

What this expression signifies at bottom when delimited ontologically, remains obscure. At the beginning of our study, moreover, we could not see any way of even making the existential-ontological meaning of "everydayness" a problem. By now, however, some light has been cast on the

[1] 'Dessen existenzial-zeitliche Konstitution ist dadurch ausgezeichnet, dass in ihm und damit auch in der "gegenwärtig" fundierten Näherung das gewärtigende Vergessen der Gegenwart nachspringt.'

meaning of Dasein's Being as temporality. Can there still be any doubt as to the existential-temporal signification of the term "everydayness"? All the same, we are far removed from an ontological conception of this phenomenon. It even remains questionable whether the explication of temporality which we have so far carried through is sufficient to delimit the existential meaning of "everydayness".

"Everydayness" manifestly stands for that way of existing in which Dasein maintains itself 'every day' ["alle Tage"]. And yet this 'every day' does not signify the sum of those 'days' which have been allotted to Dasein in its 'lifetime'. Though this 'every day' is not to be understood calendrically, there is still an overtone of some such temporal character in the signification of the 'everyday' ["Alltag"]. But what we have primarily in mind in the expression "everydayness" is a definite *"how"* of existence by which Dasein is dominated through and through 'for life' ["zeitlebens"]. In our analyses we have often used the expression 'proximally and for the most part'. 'Proximally' signifies the way in which Dasein is 'manifest' in the "with-one-another" of publicness, even if 'at bottom' everydayness is precisely something which, in an existentiell manner, it has 'surmounted'. 'For the most part' signifies the way in which Dasein shows itself for Everyman, not always, but 'as a rule'.

"Everydayness" means the "how" in accordance with which Dasein 'lives unto the day' ["in den Tag hineinlebt"], whether in all its ways of behaving or only in certain ones which have been prescribed by Being-with-one-another. To this "how" there belongs further the comfortableness of the accustomed, even if it forces one to do something burdensome and 'repugnant'. That which will come tomorrow (and this is what everyday concern keeps awaiting) is 'eternally yesterday's'. In everydayness everything is all one and the same, but whatever the day may bring is taken as diversification. Everydayness is determinative for Dasein even when it has not chosen the "they" for its 'hero'.

These manifold characteristics of everydayness, however, by no means designate it as a mere 'aspect' afforded by Dasein when 'one looks at' the things men do. Everydayness is a way *to be*—to which, of course, that which is publicly manifest belongs. But it is more or less familiar to any 'individual' Dasein as a way of existing which it may have as its own, and it is familiar to it through that state-of-mind which consists of a pallid lack of mood. In everydayness Dasein can undergo dull 'suffering', sink away in the dullness of it, and evade it by seeking new ways in which its dispersion in its affairs may be further dispersed. In the moment of vision, indeed, and often just 'for that moment', existence can even gain the mastery over the "everyday"; but it can never extinguish it.

That which is *ontically* so familiar in the way Dasein has been factically interpreted that we never pay any heed to it, hides enigma after enigma existential-ontologically. The 'natural' horizon for starting the existential analytic of Dasein is *only seemingly self-evident.*

But after the Interpretation of temporality which we have given thus far, do we find ourselves in any more promising a situation with regard to delimiting the structure of everydayness existentially? Or does this bewildering phenomenon make the inadequacy of our explication of temporality all too patent? Have we not hitherto been constantly immobilizing Dasein in certain situations, while we have, 'consistently' with this, been disregarding the fact that in living unto its days Dasein *stretches* itself *along* 'temporally' in the sequence of those days?[1] The "it's all one and the same", the accustomed, the 'like yesterday, so today and tomorrow', and the 'for the most part'—these are not to be grasped without recourse to this 'temporal' stretching-along of Dasein.

And is it not also a Fact of existing Dasein that in spending its time it takes 'time' into its reckoning from day to day and regulates this 'reckoning' astronomically and calendrically? Only if both Dasein's everyday 'historizing'[2] and the reckoning with 'time' with which it concerns itself in this historizing, are included in our Interpretation of Dasein's temporality, will our orientation be embracing enough to enable us to make a problem of the ontological meaning of everydayness as such. But because at bottom we mean by the term "everydayness" nothing else than temporality, while temporality is made possible by Dasein's *Being*,[3] an adequate conceptual delimitation of everydayness can succeed only in a framework in which the meaning of Being in general and its possible variations are discussed in principle.

[1] 'Haben wir bisher nicht ständig das Dasein auf gewisse Lagen und Situationen stillgelegt und "konsequent" missachtet, dass es sich, in seine Tage hineinlebend, in der Folge seiner Tage "zeitlich" *erstreckt*?' The older editions have 'stillgestellt' rather than 'stillgelegt.'

[2] ' "Geschehen" '. Cf. our note 1, p. 41, H. 19 above.

[3] 'Weil jedoch mit dem Titel Alltäglichkeit im Grunde nichts anderes gemeint ist als die Zeitlichkeit, diese aber das *Sein* des Daseins ermöglicht . . .'

V

TEMPORALITY AND HISTORICALITY

¶ 72. *Existential-ontological Exposition of the Problem of History*

ALL our efforts in the existential analytic serve the one aim of finding a possibility of answering the question of the *meaning of Being*[1] in general. To work out this *question*,[1] we need to delimit that very phenomenon in which something like Being becomes accessible—the phenomenon of the *understanding of Being*. But this phenomenon is one that belongs to Dasein's state of Being. Only after this entity has been Interpreted in a way which is sufficiently primordial, can we have a conception of the understanding of Being, which is included in its very state of Being; only on this basis can we formulate the question of the Being which is understood in this understanding, and the question of what such understanding 'pre-supposes'.

Even though many structures of Dasein when taken singly are still obscure, it seems that by casting light upon temporality as the primordial condition for the possibility of *care*, we have reached the primordial Interpretation of Dasein which we require. We have exhibited temporality with a view to Dasein's authentic potentiality-for-Being-a-whole. We have then confirmed the temporal Interpretation of care by demonstrating the temporality of concernful Being-in-the-world. Our analysis of the authentic potentiality-for-Being-a-whole has revealed that in care is rooted an equiprimordial connectedness of death, guilt, and conscience. Can Dasein be understood in a way that is more primordial than in the projection of its authentic existence?

Although up till now we have seen no possibility of a more radical approach to the existential analytic, yet, if we have regard for the preceding discussion of the ontological meaning of everydayness, a difficult consideration comes to light. Have we indeed brought the whole of Dasein, as regards its authentically *Being*-a-whole, into the fore-having of our existential analysis? It may be that a formulation of the question as

---

[1] Italics provided only in the later editions.

related to Dasein's totality, possesses a genuinely unequivocal character ontologically. It may be that as regards *Being-towards-the-end* the question itself may even have found its answer. But death is only the 'end' of Dasein; and, taken formally, it is just *one* of the ends by which Dasein's totality is closed round. The other 'end', however, is the 'beginning', the 'birth'. Only that entity which is 'between' birth and death presents the whole which we have been seeking. Accordingly the orientation of our analytic has so far remained 'one-sided', in spite of all its tendencies towards a consideration of *existent* Being-a-whole and in spite of the genuineness with which authentic and inauthentic Being-towards-death have been explicated. Dasein has been our theme only in the way in which it exists 'facing forward', as it were, leaving 'behind it' all that has been. Not only has Being-towards-the-beginning remained unnoticed; but so too, and above all, has the way in which Dasein *stretches along between* birth and death. The 'connectedness of life', in which Dasein somehow maintains itself constantly, is precisely what we have overlooked in our analysis of Being-a-whole.

We have regarded temporality as the meaning of the Being of Dasein's totality; must we not now take this back, even if what we have described as the 'connectedness' between birth and death is ontologically quite obscure? Or does *temporality*, as we have exhibited it, first of all give us the *basis* on which to provide an unequivocal direction for the existential-ontological question of this 'connectedness'? In the field of these investigations, it is perhaps already a gain, when we learn not to take problems too lightly.

What seems 'simpler' than to characterize the 'connectedness of life' between birth and death? It *consists of* a sequence of Experiences 'in time'. But if one makes a more penetrating study of this way of characterizing the 'connectedness' in question, and especially of the ontological assumptions behind it, the remarkable upshot is that, in this sequence of Experiences, what is 'really' 'actual' is, in each case, just that Experience which is present-at-hand 'in the current "now"', while those Experiences which have passed away or are only coming along, either are no longer or are not yet 'actual'. Dasein traverses the span of time granted to it between the two boundaries, and it does so in such a way that, in each case, it is 'actual' only in the "now", and hops, as it were, through the sequence of "nows" of its own 'time'. Thus it is said that Dasein is 'temporal'. In spite of the constant changing of these Experiences, the Self maintains itself throughout with a certain selfsameness. Opinions diverge as to how that which thus persists is to be defined, and how one is to determine what relation it may possibly have to the changing Experiences.

The Being of this perseveringly changing connectedness of Experiences remains indefinite. But at bottom, whether one likes it or not, in this way of characterizing the connectedness of life, one has posited something present-at-hand 'in time', though something that is obviously 'un-Thinglike'.

If we have regard for what we have worked out under the title of "temporality" as the meaning of the Being of care, we find that while the ordinary interpretation of Dasein, within its own limits, has its justification and is sufficient, we cannot carry through a genuine ontological analysis of the way Dasein *stretches along* between birth and death if we take this interpretation as our clue, nor can we even fix upon such an analysis as a problem.

Dasein does not exist as the sum of the momentary actualities of Experiences which come along successively and disappear. Nor is there a sort of framework which this succession gradually fills up. For how is such a framework to be present-at-hand, where, in each case, only the Experience one is having 'right now' is 'actual',[1] and the boundaries of the framework —the birth which is past and the death which is only oncoming—lack actuality? At bottom, even in the ordinary way of taking the 'connectedness of life', one does not think of this as a framework drawn tense 'outside' of Dasein and spanning it round, but one rightly seeks this connectedness in Dasein itself. When, however, one tacitly regards this entity ontologically as something present-at-hand 'in time', any attempt at an ontological characterization of the Being 'between' birth and death will break down.

Dasein does not fill up a track or stretch 'of life'—one which is somehow present-at-hand—with the phases of its momentary actualities. It stretches *itself* along in such a way that its own Being is constituted in advance as a stretching-along. The 'between' which relates to birth and death already lies *in the Being* of Dasein. On the other hand, it is by no means the case that Dasein 'is' actual in a point of time, and that, apart from this, it is 'surrounded' by the non-actuality of its birth and death. Understood existentially, birth is not and never is something past in the sense of something no longer present-at-hand; and death is just as far from having the kind of Being of something still outstanding, not yet present-at-hand but coming along. Factical Dasein exists as born; and, as born, it is already dying, in the sense of Being-towards-death. As long as Dasein factically exists, both the 'ends' and their 'between' *are*, and they *are* in the only way which is possible on the basis of Dasein's Being as *care*. Thrownness and that Being towards death in which one either flees it or anticipates

---

[1] '. . . wo doch je nur das "aktuelle" Erlebnis "wirklich" ist . . .'

it, form a unity; and in this unity birth and death are 'connected' in a manner characteristic of Dasein. As care, Dasein *is* the 'between'.

In temporality, however, the constitutive totality of care has a possible *basis* for its unity. Accordingly it is within the horizon of Dasein's temporal constitution that we must approach the ontological clarification of the 'connectedness of life'—that is to say, the stretching-along, the movement, and the persistence which are specific for Dasein. The movement [Bewegtheit] of existence is not the motion [Bewegung] of something present-at-hand. It is definable in terms of the way Dasein stretches along. The specific movement in which Dasein *is stretched along and stretches itself along*, we call its *"historizing"*.[1] The question of Dasein's 'connectedness' is the ontological problem of Dasein's historizing. To lay bare the *structure of historizing*, and the existential-temporal conditions of its possibility, signifies that one has achieved an *ontological* understanding of historicality.[2]

With the analysis of the specific movement and persistence which belong to Dasein's historizing, we come back in our investigation to the problem which we touched upon immediately before exposing temporality to view—the question of the constancy of the Self, which we defined as the "who" of Dasein.[1] Self-constancy[3] is a way of Being of Dasein, and is therefore grounded in a specific temporalizing of temporality. The analysis of historizing will lead us face to face with the problems of a thematical investigation of temporalizing as such.

If the question of historicality leads us back to these 'sources', then the *locus* of the problem of history has already been decided. This *locus* is not to be sought in historiology as the science of history. Even if the problem of 'history' is treated in accordance with a theory of science, not only aiming at the 'epistemological' clarification of the historiological way of grasping things (Simmel) or at the logic with which the concepts of historiological presentation are formed (Rickert), but doing so with an orientation towards 'the side of the object', then, as long as the question is formulated this way, history becomes in principle accessible only as the *Object* of a science. Thus the basic phenomenon of history, which is prior to any possible thematizing by historiology and underlies it, has been irretrievably put aside. How history can become a possible *object* for historiology is something that may be gathered only from the kind of Being

[1] 'Die spezifische Bewegtheit des *erstreckten Sicherstreckens* nennen wir das *Geschehen* des Daseins.' On 'Geschehen' see our note 1, p. 41, H. 19 above.
[2] On 'historicality' ('Geschichtlichkeit') see our note 2, p. 31, H. 10 above.
[3] 'Selbst-ständigkeit'. Here we follow the reading of the older editions in which the hyphen comes at the end of a line. In the newer editions the hyphen is omitted; but presumably Heidegger intends the same expanded spelling which we have already met on H. 322 and H. 332. See our notes ad loc.

which belongs to the historical—from historicality, and from the way it is rooted in temporality.

If we are to cast light on historicality itself in terms of temporality, and primordially in terms of temporality that is *authentic*, then it is essential to this task that we can carry it out only by construing it phenomenologically.[ii] The existential-ontological constitution of historicality has been covered up by the way Dasein's history is ordinarily interpreted; we must get hold of it *in spite of* all this. The existential way of construing historicality has its definite supports in the ordinary understanding of Dasein, and is guided by those existential structures at which we have hitherto arrived.

We shall first describe the ordinary ways in which history is conceived, so that we may give our investigation an orientation as to those items which are commonly held to be essential for history. Here, it must be made plain what is primordially considered as historical. The point of attack for expounding the ontological problem of historicality will thus be designated.

Our Interpretation of Dasein's authentic potentiality-for-Being-a-whole and our analysis of care as temporality—an analysis which has arisen from this Interpretation—offer us the clue for construing historicality existentially. The existential projection of Dasein's historicality merely reveals what already lies enveloped in the temporalizing of temporality. In accordance with the way in which historicality is rooted in care, Dasein exists, in each case, as authentically or inauthentically historical. It becomes plain that Dasein's inauthentic historicality lies in that which—under the title of "everydayness"—we have looked upon, in the existential analytic of Dasein, as the horizon that is closest to us.

Disclosing and interpreting belong essentially to Dasein's historizing. Out of this kind of Being of the entity which exists historically, there arises the existentiell possibility of disclosing history explicitly and getting it in our grasp. The fact that we can make history our theme—that is to say, disclose it *historiologically*—is the presupposition for the possibility of the way one 'builds up the historical world in the humane sciences'. The existential Interpretation of historiology as a science aims solely at demonstrating its ontological derivation from Dasein's historicality. Only from here can we stake out the boundaries within which any theory of science that is oriented to the factical workings of science, may expose itself to the accidental factors in its way of formulating questions.

In analysing the historicality of Dasein we shall try to show that this entity is not 'temporal' because it 'stands in history', but that, on the contrary, it exists historically and can so exist only because it is temporal in the very basis of its Being.

Nevertheless, Dasein must also be called 'temporal' in the sense of Being 'in time'. Even without a developed historiology, factical Dasein needs and uses a calendar and a clock. Whatever may happen 'to Dasein', it experiences it as happening 'in time'. In the same way, the processes of Nature, whether living or lifeless, are encountered 'in time'. They are within-time. So while our analysis of how the 'time' of within-time-ness has its source in temporality will be deferred until the next chapter,[111] it would be easy to put this before our discussion of the connection between historicality and temporality. The historical is ordinarily characterized with the help of the time of within-time-ness. But if this ordinary characterization is to be stripped of its seeming self-evidence and exclusiveness, historicality must first be 'deduced' purely in terms of Dasein's primordial temporality; this is demanded even by the way these are 'objectively' connected. Since, however, time as within-time-ness also 'stems' from the temporality of Dasein, historicality and within-time-ness turn out to be equiprimordial. Thus, within its limits, the ordinary interpretation of the temporal character of history is justified.

After this first characterization of the course of the ontological exposition of historicality in terms of temporality, do we still need explicit assurance that the following investigation does not rest upon a belief that the problem of history is to be solved by a *coup de main*? The poverty of the 'categorial' means at our disposal, and the unsureness of the primary ontological horizons, become the more obtrusive, the more the problem of history is traced to its *primordial roots*. In the following study, we shall content ourselves with indicating the ontological *locus* of the problem of historicality. The researches of Dilthey were, for their part, pioneering work; but today's generation has not as yet made them its own. In the following analysis the issue is solely one of furthering their adoption.

Our exposition of the existential problem of historicality—an exposition which is necessarily limited, moreover, in that its goal is one of fundamental ontology—is divided up as follows: the ordinary understanding of history, and Dasein's historizing (Section 73); the basic constitution of historicality (Section 74); Dasein's historicality, and world-history (Section 75); the existential source of historiology in Dasein's historicality (Section 76); the connection of the foregoing exposition of the problem of historicality with the researches of Dilthey and the ideas of Count Yorck (Section 77).

¶ *73. The Ordinary Understanding of History, and Dasein's Historizing*

Our next aim is to find the right position for attacking the primordial question of the essence of history—that is to say, for construing historicality existentially. This position is designated by that which is primordially historical. We shall begin our study, therefore, by characterizing what one has in view in using the expressions 'history' and 'historical' in the ordinary interpretation of Dasein. These expressions get used in several ways.

The most obvious ambiguity of the term 'history' is one that has often been noticed, and there is nothing 'fuzzy' about it. It evinces itself in that this term may mean the 'historical actuality' as well as the possible science of it. We shall provisionally eliminate the signification of 'history' in the sense of a "science of history" (historiology).

The expression 'history' has various significations with which one has in view neither the science of history nor even history as an Object, but this very entity itself, not necessarily Objectified. Among such significations, that in which this entity is understood as something *past*, may well be the pre-eminent usage. This signification is evinced in the kind of talk in which we say that something or other "already belongs to history". Here 'past' means "no longer present-at-hand", or even "still present-at-hand indeed, but without having any 'effect' on the 'Present' ". Of course, the historical as that which is past has also the opposite signification, when we say, "One cannot get away from history." Here, by "history", we have in view that which is past, but which nevertheless is still having effects. Howsoever the historical, as that which is past, is understood to be related to the 'Present' in the sense of what is actual 'now' and 'today', and to be related to it, either positively or privatively, in such a way as to have effects upon it. Thus 'the past' has a remarkable double meaning; the past belongs irretrievably to an earlier time; it belonged to the events of that time; and in spite of that, it can still be present-at-hand 'now'—for instance, the remains of a Greek temple. With the temple, a 'bit of the past' is still 'in the present'.

What we next have in mind with the term "history" is not so much 'the past' in the sense of that which is past, but rather *derivation* [Herkunft] from such a past. Anything that 'has a history' stands in the context of a becoming. In such becoming, 'development' is sometimes a rise, sometimes a fall. What 'has a history' in this way can, at the same time, 'make' such history. As 'epoch-making', it determines 'a future' 'in the present'. Here "history" signifies a 'context' of events and 'effects', which draws on through 'the past', the 'Present', and the 'future'. On this view, the past has no special priority.

Further, "history" signifies the totality of those entities which change 'in time', and indeed the transformations and vicissitudes of men, of human groupings and their 'cultures', as distinguished from Nature, which likewise operates 'in time'. Here what one has in view is not so much a kind of Being—historizing—as it is that realm of entities which one distinguishes from Nature by having regard for the way in which man's existence is essentially determined by 'spirit' and 'culture', even though in a certain manner Nature too belongs to "history" as thus understood.

Finally, whatever has been handed down to us is as such held to be 'historical', whether it is something which we know historiologically, or something that has been taken over as self-evident, with its derivation hidden.

If we take these four significations together, the upshot is that history is that specific historizing of existent Dasein which comes to pass in time, so that the historizing which is 'past' in our Being-with-one-another, and which at the same time has been 'handed down to us' and is continuingly effective, is regarded as "history" in the sense that gets emphasized.

The four significations are connected in that they relate to man as the 'subject' of events. How is the historizing character of such events to be defined? Is historizing a sequence of processes, an ever-changing emergence and disappearance of events? In what way does this historizing of history belong to Dasein? Is Dasein already factically 'present-at-hand' to begin with, so that on occasion it can get 'into a history'? Does Dasein first *become* historical by getting intertwined with events and circumstances? Or is the Being of Dasein constituted first of all by historizing, so that anything like circumstances, events, and vicissitudes is ontologically possible *only because Dasein is historical in its Being*? Why is it that the function of the past gets particularly stressed when the Dasein which historizes 'in time' is characterized 'temporally'?

If history belongs to Dasein's Being, and this Being is based on temporality, then it would be easy to begin the existential analysis of historicality with those characteristics of the historical which obviously have a temporal meaning. Therefore, by characterizing more precisely the remarkably privileged position of the 'past' in the concept of history, we shall prepare the way for expounding the basic constitution of historicality.

The 'antiquities' preserved in museums (household gear, for example) belong to a 'time which is past'; yet they are still present-at-hand in the 'Present'. How far is such equipment historical, when it is *not yet* past? Is it historical, let us say, only because it has become an *object* of historiological interest, of antiquarian study or national lore? But such equipment can be a *historiological object* only because it *is* in itself somehow *historical*. We repeat the question: by what right do we call this entity "historical", when it is not yet past? Or do these 'Things' have 'in themselves' 'something past', even though they are still present-at-hand today? Then *are* these, which are present-at-hand, still what they were?

Manifestly these 'Things' have altered. The gear has become fragile or worm-eaten 'in the course of time'. But that specific character of the past which makes it something historical, does not lie in this transience,[1] which continues even during the Being-present-at-hand of the equipment in the museum. What, then, is past in this equipment? What *were* these 'Things' which today they are no longer? They are still definite items of equipment for use; but they are out of use. Suppose, however, that they were still in use today, like many a household heirloom; would they then be not yet historical? All the same, whether they are in use or out of use, they are no longer what they were. What is 'past'? Nothing else than that *world* within which they belonged to a context of equipment and were encountered as ready-to-hand and used by a concernful Dasein who was-in-the-world. That *world* is no longer. But what was formerly *within-the-world* with respect to that world is still present-at-hand. As equipment belonging to a world, that which is *now* still present-at-hand can belong nevertheless to the '*past*'. But what do we signify by saying of a world that it is no longer? A world *is* only in the manner of *existing* Dasein, which *factically* i s as Being-in-the-world.[2]

Thus the historical character of the antiquities that are still preserved is grounded in the 'past' of that Dasein to whose world they belonged. But according to this, only 'past' Dasein would be historical, not Dasein 'in the present'. However, can Dasein be *past* at all, if we define 'past' as 'now *no longer either present-at-hand or ready-to-hand*'? Manifestly, Dasein can *never* be past, not because Dasein is non-transient, but because it essentially can never be *present-at-hand*. Rather, if it is, it *exists*. A Dasein which no longer exists, however, is not past, in the ontologically strict sense; it is rather "*having-been-there*" [*da-gewesen*]. The antiquities which are still present-at-hand have a character of 'the past' and of history by reason of the fact that they have belonged as equipment to a world that has been— the world of a Dasein that has been there—and that they have been derived from that world. This Dasein is what is primarily historical. But does Dasein first *become* historical in that it is no longer there? Or *is* it not historical precisely in so far as it factically exists? *Is Dasein just something that "has been" in the sense of "having been there", or has it been as something futural which is making present—that is to say, in the temporalizing of its temporality?*

From this provisional analysis of equipment which belongs to history and which is still present-at-hand though somehow 'past', it becomes plain that such entities are historical only by reason of their belonging to the world. But the world has an historical kind of Being because it makes

---

[1] 'Vergänglichkeit'. Cf. 'vergehen' ('to pass away') and 'Vergangenheit' ('the past').
[2] 'Welt *ist* nur in der Weise des *existierenden* Daseins, das a ls In-der-Welt-sein *faktisch* ist.'

up an ontological attribute of Dasein. It may be shown further that when one designates a time as 'the past', the meaning of this is not unequivocal; but 'the past' is manifestly distinct from *one's having been*, with which we have become acquainted as something constitutive for the ecstatical unity of Dasein's temporality. This, however, only makes the enigma ultimately more acute; why is it that the historical is determined *predominantly* by the 'past', or, to speak more appropriately, by the character of having-been, when that character is one that temporalizes itself equiprimordially with the Present and the future?

We contend that what is *primarily* historical is Dasein. That which is *secondarily* historical, however, is what we encounter within-the-world— not only equipment ready-to-hand, in the widest sense, but also the environing *Nature* as 'the very soil of history.' Entities other than Dasein which are historical by reason of belonging to the world, are what we call 'world-historical'. It can be shown that the ordinary conception of 'world-history' arises precisely from our orientation to what is thus secondarily historical. World-historical entities do not first get their historical character, let us say, by reason of an historiological Objectification; they get it rather *as those entities* which they are in themselves when they are encountered within-the-world.

In analysing the historical character of equipment which is still present-at-hand, we have not only been led back to Dasein as that which is primarily historical; but at the same time we have been made to doubt whether the temporal characterization of the historical in general may be oriented primarily to the Being-in-time of anything present-at-hand. Entities do not become 'more historical' by being moved off into a past which is always farther and farther away, so that the oldest of them would be the most authentically historical. On the other hand, if the 'temporal' distance from "now and today" is of no primary constitutive significance for the historicality of entities that are authentically historical, this is not because these entities are not 'in time' and are timeless, but because they exist *temporally in so primordial a manner* that nothing present-at-hand 'in time', whether passing away or still coming along, could ever—by its ontological essence—be temporal in such a way.

It will be said that these deliberations have been rather petty. No one denies that at bottom human Dasein is the primary 'subject' of history; and the ordinary conception of history, which we have cited, says so plainly enough. But with the thesis that 'Dasein is historical', one has in view not just the ontical Fact that in man we are presented with a more or less important 'atom' in the workings of world-history, and that he remains the plaything of circumstances and events. This thesis raises the problem: *to what extent and on the basis of what ontological conditions, does historicality belong, as an essential constitutive state, to the subjectivity of the 'historical' subject?*

¶ *74. The Basic Constitution of Historicality*

Dasein factically has its 'history', and it can have something of the sort because the Being of this entity is constituted by historicality. We must now justify this thesis, with the aim of expounding the *ontological* problem of history as an existential one. The Being of Dasein has been defined as care. Care is grounded in temporality. Within the range of temporality, therefore, the kind of historizing which gives existence its definitely historical character, must be sought. Thus the Interpretation of Dasein's historicality will prove to be, at bottom, just a more concrete working out of temporality. We first revealed temporality with regard to that way of existing authentically which we characterized as anticipatory resoluteness. How far does this imply an authentic historizing of Dasein?

We have defined "resoluteness" as a projecting of oneself upon one's own Being-guilty—a projecting which is reticent and ready for anxiety.[iv] Resoluteness gains its authenticity as *anticipatory* resoluteness.[v] In this, Dasein understands itself with regard to its potentiality-for-Being, and it does so in such a manner that it will go right under the eyes of Death in order thus to take over in its thrownness that entity which it is itself, and to take it over wholly. The resolute taking over of one's factical 'there', signifies, at the same time, that the Situation is one which has been resolved upon. In the existential analysis we cannot, in principle, discuss what Dasein *factically* resolves in any particular case. Our investigation excludes even the existential projection of the factical possibilities of existence. Nevertheless, we must ask whence, *in general*, Dasein can draw those possibilities upon which it factically projects itself. One's anticipatory projection of oneself on that possibility of existence which is not to be outstripped—on death—guarantees only the totality and authenticity of one's resoluteness. But those possibilities of existence which have been factically disclosed are not to be gathered from death. And this is still less the case when one's anticipation of this possibility does not signify that one is speculating about it, but signifies precisely that one is coming back to one's factical "there". Will taking over the thrownness of the Self into its world perhaps disclose an horizon from which existence snatches its factical possibilities away?[1] Have we not said in addition that Dasein never comes back behind its thrownness?[vi] Before we decide too quickly

---

[1] 'Soll etwa die Übernahme der Geworfenheit des Selbst in seine Welt einen Horizont erschliessen, dem die Existenz ihre faktischen Möglichkeiten entreisst?'

whether Dasein draws it authentic possibilities of existence from thrown-ness or not, we must assure ourselves that we have a full conception of thrownness as a basic attribute of care.

As thrown, Dasein has indeed been delivered over to itself and to its potentiality-for-Being, *but as Being-in-the-world*. As thrown, it has been submitted to a 'world', and exists factically with Others. Proximally and for the most part the Self is lost in the "they". It understands itself in terms of those possibilities of existence which 'circulate' in the 'average' public way of interpreting Dasein today. These possibilities have mostly been made unrecognizable by ambiguity; yet they are well known to us. The authentic existentiell understanding is so far from extricating itself from the way of interpreting Dasein which has come down to us, that in each case it is in terms of this interpretation, against it, and yet again for it, that any possibility one has chosen is seized upon in one's resolution.

The resoluteness in which Dasein comes back to itself, discloses current factical possibilities of authentic existing, and discloses them *in terms of the heritage* which that resoluteness, as thrown, *takes over*. In one's coming back resolutely to one's thrownness, there is hidden a *handing down* to oneself of the possibilities that have come down to one, but not necessarily *as* having thus come down.[1] If everything 'good' is a heritage, and the character of 'goodness' lies in making authentic existence possible, then the handing down of a heritage constitutes itself in resoluteness. The more authentically Dasein resolves—and this means that in anticipating death it understands itself unambiguously in terms of its ownmost distinctive possibility—the more unequivocally does it choose and find the possibility of its existence, and the less does it do so by accident. Only by the anticipation of death is every accidental and 'provisional' possibility driven out. Only Being-free *for* death, gives Dasein its goal outright and pushes existence into its finitude. Once one has grasped the finitude of one's existence, it snatches one back from the endless multiplicity of possibilities which offer themselves as closest to one—those of comfortableness, shirking, and taking things lightly—and brings Dasein into the simplicity of its *fate* [*Schicksals*]. This is how we designate Dasein's primordial historizing, which lies in authentic resoluteness and in which Dasein *hands* itself *down* to itself, free for death, in a possibility which it has inherited and yet has chosen.

---

[1] 'Die Entschlossenheit, in der das Dasein auf sich selbst zurückkommt, erschliesst die jeweiligen faktischen Möglichkeiten eigentlichen Existierens *aus dem Erbe*, das sie als *geworfene übernimmt*. Das entschlossene Zurückkommen auf die Geworfenheit birgt ein *Sichüberliefern* überkommener Möglichkeiten in sich, obzwar nicht notwendig *als* überkommener.' The grammatical structure of both sentences is ambiguous. Notice also the counterpoint of the verbs 'zurückkommen', 'überkommen', 'überliefern', 'übernehmen,' which cannot be reproduced in translation.

Dasein can be reached by the blows of fate only because in the depths of its Being Dasein *is* fate in the sense we have described. Existing fatefully in the resoluteness which hands itself down, Dasein has been disclosed as Being-in-the-world both for the 'fortunate' circumstances which 'come its way' and for the cruelty of accidents. Fate does not first arise from the clashing together of events and circumstances. Even one who is irresolute gets driven about by these—more so than one who has chosen; and yet he can 'have' no fate.[1]

If Dasein, by anticipation, lets death become powerful in itself, then, as free for death, Dasein understands itself in its own *superior power*, the power of its finite freedom, so that in this freedom, which 'is' only in its having chosen to make such a choice, it can take over the *powerlessness* of abandonment to its having done so, and can thus come to have a clear vision for the accidents of the Situation that has been disclosed.[2] But if fateful Dasein, as Being-in-the-world, exists essentially in Being-with Others, its historizing is a co-historizing and is determinative for it as *destiny* [*Geschick*]. This is how we designate the historizing of the community, of a people. Destiny is not something that puts itself together out of individual fates, any more than Being-with-one-another can be conceived as the occurring together of several Subjects.[vii] Our fates have already been guided in advance, in our Being with one another in the same world and in our resoluteness for definite possibilities. Only in communicating and in struggling does the power of destiny become free. Dasein's fateful destiny in and with its 'generation'[viii] goes to make up the full authentic historizing of Dasein.

Fate is that powerless superior power which puts itself in readiness for adversities—the power of projecting oneself upon one's own Being-guilty, and of doing so reticently, with readiness for anxiety. As such, fate requires

---

[1] This statement may well puzzle the English-speaking reader, who would perhaps be less troubled if he were to read that the irresolute man can have no 'destiny'. As we shall see in the next paragraph, Heidegger has chosen to differentiate sharply between the words 'Schicksal' and 'Geschick', which are ordinarily synonyms. Thus 'Schicksal' (our 'fate') might be described as the 'destiny' of the resolute individual; 'Geschick' (our 'destiny') is rather the 'destiny' of a larger group, or of Dasein as a member of such a group. This usage of 'Geschick' is probably to be distinguished from that which we have met on H. 16, 19, and perhaps even 379, where we have preferred to translate it by 'vicissitude'. The suggestion of an etymological connection between 'Schicksal' and 'Geschick' on the one hand and 'Geschichte' (our 'history') and 'Geschehen' (our 'historizing') on the other, which is exploited in the next paragraph, is of course lost in translation.

[2] 'Wenn das Dasein vorlaufend den Tod in sich mächtig werden lässt, versteht es sich, frei für ihn, in der eigenen *Übermacht* seiner endlichen Freiheit, um in dieser, die je nur "ist" im Gewählthaben der Wahl, die *Ohnmacht* der Überlassenheit an es selbst zu übernehmen und für die Zufälle der erschlossenen Situation hellsichtig zu werden.' It should perhaps be pointed out that 'Ohnmacht' can also mean a 'faint' or a 'swoon', and that 'Hellsichtigkeit' is the regular term for 'clairvoyance'. Thus the German reader might easily read into this passage a suggestion of the seer's mystical trance.

as the ontological condition for its possibility, the state of Being of care—that is to say, temporality. Only if death, guilt, conscience, freedom, and finitude reside together equiprimordially in the Being of an entity as they do in care, can that entity exist in the mode of fate; that is to say, only then can it be historical in the very depths of its existence.

Only an entity which, in its Being, is essentially **futural** *so that it is free for its death and can let itself be thrown back upon its factical "there" by shattering itself against death—that is to say, only an entity which, as futural, is equiprimordially in the process of* **having-been**, *can, by handing down to itself the possibility it has inherited, take over its own thrownness and be* **in the moment of vision** *for 'its time'. Only authentic temporality which is at the same time finite, makes possible something like fate—that is to say, authentic historicality.*

It is not necessary that in resoluteness one should *explicitly* know the origin of the possibilities upon which that resoluteness projects itself. It is rather in Dasein's temporality, and there only, that there lies any possibility that the existentiell potentiality-for-Being upon which it projects itself can be gleaned *explicitly* from the way in which Dasein has been traditionally understood. The resoluteness which comes back to itself and hands itself down, then becomes the *repetition* of a possibility of existence that has come down to us. *Repeating is handing down explicitly*—that is to say, going back into the possibilities of the Dasein that has-been-there.[1] The authentic repetition of a possibility of existence that has been—the possibility that Dasein may choose its hero—is grounded existentially in anticipatory resoluteness; for it is in resoluteness that one first chooses the choice which makes one free for the struggle of loyally following in the footsteps of that which can be repeated. But when one has, by repetition, handed down to oneself a possibility that has been, the Dasein that has-been-there is not disclosed in order to be actualized over again. The repeating of that which is possible does not bring again [Wiederbringen] something that is 'past', nor does it bind the 'Present' back to that which has already been 'outstripped'. Arising, as it does, from a resolute projection of oneself, repetition does not let itself be persuaded of something by what is 'past', just in order that this, as something which was formerly

3·

---

[1] 'Die *Wiederholung ist die ausdrückliche Überlieferung*, das heisst, der Rückgang in Möglichkeiten des dagewesenen Daseins'. (In the earlier editions the article 'Die', as well as the words now italicized, appears in spaced type.)

While we usually translate 'wiederholen' as 'repeat', this English word is hardly adequate to express Heidegger's meaning. Etymologically, 'wiederholen' means 'to fetch again'; in modern German usage, however, this is expressed by the cognate separable verb 'wieder . . . holen', while 'wiederholen' means simply 'to repeat' or 'do over again'. Heidegger departs from both these meanings, as he is careful to point out. For him, 'wiederholen' does not mean either a mere mechanical repetition or an attempt to reconstitute the physical past; it means rather an attempt to go back to the past and retrieve former *possibilities*, which are thus 'explicitly handed down' or 'transmitted'.

actual, may recur. Rather, the repetition makes a *reciprocative rejoinder* to the possibility of that existence which has-been-there. But when such a rejoinder is made to this possibility in a resolution, it is made *in a moment of vision; and as such* it is at the same time a *disavowal* of that which in the "today", is working itself out as the 'past'.[1] Repetition does not abandon itself to that which is past, nor does it aim at progress. In the moment of vision authentic existence is indifferent to both these alternatives.

We characterize repetition as a mode of that resoluteness which hands itself down—the mode by which Dasein exists explicitly as fate. But if fate constitutes the primordial historicality of Dasein, then history has its essential importance neither in what is past nor in the "today" and its connection' with what is past, but in that authentic historizing of existence which arises from Dasein's *future*. As a way of Being for Dasein, history has its roots so essentially in the future that death, as that possibility of Dasein which we have already characterized, throws anticipatory existence back upon its *factical* thrownness, and so for the first time imparts to *having-been* its peculiarly privileged position in the historical. *Authentic Being-towards-death—that is to say, the finitude of temporality—is the hidden basis of Dasein's historicality.* Dasein does not first become historical in repetition; but because it is historical as temporal, it can take itself over in its history by repeating. For this, no historiology is as yet needed.

Resoluteness implies handing oneself down by anticipation to the "there" of the moment of vision; and this handing down we call "fate". This is also the ground for destiny, by which we understand Dasein's historizing in Being-with Others. In repetition, fateful destiny can be disclosed explicitly as bound up with the heritage which has come down to us. By repetition, Dasein first has its own history made manifest. Historizing is itself grounded existentially in the fact that Dasein, as temporal, is open ecstatically; so too is the disclosedness which belongs to historizing, or rather so too is the way in which we make this disclosedness our own.

That which we have hitherto been characterizing as "historicality" to conform with the kind of historizing which lies in anticipatory resoluteness, we now designate as Dasein's "*authentic* historicality". From the phenomena of handing down and repeating, which are rooted in the

---

[1] 'Die Wiederholung lässt sich, einem entschlossenen Sichentwerfen entspringend, nicht vom "Vergangenen" überreden, um es als das vormals Wirkliche nur wiederkehren zu lassen. Die Wiederholung *erwidert* vielmehr die Möglichkeit der dagewesenen Existenz. Die Erwiderung der Möglichkeit im Entschluss ist aber zugleich *als augenblickliche der Widerruf* dessen, was in Heute sich als "Vergangenheit" auswirkt.' The idea seems to be that in resolute repetition one is having, as it were, a conversation with the past, in which the past proposes certain possibilities for adoption, but in which one makes rejoinder to this proposal by 'reciprocating' with the proposal of other possibilities as a sort of rebuke to the past, which one now disavows. (The punning treatment of 'wieder' and 'wider' is presumably intentional.)

future, it has become plain why the historizing of authentic history lies preponderantly in having been. But it remains all the more enigmatic in what way this historizing, as fate, is to constitute the whole 'connectedness' of Dasein from its birth to its death. How can recourse to resoluteness bring us any enlightenment? Is not each resolution just *one* more single 'Experience' in the sequence of the whole connectedness of our Experiences? Is the 'connectedness' of authentic historizing to consist, let us say, of an uninterrupted sequence of resolutions? Why is it that the question of how the 'connectedness of life' is Constituted finds no adequate and satisfying answer? Is not our investigation overhasty? Does it not, in the end, hang too much on the answer, without first having tested the legitimacy of the *question*? Nothing is so plain from the course of the existential analytic so far, as the Fact that the ontology of Dasein is always falling back upon the allurements of the way in which Being is ordinarily understood. The only way of encountering this fact methodologically is by studying the *source* of the question of how Dasein's connectedness is Constituted, no matter how 'obvious' this question may be, and by determining within what ontological horizon it moves.

If historicality belongs to the Being of Dasein, then even inauthentic existing must be historical. What if it is Dasein's *inauthentic* historicality that has directed our questioning to the 'connectedness of life' and has blocked off our access to authentic historicality and its own peculiar 'connectedness'? However this may be treated, we cannot do without a study of Dasein's inauthentic historicality if our exposition of the ontological problem of history is to be adequate and complete.

¶ *75. Dasein's Historicality, and World-history*

Proximally and for the most part, Dasein understands itself in terms of that which it encounters in the environment and that with which it is circumspectively concerned. This understanding is not just a bare taking cognizance of itself, such as accompanies all Dasein's ways of behaving. Understanding signifies one's projecting oneself upon one's current possibility of Being-in-the-world; that is to say, it signifies existing as this possibility. Thus understanding, as common sense, constitutes even the inauthentic existence of the "they". When we are with one another in public, our everyday concern does not encounter just equipment and work; it likewise encounters what is 'given' along with these: 'affairs', undertakings, incidents, mishaps. The 'world' belongs to everyday trade and traffic as the soil from which they grow and the arena where they are displayed. When we are with one another in public, the Others are encountered in activity of such a kind that one is 'in the swim' with it 'oneself'.

One is acquainted with it, discusses it, encourages it, combats it, retains it, and forgets it, but one always does so primarily with regard to *what* is getting done and *what* is 'going to come of it' [*was* . . . "herausspringt"]. We compute the progress which the individual Dasein has made—his stoppages, readjustments, and 'output'; and we do so proximally in terms of that with which he is concerned—its course, its status, its changes, its availability. No matter how trivial it may be to allude to the way in which Dasein is understood in everyday common sense, ontologically this understanding is by no means transparent. But in that case, why should not Dasein's 'connectedness' be defined in terms of what it is concerned with, and what it 'Experiences'? Do not equipment and work and every thing which Dasein dwells alongside, belong to 'history' too? If not, is the historizing of history just the isolated running-off of 'streams of Experience' in individual subjects?

Indeed history is neither the connectedness of motions in the alterations of Objects, nor a free-floating sequence of Experiences which 'subjects' have had. Does the historizing of history then pertain to the way subject and Object are 'linked together'? Even if one assigns [zuweist] historizing to the subject-Object relation, we then have to ask what kind of Being belongs to this linkage as such, if this is what basically 'historizes'. The thesis of Dasein's historicality does not say that the worldless subject is historical, but that what is historical is the entity that exists as Being-in-the-world. *The historizing of history is the historizing of Being-in-the-world.* Dasein's historicality is essentially the historicality of the world, which, on the basis of ecstatico-horizontal temporality, belongs to the temporalizing of that temporality. In so far as Dasein exists factically, it already encounters that which has been discovered within-the-world. *With the existence of historical Being-in-the-world, what is ready-to-hand and what is present-at-hand have already, in every case, been incorporated into the history of the world.* Equipment and work—for instance, books—have their 'fates'; buildings and institutions have their history. And even Nature is historical. It is *not* historical, to be sure, in so far as we speak of 'natural history';[ix] but Nature is historical as a countryside, as an area that has been colonized or exploited, as a battlefield, or as the site of a cult. These entities within-the-world *are* historical as such, and their history does not signify something 'external' which merely accompanies the 'inner' history of the 'soul'. We call such entities "the *world-historical*". Here we must notice that the expression 'world-history' which we have chosen and which is here understood ontologically, has a double signification. The expression signifies, for one thing, the historizing of the world in its essential existent unity with Dasein. At the same time, we have here in view the 'historizing' within-the-world of what is ready-to-hand and present-at-hand, in so far as entities within-the-world are, in every case, discovered with the factically existent world. The historical world is factical only as the world of entities within-the-world. That which 'happens' with equipment and work as such has its own character of movement, and this character has been completely obscure up till now. When, for instance, a ring gets 'handed over' to someone and 'worn', this is a kind of Being in which it does not simply suffer changes of location. The movement of historizing in which something 'happens to something' is not to be grasped in terms of motion as change of location. This holds for all world-historical 'processes' and events, and even, in a certain manner, for 'natural catastrophes'. Quite apart from the fact that if we were to follow up the problem of the ontological structure of world-historical historizing, we would necessarily be transgressing the limits of our theme, we can refrain from this all the more because the very aim of this exposition is to lead us face to face with the ontological enigma of the movement of historizing in general.

We need only delimit that phenomenal range which we necessarily must also have in view ontologically when we talk of Dasein's historicality. The transcendence of the world has a temporal foundation; and by reason of this, the world-historical is, in every case, already 'Objectively' there in the historizing of existing Being-in-the-world, *without being grasped historiologically*. And because factical Dasein, in falling, is absorbed in that with which it concerns itself, it understands its history world-historically in the first instance. And because, further, the ordinary understanding of Being understands 'Being' as presence-at-hand without further differentiation, the Being of the world-historical is experienced and interpreted in the sense of something present-at-hand which comes along, has presence, and then disappears. And finally, because the meaning of Being in general is held to be something simply self-evident, the question about the kind of Being of the world-historical and about the movement of historizing in general has 'really' just the barren circumstantiality of a verbal sophistry.

Everyday Dasein has been dispersed into the many kinds of things which daily 'come to pass'. The opportunities and circumstances which concern keeps 'tactically' awaiting in advance, have 'fate' as their outcome. In terms of that with which inauthentically existing Dasein concerns itself, it first computes its history. In so doing, it is driven about by its 'affairs'. So if it wants to come to itself, it must first *pull itself together*[1] from the *dispersion* and *disconnectedness* of the very things that have 'come to

---

[1] '*zusammenholen*'. The older editions have 'z u s a m m e n h o l e n'.

pass'; and because of this, it is only then that there at last arises from the horizon of the understanding which belongs to inauthentic historicality, the *question* of how one is to establish a 'connectedness' of Dasein if one does so in the sense of 'Experiences' of a subject—Experiences which are 'also' present-at-hand. The possibility that this horizon for the question should be the dominant one is grounded in the irresoluteness which goes to make up the essence of the Self's in-constancy.

We have thus pointed out the *source* of the question of the 'connectedness' of Daein in the sense of the unity with which Experiences are linked together between birth and death. At the same time, the origin of this question betrays that it is an inappropriate one if we are aiming at a primordial existential Interpretation of Dasein's totality of historizing. On the other hand, despite the predominance of this 'natural' horizon for such questions, it becomes explicable why Dasein's authentic historicality— fate and repetition—looks as if it, least of all, could supply the phenomenal basis for bringing into the shape of an ontologically grounded problem what is at bottom intended in the question of the 'connectedness' of life.

This question does not ask how Dasein gains such a unity of connectedness that the sequence of 'Experiences' which has ensued and is still ensuing can subsequently be linked together; it asks rather in which of its own kinds of Being Dasein *loses itself in such a manner[1] that it must, as it were, only subsequently pull itself together out of its dispersal, and think up for itself a unity in which that "together" is embraced.* Our lostness in the "they" and in the world-historical has earlier been revealed as a fleeing in the face of death. Such fleeing makes manifest that Being-*towards*-death is a basic attribute of care. Anticipatory resoluteness brings this Being-towards-death into authentic existence. The historizing of this resoluteness, however, is the repetition of the heritage of possibilities by handing these down to oneself in anticipation; and we have Interpreted this historizing as authentic historicality. Is perhaps the whole of existence stretched along in this historicality in a way which is primordial and not lost, and which has no need of connectedness? The Self's resoluteness against the inconstancy of distraction, is in itself a *steadiness which has been stretched along* —the steadiness with which Dasein as fate 'incorporates' into its existence birth and death and their 'between', and holds them as thus 'incorporated', so that in such constancy Dasein is indeed in a moment of vision for what is world-historical in its current Situation.[2] In the fateful repetition

---

[1] '. . . *verliert es sich so . . .*' The older editions have '. . . *verliert des sich nicht so . . .*'

[2] 'Die Entschlossenheit des Selbst gegen die Unständigkeit der Zerstreuung ist in sich selbst die *erstreckte Stätigkeit,* in der das Dasein als Schicksal Geburt und Tod in ihr "Zwischen" in seine Existenz "einbezogen" hält, so zwar, dass es in solcher Ständigkeit augenblicklich ist für das Welt-geschichtliche seiner jeweiligen Situation.' The noun

of possibilities that have been, Dasein brings itself back 'immediately'—that is to say, in a way that is temporally ecstatical—to what already has been before it. But when its heritage is thus handed down to itself, its 'birth' is *caught up into its existence* in coming back from the possibility of death (the possibility which is not to be outstripped), if only so that this existence may accept the thrownness of its own "there" in a way which is more free from Illusion.[1]

Resoluteness constitutes the *loyalty* of existence to its own Self. As resoluteness which is ready for *anxiety*, this loyalty is at the same time a possible way of revering the sole authority which a free existing can have —of revering the repeatable possibilities of existence. Resoluteness would be misunderstood ontologically if one were to suppose that it *would be* actual as 'Experience' only as long as the 'act' of resolving 'lasts'. In resoluteness lies the existentiell constancy which, by its very essence, has already anticipated [vorweggenommen] every possible moment of vision that may arise from it. As fate, resoluteness is freedom to *give up* some definite resolution, and to give it up in accordance with the demands of some possible Situation or other. The steadiness of existence is not interrupted thereby but confirmed in the moment of vision. This steadiness is not first formed either through or by the adjoining of 'moments' one to another; but these arise from the temporality of that repetition which is futurally in the process-of-having-been—a temporality which has *already been stretched along*.

In inauthentic historicality, on the other hand, the way in which fate has been primordially stretched along has been hidden. With the inconstancy of the they-self Dasein makes present its 'today'. In awaiting the next new thing, it has already forgotten the old one. The "they" evades choice. Blind for possibilities, it cannot repeat what has been, but only retains and receives the 'actual' that is left over, the world-historical that has been, the leavings, and the information about them that is present-at-hand. Lost in the making present of the "today", it understands the 'past' in terms of the 'Present'. On the other hand, the temporality of authentic historicality, as the moment of vision of anticipatory repetition,

---

'Stätigkeit', which we here translate as 'steadiness', may mean either 'continuity' or 'refractoriness'. Heidegger may have both senses in mind. Cf. our note 3, p. 475, H. 423 below.

[1] 'Mit diesem Sichüberliefern des Erbes aber ist dann die "Geburt" im Zurückkommen aus der unüberholbaren Möglichkeit des Todes *in die Existenz eingeholt*, damit diese freilich nur die Geworfenheit des eigenen Da illusionsfreier hinnehme.' Here as in H. 307 and perhaps in H. 302, Heidegger seems to be exploiting the double meaning of 'einholen' as 'to bring in' and 'to catch up with'. Dasein 'brings' its birth 'into' its existence by accepting its heritage of possibilities, and in this way it 'catches up with it'. Thus while death cannot be outstripped ('überholt'), birth can at least be 'caught up with' ('eingeholt').

deprives the "today" of its character *as present*,[1] and weans one from the conventionalities of the "they". When, however, one's existence is inauthentically historical, it is loaded down with the legacy of a 'past' which has become unrecognizable, and it seeks the modern. But when historicality is authentic, it understands history as the 'recurrence' of the possible, and knows that a possibility will recur only if existence is open for it fatefully, in a moment of vision, in resolute repetition.

The existential Interpretation of Dasein's historicality is constantly getting eclipsed unawares. The obscurities are all the harder to dispel when we have not disentangled the possible dimensions of the appropriate inquiry, and when everything is haunted by the *enigma* of *Being*, and, as has now been made plain, by that of *motion*.[2] Nevertheless, we may venture a projection of the ontological genesis of historiology as a science in terms of Dasein's historicality. This projection will serve to prepare us for the clarification of the task of destroying the history of philosophy historiologically—a clarification which is to be accomplished in what follows.ˣ

¶ *76. The Existential Source of Historiology in Dasein's Historicality.*

We need not discuss the Fact that historiology, like any science, is, as a kind of Being of Dasein, factically 'dependent' at any time on the 'prevailing world-view'. Beyond this, we must inquire into the ontological possibility of how the sciences have their source in Dasein's state of Being. This source is still not very transparent. In the context which lies before us, our analysis will acquaint us in outline with the existential source of historiology only to the extent of bringing still more plainly to light the historicality of Dasein and the fact that this historicality is rooted in temporality.

If Dasein's Being is in principle historical, then every factical science is always manifestly in the grip of this historizing. But historiology still has Dasein's historicality as its presupposition in its own quite special way.

This can be made plain, in the first instance, by the suggestion that historiology, as the science of Dasein's history, must 'presuppose' as its possible 'Object' the entity which is primordially historical. But history must not only *be*, in order that a historiological object may become accessible; and historiological cognition is not only historical, as a historizing way in which Dasein comports itself. Whether the *historiological disclosure of history* is factically accomplished or not, *its ontological structure is such that in itself this disclosure has its roots in the historicality of Dasein*. This is the connection we have in view when we talk of Dasein's historicality as the existential

[1] '. . . eine *Entgegenwärtigung* des Heute . . .'
[2] '. . . und in allem das *Rätsel* des *Seins* und, wie jetzt deutlich wurde, der *Bewegung* sein Wesen treibt.'

source of historiology. To cast light upon this connection signifies method-ologically that the *idea* of historiology must be projected ontologically in terms of Dasein's historicality. The issue here is not one of 'abstracting' the concept of historiology from the way something is factically done in the sciences today, nor is it one of assimilating it to anything of this sort. For what guarantee do we have in principle that such a factical procedure will indeed be properly representative of historiology in its primordial and authentic possibilities? And even if this should turn out to be the case—we shall hold back from any decision about this—then the concept could be 'discovered' in the Fact only by using the clue provided by the idea of historiology as one which we have already understood. On the other hand, the existential idea of historiology is not given a higher justification by having the historian affirm that his factical behaviour is in agreement with it. Nor does the idea become 'false' if he disputes any such agreement.

The idea of historiology as a science implies that the *disclosure* of historical entities is what it has seized upon as its own task. Every science is constituted primarily by thematizing. That which is familiar pre-scientifically in Dasein as disclosed Being-in-the-world, gets projected upon the Being which is specific to it. With this projection, the realm of entities is bounded off. The ways of access to them get 'managed' method-ologically, and the conceptual structure for interpreting them is outlined. If we may postpone the question of whether a 'history of the Present' is possible, and assign [zuweisen] to historiology the task of disclosing the 'past', then the historiological thematizing of history is possible only if, in general, the 'past' has in each case already been disclosed. Quite apart from the question of whether sufficient sources are available for the historiological envisagement of the past, the *way to it* must in general be *open* if we are to go back to it historiologically. It is by no means patent that anything of the sort is the case, or how this is possible.

But in so far as Dasein's Being is historical—that is to say, in so far as by reason of its ecstatico-horizonal temporality it is open in its character of "having-been"—the way is in general prepared for such thematizing of the 'past' as can be accomplished in existence. And because Dasein, *and only Dasein*, is primordially historical, that which historiological thematiz-ing presents as a possible object for research, must have the kind of Being of *Dasein which has-been-there*. Along with any factical Dasein as Being-in-the-world, there *is* also, in each case, world-history. If Dasein is there no longer, then the world too is something that has-been-there. This is not in conflict with the fact that, all the same, what was formerly ready-to-hand within-the-world does not yet pass away, but becomes something that one can, in a Present, come across 'historiologically' as something which has not passed away and which belongs to the world that has-been-there.

Remains, monuments, and records that are still present-at-hand, are *possible* 'material' for the concrete disclosure of the Dasein which has-been-there. Such things *can* turn into *historiological* material only because, in accordance with their own kind of Being, they have a *world-historical* character. And they *become* such material only when they have been understood in advance with regard to their within-the-world-ness. The world that has already been projected is given a definite character by way of an Interpretation of the world-historical material we have 're-ceived'. Our going back to 'the past' does not first get its start from the acquisition, sifting, and securing of such material; these activities pre-suppose *historical Being towards* the Dasein that has-been-there—that is to say, they presuppose the historicality of the historian's existence. This is the existential foundation for historiology as a science, even for its most trivial and 'mechanical' procedures.[xi]

If historiology is rooted in historicality in this manner, then it is from here that we must determine what the *object* of historiology 'really' is. The delimitation of the primordial theme of historiology will have to be carried through in conformity with the character of authentic historicality and its disclosure of "what-has-been-there"—that is to say, in conformity with repetition as this disclosure. In repetition the Dasein which has-been-there is understood in its authentic possibility which has been. The 'birth' of historiology from authentic historicality therefore signifies that in taking as our primary theme the historiological object we are projecting the Dasein which has-been-there upon its ownmost possibility of existence. Is historiology thus to have the *possible* for its theme? Does not its whole 'meaning' point solely to the 'facts'—to how something has factually been?

But what does it signify to say that Dasein is 'factual'? If Dasein is 'really' actual only in existence, then its 'factuality' is constituted pre-cisely by its resolute projection of itself upon a chosen potentiality-for-Being. But if so, that which authentically has-been-there 'factually' is the existentiell possibility in which fate, destiny, and world-history have been factically determined. Because in each case existence i s only as factically thrown, historiology will disclose the quiet force of the possible with greater penetration the more simply and the more concretely having-been-in-the-world is understood in terms of its possibility, and 'only' presented as such.

If historiology, which itself arises from authentic historicality, reveals by repetition the Dasein which has-been-there and reveals it in its possibility, then historiology has already made manifest the 'universal' in the once-for-all. The question of whether the object of historiology is just to put once-for-all 'individual' events into a series, or whether it also has 'laws' as its objects, is one that is radically mistaken. The theme of historiology is neither that which has happened just once for all nor something universal that floats above it, but the possibility which has been factically existent.[1] This possibility does not get repeated as such—that is to say, understood in an authentically historiological way—if it becomes perverted into the colourlessness of a supratemporal model. Only by historicality which is factical and authentic can the history of what has-been-there, as a resolute fate, be disclosed in such a manner that in repetition the 'force' of the possible gets struck home into one's factical existence—in other words, that it comes towards that existence in its futural character. The historicality of unhistoriological Dasein does not take its departure from the 'Present' and from what is 'actual' only today, in order to grope its way back from there to something that is past; and neither does historiology. Even *historiological* disclosure temporalizes itself *in terms of the future*. The '*selection*' of what is to become a possible object for historiology *has already been met with* in the factical existentiell *choice* of Dasein's historicality, in which historiology first of all arises, and in which alone it *is*.

The historiological disclosure of the 'past' is based on fateful repetition, and is so far from 'subjective' that it alone guarantees the 'Objectivity' of historiology. For the Objectivity of a science is regulated primarily in terms of whether that science can confront us with the entity which belongs to it as its theme, and can bring it, uncovered in the primordiality of its Being, to our understanding. In no science are the 'universal validity' of standards and the claims to 'universality' which the "they" and its common sense demand, *less* possible as criteria of 'truth' than in authentic historiology.

Only because in each case the central theme of historiology is the *possibility* of existence which has-been-there, and because the latter exists factically in a way which is world-historical, can it demand of itself that it takes its orientation inexorably from the 'facts'. Accordingly this research as factical has many branches and takes for its object the history of equipment, of work, of culture, of the spirit, and of ideas. As handing itself down, history is, in itself, at the same time and in each case always in an interpretedness which belongs to it, and which has a history of its own; so for the most part it is only through traditional history that

---

[1] 'Weder das nur einmalig Geschehene noch ein darüber schwebendes Allgemeines ist ihr Thema, sondern die faktisch existent gewesene Möglichkeit.'

historiology penetrates to what has-been-there itself. This is why concrete historiological research can, in each case, maintain itself in varying closeness to its authentic theme. If the historian 'throws' himself straightway into the 'world-view' of an era, he has not thus proved as yet that he understands his object in an authentically historical way, and not just 'aesthetically'. And on the other hand, the existence of a historian who 'only' edits sources, may be characterized by a historicality which is authentic.

Thus the very prevalence of a differentiated interest even in the most remote and primitive cultures, is in itself no proof of the authentic historicality of a 'time'. In the end, the emergence of a problem of 'historicism' is the clearest symptom that historiology endeavours to alienate Dasein from its authentic historicality. Such historicality does not necessarily require historiology. It is not the case that unhistoriological eras as such are unhistorical also.

The possibility that historiology in general can either be 'used' 'for one's life' or 'abused' in it, is grounded on the fact that one's life is historical in the roots of its Being, and that therefore, as factically existing, one has in each case made one's decision for authentic or inauthentic historicality. Nietzsche recognized what was essential as to the 'use and abuse of historiology for life' in the second of his studies "out of season" (1874), and said it unequivocally and penetratingly. He distinguished three kinds of historiology—the monumental, the antiquarian, and the critical—without explicitly pointing out the necessity of this triad or the ground of its unity. *The threefold character of historiology is adumbrated in the historicality of Dasein.* At the same time, this historicality enables us to understand to what extent these three possibilities must be united factically and concretely in any historiology which is authentic. Nietzsche's division is not accidental. The beginning of his 'study' allows us to suppose that he understood more than he has made known to us.

As historical, Dasein is possible only by reason of its temporality, and temporality temporalizes itself in the ecstatico-horizonal unity of its raptures. Dasein exists authentically as futural in resolutely disclosing a possibility which it has chosen. Coming back resolutely to itself, it is, by repetition, open for the 'monumental' possibilities of human existence. The historiology which arises from such historicality is 'monumental'. As in the process of having been, Dasein has been delivered over to its thrownness. When the possible is made one's own by repetition, there is adumbrated at the same time the possibility of reverently preserving the existence that has-been-there, in which the possibility seized upon has become manifest. Thus authentic historiology, as monumental, is

'antiquarian' too. Dasein temporalizes itself in the way the future and having
been are united in the Present. The Present discloses the "today" authentically, and of course as the moment of vision. But in so far as this "today"
has been interpreted in terms of understanding a possibility of existence
which has been seized upon—an understanding which is repetitive in
a futural manner—authentic historiology becomes a way in which the
"today" gets deprived of its character as present; in other words, it
becomes a way of painfully detaching oneself from the falling publicness
of the 'today'. As authentic, the historiology which is both monumental
and antiquarian is necessarily a critique of the 'Present'. Authentic
historicality is the foundation for the possibility of uniting these three
ways of historiology. But the *ground* on which authentic historiology is
founded is *temporality* as the existential meaning of the Being of care.

The existential-historical source of historiology may be presented
concretely by analysing the thematization which is constitutive for this
science. In historiological thematizing, the main point is the cultivation
of the hermeneutical Situation which—once the historically existent
Dasein has made its resolution—opens itself to the repetitive disclosure of
what has-been-there. The possibility and the structure of *historiological
truth* are to be expounded in terms of the *authentic disclosedness* ('truth') of
historical existence. But since the basic concepts of the historiological sciences
—whether they pertain to the Objects of these sciences or to the way in
which these are treated—are concepts of existence, the theory of the
humane science presupposes an existential Interpretation which has as
its theme the *historicality* of Dasein. Such an Interpretation is the constant
goal to which the researches of Wilhelm Dilthey seek to bring us closer,
and which gets illumined in a more penetrating fashion by the ideas of
Count Yorck von Wartenburg.

¶ 77. *The Connection of the Foregoing Exposition of the Problem of Historicality
with the Researches of Wilhelm Dilthey and the Ideas of Count Yorck*[1]

The analysis of the problem of history which we have just carried
through has arisen in the process of appropriating the labours of Dilthey.
It has been corroborated and at the same time strengthened, by the
theses of Count Yorck, which are found scattered through his letters to
him.[xii]

The image of Dilthey which is still widely disseminated today is that of
the 'sensitive' interpreter of the history of the spirit, especially the history

---

[1] In this section we have relaxed some of our usual conventions in view of the special
stylistic character of the quotations from Count Yorck and Heidegger's own minor
inconsistencies in punctuation. In particular, we shall now translate 'Historie' as 'History'
with a capital 'H', rather than as 'historiology.'

of literature, who 'also' endeavours to distinguish between the natural and the humane sciences, thereby assigning [zuweist] a distinctive role to the history of the latter group and likewise to 'psychology', then allowing the whole to merge together in a relativistic 'philosophy of life'. Considered superficially, this sketch is 'correct'. But the 'substance' eludes it, and it covers up more than it reveals.

We may divide Dilthey's researches schematically into three domains: studies on the theory of the humane sciences, and the distinction between these and the natural sciences; researches into the history of the sciences of man, society, and the state; endeavours towards a psychology in which the 'whole fact of man' is to be presented. Investigations in the theory of science, in historical science, and in psychological hermeneutics are constantly permeating and intersecting each other. Where any one point of view predominates, the others are the motives and the means. What looks like disunity and an unsure, 'haphazard' way of 'trying things out', is an elemental restlessness, the one goal of which is to understand 'life' philosophically and to secure for this understanding a hermeneutical foundation in terms of 'life itself'. Everything centres in psychology, in which 'life' is to be understood in the historical context of its development and its effects, and understood as the *way* in which man, as the possible *object* of the humane sciences, and *especially* as the *root* of these sciences, *is*. Hermeneutics is the way this understanding enlightens itself; it is also the methodology of historiology, though only in a derivative form.

In the contemporaneous discussions, Dilthey's own researches for laying the basis for the humane sciences were forced one-sidedly into the field of the theory of science; and it was of course with a regard for such discussions that his publications were often oriented in this direction. But the 'logic of the humane sciences' was by no means central for him—no more than he was striving in his 'psychology' 'merely' to make improvements in the positive science of the psychical.

Dilthey's friend, Count Yorck, gives unambiguous expression to Dilthey's ownmost philosophical tendency in the communications between them, when he alludes to '*our common interest in understanding historicality*' (italicized by the author).[xiii] Dilthey's researches are only now becoming accessible in their full scope; if we are to make them our own, we need the steadiness and concreteness of coming to terms with them in principle. This not the place [Ort] for discussing in detail the problems which moved him, or how he was moved by them.[xiv] We shall, however, describe in a provisional way some of Count Yorck's central ideas, by selecting characteristic passages from the letters.

In these communications, Yorck's own tendency is brought to life by the labours of Dilthey and his ways of formulating questions, and it shows itself when Yorck takes his stand as to the tasks of the discipline which is to lay the basis—analytical psychology. On Dilthey's Academy paper, 'Ideen über eine beschreibende und zergliedernde Psycholgie' (1894), he writes: 'It gets firmly laid down that the consideration of the Self is the primary means of knowing, and that the primary procedure of knowing is analysis. From this standpoint principles get formulated which are verified by their own findings. No progress is made towards critically breaking down constructive psychology and its assumptions, or towards explaining it and thus refuting it from within' (*Briefwechsel*, p. 177). '. . . your disregard for breaking things down critically (that is, for demonstrating their provenience psychologically, and carrying this out trenchantly in detail) is connected, in my opinion, with your conception of the theory of knowledge and with the position which you assign [zuweisen] to it' (p. 177). '. . . only a theory of knowledge gives the *explanation* for this inapplicability (the fact of it has been laid down and made plain). It has to render account for the adequacy of scientific methods; it has to provide the grounds for a doctrine of method, instead of having its methods taken —at a venture, I must say—from particular areas' (pp. 179 f.).

At bottom Yorck is demanding a logic that shall stride ahead of the sciences and guide them, as did the logic of Plato and Aristotle; and this demand includes the task of working out, positively and radically, the different categorial structures of those entities which *are* Nature and of those which *are* history (Dasein). Yorck finds that Dilthey's investigations *'put too little stress on differentiation generically between the ontical and the Historical'* (p. 191, italicized by the author). 'In particular, the procedure of comparison is claimed to be the method for the humane sciences. Here I disagree with you . . . Comparison is always aesthetic, and always adheres to the pattern of things. Windelband assigns [weist . . . zu] patterns to history. Your concept of the type is an entirely inward one. Here it is a matter of characteristics, not of patterns. For Windelband, history is a series of pictures, of individual patterns—an aesthetic demand. To the natural scientist, there remains, beside his science, as a kind of human tranquillizer, only aesthetic enjoyment. But your conception of history is that of a nexus of forces, of unities of force, to which the category of "pattern" is to be applicable only by a kind of transference' (p. 193).

In terms of his sure instinct for 'differentiating between the ontical and the Historical', Yorck knew how strongly traditional historical research still maintains itself in 'purely ocular ways of ascertaining' (p. 192), which are aimed at the corporeal and at that which has pattern.

'Ranke is a great ocularist, for whom things that have vanished can never become *actualities* . . . Ranke's whole tribe also provides the explanation for the way the material of history has been restricted to the political. Only the political is dramatic' (p. 60). 'The modifications which the course of time has brought appear unessential to me, and I should like to appraise this very differently. For instance, I regard the so-called Historical school as a mere sidestream within the same river-bed, and as representing only one branch of an old and thoroughgoing opposition. The name is somewhat deceptive. *That school was by no means a Historical one* (italicized by the author), but an antiquarian one, construing things aesthetically, while the great dominating activity was one of mechanical construction. Hence what it contributed methodologically—to the method of rationality—was only a general feeling' (pp. 68 f.).

'The genuine Philologus—he conceives of History as a cabinet of antiquities.[1] Where nothing is palpable—whither one has been guided only by a living psychical transposition—these gentlemen never come. At heart they are natural scientists, and they become sceptics all the more because experimentation is lacking. We must keep wholly aloof from all such rubbish, for instance, as how often Plato was in Magna Graecia or Syracuse. On this nothing vital depends. This superficial affectation which I have seen through critically, winds up at last with a big question-mark and is put to shame by the great Realities of Homer, Plato, and the New Testament. Everything that is actually Real becomes a mere phantom when one considers it as a "Thing in itself"—when it does not get Experienced' (p. 61). 'These "scientists" stand over against the powers of the times like the over-refined French society of the revolutionary period. Here as there, formalism, the cult of the form; the defining of relationship is the last word in wisdom. Naturally, thought which runs in this direction has its own history, which, I suppose, is still unwritten. The groundlessness of such thinking and of any belief in it (and such thinking, epistemologically considered, is a metaphysical attitude) is a Historical product' (p. 39). 'It seems to me that the ground-swells evoked by the principle of eccentricity,[2] which led to a new era more than four hundred years ago, have become exceedingly broad and flat; that our knowledge has progressed to the point of cancelling itself out; that man has withdrawn so far from himself that he no longer sees himself at all. The "modern man" —that is to say, the post-Renaissance man—is ready for burial' (p. 83). 'On the other hand, "All History that is truly alive and not just reflecting a tinge of life, is a critique' (p. 19). 'But historical knowledge is, for the best

---

[1] Yorck is here referring to Karl Friedrich Hermann, whose *Geschichte und System der platonischen Philosophie* (Heidelberg, 1839) he has been reading.
[2] Presumably the eccentricity of the planetary motions as described by Kepler, following on the work of Copernicus.

part, knowledge of the hidden sources' (p. 109). 'With history, what makes a spectacle and catches the eye is not the main thing. The nerves are invisible, just as the essentials in general are invisible. While it is said that "if you were quiet, you would be strong", the variant is also true that "if you are quiet, you will perceive—that is, understand" ' (p. 26). 'And then I enjoy the quietude of soliloquizing and communing with the spirit of history. This spirit is one who did not appear to Faust in his study, or to Master Goethe either. But they would have felt no alarm in making way for him, however grave and compelling such an apparition might be. For he is brotherly, akin to us in another and deeper sense than are the denizens of bush and field. These exertions are like Jacob's wrestling— a sure gain for the wrestler himself. Indeed this is what matters first of all' (p. 133).

Yorck gained his clear insight into the basic character of history as 'virtuality' from his knowledge of the character of the Being which human Dasein itself possesses, not from the Objects of historical study, as a theory of science would demand. 'The entire psycho-physical datum is not one that *is* (Here "Being" equals the Being-present-at-hand of Nature. —Author's remark) but one that lives; this is the germinal point of historicality.[1] And if the consideration of the Self is directed not at an abstract "I" but at the fulness of my Self, it will find me Historically determined, just as physics knows me as cosmically determined. Just as I am Nature, so I am history . . .' (p. 71). And Yorck, who saw through all bogus 'defining of relationships' and 'groundless' relativisms, did not hesitate to draw the final conclusion from his insight into the historicality of Dasein. 'But, on the other hand, in view of the inward historicality of self-consciousness, a systematic that is divorced from History is methodologically inadequate. Just as physiology cannot be studied in abstraction from physics, neither can philosophy from historicality—especially if it is a critical philosophy. Behaviour and historicality are like breathing and atmospheric pressure; and—this may sound rather paradoxical—it seems to me methodologically like a residue from metaphysics not to historicize one's philosophizing' (p. 69). 'Because to philosophize is to live, there is, in my opinion (do not be alarmed!), a philosophy of history—but who would be able to write it? Certainly it is not the sort of thing it has hitherto been taken to be, or the sort that has so far been attempted; you have declared yourself incontrovertibly against all that. Up till now, the question has been formulated in a way which is false, even impossible; but this is not the only way of formulating it. Thus there is no longer any

---

[1] Yorck's text reads as follows: 'Das die gesammte psychophysische Gegebenheit nicht ist sondern lebt, ist der Keimpunkt der Geschichtlichkeit'. Heidegger plausibly changes 'Das' to '. . . dass' in the earlier editions, to 'Dass' in the later ones.

actual philosophizing which would not be Historical. The separation between systematic philosophy and Historical presentation is essentially incorrect' (p. 251). 'That a science can become practical is now, of course, the real basis for its justification. But the mathematical *praxis* is not the only one. The practical aim of our standpoint is one that is pedagogical in the broadest and deepest sense of the word. Such an aim is the soul of all true philosophy, and the truth of Plato and Aristotle' (pp. 42 f.). 'You know my views on the possibility of ethics as a science. In spite of that, this can always be done a little better. For whom are such books really written ? Registries about registries! The only thing worthy of notice is what drives them to come from physics to ethics' (p. 73). 'If philosophy is conceived as a manifestation of life, and not as the coughing up of a baseless kind of thinking (and such thinking appears baseless because one's glance gets turned away from the basis of consciousness), then one's task is as meagre in its results as it is complicated and arduous in the obtaining of them. Freedom from prejudice is what it presupposes, and such freedom is hard to gain' (p. 250).

It is plain from Yorck's allusion to the kind of difficulty met with in such investigations, that he himself was already on the way to bringing within our grasp categorially the Historical as opposed to the ontical (ocular), and to raising up 'life' into the kind of scientific understanding that is appropriate to it. The aesthetico-mechanistic way of thinking[1] 'finds verbal expression more easily than does an analysis that goes behind intuition, and this can be explained by the wide extent to which words have their provenience in the ocular . . . On the other hand, that which penetrates into the basis of vitality eludes an exoteric presentation; hence all its terminology is symbolic and ineluctable, not intelligible to all. Because philosophical thinking is of a special kind, its linguistic expression has a special character' (pp. 70 f.). 'But you are acquainted with my liking for paradox, which I justify by saying that paradoxicality is a mark of truth, and that the *communis opinio* is nowhere in the truth, but is like an elemental precipitate of a halfway understanding which makes generalizations; in its relationship to truth it is like the sulphurous fumes which the lightning leaves behind. Truth is never an element. To dissolve elemental public opinion, and, as far as possible, to make possible the moulding of individuality in seeing and looking, would be a pedagogical

---

[1] Yorck is here discussing Lotze and Fechner, and suggesting that their 'rare talent for expression' was abetted by their 'aesthetico-mechanistic way of thinking', as Heidegger calls it. The reader who is puzzled by the way Yorck lumps together the 'aesthetic', the 'mechanistic', and the 'intuitive', should bear in mind that here the words 'aesthetic' and 'intuition' are used in the familiar Kantian sense of immediate sensory experience, and that Yorck thinks of 'mechanism' as falling entirely within the 'horizon' of such experience without penetrating beyond it.

task for the state. Then, instead of a so-called public conscience—instead of this radical externalization—individual consciences—that is to say, consciences—would again become powerful' (pp. 249 f.).

If one has an interest in understanding historicality, one is brought to the task of working out a 'generic differentiation between the ontical and the Historical'. *The fundamental aim of the 'philosophy of life'*[1] is tied up with this. Nevertheless, the formulation of the question needs to be radicalized *in principle.* How are we to get historicality into our grasp philosophically as distinguished from the ontical, and conceive it 'categorially', except by bringing both the 'ontical' and the 'Historical' into a *more primordial unity,* so that they can be compared and distinguished? But that is possible only if we attain the following insights: (1) that the question of historicality is an *ontological* question about the state of Being of historical entities; (2) that the question of the ontical is the *ontological* question of the state of Being of entities other than Dasein— of what is present-at-hand in the widest sense; (3) that the ontical is only *one* domain of entities. The idea of Being embraces both the 'ontical' and the 'Historical'. It is *this idea* which must let itself be 'generically differentiated'.

It is not by chance that Yorck calls those entities which are not historical, simply the "ontical". This just reflects the unbroken dominion of the traditional ontology, which, as derived from the *ancient* way of formulating the question of Being, narrows down the ontological problematic in principle and holds it fact. The problem of differentiating between the ontical and the Historical cannot be worked out as a problem for research unless *we have made sure in advance what is the clue to it,* by clarifying, through fundamental ontology, the question of the meaning of Being in general.[xv] Thus it becomes plain in what sense the preparatory existential-temporal analytic of Dasein is resolved to foster the spirit of Count Yorck in the service of Dilthey's work.

4

---

[1] ' "*Lebensphilosophie*" '. The word is italicized only in the later editions.

VI

TEMPORALITY AND WITHIN-TIME-NESS AS THE SOURCE OF THE ORDINARY CONCEPTION OF TIME

¶ *78. The Incompleteness of the Foregoing Temporal Analysis of Dasein*

To demonstrate that temporality is constitutive for Dasein's Being and how it is thus constitutive, we have shown that historicality, as a state-of-Being which belongs to existence, is 'at bottom' temporality. We have carried through our Interpretation of the temporal character of history without regard for the 'fact' that all historizing runs its course 'in time'. Factically, in the everyday understanding of Dasein, all history is known merely as that which happens 'within-time'; but throughout the course of our existential-temporal analysis of historicality, this understanding has been ruled out of order. If the existential analytic is to make Dasein ontologically transparent in its very facticity, then the factical 'ontico-temporal' interpretation of history must also be *explicitly* given its due. It is all the more necessary that the time 'in which' entities are encountered should be analysed *in principle*, since not only history but natural processes too are determined 'by time'. But still more elemental than the circumstance that the 'time factor' is one that occurs in the *sciences* of history and Nature, is the Fact that before Dasein does any thematical research, it 'reckons with time' and regulates itself *according to it*. And here again what remains decisive is Dasein's way of 'reckoning with its time'—a way of reckoning which precedes any use of measuring equipment by which time can be determined. The reckoning is prior to such equipment, and is what makes anything like the use of clocks possible at all.

In its factical existence, any particular Dasein either 'has the time' or 'does not have it'. It either 'takes time' for something or 'cannot allow any time for it'. Why does Dasein 'take time', and why can it 'lose' it? Where does it take time from? How is this time related to Dasein's temporality?

Factical Dasein takes time into its reckoning, without any existential understanding of temporality. Reckoning with time is an elemental kind of behaviour which must be clarified before we turn to the question of what it means to say that entities are 'in time'. All Dasein's behaviour is to be Interpreted in terms of its Being—that is, in terms of temporality. We must show how Dasein *as* temporality temporalizes a kind of behaviour which relates itself to time by taking it into its reckoning. Thus our previous characterization of temporality is not only quite incomplete in that we have not paid attention to all the dimensions of this phenomenon; it also is defective in principle because something like world-time, in the rigorous sense of the existential-temporal conception of the world, belongs to temporality itself. We must come to understand how this is possible and why it is necessary. Thus the 'time' which is familiar to us in the ordinary way—the time 'in which' entities occur—will be illuminated, and so will the within-time-ness of these entities.

Everyday Dasein, the Dasein which takes time, comes across time proximally in what it encounters within-the-world as ready-to-hand and present-at-hand. The time which it has thus 'experienced' is understood within the horizon of that way of understanding Being which is the closest for Dasein; that is, it is understood as something which is itself somehow present-at-hand. How and why Dasein comes to develop the ordinary conception of time, must be clarified in terms of its state-of-Being as concerning itself with time—a state-of-Being with a temporal foundation. The ordinary conception of time owes its origin to a way in which primordial time has been levelled off. By demonstrating that this is the source of the ordinary conception, we shall justify our earlier Interpretation of temporality as *primordial time.*

In the development of this ordinary conception, there is a remarkable vacillation as to whether the character to be attributed to time is 'subjective' or 'Objective'. Where time is taken as being in itself, it gets allotted pre-eminently to the 'soul' notwithstanding. And where it has the kind of character which belongs to 'consciousness', it still functions 'Objectively'. In Hegel's Interpretation of time both possibilities are brought to the point where, in a certain manner, they cancel each other out. Hegel tries to define the connection between 'time' and 'spirit' in such a manner as to make intelligible why the spirit, as history, 'falls into time'. We seem to be in accord with Hegel in the *results* of the Interpretation we have given for Dasein's temporality and for the way world-time belongs to it. But because our analysis differs in principle from his in its approach, and because its orientation is precisely the *opposite* of his in that it aims at fundamental ontology, a short presentation of Hegel's way of taking the relationship between time and spirit may serve to make plain our existential-ontological Interpretation of Dasein's temporality, of world-time. and of the source of the ordinary conception of time, and may settle this in a provisional manner.

The question of whether and how time has any 'Being', and of why and in what sense we designate it as 'being', cannot be answered until we have shown to what extent temporality itself, in the totality of its temporalizing makes it possible for us somehow to have an understanding of Being and address ouselves to entities. Our chapter will be divided as follows: Dasein's temporality, and our concern with time (Section 79); the time with which we concern ourselves, and within-time-ness (Section 80); within-time-ness and the genesis of the ordinary conception of time (Section 81); a comparison of the existential-ontological connection of temporality, Dasein, and world-time, with Hegel's way of taking the relation between time and spirit (Section 82); the existential-temporal analytic of Dasein and the question of fundamental ontology as to the meaning of Being in general (Section 83).

¶ *79. Dasein's Temporality, and our Concern with Time*

Dasein exists as an entity for which, in its Being, that Being is itself an *issue*. Essentially ahead of itself, it has projected itself upon its potentiality-for-Being *before* going on to any mere consideration of itself. In its projection it reveals itself as something which has been thrown. It has been thrownly abandoned to the 'world', and falls into it concernfully.[1] As care—that is, as existing in the unity of the pro-jection which has been fallingly thrown—this entity has been disclosed as a "there". As being with Others, it maintains itself in an average way of interpreting—a way which has been Articulated in discourse and expressed in language. Being-in-the-world has always expressed *itself*, and as *Being alongside* entities encountered within-the-world, it constantly expresses *itself* in addressing itself to the very object of its concern and discussing it. The concern of circumspective common sense is grounded in temporality—indeed in the mode of a making-present which retains and awaits. Such concern, as concernfully reckoning up, planning, preventing, or taking precautions, always says (whether audibly or not) that something is to happen '*then*', that something else is to be attended to '*beforehand*', that what has failed or eluded us '*on that former occasion*' is something that we must '*now*' make up for.[2]

In the 'then', concern expresses itself as awaiting; in the 'on that former occasion', as retaining; in the 'now', as making present. In the 'then'— but mostly unexpressed—lies the 'now-not-yet'; that is to say, this is

---

[1] 'Geworfen der "Welt" überlassen, verfällt es besorgend an sie.'
[2] '. . . "*dann*"—soll das geschehen, "*zuvor*"—jenes seine Erledigung finden, "*jezt*"— das nachgeholt werden, was "*damals*" misslang und entging.' Notice that the German 'dann', unlike its English cognate 'then', is here thought of as having primarily a future reference.

spoken in a making-present which is either awaitingly retentive or awaitingly forgetful. In the 'on that former occasion' lurks the 'now-no-longer'. With this, retaining expresses itself as a making-present which awaits. The 'then' and the 'on that former occasion' are understood with regard to a 'now'; that is to say, making present has a peculiar importance. Of course it always temporalizes itself in a unity with awaiting and retaining, even if these may take the modified form of a forgetting which does not await anything; in the mode of such forgetting, temporality ensnares itself in the Present, which, in making present, says pre-eminently 'Now! Now!' That which concern awaits as what is closest to it, gets addressed in the 'forthwith' [im "sogleich"]; what has been made proximally available or has been lost is addressed in the 'just-now' [im "soeben"]. The horizon for the retaining which expresses itself in the 'on that former occasion' is the *'earlier'*; the horizon for the 'then' is the *'later on'* ('that which is to come'); the horizon for the 'now' is the *'today'*.

Every 'then', however, is, *as such*, a 'then, when . . .'; every 'on that former occasion' is an 'on that former occasion, when . . .'; every 'now' is a 'now that . . .'.[1] The 'now', the 'then', and the 'on that former occasion' thus have a seemingly obvious relational structure which we call *"datability"* [*Datierbarkeit*]. Whether this dating is factically done with respect to a 'date' on the calendar, must still be completely disregarded. Even without 'dates' of this sort, the 'now', the 'then', and the 'on that former occasion' have been dated more or less definitely. And even if the dating is not made more definite, this does not mean that the structure of datability is missing or that it is just a matter of chance.

Wherein is such datability grounded, and to what does it essentially belong? Can any more superfluous question indeed be raised? It is 'well known' that what we have in mind with the 'now that . . .' is a 'point of time'. The 'now' is time. Incontestably, the 'now that . . .', the 'then, when . . .', and the 'on that former occasion' are things that we understand. And we also understand in a certain way that these are all connected with 'time'. But that with this sort of thing one has 'time' itself in mind, and how this is possible, and what 'time' signifies—these are matters of which we have no conception in our 'natural' understanding of the 'now' and so forth. Is it indeed obvious, then, that something like the 'then', the 'now', and the 'on that former occasion', is something we 'understand without further ado', and 'quite naturally' bring to expression? Where do we get this 'now that . . .'? Have we found this sort of thing among entities within-the-world—among those that are present-at-hand? Manifestly not. Then

[1] 'Jedes "dann" aber ist *als solches* ein "dann, wann . . .", jedes "damals" ein "damals, als . . .", jedes "jetzt" ein "jetzt, da . . .".'

have we found it at all? Have we ever set ourselves to search for this and establish its character? We avail ourselves of it 'at any time' without having taken it over explicitly, and we constantly make use of it even though we do not always make utterances about it. Even in the most trivial, offhand kind of everyday talk ('It's cold', for instance) we also have in mind a 'now that . . .'. Why is it that when Dasein addresses itself to the objects of its concern, it also expresses a 'now that . . .', a 'then, when . . .', or an 'on that former occasion, when . . .', even though it does so mostly without uttering it? First, because in addressing itself to something interpretatively, it expresses *itself* too; that is to say, it expresses its *Being alongside* the ready-to-hand—a Being which understands circumspectively and which uncovers the ready-to-hand and lets it be encountered. And secondly, because this very addressing and discussing—which interprets *itself* also—is based upon a *making-present* and is possible only as such.[1]

The making-present which awaits and retains, interprets *itself*. And this in turn is possible only because, as something which in itself is ecstatically open, it has in each case been disclosed to itself already and can be Articulated in the kind of interpretation which is accompanied by understanding and discourse. *Because temporality is ecstatico-horizonally constitutive for the clearedness of the "there", temporality is always primordially interpretable in the "there" and is accordingly familiar to us.* The making-present which interprets itself—in other words, that which has been interpreted and is addressed in the 'now'—is what we call 'time'. This simply makes known to us that temporality—which, as ecstatically open, is recognizable—is familiar, proximally and for the most part, only as interpreted in this concernful manner.[1] But while time is 'immediately' intelligible and recognizable, this does not preclude the possibility that primordial temporality as such may remain unknown and unconceived, and that this is also the case with the source of the time which has been expressed—a source which temporalizes itself in that temporality.

The fact that the structure of datability belongs essentially to what has been interpreted with the 'now', the 'then', and the 'on that former occasion', becomes the most elemental proof that what has thus been interpreted has originated in the temporality which interprets itself. When we say 'now', we always understand a 'now *that* so and

---

[1] 'Das sich auslegende Gegenwärtigen, das heisst das im "jetzt" angesprochene Ausgelegte nennen wir "Zeit". Darin bekundet sich lediglich, dass die Zeitlichkeit, als ekstatisch offene kenntlich, zunächst und zumeist nur in dieser besorgenden Ausgelegtheit bekannt ist.' The older editions have 'ausgesprochene' ('expressed') rather than 'angesprochene' ('addressed'); the comma after 'Zeitlichkeit' is missing, and the particle 'ja' appears just before 'zunächst'.

so...'[1] though we do not say all this. Why? Because the "now" interprets a *making-present* of entities. In the 'now that...' lies the *ecstatical* character of the Present. The *datability* of the 'now', the 'then', and the 'on that former occasion', *reflects* the *ecstatical* constitution of temporality, and is *therefore* essential for the time itself that has been expressed. The structure of the datability of the 'now', the 'then', and the 'on that former occasion', is evidence that these, *stemming from temporality, are themselves time.* The interpretative expressing of the 'now', the 'then', and the 'on that former occasion', is the most primordial way of *assigning a time.*[2] In the ecstatical unity of temporality—which gets understood along with datability, but unthematically and without being recognizable as such—Dasein has already been disclosed to itself as Being-in-the-world, and entities within-the-world have been discovered along with it; because of this, interpreted time has already been given a dating in terms of those entities which are encountered in the disclosedness of the "there": "now that—the door slams"; "now that—my book is missing", and so forth.[3]

The horizons which belong to the 'now', the 'then', and the 'on that former occasion', all have their source of *ecstatical* temporality; by reason of this, these horizons too have the character of datability as 'today, when...', 'later on, when...', and 'earlier, when...'[4]   4

If awaiting understands itself in the 'then' and interprets itself, and thereby, as making present, understands that which it awaits, and understands this in terms of its 'now', then the 'and-now-not-yet' is already implied when we 'assign' a 'then'. The awaiting which makes present understands the 'until-then'. This 'until-then' is Articulated by interpretation: it 'has its time' as the "*in-between*", which likewise has a relationship of datability. This relationship gets expressed in the 'during-this' or 'meanwhile' ["während dessen..."]. The 'during' can itself be Articulated awaitingly by concern, by assigning some more 'thens'. The 'until-then' gets divided up by a number of 'from-then-till-thens', which, however, have been 'embraced' beforehand in awaitingly projecting the primary 'then'. 'Enduring' gets Articulated in the understanding one has

---

[1] ' "Jetzt"-sagend verstehen wir immer auch schon, ohne es mitzusagen, ein "—*da das* und das..."'

[2] '...dass diese *vom Stamme der Zeitlichkeit, selbst Zeit sind.* Das auslegende Aussprechen der "jetzt", "dann" und "damals" ist die ursprünglichste *Zeitangabe.*' The earlier editions have 'sie' instead of 'diese'. (While we have generally tried to reserve the verb 'assign' for verbs such as 'verweisen' and 'zuweisen', it is convenient to use it in this chapter to translate such expressions as 'angeben', 'Angabe', and 'Zeitangabe'.)

[3] '...jetzt, da—die Tür schlägt; jetzt, da—mir das Buch fehlt, und dergleichen.' While the phrase 'jetzt' da...' ordinarily means 'now that...', Heidegger here seems to be interpreting it with an illusion to the 'da' which we have usually translated as 'there'—the 'da' of 'Dasein'.

[4] ' "Heute, wo...", "Späterhin, wann..." und "Früher, da...".'

of the 'during' when one awaits and makes present.[1] This lasting[Dauern], in turn, is the time which is manifest in temporality's interpretation of *itself*; in our concern this time thus gets currently, but unthematically, understood as a 'span' ["Spanne"]. The making-present which awaits and retains, lays 'out' a 'during' *with a span*, only because it has thereby disclosed *itself* as the way in which its historical temporality has been ecstatically *stretched along*, even though it does not know itself as this.[2] But here a further peculiarity of the time which has been 'assigned' shows itself. Not only does the 'during' have a span; but every 'now', 'then', and 'on that former occasion' has, with its datability-structure, its own spanned character, with the width of the span varying: 'now'—in the intermission, while one is eating, in the evening, in summer; 'then'—at breakfast, when one is taking a climb, and so forth.

The concern which awaits, retains, and makes present, is one which 'allows itself' so much time; and it assigns itself this time concernfully, even without determining the time by any specific reckoning, and before any such reckoning has been done. Here time dates itself in one's current mode of allowing oneself time concernfully; and it does so in terms of those very matters with which one concerns oneself environmentally, and which have been disclosed in the understanding with its accompanying state-of-mind —in terms of what one does 'all day long'. The more Dasein is awaitingly absorbed in the object of its concern and forgets itself in not awaiting itself, the more does even the time which it 'allows' itself remain *covered up* by this way of 'allowing'. When Dasein is 'living along' in an everyday concernful manner, it just never understands itself as running along in a Continuously enduring sequence of pure 'nows'. By reason of this covering up, the time which Dasein allows itself has gaps in it, as it were. Often we do not bring a 'day' together again when we come back to the time which we have 'used'. But the time which has gaps in it does not go to pieces in this lack-of-togetherness, which is rather a mode of that temporality which has already been disclosed and *stretched along* ecstatically. The manner in which the time we have 'allowed' 'runs its course', and the way in which concern more or less explicitly assigns itself that time, can be properly explained as phenomena only if, on the one hand, we avoid

---

[1] 'Mit dem gewärtigend-gegenwärtigenden Verstehen des "während" wird das "Währen" artikuliert.' 'Währen' of course means 'enduring' in the sense of lasting or continuing, not in that of 'suffering' or 'tolerating'.

[2] 'Das gewärtigend-behaltende Gegenwärtigen legt nur deshalb ein *gespanntes* "während" "aus", weil es dabei *sich* als die ekstatische *Erstrecktheit* der geschichtlichen Zeitlichkeit, wenngleich als solche unerkannt, erschlossen ist.' Our translation of '*gespanntes*' as '*with a span*' preserves the connection with 'Spanne' but misses the connotation of 'tenseness', which Heidegger clearly has in mind elsewhere (e.g. H. 261 f., 374) and is surely suggesting here. The pun on 'auslegen' ('interpret') and 'legt . . . "aus" ' ('lays "out" ') also disappears in translation.

the theoretical 'representation' of a Continuous stream of "nows", and if, on the other hand, the possible ways in which Dasein assigns itself time and allows itself time are to be conceived of as determined primarily in terms of *how Dasein, in a manner corresponding to its current existence, 'has' its time.*

In an earlier passage authentic and inauthentic existing have been characterized with regard to those modes of the temporalizing of temporality upon which such existing is founded. According to that characterization, the irresoluteness of inauthentic existence temporalizes itself in the mode of a making-present which does not await but forgets. He who is irresolute understands himself in terms of those very closest events and be-fallings which he encounters in such a making-present and which thrust themselves upon him in varying ways. Busily losing *himself* in the object of his concern, he *loses his time* in it too. Hence his characteristic way of talking—'I have no time'. But just as he who exists inauthentically is constantly losing time and never 'has' any, the temporality of authentic existence remains distinctive in that such existence, in its resoluteness, never loses time and 'always has time'. For the temporality of resoluteness has, with relation to its Present, the character of a *moment of vision*. When such a moment makes the Situation authentically present, this making-present does not itself take the lead, but is *held* in that future which is in the process of having-been. One's existence in the moment of vision temporalizes itself as something that has been stretched along in a way which is fatefully whole in the sense of the authentic historical *constancy* of the Self. This kind of temporal existence has its time *for* what the Situation demands of it, and it has it 'constantly'. But resoluteness discloses the "there" in this way only as a Situation. So if he who is resolute encounters anything that has been disclosed, he can never do so in such a way as to lose his time on it irresolutely.

The "there" is disclosed in a way which is grounded in Dasein's own temporality as ecstatically stretched along, and with this disclosure a 'time' is allotted to Dasein; only because of this can Dasein, as factically thrown, 'take' its time and lose it.

As something disclosed, Dasein exists factically in the way of *Being with Others*. It maintains itself in an intelligibility which is public and average. When the 'now that . . .' and the 'then when . . .' have been interpreted and expressed in our everyday Being with one another, they will be understood in principle, even though their dating is unequivocal only within certain limits. In the 'most intimate' Being-with-one-another of several people, they can say '*now*' and say it 'together', though each of them gives a different date to the 'now' which he is saying: "now that this or that has come to pass . . ." The 'now' which anyone expresses is always said in the publicness of Being-in-the-world with one another. Thus the time which any Dasein has currently interpreted and expressed has as such already been *given a public character* on the basis of that Dasein's ecstatical Being-in-the-world. In so far, then, as everyday concern understands itself in terms of the 'world' of its concern and takes its 'time', it does *not* know this 'time' *as its own*, but concernfully *utilizes* the time which 'there is' ["es gibt"]—the time with which *"they"* reckon. Indeed the publicness of 'time' is all the more compelling, the more *explicitly* factical Dasein *concerns* itself with time in specifically taking it into its reckoning.

¶ *80. The Time with which we Concern Ourselves, and Within-time-ness*

So far we have only had to understand provisionally how Dasein, as grounded in temporality, is, in its very existing, concerned with times and how, in such interpretative concern, time makes itself public for Being-in-the-world. But the sense in which time '*is*' if it is of the kind which is public and has been expressed, remains completely undefined, if indeed such time can be considered as *being* at all. Before we can make any decision as to whether public time is 'merely subjective' or 'Objectively actual', or neither of these, its phenomenal character must first be determined more precisely.

When time is made public, this does not happen just occasionally and subsequently. On the contrary, because Dasein, as something ecstatico-temporal, *is* already disclosed, and because understanding and interpretation both belong to existence, time has already made itself public in concern. One directs oneself *according to it,* so that it must somehow be the sort of thing which Everyman can come across.

Although one can concern oneself with time in the manner which we have characterized—namely, by dating in terms of environmental events—this always happens basically within the horizon of that kind of concern with time which we know as astronomical and calendrical *time-reckoning.* Such reckoning does not occur by accident, but has its existential-onto-logical necessity in the basic state of Dasein as care. Because it is essential to Dasein that it exists fallingly as something thrown, it interprets its time concernfully by way of time-reckoning. *In this,* the 'real' *making-public* of time gets temporalized, so that we must say that *Dasein's thrownness is the reason why 'there is' time publicly.*[1] If we are to demonstrate that public time has its source in factical temporality, and if we are to assure ourselves that this demonstration is as intelligible as possible, the time which has been interpreted in the temporality of concern must first be characterized,

---

[1] '*In ihr* zeitigt sich die "eigentliche" *Veröffentlichung* der Zeit, sodass gesagt werden muss: *die Geworfenheit des Daseins ist der Grund dafür, dass es öffentlich Zeit "gibt".*' Heidegger's quotation marks around 'gibt' suggest an intentional pun which would permit the alternative translation: '. . . *the reason why Dasein "gives" time publicly.*'

if only in order to make clear that the essence of concern with time does *not* lie in the application of numerical procedures in dating. Thus in time-*reckoning*, what is decisive from an existential-ontological standpoint is not to be seen in the quantification of time but must be conceived more primordially in terms of the temporality of the Dasein which reckons with time.

'Public time' turns out to be the kind of time 'in which' the ready-to-hand and the present-at-hand within-the-world are encountered. This requires that these entities which are not of the character of Dasein, shall be called entities *"within-time"*. The Interpretation of within-time-ness gives us a more primordial insight into the essence of 'public time' and likewise makes it possible to define its 'Being'.

The Being of Dasein is care. This entity exists fallingly as something that has been thrown. Abandoned to the 'world' which is discovered with its factical "there", and concernfully submitted to it, Dasein awaits its potentiality-for-Being-in-the-world; it awaits it in such a manner that it 'reckons' *on* and 'reckons' *with* whatever has an *involvement* for the sake of this potentiality-for-Being—an involvement which, in the end, is a distinctive one.[1] Everyday circum*spective* Being-in-the-world needs the *possibility of sight* (and this means that it needs brightness) if it is to deal concernfully with what is ready-to-hand within the present-at-hand. With the factical disclosedness of Dasein's world, Nature has been uncovered for Dasein. In its thrownness Dasein has been surrendered to the changes of day and night. Day with its brightness gives it the possibility of sight; night takes this away.

Dasein awaits with circumspective concern the possibility of sight, and it understands itself in terms of its daily work; in thus awaiting and understanding, it gives its time with the 'then, when it dawns . . .'[2] The 'then' with which Dasein concerns itself gets dated in terms of something which is connected with getting bright, and which is connected with it in the closest kind of environmental involvement—namely, the rising of the sun. "Then, when the sun rises, it is *time for* so and so." Thus Dasein dates the time which it must take, and dates it in terms of something it encounters within the world and within the horizon of its abandonment to the world —in terms of something encountered as having a distinctive involvement for its circumspective potentiality-for-Being-in-the-world. Concern makes use of the 'Being-ready-to-hand' of the sun, which sheds forth light and warmth. The sun dates the time which is interpreted in concern. In terms of this dating arises the 'most naural' measure of time—the day.

4

---

[1] '. . . dass es *mit* dem und *auf* das "rechnet", womit es umwillen dieses Seinkönnens eine am Ende ausgezeichnete *Bewandtnis* hat.'

[2] '. . . mit dem "dann, wann es tagt" . . .'

And because the temporality of that Dasein which must take its time is finite, its days are already numbered. Concernful awaiting takes precaution to define the 'thens' with which it is to concern itself—that is, to divide up the day. And the 'during-the-daytime' makes this possible. This dividing-up, in turn, is done with regard to that by which time is dated—the journeying sun. Sunset and midday, like the sunrise itself, are distinctive 'places' which this heavenly body occupies. Its regularly recurring passage is something which Dasein, as thrown into the world and giving itself time temporalizingly, takes into its reckoning. Dasein historizes *from day to day* by reason of its way of interpreting time by dating it—a way which is adumbrated in its thrownness into the "there".

This dating of things in terms of the heavenly body which sheds forth light and warmth, and in terms of its distinctive 'places' in the sky, is a way of assigning time which can be done in our Being with one another 'under the same sky', and which can be done for 'Everyman' at any time in the same way, so that within certain limits everyone is proximally agreed upon it. That by which things are thus dated is available environmentally and yet not restricted to the world of equipment with which one currently concerns oneself. It is rather the case that in the world the environing Nature and the public environment are always discovered along with it.[ii] This public dating, in which everyone assigns himself his time, is one which everyone can 'reckon' on simultaneously; it uses a publicly available *measure*. This dating reckons with time in the sense of a *measuring of time*; and such measuring requires something by which time is to be measured —namely, a clock. This implies that *along with the temporality of Dasein as thrown, abandoned to the 'world', and giving itself time, something like a 'clock' is also discovered—that is, something ready-to-hand which in its regular recurrence has become accessible in one's making present awaitingly.* The Being which has been thrown and is alongside the ready-to-hand is grounded in temporality. Temporality is the reason for the clock. As the condition for the possibility that a clock is factically necessary, temporality is likewise the condition for its discoverability. For while the course of the sun is encountered along with the discoveredness of entities within-the-world, it is only by making it present in awaitingly retaining, and by doing so in a way which interprets itself, that dating in terms of what is ready-to-hand environmentally in a public way is made possible and is also required.

Dasein has its basis in temporality, and the 'natural' clock which has already been discovered along with Dasein's factical thrownness furnishes the first motivation for the production and use of clocks which will be somewhat more handy; it also makes this possible. Indeed it does this in such a manner that these 'artificial' clocks must be 'adjusted' to that 'natural' one if the time which is primarily discoverable in the natural clock is to be made accessible in its turn.

Before describing the chief features in the development of time-reckoning and the use of clocks in their existential-ontological meaning, we must first characterize more completely the time with which we are concerned when we measure it. If the time with which we concern ourselves is 'really' made public only when it gets measured, then if public time is to be accessible in a way which has been phenomenally unveiled, we must have access to it by following up the way in which that which has been dated shows itself when dated in this 'reckoning' manner.

When the 'then' which interprets itself in concernful awaiting gets dated, this dating includes some such statement as "then—when it dawns—it is *time for* one's daily work". The time which is interpreted in concern is already understood as a time for something. The current 'now that so and so . . .' is as *such* either *appropriate* or *inappropriate*. Not only is the 'now' (and so too any mode of interpreted time) a 'now that . . .' which is essentially datable; but as such it has essentially, at the same time, the structure of appropriateness or inappropriateness. Time which has been interpreted has by its very nature the character of 'the time for something' or 'the wrong time for something'.[1] When concern makes present by awaiting and retaining, time is understood in relation to a "for-which";[2] and this in turn is ultimately tied up with a "for-the-sake-of-which" of Dasein's potentiality-for-Being. With this "in-order-to" relation, the time which has been made public makes manifest that structure with which we have earlier[iii] become acquainted as *significance*, and which constitutes the worldhood of the world. As 'the time for something', the time which has been made public has essentially a world-character. Hence the time which makes itself public in the temporalizing of temporality is what we designate as *"world-time"*. And we designate it thus not because it is *present-at-hand* as an entity *within-the-world* (which it can never be), but because it belongs *to the world* [zur Welt] in the sense which we have Interpreted existential-ontologically. In the following pages we must show how the essential relations of the world-structure (the *'in-order-to'*, for example) are connected with public time (the 'then, when . . .', for example) by reason of the ecstatico-horizonal constitution of temporality. Only now, in any case, can the time with which we concern ourselves be completely characterized as to its structure: it is datable, spanned, and public; and as having this structure, it belongs to the world itself. Every 'now', for

---

[1] '. . . den Charakter der "Zeit zu . . ." bzw. der "Unzeit für . . ."'

[2] '. . . ein Wozu . . .' Here English idiom calls for the expression 'for-which' rather than 'towards-which', though the latter expression has served us fairly well in similar context) such as those cited in Heidegger's note iii below. (See also our note 1, p. 109, H. 78 above.)

instance, which is expressed in a natural everyday manner, has this kind of structure, and is understood as such, though pre-conceptually and unthematically, when Dasein concernfully allows itself time.

The disclosedness of the natural clock belongs to the Dasein which exists as thrown and falling; and in this disclosedness factical Dasein has at the same time already given a distinctive *public character* to the time with which it concerns itself. As time-reckoning is perfected and the use of clocks becomes more refined, this making-public gets enhanced and strengthened. We shall not give here a historiological presentation of the historical evolution of time-reckoning and the use of clocks, with all its possible variations. We must rather ask in an existential-ontological way what mode of the temporalizing of Dasein's temporality becomes manifest in the *direction* which the development of time-reckoning and clock-using has taken. When this question is answered, there must arise a more primordial understanding of the fact that the *measurement of time*—and this means also the explicit making-public of time as an object of concern—is grounded *in the temporality* of Dasein, and indeed in a quite definite temporalizing of that temporality.

Comparison shows that for the 'advanced' Dasein the day and the presence of sunlight no longer have such a special function as they have for the 'primitive' Dasein on which our analysis of 'natural' time-reckoning has been based; for the 'advanced' Dasein has the 'advantage' of even being able to turn night into day. Similarly we no longer need to glance explicitly and immediately at the sun and its position to ascertain the time. The manufacture and use of measuring-equipment of one's own permits one to read off the time directly by a clock produced especially for this purpose. The "what o'clock is it?" is the 'what time is it?' Because the clock—in the sense of that which makes possible a public way of time-reckoning—must be regulated by the 'natural' clock, even the use of clocks as equipment is based upon Dasein's temporality, which, with the disclosedness of the "there", first makes possible a dating of the time with which we concern ourselves; this is a fact, even if it is covered up when the time is read off. Our understanding of the *natural* clock develops with the advancing discovery of *Nature*, and instructs us as to new possibilities for a kind of time-measurement which is relatively independent of the day and of any explicit observation of the sky.

But in a certain manner even 'primitive' Dasein makes itself independent of reading off the time directly from the sky, when instead of ascertaining the sun's position it measures the shadow cast by some entity available at any time. This can happen in the first instance in the simplest form of the ancient 'peasant's clock'. Everyman is constantly accompanied by a shadow; and in the shadow the sun is encountered with respect to its changing presence at different places. In the daytime, shadows have different lengths which can be paced off 'at any time'. Even if individuals differ in the lengths of their bodies and feet, the *relationship* between them remains constant within certain limits of accuracy. Thus, for example, when one is concerned with making an appointment, one designates the time publicly by saying, 'When the shadow is so many feet long, then we shall meet yonder.' Here in Being with one another within the rather narrow boundaries of an environment which is very close to us, it is tacitly presupposed that the 'locations' at which the shadow gets paced off are at the same latitude. This clock is one which Dasein does not have to carry around with it; in a certain manner Dasein itself is the clock.

The public sundial, in which the line of a shadow is counterposed to the course of the sun and moves along a numbered track, needs no further description. But why is it that at the position which the shadow occupies on the dial we always find something like time? Neither the shadow nor the divided track is time itself, nor is the spatial relationship between them. Where, then, is the time, which we thus read off directly not only on the 'sundial' but also on any pocket watch?

What does "reading off the time" signify? 'Looking at the clock' does indeed amount to more than observing the changes in some item of equipment which is ready-to-hand, and following the positions of a pointer. When we use a clock in ascertaining what o'clock it is, *we say*— whether explicitly or not—"It is *now* such and such an hour and so many minutes; *now* is the time for . . ." or "there is still time enough *now* until . . .". Looking at the clock is based on taking our time, and is guided by it. What has already shown itself in the most elementary time-reckoning here becomes plainer: when we look at the clock and regulate ourselves *according to the time*, we are essentially *saying* "*now*". Here the "now" has in each case already been understood and *interpreted* in its full structural content of datability, spannedness, publicness, and worldhood. This is so 'obvious' that we take no note of it whatsoever; still less do we know anything about it explicitly.

Saying "now", however, is the discursive Articulation of a *making-present* which temporalizes itself in a unity with a retentive awaiting. The dating which is performed when one uses a clock, turns out to be a distinctive way in which something present-at-hand is made present. Dating does not simply relate to something present-at-hand; this kind of relating has itself the character of *measuring*. Of course the number which we get by measuring can be read off immediately. But this implies that when a stretch is to be measured, we understand that our standard is, in a way, contained in it; that is, we determine the frequency of its *presence* in that stretch. Measuring is constituted temporally when a standard which has presence is made present in a stretch which has presence. The idea of a standard implies unchangingness; this means that for everyone at any time the standard, in its stability, must be present-at-hand. When the time with which one concerns oneself is dated by *measuring*, one interprets it by looking at something present-at-hand and making it present—something which would not become accessible as a standard or as something measured except by our making it present in this distinctive manner. Because the making-present of something having presence has a special priority in dating by measuring, the measurement in which one reads off the time by the clock also expresses itself with special emphasis in the "now". Thus when *time* is *measured*, it is *made public* in such a way that it is encountered on each occasion and at any time for everyone as 'now and now and now'. This time which is 'universally' accessible in clocks is something that we come across as a *present-at-hand multiplicity of "nows"*, so to speak, though the measuring of time is not directed thematically towards time as such.

The temporality of factical Being-in-the-world is what primordially makes the disclosure of space possible; and in each case spatial Dasein has—out of a "yonder" which has been discovered—allotted itself a "here" which is of the character of Dasein. Because of all this the time with which Dasein concerns itself in its temporality is, as regards its datability, always bound up with some location of that Dasein. Time itself does not get linked to a location; but temporality is the condition for the possibility that dating may be bound up with the spatially-local in such a way that this may be binding for everyone as a measure. Time does not first get coupled with space; but the 'space' which one might suppose to be coupled with it, is encountered only on the basis of the temporality which concerns itself with time. Inasmuch as both time-reckoning and the clock are founded upon the *temporality* of Dasein, which is constitutive for this entity as historical, it may be shown to what extent, ontologically, the use of clocks is itself historical, and to what extent every clock as such 'has a history'.[iv]

8 The time which is made public by our measuring it, does not by any means turn into space because we date it in terms of spatial measurement-relations. Still less is what is existential-ontologically essential in the *measuring of time* to be sought in the fact that dated 'time' is determined numerically in terms of *spatial* stretches and in changes in the *location* of some spatial Thing. What is ontologically decisive lies rather in the specific kind of *making-present* which makes measurement possible. Dating

in terms of what is 'spatially' present-at-hand is so far from a spatializing of time that this supposed spatialization signifies nothing else than that an entity which is present-at-hand for everyone in every "now" is made present in its own presence. Measuring time is essentially such that it is necessary to say "now"; but in obtaining the measurement, we, as it were, forget what has been measured as such, so that nothing is to be found except a number and a stretch.

When Dasein concerns itself with time, then the less time it has to lose, the more 'precious' does that time become, and the *handier* the clock must be. Not only should we be able to assign the time 'more precisely', but the very determining of the time should claim as little time as possible, though it must still agree with the ways in which Others assign time.

Provisionally it was enough for us to point out the general 'connection' of the use of clocks with that temporality which takes its time. Just as the concrete analysis of astronomical time-reckoning in its full development belongs to the existential-ontological Interpretation of how Nature is discovered, the foundations of historiological and calendrical 'chronology' can be laid bare only within the orbit of the tasks of analysing historiological cognition existentially.[v]

The measurement of time gives it a marked public character, so that only in this way does what we generally call 'the time' become well known. In concern every Thing has 'its time' attributed to it. It 'has' it, and, like every entity within-the-world, it can 'have' it only because after all it is 'in time'. That time 'wherein' entities within-the-world are encountered, we know as "world-time". By reason of the ecstatico-horizonal constitution of the temporality which belongs to it, this has *the same* transcendence as the world itself. With the disclosedness of the world, world-time has been made public, so that every temporally concernful Being alongside entities *within-the-world* understands these entities circumspectively as encountered 'in time'.

The time 'in which' the present-at-hand is in motion or at rest is *not 'Objective'*, if what we mean by that is the Being-present-at-hand-in-itself of entities encountered within-the-world. But *just as little* is time '*subjective*', if by this we understand Being-present-at-hand and occurring in a 'subject'. *World-time is 'more Objective' than any possible Object because, with the disclosedness of the world, it already becomes 'Objectified' in an ecstatico-horizonal manner as the condition for the possibility of entities within-the-world.* Thus, contrary to Kant's opinion, one comes across world-time *just as immediately* in the physical as in the psychical, and not just roundabout by way of the psychical. 'Time' first shows itself in the sky—precisely where one comes across it when one regulates oneself naturally *according to it*—so that 'time' even becomes identified with the sky. |*World-time, moreover, is also 'more subjective' than any possible subject; for it is what first makes possible the Being of the factically existing Self—that Being which, as is now well understood, is the meaning of care.* 'Time' is present-at-hand neither in the 'subject' nor in the 'Object', neither 'inside' nor 'outside'; and it 'is' *'earlier'* than any subjectivity or Objectivity, because it presents the condition for the very possibility of this 'earlier'. Has it then any 'Being'? And if not, is it then a mere phantom, or is it something that has 'more Being' ["seiender"] than any possible entity? Any investigation which goes further in the direction of questions such as these, will come up against the same 'boundary' which has already set itself up to our provisional discussion of the connection between truth and Being.[vi] In whatever way these questions may be answered in what follows—or in whatever way they may first of all get primordially formulated—we must first understand that temporality, as ecstatico-horizonal, temporalizes something like *world*-time, which constitutes a within-time-ness of the ready-to-hand and the present-at-hand. But in that case such entities can never be designated as 'temporal' in the strict sense. Like every entity with a character other than that of Dasein, they are non-temporal, whether they Really occur, arise and pass away, or subsist 'ideally'.

If world-time thus belongs to the temporalizing of temporality, then it can neither be volatilized 'subjectivistically' nor 'reified' by a vicious 'Objectification'. These two possibilities can be avoided with a clear insight—not just by wavering insecurely between them—only if we can understand how everyday Dasein conceives of 'time' theoretically in terms of an understanding of time in the way which is closest to it, and if we can also understand to what extent this conception of time and the prevalence of this concept obstruct the possibility of our understanding in terms of primordial time what is meant by this conception—that is, the possibility of understanding it *as temporality*. The everyday concern which gives itself time, finds 'the time' in those entities within-the-world which are encountered 'in time'. So if we are to cast any light on the genesis of the ordinary conception of time, we must take within-time-ness as our point of departure.

¶ *81. Within-time-ness and the Genesis of the Ordinary Conception of Time*

How does something like 'time' first show itself for everyday circumspective concern? In what kind of concernful equipment-using dealings does it become explicitly accessible? If it has been made public with the disclosedness of the world, if it has always been already a matter of concern with the discoveredness of entities within-the-world—a discoveredness which belongs to the world's disclosedness—and if it has been a matter of such concern in so far as Dasein calculates time in reckoning with *itself*, then the kind of behaviour in which 'one' explicitly regulates oneself *according to time*, lies in the use of clocks. The existential-temporal meaning of this turns out to be a making-present of the travelling pointer. By *following* the positions of the pointer in a way which makes present, one *counts* them. This making-present temporalizes itself in the ecstatical unity of a retention which awaits. To *retain* the 'on that former occasion' and to retain it by *making it present*, signifies that in saying "now" one is open for the horizon of the earlier—that is, of the "now-no-longer". To *await* the 'then' by *making it present*, means that in saying "now" one is open for the horizon of the later—that is, of the "now-not-yet". *Time is what shows itself in such a making-present.* How then, are we to define the *time* which is manifest within the horizon of the circumspective concernful clock-using in which one takes one's time? *This time is that which is* **counted** *and which shows itself when one follows the travelling pointer, counting and making present in such a way that this making-present temporalizes itself in an ecstatical unity with the retaining and awaiting which are horizonally open according to the "earlier" and "later".* This, however, is nothing else than an existential-ontological interpretation of Aristotle's definition of "time": τοῦτο γάρ ἐστιν ὁ χρόνος, ἀριθμὸς κινήσεως κατὰ τὸ πρότερον καὶ ὕστερον. "For this is time: that which is counted in the movement which we encounter within the horizon of the earlier and later."[vii] This definition may seem strange at first glance; but if one defines the existential-ontological horizon from which Aristotle has taken it, one sees that it is as 'obvious' as it at first seems strange, and has been genuinely derived. The source of the time which is thus manifest does not become a problem for Aristotle. His Interpretation of time moves rather in the direction of the 'natural' way of understanding Being. Yet because this very understanding and the Being which is thus understood have in principle been made a problem for the investigation which lies before us, it is only *after* we have found a solution for the question of Being that the Aristotelian analysis of time can be Interpreted thematically in such a way that it may indeed gain some signification in principle, if the formulation of this question in ancient ontology, with all its critical limitations, is to be appropriated in a positive manner.[viii]

Ever since Aristotle all discussions of the concept of time have clung *in principle* to the Aristotelian definitions; that is, in taking time as their theme, they have taken it as it shows itself in circumspective concern. Time is what is 'counted'; that is to say, it is what is expressed and what we have in view, even if unthematically, when the *travelling* pointer (or the shadow) is made present. When one makes present that which is moved in its movement, one says 'now here, now here, and so on'. The "nows" are what get counted. And these show themselves 'in every "now"' as "nows" which will 'forthwith be no-longer-now' and "nows" which have 'just been not-yet-now'.[1] The world-time which is 'sighted' in this manner in the use of clocks, we call the *"now-time"* [*Jetzt-Zeit*].

When the concern which gives itself time reckons with time, the more 'naturally' it does so, the less it dwells at the expressed time as such; on the contrary, it is lost in the equipment with which it concerns itself, which in each case has a time of its own. When concern determines the time and assigns it, the more 'naturally' it does so—that is, the less it is directed towards treating time as such thematically—all the more does the Being which is alongside the object of concern (the Being which falls as it makes present) say unhesitatingly (whether or not anything is uttered) "now" or "then" or "on that former occasion". Thus for the ordinary understanding of time, time shows itself as a sequence of "nows" which are constantly 'present-at-hand', simultaneously passing away and coming along. Time is understood as a succession, as a 'flowing stream' of "nows", as the 'course of time'. *What is implied by such an interpretation of the world-time with which we concern ourselves?*

We get the answer if we go back to the *full* essential structure of world-time and compare this with that with which the ordinary understanding of time is acquainted. We have exhibited *datability* as the first essential item in the time with which we concern ourselves. This is grounded in the ecstatical constitution of temporality. The 'now' is essentially a "now that . . .". The datable "now", which is understood in concern even if we cannot grasp it as such, is in each case one which is either appropriate or inappropriate. *Significance* belongs to the structure of the "now". We have accordingly called the time with which we concern ourselves *"world*-time". In the ordinary interpretations of time as a sequence of "nows", both datability and significance are *missing*. These two structures are *not* permitted to 'come to the fore' when time is characterized as a pure succession. The ordinary interpretation of time *covers them up*. When these are covered up, the ecstatico-horizonal constitution of temporality, in which the datability and the significance of the "now" are grounded, gets *levelled off*. The "nows" get shorn of these relations, as it were; and, as thus shorn, they simply range themselves along after one another so as to make up the succession.

It is no accident that world-time thus gets levelled off and covered up by the way time is ordinarily understood. But just *because* the everyday

---

[1] 'Und diese zeigen sich "in jedem Jetzt" als "sogleich-nicht-mehr . . ." und "eben-noch-nicht-jetzt".' It is possible to read the hyphenated expressions in other ways.

interpretation of time maintains itself by looking solely in the direction of concernful common sense, and understands only what 'shows' itself within the common-sense horizon, these structures must escape it. That which gets counted when one measures time concernfully, the "now", gets co-understood in one's concern with the present-at-hand and the ready-to-hand. Now so far as *this* concern with time comes back to the time itself which has been co-understood, and in so far as it 'considers' that time, it sees the "nows" (which indeed are also somehow 'there') within the horizon of that understanding-of-Being by which this concern is itself constantly guided.[ix] Thus the "nows" are in a certain manner *co-present-at-hand*: that is, entities are encountered, *and so too* is the "now". Although it is not said explicitly that the "nows" are present-at-hand in the same way as Things, they still get 'seen' ontologically within the horizon of the idea of presence-at-hand. The "nows" *pass away*, and those which have passed away make up the past. The "nows" *come along*, and those which are coming along define the 'future'. The ordinary interpretation of world-time as now-time never avails itself of the horizon by which such things as world, significance, and datability can be made accessible. These structures necessarily remain covered up, all the more so because this covering-up is reinforced by the way in which the ordinary interpretation develops its characterization of time conceptually.

The sequence of "nows" is taken as something that is somehow present-at-hand, for it even moves 'in to time'.[1] We say: '*In* every "now" is now; *in* every "now" it is already vanishing.' In *every* "now" the "now" is now and therefore it constantly has presence *as something selfsame*, even though in every "now" another may be vanishing as it comes along.[2] Yet as *this* thing which changes, it simultaneously shows its own constant presence. Thus even Plato, who directed his glance in this manner at time as a sequence of "nows" arising and passing away, had to call time "the image of eternity": εἰκὼ δ' ἐπενόει κινητόν τινα αἰῶνος ποιῆσαι, καὶ διακοσμῶν ἅμα οὐρανὸν ποιεῖ μένοντος αἰῶνος ἐν ἑνὶ κατ' ἀριθμὸν ἰοῦσαν αἰώνιον εἰκόνα, τοῦτον ὃν δὴ χρόνον ὠνομάκαμεν.[x]

The sequence of "nows" is uninterrupted and has no gaps. No matter how 'far' we proceed in 'dividing up' the "now", it is always now. The continuity[3] of time is seen within the horizon of something which is indissolubly

---

[1] '... denn sie rückt selbst "in die Zeit".'

[2] 'In *jedem* Jetzt ist das Jetzt Jetzt, mithin ständig *als Selbiges* anwesend, mag auch in jedem Jetzt je ein anderes ankommend verschwinden.'

[3] 'Stetigkeit'. In the earlier editions this appears as 'Stätigkeit'—a spelling which we find on H. 390 f. and 398 in both earlier and later editions. It is not clear how seriously this 'correction' is to be taken here; but we have decided, with some hesitation, to translate 'Stätigkeit' as 'steadiness', and 'stetig' and 'Stetigkeit' as 'continuous' and 'continuity' respectively, saving 'Continuous' and 'Continuity' for 'kontinuierlich' and 'Kontinuität'.

present-at-hand. When one takes one's ontological orientation from something that is constantly present-at-hand, one either looks for the problem of the Continuity of time or one leaves this impasse alone. In either case the specific structure of world-time must remain *covered up*. Together with datability (which has an ecstatical foundation) it has been *spanned*. The spannedness of time is not to be understood in terms of the horizonal *stretching-along* of the ecstatical unity of that temporality which has made itself public in one's concern with time. The fact that in every "now", no matter how momentary, it is *in each case already* now, must be conceived in terms of something which is 'earlier' *still* and from which every "now" stems: that is to say, it must be conceived in terms of the ecstatical stretching-along of that temporality which is alien to any Continuity of something present-at-hand but which, for its part, presents the condition for the possibility of access to anything continuous[1] that is present-at-hand.

The principal thesis of the ordinary way of interpreting time—namely, that time is 'infinite'—makes manifest most impressively the way in which world-time and accordingly temporality in general have been levelled off and covered up by such an interpretation. It is held that time presents itself proximally as an uninterrupted sequence of "nows". Every "now", moreover, is already either a "just-now" or a "forthwith".[2] If in characterizing time we stick primarily and exclusively *to such a sequence*, then in principle neither beginning nor end can be found in it. Every last "now", *as "now"*, is always *already* a "forthwith" that is no longer [ein Sofort-nicht-mehr]; thus it is time in the sense of the "no-longer-now"—in the sense of the past. Every first "now" is a "just-now" that is not yet [ein Soeben-noch-nicht]; thus it is time in the sense of the "not-yet-now"—in the sense of the 'future'. Hence time is endless 'on both sides'. This thesis becomes possible only on the basis of an orientation *towards a free-floating "in-itself" of a course of "nows" which is present-at-hand*—an orientation in which the full phenomenon of the "now" has been covered up with regard to its datability, its worldhood, its spannedness, and its character of having a location of the same kind as Dasein's, so that it has dwindled to an unrecognizable fragment. If one directs one's glance towards Being-present-at-hand and not-Being-present-at-hand, and thus 'thinks' the sequence of "nows" through 'to the end', then an end can never be found. In *this* way of *thinking* time through to the end, one *must* always *think* more time; from this one infers that time *is* infinite.

But wherein are grounded this levelling-off of world-time and this

---

[1] '. . . Stetigen . . .' The earlier editions have 'Stätigen'.
[2] 'Jedes Jetzt ist auch schon ein Soeben bzw Sofort.'

covering-up of temporality? In the Being of Dasein itself, which we have, in a preparatory manner, Interpreted as *care*.[xi] Thrown and falling, Dasein is proximally and for the most part lost in that with which it concerns itself. In this lostness, however, Dasein's fleeing in the face of that authentic existence which has been characterized as "anticipatory resoluteness", has made itself known; and this is a fleeing which covers up. In this concernful fleeing lies a fleeing *in the face of* death—that is, a looking-away *from* the end of Being-in-the-world.[xii] This looking-away from it, is in itself a mode of that Being-*towards*-the-end which is ecstatically *futural*. The inauthentic temporality of everyday Dasein as it falls, must, as such a looking-away from finitude, fail to recognize authentic futurity and therewith temporality in general. And if indeed the way in which Dasein is ordinarily understood is guided by the "they", only so can the self-forgetful 'representation' of the 'infinity' of public time be strengthened. The "they" never dies because it cannot die; for death is in each case mine, and only in anticipatory resoluteness does it get authentically understood in an existentiell manner. Nevertheless, the "they", which never dies and which misunderstands Being-towards-the-end, gives a characteristic interpretation to fleeing in the face of death. To the very end 'it always has more time'. Here a way of "having time" in the sense that one can lose it makes itself known. 'Right now, this! then that! And that is barely over, when. . .'[1] Here it is not as if the finitude of time were getting understood; quite the contrary, for concern sets out to snatch as much as possible from the time which still keeps coming and 'goes on'. Publicly, time is something which everyone takes and can take. In the everyday way in which we are with one another, the levelled-off sequence of "nows" remains completely unrecognizable as regards its origin in the temporality of the individual Dasein. How is 'time' in its course to be touched even the least bit when a man who has been present-at-hand 'in time' no longer exists?[2] Time goes on, just as indeed it already 'was' when a man 'came into life'. The only time one knows is the public time which has been levelled off and which belongs to everyone—and that means, to nobody.

But just as he who flees in the face of death is pursued by it even as he evades it, and just as in turning away from it he must see it none the less, even the innocuous infinite sequence of "nows" which simply runs its course, imposes itself 'on' Dasein in a remarkably enigmatical way.[3]

---

[1] '. . . "jetzt erst noch das, dann das, und nur noch das und dann . . ." '

[2] 'Die nivellierte Jetztfolge bleibt völlig unkenntlich bezüglich ihrer Herkunft aus der Zeitlichkeit des einzelnen Daseins im alltäglichen Miteinander. Wie soll das auch "die Zeit" im mindesten in ihrem Gang berühren, wenn ein "in der Zeit" vorhandener Mensch nicht mehr existiert?'

[3] '. . . so legt sich auch die lediglich ablaufende, harmlose, unendliche Folge der Jetzt doch in einer merkwürdigen Rätselhaftigkeit "über" das Dasein.'

Why do we say that time *passes away*, when we do not say with *just as much* emphasis that it arises? Yet with regard to the pure sequence of "nows" we have as much right to say one as the other. When Dasein talks of time's *passing away*, it understands, in the end, more of time than it wants to admit; that is to say, the *temporality* in which world-time temporalizes itself has *not been completely closed off*, no matter how much it may get covered up. Our talk about time's passing-away gives expression to this 'experience': time does not let itself be halted. This 'experience' in turn is possible only because the halting of time is something that we want. Herein lies an inauthentic *awaiting* of 'moments'—an awaiting in which these are already *forgotten* as they glide by. The *awaiting* of inauthentic existence—the awaiting which forgets as it makes present—is the condition for the possibility of the ordinary experience of time's passing-away. Because Dasein is futural in the "ahead-of-itself", it must, in awaiting, understand the sequence of "nows" as one which *glides by* as it passes away. *Dasein knows fugitive time in terms of its 'fugitive' knowledge about its death.* In the kind of talk which emphasizes time's passing away, the *finite futurity* of Dasein's temporality is publicly reflected. And because even in talk about time's passing away, death can remain covered up, time shows itself as a passing-away 'in itself'.

But even in this pure sequence of "nows" which passes away in itself, primordial time still manifests itself throughout all this levelling off and covering up. In the ordinary interpretation, the stream of time is defined as an *irreversible* succession. Why cannot time be reversed? Especially if one looks exclusively at the stream of "nows", it is incomprehensible in itself why this sequence should not present itself in the reverse direction. The impossibility of this reversal has its basis in the way public time originates in temporality, the temporalizing of which is primarily futural and 'goes' to its end ecstatically in such a way that it 'is' already towards its end.

The ordinary way of characterizing time as an endless, irreversible sequence of "nows" which passes away, arises from the temporality of falling Dasein. *The ordinary representation of time has its natural justification.* It belongs to Dasein's average kind of Being, and to that understanding of Being which proximally prevails. Thus proximally and for the most part, even *history* gets understood *publicly* as happening *within-time*.[1] This interpretation of time loses its exclusive and pre-eminent justification only if it claims to convey the 'true' conception of time and to be able to prescribe the sole possible horizon within which time is to be Interpreted. On the contrary, it has emerged that *why and how world-time belongs to Dasein's*

---

[1] 'Daher wird auch zunächst und zumeist die *Geschichte öffentlich als innerzeitiges* Geschehen verstanden.' The words 'öffentlich als' are italicized only in the later editions.

temporality is intelligible only in terms of that temporality and its temporalizing. From temporality the full structure of world-time has been drawn; and only the Interpretation of this structure gives us the clue for 'seeing' at all that in the ordinary conception of time something has been covered up, and for estimating how much the ecstatico-horizonal constitution of temporality has been levelled off. This orientation by Dasein's temporality indeed makes it possible to exhibit the origin and the factical necessity of this levelling off and covering up, and at the same time to test the arguments for the ordinary theses about time.

On the other hand, within the horizon of the way time is ordinarily understood, *temporality is inaccessible in the reverse direction*.[1] Not only must the now-time be oriented primarily by temporality in the order of possible interpretation, but it temporalizes itself only in the inauthentic temporality of Dasein; so if one has regard for the way the now-time is derived from temporality, one is justified in considering temporality as the *time which is primordial*.

Ecstatico-horizonal temporality temporalizes itself *primarily* in terms of the *future*. In the way time is ordinarily understood, however, the basic phenomenon of time is seen in the "*now*", and indeed in that pure "now" which has been shorn in its full structure—that which they call the 'Present'. One can gather from this that there is in principle no prospect that *in terms of this kind of* "*now*" one can clarify the ecstatico-horizonal phenomenon of the *moment of vision* which belongs to temporality, or even that one can derive it thus. Correspondingly, the future as ecstatically understood—the datable and significant 'then'—does not coincide with the ordinary conception of the 'future' in the sense of a pure "now" which has not yet come along but is only coming along. And the concept of the past in the sense of the pure "now" which has passed away, is just as far from coinciding with the ecstatical "having-been"—the datable and significant 'on a former occasion'. The "now" is not pregnant with the "not-yet-now", but the Present arises from the future in the primordial ecstatical unity of the temporalizing of temporality.[xiii]

Although, proximally and for the most part, the ordinary experience of time is one that knows only 'world-time', it always gives it a *distinctive* relationship to 'soul' and 'spirit', even if this is still a far cry from a philosophical inquiry oriented explicitly and primarily towards the 'subject'. As evidence for this, two characteristic passages will suffice. Aristotle says: εἰ δὲ μηδὲν ἄλλο πέφυκεν ἀριθμεῖν ἢ ψυχὴ καὶ ψυχῆς νοῦς, ἀδύνατον εἶναι χρόνον ψυχῆς μὴ οὔσης. . . .[xiv] And Saint Augustine writes:

---

[1] 'Dagegen bleibt *umgekehrt* die Zeitlichkeit im Horizont des vulgären Zeitverständnisses *unzugänglich*.'

"*inde mihi visum est, nihil esse aliud tempus quam distentionem; sed cuius rei nescio; et mirum si non ipsius animi.*"[xv] Thus in principle even the Interpretation of Dasein as temporality does not lie beyond the horizon of the ordinary conception of time. And Hegel has made an explicit attempt to set forth the way in which time as ordinarily understood is connected with spirit. In Kant, on the other hand, while time is indeed 'subjective', it stands 'beside' the 'I think' and is not bound up with it.[xvi] The grounds which Hegel has explicitly provided for the connection between time and spirit are well suited to elucidate indirectly the foregoing Interpretation of Dasein as temporality and our exhibition of temporality as the source of world-time.

¶ *82. A Comparison of the Existential-ontological Connection of Temporality, Dasein, and World-time, with Hegel's Way of Taking the Relation between Time and Spirit*

History, which is essentially the history of spirit, runs its course 'in time'. Thus 'the development of history falls into time'.[xvii] [1] Hegel is not satisfied, however, with averring that the within-time-ness of spirit is a Fact, but seeks to understand how it is *possible* for spirit to fall into time, which is 'the non-sensuous sensuous'.[xviii] Time must be able, as it were, to take in spirit. And spirit in turn must be akin to time and its essence. Accordingly two points come up for discussion: (1) how does Hegel define the essence of time? (2) what belongs to the essence of spirit which makes it possible for it to 'fall into time'? Our answer to these questions will serve merely to *elucidate* our Interpretation of Dasein as temporality, and to do so by way of a comparison. We shall make no claim to give even a relatively full treatment of the allied problems in Hegel, especially since 'criticizing' him will not help us. Because Hegel's conception of time presents the most radical way in which the ordinary understanding of time has been given form conceptually, and one which has received too little attention, a comparison of this conception with the idea of temporality which we have expounded is one that especially suggests itself.

(a) Hegel's Conception of Time

When a philosophical Interpretation of time is carried out, it gets a 'locus in a system'; this locus may be considered as criterial for the basic way of treating time by which such an Interpretation is guided. In the

---

[1] 'Also fällt die Entwicklung der Geschichte in die Zeit".' Throughout this section it will be convenient to translate Hegel's verb 'fallen' by 'fall', though elsewhere we have largely pre-empted this for Heidegger's 'verfallen'. 'Verfallen' does not appear until H. 436, where we shall call attention to it explicitly. (In this quotation, as in several others, Heidegger has taken a few minor liberties with Hegel's text, which are too trivial for any special comment.)

'physics' of Aristotle—that is, in the context of an ontology of *Nature*—the ordinary way of understanding time has received its first thematically detailed traditional interpretation. 'Time', 'location', and 'movement' stand together. True to tradition, Hegel's analysis of time has its locus in the second part of his *Encyclopedia of the Philosophical Sciences*, which is entitled 'Philosophy of Nature'. The first portion of this treats of mechanics, and of this the first division is devoted to the discussion of 'space and time'. He calls these 'the abstract "outside-of-one-another" '.xix

Though Hegel puts space and time together, this does not happen simply because he has arranged them superficially one after the other: space, 'and time also'. 'Philosophy combats such an "also".' The transition from space to time does not signify that these are treated in adjoining paragraphs; rather 'it is space itself that makes the transition'.[1] Space 'is' time; that is, time is the 'truth' of space.xx If space is *thought* dialectically in that *which it is*, then according to Hegel this Being of space unveils itself as time. How must space be thought?

Space is 'the unmediated indifference of Nature's Being-outside-of-itself'.xxi This is a way of saying that space is the abstract multiplicity [Vielheit] of the points which are differentiable in it.[2] Space is not interrupted by these; but neither does it arise from them by way of joining them together. Though it is differentiated by differentiable points which are space themselves, space remains, for its part, without any differences. The differences themselves are of the same character as that which they differentiate. Nevertheless, the point, in so far as it differentiates anything in space, is the *negation* of space, though in such a manner that, as this negation, it itself remains in space; a point is space after all. The point does not lift itself out of space as if it were something of another character. Space is the "outside-of-one-another" of the multiplicity of points [Punktmannigfaltigkeit], and it is without any differences. But it is not as if space were a point; space is rather, as Hegel says, 'punctuality' ["Punktualität"]. xxii This is the basis for the sentence in which Hegel thinks of space in its truth—that is, as time: 'Negativity, which relates itself as point to space, and which develops in space its determinations as line and surface, is, however, just as much *for itself* in the sphere of Being-outside-of-itself, and so are its determinations therein, though while it is

---

[1] '. . . sondern "der Raum selbst geht über".'
[2] '. . . in ihm unterscheidbaren Punkte.' We have often translated 'unterscheiden' as 'distinguish' or 'discriminate', and 'Unterschied' as 'distinction' or 'difference', leaving 'differentiate' and 'differentiation' for such words as 'differenzieren' and 'Differenz', etc. In this discussion of Hegel, however, it will be convenient to translate 'unterscheiden' as 'differentiate', 'Unterschied' as 'difference', 'unterscheidbar' as 'differentiable', 'unterschiedslos' as 'without differences'. (We shall continue to translate 'gleichgültig as 'indifferent'.)

positing as in the sphere of Being-outside-of-itself, it appears indifferent as regards the things that are tranquilly side by side. As thus posited for itself, it is time.'[xxiii]

If space gets represented—that is, if it gets intuited immediately in the indifferent subsistence of its differences—then the negations are, as it were, simply given. But by such a representation, space does not get grasped in its Being. Only in thinking is it possible for this to be done—in thinking as the synthesis which has gone through thesis and antithesis and transmuted them. Only if the negations do not simply remain subsisting in their indifference but get transmuted—that is, only if they themselves get negated—does space get *thought* and thus grasped in its Being. In the negation of the negation (that is, of punctuality) the point posits itself *for itself* and thus emerges from the indifference of subsisting. As that which is posited for itself, it differentiates itself from this one and from that one: it is *no longer* this and *not yet* that. In positing itself for itself, it posits the succession in which it stands—the sphere of Being-outside-of-itself, which is by now the sphere of the negated negation. When punctuality as indifference gets transmuted, this signifies that it no longer remains lying in the 'paralysed tranquillity of space'. The point 'gives itself airs' before all the other points.[1] According to Hegel, this negation of the negation as punctuality is time. If this discussion has any demonstrable meaning, it can mean nothing else than that the positing-of-itself-for-itself of every point is a "now-here", "now-here", and so on. Every point 'is' posited for itself as a now-point. 'In time the point thus has actuality.' *That through which* each point, as this one here, can posit itself for itself, is in each case a "now". The "now" is the condition for the *possibility* of the point's positing itself for itself. This possibility-condition makes up the *Being* of the point, and Being is the same as having been thought. Thus in each case the pure thinking of punctuality—that is, of space—'thinks' the "now" and the Being-outside-of-itself of the "now"; because of this, space 'is' *time*. How is time itself defined?

'Time, as the negative unity of Being-outside-of-itself, is likewise something simply abstract, ideal. It is that Being which, in that it is, is not, and which, in that it is not, is: it is intuited becoming. This means that those differences which, to be sure, are simply momentary, transmuting themselves immediately, are defined as external, yet as external to themselves.'[xxiv] For this interpretation, time reveals itself as 'intuited becoming'. According to Hegel this signifies a transition from Being to nothing or from nothing to Being.[xxv] Becoming is both arising and passing away.

---

[1] 'Der Punkt "spreizt sich auf" gegenüber allen anderen Punkten.' The verb 'spreizen' means 'to spread apart'; but when used reflexively, as here, it takes on the more specific connotation of swaggering, giving oneself airs.

Either Being 'makes the transition', or not-Being does so. What does this mean with regard to time? The Being of time is the "now". Every "now", however, either 'now' is-*no*-longer, or now is-*not*-yct; so it can be taken also as not-Being.[1] Time is '*intuited*' becoming—that is to say, it is the transition which does not get thought but which simply tenders itself in the sequence of "nows". If the essence of time is defined as 'intuited becoming', then it becomes manifest that time is primarily understood in terms of the "now", and indeed in the very manner in which one comes across such a "now" in pure intuition.

No detailed discussion is needed to make plain that in Hegel's Interpretation of time he is moving wholly in the direction of the way time is ordinarily understood. When he characterizes time in terms of the "now", this presupposes that in its full structure the "now" remains levelled off and covered up, so that it can be intuited as something present-at-hand, though present-at-hand only 'ideally'.

That Hegel Interprets time in terms of this primary orientation by the "now" which has been levelled off, is evidenced by the following sentences: 'The "now" is monstrously privileged: it 'is' nothing but the individual "now"; but in giving itself airs, this thing which is so exclusive has already been dissolved, diffused, and pulverized, even while I am expressing it.'[xxvi] 'In Nature, moreover, where time is now, no "stable" ["bestehend"] difference between these dimensions' (past and future) 'ever comes about'.[xxvii] 'Thus in a positive sense one can say of time that only the Present is; the "before" and "after" are not; but the concrete Present is the result of the past and is pregnant with the future. Thus the true Present is eternity.'[xxviii]

If Hegel calls time 'intuited becoming', then neither arising nor passing away has any priority in time. Nevertheless, on occasion he characterizes time as the 'abstraction of consuming' ["Abstraktion des Verzehrens"]— the most radical formula for the way in which time is ordinarily experienced and interpreted.[xxix] On the other hand, when Hegel really defines "time", he is consistent enough to grant no such priority to consuming and passing away as that which the everyday way of experiencing time rightly adheres to; for Hegel can no more provide dialectical grounds for such a priority than he can for the 'circumstance' (which he has introduced as self-evident) that the "now" turns up precisely in the way the point posits itself for itself. So even when he characterizes time as "becoming", Hegel understands this "becoming" in an 'abstract' sense, which goes well beyond the representation of the 'stream' of time. Thus

---

[1] 'Das Sein der Zeit ist das Jetzt; sofern aber jedes Jetzt "jetzt" auch schon *nicht-mehr*- bzw. je jetzt zuvor noch-*nicht*-ist, kann es auch als Nichtsein gefasst werden.'

the most appropriate expression which the Hegelian treatment of time receives, lies in his defining it as "the *negation of a negation*" (that is, of punctuality). Here the sequence of "nows" has been formalized in the most extreme sense and levelled off in such a way that one can hardly go any farther.ˣˣˣ Only from the standpoint of this formal-dialectical conception of time can Hegel produce any connection between time and spirit.

(b) Hegel's Interpretation of the Connection between Time and Spirit

If Hegel can say that when spirit gets actualized, it accords with it to fall into time, with "time" defined as a negation of a negation, how has spirit itself been understood? The essence of spirit is the *concept*. By this Hegel understands not the universal which is intuited in a genus as the form of something thought, but rather the form of the very thinking which thinks itself: the conceiving of *oneself—as the grasping* of the not-I. Inasmuch as the grasping of the *not*-I presents a differentiation, there lies in the pure concept, as the grasping of *this* differentiation, a differentiation of the difference. Thus Hegel can define the essence of the spirit formally and apophantically as the negation of a negation. This 'absolute negativity' gives a logically formalized Interpretation of Descartes' "*cogito me cogitare rem*", wherein he sees the essence of the *conscientia*.

The concept is accordingly a self-conceiving way in which the Self has been conceived; as thus conceived, the Self is authentically as it can be— that is *free*.[1] 'The "*I*" is the pure concept itself, which as concept has come into *Dasein*.'ˣˣˣⁱ 'The "I", however, is this *initially* pure unity which relates itself to itself—not immediately, but in that it abstracts from all determinateness and content, and goes back to the freedom of its unrestricted self-equality.'ˣˣˣⁱⁱ Thus the "I" is '*universality*', but it is 'individuality'[2] *just as* immediately.

This negating of the negation is both that which is 'absolutely restless' in the spirit and also its *self-manifestation*, which belongs to its essence. The 'progression' of the spirit which actualizes itself in history, carries with it 'a principle of exclusion'.ˣˣˣⁱⁱⁱ In this exclusion, however, that which is excluded does not get detached from the spirit; it gets *surmounted*. The kind

---

[1] 'Der Begriff ist sonach die sich begreifende Begriffenheit des Selbst, als welche das Selbst eigentlich ist, wie es sein kann, das heisst *frei*.' The noun 'Begriffenheit' is of course derived from 'begriffen', the past participle of 'begreifen' ('to conceive' or 'to grasp'). 'Begriffen', however, may also be used when we would say that someone is 'in the process of' doing something. This would suggest the alternative translation: 'The concept is accordingly a self-conceiving activity of the Self—an activity of such a nature that when the Self performs it, it is authentically as it can be—namely, *free*.'

[2] ' "Einzelheit" '. We take this reading from Lasson's edition of Hegel, which Heidegger cites. The older editions of Heidegger's work have 'Einzelnheit'; the newer ones have 'Einzenheit'. Presumably these are both misprints.

of making-itself-free which overcomes and at the same time tolerates, is characteristic of the freedom of the spirit. Thus 'progress' never signifies a merely quantitative "more", but is essentially qualitative and indeed has the quality of spirit. 'Progression' is done knowingly and knows itself in its goal. In every step of its 'progress' spirit has to overcome 'itself' "as the truly malignant obstacle to that goal".xxxiv In its development spirit aims 'to reach its own concept'.xxxv The development itself is 'a hard, unending battle against itself'.xxxvi

Because the restlessness with which *spirit* develops in bringing itself to its concept is the *negation of a negation*, it accords with spirit, as it actualizes itself, to fall 'into *time*' as the immediate *negation of a negation*. For '*time* is the *concept* itself, which *is there* [*da ist*] and which represents itself to the consciousness as an empty intuition; because of this, spirit necessarily appears in time, and it appears in time as long as it does not *grasp* its pure concept—that is, as long as time is not annulled by it. Time is the pure Self-*external*, intuited, *not grasped* by the Self—the concept which is merely intuited.'xxxvii Thus *by its very essence* spirit necessarily appears in time. 'World-history is therefore, above all, the interpretation of spirit in time, just as in space the idea interprets itself as Nature.'xxxvii The 'exclusion' which belongs to the movement of development harbours in itself a relationship to not-Being. This is time, understood in terms of the "now" which gives itself airs.

Time is 'abstract' negativity. As 'intuited becoming', it is the differentiated self-differentiation which one comes across immediately; it is the concept which 'is there' ["daseiende"]—but this means present-at-hand. As something present-at-hand and thus external to spirit, time has no power over the concept, but the concept is rather 'the power of time'.xxxix

By going back to *the selfsameness of the formal structure which both spirit and time possess as the negation of a negation*, Hegel shows how it is possible for spirit to be actualized historically 'in time'. Spirit and time get disposed of with the very emptiest of formal-ontological and formal-apophantical abstractions, and this makes it possible to produce a kinship between them. But because time simultaneously gets conceived in the sense of a world-time which has been utterly levelled off, so that its origin remains completely concealed, it simply gets contrasted with spirit—contrasted as something that is present-at-hand. Because of this, spirit *must first of all fall* 'into time'. It remains obscure what indeed is signified ontologically by this 'falling' or by the 'actualizing' of a spirit which has power over time and really 'is' ["seienden"] outside of it. Just as Hegel casts little light on the source of the time which has thus been levelled off, he leaves totally unexamined the question of whether the way in which spirit is essentially constituted as the negating of a negation, is possible in any other manner than on the basis of primordial temporality.

We cannot as yet discuss whether Hegel's Interpretation of time and spirit and the connection between them is correct and rests on foundations which are ontologically primordial. But the very *fact that* a formal-dialectical 'construction' of this connection can be ventured *at all*, makes manifest that these are primordially akin. Hegel's 'construction' was prompted by his arduous struggle to conceive the 'concretion' of the spirit. He makes this known in the following sentence from the concluding chapter of his *Phenomenology of the Spirit*: 'Thus time appears as the very fate and necessity which spirit has when it is not in itself complete: the necessity of its giving self-consciousness a richer share in consciousness, of its setting in motion the *immediacy* of the *"in-itself"* (the form in which substance is in consciousness), or, conversely, of its realizing and making manifest the "in-itself" taken as the *inward* (and this is what first is *inward*) —that is, of vindicating it for its certainty of itself.'[xl]

Our existential analytic of Dasein, on the contrary, starts with the 'concretion' of factically thrown existence itself in order to unveil temporality as that which primordially makes such existence possible. 'Spirit' does not first fall into time, but it *exists as* the primordial *temporalizing* of temporality. Temporality temporalizes world-time, within the horizon of which 'history' can 'appear' as historizing within-time. 'Spirit' does not fall *into* time; but factical existence 'falls' as falling *from* primordial, authentic temporality.[1] This 'falling' ["Fallen"], however, has itself its existential possibility in a mode of its temporalizing—a mode which belongs to temporality.

¶ 83. The Existential-temporal Analytic of Dasein, and the Question of Fundamental Ontology as to the Meaning of Being in General

In our considerations hitherto, our task has been to Interpret the *primordial whole* of factical Dasein with regard to its possibilities of authentic and inauthentic existing, and to do so in an existential-ontological manner *in terms of its very basis. Temporality* has manifested itself as this basis and accordingly as the meaning of the Being of care. So that which our *preparatory* existential analytic of Dasein contributed *before* temporality was laid bare, has now been *taken back* into temporality as the primordial structure of Dasein's totality of Being. In terms of the possible ways in which primordial time can temporalize itself, we have provided the

---

[1] 'Der "Geist" fällt nicht *in* die Zeit, sondern: die faktische Existenz "fällt" als verfallende *aus* der ursprünglichen, eigentlichen Zeitlichkeit.' The contrast between Hegel's verb 'fallen' and Heidegger's 'verfallen' is obscured by our translating them both as 'fall'. Cf. our note 1, p. 480, H. 428.

'grounds' for those structures which were just 'pointed out' in our earlier treatment. Nevertheless, our way of exhibiting the constitution of Dasein's Being remains only *one way* which we may take. Our *aim* is to work out the question of Being in general. The *thematic* analytic of existence, however, first needs the light of the idea of Being in general, which must be clarified beforehand. This holds particularly if we adhere to the principle which we expressed in our introduction as one by which any philosophical investigation may be gauged: that philosophy "is universal phenomenological ontology, and takes its departure from the hermeneutic of Dasein, which, as an analytic of *existence*, has made fast the guiding-line for all philosophical inquiry at the point where it *arises* and to which it *returns*."[xii] This thesis, of course, is to be regarded not as a dogma, but rather as a formulation of a problem of principle which still remains 'veiled': can one provide *ontological* grounds for ontology, or does it also require an *ontical* foundation? and *which* entity must take over the function of providing this foundation?

The distinction between the Being of existing Dasein and the Being of entities, such as Reality, which do not have the character of Dasein, may appear very illuminating; but it is still only the *point of departure* for the ontological problematic; it is nothing with which philosophy may tranquillize itself. It has long been known that ancient ontology works with 'Thing-concepts' and that there is a danger of 'reifying consciousness'. But what does this "reifying" signify? Where does it arise? Why does Being get 'conceived' 'proximally' in terms of the present-at-hand *and not* in terms of the ready-to-hand, which indeed lies *closer* to us? *Why* does this reifying always keep coming back to exercise its dominion? What *positive* structure does the Being of 'consciousness' have, if reification remains inappropriate to it? Is the 'distinction' between 'consciousness' and 'Thing' sufficient for tackling the ontological problematic in a primordial manner? Do the answers to these questions lie along our way? And can we even *seek* the answer as long as the *question* of the meaning of Being remains unformulated and unclarified?

One can never carry on researches into the source and the possibility of the 'idea' of Being in general simply by means of the 'abstractions' of formal logic—that is, without any secure horizon for question and answer. One must seek a *way* of casting light on the fundamental question of ontology, and this is the way one must *go*. Whether this is the *only* way or even the right one at all, can be decided only *after one has gone along it*. The conflict as to the Interpretation of Being cannot be allayed, *because it has not yet been enkindled*. And in the end this is not the kind of conflict one can 'bluster into'; it is of the kind which cannot get enkindled unless preparations are made for it. Towards this alone the foregoing investigation is *on the way*. And where does this investigation stand?

Something like 'Being' has been disclosed in the understanding-of-Being which belongs to existent Dasein as a way in which it understands. Being has been disclosed in a preliminary way, though non-conceptually; and this makes it possible for Dasein as existent Being-in-the-world to comport itself *towards entities*—towards those which it encounters within-the-world as well as towards itself as existent. *How is this disclosive understanding of Being at all possible for Dasein?* Can this question be answered by going back to the *primordial constitution-of-Being* of that Dasein by which Being is understood? The existential-ontological constitution of Dasein's totality is grounded in temporality. Hence the ecstatical projection of Being must be made possible by some primordial way in which ecstatical temporality temporalizes. How is this mode of the temporalizing of temporality to be Interpreted? Is there a way which leads from primordial time to the meaning of *Being*? Does *time* itself manifest itself as the horizon of *Being*?

AUTHOR'S NOTES

Foreword

i. (H. 1) Plato, *Sophistes* 244a.

Introduction, Chapter One

i. (H. 3) Aristotle, *Metaphysica B* 4, 1001 a 21.
ii. (H. 3) Thomas Aquinas, *Summa Theologica* 11¹ Q .94 art. 2.
iii. (H. 3) Aristotle, *Metaphysica B* 3, 998 b 22.
iv. (H. 4) Cf. Pascal, *Pensées et Opuscules* (ed. Brunschvicg),⁶ Paris, 1912, p. 169; 'On ne peut entreprendre de définir l'être sans tomber dans cette absurdité: car on ne peut définir un mot sans commencer par celui-ci, *c'est*, soit qu'on l'exprime ou qu'on le sous-entende. Donc pour définir l'être, il faudrait dire *c'est*, et ainsi employer le mot défini dans sa définition.'
v. (H. 6) Plato, *Sophistes* 242c.
vi. (H. 14) Aristotle, *De Anima Γ* 8, 431 b 21; cf. *ibid. Γ* 5, 430 a 14 ff.
vii. (H. 14) Thomas Aquinas, *Quaestiones de Veritate*, q. I, a 1 c; cf. the somewhat different and in part more rigorous way in which he carries out a 'deduction' of the *transcendentia* in his opuscule '*De Natura Generis*'.

Introduction, Chapter Two

i. (H. 23) I. Kant, *Critique of Pure Reason*,² pp. 180 f.
ii. (H. 26) Aristotle, *Physica Δ* 10–14 (217b 29–224a 17).
iii. (H. 26) I. Kant, *op. cit.*, p. 121.
iv. (H. 32) Cf. Aristotle, *De Interpretatione* 1–6; also *Metaphysica Z* 4, and *Ethica Nicomachea Z*
v. (H. 38) If the following investigation has taken any steps forward in disclosing the 'things themselves', the author must first of all thank E. Husserl, who, by providing his own incisive personal guidance and by freely turning over his unpublished investigations, familiarized the author with the most diverse areas of phenomenological research during his student years in Freiburg.

Division One, Chapter One

i. (H. 44) St. Augustine, *Confessiones*, X, 16. ['But what is closer to me than myself? Assuredly I labour here and I labour within myself; I have become to myself a land of trouble and inordinate sweat.'—Tr.]
ii. (H. 47) Edmund Husserl's investigations of the 'personality' have not as yet been published. The basic orientation of his problematic is apparent as early as his paper 'Philosophie als strenge Wissenschaft', *Logos*, vol. I, 1910, p. 319. His investigation was carried much further in the second part of his *Ideen zu einer reinen Phänomenologie und phänomenologischen Philosophie* (*Husserliana IV*), of which the first part (Cf. this *Jahrbuch* [*Jahrbuch für Philosophie und phänomenologische Forschung*—Tr.] vol. I, 1913), presents the problematic of 'pure consciousness' as the basis for studying the Constitution of any Reality whatsoever. His detailed Constitutional analyses are to be found in three sections of the second part, where he treats: 1. the Constitution of material Nature; 2. the Constitution of animal Nature; 3. the Constitution of the spiritual world (the personalistic point of view as opposed to the naturalistic). Husserl begins with the words: 'Although Dilthey grasped the problems which point the way, and saw the directions which the work to be done would have to take, he still failed to penetrate to any decisive formulations of these problems, or to any solutions of them which are methodologically correct.' Husserl has studied these problems still more deeply since this first treatment of them; essential portions of his work have been communicated in his Freiburg lectures.

iii. (H. 47) This *Jahrbuch*, vol. I, 2, 1913, and II, 1916; cf. especially pp. 242 ff.

iv. (H. 47) *Ibid.*, II, p. 243.

v. (H. 47) Cf. *Logos* I, *loc. cit.*

vi. (H. 48) *Ibid.*, p. 246.

vii. (H. 48) *Genesis* I, 26. ['And God said, "Let us make man in our image, after our likeness." '—Tr.]

viii. (H. 49) Calvin, *Institutio* I, XV, Section 8. ['Man's first condition was excellent because of these outstanding endowments: that reason, intelligence, prudence, judgment should suffice not only for the government of this earthly life, but that by them he might *ascend beyond*, even unto God and to eternal felicity.'—Tr.]

ix. (H. 49) Zwingli. *Von der Klarheit des Wortes Gottes* (*Deutsche Schriften* I, 56). ['Because man *looks up* to God and his Word, he indicates clearly that in his very Nature he is born somewhat closer to God, is something more *after his stamp*, that he has something that *draws him to God*—all this comes beyond a doubt from his having been created in God's *image*.'—Tr.]

x. (H. 50) But to disclose the *a priori* is not to make an *'a-prioristic'* construction. Edmund Husserl has not only enabled us to understand once more the meaning of any genuine philosophical empiricism; he has also given us the necessary tools. *'A-priorism'* is the method of every scientific philosophy which understands itself. There is nothing constructivistic about it. But for this very reason *a priori* research requires that the phenomenal basis be properly prepared. The horizon which is closest to us, and which must be made ready for the analytic of Dasein, lies in its average everydayness.

xi. (H. 51) Ernst Cassirer has recently made the Dasein of myth a theme for philosophical Interpretation. (See his *Philosophie der symbolischen Formen*, vol. II, *Das mythische Denken*, 1925.) In this study, clues of far-reaching importance are made available for ethnological research. From the standpoint of philosophical problematics it remains an open question whether the foundations of this Interpretation are sufficiently transparent— whether in particular the architectonics and the general systematic content of Kant's *Critique of Pure Reason* can provide a possible design for such a task, or whether a new and more primordial approach may not here be needed. That Cassirer himself sees the possibility of such a task is shown by his note on pp. 16 ff., where he alludes to the phenomenological horizons disclosed by Husserl. In a discussion between the author and Cassirer on the occasion of a lecture before the Hamburg section of the *Kantgesellschaft* in December 1923 on 'Tasks and Pathways of Phenomenological Research', it was already apparent that we agreed in demanding an existential analytic such as was sketched in that lecture.

Division One, Chapter Two

i. (H. 54) Cf. Jakob Grimm, *Kleinere Schriften*, vol. VII, p. 247.

ii. (H. 56) Cf. Section 29.

Division One, Chapter Three

i. (H. 72) The author may remark that this analysis of the environment and in general the 'hermeneutic of the facticity' of Dasein, have been presented repeatedly in his lectures since the winter semester of 1919–1920.

ii. (H. 77) Cf. E. Husserl, *Ideen zu einer reinen Phänomenologie und phänomenologischen Philosophie*, I. Teil, this Yearbook [*Jahrbuch für Philosophie und Phänomenologische Forschung*] vol. I, Section 10 ff., as well as his *Logische Untersuchungen*, vol. I, Ch. 11. For the analysis of signs and signification see *ibid.*, vol. II, I, Ch. 1.

iii. (H. 90) Descartes, *Principia Philosophiae*, I, Pr. 53. (*Œuvres*, ed. Adam and Tannery, vol. VIII, p. 25.) ['And though substance is indeed known by some attribute, yet for each substance there is pre-eminently one property which constitutes its nature and essence, and to which all the rest are referred.'—Tr.]

iv. (H. 90) *Ibid.* ['Indeed *extension* in length, breadth, and thickness constitutes the nature of corporeal substance.' The emphasis is Heidegger's.—Tr.]

v. (H. 90) *Ibid.* ['For everything else that can be ascribed to body presupposes extension.' —Tr.]

vi. (H. 90) *Ibid.*, Pr. 64, p. 31. ['And one and the same body can be extended in many different ways while retaining the same quantity it had before; surely it can sometimes be greater in length and less in breadth or thickness, while later it may, on the contrary, be greater in breadth and less in length.'—Tr.]

vii. (H. 91) *Ibid.*, Pr. 65, p. 32. ['. . . if we think of nothing except what has a place, and do not ask about the force by which it is set in motion . . .'—Tr.]

viii. (H. 91) *Ibid.*, II, Pr. 4. p. 42. ['For, so far as hardness is concerned, the sense shows us nothing else about it than that portions of hard bodies resist the movement of our hands when they come up against those portions. For if whenever our hands are moved towards a certain portion, all the bodies there should retreat with the same velocity as that with which our hands approach, we should never feel any hardness. Nor is it in any way intelligible that bodies which thus recede should accordingly lose their corporeal nature; hence this does not consist in hardness.'—Tr.]

ix. (H. 91) *Ibid.* ['And by the same reasoning it can be shown that weight and colour and all the other qualities of this sort which are sensed in corporeal matter, can be taken away from it, while that matter remains entire; it follows that the nature of this <viz. of extension> depends upon none of these.'—Tr.]

x. (H. 92) *Ibid.*, I, pr. 51, p. 24. ['Indeed we perceive that no other things exist without the help of God's concurrence.'—Tr.]

xi. (H. 92) *Ibid.* ['. . . only one substance which is in need of nothing whatsoever, can be understood, and this indeed is God.'—Tr.]

xii. (H. 92) *Ibid.* ['Indeed we perceive that other things cannot exist without the help of God's concurrence.'—Tr.]

xiii. (H. 93) *Ibid.* [The complete passage may be translated as follows: 'The name "substance" is not appropriate to God and to these *univocally*, as they say in the Schools; that is, no signification of this name which would be common to both God and his creation can be distinctly understood.'—Tr.]

xiv. (H. 93) In this connection, cf. *Opuscula omnia Thomae de Vio Caietani Cardinalis, Lugduni*, 1580, *Tomus* III, *Tractatus* V; '*de nominum analogia*', pp. 211–219.

xv. (H. 93) Descartes, *op. cit.*, I, Pr. 51, p. 24. ['No signification of this name<"substance"> which would be common to God and his creation can be distinctly understood.'—Tr.]

xvi. (H. 94) *Ibid.*, I, Pr. 52, p. 25. ['Yet substance cannot first be discovered merely by the fact that it is a thing that exists, for this alone by itself does not affect us.'—Tr.]

xvii. (H. 94) *Ibid.*, I, Pr. 63, p. 31. ['Indeed we understand extended substance, or thinking substance more easily than substance alone, disregarding that which thinks or is extended.'—Tr.]

xviii. (H. 96) *Ibid.*, II, Pr. 3, p. 41. ['It will be enough if we point out that the perceptions of the senses are not referred to anything but the union of the human body with the mind, and that indeed they ordinarily show us in what way external bodies can be of help to it or do it harm.'—Tr.]

xix. (H. 97) *Ibid.*, II, Pr. 3, pp. 41–42. ['. . . but they do not teach us what kinds of things <bodies> exist in themselves.'—Tr.]

xx. (H. 97) *Ibid.*, II, Pr. 4, p. 42. ['If we do this, we shall perceive that the nature of matter, or of body as regarded universally, does not consist in its being something hard or heavy or coloured or affecting the senses in some other way, but only in its being something extended in length, breadth, and thickness.'—Tr.]

xxi. (H. 109) Immanuel Kant: 'Was Heisst: Sich im Denken orientieren?' (1786) *Werke* (*Akad. Ausgabe*), Vol. VIII, pp. 131–147.

xxii. (H. 112) Cf. O. Becker, *Beiträge zur phänomenologischen Begründung der Geometrie und ihrer physikalischen Anwendungen*, in this Year book [*Jahrbuch für Philosophie und phänomenologische Forschung*], vol. VI (1923), pp. 385 ff.

Division One, Chapter Four

i. (H. 116) Cf. what Max Scheler has pointed out phenomenologically in his *Zur Phänomenologie und Theorie der Sympathiegefühle*, 1913, Anhang, pp. 118 ff.; see also his second edition under the title *Wesen und Formen der Sympathie*, 1923, pp. 244 ff.

ii. (H. 119) 'Über die Verwandtschaft der Ortsadverbien mit dem Pronomen in einigen Sprachen' (1829), *Gesammelte Schriften* (published by the Prussian Academy of Sciences), vol. VI, Part 1, pp. 304–330.

Division One, Chapter Five

i. (H. 131) Cf. Section 12, H. 52 ff.

ii. (H. 131) Cf. Section 13, H. 59–63.

iii. (H. 137) Cf. Section 18, H. 83 ff.

iv. (H. 138) Cf. Aristotle, *Metaphysica* A 2, 982 b 22 *sqq.* ['comfort and recreation'—Ross].

v. (H. 139) Cf. Pascal, *Pensées*, [ed. Brunschvicg, Paris, p. 185]. '*Et de là vient qu'au lieu qu'en parlant des choses humaines on dit qu'il faut les connaître avant que de les aimer, ce qui a passé en proverbe, les saints au contraire disent en parlant des choses divines qu'il faut les aimer pour les connaître, et qu'on n'entre dans la vérité que par la charité, dont ils ont fait une de leurs plus utiles sentences.*' ['And thence it comes about that in the case where we are speaking of human things, it is said to be necessary to know them before we love them, and this has become a proverb; but the saints, on the contrary, when they speak of divine things, say that we must love them before we know them, and that we enter into truth only by charity; they have made of this one of their most useful maxims'.—Tr.] Cf. with this, Augustine, *Opera*, (Migne *Patrologiae Latinae*, tom. VIII), *Contra Faustum, lib.* 32, *cap.* 18: '*non intratur in veritatem, nisi per charitatem.*' ['one does not enter into truth except through charity'.—Tr.]

vi. (H. 140) Cf. Aristotle, *Rhetorica B* 5, 1382 a 20–1383 b 11.

vii. (H. 143) Cf. Section 18, H. 85 ff.

viii. (H. 147) Cf. Section 4, H. 11 ff.

ix. (H. 156) Cf. Section 13, H. 59 ff.

x. (H. 166) On the doctrine of signification, cf. Edmund Husserl, *Logische Untersuchungen*, vol. II, Investigations I, IV-VI. See further the more radical version of the problematic in his *Ideen* I, Sections 123 ff., pp. 255 ff.

xi. (H. 171) Aristotle, *Metaphysica A* 1, 980 a 21.

xii. (H. 171) Augustine, *Confessiones*, X, 35.

xiii. (H. 175) Cf. Section 9, H. 42 ff.

Division One, Chapter Six

i. (H. 180) Cf. Section 12, H. 52 ff.

ii. (H. 188) Cf. Section 12, H. 53 ff.

iii. (H. 189) Cf. Section 27, H. 126 ff.

iv. (H. 190) It is no accident that the phenomena of anxiety and fear, which have never been distinguished in a thoroughgoing manner, have come within the purview of Christian theology ontically and even (though within very narrow limits) ontologically. This has happened whenever the anthropological problem of man's Being towards God has won priority and when questions have been formulated under the guidance of phenomena like faith, sin, love, and repentance. Cf. Augustine's doctrine of the *timor castus* and *servilis*, which is discussed in his exegetical writings and his letters. On fear in general cf. his *De diversis quaestionibus octoginta tribus, qu.* 33 (*de metu*); *qu.* 34 (*utrum non aliud amandum sit, quam metu carere*); *qu.* 35 (*quid amandum sit*). (Migne, *Patrologiae Latinae* tom. VII, pp. 23 ff.)

Luther has treated the problem of fear not only in the traditional context of an Interpretation of *poenitentia* and *contritio*, but also in his commentary on the Book of *Genesis*, where, though his treatment is by no means highly conceptualized, it is all the more impressive as edification. Cf. *Enarrationes in genesin, cap.* 3, *Werke* (Erlanger Ausgabe), *Exegetica opera latina, tom.* I, pp. 177 ff.

The man who has gone farthest in analysing the phenomenon of anxiety—and again in the theological context of a 'psychological' exposition of the problem of original sin—is Søren Kierkegaard. Cf. *Der Begriff der Angst* [*The Concept of Dread*], 1844, *Gesammelte Werke* (Diederichs), vol. 5.

v. (H. 197) The author ran across the following pre-ontological illustration of the existential-ontological Interpretation of Dasein as care in K. Burdach's article. 'Faust und die Sorge' (*Deutsche Vierteljahrschrift für Literaturwissenschaft und Geistesgeschichte*, vol. I, 1923, pp. 1 ff.). Burdach has shown that the fable of Cura (which has come down to us as No. 220 of the Fables of Hyginus) was taken over from Herder by Goethe and worked up for the second part of his *Faust*. Cf. especially pp. 40 ff. The text given above is taken from F. Bücheler (*Rheinisches Museum*, vol. 41, 1886, p. 5); the translation is from Burdach, *ibid.*, pp. 41 ff.

vi. (H. 198) Cf. Herder's poem: 'Das Kind der Sorge' (Suphan XXIX, 75).

vii. (H. 199) Burdach, *op. cit.*, p. 49. Even as early as the Stoics, μέριμνα was a firmly established term, and it recurs in the New Testament, becoming "*sollicitudo*" in the Vulgate. The way in which 'care' is viewed in the foregoing existential analytic of Dasein, is one which has grown upon the author in connection with his attempts to Interpret the Augustinian (i.e., Helleno-Christian) anthropology with regard to the foundational principles reached in the ontology of Aristotle.

viii. (H. 201) Cf. H. 89 ff. and H. 100.

ix. (H. 203) Cf. Kant, *Critique of Pure Reason*,[2] pp. 274 ff., and further the corrections added in the preface to the second edition, p. xxxix, note: see also 'On the Paralogisms of the Pure Reason', *ibid.*, pp. 399 ff., especially p. 412.

x. (H. 203) *Ibid.*, Preface, note.

xi. (H. 203) *Ibid.*, p. 275.

xii. (H. 203) *Ibid.*, p. 275.

xiii. (H. 204) *Ibid.*, p. 275.

xiv. (H. 205) *Ibid.*, Preface, note.

xv. (H. 205) Cf. W. Dilthey, 'Beiträge zur Lösung der Frage vom Ursprung unseres Glaubens an die Realität der Aussenwelt und seinem Recht' (1890), *Gesammelte Schriften*, Vol. V, 1, pp. 90 ff. At the very beginning of this article Dilthey says in no uncertain terms: 'For if there is to be a truth which is universally valid for man, then in accordance with the method first proposed by Descartes, thought must make its way from the facts of consciousness rather than from external actuality.' (*Ibid.*, p. 90.)

xvi. (H. 208) Following Scheler's procedure, Nicolai Hartmann has recently based his ontologically oriented epistemology upon the thesis that knowing is a 'relationship of Being'. Cf. his *Grundzüge einer Metaphysik der Erkenntnis*, second enlarged edition, 1925. Both Scheler and Hartmann, however, in spite of all the differences in the phenomenological bases from which they start, fail to recognize that in its traditional basic orientation as regards Dasein, 'ontology' has been a failure, and that the very 'relationship of Being' which knowing includes (see above, H. 59 ff.), compels such 'ontology' to be revised *in its principles*, not just critically corrected. Because Hartmann underestimates the unexpressed consequences of positing a relationship-of-Being without providing an ontological clarification for it, he is forced into a 'critical realism' which is at bottom quite foreign to the level of the problematic he has expounded. On Hartmann's way of taking ontology, cf. his 'Wie ist kritische Ontologie überhaupt möglich ?', *Festschrift für Paul Natorp*, 1924, pp. 124 ff.

xvii. (H. 209) Cf. especially Section 16, H. 72 ff. ('How the Worldly Character of the Environment Announces itself in Entities Within-the-world'); Section 18, H. 83 ff. ('Involvement and Significance; the Worldhood of the World'); Section 29, H. 134 ff. ('Dasein as State-of-Mind'). On the Being-in-itself of entities within-the-world, cf. H. 75 f.

xviii. (H. 209) Dilthey, *op. cit.*, p. 134.

xix. (H. 210) Cf. Scheler's lecture, 'Die Formen des Wissens und die Bildung', 1925, notes 24 and 25. In reading our proofs we notice that in the collection of Scheler's treatises which has just appeared (*Die Wissensformen und die Gesellschaft*, 1926) he has published his long-promised study 'Erkenntnis und Arbeit' (pp. 233 ff.). Division VI of this treatise (p. 455) brings a more detailed exposition of his 'voluntative theory of Dasein', in connection with a evaluation and critique of Dilthey.

xx. (H. 212) Diels, Fragment 5. [This passage may be translated in more than one way: e.g., 'for thought and being are the same thing' (Fairbanks); 'it is the same thing that can be thought and that can be' (Burnet).—Tr.]

xxi. (H. 212) Aristotle, *Metaphysica A*.

xxii. (H. 213) *Ibid.*, *A*, 984a 18 ff. ['. . . the very fact showed them the way and joined in forcing them to investigate the subject.' (Ross)—Tr.]

xxiii. (H. 213) *Ibid.*, *A*, 986b 31.

xxiv. (H. 213) *Ibid.*, *A*, 984b 10.

xxv. (H. 213) *Ibid.*, *A*, 983b 2. Cf. 988a 20.

xxvi. (H. 213) *Ibid.*, *aI*, 993b 17.

xxvii. (H. 213) *Ibid.*, *aI*, 993b 20.

xxviii. (H. 213) *Ibid.*, *Γ* 1, 1003a 21.

xxix. (H. 214) Aristotle, *De interpretatione* 1, 16a. 6. [This is not an exact quotation.—Tr.]

xxx. (H. 214) Cf. Thomas Aquinas, *Quaestiones disputatae de veritate*, qu. 1, art. 1.

xxxi. (H. 215) Kant, *Critique of Pure Reason*,[2] p. 82.

xxxii. (H. 215) *Ibid.*, p. 83. [Two trivial misprints in this quotation which appear in the earlier editions have been corrected in the later editions.—Tr.]

xxxiii. (H. 215) *Ibid.*, p. 350. [Another trivial misprint has been corrected in the later editions.—Tr.]

xxxiv. (H. 218) On the idea of demonstration as 'identification' cf. Husserl, *Logische Untersuchungen*,[2] vol. II, part 2, *Untersuchung* VI. On 'evidence and truth' see *ibid.*, Sections 36-39, pp. 115 ff. The usual presentations of the *phenomenological* theory of truth confine themselves to what has been said in the *critical* prolegomena (vol. I), and mention that this is connected with Bolzano's theory of the proposition. But the *positive* phenomenological Interpretations, which differ basically from Bolzano's theory, have been neglected. The only person who has taken up these investigations positively from outside the main stream of phenomenological research, has been E. Lask, whose *Logik der Philosophie* (1911) was as strongly influenced by the sixth *Untersuchung* (Über sinnliche und kategoriale Anschauungen', pp. 128 ff.) as his *Lehre vom Urteil* (1912) was influenced by the above-mentioned sections on evidence and truth.

xxxv. (H. 219) Cf. Diels, *Die Fragmente der Vorsokratiker*, Heracleitus fragment B 1.

xxxvi. (H. 220) Cf. H. 32 ff.

xxxvii. (H. 221) Cf. H. 134 ff.

xxxviii. (H. 221) Cf. H. 166 ff.

xxxix. (H. 223) Karl Reinhardt (Cf. his *Parmenides und die Geschichte der grieschischen Philosophie*, 1916) was the first to conceptualize and solve the hackneyed problem of how the two parts of Parmenides' poem are connected, though he did not explicitly point out the ontological foundation for the connection between ἀλήθεια and δόξα, or its necessity.

xl. (H. 223) Cf. Section 33 above, H. 153 ff. ('Assertion as a derivative mode of interpretation.')

xli. (H. 223) Cf. Section 34, H. 160 ff.

xlii. (H. 225) Cf. Aristotle, *Ethica Nicomachea* Z and *Metaphysica* Θ 10.

Division Two, Section 45

i. (H. 231) Cf. Section 9, H. 41 ff.

ii. (H. 231) Cf. Section 6, H. 19 ff.; Section 21, H. 95 ff.; Section 43, H. 201.

iii. (H. 232) Cf. Section 32, H. 148 ff.

iv. (H. 232) Cf. Section 9, H. 41 ff.

v. (H. 233) Cf. Section 41, H. 191 ff.

vi. (H. 235) In the nineteenth century, Søren Kierkegaard explicitly seized upon the problem of existence as an existentiell problem, and thought it through in a penetrating fashion. But the existential problematic was so alien to him that, as regards his ontology, he remained completely dominated by Hegel and by ancient philosophy as Hegel saw it.[1] Thus, there is more to be learned philosophically from his 'edifying' writings than from his theoretical ones—with the exception of his treatise on the concept of anxiety. [Here Heidegger is referring to the work generally known in English as *The Concept of Dread.*—Tr.]

Division Two, Chapter One

i. (H. 240) Cf. Section 9, H. 41 ff.

ii. (H. 241) Cf. Section 10, H. 45 ff.

iii. (H. 244) The distinction between a whole and a sum, ὅλον and πᾶν, totum and compositum, has been familiar since the time of Plato and Aristotle. But admittedly no one as yet *knows* anything about the systematics of the categorial variations which this division already embraces, nor have these been conceptualized. As an approach to a thorough analysis of the structures in question, cf. Edmund Husserl, *Logische Untersuchungen*, vol. II, *Untersuchung* III: 'Zur Lehre von den Ganzen und Teilen'.

iv. (H. 245) *Der Ackermann aus Böhmen*, edited by A. Bernt and K. Burdach. (*Vom Mittelalter zur Reformation. Forschungen zur Geschichte der deutschen Bildung*, edited by K. Burdach, vol. III, 2. *Teil*) 1917, chapter 20, p. 46.

v. (H. 246) On this topic, cf. the comprehensive presentation in E. Korschelt's *Lebensdauer, Altern und Tod*, 3rd Edition, 1924. Note especially the full bibliography, pp. 414 ff.

vi. (H. 249) In its Interpretation of 'life', the anthropology worked out in Christian theology—from Paul right up to Calvin's *meditatio futurae vitae*—has always kept death in view. Wilhelm Dilthey, whose real philosophical tendencies were aimed at an ontology of 'life', could not fail to recognize how life is connected with death: '. . . and finally, that relationship which most deeply and universally determines the feeling of our Dasein—the relationship of life to death; for the bounding of our existence by death is always decisive for our understanding and assessment of life.' (*Das Erlebnis und die Dichtung*, 5th Edition, p. 230.) Recently, G. Simmel has also explicitly included the

[1] Here we follow the older editions in reading '. . . und der durch diesen gesehenen antiken Philosophie . . .' In the new editions 'gesehenen' has been changed to 'geschehenen'.

phenomenon of death in his characterization of 'life', though admittedly without clearly separating the biological-ontical and the ontological-existential problematics. (Cf. his *Lebensanschauung: Vier Metaphysische Kapitel*, 1918, pp. 99-153.) For the investigation which lies before us, compare *especially* Karl Jaspers' *Psychologie der Weltanschauungen*, 3rd Edition, 1925, pp. 229 ff., especially pp. 259-270. Jaspers takes as his clue to death the phenomenon of the 'limit-situation' as he has set it forth—a phenomenon whose fundamental significance goes beyond any typology of 'attitudes' and 'world-pictures'.
　　Dilthey's challenges have been taken up by Rudolf Unger in his *Herder, Novalis und Kleist. Studien über die Entwicklung des Todesproblems im Denken und Dichten von Sturm und Drang zur Romantik*, 1922. In his lecture 'Literaturgeschichte als Problemgeschichte. Zur Frage geisteshistorischer Synthese, mit besonderer Beziehung auf Wilhelm Dilthey' (*Schriften der Königsberger Gelehrten Gesellschaft, Geisteswissenschaftliche Klasse*, 1. Jahr, Heft 1, 1924), Unger considers the principles of Dilthey's way of formulating the question. He sees clearly the significance of phenomenological research for laying the foundations of the 'problems of life' in a more radical manner. (*Op. cit.*, pp. 17 ff.)

vii. (H. 249) Cf. Section 41, H. 192.

viii. (H. 251) Cf. Section 40, H. 184 ff.

ix. (H. 252) Cf. Section 27, H. 126 ff.

x. (H. 253) Cf. Section 16, H. 72 ff.

xi. (H. 253) Cf. Section 38, H. 177 ff.

xii. (H. 254) In his story 'The Death of Ivan Ilyitch' Leo Tolstoi has presented the phenomenon of the disruption and breakdown of having 'someone die'.

xiii. (H. 255) In connection with this methodological possibility, cf. what was said on the analysis of anxiety, Section 40, H. 184.

xiv. (H. 256) Cf. Section 44, H. 212 ff., especially H. 219 ff.

xv. (H. 257) Cf. Section 44 *b* H. 222.

xvi. (H. 259) The inauthenticity of Dasein has been handled in Section 9 (H. 42 ff.), Section 27 (H. 130), and especially Section 38 (H. 175 ff.).

xvii. (H. 263) Cf. Section 31, H. 142 ff.

xviii. (H. 265) Cf. Section 62, H. 305 ff.

xix. (H. 265) Cf. Section 29, H. 134 ff.

xx. (H. 266) Cf. Section 40, H. 184 ff.

Division Two, Chapter Two

i. (H. 267) Cf. Section 25, H. 114 ff.

ii. (H. 267) Cf. Section 27, H. 126 ff., especially H. 130.

iii. (H. 268) These observations and those which follow after were communicated as theses on the occasion of a public lecture on the concept of time, which was given at Marburg in July 1924.

iv. (H. 270) Cf. Section 28 ff., H. 130 ff.

v. (H. 271) Cf. Section 34, H. 160 ff.

vi. (H. 272) Besides the Interpretations of conscience which we find in Kant, Hegel, Schopenhauer, and Nietzsche, one should notice M. Kähler's *Das Gewissen, erster geschichtlicher Teil* (1878) and his article in the *Realenzyklopädie für Protestantische Theologie und Kirche*. See too A. Ritschl's 'Über das Gewissen' (1876), reprinted in his *Gesammelte Aufsätze, Neue Folge* (1896), pp. 177 ff. See finally H. G. Stoker's monograph, *Das Gewissen*, which has recently appeared in *Schriften zur Philosophie und Soziologie*, vol. II (1925), under the editorship of Max Scheler. This is a wide-ranging investigation; it brings to light a rich multiplicity of conscience-phenomena, characterizes critically the different possible ways of treating this phenomenon itself, and lists some further literature, though as regards the history of the concept of conscience, this list is not complete. Stoker's monograph differs from the existential Interpretation we have given above in its approach and accordingly in its results as well, regardless of many points of agreement. Stoker underestimates from the outset the hermeneutical conditions for a 'description' of 'conscience as something which subsists Objectively and actually' (p. 3). This leads to blurring the boundaries between phenomenology and theology, with damage to both. As regards the anthropological foundation of this investigation, in which the personalism of Scheler has been taken over, cf. Section 10 of the present treatise, H. 47 ff. All the same, Stoker's monograph signifies notable progress as compared with previous Interpretations of conscience, though more by its comprehensive treatment of the conscience-phenomena and their ramifications than by exhibiting the ontological roots of the phenomenon itself.

vii. (H. 277) Cf. Section 40, H. 189.

viii. (H. 291) Cf. Max Scheler, *Der Formalismus in der Ethik und die materiale Wertethik*, Part Two, *Jahrbuch für philosophie und phänomologische Forschung*, vol. II (1916), p. 192. [This passage is found on page 335 of the fourth edition, Francke Verlag, Bern, 1954 —Tr.]

ix. (H. 296) Cf. Section 34, H. 164.

x. (H. 297) Cf. Section 44, H. 212 ff.

xi. (H. 297) Cf. *ibid.*, H. 221.

xii. (H. 297) Cf. Section 18, H. 83 ff.

xiii. (H. 298) Cf. Section 44b, H. 222.

xiv. (H. 299) Cf. Sections 23 and 24, H. 104 ff.

xv. (H. 301) In the direction of such a problematic, Karl Jaspers is the first to have explicitly grasped the task of a doctrine of world-views and carried it through. Cf. his *Psychologie der Weltanschauungen*, 3rd edition, 1925. Here the question of 'what man is' is raised and answered in terms of what he essentially can be. (Cf. the foreword to the first edition.) The basic existential-ontological signification of 'limit-situations' is thus illumined. One would entirely miss the philosophical import of this 'psychology of world-views' if one were to 'use' it simply as a reference-work for 'types of world-view'.

Division Two, Chapter Three

i. (H. 302) Cf. Section 58, H. 280 ff. [This reference, which appears in both earlier and later editions seems to be incorrect. Cf. Section 53, H. 260 ff.—Tr.]

ii. (H. 306) The Being-guilty which belongs primordially to Dasein's state of Being, must be distinguished from the *status corruptionis* as understood in theology. Theology can find in Being-guilty, as existentially defined, an ontological condition for the factical possibility of such a *status*. The guilt which is included in the idea of this *status*, is a factical indebtedness of an utterly peculiar kind. It has its own attestation, which remains closed off in principle from any philosophical experience. The existential analysis of Being-guilty, proves nothing either *for* or *against* the possibility of sin. Taken strictly, it cannot even be said that the ontology of Dasein *of itself* leaves this possibility open; for this ontology, as a philosophical inquiry, 'knows' in principle nothing about sin.

iii. (H. 309) Cf. Section 45, H. 231 ff.

iv. (H. 310) Cf. Section 45, H. 232.

v. (H. 311) Cf. Section 5, H. 15.

vi. (H. 314) Cf. Section 43, H. 200 ff.

vii. (H. 314) Cf. H. 212 and H. 117.

viii. (H. 314) Cf. Section 32, H. 152 ff.

ix. (H. 316) Cf. Section 44b, H. 219 ff.

x. (H. 317) Cf. Section 41, H. 191 ff.

xi. (H. 317) Cf. Section 45, H. 231 ff.

xii. (H. 318) Cf. Section 25, H. 114 ff.

xiii. (H. 318) Cf. Section 43c, H. 211.

xiv. (H. 318) Cf. Section 41, H. 193.

xv. (H. 318) Cf. Kant, *Critique of Pure Reason*, second edition, p. 399; and especially the treatment in the first edition, pp. 348 ff.

xvi. (H. 319) On the analysis of transcendental apperception, one may now consult Martin Heidegger, *Kant und das Problem der Metaphysik* (zweite unveränderte Auflage, 1951), Division III. [This note replaces the following note in the earlier editions, referring to a portion of *Being and Time* which has never appeared: 'The first division of the second part of this treatise will bring the concrete phenomenologico-critical analysis of transcendental apperception and its ontological signification.'—Tr.]

xvii. (H. 319) Kant, *op. cit.*, second edition, p. 404.

xviii. (H. 319) Kant, *op. cit.*, first edition p. 354.

xix. (H. 320) The fact that in taking the ontological character of the personal Self as something '*substantial*', Kant has still kept basically within the horizon of the inappropriate ontology of what is present-at-hand within-the-world, becomes plain from the material which H. Heimsoeth has worked over in his essay 'Persönlichkeitsbewusstsein und Ding an sich in der Kantischen Philosophie' (reprinted from *Immanuel Kant*.

Festschrift zur zweiten Jahrhundertfeier seines Geburtstages, 1924). The line taken in the essay goes beyond giving a mere historiological report, and is aimed towards the 'categorial' problem of personality.

Heimsoeth says: 'Too little note has been taken of the intimate way in which the theoretical and the practical reason are worked into one another in Kant's practice and planning; too little heed has been given to the fact that even here the categories (as opposed to the way in which they are filled in naturalistically in the 'principles') explicitly retain their validity and, under the primacy of the practical reason, are to find a new application detached from naturalistic rationalism (substance, for instance, in the 'person' and personal immortality; causality as the 'causality of freedom'; and reciprocity in the 'community of rational creatures'; and so forth). They serve as intellectual fixatives for a new way of access to the unconditioned, without seeking to give any ratiocinative knowledge of it as an object.' (pp. 31 f.)

But here the real ontological problem has been *passed over.* We cannot leave aside the question of whether these 'categories' can retain their primordial validity and only need to be applied in another way, or whether they do not rather *pervert* the ontological problematics of Dasein from the ground up. Even if the theoretical reason has been built into the practical, the existential-ontological problem of the Self remains not merely unsolved; it has not even been *raised*. On what ontological basis is the 'working into one another' of the theoretical and the practical reason to be performed? Is it theoretical or practical behaviour that determines the kind of Being of a person, or neither of them—and if neither, then what is it? In spite of their fundamental significance, do not the paralogisms make manifest how ontologically groundless are the problematics of the Self from Descartes' *res cogitans* right up to Hegel's concept of spirit? One does not need to think either 'naturalistically' or 'rationalistically', and yet one may be under the domination of the ontology of the 'substantial'—a domination which is only more baleful because it is seemingly self-evident.

See what is essentially a supplement to the above-mentioned essay: Heimsoeth, 'Die metaphysischen Motive in der Ausbildung des Kritischen Idealismus', *Kantstudien,* XXIX, (1924), pp. 121 ff. For a critique of Kant's conception of the "I", see also Max Scheler, *Der Formalismus in der Ethik und die materiale Wertethik,* Part Two, in this *Yearbook* [*Jahrbuch für Philosophie und phänomenologische Forschung*] vol. II, 1916, pp. 246 ff. ('Person und das "Ich" der transzendentalen Apperzeption'). [This section is to be found on pp. 384 ff. of the fourth edition of Scheler's work, Bern, 1954.—Tr.]

xx. (H. 321) Cf. our phenomenological critique of Kant's 'Refutation of Idealism'. Section 43a, H. 202 ff.
xxi. (H. 321) Cf. Sections 12 and 13, H. 52 ff.
xxii. (H. 324) Cf. Section 32, H. 148 ff., especially H. 151 f.
xxiii. (H. 327) Cf. Section 41, H. 196.
xxiv. (H. 332) Cf. Section 9, H. 43.
xxv. (H. 332) Cf. Sections 25 ff., H. 113 ff.

Division Two, Chapter Four

i. (H. 334) Cf. Division One, H. 41-230.
ii. (H. 336) Cf. Section 31, H. 142 ff.
iii. (H. 338) S. Kierkegaard is probably the one who has seen the *existentiell* phenomenon of the moment of vision with the most penetration; but this does not signify that he has been correspondingly successful in Interpreting it existentially. He clings to the ordinary conception of time, and defines the "moment of vision" with the help of "now" and "eternity". When Kierkegaard speaks of 'temporality', what he has in mind is man's 'Being-in-time' ["In-der-Zeit-sein"]. Time as within-time-ness knows only the "now"; it never knows a moment of vision. If, however, such a moment gets experienced in an existentiell manner, then a more primordial temporality has been presupposed, although existentially it has not been made explicit. On the 'moment of vision', cf. K. Jaspers, *Psychologie der Weltanschauungen,* third unaltered edition, 1925, pp. 108 ff., and further his 'review of Kierkegaard' (*ibid.*, pp. 419-432).
iv. (H. 339) Cf. Section 29, H. 134 ff.
v. (H. 341) Cf. Section 30, H. 140 ff.
vi. (H. 342) Cf. Aristotle, *Rhetorica B* 5, 1382a 21.
vii. (H. 342) Cf. Section 40, H. 184 ff.
viii. (H. 346) Cf. Section 38, H. 175 ff.

ix. (H. 346) Cf. Sections 35 ff., H. 167 ff.
x. (H. 346) Cf. Section 36, H. 170 ff.
xi. (H. 349) Cf. Section 34, H. 160 ff.
xii. (H. 349) Cf., among others, Jakob Wackernagel, *Vorlesungen über Syntax*, vol. I, 1920, p. 15, and especially pp. 149-210. See further G. Herbig, 'Aktionsart und Zeitstufe' in *Indogermanische Forschung*, vol. VI, 1896, pp. 167 ff.
xiii. (H. 349) Cf. Division Three, Chapter II of this treatise. [Since Division Three has never been published, this footnote has been deleted in the later editions.—Tr.]
xiv. (H. 350) Cf. Section 28, H. 133.
xv. (H. 352) Cf. Section 15, H. 66 ff.
xvi. (H. 352) Cf. Section 12, H. 56 ff.
xvii. (H. 353) Cf. Section 18, H. 83 ff.
xviii. (H. 354) Cf. Section 16, H. 72 ff.
xix. (H. 357) Cf. Section 44, H. 212 ff.
xx. (H. 357) Cf. Section 7, H. 27 ff.
xxi. (H. 358) Kant, *Critique of Pure Reason*, second edition p. 33.
xxii. (H. 360) Cf. Section 32, H. 151.
xxiii. (H. 363) The thesis that all cognition has 'intuition' as its goal, has the temporal meaning that all cognizing is making present. Whether every science, or even philosophical cognition, aims at a making-present, need not be decided here.

Husserl uses the expression 'make present' in characterizing sensory perception. Cf. his *Logische Untersuchungen*, first edition, 1901, vol. II, pp. 588 and 620. This 'temporal' way of describing this phenomenon must have been suggested by the analysis of perception and intuition in general in terms of the idea of *intention*. That the intentionality of 'consciousness' is *grounded* in [Italics in newer editions only.—Tr.] the ecstatical unity of Dasein, and how this is the case, will be shown in the following Division. [This Division has never been published.—Tr.]

xxiv. (H. 364) Cf. Section 18, H. 87 ff.
xxv. (H. 367) Cf. Sections 22-24, H. 101 ff.
xxvi. (H. 370) Cf. Section 9, H. 42 ff.

Division Two, Chapter Five

i. (H. 375) Cf. Section 64, H. 316 ff.
ii. (H. 375) Cf. Section 63, H. 310 ff.
iii. (H. 377) Cf. Section 80, H. 411 ff.
iv. (H. 382) Cf. Section 60, H. 295 ff.
v. (H. 382) Cf. Section 62, H. 305 ff.
vi. (H. 383) Cf. H. 284.
vii. (H. 384) Cf. Section 26, H. 117 ff.
viii. (H. 385) On the concept of the 'generation', cf. Wilhelm Dilthey, 'Über das Studium der Geschichte der Wissenschaften vom Menschen, der Gesellschaft und dem Staat' (1875). *Gesammelte Schriften*, vol. V (1924), pp. 36-41.
ix. (H. 388) On the question of how 'natural happening' is to be distinguished ontologically from the movement of history, cf. the studies of F. Gottl, which for a long time have not been sufficiently appreciated: *Die Grenzen der Geschichte* (1904).
x. (H. 392) Cf. Section 6, H. 19 ff.
xi. (H. 394) On the Constitution of historiological understanding, cf. Eduard Spranger, 'Zur Theorie des Verstehens und zur geisteswissenschaftlichen Psychologie', *Festschrift für Johannes Volkelt*, 1918, pp. 357 ff.
xii. (H. 397) Cf. *Briefwechsel zwischen Wilhelm Dilthey und dem Grafen Paul Yorck von Wartenburg 1877-1897*, Halle-an-der-Saale, 1923.
xiii. (H. 398) *Briefwechsel*, p. 185.
xiv. (H. 399) We can forgo this all the more because we are indebted to G. Misch for a concrete presentation of Dilthey which is aimed at his central tendencies, and which is indispensable for coming to terms with Dilthey's work. Cf. his introduction to Wilhelm Dilthey, *Gesammelte Schriften*, vol. V (1924), pp. vii-cxvii.
xv. (H. 403) Cf. Sections 5 and 6, H. 15 ff.

Division Two, Chapter Six

i. (H. 408) Cf. Section 33, H. 154 ff.
ii. (H. 413) Cf. Section 15, H. 66 ff.

iii. (H. 414) Cf. Section 18, H. 83 ff., and Section 69c, H. 364 ff.

iv. (H. 417) Here we shall not go into the problem of the *measurement* of time as treated in the theory of relativity. If the ontological foundations of such measurement are to be clarified, this presupposes that world-time and within-time-ness have already been clarified in terms of Dasein's temporality, and that light has also been cast on the existential-temporal Constitution of the discovery of Nature and the temporal meaning of measurement. Any axiomatic for the physical technique of measurement must *rest upon* such investigations, and can never, for its own part, tackle the problem of time as such.

v. (H. 418) As a first attempt at the Interpretation of chronological time and 'historical numeration' ["Geschichtszahl"], cf. the author's habilitation-lecture at Freiburg in the summer semester of 1915: 'Der Zeitbegriff in der Geschichtswissenschaft' (published in *Zeitschrift für Philosophie und Philosophische Kritik*, vol. 161, 1916, pp. 173 ff.) The connections between historical numeration, world-time as calculated astronomically, and the temporality and historicality of Dasein need a more extensive investigation.

Cf. further G. Simmel, 'Das Problem der historischen Zeit' in *Philosophische Vorträge*, *veröffentlicht von der Kantgesellschaft*, No. 12, 1916. The two works which laid the basis for the development of historiological chronology are Josephus Justus Scaliger, *De emendatione temporum* (1583) and Dionysius Petavius, S. J., *Opus de doctrina temporum* (1627). On time-reckoning in antiquity cf. G. Bilfinger, *Die antiken Stundenangaben* (1888) and *Der bürgerliche Tag. Untersuchungen über den Beginn des Kalendertages im klassischen Altertum und in der christlichen Mittelalter* (1888). See also H. Diels, *Antike Technik*, second edition, 1920, pp. 155-232: 'Die antike Uhr'. More recent chronology is handled by Fr. Rühl in his *Chronologie des Mittelalters und der Neuzeit* (1897).

vi. (H. 420) Cf. Section 44c, H. 226 ff.

vii. (H. 421) Cf. Aristotle, *Physica Δ* 11, 219b 1 ff.

viii. (H. 421) Cf. Section 6, H. 19-27.

ix. (H. 423) Cf. Section 21, especially H. 100 f.

x. (H. 423) Cf. Plato, *Timaeus* 37 d. ['But he decided to make a kind of moving image of the eternal; and while setting the heaven in order, he made an eternal image, moving according to number—an image of that eternity which abides in oneness. It is to this image that we have given the name of "time".'—Tr.]

xi. (H. 424) Cf. Section 41, H. 191 ff.

xii. (H. 424) Cf. Section 51, H. 252 ff.

xiii. (H. 427) The fact that the traditional conception of "eternity" as signifying the "standing 'now'" (*nunc stans*), has been drawn from the ordinary way of understanding time and has been defined with an orientation towards the idea of 'constant' presence-at-hand, does not need to be discussed in detail. If God's eternity can be 'construed' philosophically, then it may be understood only as a more primordial temporality which is 'infinite'. Whether the way afforded by the *via negationis et eminentiae* is a possible one, remains to be seen.

xiv. (H. 427) Aristotle, *Physica Δ* 14, 223 a 25; cf. *ibid.*, 11, 218 b 29-219 a 1, 219 a 4-6. ['But if nothing other than the soul or the soul's mind were naturally equipped for numbering, then if there were no soul, time would be impossible.'—Tr.]

xv. (H. 427) Augustine, *Confessiones* XI, 26. ['Hence it seemed to me that time is nothing else than an extendedness; but of what sort of thing is it an extendedness, I do not know; and it would be surprising if it were not an extendedness of the soul itself.'—Tr.]

xvi. (H. 427) On the other hand, the extent to which an even more radical understanding of time than Hegel's makes itself evident in Kant, will be shown in the first division of the second part of this treatise. [This portion of the work has not been published.—Tr.]

xvii. (H. 428) Hegel, *Die Vernunft in der Geschichte. Einleitung in die Philosophie der Weltgeschichte* (ed. G. Lasson, 1917), p. 133.

xviii. (H. 428) Hegel, *loc. cit.* [This phrase ('das unsinnliche Sinnliche') does not occur in this section of Hegel's work as presented in Lasson's 1920 edition, though we do find: 'Die Zeit ist dies ganz Abstrakte, Sinnliches.' And in the *addendum* to Section 254 of Hegel's *Encyclopedia*, which Heidegger cites in the following note, we read that *space* is 'eine unsinnliche Sinnlichkeit, und eine sinnliche Unsinnlichkeit'.—Tr.]

xix. (H. 429) Cf. Hegel, *Encyklopädie der philosophischen Wissenschaften im Grundrisse* (ed. G. Bolland, Leiden, 1906), Sections 254 ff. This edition also includes the '*addenda*' from Hegel's lectures.

xx. (H. 429) *Op. cit.*, Section 257, *addendum*.

xxi. (H. 429) *Ibid.*, Section 254. [Here Heidegger has again somewhat rearranged Hegel's words.—Tr.]

xxii. (H. 429) *Ibid.*, Section 254, *addendum.* [The passage reads as follows: 'Space is thus punctuality, but a punctuality which is null—complete Continuity.'—Tr.]

xxiii. (H. 430) Cf. Hegel, *Encyklopädie*, Hoffmeister's critical edition, 1949, Section 257. [In the later editions Heidegger quotes this passage as follows: 'Die Negativität, die sich als Punkt auf den Raum bezieht und in ihm ihre Bestimmungen als Linie und Fläche entwickelt, ist aber in der Sphäre des Aussersichseins ebensowohl *für sich* und ihre Bestimmungen darin, aber zugleich als in der Sphäre des Aussersichseins setzend, dabei als gleichgültig gegen das ruhige Nebeneinander erscheinend. So für sich gesetzt, ist sie die Zeit.' This version differs somewhat from that given in the earlier editions of Heidegger's work, in which this footnote does *not* include the reference to Hoffmeister's edition of the *Encyclopedia.* Neither version entirely matches those found in the earlier editions of Hegel, and similar discrepancies are found in Heidegger's other quotations from the *Encyclopedia.*—Tr.]

xxiv. (H. 430) *Ibid.*, Section 258.

xxv. (H. 431) Cf. Hegel, *Wissenschaft der Logik*, Book I, Division I, chapter 1 (ed. G. Lasson, 1923), pp. 66 ff.

xxvi. (H. 431) Cf. Hegel, *Encyklopädie*, Section 258, *addendum.*

xxvii. (H. 431) *Ibid.*, Section 259. [' "Übrigens kommt es in der Natur, wo die Zeit Jetzt ist, nicht zum *'bestehenden'* Unterschiede von jenen Dimensionen" (Vergangenheit und Zukunft).' The quotation appears in a considerably less accurate form in the earlier editions of Heidegger's work.—Tr.]

xxviii. (H. 431) *Ibid.*, Section 259, *addendum.*

xxix. (H. 431) *Ibid.*, Section 258, *addendum.* [The passage from Hegel reads as follows: 'Time is not, as it were, a receptacle in which everything has been put in a stream, and from which it gets swept away and swept under. Time is only this abstraction of such consuming.'—Tr.]

xxx. (H. 432-433) The priority which Hegel has given to the "now" which has been levelled off, makes it plain that in defining the concept of time he is under the sway of the manner in which time is *ordinarily* understood; and this means that he is likewise under the sway of the *traditional* conception of it. It can even be shown that his conception of time has been drawn *directly* from the 'physics' of Aristotle.

In the *Jena Logic* (Cf. G. Lasson's 1923 edition), which was projected at the time of Hegel's habilitation, the analysis of time which we find in his *Encyclopedia* has already been developed in all its essential parts. Even the roughest examination reveals that the section on time (pp. 202 ff.) is a *paraphrase* of Aristotle's essay on time. In the *Jena Logic* Hegel has already developed his view of time within the framework of his philosophy of Nature (p. 186), the first part of which is entitled 'System of the Sun' (p. 195). Hegel discusses the concept of time in conjunction with defining the concepts of aether and motion. Here too his analysis of space comes later. Though the dialectic already emerges, it does not have as yet the rigid schematic form which it will have afterward, but still makes it possible to understand the phenomena in a fairly relaxed manner. On the way from Kant to Hegel's developed system, the impact of the Aristotelian ontology and logic has again been decisive. The Fact of this impact has long been well known. But the kind of effect it has had, the path it has taken, even its limitations, have hitherto been as obscure as the Fact itself has been familiar. A *concrete philosophical* Interpretation comparing Hegel's *Jena Logic* with the 'physics' and 'metaphysics' of Aristotle will bring new light. For the above considerations, some rough suggestions will suffice.

Aristotle sees the essence of time in the νῦν, Hegel in the "now". Aristotle takes the νῦν as ὅρος; Hegel takes the "now" as a 'boundary'. Aristotle understands the νῦν as στιγμή; Hegel interprets the "now" as a point. Aristotle describes the νῦν as τόδε τι; Hegel calls the "now" the 'absolute this' Aristotle follows tradition in connecting χρόνος with the σφαῖρα; Hegel stresses the 'circular course' of time. To be sure, Hegel escapes the central tendency of the Aristotelian analysis—the tendency to expose a foundational connection (ἀκολουθεῖν) between the νῦν, the ὅρος, the στιγμή, and the τόδε τι.

In its results, Bergson's view is in accord with Hegel's thesis that space 'is' time, in spite of the very different reasons they have given. Bergson merely says the reverse: that time *(temps)* is space. Bergson's view of time too has obviously arisen from an Interpretation of the Aristotelian essay on time. That a treatise of Bergson with the title

Quid Aristoteles de loco senserit should have appeared at the same time as his *Essai sur les données immédiates de la conscience*, where the problem of *temps* and *durée* is expounded, is not just a superficial literary connection. Having regard to Aristotle's definition of time as the ἀριθμός κινήσεως, Bergson prefaces his analysis of time with an analysis of *number*. Time as space (Cf. *Essai*, p. 69) is *quantitative* Succession. By a counterorientation to this conception of time, duration gets described as *qualitative* Succession. This is not the place [Ort] for coming to terms critically with Bergson's conception of time or with other Present-day views of it. So far as anything essential has been achieved in to-day's analyses which will take us beyond Aristotle and Kant, it pertains more to the way time is grasped and to our 'consciousness of time'. We shall come back to this in the first and third divisions of Part Two. [The preceding sentence has been deleted in the later editions.—Tr.]

In suggesting a direct connection between Hegel's conception of time and Aristotle's analysis, we are not accusing Hegel of any 'dependence' on Aristotle, but are calling attention to *the ontological import which this filiation has in principle* for the Hegelian logic.

On 'Aristotle and Hegel', cf. Nicolai Hartmann's paper with this title in *Beiträge zur Philosophie des deutschen Idealismus*, vol. 3, 1923, pp. 1-36.

xxxi. (H. 433) Cf. Hegel, *Wissenschaft der Logik*, vol. II (ed. Lasson, 1923)' Part 2, p. 220.

xxxii. (H. 434) *Ibid.*

xxxiii. (H. 434) Cf. Hegel, *Die Vernunft in der Geschichte. Einleitung in die Philosophie der Weltgeschichte* (ed. G. Lasson, 1917), p. 130.

xxxiv. (H. 434) *Ibid.*, p. 132.

xxxv. (H. 434) *Ibid.*

xxxvi. (H. 434) *Ibid.*

xxxvii. (H. 434) Cf. Hegel, *Phänomenologie des Geistes*, *Werke* vol. II, p. 604. [In italicizing the word 'time', we have followed Heidegger's earlier editions and the principal editions of Hegel's works; these italics are not found in the later editions of *Sein und Zeit*. The italicization of 'is' has been introduced by Heidegger, and does not appear in the edition of Hegel which he has apparently used.—Tr.]

xxxviii. (H. 434) Cf. Hegel, *Die Vernunft in der Geschichte*, p. 134.

xxxix. (H. 435) Cf. Hegel, *Encyklopädie*, Section 258.

xl. (H. 435) Cf. Hegel, *Phänomenologie des Geistes*, p. 605.

xli. (H. 436) Cf. Section 7, H. 38.

NOTE ON THE INDEX AND GLOSSARY

Being and Time is a work of many interwoven themes, where words are used in strange ways made stranger still by the shift to another language. The reader must constantly remind himself of how specific expressions are used, and he must recall the contexts in which they have appeared before. In our index of English expressions we have tried to list most of those which he may have occasion to look up, indicating which German expressions they have been used to translate and the chief passages in which they appear. We have also provided a German-English glossary for the benefit of the reader who needs a translation as an aid in studying the German text, or who has read other works of Heidegger or discussions of his theories and wants to know how we have handled specific problems. We have taken the reader into our confidence, as it were, exposing not only the pedantic consistency with which many expressions have been treated but also our many departures from consistency when a little more pedantry might have been warranted.

Rather than overloading the index and glossary with trivial details, we have made no effort to list all the important expressions which belong to the same family, but have usually chosen one or two to serve as representatives for the rest. We have, however, used the expression '*But cf.*' to introduce members of the family which have been handled in ways other than those which our main entry suggests; we have done so even in some cases where these exceptions are quite trivial.

In both the index and the glossary we have usually tried to list *all* the 'equivalents' for expressions of each family for which an entry is made. In those cases where our list is incomplete, we have usually indicated this by an '*etc.*'; and we can assure the reader that most of the expressions covered by this abbreviation are of little philosophical importance. In the *index*, an asterisk (*) attached to a *German* expression means that to the best of our knowledge this expression has *always* been translated by some member of the family for which the entry is made. Similarly, in the *glossary* we have used asterisks to indicate those *English* expressions which (again to the best of our knowledge) have been used *solely* to translate the corresponding German expression and its cognates. When several 'equivalents' are listed, we have put the more frequent ones first. If a word *not* marked with an asterisk is given as an 'equivalent' for an expression listed in the glossary, but is not itself listed in the index (or *vice versa*), we have sometimes indicated in parentheses the other expressions to which it corresponds.

When an English expression has been used to translate several German words of which only one or two are of philosophical interest, we have often confined our index references explicitly to these. When two or more English expressions have been used to translate the same German word, we have sometimes found it convenient to put all the references together under a single entry. See, for example, our entries for 'assign' and 'refer'.

In the index we have usually made no attempt to indicate *all* the passages in which an expression occurs. Indeed there are several expressions of the utmost importance, occurring nearly on every page, for which we have been content to list only a few key passages or even none at all. When, however, we have some reason to suppose that our list is complete, we have indicated this with a dagger (†). In general, the less frequently a word appears, the fuller our coverage.

In both the index and the glossary we have used the abbreviation '*ftn.*' to indicate the pages on which our relevant footnotes are to be found. In the index we have sometimes used the abbreviation '*df.*' to designate the chief passages in which the author has discussed the meaning of an expression, if these do not coincide with those in which it first appears; we have done so even in some cases where the author would probably not feel that he has given a full or official 'definition'.

The fullness and accuracy of both index and glossary are due in large measure to the extensive and careful records prepared by Miss Marjorie Ward. She is not responsible, however, for any errors we have made in supplementing her records or reducing them to a more compact form.

All references are to the pagination of the later German editions as indicated in our margins.

GLOSSARY OF GERMAN EXPRESSIONS

abblenden: *dim down
Abgeschlossenheit: (*See* abschliessen.)
Abgrund: *abyss
(*ftn.* H. 152)
abkünftig: derivative
(*ftn.* H. 329)
ableben: *demise
(*ftn.* H. 247)
abschliessen, Abschluss: *settle; conclude (H. 184, 259)
Abstand: distance
abstandmässig, Abständigkeit: *distantial, *distantiality
Absturz: *downward plunge
abträglich: *detrimental
Abwesenheit: absence (Fehlen; Mangel, H. 9; *etc.*)
Aktionsart: aspect
alltäglich, Alltäglichkeit; Alltag: *everyday, *everydayness
But *cf.* alle Tage (every day, H. 370)
(*ftn.* H. 16)
an: at; to; *etc.*
(*ftn.* H. 54)
Analyse: analysis, analyse
Analytik: *analytic
der Andere: the Other, *etc.*
Angabe, angeben: assign; tell (erzählen, Aufschluss geben, sagen, Anweisung, *etc.*); cite (anführen); *etc.*
(*ftn.* H. 408)
Angänglichkeit, angehen: matter (*verb*); be feasible (*tunlich, H. 337)
angleichen: *liken; *assimilate
(*ftn.* H. 214)
Angst: *anxiety; dread (H. 190 n. iv)
(*ftn.* H. 182, 277)
anhalten: persist (H. 134); persevere (H. 354)
But *cf.* Anhalt (support, foothold); ansichhalten (hold itself in, H. 75, 80)
(*ftn.* H. 354)
ankommen, ankünftig: *come along, *come on, *oncoming; *etc.*
But *cf.* Ankunft (*arrival, H. 250)
Anruf, anrufen: appeal
(*ftn.* H. 269, 273)

Ansatz, ansetzen: *approach; regard; start; posit; *etc.*
anschauen. Anschauung: behold (schauen, H. 37, 169); intuit, intuition
(*ftn.* H. 27, 402)
anschneiden: *take the first cut
(*ftn.* H. 150)
ansichhalten: hold itself in
But *cf.* entry for 'anhalten' above.
(*ftn.* H. 75)
An-sich-sein: Being-in-itself, Being-in-themselves (An-ihm-selbst-sein, H. 90)
(*ftn.* H. 75)
ansprechen: address; consider
(*ftn.* H. 37, 408)
Anthropologie: *anthropology
(*ftn.* H. 17)
anvisieren: *set our sights
anweisen, angewiesen, Angewiesenheit: submit, submission; *enjoin, *injunction; allot; assign; dependent (*abhängig; *etc.*); *instruct, *instruction; tell (H. 19, 43, 115); provide (H. 19)
(*ftn.* H. 68, 87)
anwesend: *having presence
But *cf.* Anwesenheit (presence).
(*ftn.* H. 326)
Anwesenheit: presence
But *cf.* anwesend (*having presence).
(*ftn.* H. 25, 326)
anzeigen, Anzeige: indicate; call attention
(*ftn.* H. 77)
apophantisch: *apophantical
artikulieren: *Articulate
(*ftn.* H. 153)
ästhetisch: *aesthetic
auf: to; for; *etc.*
(*ftn.* H. 84, 329)
aufdecken: uncover; expose (freilegen, H. 375; sich aussetzen, H. 376)
aufdringlich: *obtrusive
(*ftn.* H. 74)
Aufenthalt: dwelling; sojourn (H. 24); *stop for a while H. 303)
(*ftn.* H. 61)

auffällig, auffallend: *conspicuous
(*ftn.* H. 74)
aufgehen: *be absorbed; rise (H. 412)
(*ftn.* H. 54)
aufhalten: dwell; hold up (vorhalten,
H. 266)
(*ftn.* H. 61, 354)
aufrufen, Aufruf: *summon
(*ftn.* H. 269, 273)
Aufsässigkeit: *obstinacy
(*ftn.* H. 74)
aufschliessen: *lay open
But *cf.* Aufschluss (information; tell;
etc.)
(*ftn.* H. 75)
das "Auf-sich-zu": *the 'towards-
oneself'
(*ftn.* H. 329)
sich aufspreizen: *give itself airs
(*ftn.* H. 430)
aufweisen: exhibit; point out; point to
(*ftn.* H. 53)
aufzeigen: point out; exhibit; point to
(H. 71); *point at (H. 215)
Augenblick: moment; *moment of
vision
(*ftn.* H. 328, 338)
ausdrücken, Ausdruck: express, expression
But *cf.* ausdrücklich (explicit; etc.)
(*ftn.* H. 149)
ausdrücklich: explicit
But *cf.* unausdrücklich (tacit, unexpressed, not explicit, etc.)
(*ftn.* H. 149)
auseinanderlegen: analyse; take apart
(*ftn.* H. 149)
ausgleichen: balance off; *even out
(H. 126)
auslegen: *interpret; lay out (H. 409)
(*ftn.* H. 1, 148, 149, 409)
ausliefern: *surrender
ausrichten, ausgerichtet: direct, *directional, *directionality; contribute (H. 82)
(*ftn.* H. 102)
(*Note:* while 'Ausrichtung' is translated
as 'directionality', 'Ausgerichtetheit'
is translated as *'directedness'*.)
ausrücken: *back away
(*ftn.* H. 339)
*ausrufen: proclaim
aussagen, Aussage: *assert, *assertion;
*deposition (H. 197)

But *cf.* Aussagesatz (statement);
Heraussage (*speaking forth).
(*ftn.* H. 62, 149)
Aussein auf . . . : *Being out for . . ;
*Being out to get . . . (H. 261)
äusserlich: *superficial; external
(*ftn.* H. 339)
das Ausser-sich: *the "outside-of-itself"
Aussersichsein: *Being-outside-of-itself
aussprechen: express; *speak out (H.
168f)
But *cf.* unausgesprochen (tacit; unexpressed); Ausspruch (pronouncement; *etc.*); Aussprache
(pronouncing; *etc.*).
(*ftn.* H. 149, 167, 224, 408)
Ausstand, ausstehen: *outstanding;
has yet to be given (H. 205, 230)
(*ftn.* H. 236, 250)
ausweisen: demonstrate
(*ftn.* H. 53)

bedeuten, Bedeutung, Bedeutsamkeit:
*signify, signification, *significance
(*ftn.* H. 1, 87)
(*Note; 'Bedeutsamkeit'* has always been
translated as 'significance', which,
however, has also been used occasionally
for 'Bedeutung'.)
bedrohen: threaten
befinden, befindlich, Befindlichkeit:
*state-of-mind; to be found; find
But *cf.* Befund (findings; datum,
H. 53; find)
(*ftn.* 134, 137, 328)
(*Note: 'Befindlichkeit'* has always been
translated as 'state-of-mind', which
has also been used occasionally for
'befinden' and 'befindlich'.)
befragen: *interrogate
befreien: *liberate
befürchten: *be apprehensive
But *cf.* Furcht, fürchten (*fear); sich
fürchten (*be afraid).
begegnen: *encounter
(*ftn.* H. 31, 44, 329)
(*Note; while 'Begegnisart'* is translated
as 'way of encountering', 'Begegnis' is
translated as 'mishap' in H. 252.)
begreifen, Begriff: Begrifflichkeit: *conceive, *concept, *conception,
*conceptual; include; *etc.*
But *cf.* Inbegriff (aggregate).
(*ftn.* H. 150, 433)

behalten: retain, *retention, *retentive; keep (H. 132)
But cf. Recht behalten (is right, is justified); vorbehalten (reserve) (*ftn.* H. 354)
bei: *alongside; in; in spite of; etc. (*ftn.* H. 54, 84, 85, 141, 239, 329)
belegen: reserve (H. 368), *pre-empt (H. 19); evidence (H. 431) (*ftn.* H. 368)
benommen: *fascinated
But cf. benehmen (take away; deprive).
(*ftn.* H. 344)
berechnen: calculate
bereden: *talk about
But cf. Rede (*discourse, talk)
berufen: *invoke; appeal (H. 150)
But cf. Beruf (*occupation).
beruhigen: *tranquillize; tranquillity (Ruhe, H. 254, 430)
berühren: touch
besagen: mean; say; amount to; be tantamount to
(*ftn.* H. 1)
beschliessen: include; imply; embrace; comprise; make a decision (H. 299) (*ftn.* H. 299, 300)
besinnen: consider
(*ftn.* H. 15)
besorgen: *concern; provide (H. 253); *make provision (H. 106)
But cf. Besorgnis (*worry); Sorge (care) and its other compounds.
(*ftn.* H. 57)
besprechen: discuss
But cf. sprechen (speak, etc.) and its other compounds.
(*ftn.* H. 34)
Bestand: content; *stock; subsistence; etc.
But cf. Lehrbestand (*body of doctrine, H. 22); Tatbestand (*facts of the case; *how things stand, H. 242); Bestandstuck (*component); Bestandart (what . . . consists in); beständig (*q.v.*).
(*ftn.* H. 36, 303)
beständig, Beständigkeit: steadiness; stability (H. 417); permanent (H. 98)
But cf. Bestand (*q. v.*).
bestehen: be; consist; subsist; remain; persist (H. 174); etc.
(*ftn.* H. 303)

bestimmen: *determine; define; *make definite; *give a definite character; characterize (*charakterisieren, etc.; kennzeichnen); attribute (*Attribut; zusprechen); ascertain (festlegen; feststellen); *destine
(*ftn.* H. 15, 344)
(*Note:* this verb and its derivatives are by no means technical terms for Heidegger, but are ubiquitous in German philosophical writing. While we have found it impossible to adopt any standard policy for translating them, we have tried to use forms of 'determine' or 'define' whenever we can do so without awkwardness.)
bevorstehen, Bevorstand: *impend, *impendence; stand before; etc.
(*ftn.* H. 250)
Bewandtnis: involvement (bewenden) (*ftn.* H. 84)
bewegen: move; operate; etc.
Bewegtheit: movement
Bewegung: *motion; movement; etc.
bewenden: *involve, involvement (Bewandtnis)
(*ftn.* H. 84)
bezeugen: *attest
But cf. Zeugnis (*testimony; document); Zeug (*equipment, etc.) and its compounds.
beziehen, Beziehung, Bezogenheit, Bezug, bezüglich: relate, relation, relationship, relational, etc.
(*Note:* 'Bezug' and 'bezüglich' have been translated very freely, but 'unbezüglich' is always translated as 'non-relational'.)
Bild: picture; image (H. 397)
(*ftn.* H. 217)
(*Note:* compounds such as 'Gebild', 'bilden', etc. have been translated in other ways.)
bin: *am
(*ftn.* H. 54)

Charakter, Charakteristik, charakterisieren: character, characterize, characteristic; factor (H. 5)
(*Note:* while these words appear quite frequently, we have used their English cognates even more freely.)

da: there; that; as; here (H. 102, 430)
(*ftn.* H. 7, 135, 408)
dabei: there alongside; thereby, *etc.*
But *cf.* Mit-dabei-sein (Being "in on it" with someone).
(*ftn.* H. 85, 119, 239)
dagewesen: *has-been-there
damals: *on that former occasion
But *cf.* damalig (of that time).
dann: then; than; in that case; *etc.*
(*ftn.* H. 406)
Dasein: *Dasein
(*ftn.* H. 7, 25, 41, 58, 63, 184)
Da-sein: *Being-there
(*ftn.* H. 7)
daseinsmässig: *of the character of Dasein; *of the kind which belongs to Dasein; *on the part of Dasein; Dasein's; *etc.*
(*Note: see entry on '-mässig' below.*)
das Dass: *the "that-it-is"
(*ftn.* H. 135)
das "Dass es ist": *the 'that it is'
(*ftn.* H. 135)
datieren: *date (verb)
Dauer: *duration
But *cf.* Lebensdauer (*longevity); Unsterblichkeitsdauer (*immortality); dauern (*q.v.*)
dauern: *to last
But *cf.* Dauer (*q.v.*)
das Dazu: *the "towards-this"
defizient: *deficient
(*ftn.* H. 20)
determinieren: *Determine
deuten: point to; explain
But *cf.* andeuten (intimate; suggest; *hint); Ausdeutung (*exegesis); bedeuten (signify; *etc.*)
(*ftn.* H. 87)
dienen: serve; *etc.*
(*ftn.* H. 78)
Dienlichkeit: *serviceability
(*ftn.* H. 78)
Differenz, differenzieren: differentiate
But *cf.* indifferent (*Indifferent, *undifferentiated; *etc.*)
(*ftn.* H. 429)
Ding: *Thing
But *cf.* verdinglichen (*reify)
das Dort: *the "yonder"
But *cf.* das Dorther (*the "thence"); das Dorthin (the "thither").

Drang: urge
(*Note: while 'urge' has been reserved for 'Drang' and for 'drängen' and some of its compounds, most of these have usually been translated in other ways.*)
drohen: threaten
Durchschnitt, durchschnittlich: *average
durchsichtig: *transparent
But *cf.* undurchsichtig (*opaque).
(*ftn.* H. 5)

echt: genuine
But *cf.* unecht (*bogus; not genuine).
(*ftn.* H. 5)
eigen; eigenst: own; *ownmost, *most its own
But *cf.* eigentlich (*q.v.*); Eigenschaft (*q.v.*); eignen (*have as its own; belong; *etc.*); geeignet (*q.v.*).
(*ftn.* H. 42)
Eigenschaft: *property
(*ftn.* H. 83)
eigentlich: *authentic; *real; properly (H. 171); *etc.*
(*ftn.* H. 5, 42, 329)
einebnen: *level down
Einfühlung: *empathy
einholen: catch up
(*ftn.* H. 302)
einmalig: once for all
einnehmen: occupy; take in (H. 368f)
(*ftn.* H. 368)
einräumen: *make room
(*ftn.* H. 111, 368)
einschränken: confine; restrict
(*ftn.* H. 155)
einspringen: *leap in; *intervene (H. 100)
(*ftn.* H. 100, 122)
einwohnen
(*ftn.* H. 54)
Ekstase, ekstatisch: *ecstasis, *ecstatical.
(*ftn.* H. 329, 338)
Ende: *end (*noun*) *etc.*
But *cf.* enden (*q.v.*); endgültig (*q.v.*); endlich (*q.v.*); unendlich (*q.v.*).
(*Note: 'Ende' is usually translated as 'end' except in the expression 'am Ende', which is translated not only as 'in the end' but also as 'ultimately', 'in the long run', etc.*)

enden: end (*verb*)
But *cf.* Beendigung (*termination);
verenden (*perish); vollenden (fulfil; complete)
endgültig: final
endlos: *endless
entdecken: *discover; uncover
(*ftn.* H. 33, 218)
entfernen: *desever; *remove
But *cf.* ent-fernen (*q.v.*).
(*ftn.* H. 103, 105)
ent-fernen: *de-sever
But *cf.* entfernen (*q.v.*)
(*ftn.* H. 105)
entfremden: *alienate
But *cf.* befremden (*seem strange).
entgegenkommen: accommodate (H. 127f); confront . . . as coming from (H. 337); come its way (H. 384)
entgegenwärtigen: *deprive of its character as present
entgegenwerfen: *throw against
(*ftn.* H. 363)
enthalten: *contain; include; hold back (*retardieren, H. 169)
But *cf.* vorenthalten (*withhold, H. 281)
(*ftn.* H. 61)
enthüllen: *reveal; *unveil; patent (H. 141)
entrücken, Entrückung: *carry away; *rapture; withdraw (H. 401, *Yorck*)
(*ftn.* H. 338, 339)
entschliessen: *resolve
(*ftn.* H. 299, 300)
Entschlossenheit: *resoluteness
(*ftn.* H. 297)
Entschluss: *resolution
entspringen: arise; *spring from; *leap away; source (H. 45, 70); *etc.*
(*ftn.* H. 347, 348)
entweltlichen: *deprive of its worldhood
entwerfen, Entwurf: *project, *projection
(*ftn.* H. 124, 145, 285, 315)
Ereignis: event
erfahren: *experience; undergo; *etc.*
(*ftn.* H. 46)
erfassen: grasp: *get in one's grasp; *apprehend; *comprehension (H. 49)

erfüllen: *fill in; fulfill; complete (*verb*)
But *cf.* Normerfüllung (*satisfying a norm)
(*ftn.* H. 151)
ergreifen: *seize upon; *take hold of; grasp (H. 332, 384); *etc.*
erinnern: *remember; *recall
(*ftn.* H. 339)
erkennen, Erkenntnis: know, knowledge; *cognize, *cognition; recognize (anerkennen, *wiedererkennen, kennen, *etc.*)
But *cf.* anerkennen (recognize; acceptance, H. 32); Erkenntnistheorie (*theory of knowledge; *epistemology). ·
(*ftn.* H. 36, 123, 124, 146)
(*Note:* 'verkennen' and 'verfehlen' have both been translated as 'fail to recognize'; 'kenntlich' as 'recognizable' and *'unrecognizable'.)
erleben, Erlebnis: *Experience
But *cf.* Er-leben (*living-through).
(*ftn.* H. 46)
errechnen: compute
(*ftn.* H. 48)
erscheinen, Erscheinung: *appear, *appearance; *apparition (H. 402, *Yorck*)
But *cf.* Krankheitserscheinung (*symptom of a disease).
(*ftn.* H. 29)
erschliessen: *disclose; infer (H. 318)
(*ftn.* H. 75, 151, 297, 298, 300, 315)
erschrecken: *alarm
erstrecken: *stretch along; stretch (Strecke); extend
erwarten: *expect
erwidern: *rejoin, *rejoinder
(*ftn.* H. 386)
das "es gibt": the 'there is'
(*ftn.* H. 212, 412)
Essenz: *Essence
(*ftn.* H. 117)
essentiell: *Essential
(*ftn.* H. 117)
existent, Existenz, existieren: *existent, *existence, *exist
But *cf.* Existenzverfassung (existential constitution, H. 43)
(*ftn.* 303)
Existenzial (*noun*): *existentiale

existenzial (*adj.*): *existential
(*ftn.* H. 12)
existenziell: *existentiell
(*ftn.* H. 12)
explizit: explicit
But *cf.* explizieren (explain).
(*ftn.* H. 149)

faktisch: *factical
(*ftn.* H. 7, 56)
Faktizität: *facticity
(*ftn.* H. 7, 56)
Faktum: *Fact
(*ftn.* H. 56)
fallen: fall; *etc.*
(*ftn.* H. 134, 428)
(*Note: in general verbs terminating in '-fallen' have been translated by variants of 'fall'. Exceptions: auffallend (conspicuous); ausfallen (drop out); beifallen (help); entfallen (drop out); überfallen (*assail); zerfallen (*disintegrate; collapse; etc.); zurückfallen (*fall back; *relapse); zusammenfallen (coincide; collapse).)*
fern: far
(*ftn.* H. 105)
(*Note: while the adjective 'fern' and the derivative noun 'Ferne' have generally been translated by some form of 'far', this is not usually the case with compounds based on this stem.)*
festhalten: *hold fast; adhere (*anhaften); keep in mind; reserve; *etc.*
(*ftn.* H. 354)
finden: find
(*ftn.* H. 135)
fliehen, Flucht: flee (flüchtig)
But *cf.* Zuflucht (*refuge; *resort to),
(*ftn.* H. 184)
flüchtig: *fugitive; *fleeting; flee (*fliehen, *Flucht)
But *cf.* verflüchtigen (*volatilize).
fortlaufend: continuing
(*ftn.* H. 243)
frei: free (*adj.*)
But *cf.* befreien (*liberate); freilegen (*lay bare; *expose to view, H. 375); Freimut (*ingenuousness); freihalten (*hold free; *steer clear, H. 33; *keep open, H. 101; *etc.*); freschwebend (*q.v.*); wahlfrei (*options of choice).

freigegen, Freigabe: *free (*verb)
(*ftn.* H. 83)
freischwebend: *free-floating; soaring
(*überfliegend, H. 310)
Fundament: foundation (fundieren, *fundamentieren)
But *cf.* fundamental (*q.v.*); fundamentieren (*q.v.*).
fundamental: *fundamental
But *cf.* Fundament (*q.v.*); fundamentieren (*q.v.*).
fundamentieren: *lay the foundations
But *cf.* Fundament (*q.v.*); fundamental (*q.v.*).
fundieren: *to found; foundation (*Fundament; *fundamentieren)
(*ftn.* H. 34, 59)
für: for, *etc.*
(*ftn.* H. 84)
Furcht, fürchten: fear (*noun and verb)
But *cf.* befürchten (*be apprehensive); sich fürchten (*q.v.*).
(*ftn.* H. 141, 142)
with für: *fear for . . .
with um: *fear about . . .
with vor: fear in the face of . . .
sich fürchten: *be afraid
(*ftn.* H. 142)
furchtbar: *fearsome
furchtsam: *fearful
Fürsorge: *solicitude; *welfare work
(H. 121)
But *cf.* Sorge (*care); besorgen (*concern; *etc.*)
(*ftn.* H. 121)

ganz: whole (Ganze), *wholly; completely; quite; altogether; *etc.*
But *cf.* Ganzheit (*q.v.*); ergänzen (*round out).
Ganze: whole (ganz); totality (*Ganzheit; Gesamtheit, H. 28; das All)
(*ftn.* H. 236)
Gänze: *wholeness
(*ftn.* H. 236)
Ganzheit: totality (Ganze; das All; Gesamtheit, H. 28)
But *cf.* ganz (*q.v.*).
(*ftn.* H. 236)
Ganzzein: *Being-a-whole
Ganzseinkönnen: *potentiality-for-Being-a-whole
geeignet: appropriate; suited
(*ftn.* H. 83)

das Gegen: *the "counter to" H. 210)
 (*ftn.* H. 255)
 (*Note: while the prefix 'Gegen-' has often been translated by 'counter', this is not always the case; the preposition 'gegen' is usually translated in other ways.*)
Gegend : *region
 But cf. Region (*realm).
 (*ftn.* H. 103)
Gegenstand: object
 But cf. Objekt (*Object).
Gegenwart: *Present; *Present-day (H. 432 n. xxx)
 But cf. gegenwärtig (*q.v.*); gegenwärtigen, *etc.* (*q.v.*).
 (*ftn.* H. 25, 26, 326, 329, 338, 347)
gegenwärtig: *in the present
 But cf. Gegenwart (*q.v.*).
 (*ftn.* H. 326)
gegenwärtigen: *make present
 But cf. Gegenwart (*q.v.*); entgegenwärtigen (*deprive of its character as present); Nichtgegenwärtigen (*not-making-present); Ungegenwärtigen (*making-unpresent); vergegenwärtigen (*envisage).
 (*ftn.* H. 326, 347, 359)
Gehalt: content (*Inhalt; Bestand)
gehören: belong; *etc.*
 But cf. sich gehören (*be fitting).
 (*ftn.* H. 284)
Geist, geistig: spirit, *spiritual; intellectual
 But cf. Geisteswissenschaft (*q.v.*).
Geisteswissenschaft: *humane science
 But cf. Geist (*q.v.*).
gelten, Geltung: valid, validity (gültig, Gültigkeit); be accepted as . . .; be regarded as . . .; hold, *etc.*
 (*ftn.* H. 155)
genuin: genuine (echt)
 (*ftn.* H. 5)
Gerede: *idle talk
 But cf. das Geredete (*what is said in the talk).
geschehen: *historize; happen
 (*ftn.* H. 19, 371, 384)
Geschichte, geschichtlich: *history, *historical; story (H. 6)
 But cf. Historie (*historiology, *History), *etc.*
 (*ftn.* H. 10)

Geschichtlichkeit: *historicality
 But cf. Historizität (*historicity).
Geschick: *destiny; *vicissitude
 (*ftn.* H. 384)
Gestalt: form; pattern; *shape; *etc.*
gestimmt, Gestimmtheit, Gestimmtsein: (*See* stimmen.)
gewärtig, gewärtigen: await
 (*ftn.* 337, 347)
das Gewesen: *the "been"
gewesen: having been, have been; *etc.*
 (*ftn.* H. 326)
gewesend: *in the process of having been
 (*ftn.* H. 326)
Gewesenheit: having been; *the character of having been; *etc.*
 (*ftn.* H. 326, 328, 329)
gewesen sein: *be as having been
 (*ftn.* H. 326)
gewiss: certain (bestimmt; *etc.*)
 But cf. Gewissen (*q.v.*).
 (*ftn.* H. 291)
Gewissen: *conscience
 But cf. gewiss (*q.v.*).
 (*ftn.* H. 291)
Gewissenhabenwollen: *wanting to have a conscience
Geworfenheit: *thrownness
 (*ftn.* H. 135)
Gier: *craving
 (*ftn.* H. 346)
gleichgültig: *indifferent
 But cf. indifferent (*Indifferent; *undifferentiated, *etc.*).
 (*ftn.* H. 42, 255, 429)
Gleichmut: *equanimity
 (*ftn.* H. 134)
gleichursprünglich: *equiprimordial; *with equal primordiality
gliedern: *articulate; divide
 But cf. zergliedern (*dissect); artikulieren (*Articulate).
 (*ftn.* H. 153)
Grenzsituation: *limit-situation
Grund, gründen: ground (Boden; *etc.*); *base; basis (*Basis; Boden, *etc.*); reason (Vernunft; *etc.*); *bottom; *etc.*
 (*ftn.* H. 34, 152)
 (*Note: most of the compounds in which the stem 'grund-' or the termination '-grund' appears have been translated with the aid of either 'base', 'basic',*

Grund—*cont.*
or '*basis*'. *Exceptions:* '*Abgrund*',
'*begründen*', '*grundlage*', '*gründlich*',
'*Grundsatz*', '*grundsätzlich*', '*grund-
verschieden*', '*Hintergrund*', '*Rechts-
grund*', '*zugrundeliegen*'.)
Grundsein: *Being the basis, *Being a
basis
Grundverfassung: *basic constitution,
*basic state, *basically constituted
gültig, Gültigkeit: valid, valid character (gelten, Geltung)
But cf. endgültig (finally, finality);
gleichgültig (*indifferent).
(*ftn.* H. 155)

halten: hold; maintain; *etc.*
(*ftn.* H. 75, 256, 347, 354)
(*Note: we have made no effort to translate
'halten' and its numerous compounds
in any systematic fashion.*)
zur Hand: *to hand
But cf. zuhanden (*ready-to-hand).
handeln: *take action; handle; act,
action; be a matter of
But cf. abhandeln, Abhandlung
(treat, *treatise); behandeln
(treat, handle); verhandeln (discuss; *plead one's cause; *etc.*).
(*ftn.* H. 300)
handlich: *handy; *manual (*adj.* H.
109); manipulable
But cf. unhandlich (*unmanageable,
H. 355); leichthandlich (facile,
H. 78)
Hang: *addiction
hantieren: manipulate
heissen: mean; *etc.*
(*ftn.* H. 1)
hellsichtig: *have clear vision
(*ftn.* H. 384)
herannahen: *draw close
hereinstehen: *enter into
Hermeneutik, hermeneutisch: *hermeneutic, *hermeneutical
hervorbringen: bring forth
(*ftn.* H. 29)
hinhören: *listen away
(*ftn.* H. 271)
Historie: *historiology; *History
But cf. Geschichte (*history; story)
(*ftn.* H. 10, 397)
historisch: *historiological; *Historical
But cf. geschichtlich (*historical)
(*ftn.* H. 10, 397)

Historizität: *historicity
But cf. Geschichtlichkeit (*historicality)
(*ftn.* H. 10, 20)
horchen: *hearken
hören: *hear; *listen
(*ftn.* H. 164, 271, 284)
(*Note: most compounds in which 'hören'
appears have been translated with
variants of 'hear' and 'listen'. But cf.
'aufhören' ('stop'); 'gehören' ('belong'); 'unerhört' ('unprecedented').*)
hörig: *thrall to . . .
But cf. zugehörig (belonging);
Gehörigkeit (*belongingness, H.
111)
Horizont, horizontal: *horizon, *horizonal
(*ftn.* H. 1)

das Ich: *the "I"
Ichheit: *"I"-hood
identifizieren: identify (feststellen, H.
79)
identisch: *identical
(*ftn.* H. 114)
Illusion: *Illusion
But cf. Schein (*illusion; *semblance;
etc.)
in der Welt: *in the world
But cf. innerweltlich (*q.v.*); innerhalb
der Welt (*q.v.*).
(*ftn.* H. 13)
indifferent, Indifferenz: *Indifferent;
*undifferentiated; *etc.*
But cf. gleichgültig (*Indifferent;
*undifferentiated; *etc.*
But cf. gleichgültig (*Indifferent).
(*ftn.* H. 42)
innerhalb der Welt: *within the world
But cf. innerweltlich (*q.v.*); in der
Welt (*q.v.*).
(*ftn.* H. 13)
innerweltlich: *within-the-world
But cf. in der Welt (*q.v.*); innerhalb
der Welt (*q.v.*).
(*ftn.* H. 13)
innerzeitig: *within-time
In-Sein, In-sein: *Being-in
intendieren: *intend
(*ftn.* H. 5)
intentional: *intentional

interpretieren, Interpretation: *Interpret, *Interpretation
But *cf.* auslegen (*interpret; lay out) (*ftn.* p. 1)
Inwendigkeit: *insideness
isolieren: *isolate (*ftn.* H. 142)

je meines, Jemeinigkeit: *in each case mine, *mineness
jeweilig: *current; at the time; particular; any, *etc.*
jeweils: in every case; on each occasion; always; any; sometimes (H. 60); *etc.*

kennen: know; be acquainted; acquaintance (der Bekannte, H. 107, 118)
But *cf.* kenntlich (*q.v.*); Kenntnis (*q.v.*); erkennen (*q.v.*). (*ftn.* H. 124, 146)
kenntlich: recognizable
But *cf.* kenntlich machen (designate, H. 151, 351; acquaint, H. 392); kennen (*q.v.*); Kenntnis (*q.v.*).
Kenntnis: information; acquaintance; knowledge; *etc.*
But *cf.* Kenntnisnahme, Kenntnis nehmen (*take cognizance; acquire information; *etc.*); Kennen (*q.v.*); Erkenntnis (*q.v.*). (*ftn.* H. 46, 58)
-können: *potentiality for . . .; *etc.*
(*Note: compounds ending in '-können' are very numerous and have usually been translated by 'potentiality for . . .'. In other contexts the verb 'können' has been translated more freely.*)
Konstitution: *Constitution
But *cf.* Verfassung (*constitution) (*ftn.* H. 8)
Konstituens, konstituieren, Konstitutivum, konstitutiv: *constituent, constitute, constitutive (Verfassungs-)
Kontinuität, kontinuierlich: *Continuity, *Continuous
But *cf.* Stetigkeit, stetig (*continuity, *continuous). (*ftn.* H. 423)

Lage: *situation (*ftn.* H. 299)
(*Note: compounds terminating in '-lage' are always translated in other ways.*)

laufen, Lauf: run; course (*ftn.* H. 243)
(*Note: most words terminating in '-laufen' or '-lauf' have been translated with either 'run' or 'course'. Exceptions: Anlauf, anlaufen, durchlaufen, fortlaufen, verlaufen, zuwiderlaufen.*)
Leben, leben: *life, *live
But *cf.* ableben (*demise); erleben, Erlebnis (*Experience); lebendig (alive; *lively; *vital; *etc.*); Lebensalter (*age); Lebensdauer (*longevity); Nur-noch-leben (mere aliveness). (*ftn.* H. 46, 58)
leicht: light; easy (*ftn.* H. 360)
Leitfaden: *clue; *guiding-line,
Licht: light, *etc.*
But *cf.* lichten, Lichtung (*q.v.*). (*ftn.* H. 133)
lichten, Lichtung, Gelichtetheit: *clear (*verb*), *clearing (*noun*), *clearedness; *etc.*
But *cf.* Licht (*q.v.*). (*ftn.* H. 133).

das Man: *the "they" (*ftn.* H. 113, 129, 253)
das Man-selbst: *the they-self (*ftn.* H. 129)
Mannigfaltigkeit: multiplicity; manifold
-mässig
(*Note: Heidegger uses at least twenty-three compounds terminating in '-mässig', some of them (notably 'daseinsmässig' and 'nichtdaseinsmässig') very frequently. The original meaning of this suffix is roughly 'after the measure of', but Heidegger seems to use it primarily as just a device for constructing adjectives or adverbs from nouns. We have made no effort to translate it systematically, though in a few cases we have used 'in accordance with' (e.g. 'bedeutungsmässig', 'bewandtnismässig', 'situationsmässig', 'stimmungsmässig', 'weltmässig').*)
meinen: mean; have in view; have in mind; suppose; stand for; *etc.*
But. *cf.* Meinung (opinion; suppose; *etc.*); vermeinen *etc.* (suppose;

meinen—*cont.*
presume; *etc.*); Vormeinung (assumption); das Mitgemeinte (*connotation).
(*ftn.* H. 1)
melden: *announce
(*ftn.* H. 29)
Methode, methodisch: *method; *methodological; *methodical (H. 49, 362)
But *cf.* Methodik, Methodologie (*q.v.*).
Methodik, Methodologie: *methodology
But *cf.* Methode, methodisch (*q.v.*).
Missmut: *ill-humour
(*ftn.* H. 134)
mit: with; *etc.*
(*ftn.* H. 84)
(*Note: there are overy forty compounds in which 'mit-' has been used as a prefix. With about a dozen rather unimportant exceptions, we have translated these with the help of 'with', 'too', or the prefix 'co-'.*)
Mit-dabei-sein: *Being "in on it" with someone
Mitdasein: *Dasein-with
But *cf.* mit-da-sein.
mit-da-sein: *be there with us
But *cf.* Mitdasein.
miteinander: *with one another
But *cf.* miteinanderteilen (mutual sharing, H. 155).
mitnehmen: *take along; *carry along
Mitsein: Being-with (Sein mit . . ., H. 263)
(*Note: this expression is usually followed by a prepositional phrase introduced by 'mit'. Rather than writing 'Being-with with . . .', we have usually omitted the second 'with'.*)
mitteilen: communicate (*Kommunikation, H. 398f); present (H. 26, 72 n. i)
But *cf.* teilen mit . . . (*share with . . .; impart, H. 168).
Mitwelt: *with-world
Modus: *mode
(*ftn.* H. 20, 59)
Moment: *item; *momentum (H. 271)
But *cf.*: momentan (*momentary); momentweise (*from moment to moment).

nacheinander: *successive, *succession
But *cf.* Sukzession (*Succession); Sich-jagen (*rapid succession, H. 322).
nachhängen: *hanker
nachreden: *gossip
Nachsehen: inspection; *perfunctoriness (H. 123)
(*ftn.* H. 123)
Nachsicht: *forbearance
But *cf.* unnachsichtig (relentless, H. 307).
(*ftn.* H. 123)
nachspringen: *leap after
(*ftn.* H. 347)
nah: close (*adj.*); *etc.*
But *cf.* zunächst (*proximally; *in the first instance; *etc.*)
(*ftn.* H. 6)
(*Note: while we have usually translated this expression and its derivatives by variants of 'close', the superlative 'nächst' occasionally appears as 'next', 'first', 'proximate', 'most intimate', etc. Exceptions: 'nahelegen'; 'naheliegen'.*)
Nähe: closeness; *etc.*
(*ftn.* H. 102)
(*Note: with a few trivial exceptions, the phrase 'in der Nähe' and 'innerhalb der Nähe' are translated as 'close by'.*)
Natur: *Nature; natural (natürlich)
nebeneinander: *side by side
Neugier: *curiosity
(*ftn.* H. 346, 347)
Nichtheit: *notness
nichtig: *null; *nugatory (H. 237); *which count for nothing (H. 344)
But *cf.* vernichten (*annihilate; *nullify).
(*ftn.* H. 283)
Nichtmehrdasein: *no-longer-Dasein
But *cf.* Nicht-mehr-da-sein (*no-longer-Being-there); Nicht-mehr-dasein-können (*no-longer-being-able-to-be-there).
(*ftn.* H. 250)
das Niemand: *the "nobody"
nivellieren: *level off
das Noch-nicht: *the "not-yet"
But *cf.* vorläufig noch nicht (*not right away).
(*ftn.* H. 259)
Nur-immer-schon-bei: *just-always-already-alongside
(*ftn.* H. 195)

nur-noch-vorhanden: *just present-at-hand-and-no-more
(*ftn.* H. 74)

Objekt: *Object
But cf. Gegenstand, *etc.* (object).
(*ftn.* H. 363)
Offenbar, offenbaren; manifest; open up (H. 124)
öffentlich, Öffentlichkeit: *public; *publicness
But cf. veröffentlichen (*make public; *give a public character).
Ohnmacht: *powerlessness
(*ftn.* H. 384)
ontisch: *ontical, *ontico-
(*ftn.* H. 11, 12)
Ontologie, ontologisch: *ontology, *ontological, *ontologico-
(*ftn.* H. 11, 12)
Ort: *locus; *location; *locative; place (H. 399, 432 n. xxx); *etc.*
(*ftn.* H. 44)

pflegen: be accustomed to . . .; *look after; *etc.*
(*ftn.* H. 54)
Platz, platzieren: place
But cf. Schauplatz (*arena, H. 388)
praktisch: *practical
(*ftn.* H. 69)
Privation, privativ: *privation, *privative
(*ftn.* H. 58)
Projektion: *Projection
But cf. entwerfen, Entwurf (*projection, *etc.*)
(*ftn.* H. 124)

Raum, räumlich: *space; *spatial, *spatio-; room (H. 103)
But cf. Spielraum (*leeway); einräumen (*make room); umräumen (*move around: *rearrange); wegräumen (*move out of the way; clear away).
(*ftn.* H. 111, 368)
Raum-geben: *give space
(*ftn.* H. 111)
real: *Real; *realia (H. 68)
But cf. eigentlich (*real, *authentic; *etc.*).
rechnen: *reckon; account; *calculus (H. 159)
But cf. anrechnen (deem); ausrechnen, berechnen (*calculate);

errechnen, rechnerisch (*compute); vorrechnen (*accuse).
Rede, reden: talk; *discourse; words (H. 30); say (H. 32)
But cf. Ausrede (*subterfuge); nachreden (*gossip); überreden (*persuade); verabreden (*stipulate; *make an appointment); Vorrede (*preface); weiterreden (*pass the word along). *Cf. also* bereden (*talk about); aufreden, einreden (*talk into); *etc.*
(*ftn.* H. 25, 160)
Region: *realm
But cf. Gegend (*region).
(*ftn.* H. 103)
Reife, reifen: *ripeness, *ripen
(*ftn.* H. 244)
Relation: *Relation
But cf. Beziehung, Bezug, Verhältnis (*relation, *relationship, *etc.*)
richten: direct (*verb*); regulate
But cf. aufrichten (set up, H. 420); ausrichten (*q.v.*); berichten (report); einrichten (arrange; *etc.*); Richtung (*q.v.*) verrichten (perform); zurichten (*adapt).
(*ftn.* H. 102)
Richtung: direction; direct (H. 114); movement (H. 38, 47); field (H. 131)
Rücksicht: regard; *considerateness; *etc.*
But cf. rücksichtslos (*inconsiderate; relentless, H. 333).
(*ftn.* H. 123)
Ruf, rufen: call
But cf. Anruf, anrufen (*q.v.*); Aufruf, aufrufen (*q.v.*); ausrufen (*q.v.*); Beruf, berufen (*q.v.*); hervorrufen (*conjure up. H. 175); *evoke, H. 401); Widerruf (*q.v.*).
(*ftn.* H. 269, 273, 291)
rügen: *reprove
rühren: touch

Sache: thing; matter; affair; *etc.*
(*ftn.* H. 27)
(*Note: most of the compounds based on this stem have been translated with the aid of one of the three expressions listed, or with 'fact' or 'subject-matter'. Exceptions: 'sachlich' (*q.v.*); 'Ursache' ('cause').*).
die Sachen selbst: *the things themselves
(*ftn.* H. 27)

sachlich: *objective
But cf. Sache (q.v.); objectiv (*Objective).

Satz: *proposition; *sentence; principle (*Prinzip; Grundsatz)
(*Note: compounds beginning with 'Satz' have been translated with the aid of 'proposition' or 'propositional', but compounds with '-satz' as a suffix have always been handled in other ways.*)

Schein: *semblance; *illusion; seem (H. 176)
But cf. Illusion (*Illusion).
(*Note: except for the adjective 'scheinbar', compounds based on this stem are not translated by any of the expressions here listed.*)

scheinen: seem
(ftn. H. 29)

Schicksal: *fate
But cf. fatal (*fatal)
(ftn. H. 384)

schliessen, Schluss: include; conclude; infer; close; etc.
But cf. abschliessen, Abschluss (q.v.); anschliessen, Anschluss (attach; etc.); aufschliessen, Aufschluss (q.v.); ausschliessen (exclude, rules out, prevent); beschliessen (q.v.); einschliessen (include; *enclose, H. 60); entschliessen, Entschluss (q.v.); erschliessen (q.v.); umschliessen (*close round); verschliessen (q.v.); zusammenschliessen (fit together).
(ftn. H. 330)

Schon-sein-bei: *Being-already-alongside
(ftn. H. 195)

Schon-sein-in: *Being-already-in
(ftn. H. 329)

Schuld: *guilt; *debt; *responsibility
But cf. Unschuld (innocence, H. 292); Verschuldung *indebtedness).
(ftn. H. 242, 280)

Schuld haben an . . . : *have responsibility for . . .

schuld sein an . . . : be responsible for (schuldig)

Schulden haben: *have debts

Schulden machen: *incur debts

schulden: owe
(ftn. H. 281)

schuldig: *guilty; responsible
But cf. schuldig werden (q.v.).
(ftn. H. 280, 281, 282, 287)

sich schuldig machen: *make oneself guilty; *make oneself responsible

Schuldigsein: *Being-guilty
(ftn. H. 281)

schuldig werden: *come to owe; *become guilty

schweigen: *keep silent; *silence
But cf. stillschweigend (tacit); verschwiegen (*reticent)

schwer: heavy, etc.
(ftn. H. 360)

sehen: see; look; etc.
But cf. Nachsehen (q.v.), etc.
(ftn. H. 69, 171)
(*Note: in most cases where Heidegger seems to be concerned with seeing or looking when he uses compounds involving 'sehen', we have translated them accordingly, but not otherwise.*)

seiend: being (sein; etc.); entity (H. 130); is; are
(ftn. H. 1, 3)

Seiendes: entity (seiend, H. 130); *entities; that which is (H. 154); what is (H. 96)
(ftn. H. 1, 3)

sein: be; being (seiend)
(ftn. H. 1, 326)

Sein: *Being
(ftn. H. 1, 4)
(*Note: we have counted 48 compounds beginning with 'Sein-' and as many as 106 terminating with '-Sein', or more frequently '-sein'. With very few exceptions these have been handled with 'Being' or occasionally 'being'. Except for 'Bewusstsein' and 'Dasein' and some of their compounds, none of the exceptions occurs more than once, and we have usually indicated the German reading. Cf. 'Enthaltensein' ('is contained'); 'Enthobensein' ('has been *alleviated'); 'Hingegebensein' ('devotion'); 'In-der-Welt-gewesensein' (*having-been-in-the-world'); Nicht-mehr-sein ('is *no longer'); 'Noch-nicht-zugänglich-geworden-sein' ('has not yet become *accessible'); 'Überfallensein' ('is *assailed'); 'Nochnichtbeisammensein' ('is not yet all together').*)

Sein-bei, Sein bei . . . : *Being alongside
(ftn. H. 54, 141, 329)

Seinkönnen: *potentiality-for-Being (*ftn.* H. 250)

Seinssinn, Sinn des Seins: *meaning of Being

Seinsverfassung: *constitution of Being; *state of Being; *constitutive state of Being; *etc.*

Sein zu . . .: *Being towards (*ftn.* H. 4)

Sein zum Ende: *Being-towards-the-end)
But cf. Zu-Ende-sein (*Being-at-an-end)
(*ftn.* H. 234)

Sein sum Tode: *Being-towards-death (*ftn.* H. 4, 262)

selbig: *selfsame (*ftn.* H. 114)

Selbst: *Self
But cf. sich, selbst (itself, oneself, *etc.*) (*ftn.* H. 114)
(*Note: most of the compounds based on 'Selbst' have been translated with either 'Self' or 'self' or, more rarely, 'itself', 'oneself', etc. Exceptions: 'Selbstgespräch' (*'soliloquy'); 'Selbstmord' (*'suicide'); 'Selbstverhalten' ('behaviour'); 'selbstverständlich' (*'self-evident'; 'obvious').)*

selbständig: *self-subsistent
But cf. Selbst-ständigkeit (*Self-con-constancy); Unselbständigkeit (*failure to stand by one's Self; *etc.*); Unselbst-ständigkeit (*non-Self-constancy).
(*ftn.* H. 117, 128, 291, 303, 322, 332 375)

Selbsterkenntnis: *knowledge of the Self (*ftn.* H. 124, 146)

Selbstsein: *Being-one's-Self; *Being-its-Self; *etc.*

Sichkennen: knowing-oneself (*ftn.* H. 124, 146)

Sicht: sight (*noun*) sichtbar (*q.v.*);
But cf. sichten (*q.v.*); sichtbar (*q.v.*); Nachsicht (*q.v.*); Rücksicht (*q.v.*), Umsicht (*q.v.*).
(*ftn.* H. 69, 123)
(*Note: with a few obvious exceptions, the word 'sight' is not used in translating compounds involving 'Sicht'.)*

sichtbar: visible (*sichtig, H. 149); see; *etc.*

sichten: *sight (*verb*); *sift (H. 51, 394)

Sichtlosigkeit: *sightlessness (*ftn.* H. 69)

Sich-vorweg: (*See* vorweg.)

Sinn: *meaning; *sense (*noun*); *etc.*
(*ftn.* H. 1, 137, 151)
(*Note: most compounds based on 'Sinn' have been translated with some derivative of 'sense' or 'mean'. Exceptions: 'sinnend' ('thoughtfully'); 'besinnen' (*q.v.*); 'einsinnig' (*'univocal'); 'tiefsinnig' (*'deep'); 'widersinnig' (*'absurd'); 'sinnlich' (*'sensory'; *'sensuous').)*

Situation: *Situation
But cf. Grenzsituation (*limit-situation).
(*ftn.* H. 299)
(*Note: see note on 'situation' in the Index of English Expressions.)*

Sorge: *care
But cf. besorgen (*q.v.*); Besorgnis (*q.v.*); Fürsorge (*q.v.*); vorsorgen (take precautions, H. 406, 413).
(*ftn.* H. 57, 121, 171)

Spanne, spannen: *span
But cf. gespannt (*spanned; *intent; *drawn tense, H. 374); umspannen (*span round, H. 374; encompass, H. 64); weitgespannt (broad, H. 242).
(*ftn.* H. 409)

Spielraum: *leeway (*ftn.* H. 368)

Sprache, Sprach-, sprachlich: *language; *linguistic
But cf. Aussprache (discussion, H. 51 n. xi; pronouncing, H. 161); Fürsprache (*interceding, H. 161f); Rücksprache (consulting, H. 161); Selbstgespräch (*soliloquy); Sprachgebrauch (usage).
(*ftn.* H. 25)

spreizen: (*See* aufspreizen.)

ständig: constant (*konstant, H. 416)
But cf. Abständigkeit (*q.v.*); Bodenständigkeit (*indigenous character, H. 36; *grounds to stand on, H. 168); eigenständig (*autonomous; in its own right; *etc.*); selbständig (*q.v.*); vollständig (complete).
(*ftn.* H. 117, 128, 291, 303, 322, 332, 375)

Stätigkeit: steadiness
But cf. Stetigkeit (*q.v.*).
(*ftn.* H. 423)

Stelle: position; *etc.*
stellen: put; set; formulate; raise, *etc.*
(*ftn.* H. 300)
(*Note: the numerous compounds of 'stellen' do not call for any uniform policy of translation.*)
sterben: *die
But *cf.* absterben, ersterben (*die away); der Gestorbene (the dead person, H. 238; *etc.*); der Verstorbene (*the deceased); sterblich (*mortal); unsterblich (*immortal).
stetig, Stetigkeit: *continuous, *continuity
But *cf.* Stätigkeit (*q.v.*); kontinuierlich, Kontinuität (*Continuous; *Continuity).
(*ftn.* H. 423)
stilllegen: *immobilize
(*ftn.* H. 371)
Stimme- *voice
But *cf.* stimmen (*q.v.*); Stimmung (*q.v.*); einstimmig (agreed), *etc.*
stimmen: *attune; fit (H. 78); mood (*See note.*)
But *cf.* bestimmen (*q.v.*); übereinstimmen, zustimmen, zusammenstimmen, einstimmig (*agree); Ungestimmtheit (*lack of mood').
(*ftn.* H. 134)
(*Note: while the participle 'gestimmt' is occasionally translated by some form of 'attune', it is far more often translated by variants of 'have a mood', as are its derivatives 'Gestimmtheit' and 'Gestimmtsein'.*)
Stimmung: *mood
But *cf.* Verstimmung (*bad mood).
(*ftn.* H. 134, 144)
Struktur: *structure
Subjekt: *subject (*noun*)
(*Note: all compounds based on 'Subjekt' have been translated with the help of the noun 'subject' or the adjective 'subjective'; but the verb 'subject' has been used only in translating other [expressions, and the noun 'subject matter' has been reserved for expressions derived from 'Sache'—chiefly 'sachhaltig'.*)
Substanz: *substance
(*ftn.* H. 303)

tasten: touch, *grope; *feel one's way by touch

But *cf.* antasten (impair, H. 227); unantastbar (*unimpeachable, H. 59).
Tatbestand: *facts of the case; *how things stand (H. 242)
But *cf.* Bestand (*q.v.*)
Tatsache: fact
But *cf.* Faktum (*Fact).
tatsächlich: *factual
(*ftn.* H. 7, 56, 135)
temporal: *Temporal
But *cf.* tempora (*tenses, H. 349)
(*ftn.* H. 17)
Thema, thematisch, thematisieren: *theme, *thematic, *thematize
(*ftn.* H. 2)
tilgen: *pay off; annul (H. 434)

überantworten: *deliver over
(*ftn.* H. 21)
übereinstimmen: agree
überfallen: *assail
übergeben: transmit
(*ftn.* H. 21)
übergehen, Übergang: pass over; *transition; *etc.*
überholen: *outstrip
überhören: *fail to hear
(*ftn.* H. 271)
überkommen: come down; traditional
(*ftn.* H. 21, 383)
überlassen: abandon; *etc.*
überlegen: *deliberate (*verb*)
But *cf.* the adjective 'überlegen' ('superior').
überliefern: *hand down; come down; traditional
(*ftn.* H. 21, 383)
übernehmen, Übernahme: take over (entnehmen, H. 61, 259); *etc.*
(*ftn.* H. 383)
überspringen: pass over
überwinden: *overcome; *surmount; *conquest (H. 105)
Überzeugung: *conviction
(*ftn.* H. 256)
um: around; about; in order to; *etc.*
(*ftn.* H. 8, 65, 69, 11, 141)
Umgang, umgehen: *dealings; *deal; *etc.*
But *cf.* unumgänglich (inevitable; indispensable; unsociable, H. 125); es geht . . . um - - - (*- - - is an issue for . . .)
(*ftn.* H. 8, 65, 66)

das Umhafte: *the aroundness
(*ftn.* H. 101)
Umkreis: range (*noun*)
(*Note: the noun 'range' has been reserved for 'Umkreis' and a few infrequent compounds in '-kreis' or '-weite'; the verb 'range' translates a few other expressions of little importance.*)
umschlagen, Umschlag: *change over
Umsicht: *circumspection
(*ftn.* H. 65, 69, 123)
Umwelt: *environment
(*ftn.* H. 65)
das Umwillen: *the "for-the-sake-of"
das Um-zu: *the "in-order-to"
(*ftn.* H. 65, 78)
unausdrücklich: tacit; unexpressed; inexplicit
unbestimmt: *indefinite; *undetermined; *indeterminate (H. 3)
unbezüglich: *non-relational
(*ftn.* H. 250)
undurchsichtig: *opaque
But *cf.* durchsichtig (*transparent)
unendlich: *infinite; *unending (H. 434)
But *cf.* un-endlich (*in-finite).
(*ftn.* H. 330)
ungehalten: *indignant; *not held on to
(*ftn.* H. 347)
unheimlich: *uncanny
But *cf.* heimlich (secret).
(*ftn.* H. 188)
Unselbständigkeit: *failure to stand by itself
But *cf.* Unselbst-ständigkeit (*non-Self-constancy).
(*ftn.* H. 117, 322)
unterscheiden: differentiate; discriminate; distinguish; differ; *etc.*
(*ftn.* H. 429)
Unterschied: difference; distinction; *etc.*
(*ftn.* H. 429)
unüberholbar: *not to be outstripped
Ursprung: source
But *cf.* ursprünglich (*q.v.*).
(*ftn.* H. 348)
ursprünglich: *primordial
But *cf.* Ursprung (*q.v.*).
(*ftn.* H. 348)

verantwortlich: *answerable
verbrauchen: use up (*aufbrauchen, H. 245)
(*ftn.* H. 333)
verdecken: conceal; *cover up
verdinglicien: *reify
But *cf.* dinglich (*Thinglike).
vereinzeln: *individualize
(*ftn.* H. 142)
verenden: *perish
verfallen: fall; deteriorate (verderben, H. 134)
(*ftn.* H. 21, 134, 175, 428)
verfangen: *entangle
Verfassung: *constitution; *constitutive state; state
But *cf.* Verfassungsmoment (constitutive item); Verfassungsganzheit (*constitutive totality).
(*ftn.* H. 8)
Vergangenheit: past (vergangen)
But *cf.* Vergänglichkeit (*q.v.*); vergehen (*q.v.*).
(*ftn.* H. 326, 380)
Vergänglichkeit: *transience
But *cf.* Vergangenheit (*q.v.*).
vergegenwärtigen: *envisage
But *cf.* Gegenwart (*Present, *etc.*); gegenwärtigen (*make present).
(*ftn.* H. 359)
vergehen: *pass away; transgress (überschreiten)
But *cf.* Vergangenheit (*q.v.*).
(*ftn.* H. 380)
Note: the participle 'vergangen' is sometimes translated as 'passed away', but more often simply as 'past'.)
vergewissern: *make certain
(*ftn.* H. 291)
verhalten: behave, behaviour (*sich gebärden, H. 128); *comport; relate; inhibit (H. 253); attitude
But *cf.* Verhältnis (*q.v.*).
(*ftn.* H. 34)
Verhältnis: relationship, relation
But *cf.* verhalten (*q.v.*).
(*ftn.* H. 34)
verhüllen: to veil; to conceal
verlassen: abandon; *forsake
Verlauf: course; *etc.*
But *cf.* verlaufen (run its course; go astray; etc.).
(*ftn.* H. 243)
verlegen: *divert; *block; *shift; misplace (H. 352); defer (H. 377)

vernehmen: perceive; be aware; *etc.*
vernichten: *annihilate; *nullify
Vernunft, vernünftig: reason; rational;
*reasonable (H. 204)
(*ftn.* H. 34)
veröffentlichen: *make public; *give
a public character; *publish;
*publication
verräumlichen: *spatialize
verrechnen: *reckon up
But *cf.* rechnen, *etc.* (*q.v.*).
(*ftn.* H. 48, 300)
Verschliessen: *close off
Verschuldung: *indebtedness
But *cf.* Schuld, schuldig, *etc.* (*q.v.*).
verschwiegen, Verschwiegenheit:
*reticent, *reticence
Verstand, Verständnis, verstehen:
*understanding; *understand
But *cf.* verständig (*q.v.*); verständlich
(*q.v.*); verstandesmässig (*intellective, H. 98); Verstandeswesen
(*something endowed with intelligence, H. 49).
(*ftn.* H. 143, 151)
verständig, Verständigkeit: *common-
sense, *common sense
But *cf.* Verstand, *etc.* (*q.v.*); unver-
ständig (*lacking in understand-
ing, H. 219); Vorverständigung
(*first came to an understanding,
H. 11).
verständlich, Verständlichkeit: *intelligible, *intelligibility
But *cf.* Verstand, etc. (*q.v.*);
selbstverständlich (*self-evident;
obvious); unmissverständlich (unmistakable; *etc.*).
verstellen: *disguise; obstruct (ver-
bauen)
Verstimmung: *bad mood
(*ftn.* H. 134)
der Verstorbene: *the deceased
vertraut: familiar; aware (H. 1)
vertreten: represent; *etc.*
(*ftn.* H. 239)
verweilen: *tarry
verweisen: *refer; assign
(*ftn.* H. 31, 68, 70, 84, 408)
verwenden: use; utilize (H. 333);
make use; put to use
(*ftn.* H. 333)
verwirklichen: *actualize
verwirren:*bewilder; confuse (*zusammenwerfen; verwechseln, H. 138)

vollenden: fulfill; complete (*verb*)
(*ftn.* H. 243, 244)
vor, vor-: *in the face of; *face to face
with; fore-; pre-; forth; before;
in advance; *etc.*
(*ftn.* H. 150, 184, 291, 327)
vorausspringen: *leap ahead
(*ftn.* H. 122)
vorfallen: *befall
But *cf.* zu-fallen, Zu-fall (*be-fall).
vorfinden, vorfindlich: come across;
*show up (H. 108)
Vorgabe: (*See* vorgeben.)
vorgängig: previous; preliminary;
prior; beforehand; first; *etc.*
vorgeben, Vorgabe: present (*verb*);
give; H. 204; *etc.*
(*ftn.* H. 150)
vorgreifen: anticipate
(*ftn.* H. 150)
Vorgriff: *fore-conception; *something
we grasp in advance
(*ftn.* H. 150, 327)
Vorhabe: *fore-having; something we
have in advance
(*ftn.* H. 150, 327)
vorhaben: *have before us; *purpose
(H. 1)
vorhanden, Vorhandenheit: *present-
at-hand, *presence-at-hand
(*ftn.* H. 7, 25, 74, 106)
vorkommen: *occur; *come before us
(H. 106)
(*ftn.* H. 106)
vorlagern: *lie ahead of
(*ftn.* H. 259, 264, 302)
vorlaufen: anticipate
But *cf.* vorläufig (*q.v.*).
(*ftn.* H. 262, 264, 302)
vorläufig: *provisional
But *cf.* Vorläufigkeit (*anticipatoriness, H. 302); vorläufig noch nich
(*not right away, H. 255, 258);
vorlaufen (*q.v.*).
vorrufen: *call forth
(*ftn.* H. 273, 291)
Vorsicht, Vor-sicht: *fore-sight;
*something we see in advance
But *cf.* vorsichtig (*foresightedly, H.
150; *with foresight, H. 257).
(*ftn.* H. 150, 327)
vorspringen: *leap forth
(*ftn.* H. 122)

vorstehen: manage (H. 143); foregoing; preceding; etc.
(*ftn.* H. 143)

vorstellen, Vorstellung: represent, representation; *lay before (H. 83); put before (H. 300); *ideation (H. 139)
(*ftn.* H. 217, 239, 300)

Vor-struktur: *fore-structure
(*ftn.* H. 327)

vorweg: *ahead, in advance
But *cf.* Vorwegnahme (*foreseen, H. 131); vorwegnehmen (take for granted, H. 147); *take in advance, (H. 264); anticipate, H. 391).
(*ftn.* H. 329)

vorwerfen: *reproach; *throw before
(*ftn.* H. 145)

Wahl, wählen: *choose, *choice
But *cf.* Auswahl, auswählen (*select, *selection).

Wahr, Wahrheit: *true, *truth
But *cf.* wahren, *etc.* (*q.v.*); währen, *etc.* (*q.v.*). wahrnehmen (*q.v.*).

wahren: preserve (aufbewahren, H. 380; bewahren; *verwahren; erhalten, H. 380; Sichretten, H. 342)
But *cf.* wahr (*q.v.*); währen, *etc.* (*q.v.*).

währen: endure (*fortwährend; *immerwährend)
But *cf.* wahr (*q.v.*); wahren, *etc.* (*q.v.*); während (*q.v.*); bewähren (confirm; prove, H. 72; *substantiation, H. 209; *etc.*); Gewähr, gewähren, gewährleisten (guarantee, assure, grant, *etc.*)

das "während": *the 'during'
But *cf.* währen, *etc.* (*q.v.*).

wahrnehmen: perceive
But *cf.* wahr (*q.v.*).

wegräumen: *move out of the way; clear away (lichten)

weitersagen: *pass along in further retelling; *further retelling

Welt: *world
But *cf.* Umwelt (*environment).
(*ftn.* H. 63, 73)

weltlich: *worldly; *after the manner of the world; *in a worldly way (H. 276)

But *cf.* Weltlichkeit (*q.v.*); innerweltlich (*q.v.*); entweltlichen (*q.v.*).
(*ftn.* H. 63)

Weltlichkeit: *worldhood
But *cf.* weltlich (*q.v.*); Innerweltlichkeit (*q.v.*); entweltlichen (*q.v.*).
(*ftn.* H. 63)

Weltmässigkeit: *worldly character
But *cf.* weltmässig (in-accordance-with-the-world, H. 104); Weltcharakter (*world-character).
(*ftn.* H. 63)

werfen, Wurf: *throw; cast H. 415)
But *cf.* entwerfen, Entwurf (*q.v.*); hinwerfen (*put forward casually, H. 311); hinauswerfen (*emit, H. 111); unterwerfen (subject, H. 78); verwerfen (rejection, H. 32); vorwerfen (*q.v.*); zusammenwerfen (confuse).
(*ftn.* H. 135, 145)

Werk: work
But *cf.* bewerkstelligen (accomplish; *etc.*); handwerklich (mechanical, H. 394); Werkzeug, *etc.* (*tool, *etc.*; *equipment for working, H. 68).
(*ftn.* H. 70)

Wesen, wesenhaft, wesentlich: *essence *essential; creature (Gebild)
But *cf.* sein Wesen treibt (*is haunted by, H. 392); Lebewesen (*something living); Nachrichtenwesen (*information service, H. 126); Verstandeswesen (*something endowed with intelligence, H. 49); Essenz (*Essence).
(*ftn.* H. 117)

das Wider: the "against" (H. 210)

Widerruf: *disavowal
(*ftn.* H. 386)

widerstehen, Widerstand: resist, resistance

das Wie: *the "how"

wiederholen: *repeat; *restate; *recapitulate (H. 51, 234); *over again (H. 17, 332); raise again (H. 4)
(*ftn.* H. 308, 339, 385, 386)

wirklich: *actual
But *cf.* aktuell (right now, H. 374).
(*ftn.* H. 7)

wissen: know
But *cf.* Nichtwissen (*ignorance).

Wissenschaft,wissenschaftlich:*science,
*scientific; *scholarly (H. 32);
learned (*adj.*) (H. 171); *as a
branch of knowledge (H. 225)
But *cf.* vorwissenschaftlich (*pre-
scientific; *colloquial, H. 52).
das Wobei: *the "in-which"; *the
"whereat" (H. 107); *etc.*
(*Note: see our entry on 'bei' above.*)
das Wofür: the "for-which" (das
Wozu, H. 414)
das Woher: *the 'whence'
das Wohin: *the 'whither'
wohnen: *reside; accustom (pflegen)
(*ftn.* H. 54)
wollen: *want; will; *volition (H. 136,
139); insist upon (H. 253, 265);
seek; *etc.*
das Womit: *the 'with-which'; *etc.*
das Woraufhin: *the 'upon-which' etc.
(*Note: 'woraufhin' has been translated
in many ways, depending on the
contexts.*)
das Woraus: *the "whereof"
das Worin: *the "wherein"; *etc.*
das Worinnen: *the "inside-which";
etc.
das Worüber, das Worum; about
which; *etc.*
(*ftn.* H. 141)
das Worumwillen: *the "for-the-sake-
of-which"; *etc.*
das Wovor: that in the face of which;
etc.
das Wozu: *the "towards-which"; the
"for-which" (H. 414)
(*ftn.* H. 78, 84, 414)
Wurf: throw (werfen)
But *cf.* Entwurf (projection).

Zeichen: sign
But *cf.* Anzeichen (symptom; *be-
token, H. 185); Anführungszei-
chen (*quotation mark); Frage-
zeichen (*question mark); Vor-
zeichen (*warning signal).
zeigen: show; indicate
But *cf.* Anzeige, anzeigen (indicate;
call attention); aufzeigen (exhibit;
point out; point to; *point at, H.
215); Zeiger (*pointer).
(*ftn.* H. 29, 77, 122, 178, 304)
Zeit: time; era (H. 401)
But *cf.* Zeitbestimmtheit (*temporal
character, H. 203, 370; *temporal

attribute, H. 333); zeitgenössisch
(*contemporaneous); Zeitigen
(*q.v.*); zeitlebens (*for its lifetime;
*for life, H. 370); zeitlich (*q.v.*);
Zeitstufe (*temporal stage); Folge-
zeit (*posterity); Zeitalter (era);
unzeitgemäss (*out of season).
(*ftn.* H. 304, 329)
Zeitablesung, Ablesung der Zeit:
*reading off the time; *telling the
time (H. 70)
Zeitangabe, Zeit angeben: *assigning
a time
(*ftn.* H. 408)
zeitigen: *temporalize; *bring to
maturity; bring about (*her-
beiführen, H. 261)
(*ftn.* H. 22, 122, 178, 235, 403)
zeitlich: *temporal
But *cf.* neuzeitlich (of modern times,
H. 49); temporal (*Temporal).
(*ftn.* H. 17, 304)
sich zeitnehmen: *take one's time
Zeitrechnung: *time-reckoning
zergliedern: *dissect
zerstreuen: *disperse; *distract
Zeug: *equipment; *item of equipment
But *cf.* Schreibzeug (*inkstand;
*equipment for writing); Schuh-
zeug (*footgear); Werkzeug (*q.v.*);
Zeugnis (*q.v.*).
(*ftn.* H. 68, 74)
Zeugganze, Zeugganzheit: *equipmental totality, *totality of equipment
Zeugnis: *testimony; document
(*Dokument, *dokumentieren)
das zu: the "towards"
(*ftn.* H. 84, 329)
(*Note: the preposition 'zu' has of
course been translated in many other
ways.*)
Zu-Ende-sein: *Being-at-an-end
But *cf.* Sein zum Ene (*Being-
towards-the-end)
(*ftn.* H. 234)
Zufall, zufällig: *accident, *accidental;
*chance; *haphazard (H. 37,
398); *incidental (H. 310)
But *cf.* Zu-fall, zu-fallen (*q.v.*).
(*ftn.* H. 300)
Zu-fall, zu-fallen: *be-falling, *be-fall
But *cf.* Zufall, sufallen (*q.v.*).
(*ftn.* H. 300)

Zugang, zugänglich: *access, *accessible
(*ftn.* H. 44)
zugehörig, zugehören: belong to
(*ftn.* H. 163)
zuhanden, Zuhandenheit: *ready-to-hand, *readiness-to-hand
But *cf.* zur Hand (*q.v.*).
(*ftn.* H. 25, 74, 104, 106)
das Zuhause: *the "at-home"
zukommen: come towards; belong to; go with *etc.*
(*ftn.* H. 325, 329)
(*Note: whenever 'zukommen' is used with the preposition 'auf', it is translated by 'come towards'; but when it is used with the dative, it is translated in other ways. It is apparently not used in other constructions.*)
Zukunft: *future (*noun*)
But *cf.* Zu-kunft (*q.v.*); zukünftig (*q.v.*).
(*ftn.* H. 325, 329)
Zu-kunft: *the future as coming towards
But *cf.* Zukunft (*q.v.*).
(*ftn.* H. 325)
zukünftig: *futural *future (*adj.* H. 141, 341, 343)
But *cf.* Zukunft (*q.v.*); Zukünftigkeit (*futural character, H. 395; *futurity, H. 424f).
(*ftn.* H. 329)
zumeist: *for the most part; *mostly
(*ftn.* H. 16)
zumuten: *exact (*verb*); impose (H. 39)

But *cf.* rächen sich (*exact their penalty, H. 174).
zunächst: *proximally; *in the first instance; first; right now (H. 253); *etc.*
But *cf.* nächst. (*See entry on 'nah' above.*)
(*ftn.* H. 6, 16)
zur Hand: *to hand
But *cf.* zuhanden (*q.v.*).
das Zurück auf: *the "back to"
(*ftn.* H. 329)
zurückkommen: *come back
(*ftn.* H. 329, 383),
zurücknehmen, Zurücknahme: *take back
(*ftn.* H. 308, 344)
Zusammenhang, zusammenhängen: *connection, *connect; *interconnection, *interconnect; *context; *hang together
Zu-sein; to be
(*ftn.* H. 42)
zuweisen: assign; allot; give (H. 154)
(*ftn.* H. 68, 408)
zweideutig: *ambiguous
But *cf.* doppeldeutig (*gets used in two ways; double signification); Doppelsinn (*double meaning); Doppelbedeutung (double signification); vieldeutig (*has many significations; *is used in several ways).
das Zwischen: *the "between"
(*Note: in compounds 'Zwischen-' is often translated as 'intermediate'!*)

INDEX OF ENGLISH EXPRESSIONS

observe—*cont.*
 *beobachten: H. 340, 358, 362, 415
†obstinacy: *Aufsässigkeit
 (*ftn.* H. 74)
 H. 74f, 186, 354
†obtrusiveness: *Aufdringlichkeit
 (*ftn.* H. 74)
 H. 73-75, 81, 189, 354, 377
obvious: selbstverständlich (*self-evident); offensichtlich (open, H.
 128); *etc.*
occasion, occasionally, on occasion:
 *Veranlassung; *gelegentlich;
 jeweils; zuweilen; *etc.*
 (*See also* on that former occasion.)
†occupy: einnehmen (take in, H. 368f);
 *besetzbar (H. 103)
 But cf. occupation (*Beruf, H. 239)
 (*ftn.* H. 368)
 H. 103, 107f, 413, 416
occur: *vorkommen
 (*ftn.* H. 106)
 H. 12, 29, 33, 48, 54-56, 63, 69f, 73,
 79-81, 102, 104, 117, 119-121,
 125, 128, 154, 170, 173, 177,
 179, 188, 194, 252-254, 257, 269,
 278, 291, 299f, 327, 332, 338,
 344, 367, 384, 404f, 419f
†ocular: *okular
 400 (*Torck*), 402 (*Torck*)
†on that former occasion: *damals
 H. 406-409, 421f
on the basis of: auf dem Grunde (by
 reason of; because of); auf dem
 Boden; woraufhin (with regard
 to which; upon which; whereupon; *etc.*)
 woraufhin: H. 6, 85f, 110, 143
†on its way: *unterwegs
 H. 79
†once for all: *einmalig
 H. 395
oncoming (*See* come along.)
†'one dies': "man stirbt"
 H. 253-255
ontical: *ontisch
 (*ftn.* H. 11)
 H. 11-15 (Section 4), 19, 43, 92, 63,
 94, 114; 116, 182, 199, 201, 266,
 279, 293, 312, 324, 371, 382,
 399f (*Torck*), 402f, *et passim*
ontology, ontological: *Ontologie,
 *ontologisch
 (*ftn.* H. 11, 12) (*df.* H. 11, 12, 27, 35,
 38, 231, 232, 248)

H. 8-11 (Section 3), 12, 15f, 27, 43,
 52, 94, 116, 182, 199, 201, 204,
 210, 301-333 (II, III), 266,
 295, 311f, 403, 436, *et passim*
 (*See also* ancient o., fundamental o.,
 medieval o.)
†opaque: *undurchsichtig
 H. 11, 44, 146, 156
open: *offen; *öffnen; *etc.*
 H. 137, 163, 169, 265, 307f, 341, 350,
 369, 392f, 396f, 408, 421
†opportunity: *Gelegenheit
 H. 172, 174, 300, 359, 389
ordinary: *vulgär
 (*df.* H. 289)
o. conception of Being: H. 387, 389
o. conception of Being guilty: H. 282
o. conception of conscience: H. 269f,
 279, 289-295 (Section 59)
o. conception of the 'connectedness
 of life': H. 374
o. conception of Dasein: H. 374, 378,
 427
o. conception of historicality: H. 377
o. conception of history: H. 376f,
 378-382 (Section 73)
o. conception of phenomenon: H.
 31, 35, 37
o. conception of time: H. 17f, 24,
 235, 304, 326, 329f, 333, 338 n.
 iii, 404-437 (II, VI)
origin, orginate: Herkunft (derivation)
†original: *originär
 But cf. original sin (Erbsünde, H.
 190, n. iv.)
 H. 37, 62, 224
Other: Andere; fremd (H. 124)
 (*df.* H. 118)
Being towards Others: H. 124f, 177
Being-with Others (*See* Being-with.)
coming to owe something to Others:
 H. 282
conscience of Others: H. 298
Dasein-with of Others (*See* Dasein-
 with.)
death of Others: H. 237-241 (Section
 47), 254, 257
encountering of Others: H. 117, 120,
 125
fearing for Others: H. 141f
potentiality-of-Being of Others: H.
 264, 298
solicitude for Others (*See* solicitude.)
understanding Others: H. 123

Self—*cont.*
potentiality-for-Being-one's-Self
(*See entry for this expression above.*)
S. *as* disinterested spectator: H. 293
S. *as* subject *or* substance: H. 129f,
317, 320 n. xix, 323, 332
(*See also* subject *and* substance.)
Self *and* the "I": H. 129f, 317-323,
348
Self-Thing: H. 323
S. *as* thrown: H. 277, 284, 339, 383
S. *as* lost in the "they": H. 271, 274,
383 (*Cf.* H. 116, *and see* they-
self.)
S. *as* factically existing: H. 419
selfsameness of the Self: H. 114, 130,
320, 373
constancy, inconstancy, and non-
Self-constancy of the Self
(*See entry above under 'constant'.*)
failure to stand by one's Self
(*See entry for this expression above.*)
†Self-subsistence: *Selbständigkeit
(*ftn.* H. 291, 303, 322, 375)
H. 303, 332 (*Cf.* H. 291f.)
S. *and* the Other: H. 124, 128 (*Cf.*
also they-self.)
S. *as* being-ahead-of-itself: H. 193
S. *and* care: H. 193, 304, 316-323
(Section 64)
S. *and* the call of conscience, *etc.*:
H. 273f, 277, 280, 288, 296
S. *and* resoluteness: H. 298, 300, 310,
391
S. *and* rapture: H. 348
Dasein's understanding of the S.: H.
72
(*See entry under 'self' below.*)
'knowledge of the Self': *"Selbster-
kenntnis"
(*ftn.* H. 124, 146)
H. 146
The S. must lay the basis for itself:
H. 284
The S. must forget itself: H. 354
Hegel on the S.: H. 433f
Kant on the S.: H. 318-321, 320 n.
xix, 323
Yorck on the consideration of the Self:
H. 399, 401
self, oneself, itself: selbst; Selbst—(*in
certain compounds*); sich
†self-consciousness: *Selbstbewusst-
sein
H. 401 (*Yorck*), 435 (*Hegel*)

†self-dissection: *Selbstzergliederung
H. 178
self-evidence: Selbstverständlichkeit
(obviousness)
H. 4, 16, 43, 49, 93, *et passim*
self-forgetful: selbstvergessen
H. 322, 424 (*Cf. also* H. 277, 342,
354.)
self-interpretation, interpretation of
the Self, *etc.*: *selbstauslegung
H. 51, 116, 184, 196f, 200, 312, 318
self-subsistent: *selbständig
(*ftn.* H. 291)
H. 291f (*See entry for 'Self-subsistence' above.*)
(*Note: this list includes only a few of
the more interesting expressions in
which 'self', 'oneself', etc. appear.*)
†selfsame: *selbig
(*ftn.* H. 114)
H. 114, 130, 188, 218, 320, 322, 373,
423, 435
†semblance: Schein
H. 29-32, *et passim*
†sense (*verb*), sensation: *empfinden;
*Sinnlichkeit (H. 97)
H. 137, 152, 163f
sense (*noun*): Sinn
But *cf.* common sense (*Verständig-
keit).
(*ftn.* H. 1, 137)
H. 91, 96, 107, 137, 147
(*Note: cf.* our entry for 'meaning' above
and our glossary-entry for 'Sinn'.
This list includes only passages referring to 'senses' such as vision or
touch, not to the 'senses' of words or
other expressions.*)
sentence: Satz
separation: Trennung (distinguishing;
etc.); Scheidung (distinguishing,
division, *etc.*)
H. 159, 217, *et passim*
sequence: Folge; *Abfolge
s. of days: H. 371
s. of Experiences: H. 291, 293, 355,
373, 387f, 390
s. of "nows": H. 329, 373, 409, 422-
426, 431f
s. of processes: H. 379
s. of resolutions: H. 387
†serviceability: *Dienlichkeit
(*ftn.* H. 78)
H. 68, 78, 82-84, 137, 144

use—*cont.*
  using up: *verbrauchen, *auf-
    brauchen: H. 244f, 333
  unusable: *unverwendbar, *un-
    brauchbar: H. 73f, 355
  Thing of use: *Gebrauchsding: H. 99
†utilitarianism: *Nützlichkeitsmoral
    H. 293
utilize: verwenden (H. 333); nutzen
    (H. 61); ausnützen (H. 411);
    etc.
  (*ftn.* H. 333)
utter (*verb*), utterance: Verlautbarung
    H. 32f, 163-165, 271-273, 277, 296
utter (*adj.*): völlig: schlechthin; schlech-
    thinnig
†uttermost: äusserst
    H. 250, 255, 259, 262-264, 266, 302f,
    326

valid, validity: gelten, Geltung; gül-
    tig, Gültigkeit
  (*ftn.* H. 155)
    H. 7, 99, 127, 155f, 227, 357, 395
value: Wert; *etc.*
    H. 63, 69, 80, 99f, 150, 152, 227,
    286, 293f
veil: verhüllen; einhüllen; versch-
    leiern (H. 136)
†velocity: Geschwindigkeit (speed,
    H. 105)
    H. 91, 97
†vicissitude: Geschick
    (*ftn.* H. 384)
    H. 16, 19, 379)
†violent: gewaltsam (drastic, H. 219)
    H. 183, 287, 311, 313, 315, 327
†virtuality: *Virtualität
    H. 401
vision: (*See* clear vision, moment of
    vision.)
†vitalism: *Vitalismus (H. 10)
    But *cf.* vital (lebendig, H. 400, 402).
†volition: Wollen
    H. 136, 139
voice: *Stimme
  alien voice: H. 277
  mysterious voice: H. 274
  voice of conscience: H. 268f, 271,
    275, 280, 290-292, 294, 300
  voice of the friend: H. 163
  voice of the "they": H. 278
  voice which is universally binding:
    H. 278

†volatilize: *verflüchtigen
    H. 87f, 117, 177, 420
†voluntative: *voluntativ
    H. 210, 210 n. xix

wait: warten; *etc.*
  (*ftn.* H. 25, 26, 338)
    H. 262, 337f, *et passim*
want: wollen
  wanting to have a conscience: (*See*
    entry under 'conscience' above.)
†warn: *warnen
  But *cf.* warning signal (H. 78, 80).
    H. 161, 279, 281, 290, 292, 294
way of conceiving: Bergrifflichkeit
the 'we': das "wir"
    H. 227f
†the we-world: *das Wir-welt
    H. 65
weak, weakness: *schwach, *Schwäche
  But *cf.* weaken (*abschwächen).
    H. 251, 254
†welfare work: Fürsorge
  (*ftn.* H. 121)
    H. 121
the "what": das Was
    H. 12, 27, 42, 45, 122, 143, 158, 274
the "when": das Wann
    H. 258, 265
†the 'then, when . . .': *das "dann,
    wann . . .": H. 407, 410, 412,
    414
†the "whence": *das Woher
    H. 134-136, 280, 348
the "where": das Wo
    H. 102f, 107
†the "whereat": das Wobei
    H. 107
the "wherein": das Worin
    H. 30, 65, 76, 80, 86f, 110, 151, 198,
    202
  (*Note: this list also includes some
    passages in which 'das Worin' or
    'worin' has been translated some-
    what more freely.*)
the "whereof": das Woraus
    H. 70
  (*Note: cf. also H. 198.*)
†the "whereupon": das Woraufhin
    H. 365
  (*Note: cf. our entry for 'the "upon-
    which" '.*)
the "whither": das Wohin
    H. 103, 108, 110f, 134-136, 280, 365,
    368

INDEX OF LATIN EXPRESSIONS

INDEX OF GREEK EXPRESSIONS

INDEX OF PROPER NAMES

CPSIA information can be obtained
at www.ICGtesting.com
Printed in the USA
BVHW051145181022
649721BV00001B/5